D1601626

This volume of essays by German and American historians deals with the most important issues of the United States' policy toward Germany in the decade following World War II: constitutional problems, political and economic democratization, higher education, urban reconstruction, questions of industry, demilitarization and rearmament, treatment of war criminals, problems of German and European security, and integration of the Federal Republic of Germany into the Western Alliance. All of the contributions to this volume are based upon research in German and American archives, including two comprehensive essays on archival sources in the Federal Republic and the United States for the Occupation period and the era of the Allied High Commission.

PUBLICATIONS OF THE GERMAN HISTORICAL INSTITUTE,
WASHINGTON, D.C.

Edited by Hartmut Lehmann
with the assistance of Kenneth F. Ledford

*American Policy and the Reconstruction of
West Germany, 1945–1955*

THE GERMAN HISTORICAL INSTITUTE, WASHINGTON, D.C.

The German Historical Institute is a center for advanced study and research whose purpose is to provide a permanent basis for scholarly cooperation between historians from the Federal Republic of Germany and the United States. The Institute conducts, promotes, and supports research into both American and German political, social, economic, and cultural history, into transatlantic migration, especially in the nineteenth and twentieth centuries, and into the history of international relations, with special emphasis on the roles played by the United States and Germany.

American Policy and the
Reconstruction of
West Germany, 1945–1955

Edited by

JEFFRY M. DIEFENDORF

AXEL FROHN

HERMANN-JOSEF RUPIEPER

GERMAN HISTORICAL INSTITUTE

Washington, D.C.

and

CAMBRIDGE
UNIVERSITY PRESS

Published by the Press Syndicate of the University of Cambridge
The Pitt Building, Trumpington Street, Cambridge CB2 1RP
40 West 20th Street, New York, NY 10011-4211, USA
10 Stamford Road, Oakleigh, Victoria 3166, Australia

First published 1993

Printed in the United States of America

Library of Congress Cataloging-in-Publication Data

American policy and the reconstruction of West Germany, 1945–1955 /
edited by Jeffry M. Diefendorf, Axel Frohn, Hermann-Josef Rupieper.

    p.   cm. – (Publications of the German Historical Institute)

    Includes bibliographical references.

    ISBN 0-521-43120-4

    1. United States – Foreign relations – Germany.   2. Germany – Foreign
relations – United States.   3. Reconstruction (1939–1951) – Germany.
4. Germany – History – 1945–1955.   I. Diefendorf, Jeffry M., 1945–   .
II. Frohn, Axel, 1934–   .   III. Rupieper, Hermann-Josef, 1942–   .
IV. Series.

                    E183.8.G3A44   1993
327.73043 – dc20   93-12939
                                                        CIP

A catalog record for this book is available from the British Library.

ISBN 0-521-43120-4 hardback

Contents

Introduction

In its broad outlines, the United States' policy toward Germany after World War II has long been known. Its structure was first determined by the Potsdam Agreement and by such documents as the Joint Chiefs of Staff directive 1067. Initial U.S. policy was punitive, stressing denazification, demilitarization, deindustrialization, prolonged Allied occupation, a minimal standard of living for the Germans, and tutelage in democracy. Even if this bundle of policies was not as draconic as the Morgenthau Plan, designed to pastoralize Germany, it was still ill suited to deal with the complex realities of a destroyed and divided postwar Germany and the onset of the Cold War.

Consequently Americans changed their thinking about Germany, in the process reversing the policies of deindustrialization and demilitarization, deemphasizing denazification, and encouraging German economic recovery within a framework of European recovery, all the while insisting on democratization of the German polity. These and other changes in American policy are the subject of the research presented in this book. The founding of the Federal Republic of Germany, the recovery that came to be called the Economic Miracle, and West Germany's integration into Western Europe within the Coal and Steel Community, North Atlantic Treaty Organization, and European Economic Community all took place in close consultation with the United States, and the Federal Republic of Germany and America became close friends and allies. That, at least, is the outline of a happy success story. Moreover, there can be little doubt that West European integration, even if still incomplete, has been a dominant force in shaping domestic and international relations during the past forty years.

The contrast between West European, and particularly West German, prosperity and democracy and the absence of both in what used to be called the Soviet Bloc could hardly have been made sharper than by the events that transpired at the very moment that the essays in this book were being presented and discussed: Thousands of citizens of the German Democratic Republic fled to the West via Poland or Hungary or Czechoslovakia in a migration resembling that of the months just before the erection of the Berlin Wall.

As it turned out, that flight of East Germans to the West was the harbinger of even more dramatic events to come. The opening of the Berlin Wall, the progressive collapse of the Socialist Unity Party's monopoly of power in East Germany, the first free elections, the participation of opposition groups in a transitional government, and the growing clamor for some form of unification between the two German states made Germany the center of world attention. Questions that seemed closed by 1955 were suddenly open once again – for example, whether Germany should become a neutral state or belong to NATO. The United States, the Soviet Union, Great Britain, and France were forced by the rapid changes in the German Democratic Republic and in other Eastern European states to reconsider policies toward Germany that had been set long ago. Suddenly it was not even clear to what extent the victorious powers from World War II would be able to shape, much less control, events in Germany, although greater European integration, or to use the expression now current, the "common house of Europe" from the Atlantic to the Urals, still depended in good part on a resolution of the German question.

All the more reason, then, for a scholarly reexamination of American policy toward Germany during the decade after 1945. A great many of the issues discussed in the essays in this volume – for example, the shape of a united Germany, the place of the two German states in their respective military alliances, the presence of foreign troops on German soil, and the treatment of the members of a discredited military force – were major issues during the first decade after the war and were also being discussed by politicians, journalists, and commentators during the dramatic period from mid-1989 to autumn 1990, a year that saw the final collapse of the German Democratic Republic and the unification of Germany with the consent of the victors in World War II. The same is true for the relationship between the economies of Western and Eastern Europe, the possibility and legality of technology transfers, major currency reforms, the rooting out of authoritarian institutions and behavior, the creation of democratic institutions and the learning of democratic ways of acting and thinking, Western aid for a German economy, and Western help in building new housing and shoring up a deteriorating urban infrastructure. After the war a trustee administration was created to supervise the deconcentration of the coal and steel industry; today a trustee administration is supervising the privatization of the large state-owned enterprises of East Germany. When the planning for this scholarly undertaking was begun in autumn 1987, we had no idea that our historical research would be so relevant for the 1990s.

Although the allied responsibilities for Germany officially ended with the signing of a treaty between the United States, the Soviet Union, France, Great Britain, and the two German states on September 13, 1990, the United States still has an important role to play in German and European affairs. In 1989–90 it was frequently said that American policymakers were busily digging out old postwar position papers long buried in the backs of drawers in the State and Defense departments. If Americans and Germans are not to be trapped in the logic and formulas of the first postwar decade, when America's German policy was formulated, it is essential to understand in detail the history of that policy. The historical record, however, proves not to be as simple as the broad outline of American policy might suggest. In the 1980s, a mountain of documents in American and German archives from the first decade after the war were made available for scholarly examination, though many documents remain inaccessible, classified, or extremely difficult to use because of their chaotic condition. In growing numbers German and American historians have been burrowing into this mountain to trace the origins and course of American policy. In most areas, the results of this scholarly activity demonstrate that American policy was more often complex and serpentine than linear and straightforward.

The conference on which this book is based was conceived as a forum for presenting new historical scholarship on the period between 1949 and 1955 – in other words, between the founding of the Federal Republic and its regaining sovereignty and its entry into NATO. Most of the contributions were to focus on what is usually considered grand policy (*Grosse Politik*): defense issues and questions of West European integration in economic and political terms. Contributors were selected by the editors of this volume because they were actively engaged in research on this period. Undoubtedly some readers will feel that they should also have had the opportunity to present their work here. We could not include everyone, and we ask their understanding. Certain themes were chosen to give the conference coherence, but we made no attempt to be comprehensive. Many subject areas were necessarily left out. For example, the experiences of everyday life, where there were many contacts between Americans and Germans, were excluded because, rightly or wrongly, we felt that would take us too far from the larger issues in American policy. We did not include a section on denazification because, as far as the Americans were concerned, it no longer played a major role in their policy after 1949.

Once the invitations were issued, however, the conference took on a life of its own. Half of the contributors took their researches back at least to 1945, mainly because 1949 did not in fact prove to be a clear dividing line or starting point for the formulation of policy. American policy toward the Federal Republic grew out of the policies of wartime and occupation, and thus in certain areas the first postwar decade needs to be seen as a whole. Had we conceived of the conference as dealing with that entire first decade, we might have organized things somewhat differently and included other topics and other participants. Nevertheless, in our view the essays presented here make an important contribution to the understanding of that crucial decade of America's relations with her former enemy.

The contribution is weighty in another sense too. The twenty-three essays make up a very substantial volume. For that reason, and because we want readers to turn quickly to those essays, we decided against a long introduction that would attempt to summarize either the field in general or the essays here. This is not a book for complete beginners in postwar history, and we assume that most readers have some familiarity with the period. The essays are grouped thematically, but some overlap more than one category. The final two chapters, surveying relevant archival collections in West Germany and the United States, will be particularly useful to advanced students and scholars, who, we hope will find this book an aid in further research.

Finally, we wish to express our appreciation to the German Historical Institute in Washington, its director, Dr. Hartmut Lehmann, and its Academic Advisory Council for providing the financial support that made both the conference and the publication of the papers possible, and to Dr. Kenneth Ledford for his contribution to the editorial process. We also wish to thank Professor Dietrich Simon, president of the Philipps-University of Marburg, for providing the facilities for the conference, and Oliver Bauer, Anjana Buckow, Udo Muras, and Bernd Obermeier of the *Seminar für neuere Geschichte* for their help in preparing the conference.

The editors

Contributors

Rebecca Boehling: Ph.D. University of Wisconsin, Madison; Assistant Professor of History, University of Maryland, Baltimore County.

Christoph Buchheim: Ph.D. Munich University; Professor of Economic History, Mannheim University, Germany.

Werner Bührer: Ph.D. Hamburg University; Research Fellow, Institut für Zeitgeschichte, Munich, Germany.

Jeffry M. Diefendorf: Ph.D. University of California, Berkeley; Professor of History, University of New Hampshire, Durham.

Albert Diegmann: Ph.D. candidate, Department of History, Aachen University, Germany.

James M. Diehl: Ph.D. University of California, Berkeley; Professor of History, Indiana University, Bloomington.

Michael Fichter: Ph.D. Free University Berlin; Research Associate, Zentralinstitut für sozialwissenschaftliche Forschung der Freien Universität Berlin, Germany.

Axel Frohn: Ph.D. Cologne University; Senior Research Fellow, German Historical Institute, Washington, D.C.

John Gillingham: Ph.D. University of California, Berkeley; Professor of History, University of Missouri – St. Louis.

John Gimbel (deceased): Ph.D. University of Oregon; former Professor of History, Humboldt State University, Arcata, California.

Erich J. Hahn: Ph.D. Yale University; Associate Professor of History, University of Western Ontario, London, Ontario, Canada.

Josef Henke: Ph.D. Cologne University; Senior Archivist, *Bundesarchiv,* Koblenz, Germany.

Ulrich Kluge: Ph.D. Free University Berlin; Professor of History, Freiburg University, Germany.

David Clay Large: Ph.D. University of California, Berkeley; Associate Professor of History, Montana State University, Bozeman.

Gunther Mai: Ph.D. Marburg University; Professor of History, Marburg University, Germany.

Klaus A. Maier: Ph.D. Tübingen University; Lt. Col., Militärgeschichtliches Forschungsamt, Freiburg, Germany.

Diethelm Prowe: Ph.D. Stanford University; Professor of History, Carleton College, Northfield, Minnesota.

Hermann-Josef Rupieper: Ph.D. Stanford University; Professor of History, Marburg University, Germany.

Thomas Alan Schwartz: Ph.D. Harvard University; Assistant Professor of History, Vanderbilt University, Nashville, Tennessee.

Raymond G. Stokes: Ph.D. Ohio State University; Assistant Professor of History, Rensselaer Polytechnic Institute, Troy, New York.

James F. Tent: Ph.D. University of Wisconsin, Madison; Professor of History, University of Alabama at Birmingham.

Bruno Thoss: Ph.D.; Senior Research Fellow, Militärgeschichtliches Forschungsamt, Freiburg, Germany.

Michael Wala: Ph.D. Hamburg University; Assistant Professor of History, University of Erlangen-Nürnberg, Germany.

Robert Wolfe: Director, Captured German Records Staff, National Archives and Records Administration, Washington, D.C.

Abbreviations

a.D.	*ausser Dienst*
ABC	American/British conversations
ABC weapons	atomic, biological, chemical weapons
ACA	Allied Control Authority
ACC	Allied Control Council
AE	Aid to Europe (a Council on Foreign Relations study group)
AFL	American Federation of Labor
A.G.	*Aktiengesellschaft*
AGWAR	The Adjutant General, War Department
AHC	Allied High Commission
AIHK-Hess	Arbeitsgemeinschaft der hessischen Industrie- und Handelskammern
AKB	Allied Kommandatura for Berlin
AKEC	Allied Kommandatura's Education Committee
AN	Archives Nationales de France, Paris
Antifa	anti-Fascist committees or their members
AOFAA	Archives de l'Occupation Française en Allemagne et en Autriche, Colmar
API	American Petroleum Institute
AStA	Allgemeiner Studentenausschuss
BA	Bundesarchiv, Koblenz
BA/MA	Bundesarchiv, Militärarchiv, Freiburg
BASF	Badische Anilin- & Sodafabrik A.G.
Bd.	*Band*
BDC	Berlin Document Center
BDI	Bundesverband der Deutschen Industrie
BELF	Bundesministerium für Ernährung, Landwirtschaft und Forsten
BICO	Bipartite Control Office
BIOS	British Intelligence Objectives Subcommittee

BML	Bundesministerium für Landwirtschaft
BMW	Bayerische Motoren Werke
BuR	Bürgermeister und Rat
BVP	Bayerische Volkspartei
CCCG	Combined Coal Control Group
CCS	Combined Chiefs of Staff
CDU	Christlich-Demokratische Union
CEA	Commissariat à l'Energie Atomique
CEEC	Conference of European Economic Cooperation
CEN	*Chemical and Engineering News*
CENTAG	Central Army Group
CFM	Council of Foreign Ministers
CFR	Council on Foreign Relations
CG	Commanding General
CIC	Combined Intelligence Committee
CIO	Congress of Industrial Organizations
CIOS	Combined Intelligence Objectives Subcommittee
C/S	Chief of Staff
CSC	Coal and Steel Community
CSG	Combined Steel Group
CSU	Christlich-Soziale Union
DD	Digest of Discussion
DEF	Disarmed Enemy Forces
desp.	despatch
DGB	Deutscher Gewerkschaftsbund
DIHT	Deutscher Industrie- und Handelstag
DISCC	District Information Services Control Command
DKBL	Deutsche Kohlenbergbauleitung
DKV	Deutscher Kohlenverkauf
DM	Deutsche Mark
DP	Deutsche Partei
EAC	European Advisory Commission
EC	Erdölchemie GmbH
ECA	Economic Cooperation Administration
ECE	Economic Commission for Europe
ECSC	European Coal and Steel Community
EDC	European Defense Community
EL	Dwight D. Eisenhower Library, Abilene, Kansas
EPC	European Political Community
EPU	European Payments Union
ERP	European Recovery Program
ETO	European Theater of Operations
EUCOM	European Command

EVG	Europäische Verteidigungsgemeinschaft
FBI	Federal Bureau of Investigation
FDP	Freie Demokratische Partei
FEA	Foreign Economic Administration
FIAT	Field Information Agency, Technical
FO	Foreign Office
FRUS	*Foreign Relations of the United States*
FTUC	Free Trade Union Committee, AFL
FU	Freie Universität
FU-ZI SOWIFO	Freie Universität Berlin, Zentralinstitut für sozialwissenschaftliche Forschung
GARIOA	Government and Relief in Occupied Areas
GATT	General Agreement on Tariffs and Trade
GDR	German Democratic Republic
GEORG	Gemeinschaftsorganisation Ruhrkohle
GmbH	*Gesellschaft mit beschränkter Haftung*
HBS	Hans-Böckler-Stiftung
HICOG	U.S. High Commissioner for Germany
HSA FUB	Hochschularchiv der Freien Universität Berlin
HStA	Hauptstaatsarchiv
IAA	Inter-American Affairs (a Council on Foreign Relations study group)
IARA	Inter-Allied Reparations Agency
ICD	Information Control Division
IfZ	Institut für Zeitgeschichte
IHK	Industrie- und Handelskammer
INT/FIAT	Intelligence/Field Information Agency, Technical
ITT	International Telephone and Telegraph Company
JCS	Joint Chiefs of Staff
JEIA	Joint Export–Import Agency
JIC	Joint Intelligence Committee
JIOA	Joint Intelligence Objectives Agency
JM	Archives Jean Monnet pour l'Europe
KPD	Kommunistische Partei Deutschlands
LC	Library of Congress, Washington, D.C.
LDP	Liberal-Demokratische Partei
MdAE	Ministère des Affaires Etrangères
MG	Military Government
MGM	*Militärgeschichtliche Mitteilungen*
MGO	Military Government Officer [head of MG detachment]
MML	Seeley G. Mudd Manuscript Library, Princeton University, Princeton, New Jersey

MSA	Mutual Security Agency
NA	National Archives
NARA	National Archives and Records Administration
NATO	North Atlantic Treaty Organization
NBC weapons	nuclear, biological, chemical weapons
NGCC	North German Coal Control
NGCDO	North German Coal Distribution Office
NGISC	North German Iron and Steel Control
NL	*Nachlass*
NORTHAG	Northern Army Group
NRW	Nordrhein-Westfalen
NSC	National Security Council
NSDAP	Nationalsozialistische Deutsche Arbeiterpartei
OB	Oberbürgermeister
ODDI	Office of Deputy Director for Intelligence
OEEC	Organization for European Economic Cooperation
OLA	Office of Labor Affairs, HICOG
OMG	Office of Military Government
OMGUS	Office of Military Government for Germany (U.S.)
OPB	Office of the Publications Board
OSS	Office of Strategic Services
OTS	Office of Technical Services
PofG	The Problem of Germany (a Council on Foreign Relations study group)
POLAD	Political Advisor
POW	Prisoner of War
PPS	Policy Planning Staff, U.S. Department of State
PRO	Public Record Office, London
ret.	retired
RG	Record Group
RGCFR	Records of Groups, Council on Foreign Relations
RM	Reichsmark
ROW	Rheinische Olefinwerke
SAC	Strategic Air Command
SACEUR	Supreme Allied Commander, Europe
SecState	Secretary of State
SecWar	Secretary of War
SED	Sozialistische Einheitspartei Deutschlands
SEP	Surrendered Enemy Personnel
SFP	Soviet Foreign Policy (a Council on Foreign Relations study group)
SHAEF	Supreme Headquarters, Allied Expeditionary Forces
SHAPE	Supreme Headquarters, Allied Powers Europe

SPD	Sozialdemokratische Partei Deutschlands
St. A.	Studentische Arbeitsgemeinschaft zur Bekämpfung von Faschismus und Militarismus
StA	Stadtarchiv
STV	Stahltreuhändervereinigung
SWNCC	State–War–Navy Coordinating Committee
tel.	telegram
telecon.	teleconference
T-Forces	Technical Forces
TIIC	Technical Industrial Intelligence Committee
TIID	Technical Industrial Intelligence Division
TL	Harry S. Truman Library, Independence, Missouri
TWI	training-within-industry
UK/US CCG	United Kingdom/United States Coal Control Group
UNRRA	United Nations Relief and Rehabilitation Administration
USAREUR	United States Army, Europe
USFET	United States Forces European Theater
USGCC	United States Group, Control Council for Germany
USR	United States' Relations with Russia (a Council on Foreign Relations study group)
VELF	Verwaltungsrat für Ernährung, Landwirtschaft und Forsten
VfZG	*Vierteljahrshefte für Zeitgeschichte*
WAB-W	Stiftung Wirtschaftsarchiv Baden-Württemberg
WDSCA	War Department Staff, Civil Affairs
WEA	Western European Affairs (a Council on Foreign Relations study group)
WEU	Western European Union
WRK	Westdeutsche Rektorenkonferenz
WWA	Stiftung Westfälisches Wirtschaftsarchiv

American Policy and the Reconstruction of West Germany, 1945–1955

1

"Ripping Holes in the Iron Curtain": The Council on Foreign Relations and Germany, 1945–1950

MICHAEL WALA

Allied troops were still fighting in Europe when the Council on Foreign Relations (CFR) began to discuss and to study possibilities for economic and political rehabilitation of the liberated countries after the fighting ceased. The war in Europe was almost won – but in March 1945, peace remained a task of the future. Walter Mallory, executive director of the CFR, put it more bluntly a couple of months later: "As the struggle to make a just and lasting peace proceeds, it becomes clear that few problems have been finally resolved by the cessation of hostilities, and that peace will need to be worked out as diligently as war has been."[1]

Officers and members of the council were certain that they were to play a major part in this process. Together they represented a great wealth of experience, knowledge, and influence in domestic affairs and, even more, in foreign affairs. Authorities in banking and finance, experts on foreign policy, former politicians and government aides, clergymen, and professors, they believed in commitment to international organizations and in a strong and active American foreign policy. They were certain that the United States, in its capacity as the most powerful industrial and military nation, had no choice but to play a major role in the international arena.

---

1 CFR, *Report of the Executive Director, 1944–1945* (New York, n.d.), 9, marked "Confidential for Members." These annual reports can be found in the Council on Foreign Relations' Library, Harold Pratt House, New York. Publications on the Council include: Robert D. Schulzinger, *The Wise Men of Foreign Affairs: The History of the Council on Foreign Relations* (New York, 1984), a good overview of the council's history since 1921 but rather sketchy and unsubstantial on the beginning Cold War and the council's role in American society; Elisabeth Jakab, "The Council on Foreign Relations," *Book Forum* 3 (1976): 418–72, informative but of little analytical value; and Laurence H. Shoup and William Minter, *Imperial Brain Trust: The Council on Foreign Relations and United States Foreign Policy* (New York, 1977), with an emphasis on the World War II period. The most recent study is Michael Wala, *Winning the Peace: Amerikanische Aussenpolitik und der Council on Foreign Relations, 1945–1950* (Stuttgart, 1990).

Developments after World War I, they believed, left no trace of doubt that, as council member and World War II Secretary of War Henry L. Stimson phrased it in 1947 in the council's periodical *Foreign Affairs,* "The attitude of isolationism – political and economic – must die." Council members saw Germany as a possible European bridgehead in the imminent ideological war with the USSR and even as a potential future ally. Germany's drive for self-determination and unification, they thought, might break the "iron curtain" wide open.[2]

Composed today of some 2,500 carefully chosen members, the Council on Foreign Relations was founded in 1921 through the merger of an "old" council (created in 1918 in New York City by a group of businessmen) and the American Institute of International Affairs. The latter organization was established in Paris in 1919 by members of the American delegation to the Paris Peace Conference as a counterpart of what today is known as the Royal Institute for International Affairs in London.[3]

Since the 1950s critics from both political right and left have attacked the council fiercely; in some cases with outrageous accusations. In *Rockefeller "Internationalist,"* Emmanuel M. Josephson even speculated about the existence of secret pathways beneath Sixty-eighth Street connecting the council's headquarters with the Soviet consulate, tunnels where council members were alleged to meet with Soviet agents to receive directives from the Kremlin and bags full of gold.[4]

Despite the critics' claims, the council as an organization never advocated specific policies and did not devise new approaches to American foreign policy during the beginning Cold War. There is no evidence that council members ever pressured the administration into a foreign policy measure that ran counter to State Department

2 Henry L. Stimson, "The Challenge to Americans," *Foreign Affairs* 26 (Oct. 1947):6.
3 M. L. Dockrill, "Historical Note: The Foreign Office and the 'Proposed Institute of International Affairs 1919,' " *International Affairs* 56 (1980):665–72; Whitney H. Shepardson, *Early History of the Council on Foreign Relations* (Stamford, Conn., 1960), 1–8; Hamilton Fish Armstrong, *Peace and Counterpeace: From Wilson to Hitler* (New York, 1971).
4 Emmanuel M. Josephson, *Rockefeller "Internationalist": The Man Who Misrules the World* (New York, 1952), 4. The council came to the attention of the broader public only in 1971, when a number of newspaper articles appeared in the wake of the unpopular decision to make William P. Bundy successor to Hamilton Fish Armstrong as editor of *Foreign Affairs;* Carl Gershman, "The Rise and Fall of the New Foreign Policy Establishment," *Commentary* 70 (Aug. 1951):13–24; J. Anthony Lukas, "The Council on Foreign Relations – Is It a Club? Seminar? Presidium? 'Invisible Government'?" *New York Times Magazine,* Nov. 21, 1971, pp. 43, 123–32, 142.

officials' ideas. The council did, however, consider and examine anticipated or conceivable policies in order to explore the possibility of reaching a consensus.[5]

The council's weekly discussion and study group meetings, its less frequent dinner meetings, and a few full-membership meetings at the Harold Pratt House in New York City were often used as forums to discuss policy. Speakers could transmit their ideas to an interested public, advocate their causes, and further the development of public opinion. Council members received information and could in turn convey their impressions through manifold channels of communication.

In addition, the council served as recruiting ground for the State Department and other government agencies. Between 1945 and 1950, council members increasingly secured appointment to high executive posts, at the assistant secretary level and above, and participated in committees such as the President's Committee on Foreign Aid or the House Select Committee on Foreign Aid during the deliberations prior to the Marshall Plan.[6]

The council provided an abundant supply of long-range concepts that could be developed by those who did not face the pressure of daily chores of State Department officials. These ideas "floated around" and could be employed to act more speedily and effectively.[7] These recommendations were not particularly original or altogether different from already existing policies: Council members and State Department officials to a large degree shared a common weltanschauung and structure of thought after World War II.

5 Individual members, nevertheless, quite often participated in ad hoc committees supposedly founded to vocalize public sentiment or to induce the administration to initiate a certain policy. For some of these committees that were external propaganda agencies of the State Department rather than just voluntary organizations of concerned citizens, see Michael Wala, "Selling War and Selling Peace," *Amerikastudien/American Studies* 30 (1985):91–105; Walter Johnson, *The Battle against Isolation* (New York, 1944); Michael Wala, "Selling the Marshall Plan at Home: The Committee for the Marshall Plan to Aid European Recovery," *Diplomatic History* 10 (Summer 1986):247–65.

6 Of the upper echelons (assistant secretary level and above) of the State Department and related agencies in the Truman administration 42 percent were council members. In the Eisenhower years, this number declined to 40 percent; it increased to 51 percent under Kennedy and 57 percent under Johnson; William M. Minter, "The Council on Foreign Relations: A Case Study in the Societal Bases of Foreign Policy Formulation," Ph.D. diss., University of Wisconsin – Madison, 1973, p. 122. "Whenever we needed a man," recalled John J. McCloy, high commissioner for Germany, somewhat exaggeratedly, "we thumbed through the roll of council members and put through a call to New York"; cited in Joseph Kraft, "School for Statesmen," *Harper's Magazine* (July 1958):67.

7 Willard L. Thorp, assistant secretary of state for economic affairs, 1946–52, recalled this for the situation in the State Department generally; Thorp Oral History Interview, p. 32, TL.

Officers of the council tried to draw into the CFR's membership experts not only from business and academia. Journalists, editors, and clergymen were regarded as equally vital for a foreign policy supported by all elites. The relationship between organized labor and council officers remained ambivalent. In May 1946, the board of directors of the CFR decided that the added importance of labor after World War II warranted the inclusion of more labor officials in the council membership. But merely a few carefully chosen and trustworthy, that is, conservative, union leaders were asked to join. Just two, Solomon Barkin of the Textile Workers' Union of America and the CIO's Michael Ross accepted the council's invitation, and four years later, David Dubinsky of the International Ladies Garment Workers Union was the sole union member still among the members.[8]

It would thus be easy to conclude that businessmen utilized politicians, labor officials, and their peers at the council to advance their personal economic interests. The sources show, however, that these business leaders were first and foremost internationalists and not preeminently interested in short-term profits. They regarded the American decision not to join the League of Nations as a grave error, an error that had made possible the developments of the 1930s and World War II. They placed their hopes in the newly-founded United Nations to provide a stable system of defined and enforceable rules. The stability of such a system would further international trade, and all countries would benefit. The United States, they demanded, should play a major role in world politics, a role that would pay tribute to the military, economic, and moral strength of the nation.

From the council's founding until the end of World War II, the organization developed from an elitist men's club to a renowned forum for high-level discussions of experts on international affairs. During World War II, the council worked closely with the State Department. Only a few days after Germany attacked Poland, Council

8 "Suggested Labor Members for the Council on Foreign Relations," May 17, 1946, encl., Mallory to John W. Davis, June 25, 1946, and Davis to Mallory, July 8, 1946, John W. Davis Papers, box 133, Sterling Library, Yale University, New Haven, Conn. Female membership, by the way, was not considered until 1970. Even then, some honorable council members complained that accepting women would make it hard for them "to keep their own wives from joining" and that meetings until very late at night could now generate jealousy; Lukas, "The Council on Foreign Relations," 130; John Franklin Campbell, "The Death Rattle of the Eastern Establishment," *New York*, Sept. 20, 1971, p. 48; William Diebold, Jr., interview, Century Club, New York, Sept. 20, 1988.

members offered the Department help in developing war and peace aims. War and Peace Studies was set up, resulting in more than 600 memoranda for the State Department. During this period, the Council grew into the role of respected adviser and listening post.[9] But these special projects only supplemented the regular concern of the council. Thus, in March 1945, the council continued a system of study groups on the European situation begun in the 1920s.[10]

Allen W. Dulles, better known today for his services as director of the Central Intelligence Agency under presidents Eisenhower and Kennedy, headed such a study group titled Western European Affairs. He had been an expert on Germany since his service with the American legation in Bern in 1917. In World War II, he again was in Bern, this time as head of the Office of Strategic Services (OSS) station and responsible for Operation Sunrise, the surrender of German forces in Italy under SS-General Karl Wolff.[11]

After Nazi Germany's unconditional surrender, Dulles headed the OSS in Germany. His task was to help implement American denazification policy. Here he was hindered in his pursuits and falsely accused of being pro-Nazi and anti-Semitic in a propaganda campaign launched by his Soviet colleagues. Americans could hardly move freely in the Soviet occupational zone, but they nevertheless discovered that many moderate German socialists returning to their homes disappeared – possibly dead or sent to Siberia. "An iron curtain has descended over the fate of these people," Dulles said in the first study group meeting in early December 1945 about the situation of Germans in the Soviet zone, "and likely conditions are truly terrible."[12]

Earlier than many of their colleagues and peers in the United States, Dulles and his friends at the council reached the conclusion that Germany was at the focal point of a number of important

9 Shoup and Minter, *Imperial Brain Trust*. Official accounts are CFR, *The War and Peace Studies of the Council on Foreign Relations* (New York, 1946); U.S. Department of State, ed., *Postwar Foreign Policy Preparations, 1939–1945* (Washington, D.C., 1949).
10 Percy W. Bidwell to Carl W. Ackerman (Dean of Columbia University), March 22, 1945, study group on The Economic and Political Reconstruction of Liberated Areas in Europe (ERP), Records of Groups, vol. XVIB, CFR Archives, Harold Pratt House [hereafter: RGCFR with the appropriate volume number].
11 "Memorandum for the Secretary," March 13, 1945, Charles E. Bohlen Papers, box 4, LC.
12 Digest of Discussion (DD), Dec. 3, 1945, p. 4, study group on Western European Affairs (WEA), RGCFR-XVIIIE; Dulles's subject was "The Present Situation in Germany." Better known for use of the "iron curtain" metaphor is certainly Winston Churchill, who used it a few months later in his famous speech in Fulton, Missouri, on March 5, 1946.

decisions determining the future political, strategic, and economic situation of Europe – if not the world. Germany was vitally important for European economic restoration, and it was the site at which the future predominance of the Soviet or of the American economic and political system in Europe would be decided. Dulles was certain that clashes between the USSR and the United States were almost inevitable, and only "insulating the two systems" promised a chance for lasting peace.[13] European infrastructure – roads, waterways, railroads – had to a large part been destroyed by the war. Staple foods could be transported to areas of need only with great difficulty, and some council members doubted that the military was the best choice to organize and structure the economic recovery of Europe.

The exceptionally large membership of the Western European Affairs study group – nearly one hundred, rather than the more typical twenty – drawn from all quarters of the council's elite membership, demonstrated the council's tremendous interest in this topic. It also reveals the strategy Dulles and his council friends used: As was common practice, all group members received digests of the proceedings; even if only a fraction of the members attended, this assured that the important information, the message Dulles and his friends wanted to get across, reached all one hundred group members and could be disseminated further. Dulles used the study group to spread the conviction that economic reconstruction of Germany was imperative, and that only the degree of rehabilitation was up for debate. Germany undoubtedly had to be prevented from ever being able again to attack her neighbors. But she also had to be put back to work to help the rehabilitation of the European economy as a whole.[14]

The Joint Chiefs of Staff directive 1067 (JCS 1067) – issued to General Eisenhower in early 1945 and providing for firm demilitarization and denazification – Dulles told the group members at their first meeting, hampered adequate improvement of the German economy. Dulles was by no means a "friend of Germany"; he detested Nazism fervently and was, like most of his peers at the council, an Anglophile. He simply wanted to put Germany back to work "for the benefit of Europe and particularly for the benefit of those

13 "Memorandum for J. F. D. [John Foster Dulles]," May 14, 1946, John Foster Dulles Papers, box 28, Mudd Manuscript Library, Princeton University, Princeton, N.J.
14 Only for the meeting on May 28, 1948, when twenty-five members attended, were the names of the members present recorded.

countries plundered by the Nazis. . . . Europe as a whole," he argued, "cannot get back to anything like normal conditions, not to speak of any prosperity, with a completely disorganized Germany."[15]

Many council members agreed with Dulles's assessment that stern deindustrialization as a security measure against Germany was a flawed concept. DeWitt C. Poole, a member of the staff of the American embassy in Moscow during the Russian Revolution and until recently involved in the interrogation of German politicians, argued that it was time to free Germany from "indiscriminate de-Nazification + unrelenting de-industrialization." And Chicago lawyer Laird Bell, who had been deputy director of the Economic Division of the U.S. Office of Military Government for Germany (OMGUS), maintained that JCS 1067, as the guideline for occupation policy in Germany, was ill advised and based on political presumptions long surpassed by events.[16]

Nevertheless, Bell maintained, "Our essential objective in Germany is to prevent the Germans from plunging the world into another war. We could have done this by killing off the sixty-five or seventy million Germans still left, a course we fortunately have no intention of adopting." Another possibility, he had learned from his talks in Washington, was to "police the Germans more or less indefinitely." Both prospects were unfeasible, and crushing Germany would only induce bitterness, resentment, and revenge – feelings that might lead to merely another war, thus achieving just the opposite of the effect intended.[17]

Among Americans, in the general public as well as among the interested and attentive public, the attitude toward Germany, Bell believed, was still guided mainly by "war hysteria with vengeance as its principal ingredient." Something had to be done to change this perspective to allow for modification of U.S. policy. Thus, after

15 DD, Dec. 3, 1945, p. 5, WEA/RGCFR-XVIIIE; manuscript, "Talk at CFR, 113/45," Allen W. Dulles Paper, box 21, MML. As early as October 1944, Thomas W. Lamont, internationalist chairman of the board of J. P. Morgan & Co., had argued similarly against the deindustrialization of Germany. His friend and colleague at J. P. Morgan, Russell C. Leffingwell, a member of the study group on Western European Affairs, had disagreed at that time. He wanted Germany "defeated and crushed to lick her wounds" and rather to foster "our entente and alliance with Great Britain and Russia"; Lamont to Leffingwell, Oct. 9, 1944, and Leffingwell to Lamont, Oct. 25, 1944, Lamont Papers, box 104, Baker Library, Harvard University, Cambridge, Mass.
16 Poole to Dulles, Feb. 8, 1946, Allen Dulles Papers, box 21, MML. Bell claimed to fight a "one man crusade against [directive JCS] 1067"; Bell to Dulles, Jan. 28, 1946, Allen Dulles Papers, box 23, MML.
17 DD, Feb. 6, 1946, pp. 1–5, WEA/RGCFR-XVIIE.

the study group's meeting on February 6, 1946, Bell, Dulles, and a few other members got together to "see whether there was anything we could do to help get the right slant to public opinion on Germany."[18]

Through the good offices of Dean G. Acheson, then under secretary of state, Bell also met with State Department officials James Riddleberger, Charles P. Kindleberger, and John Kenneth Galbraith.[19] JCS 1067 was not very helpful, all agreed, and the State Department wanted to implement changes. Officials feared, however, that to do so openly would arouse the "residual power of the Morgenthau group" within the administration. The State Department was uncertain about its future policy toward the Soviet Union and Germany, but it wanted to avoid unnecessary tension. Riddleberger indicated that the department's political advisors agreed with him on the necessity of change in the deindustrialization policy and that the "youngsters on the economic side" would do what they were ordered to do, leaving only the president and Secretary of State Byrnes to be won over.[20]

A group discussion on May 28, 1946, was considered what almost amounted to a nucleus of future American policy in Europe. European reconstruction, it was maintained, was important to the fabric of international economic ties and for the well-being of the United States. A speedy and effective restoration of the European economies depended on German economic rehabilitation, which in turn was achievable only if Germany could be treated as an economic unit. Russia, however, would not permit the unification of Germany. The division of Germany was a fact, members stated, and a Western European federation, including the three western zones of Germany, should be established. Asked if this would not violate the Potsdam Agreement, the council members were informed by Dulles that if unification of Germany was offered "to Russia and she turned it down, then Russia and not the United States would be in the position of rejecting the Potsdam formula." He suggested to "offer the

---

18 Dulles to Bell, Jan. 3, 1946, and Bell to Dulles, Feb. 9, 1946, Allen Dulles Papers, box 23, MML.
19 Riddleberger was chief of the Division of Central European Affairs; Kindleberger chief of the Division of German and Austrian Economic Affairs; and Galbraith was director of Economic Security Policy.
20 Riddleberger to Poole, Feb. 5, 1946, Hamilton F. Armstrong Papers, box 40, MML; Poole to Dulles, Feb. 8, 1946, Allen Dulles Papers, box 21, MML.

Soviets a feasible plan," but in case they did not accept it, "work out a constructive policy for western Germany" and "cooperation between the three western zones of Germany."[21]

Well before the United States in July 1946 offered economic unification with any other zone, the council members advocated unification of the three Western occupation zones of Germany. And long before Secretary of State Byrnes's well-known speech in Stuttgart in September 1946, the Council called for the revitalization of German industry. The future treatment of Germany, council members knew quite well, was the major issue in the beginning of the Cold War and forced decisions upon the American government that would necessarily lead to discord with the Soviet Union.

In the fall of 1946, the council's focus upon Germany rose considerably. Two study groups were founded for the years 1946–47. Under the leadership of Charles M. Spofford, former member of the Allied Military Government in Italy, a group addressed the topic Reconstruction of Western Europe and Allen Dulles continued his work in the study group The Problem of Germany.

At the same time the council, aided by the Department of State, conducted an opinion poll among members of its local chapters, the Committees on Foreign Relations.[22] Most respondents believed that a unified and prosperous Germany would not be a threat to future peace, provided "demilitarization takes place and . . . the German people establish and support democratic institutions." Germany should be encouraged to participate in international trade, and American policy should assist development of German industry to that end. But the poll also revealed that revival of the German economy should not take precedence over denazification. One respondent cautioned that "anyone who entertains the idea, twenty-one months after the surrender, that the German people have become sufficiently denazified, is sadly deluded." Similarly emphatic were the arguments against thorough denazification at the expense of the revival of the German industry. One member was ahead of his time when he

---

21 DD, March 28, 1946, pp. 3–4, WEA/RGCFR-XVIIIE.
22 The council had started in 1938 to organize these local chapters throughout the United States. In 1946, twenty-two committees with about 1,000 members had been set up. Joseph Barber, responsible for the poll, had written to Francis H. Russell of the State Department for help in drafting the questionnaires. He was put in contact with Shepard S. Jones, acting chief of Division of Public Studies; Barber to Russell, Nov. 27, 1946, and Russell to Barber, Dec. 12, 1946, NA, RG 59, 811.43, Council on Foreign Relations/11-2746.

argued, "We are no longer fighting nazism; we are fighting communism and [a more lenient denazification policy] is the only way to
combat that." Council staff members summarized the poll's findings
thusly: "Denazification and the revival of the German economy are
[regarded as] equally essential."[23]

The council considered these findings important enough to war-
rant publication and general distribution. Just in time for the Moscow Conference in March 1947, advance copies of the report titled
American Policy toward Germany were directed to the State Department and to OMGUS officials in Germany. "Copies were available
at the Moscow Conference and were found to be helpful, according
to individuals who were present," claimed the Council's *Annual Report* for 1946–47 proudly.[24]

During the winter of 1947, the economic situation in Europe
worsened much more than had been anticipated. Severe weather
conditions hampered rehabilitation, coal mining broke down almost
completely, and supply of food, especially in Germany, was cata-
strophically low. People froze and starved to death. Many council
members agreed that reconstruction without American help was impossible. Only the kind of help and its allocation was still debatable.
Questions such as "What are the causes of the slow progress . . . toward political stability and better business conditions? What American policies can help most?" and "How can these policies be framed
so as to safeguard and advance the interest of the United States?"
show this concern clearly. These questions also revealed, however,
the council's inclination to give special attention to advantages and
concerns of the United States.[25]

In this situation, Dulles's group had a special task. During the
summer of 1946, the newly founded Nederlandsch Genootschap
voor Internationale Zaken had invited the council to participate in a
conference of preeminent foreign affairs institutes in Europe on the
topic of postwar Germany to be held at Baarn in early October 1947.
Percy Bidwell, director of studies of the CFR, was to represent the

23 Of the respondents, 44 percent considered it pivotal "to make sure of thorough denazification, perhaps at the expense of delaying the revival of the German economy," whereas 45
percent deemed it more critical "to pursue a more lenient policy in the belief that the defeat
of Germany has so discredited Nazism that its reconstitution is no longer an appreciable
danger"; 10 percent were uncertain and only 1 percent had no answer; Joseph Barber, ed.,
American Policy toward Germany (New York, 1947), 4–5, 15.
24 CFR, *Annual Report of the Executive Director, 1946–1947* (New York, 1947), 52.
25 Ibid., 15.

council, and the Committee on Studies wanted to give him thoroughly researched background information for his preparations.[26]

In its effort to gather data on the economic situation of Germany, the group swiftly addressed the question of supply of food. Kenneth Galbraith told his captive audience that the infrastructure was no longer the chief problem and that the main cause of the slow process of rehabilitation was now, aside from the shortage of money, the lack of food. Galbraith had argued already in fall of 1946 that credits to Europe could be a main foreign policy instrument. At the core of this policy, he had mentioned, was the reconstruction of German industry in the interest of Europe as a whole. Coal production in the Ruhr, he wrote, was a major bottleneck.[27]

"It will require imports of food, and several years of credit, to prime the pump with raw materials and some machinery" to revitalize German industry, economist Karl Brand of Stanford University's Food Research Institute wrote to Shepard Morgan after the group's meeting on November 12, 1946. "Recovery in Denmark, Holland, France and Switzerland particularly is impeded and delayed so long as the cadaver of Germany sends its stench of decay into all these countries."[28]

Others advanced arguments for a thorough reindustrialization and debated whether the eastern parts of Germany now under Soviet or Polish jurisdiction should be reunited with the rest of the nation. John J. McCloy, assistant to Henry Stimson during the war and a member of the group since autumn 1946, argued that to render Germany incapable of aggression in the eyes of Europe, it would be necessary to "restore Germany but prevent her from becoming dominant economically in Europe." Theologian Reinhold Niebuhr added that "a viable economy in Germany would do more to eliminate communism than anything else." When reunification of Germany again became a topic of discussion, DeWitt Poole maintained that there was no prospect of cooperation with the Soviet Union in this respect. "Germany had been unified only since 1870," he

---

26 Financing of the group work and the travel of two council representatives to Europe was provided by the Rockefeller Foundation. The conference was sponsored with $25,000 of the foundation's money. RFE to Willits and ME, March 4, 1947; "Inter-Office Correspondence," March 5, 1947; 1/100/97/889; and RA SS 4725, Apr. 25, 1947, 1/100/98/889; all, Rockefeller Archives Center, North Tarrytown, N.Y.
27 John K. Galbraith, "Recovery in Europe," *Planning Pamphlets* 53 (Nov. 1946): 28, 30–5.
28 Brandt to Shepard Morgan, Nov. 22, 1946, study group on The Problem of Germany (PofG), RGCFR-XXIC.

argued, and "United States' policy should favor the partition of Germany . . . the public should be weaned away from the idea of the necessity of unification."[29]

But the group's work soon expanded beyond the exclusive task of providing background material for the conference at Baarn. Rapporteurs Carl E. Schorske and Hoyt Price had been assigned to write an informative account of the basic facts and principles of American policy toward Germany for general circulation in the United States as well as a policy statement for the State Department.[30] Percy Bidwell considered neither Schorske nor Price competent to write such a sensitive document. Several drafts were discussed and rejected before group members agreed to use Allen Dulles's introduction for the meeting on January 10 as a basis for the group's statement for the Department.[31]

Dulles had outlined the danger of domination of Western Europe by the Soviet Union if Germany became a satellite state of the USSR. "Germany belongs predominantly to the culture of the West and not to the area of Slav civilization," he maintained. Fear of disturbing the uneasy balance in the relations between the Soviet Union and the Western Allies had delayed settlement of the main issues until rapid deterioration of the situation in Europe threatened. It would be essential, Dulles emphasized, that at the forthcoming conference of foreign ministers in Moscow, "a beginning be made toward measures of reconstruction and toward tracing out a program for the future." A disarmed and neutralized Germany should be established, which "although a part of western Europe, would not be a legitimate cause of apprehension to Russia."[32]

Group members discussed Dulles's manuscript and made a few suggestions and changes to sharpen the statement, which, as one

29 DD, Dec. 11, 1946, PofG/RGCFR-XXIC, pp. 4–6.
30 DD, Jan. 10, 1948, PofG/RGCFR-XXIC, p. 1. Economist Price had worked with Robert Murphy, political advisor to Lucius D. Clay; Schorske had been chief of the Central European Section of the OSS. Their account was published in Hoyt Price and Carl E. Schorske, *The Problem of Germany* (New York, 1947). An advance copy reached George F. Kennan at the State Department, and he advised the Research and Analysis Department to urgently prepare a summary; documents and correspondence in NA, RG 59, 862.00/9-2547.
31 Bidwell to Dulles, Dc. 12, 1946, PofG/RGCFR-XXIC; DD, Jan. 10, 1947, PofG/RGCFR-XXIC, p. 1.
32 Dulles, "United States Policy with Respect to Germany: I. Introductory Statement," Jan. 10, 1946 [sic, 1947]; DD, Jan. 10, 1947; and DD, Jan. 29, 1947; all, PofG/RGCFR-XXIC. Dulles's "Introductory Statement" served as basis for his article "Alternatives for Germany," in *Foreign Affairs* 25 (April 1947), see note on p. 421.

council member believed, "would have a good chance of being read top-side in the State Department as an exposition by a representative and highly informed group." Time was running out, and group members were pressed to submit their comments by February 28, to assure that "the final draft [is] in the hands of the Secretary of State shortly after the first of March, at the latest."[33]

When Secretary of State George C. Marshall returned from Moscow, he was disappointed by the conference's outcome and launched a new U.S. policy, a policy that would implement all requirements the council members thought necessary. The principles of the American economic aid program, proposed by Marshall at Harvard University on June 5, 1947, were very well received by the council membership. Again, the council polled the local chapters, and 95 percent of all respondents agreed with the secretary of state that the United States should undertake a long-term aid program. The committee members did not, however, accept at face value his statement that this "policy is directed not against any country or doctrine." They were certain that "American policy is, and should be, directed against communism."[34]

Members of the committees considered the revival of the European economy and success of the Marshall Plan of such importance to the well-being of the nation that they were even "willing to put up with necessary consumer and production control" in the United States. They rejected Marshall's cautious statement that the role of the United States should only "consist of friendly aid in drafting of a European Program and of later support . . . by financial and other means." The United States should avoid controls that recipient countries might interpret as unwarranted intervention in internal affairs, but since the United States provided the aid, it would be "entitled to adequate guarantees of its proper use." Use of the scientific knowledge and skills of the Germans, as well as the inclusion of Germany in the Marshall Plan, was regarded as of prime importance to European recovery.[35]

Percy Bidwell was surprised at the lack of serious disagreement about including Germany in the Marshall Plan. The same lack of

33 Poole to Bidwell, Feb. 4, 1947, and Price to members, Feb. 24, 1947, PofG/RGCFR-XXIB.
34 Joseph Barber, ed., *The Marshall Plan as American Policy: A Report on the Views of Community Leaders in 21 Cities* (New York, 1948), 4–5.
35 Ibid., 5.

opposition was to be found among the European nations. The only explanation he could think of was that these nations hoped to obtain assurance of receiving a certain share of the goods Germany produced. Some group members considered the question of future control of the Ruhr area more urgent than German participation. During the war, American and international policy had tended to favor internationalization of the Ruhr as a precautionary measure of control over Germany's war potential.[36]

Now, in early 1948, with German and, more broadly, European recovery depending on coal production in this area, the Ruhr had become an issue of discord among the Allies. The Foreign Ministers' Conference in late 1947 had revealed definitively that no unified Allied program for Germany could be expected. The Soviet Union was asking for participation in the control of the Ruhr, and the United States feared that a possible Soviet-inspired revolt in this region would immensely impede German and European reconstruction. Council members discussed different measures of internationalization, decartelization, decentralization, socialization, and control. Eminent historian George N. Shuster caught the gist of the discussion when he opted for the Ruhr to be closely linked politically and economically to the three Western zones. If Communists tried to gain control, the area could easily be cut off from the rest of Germany to ensure that the industrial potential would not be used against the democratic nations. To assure economic rehabilitation, "the Ruhr should be granted priority to the fullest extent possible." Nevertheless, Reinhold Niebuhr wondered "whether the issue [of controlling the Ruhr area] was a real one." To him, it seemed that "the dividing line between Russia and the United States runs right down the middle of German[y]." As long as that was true, he maintained, the United States would likely remain in Germany, and there would be "no need for a special regime to keep the Ruhr out of Russian hands."[37]

DeWitt Poole, who had already in December 1946 insisted that there was no way to prevent the division of Germany, again outlined a hard-nosed course for the future. The development of the last couple of years and policies that the Marshall Plan would soon put into

36 DD, Feb. 11, 1948, p. 4, PofG/RGCFR-XXVA.
37 DD, Feb. 11, 1948, pp. 4–5; PofG/RGCFR-XXVA. Shuster to Bidwell, Feb. 24, 1948, and Sherman to Bidwell, Feb. 16, 1948, PofG/RGCFR-XXVA. Shuster at the time taught at Hunter College, New York City.

effect, would certainly advance the division of Germany. Both of her parts were already isolated from each other more drastically than Germany and France had been before the war. The cohesion of the German people, he claimed, would nourish a political force "to bridge the Elbe . . . Fine! Some day that force will be ripping holes in the Iron Curtain. Given a West European confederation of the kind suggested [by the American government], later adherence by trans-Elbian components will be highly desirable."[38]

The European Recovery Program (ERP), the members of the Council study group were certain, would foster German and European economic rehabilitation, preserve democratic institutions in France, Italy, and Great Britain, and assure that Western Europe would not fall prey to communism and the Soviet Union. The Marshall Plan, Allen Dulles wrote in an unpublished manuscript in January 1948, "is not a philanthropic enterprise. . . . It is based on our views of the requirements of American security . . . this is the only peaceful avenue now open to us which may answer the Communist challenge to our way of life and our national security."[39]

Discussions among council members in these study groups clearly show that whatever spirit of cooperation with the Soviet Union may have existed among its elite membership was displaced by an inclination toward conflict. Old anxieties, covered only slightly by the common fight against Nazi Germany, surfaced again. In March 1945, a council member had still believed that "Russia is moving toward democracy and may intend to take her place among the great trading nations of the world." Only a year later, another member of the same discussion group claimed that "THE 3RD WORLD WAR – the war between the U.S.S.R and Western Christendom – IS ALREADY VIGOROUSLY BEING WAGED AGAINST US!"[40]

It was no wonder then that George F. Kennan's suggestions about containing Soviet expansion were readily accepted among council members. He had been invited to address the study group Soviet Foreign Policy and developed ideas he had expressed already in his "long telegram" from Moscow. Kennan's discourse titled "The

---

38 Poole to Diebold, March 2, 1948, PofG/RGCFR-XXVA.
39 Manuscript, "Book on Marshall Plan, draft, Chapter VIII," p. 1, Jan. 6, 1948, Allen Dulles Papers, box 36, MML.
40 DD, March 21, 1945, study group United States' Relations with Russia (USR), USR/ RGCFR-XVID; Switz to Schubart, June 13, 1946, USR/RGCFR-XVIIA.

Soviet Way of Thought and Its Effect on Foreign Policy" intrigued
council members so much that they asked Hamilton F. Armstrong,
editor of *Foreign Affairs,* to approach Kennan for a contribution to the
periodical. Kennan took some time to get around to an answer, and
more weeks elapsed to clear State Department red tape before his
treatise appeared anonymously as "Sources of Soviet Conduct" in
the July 1947 issue of *Foreign Affairs.* His essay brought relief to a
puzzled public: The trend of American foreign policy toward a more
aggressive stance with the USSR was now based on intellectual analysis; the uncertainties of past attitudes toward the USSR could finally be cast aside.[41]

Meanwhile Robert M. Lovett, designated successor to Dean
Acheson as under secretary of state, had established contacts with the
council. He asked Walter Mallory to assemble a group of council
members to brief him on possible foreign policy strategies. The
council could hardly decline such an opportunity to prove its excellence as research institution and community of experts whose advice
was in high regard at the Department of State.[42]

When the meeting took place on May 12, 1947, the council members told Lovett that the political interests of the United States had
become global. The main objective of U.S. foreign policy was to
prevent the USSR from extending her influence to all of Europe.
Grayson Kirk summarized the United States' political responsibilities: to give priority to Germany, to secure Western influence in
Greece and Turkey, and to safeguard China against "Sovietization."

41 DD, Jan. 7, 1947, p. 1, study group Soviet Foreign Policy (SFP), SFP/RGCFR-XXIIC.
   Armstrong to Kennan, Jan. 10, 1947, George F. Kennan Papers, box 28, MML; Kennan to
   Armstrong, Feb. 4, 1947, Armstrong Papers, box 33; MML; Kennan to Michael Wala, Oct.
   24, 1986, in my possession. Kennan to John T. Connor (special assistant to Secretary Forrestal), March 10, 1947; Marx Leva (successor to Connor) to Kennan, Mar. 12, 1947; Kennan to E. Eilder Spaulding (chairman, Committee of Unofficial Publications, State
   Department) March 13, 1974; and Spaulding to Kennan, Apr. 8, 1947; all, Kennan Papers,
   box 28, MML. Galley proofs Armstrong sent to Kennan on May 15, 1947, to offer, at the
   same time, his participation in the "projected planning committee," Armstrong to Kennan, May 15, 1947, Kennan Papers, Box 28, MML. Armstrong was too late: the Policy
   Planning Staff had already been officially set up on May 5, 1947 [*FRUS 1947,* vol. 3, *The
   British Commonwealth; Europe* (Washington, D.C., 1972), 220; *Department of State Bulletin* 16
   (1947):1007].
42 DD, May 12, 1947, pp. 1–2, Records of Meetings, vol. XXII, CFR Archives; Kraft,
   "School for Statesmen," 68. Members attending this dinner meeting were Hamilton F.
   Armstrong; Hanson W. Baldwin, military editor of the *New York Times;* Percy Bidwell;
   Grayson Kirk, Professor of Government at Columbia University; James Grafton Rogers,
   former assistant secretary of state and now with Foreign Bondholders' Protective Council;
   and Joseph H. Willits of the Rockefeller Foundation.

"I came away from the session," Lovett later recalled, "with the firm conviction that it would be our principal task at State to awaken the nation to the dangers of Communist aggression."[43]

Future President Dwight D. Eisenhower led another study group to research political and military implications of the Marshall Plan. The general, although busy as president of Columbia University, missed only one of the twenty meetings of the study group. "Whatever General Eisenhower knows about economics," one member of the Aid to Europe group later claimed, "he has learned at the study group meetings." The Rockefeller Foundation, sponsor of the council's meeting and research program, went even further to suggest that the study group had "served as a sort of education in foreign affairs for the future President of the United States."[44]

The group had been founded when Frank A. Lindsay, assistant to Administrator Paul G. Hoffman of the Economic Cooperation Administration (ECA), asked his friends at the council to conduct a large-scale research program for the European Recovery Program in March 1948. Lindsay did not believe the administration would conduct such a program itself and counted on Allen Dulles to help the ECA to develop long-range plans.[45] Theodore Geiger of ECA was contacted and discussed the plans with Richard M. Bissell, Jr., assistant deputy administrator of ECA, and with Lincoln Gordon, head of the ECA-internal study department. All three, proclaiming "keen interest," liked the concept of a council investigation, and Hoffman wrote Dulles in mid-June in support of the idea.[46] Summer intervened, however, and it took almost half a year before the group actually was set up.

Meanwhile, the Communist coup in Czechoslovakia in February, the Vandenberg Resolution in June 1948, and the beginnings of consultations about the envisioned North Atlantic Treaty Organization had shifted the attention away from economic issues. With General Eisenhower as chairman of the group, the discussion very rapidly

---

43 Lovett to Mallory (copy), March 23, 1947, encl., Mallory to Willits, May 26, 1947, Rockefeller Foundation Records, 1/100/97/879; Kraft, "School for Statesmen," 68.

44 Kraft, "School for Statesmen," 64–8; "Excerpts from Trustees' Confidential Monthly Report," Jan. 1, 1953, pp. 39–40, Rockefeller Foundation Records, 1.2/57/440.

45 Lindsay to Dulles, May 1, 1948, Allen Dulles Papers, box 36, MML.

46 Memo, Dulles to Mallory, May 4, 1948; Geiger, Special Assistant for Programming Policy and Procedures, to Dulles, June 3, 1948; Dulles to Hoffman (copy), June 15, 1948; Hoffman to Dulles, June 22, 1948; Bissell to Dulles, July 7, 1948; and Dulles to Bissell, July 12, 1948; all, study group on Aid to Europe (AE), RGCFR-XXXA.

moved away from economic and political questions to discussions of military aspects.[47]

In the first meeting, the general already found strong interrelations between the Marshall Plan and the North Atlantic Treaty. ECA and the Atlantic Pact, he maintained, were interrelated programs to defend "democracy and the [free] enterprise system." If Western Europe would be "overrun by the Russians," claimed Eisenhower, "we are on the way to extinction. . . . If western Europe goes, Africa is in danger, then South America. Much of Asia is already lost or in jeopardy." This made economic recovery of Western Europe all the more pressing; it would serve to "strengthen the war potential of these countries against an overt military attack, and at the same time to keep their economies strong enough so that they may not be susceptible to Communist infiltration from within."[48]

Even rearmament of Germany was considered reasonable to avert this danger. McGeorge Bundy, assistant to Henry L. Stimson and ghostwriter of his memoirs *On Active Service in Peace and War,* had prepared a working paper on the political equilibrium in Western Europe. "Irresponsible men," Bundy wrote, were proposing rearmament of Germany, an assessment other group members protested vehemently.[49]

Hanson Baldwin, military editor of the *New York Times,* judged Bundy's evaluation as hardly realistic. The Federal Republic of Germany had been established, and Baldwin found it inconceivable that an independent nation could be prevented from establishing an army. Eisenhower pursued a somewhat different line of argument. The question was whom the United States feared more, the Germans or the Russians. Treating Germany as a neutral power would necessarily drive her into the arms of the Soviet Union, and thus would increase unnecessarily the number of enemies. Jacob Viner of

47 "Minutes of Meeting of Subcommittee of the Committee on Studies of the CFR," Aug. 4, 1948, AE/RGCFR-XXXA; "Committee on Studies Meeting," Nov. 29, 1948, Rockefeller Foundation Records, 1.2/58/444. The Rockefeller Foundation supplied $50,000 to cover the expenses for the study group (Mallory to Eisenhower, Dec. 31, 1948; Bidwell to Mallory, May 3, 1949; and Resolution 49010, 1.2/57/440; all, Rockefeller Foundation Records).
48 Memo, "Studies on Aid to Europe," n.d., encl., Mallory to Eisenhower, Nov. 26, 1948, Rockefeller Foundation Records, 1.2/57/440; DD, Jan. 10, 1949, pp. 4, 5, 11, 13, AE/RGCFR-XXXA. Banker Russell C. Leffingwell argued that it was "impossible to talk of the economic and military programs as separate items," DD, Apr. 4, 1949, p. 14, AE/RGCFR-XXXA.
49 DD, June 27, 1949, pp. 14–17, AE/RGCFR-XXXA. McGeorge Bundy, "Working Paper on the Problem of Political Equilibrium," memo M-13, June 16, 1949, AE/RGCFR-XXXIIA.

Columbia University summarized the problem as follows: "We fear a possible German menace, but we also have thoughts about Germany as a potential ally." Eisenhower counseled patience. If in some time the emotional background of fear of the Germans had eased, everyone would agree to embrace Germany as an ally. While group members Allen Dulles and Hamilton Armstrong advised a slower pace in the change of political attitude toward the former enemy, and economist Emil Després could hardly envision Germany as ally of the United States at all, Ford International Corporation manager Graeme K. Howard wanted West Germany immediately accepted as a member of NATO, "part and parcel."[50]

With the Korean War escalating in 1950, the study group thought of means to convey to President Truman the importance of military readiness. Averell Harriman, then special assistant to the president, had participated in an earlier meeting. Now he was called upon to help with last minute corrections and delivery of a council memorandum sent to the president on December 12, 1950.[51]

In his cover letter to Truman, Harriman stressed the importance of the council "among thoughtful people in New York . . . and in helping to mobilize public opinion." The group members claimed, "If our potential enemies choose to attack us in our present posture we face disastrous consequences" and that "today we run the risk of global war." National security was at stake; the military forces had to be built up speedily and effectively with minimal costs (through universal military training); all government spending not related to military build-up should be minimized; and a large number of American troops must be stationed in Europe. The last paragraph of this memorandum read almost like a call for general mobilization: "Do all things that will produce the strength necessary to carry us through the tensions of an indefinite future, without war if possible, but be prepared to wage it effectively if it is thrust upon us." Truman's comment to Harriman, in face of this dramatic analysis, was rather calm: "Thanks for your memorandum of the

---

50 DD, June 27, 1949, pp. 14–15, AE/RGCFR-XXXA. In a *New York Times* article of December 29, 1949, Baldwin displayed more concern about a revival of German militarism: "The moment we put arms in the hands of any great numbers of Germans," he wrote, "that moment Germany will be calling the tune, not we. The moment Germany is rearmed, she holds the balance of power – not we." On the basis of the study group's deliberations and background papers, Howard S. Ellis wrote *The Economics of Freedom: The Progress and Future of Aid to Europe* (New York, 1950).

51 Dulles to Wriston, Dec. 29, 1950, Allen Dulles Papers, box 44, MML.

thirteenth, enclosing me a copy of the letter from the Council on
Foreign Relations in New York. It is an interesting document and I
read it with a lot of pleasure."[52]

The council participated in a network of government agencies
and private organizations bound together through formal and informal ties. They cooperated to devise foreign policy through self-
regulation and by attempting to mediate a consensus supported by a
large part of societal elites. The council played an important role in
this strategy; it helped to reach a consensus even before a decision on
policy was reached, and it served as a pool for recruitment for high-
level posts in State Department and other governmental agencies.

The "ideological war" between the United States and the Soviet
Union led the Council on Foreign Relations to a myopic view of international relations, reducing all its aspects to this confrontation.
Arguments and political ideas advanced by council members were
quite often a mixture of expertise, arrogance, and naiveté, and conveyed an almost messianic belief in the advantages of the "American
way of life." Or, in the words of council members, "We must bend
every effort to make this country strong, prosperous, and happy . . .
to show the world a way of life that people everywhere will wish to
emulate," and "our main objective is to guide thoughts to government in order to preserve American security, private enterprise, and
our way of life." Council members perceived the Truman Doctrine,
the containment policy, and the Marshall Plan to be suitable weapons in this confrontation. The battleground was Western Europe –
and at its very heart was Germany. "If in two decades Western
Europe gradually slides into the Russian political and economic or-
bit," one member argued, "the decision on it matures nowhere else
but in Germany."[53]

52 DD, Dec. 11, 1950, AE/RGCFR-XXXIA, Armstrong et al. to President Truman, Dec. 12,
   1950, "Memorandum for the President," Averell Harriman, Dec. 13, 1950; and memo, The
   President to Averell Harriman, Dec. 15, 1950, signed "H. S. T." all, Harry S Truman Papers, Papers as President of the United States, President's Secretary's Files, 1945–53, box
   114, TL.
53 George S. Franklin, "United States' Relations with the USSR," Apr. 8, 1946, USR/
   RGCFR-XVIIA; DD, Oct. 13, 1948, p. 12, study group Inter-American Affairs (IAA),
   RGCFR-XXVIIB; Brandt to Shepard Morgan, Nov. 22, 1946, PofG/RGCFR-XXIC.

2

U.S. Policy on a West German Constitution, 1947–1949

ERICH J. HAHN

When the Basic Law, the constitution of the Federal Republic of Germany, was drawn up in 1948–49, the occupying powers still held the "supreme authority" that they had assumed upon Germany's unconditional surrender in 1945. At that time, the four victors had committed themselves to the eventual establishment of a decentralized democratic Germany.[1] In the interim, during a period of political tutelage, Germans were to develop democratic attitudes through self-government at the local, regional, and state levels. However, the victors failed to specify what democratic norms had to be met before they would relinquish supreme authority. Their tutelage appeared to be without term. Could the Germans learn democratic habits under military government? In 1946 an American official summed up the problem: "How can we foster adoption of [a] constit[ution] which is based on [the] principle that *'alle Gewalt geht vom Volke aus'* [all power issues from the people] when it is actually ours?"[2]

At that time, military government in the U.S. Zone of Occupation was taking steps to return political responsibility to the people. In 1945 the U.S. Office of Military Government for Germany (OMGUS) had appointed all German officials from the local to the state level. The American deputy military governor, General Lucius D. Clay, quickly introduced democratic elections at all levels. Many years later, Clay recalled that he had not had a specific model of

I gratefully acknowledge grants from the Social Sciences and Humanities Research Council, Ottawa, which helped make the archival research for this essay possible, and the cordial help that Dr. and Mrs. H. von Moltke and Dr. and Mrs. G. von Moltke extended to me while I worked in Washington, D.C.

1 "Declaration Regarding the Defeat of Germany . . . ," June 5, 1945, in *Treaties and Other International Agreements of the United States of America, 1776–1949*, ed. U.S. Department of State, vol. 3 (Washington, D.C., 1969), 1141.

2 Marginal comment by [?], June 3, 1946, on "Vorläufiger Entwurf einer Verfassung," by Prof. Carlo Schmid, NA, RG 260, OMGUS, 3/153–2/9.

democracy, but had thought that local self-government, once entrenched, would stand up to a state government in the future.[3] Clay wanted barriers against centralization and believed that democracy was best learned through practice. But he was also keeping up with reforms in the Soviet zone and preparing to meet a shortage of U.S. personnel due to rapid demobilization.[4] In February 1946 Clay ordered the preparation of constitutions for the states in the U.S. zone. The state constitutions of Bavaria, Hesse, Württemberg-Baden were to be drawn up by special commissions, voted on in popularly elected constituent assemblies, referred for approval to the U.S. military government, and ratified by referendum in each state.[5] U.S. liaison officials informally and discreetly followed and guided the deliberations of the constituent assemblies, which were told that OMGUS would reject any charter that did not accord with democratic principles and occupation policy or hindered a unified Germany.[6] But in general, the formalities of self-determination were respected, although Clay eventually disallowed specific provisions of the Bavarian and Hessian constitutions that he deemed contrary to German national interest.[7] The state constitutions in the U.S. zone could not be disavowed as imposed charters, even though OMGUS had begun, scheduled, and monitored the constituent process.

Thus, within eight months after assuming supreme authority, OMGUS was devising and testing procedures to found democratic institutions under military government. Well before that work was completed, Clay wanted to proclaim that the constituent process under way in the U.S. zone would be adopted when a German national constitution was drawn up. In addition, Clay wanted to issue a checklist of democratic principles that the national constitution

3 Lucius D. Clay, "Proconsul of a People, by Another People, for Both Peoples," in Robert Wolfe, ed., *Americans as Proconsuls: United States Military Government in Germany and Japan, 1944–1953* (Carbondale, Ill., 1984), 105.
4 Clay to McCloy, Sept. 16, 1945, in Jean Edward Smith, ed., *The Papers of General Lucius D. Clay: Germany 1945–1949*, 2 vols. (Bloomington, Ind., 1974), 1:77; Michael Balfour and John Maier, *Four Power Control in Germany and Austria, 1945–1946* (New York, 1972), 186–7. The reforms are summarized in T. F. J. Gillen, *State and Local Government in West Germany, 1945–1953*, Historical Division of the Office of HICOG (n.p., 1953), 6–16.
5 Directive, "Election Schedule," Clay to OMG Land Directors, Feb. 4, 1946, in James K. Pollock et al., eds., *Germany under Occupation: Illustrative Materials and Documents* (Ann Arbor, Mich., 1947), 120–1.
6 Barbara Fait, " 'In einer Atmosphäre der Freiheit': Die Rolle der Amerikaner bei der Verfassungsgebung in den Ländern der US-Zone 1946," *VfZG* 33 (1985):431. Cf. idem, "Auf Befehl der Besatzungsmacht? Der Weg zur Bayerischen Verfassung," in Wolfgang Benz, ed., *Neuanfang in Bayern 1945 bis 1949* (Munich, 1988), 36–63.
7 Balfour and Mair, *Four Power Control*, 195–6; Gillen, *State and Local Government*, 47–52.

would have to guarantee. By committing the United States to a procedure that allowed Germans broad self-determination, Clay hoped to rebut a much publicized but vague call for German unity by Soviet Foreign Minister Vyacheslav Molotov.[8] Clay was denied permission to issue his program. But Secretary of State James F. Byrnes included in his Stuttgart speech of September 6, 1946, a proposal that closely followed Clay's ideas on how Germans should draw up a constitution and form a central government: The ministers president (heads of the state governments) from the four zones would form a national council or provisional government. The council would draft a constitution and submit it first to the Allied Control Council, then to an elected constituent assembly, and finally to a popular referendum for ratification. Byrnes specified only that the charter "should insure the democratic character of the new Germany and the human rights and fundamental freedoms of all inhabitants."[9]

In late September 1946, Clay reiterated the Byrnes plan for a German government in a directive defining the reserve powers that OMGUS would keep after the democratic state constitutions were enacted. The directive included a list of democratic principles to which the new state constitutions and, by inference, a German constitution would have to adhere: free and frequent elections, independent political parties, freedom of the press, civil liberties, and the rule of law. The directive also took up the distribution of powers between the states and a future German national government. Clay seized an opportunity to set out an OMGUS plan for a democratic Germany. The directive specified a federal Germany or "Bundesstaat" made up of "states" (*Staaten* not *Länder*), which was "decentralized . . . to the maximum degree consistent with the modern economic life."[10] The fact that the central government was to ensure economic unity reflects the United States' concern with the high cost of zonal particularism.

In two places Clay's directive proclaimed: "All political power is recognized as originating with the people and subject to their

8 Clay to Echols, July 19, 1946, *Clay Papers*, 1.240–1, cf. 212–17, 257. Wolfgang Krieger, *General Lucius D. Clay und die amerikanische Deutschlandpolitik 1945–1949* (Stuttgart, 1987), 157–60.

9 Stuttgart speech by James F. Byrnes, September 6, 1946, in Beate Ruhm von Oppen, ed., *Documents on Germany under Occupation, 1945–1954* (London, 1955), 158; cf. 156–7. On the origins and intent of the Byrnes speech see Krieger, *Clay*, 160–5.

10 Directive, "Relationship between Military and Civil Government (U.S. Zone) Subsequent to the Adoption of Land Constitutions," Sept. 30, 1946, in Edward H. Litchfield et al., eds., *Governing Postwar Germany*, (Ithaca, N.Y., 1953), 540.

control." That was patently untrue. However, if German institutions were to have sound democratic foundations, then the people had to be the source of all power. In accordance with the theory of dual sovereignty, they were said to grant it first of all to the states which, in turn, delegated governmental functions to local authority. Second, the people also granted power to the federal government, but only "in specifically enumerated and limited instances."[11] If all power came directly from the people and federal powers were strictly enumerated, the central government could not expand its authority at the expense of the states. Clay's directive invoked the principle of dual sovereignty to protect the states from federal encroachments. Byrnes's speech and Clay's directive of September 1946 committed the United States to a democratic federal government in Germany as a whole. Their program also gave Germans a standard to judge the rhetoric and reality of democratization in other zones and challenged the other powers to match the democratic standards of the U.S. zone.

The chances that the other powers would adopt the U.S. program for a German government were small in 1946–47. This was clear at the meetings of the Council of Foreign Ministers (CFM), which showed that the Allies disagreed profoundly about when Germans should set up a government and how it should be structured. Britain was skeptical of the German aptitude for democracy and advocated a provisional not a permanent government. France resolutely blocked every proposal in the direction of a democratic federal Germany. The Soviets were not committed to independent political parties, civil liberties, or the rule of law in their zone or for Germany as a whole. The United States, which paid heavily to relieve the hardships of political and economic disunity imposed by the zonal separatism of France and the Soviet Union, considered it all important that the Germans be responsible for their condition and take initiatives to improve it.

For the Moscow CFM (March–April 1947), the State Department took the position that a permanent German government should be set up within one year. Germans would not need detailed instructions, since the Allies retained final approval.[12] According to an

11 Ibid., 539–40.
12 Policy Paper, State Dept., Feb. 1947, in *FRUS 1947*, vol. 2, *Council of Foreign Ministers; Germany and Austria* (Washington, D.C., 1972), 203–4; memo, OMGUS, March 5, 1947, ibid., 230.

OMGUS paper, "The specific structures of government may have considerable mechanical significance but for the most part, do not affect its character or a democratic organization. For this reason those structures . . . may therefore be left to the Germans themselves to decide."[13] An OMGUS paper for the London CFM (November–December 1947), required that the constitution be drafted by "persons clearly responsive to the public and who have been selected for the exclusive purpose of preparing that document. The election of the constitutional assembly . . . is to be an important method of insuring both the democratic character of the permanent constitution and also the popular support which such a document must enjoy." Moreover, the victors would have to "unequivocally commit themselves to the same observance of the rights of free men which we require of the German government."[14] This meant that the laws of the new German government would take effect routinely, unless disallowed by a majority of the Control Council. Thus, the supreme authority each power held in its zone would be curtailed, and the veto that had destroyed German unity would be suspended.

Before the London CFM turned to plans for a German government, the conference broke up in mid-December over reparations. Thereupon, the three Western powers immediately agreed to work out common solutions to the economic and political problems of their zones. Their talks began in London in late February 1948 and adjourned in early March, to continue in Berlin among the Western military governors and their staffs. The final session of the London conference was held from late April to June 1, 1948.

The United States entered the London talks with the program it had tested in its zone and refined in the CFM proposals. The Allies would initiate and monitor the constituent process, but they would adhere to the formalities of self-determination. To provide the new German government with an unassailable democratic basis, an elected constituent assembly and a popular referendum were essential. The assembly would have general guidelines for a constitution that adhered to democratic principles, assured the rule of law, and guaranteed the independence of the states against the

13 "Permanent Government – Structure, Tab 13," March [?] 1947, NA, RG 260, OMGUS, microfiche, 3/162–3/6, fiche 2.
14 Litchfield to Clay, submitting memo, "British Paper on Governmental Organization. Proposed Statement for Secretary [Marshall]," [Dec. 3, 1947], NA, RG 260, OMGUS, microfiche, 3/162–1/20, fiche 1.

central government. Because the Allies would approve the constitution and watch over its application, the details could be left largely to
the Germans.

When the London conference on Germany opened in late February
1948, Britain agreed with the United States that all Germans in the
Western zones should quickly elect a national constituent assembly
that would proceed with a few general guidelines. But the French objected strongly to popular sovereignty, claiming that the individual
states had to hold sovereignty, and that their legislatures had to
choose the constituent assembly and ratify the constitution. The
French wanted to rule out national elections for all time by prescrib-
ing a confederate constitution, because, they alleged, Germans were
predisposed to radical nationalism. The state governments would
choose the upper chamber and the state assemblies elect the lower.[15]
In short, while the United States, now backed by Britain, favored a
laissez-faire approach based on popular sovereignty and self-
determination, the French were determined to impose a confederate
solution. These disagreements had been fully aired when the London
talks recessed in early March 1948.

The United States opened the next round of talks in Berlin with a
maneuver to circumvent the London impasse. Clay's civil affairs advisor, Edward H. Litchfield, demanded that the content of the German constitution be discussed only after a timetable for setting up a
German government had been adopted. He suggested an immediate
merger of the three Western zones. The French zone would join the
economic union of the U.S.–British bizone. Its administration would
be transformed into a provisional West German government by September 1948. A constituent assembly would be elected by November
and a constitution submitted for approval to the military governors
in March 1949. Elections for the West German government would
follow in May. This tight schedule, along with a promise to define
the reserve powers of the Allies in an occupation statute, would be
proclaimed "as the Military Government's contribution to the Cen-
tennial of the Revolution of 1848" in St. Paul's Cathedral, Frankfurt,
on May 18, 1948.[16]

---

15 Douglas to SecState, Mar. 1, 1947, *FRUS 1948,* vol. 2, *Germany and Austria* (Washington,
D.C., 1973), 108–9.
16 Litchfield to Tripartite Working Party, "Proposed Schedule for Political Development of
Western Germany," March 22, 1948, and "Draft of Proposed Statement . . . Concerning . . . West German Government," March 23, 1948, NA, RG 59, 740.00119 Control

The U.S. proposal presented no difficulty to the British.[17] German officials had been working routinely for more than a year with British and U.S. officials in the agencies of the U.S.–British bizone. But France could have only a minor role as a latecomer in an economic trizone. Threatened with marginalization, France had to reconsider its firm opposition to an effective central government. The U.S. officials in Berlin held a strong bargaining position when they hinted that French counterproposals would be welcome.[18] The French Foreign Ministry quickly sent Maurice Couve de Murville to Berlin to negotiate with Clay.[19] They agreed on a document that Clay drew up: A constituent assembly, popularly elected through procedures to be set by the states, would meet by September 1, 1948, to "draft a democratic constitution which will establish a federal-type governmental structure for the participating states which will protect the rights of the participating states and which will contain guarantees of individual rights and freedoms."[20] If the occupiers found that the constitution satisfied these general guidelines, it would be ratified by the individual states according to their own procedures. Thus, Couve gained for the states an imprecise role at the start and the end of the constituent process. Clay won French acceptance for U.S. timing – a major gain – but yielded on strictly democratic procedures, such as national elections for the constituent assembly and a popular referendum on the constitution.

The three-power talks resumed in London in late April and concluded on June 1, 1948, with a package of agreements on the future control of the Ruhr industries and resources, the continued Allied occupation in Germany, German demilitarization, and a future West German government. On the latter subject, there were three major papers. They developed the Clay–Couve agreement into instructions for the military governors to begin the constituent process and guide it to the formation of a West German government.

(Germany)/3-3048. Litchfield explained the plan to his French counterpart Seydoux, note no. 1566, March 24, 1948, AOFAA, Cabinet Civil Pol V, E 3, Groupe d'études no. 5. Earlier, Clay had made a very similar proposal, cf. Clay to Draper, Feb. 7 [6?], 1948, *Clay Papers*, 2:556–8.

17 Minutes, Leishman, Apr. 13, 1948, and Steel to Dean, March 26 and 31, 1948, PRO, FO 371/70584.
18 Klévanski, Baden-Baden, to Paris, note 74, April 4, 1948, MdAE, Série Y Internationale 1944–49, vol. 302, fol. 184.
19 Krieger, *Clay*, 355–6, links French willingness to negotiate to the beginning Berlin crisis.
20 *Clay Papers*, 2:631.

One paper titled "Political Organization" outlined the process by which the West German constitution would be drawn up, in particular how the constituent assembly would be selected and instructed. The discussion of these issues was most controversial. The United States and Britain still wanted the assembly to be elected directly by universal suffrage. The French dreaded a lower house based on that franchise. According to Couve: "German democracy was not yet sufficiently developed to be able to trust a popularly elected Assembly."[21] The United States would not constrain German self-determination but agreed to let the state legislatures decide how the delegates to the constituent assembly would be "chosen."[22] In a further concession to the French view that the states, not the people, should build the new polity, the powers agreed that the constitution would be ratified by a separate referendum in each state instead of the national referendum favored by the United States.[23] Eventually, the Germans themselves opposed a referendum and were permitted to ratify the constitution in the state legislatures.

The instructions to the constituent assembly were equally controversial. In order to preserve the spirit and appearance of self-determination, the United States wanted the Germans to receive minimal and discreet guidance. The French expected to dictate provisions central to any constitution. Couve, for instance, declared that France "could not agree to popular election of the Lower House." The French Ambassador René Massigli predicted: "Most unfortunate results might emerge if the Germans were free to choose the form of Executive."[24] The conference could not define instructions that were specific enough to suit the French yet so vague that the Germans did not cry out "Versailles!" Therefore, the conference reiterated the vague Clay–Couve agreement for "a democratic constitution . . . [and] a governmental structure of federal type which is best adapted to the eventual re-establishment of German unity at present disrupted, and which will protect the rights of the participating states, provide adequate central authority, and contain guar-

---

21 Minutes, "Talks on Germany," May 26, 1948, U.K. Circular no. 99, p. 4, PRO FO 371/71113.
22 "Political Organization," May 31, 1948, *FRUS 1948,* 2:305, para. 4.
23 Ibid., para. 7.
24 Minutes, "Talks on Germany," Apr. 29, 1948, UK Circular no. 53, p. 2, and Minutes, "Talks on Germany," Apr. 30, 1948, UK Circular no. 54, p. 1, PRO FO 371/70589.

antees of individual rights and freedom."[25] Because the Allies could not agree on more specific instructions, the Germans gained in self-determination by default.

In fact, the Allies did adopt further constitutional requirements in a confidential "Letter of Advice" to the military governors, who would review and approve the constitution. This letter conceded that there were many ways to achieve decentralized federalism. An acceptable constitution had to provide for a bicameral legislature in which the upper house would represent and protect the states; an executive with enumerated powers; a federal government with enumerated fields of competence, limited powers to tax and spend, and a small administration for tasks the states could not readily assume; and an independent judiciary to review the constitutionality of federal and state laws and actions, and to safeguard civil liberties. The unstated presumption was that all residual powers would stay with the states. The fields expressly reserved for them were education, cultural and religious affairs, local government, and health and welfare. However, mindful that exceptional situations could arise, the United States insisted that federal power could extend to health and welfare whenever uniform national policy was needed; and that a federal police force should be permitted to ensure security.[26] Since these instructions were confidential, they could not guide or hamper the constituent assembly. Clay suggested that the three powers appoint liaison officers, as he had done in 1946, to ensure that the assembly knew Allied thinking and did not draw up an unacceptable constitution.[27]

Another "Letter of Advice" instructed the military governors on the occupation statute that would define the reserve powers of military government after the constitution was enacted.[28] In London Clay recommended that the victors enact the statute before the constitution came into effect, so that Germans would know both the powers and limitations of their new government. Their referendum on the constitution would then also encompass the occupation stat-

---

25 "Political Organization," *FRUS 1948*, 2:305, para. 6.
26 "Letter of Advice . . . Regarding German Constitution," May 12, 1948, *FRUS 1948*, 240–1; cf. 220–1.
27 Minutes, "Talks on Germany," Apr. 27, 1948, UK Circular no. 41, pp. 6–7, PRO FO 371/70589.
28 "Letter of Advice . . . Regarding Powers of Civil and Military Government, *FRUS 1948*, 2:260–2.

ute, to preclude charges that the victors had imposed a system of partial sovereignty.[29] In the subsequent arduous negotiations, Clay, supported by the British, tried to ensure the German government maximum freedom of action, while France intended to retain maximum controls. Clay believed that Germans would be reluctant to accept governmental responsibility if the Allies remained above the law. Therefore, he wanted an Allied court of appeal, including German judges, as proof that unchecked military government authority had ended.[30] A similar right of appeal against administrative decisions was well established in the German Rechtsstaat tradition. Officials in the State Department believed that a German judge on the Allied court would give Germans a measure of respectability and equality, encourage them to take on political responsibility, and provide them with lessons in the rule of law.[31] But France would not tolerate a German judge ruling on decisions of the commanders in chief.[32] Eventually, in April 1949, the foreign ministers in Washington adopted a simplified occupation statute that omitted the court entirely. Clay's firm stand for a German judge on the appeal court shows how committed he was to building up German self-esteem and dismantling the appearance of subjugation.

The practical result of the vagueness and confidentiality of the London agreements was that the West German constituent assembly would have the freedom Byrnes and Clay had recommended in 1946. Moreover, the military governors had to resolve ambiguities in the London agreements. The arrangement favored U.S. policy as interpreted by Clay. He could act more freely than his British and French colleagues because in distant Washington, American policy-making was a cumbersome process of consultations between the State and War departments. Clay used his personal authority and relative independence with great skill to keep up the common front among the Allies, and to engage the Germans fully. More than anyone, he helped fulfill the U.S. goal of the London conference, to attain a consensus for a West German political order.

29 Minutes, "Talks on Germany," May 4 [5?], 1948, UK Circular 59, pp. 1–3, PRO FO 371/70589; Douglas to SecState, May 5, 1948, *FRUS 1948*, 2:224; Minutes, May 5, 1948, MdAE, Série Y Internationale 1944–49, vol. 308, fol. 97.
30 Clay to Draper, Aug. 19, 1948, *Clay Papers*, 2:775.
31 Lovett to Douglas, Jan. 19, 1949, *FRUS 1949*, vol. 3, *Council of Foreign Ministers; Germany and Austria* (Washington, D.C., 1974), 13–14, cf. 23, 27, 31.
32 French note no. 374, Dec. 3, 1948, NA, RG 59, 740.00119 Control (Germany)/12–348; cf. Murphy to Saltzman, Dec. 3, 1948, p. 5; both, NA, RG 59, 740.00119 Control (Germany) 12–348.

According to the London agreements, the ministers president were to begin the constituent process. On July 1, 1948, the military governors handed the ministers president the London terms in three documents. This ceremony in Frankfurt reminded one observer of the delivery of the Versailles Treaty.[33] One document "authorized" the ministers president to convene a constituent assembly; another "asked" them to review state boundaries; the third promised the occupation statute. The ministers president did not want to risk charges of collaborating with the victors and dividing Germany. So they chose to interpret the Frankfurt documents as an occasion to negotiate.[34] After consulting with their legislatures and the major parties, they offered to draw up only a provisional arrangement, hoping to reduce their own political risks by exposing the dominant role of the Allies. Thus, the ministers president offered to "collaborate creatively," to implement reforms that were "ultimately based on the will of the Occupying Powers," and were not "an act of self-determination of the German people." They would set up a provisional administration, not a permanent government; they would prepare a "Basic Law" approved by the state legislatures, not a constitution ratified by popular referendum. Their reason was that "a referendum would give the basic law a kind of weight which should be reserved to a final constitution."[35]

This reply infuriated Clay. In a "heart-to-heart talk" with his ministers president, he deplored their refusal to accept political responsibility for a permanent government, and accused them of helping the French and Soviets by rejecting a unique opportunity that tenacious U.S. diplomacy had won for them in London.[36] Clay's vehement reaction was shared neither by his advisors nor by the British and French military governors, Sir Brian Robertson and Pierre Koenig. They found the Koblenz reply a useful basis for further talks. But Clay insisted that the London terms were absolutely not negotiable and persuaded his colleagues to be firm.[37] When both sides met again on July 20, the military governors pointed out where

---

33 Hans Simons, "The Bonn Constitution and its Government," in Hans J. Morgenthau, ed., *Germany and the Future of Europe* (Chicago, 1951), 120.
34 Murphy to SecState, July 14, 1948, *FRUS 1948*, 2:395.
35 Ministers President to Military Governors, July 10, 1948, *FRUS 1948*, 2:385–6.
36 Minutes, Meeting between Clay and Ministers President, July 14, 1948, in *Der Parlamentarische Rat 1948–1949: Akten und Protokolle*, ed. Deutscher Bundestag and Bundesarchiv, vol. 1, *Vorgeschichte*, ed. Johannes Volker Wagner (Boppard, 1975), 151–6.
37 Murphy to SecState, July 15, 1948, *FRUS 1948*, 2:399.

the German proposals departed from the London terms and explained that these were governmental agreements they could not alter. The ministers president had to choose. If they accepted the
London terms, they took responsibility for setting up a West German government. If they insisted that their plan for a provisional
government be referred back to London, they would be responsible
for all delays.

After reviewing the situation, the ministers president countered
with two requests (one departed only from the London terms, the
other also from democratic principle): first, that the constitution be
labeled "Basic Law" (Provisional Constitution), to emphasize that
the West German state was transitional, not permanent; second, that
the Basic Law be ratified by the state legislatures, because a coalition
of communists and political malcontents could turn a popular referendum into a plebiscite against military government.[38] The generals
withdrew to confer privately. Clay was intransigent: Any change to
the London terms had to be approved by the governments. Thereupon the Germans gave in. In another huddle among the generals,
Clay found "that everything was now fine since the Ministers President had accepted London." But Koenig was uneasy about Clay's
rigidity. Robertson warned that it was "very unwise that we should
force the London decisions down unwilling throats." At their urging,
Clay conceded the term Basic Law, and agreed that the method of
ratification and the redrawing of state boundaries might be decided
later. A "chorus of assent" greeted these concessions.[39]

Clay's unyielding demand that the Germans had to adopt the full
London program came close to a _Diktat_. He yielded to his colleagues
and conceded the label Basic Law, but only after the ministers president had "accepted unconditionally [sic!] the London Conference
proposals and the responsibility to set them in motion."[40] By defending the integrity of the London terms, Clay safeguarded the whole
enterprise against early failure. When the ministers president accepted the London terms in toto, he had won an important prece-
dent. Now the British, French, and Germans had notice that the
London agreements, unlike the Potsdam Protocol, would not be

38 Murphy to SecState, July 26, 1948, _FRUS 1948_, 2:410–11.
39 Tel. 240, Frankfurt to Foreign Office, July 26, 1948, PRO FO 371/70596B. Two other reports of the meeting suggest that the military governors did not force the ministers president to capitulate before granting the term "basic law," cf. _Der Parlamentarische Rat_, 1:273–
82, and Litchfield, _Governing Postwar Germany_, 552–61.
40 Clay to Noce, July 27, 1948, _Clay Papers_, 2:746.

tampered with. Robertson and Koenig rightly protested that unconditional acceptance of the London terms was not a propitious start. But the alternative, acceptance tainted by compromise, could spawn further amendments whenever one side might wish to delay or scuttle a West German government.

When the Parliamentary Council, the constituent assembly of the Western zones, convened in Bonn in September 1948, it had minimalist guidelines and, thus, wide scope for drafting the Basic Law. As the council's work advanced, it became clear that the financial provisions in the Basic Law would not accord with the confidential Letter of Advice to the military governors. The council envisaged federal administration of taxes to minimize bureaucratic expense, and federal grants-in-aid to poorer states to ensure social justice. In order to meet these obligations, the federal government would control most taxes and be tempted to coerce the states by making or denying them grants-in-aid. To protect the states from the threat of creeping centralization, the Letter of Advice specified that the central government could raise revenues only to fulfill its constitutional obligations. It could set the rates for taxes that had to be levied uniformly, but could neither collect nor disburse them. The same principle of separate powers applied to the federal administration. It could extend only to fields where state administration was impractical.[41] The federation could not administer any taxes for the states, whatever the saving.

The Parliamentary Council did not know the stipulations of the Letter of Advice until the liaison officers gave notice that the financial powers of the federal government were becoming too great. On November 22, after one warning had already failed, the officers handed the president of the Parliamentary Council, Konrad Adenauer, an *aide mémoire* with the main points of the Letter of Advice.[42] A further warning came on December 17, at a meeting of the military governors and a Parliamentary Council delegation headed by Adenauer.[43] Yet the council was not moved to revise the financial provisions because these rested on a fragile compromise among the

---

41 *FRUS 1948*, 2:240–1, para. 1, d, f.
42 Memo by Hans Simons, Oct. 22, 1948, and "Statement to the [Vice-] President of the Parliamentary Council on the Distribution of Powers in the Financial Field," [Oct. 20, 1948], NA, RG 260, OMGUS, 17/254–2/5. Tel. 41, British Liaison Staff Bonn to Berlin, Nov. 22, 1948, PRO FO 1030/85; for the text of the *aide mémoire*, see *FRUS 1948*, 2:442–3.
43 Minutes, Meeting of Military Governors and Parliamentary Council Delegation, Dec. 17, 1948, *FRUS 1948*, 2:648–9.

major parties. The SPD had agreed to a federalist upper chamber
(Bundesrat) made up of appointed representatives of state governments and endowed with a veto. In turn, the CDU/CSU had conceded greater financial authority to the federal government.[44] This
delicate balance between the centralism of the SPD and the federalism
of the CDU/CSU assured the Basic Law broad support.

In early February 1949, the draft of the Basic Law passed the committee stage and was sent to the Allies for approval before it was ta-
bled in the full Parliamentary Council.[45] In their review the liaison
officers found the draft met many, but by no means all, conditions in
the *aide mémoire* of November 22. The federal authority could regulate too many taxes and legislate in public health and welfare, fields
that were reserved for the states. The draft also extended the Basic
Law to greater Berlin as a twelfth state, which the London agreements did not allow.[46] But the most serious flaw was that the federal
government could still collect more revenues than it needed for its
constitutional obligations, and fund policies beyond its jurisdictions
through transfer payments to the states.

Despite these shortcomings, U.S. liaison officials believed "that
the Germans have gone about as far as we can expect them to go in
producing a Basic Law that meets the requirements for a federal state
with a sufficiently strong central government while protecting the
rights of the laender [states]." They recommended compromise because the draft Basic Law, as it stood, had the support of every major
party. If amendments were required at this late stage, especially in
the division and administration of taxes, the SPD could "seize the
opportunity to abandon the whole business and proceed to make the
maximum political capital out of it at the expense of the CDU."[47]
This was ominous. The Weimar Republic had failed, in part because
not all major parties had backed the new order. Without the support
of the SPD, the Basic Law could not be a sound foundation for a
West German state.

44 Hans-Jürgen Grabbe, "Die deutsch-alliierte Kontroverse um den Grundgesetzentwurf im
   Frühjahr 1949," *VfZG* 26 (1978):397–8. See John Ford Golay, *The Founding of the Federal
   Republic of Germany* (Chicago, 1958), 44–50, for the compromise on the Bundesrat; on finances, see ibid., 74–86.
45 Wolfgang Benz, *Von der Besatzungsherrschaft zur Bundesrepublik: Stationen einer Staatsgründung 1946–49* (Frankfurt am Main, 1984), 218–19.
46 "Comparison de l'aide mémoire . . . avec la loi fondamentale . . . ," Feb. 14, 1949,
   AOFAA, Cabinet Civil, Pol V, F 1/17.
47 Wendelin to Beam, Feb. 14, 1949, NA, RG 59, 862.00/2-1449.

When the military governors reviewed the draft Basic Law on March 1 and 2, 1949, they spent much time on its financial provisions. Only Robertson had already said that Britain would accept the draft as it stood. Koenig upheld the French view that federalism entailed decentralization; he maintained that the states should collect federal revenues and administer federal laws wherever possible. In Clay's opinion, federalism required a clear division of powers. Thus, the federation could administer only the exclusive federal taxes and that portion of concurrent taxes it needed to meet its obligations. The states would administer the rest.[48] The obvious drawback of this arrangement was that it required parallel federal and state tax administrations, a costly duplication that the Parliamentary Council was determined to avoid. On March 2, the military governors gave the council their "comments" on the draft Basic Law. These included revised Basic Law articles that reassigned taxes and legislative fields, approximating the principles of dual sovereignty. Unless the federation commissioned the states to administer all its taxes, to which the SPD would never agree, the states and the federal government would have separate finance authorities to collect their respective revenues. In addition, equalization payments were ruled out, to block the growth of the central power.[49]

These comments threatened the constitutional compromise among the major parties. The SPD was not ready to accept the trimming of federal finance powers and the denial of equalization payments. It was not convincing to say that sound federalism required costly duplicate tax administrations, but that it ruled out equalization payments that furthered social justice. Robertson warned that the SPD might reject a Basic Law that had been amended under Allied pressure. But Clay and Koenig found the division of financial powers that the draft proposed to be unacceptable. Clay insisted that the Parliamentary Council come up with a solution.[50] On March 25, after repeated, fruitless meetings among Allied and German finance experts, the Germans were told bluntly to complete the Basic Law

48 "Verbatim of the Ninth Meeting of the . . . Military Governors," March 1, 1949, NA, RG 260, OMGUS, COS Tripartite Secretariat, 17/8185/3, pp. 41–5.
49 Murphy to SecState, March 2, 1949, *FRUS 1949*, 3:217–21.
50 Tels. 970 and 973, Noiret to Paris, March 24, 1949, fols. 249, 252–3, and tel. 266–72, Sauvanargues to Paris, March 26, 1949, fols., 279–81, MdAE, Série Y Internationale 1944–49, vol. 322.

"in full knowledge of the observations" they had received.[51] Thus, in late March 1949, the military governors were deadlocked with the Parliamentary Council and disagreed among themselves whether the draft Basic Law could be accepted. The Frankfurt impasse was solved in early April when the three Western foreign ministers conferred in Washington after signing the North Atlantic Treaty. This new defense pact made concessions to the Germans easier. Concessions were urgently needed. The possibility of talks with the Soviets to end the Berlin blockade could upset the whole project for a West German government.

The U.S. government had begun a full review of its German policy in early 1949, in a subcommittee of the National Security Council. According to George Kennan, who represented the State Department, the goal of U.S. policy in Europe was to integrate a sovereign Germany into a future European community. Thus, the German attitude toward European integration was more important than the structure of a German government, so long as it could ensure stability and "have real foundation in the psychology and tradition of the German population."[52] From this olympian perspective constitutional details lost significance. Kennan advocated generous acceptance of the work of the Parliamentary Council in order to help put Germans into a positive frame of mind for the greater task: the Europeanization of the German problem. A trip to Germany in mid-March 1949 convinced Kennan that "the moment of decision" was near in Germany. Under more pressure, the SPD could balk, and "the theory of German authorship of the constitution, as distinct from Allied dictation, will therefore be destroyed." Germans should not be pressured to adopt further decentralization and if they "make a real issue of it, we should not insist on the recent demands we made of them on the constitutional financial questions."[53]

The State Department incorporated Kennan's views into a report it submitted on March 31, 1949, to President Truman. The paper set down U.S. policy for the foreign ministers' discussions a week later.

51 Minutes, CFR/LOPC, 10ème séance, March 25, 1949, AOFAA, Cabinet Civil, Pol V, K 4, pp. 1–3; cf. Riddleberger to SecState, March 2, 1949, *FRUS 1949*, 3:231–2.
52 Paper by Kennan, Feb. 7, 1949, *FRUS 1949*, 3:92; cf. Grabbe, "Die deutsch-alliierte Kontroverse," 399–400.
53 Letter [not sent], Kennan to Dean [Acheson], March 29, 1949, Princeton University, Seeley G. Mudd Library, George F. Kennan Papers, box 23, folder: Papers relating to George Kennan's visit to Germany, 1949. Cf. *FRUS 1949*, 3:137–8.

Using the most general terms, it proposed for West Germany "a governmental system dedicated to uphold the basic civil and human rights of the individual in which the German people function in accordance with democratic procedure."[54] In closing, the report recommended that the foreign ministers "consider carefully the delicate balance of German political forces represented in that document [the draft Basic Law] and should be aware that insistence upon changes beyond those now proposed by the Germans will incur the risk of placing on the Allies themselves the onus for future difficulties encountered in the working of the constitution."[55] All-party support to ensure that Germans accepted political responsibility under the Basic Law had become more important than strict fulfillment of the London terms.

Clay was only consulted on this new U.S. policy. It appears to abandon his long-standing commitment to establish the nearest thing possible to a full-fledged West German state. Yet his first reactions were favorable. He was, however, determined that the Parliamentary Council would put forward a compromise that incorporated the military governors' "observations" of March 2 so that no party would be able to claim in the upcoming elections that it had defended the Basic Law against Allied pressures. Clay's campaign to extract consensus from the Parliamentary Council started on April 5, a day before the foreign ministers in Washington turned to the German question. At noon, the U.S. liaison officer Hans Simons gave representatives of the Parliamentary Council a note from the foreign ministers. He astonished his French and British colleagues when he informed them of his unprecedented solo mission only after the fact. Clay probably solicited the note from Washington on the suggestion of Simons.[56]

The note of April 5, the first of three from the foreign ministers to the Parliamentary Council, contained a pat on the back and a veiled threat. The ministers commended the council for "pressing forward" with the Basic Law, but also told it to

give due consideration to the recommendations of the Military Governors, which conform with the provisions of the London Agreement. . . . The Foreign Secretaries desire that the decisions of the Parliamentary Council will be taken in a spirit of facilitating a mutually cooperative attitude

54 "U.S. Policy Respecting Germany," March 31, 1949, *FRUS 1949*, 3:144.
55 Ibid., 155.
56 Tel. 14, Cheysson to Baden-Baden, Apr. 5, 1949, AOFAA, Cabinet Civil, Pol V, K 4.

between the future German federal authorities and the occupying powers, which is one of the important objectives being sought in the current talks in Washington regarding Germany.[57]

The message was plain: There would be no concessions on the London terms; German intransigence was vain and would forfeit Allied goodwill toward the future government.

The purpose of this unprecedented hasty message was certainly to deal the SPD a setback. U.S. officials in Germany believed that the SPD stood firm because it expected the foreign ministers to yield on the division of finances in order to win broad consent for the Basic Law.[58] The resolute SPD caucus had sounded a nationalist note on March 30, when it resolved to uphold the distribution of fiscal powers according to "the thoroughly considered German conception of the conditions of a Federal Government's ability to function." By contrast, the CDU/CSU caucus voted to find a formula to satisfy both German interests and meet the observations of the military governors.[59]

It has been suggested that Clay wanted to thwart the SPD because he opposed the party's nationalization policies, found its structure insufficiently democratic, and wanted to bolster the chances of the CDU/CSU in the coming elections.[60] OMGUS officials were certain that the British were encouraging the SPD to stand firm. If the foreign ministers made concessions, the SPD would claim credit for them and accuse the CDU/CSU of collaborationist tendencies. The OMGUS experts feared that such a split over the Basic Law could become as destructive as the political divisions of the Weimar Republic.[61] Clay shared these premonitions. To him the extensive federal powers to tax and legislate envisaged in the draft Basic Law were contrary to the London terms and could threaten the states. He also suspected that the SPD wanted large federal revenues because it had long-term plans for socialization that would require compensation payments. However, if the Allies were firm, Clay calculated

57 *FRUS 1949*, 3:236–7; Simons handed the note to Konrad Adenauer (CDU), Walter Menzel (SPD), and Hermann Schäfer (FDP) [Schaeffer or Schaffer in the French documents]. The suggestion that all three liaison officers delivered the message appears to be wrong.
58 Riddleberger to SecState, March 28, 1949, *FRUS 1949*, 3:231–2.
59 Ibid., 232–3; cf. Grabbe, "Die deutsch-alliierte Kontroverse," 400–1.
60 Grabbe suggests that Clay's policy was dominated by the concern that in future an SPD government would be a difficult partner; cf. ibid., 403–5, 416–18. Krieger sees Clay determined to block only a triumph of the authoritarian, nationalist Schumacher over more moderate elements in the SPD; Krieger, *Clay*, 462–3, 465–6.
61 Clay to Voorhees, Apr. 4, 1949, *Clay Papers*, 2:1085–7; cf. 1102, 1114.

that the SPD would not choose isolation but would seek compromise.[62] Clay's strategy succeeded. On April 6, the SPD moved in committee to forward the draft Basic Law unamended to the full Parliamentary Council. The motion failed. Instead the committee voted to review the finance provisions once again, in order to find an all-party compromise. Thus, for the moment, the danger that the Basic Law could become a topic of divisive nationalistic electioneering was lessened.[63]

Actually, on April 6–7, the foreign ministers in Washington accepted the Basic Law much as it stood and also adopted a streamlined occupation statute. The French foreign minister, Robert Schuman, conceded equalization payments in the Basic Law when his British colleague, Ernest Bevin, said that such fiscal transfers, limited to specified social programs, were needed to prevent communist gains. Secretary of State Dean Acheson agreed. This consensus meant that the federal financial powers would not be reduced. On behalf of the foreign ministers, the military governors could inform the Parliamentary Council at an "appropriate" time, but "before opinion in the Parliamentary Council has crystallized" that a Basic Law which balanced federal and state power and guaranteed each side legislative authority and independent finances to meet its obligations would get "sympathetic consideration." The Basic Law could also provide for federal payments to the states through "grants for education, health, and welfare purposes, subject in each case to specific approval by the Bundesrat."[64] The military governors could choose the moment to give these concessions to the Council. Clay exploited that latitude to the utmost in order to assure that the Basic Law had the full support of the major parties.

On April 10 the Parliamentary Council received the streamlined occupation statute. The victors kept control over specified fields and they reserved the right to resume supreme authority, if they explained the need for such action. Otherwise the civil liberties and legal rights of Germans would be respected. The statute was to be phased out gradually after twelve to eighteen months.[65] To emphasize that these self-restricting pledges were binding, the foreign

62 Clay to Voorhees, March 31, 1949, *Clay Papers*, 2:1067.
63 Telecon., Clay-Crook, Apr. 6, 1949, ibid., 1087. Riddleberger to SecState, Apr. 7, 1949, *FRUS 1949*, 3:235–6.
64 "Message to the Military Governors," Apr. 8, 1949, *FRUS 1949*, 3:185.
65 "Occupation Statute," Apr. 8, 1949, *FRUS 1949*, 3:179–81.

ministers announced in their cover letter that military government itself would be replaced by a civilian high commission with a minimal staff. The letter concluded pointedly that now the Parliamentary Council's agreement on the Basic Law was the last obstacle to implementing this program.[66] The military governors themselves were standing by "to discuss every proposal that could be made in light of these documents."[67] With their two messages in five days the foreign ministers had proven their goodwill and had urged the Parliamentary Council to follow suit and compromise on the Basic Law. But the council was not so inclined. The British believed that now the moment had come to give the council the foreign ministers concessions on federal grants-in-aid. Clay, however, absolutely refused.

This situation resembled the July 1948 confrontation over the Frankfurt documents, and Clay resorted to his former strategy. By protecting the integrity of the London accords in July 1948, he had done much to assure that a constitution was nearly completed on schedule. That had been a major goal of U.S. policy in London. Now it was at risk. Unless the Basic Law was carried by a broad coalition, it would not be a firm basis for a new political order, as the Weimar experience showed. Therefore, Clay insisted that the Council work out a compromise that satisfied Allied demands on the division of financial powers before it would get the Washington concessions on grants-in-aid.

On April 14 the military governors met delegates of the Parliamentary Council to answer questions about the occupation statute. The generals barely managed to present a common front. To coax the Germans into compromise, Clay stressed the opportunities that awaited them once the Basic Law was agreed. The occupation statute, enacted "as a living document," would give a German government maximum autonomy. In reply to a remark by Carlo Schmid, the ranking SPD constitutional expert, Clay even suggested that "the Occupation Statute in many ways can be considered as de facto removal of the state of war."[68] Certainly, the foreign ministers had no

66 "Message to the Parliamentary Council," Apr. 8, 1949, *FRUS 1949*, 3:186.
67 Minutes, CRF/LOCP 12ème Séance, Apr. 10, 1949, AOFAA, Cabinet Civil, Pol V, K 4.
68 "Verbatim Minutes of Meeting of Three Military Governors with Representatives of the Parliamentary Council," Apr. 14, 1949, AOFAA, Cabinet Civil, Pol V, K 3, quotations pp. 7, 12. Cf. *FRUS 1949*, 3:237–42.

such intention. As Clay well knew, the opening sentence of the statute reaffirmed supreme Allied authority. He wanted to persuade Schmid, an influential SPD moderate who had long advocated an occupation statute, to seize the opportunity and accept the closest thing to a full West German government.[69] Offering to be the honest broker, Clay urged the Parliamentary Council members to come forward quickly with final proposals and clear up any differences with the help of the military governors. The sides agreed to meet again on April 25. The SPD members could not come earlier, as Clay wanted, because of a party convention on April 19–20 in Hanover. They would come, however, seemingly accepting Clay's challenge to reach agreement.

Now the British wanted the foreign ministers' compromise delivered immediately to encourage compromise in the council. But Clay balked. He did not object to the compromise as such. As his prescient comments on early drafts show, he believed it to be constructive and a useful basis for negotiation, but only after the parties in Bonn had fought out their battle over financial powers: "We must await German proposal or else we are most apt to upset the bucket. In other words, let us not tell the Germans we will compromise until they have offered some new proposal using the instructions then as our guide." If the foreign ministers' compromise was delivered prematurely, the SPD would be triumphant.[70]

When Clay would not forward the foreign ministers' compromise on grants-in-aid, he was not obstructing the new policy, but questioning the timing of its release. If premature, it threatened to ruin his plan to force agreement in the Parliamentary Council, so that all major parties stood behind the Basic Law. Clay had a report that the British liaison officer was letting Germans know that Britain would not accept a Basic Law against the SPD.[71] If the British had broken rank, and even offered to share their veto, the SPD had no reason to compromise. On the contrary, the SPD meeting in Hanover on April 19–20 escalated tensions by voting its own draft of the Basic Law. Yet the party did not rule out further talks on April 25, as pre-

---

69 For Schmid's thoughts on an occupation statute, see Carlo Schmid, *Erinnerungen* (Bern, 1979), 327–30; Hellmuth Auerbach, "Die politischen Anfänge Carlo Schmids: Kooperation und Konfrontation mit der französischen Besatzungsmacht 1945–1948," *VfZG* 36 (1988):643–4.

70 Telecon., Clay–Voorhees, Apr. 7, 1949, *Clay Papers*, 2:1093–9, quotation p. 1098.

71 Telecon., Clay–Voorhees, Apr. 12, 1949, *Clay Papers*, 2:1105.

viously agreed.[72] Meanwhile, on April 22, after Acheson personally overruled Clay, the Council received the foreign minister's concession on grants-in-aid.

Under Clay's masterful direction, the meeting on April 25, between the military governors and the Parliamentary Council representatives, achieved the compromise he sought. The Germans came with a joint proposal on the distribution of financial powers. The federation would legislate in concurrent fields (those shared with the states), whenever legal and economic unity had to be upheld. Clay and Robertson objected to this formula because it would allow the federation to encroach on the states. An appeal to the constitutional court would not help them, because national unity was not a strict legal concept but a volatile political idea. After some coaching by Clay, the Germans came up with a restrictive formula. The federation would ensure "homogeneity of living conditions," or equal economic opportunity when the states failed to do so.[73] But for such extra grants-in-aid the federation had to draw revenue out of the tax base of the states. The Germans thought that only the federal finance administration would be competent enough to handle the transfers. But thereby the federation would accumulate fiscal power. Clay was against "giving the Federal Government the right to interfere with State revenue."[74] A formula was needed to give the federation access to the taxes of the states without giving it more authority over them. After conferring with his colleagues, Clay set out a winning formula that maintained the federal–state balance. The federal government could legislate that a certain portion of specified state taxes would be reallocated for equalization grants. The states could defend their tax base against federal tax grabs in the upper house (Bundesrat), which had to approve such laws.[75] Thanking Clay, Adenauer accepted this suggestion. Then Clay exploited the propitious moment and urged the Germans to settle their last differences, now that those with the Allies were resolved. After a recess of more than one hour, Adenauer announced that the parties were agreed, and that "the Basic Law would soon be passed by a great majority in the Parliamentary Council." Adenauer acknowledged that the guidance and under-

72 Riddleberger to SecState, Apr. 12, 1949, *FRUS 1949*, 3:246–7.
73 "Meeting of Military Governors and Delegation of Parliamentary Council," Apr. 26 [sic., 25?], 1949, *FRUS 1949*, 3: ibid., 254, 257–9.
74 Ibid., 256.
75 Ibid., 259. Clay's suggestion was based on a formula in the foreign minister's letter delivered on April 22, 1949. The text was originally British; *Clay Papers*, 3:1094–5.

standing of the military governors and the letters from the foreign
ministers "had now brought their work to a happy conclusion."[76]
But that outcome was mostly due to Clay's perseverance. He understood that a Basic Law had to be supported by a great majority,
which would then be irrevocably committed to making the new political order a success.

The agreement of April 25 between the military governors and the
Parliamentary Council fulfilled in a large measure the constitutional
program that Clay had applied in the U.S. zone in 1946 and that the
United States had set out in the Council of Foreign Ministers meetings in 1946–47. A broad popular base, a short list of democratic essentials to guide Germans, a quick pace, and a fixed schedule had
been features of U.S. policy since 1945. The goal of that policy was
to establish institutions with sound democratic credentials that
would be widely accepted, would engage German political commitment, and would become the basis for an enduring political order.
Democratic legitimacy at all levels of government would facilitate
the reduction of U.S. involvement in German affairs. In the London
terms of 1948, the United States made concessions on democratic
principles it had upheld since 1946 in order to win agreement from
France. The elected constituent convention and popular referendum
on the constitution were sacrificed. The states were allowed a greater
role in the constituent process. In Frankfurt, in June 1948, the cosmetic concession on "Basic Law" helped Germans to begin the constituent process with goodwill. In Washington, in April 1949, the
Western foreign ministers made further concessions in order to help
the parties in the Parliamentary Council achieve agreement on the
Basic Law.

General Clay would disregard his own advisors, his British and
French colleagues, and even his State Department, in order to get
agreement from the Germans. In July 1948, he upheld the London
accords, not to defend any constitutional principle, but to prevent a
crippling compromise. In April 1949, when the Basic Law was
within reach, Clay again looked to the future success of the enterprise. To assure that the Basic Law had all-party support he even
stood up to his secretary of state. Thereby Clay helped to avert the
Western German polity's getting off to a rocky start, a predictable
beginning if the major parties had split over the Basic Law before it

76 *FRUS 1949*, 3:260.

was even promulgated. In both instances, Clay showed uncompromising political toughness to Germans and Allies alike. He was, in fact, defending to the utmost the long-term goals of U.S. policy on the German constitution: to block crippling delay; to assure that the constitution had a broad democratic base so its legitimacy could not be called into question; to avoid undue intervention and allow the constituent process maximum self-determination; and finally, to permit German political forces to play out their quarrels. Only then would the Basic Law have broad acceptance before responsibility passed to the new West German democracy.

3

American Policy toward German Unification, 1949–1955

HERMANN-JOSEF RUPIEPER

When U.S. Secretary of State Dean Acheson explained to British Foreign Minister Ernest Bevin the goals of American policy toward Germany after the end of the Berlin Blockade in May 1949, he pointed toward two troublesome interconnected problems: European integration and German unification. However, he made it clear beyond doubt that American support for reunification was dependent upon a general relaxation of East–West tensions: "If we can integrate a greater part of Germany than we now control under conditions which help and do not retard what we are now doing, we favor; but only if the circumstances are right."[1] After his return from the Geneva summit meeting, U.S. Secretary of State John Foster Dulles declared on July 28, 1955, before the National Security Council (NSC), "The West must keep pressing the German unification issue." He predicted, but did not wish to be held to his prediction, that "we might get a unification in the next two years."[2]

Both the Democratic and the Republican secretaries of state addressed themselves in their statements to difficult problems and expectations that influenced American policy from the foundation of the Federal Republic of Germany to its integration into the NATO alliance. Both statements also show that German reunification remained one of the principal goals of U.S. policy. While Acheson was rather cautious in his approach a few months before the first West German government was formed under Chancellor Konrad Adenauer, Dulles apparently believed that after West Germany's admission to NATO, fundamental U.S. preconditions for the peaceful

---

1 *FRUS 1949*, vol. 3, *Council of Foreign Ministers; Germany and Austria* (Washington, D.C., 1974), 873.
2 Memorandum of Discussion at the 256th Meeting of the National Security Council, July 28, 1955, EL, Ann Whitman File, NSC Records.

solution of the German question had been met. There was another difference. While Acheson was not quite clear about what was to be united, by 1955 there was no doubt that the term "unity" applied only to the territory of the Federal Republic, the German Democratic Republic (GDR), and Greater Berlin. Another remarkable difference also stands out. Dulles was indeed convinced between the Geneva summit meeting and the Foreign Ministers' Conference (July and October 1955) that a significant change had taken place in Soviet foreign policy, which had opened the possibility for an agreement between East and West on Germany. In a meeting with President Dwight D. Eisenhower, Dulles even ridiculed the cautious German Chancellor Konrad Adenauer who did not believe in the "Spirit of Geneva":

I [Dulles] said that I felt confident that Adenauer was wrong and had not yet adjusted to the new possibilities which I felt more likely than ever before the unification of Germany. I said that it was difficult for a man of Adenauer's age – about 80 – to adjust himself to a new line of thinking after he had been dedicated to another line for so long.[3]

Adenauer's expectations about the chances for overcoming the division of Germany proved to be correct at the time. It is necessary to remember that the policy of both the Truman and the Eisenhower administration toward Germany was the result of three interconnected problems: (1) the development of the East–West conflict and thus the global U.S.–Soviet confrontation; (2) any solution of the German problem was of crucial importance for the stabilization of Europe and the concept of Western European integration, which had started with the Marshall Plan; and (3), considering Western experiences with a united Germany and especially U.S. intervention in two world wars to prevent the domination of the continent by Germany, the future Germany also affected U.S. national security interests.

While the democratization of German society and the acceptance of Western values remained the undisputed preconditions and bases for American policy, reunification and European integration remained a source of permanent insecurity, agonizing doubts, and complex deliberations. German unity was not only of concern for the German people, but it also had to be analyzed in the wider context of

3 Memorandum of a Conversation between the President and the Secretary of State, Aug. 11, 1955, EL, John Foster Dulles Papers.

European and American security interests. In this essay, I address the development of the relationship between unification, integration, and security.

Although for the majority of the German people the quest for unification probably remained the most important national issue until the 1960s, American foreign policy had other priorities. As early as May 1949, Ambassador-at-Large Philipp C. Jessup summarized discussions in the Policy Planning Staff (PPS) of the Department of State:

> It is a major premise that the problem we are considering is not Germany in itself but the future of Europe as a whole. Germany is merely part of this problem. Thus the main objective is not the unification of Germany as an end in itself. The end in view is to support the Western European strength which has already been achieved and to expand it.[4]

George Kennan, director of the PPS and a sometime maverick as far as Germany was concerned, argued: "There is no solution to the German problem in terms of Germany. There is only a solution in terms of Europe."[5] Robert Murphy, formerly political advisor to General Lucius D. Clay and a highly regarded expert on German and European affairs, also stressed the European dimension of the German problem.[6]

The idea of taming the German "colossus" through European integration and a close connection with the Western powers was nothing new at the time. However, European integration was a far-off dream, although the European Council, the Organization for European Economic Cooperation (OEEC), and other organizations had been formed. According to American and European politicians, even the Federal Republic could pose a problem for West European equilibrium if the new state was not bound politically, economically, and militarily to the West. It might even be necessary to complete the process of integration before a new Germany could be permitted, one argument ran. After a meeting of American ambassadors in Europe, Charles Bohlen, counsellor of the American embassy in Paris, informed Washington that his colleagues believed that the members

---

4 Memo by Jessup on a discussion in the presence of Acheson May 5/6, 1949, NA, RG 59, Records of the Policy Planning Staff, 1947–1953, box 16, folder: Germany 1949 [hereafter: PPS Records].
5 *FRUS 1949*, 3:96 (March 8, 1949).
6 Ibid., 3:118ff. ("U.S. Policy respecting Germany," March 23, 1949).

of a "European Union" would have to be stronger than the Federal Republic "as to preclude the real possibility that Germany would dominate the Union."[7]

Another line of argument was influential as well. Immediately after the foundation of the Federal Republic, planners in Washington were convinced that the Western powers were working under a time limit, because the newly created Occupation Statute would have to be significantly revised soon in order to grant the Bonn government more political freedom. The basic argument was that four years after World War II the presence of occupation troops would lead to resentment and would in the long run be a heavy burden for the improvement of German–Allied relations. But there was another and equally important aspect of U.S. policy toward Germany: the relationship between security and unity. In Acheson's view, NATO was not only a defensive alliance against the Soviet Union, but it was also of crucial importance in order to influence and overcome a restrictive French policy toward Germany:

It is doubtful that, without some pact, the French would ever be reconciled with the inevitable diminution of direct allied control over Germany and the progressive reduction of occupation troops, that a pact of this nature would give France a greater sense of security against Germany as well as the Soviet Union and should considerably help in the realistic consideration of the problem of Germany.[8]

Besides the military control of Germany with its political as well as military advantages for the West, there existed another reason for the urgency of European integration. The Western powers had to prevent a future German–Russian alliance, a return to the Rapallo policy, or the reestablishment of an independent state that might act as an intermediary between East and West.[9] Although these basic concepts of American policy toward Europe and Germany had been formulated by 1949, there existed considerable insecurity with regard to their implementation. A number of important questions had not been solved satisfactorily. Should a European Union include Great Britain? Did the British refusal to bind the country to the continent

7 Bohlen to Kennan, Oct. 29, 1949, NA, RG 59, Charles E. Bohlen Papers, box 2, folder: Correspondence 1949–1953
8 Talk with Senators Connally and Vandenberg, Feb. 14, 1949, TL, Dean Acheson Papers, Memoranda of Conversations, folder: Jan.–Feb. 1949.
9 Memo, Bissell to Bruce, Oct. 15, 1949, NA, RG 59, Charles E. Bohlen Papers, box 6, folder: European Integration; NA, RG 59, Records of the Central European Division, 1944–53, box 1, folder: CE-Files; NA, RG 59, PPS Records, box 28, with several examples.

mean that it was preferable to demand a continental union? Would it be possible to bring about unity before the German problem had been solved? The answer to these questions of course depended partially on Soviet policy toward Germany.

Under these circumstances, the State Department adopted a two-track strategy: (1) to continue current attempts to create European unity and (2) to develop contingency plans in case the Soviet Union raised the issue of German unity at a four-power conference. The goal of this policy was to prevent Soviet exploitation of the theme of unity while the Western powers pushed for German integration. It was John J. McCloy, the first American high commissioner for Germany, who was especially concerned about this aspect of U.S. policy. When McCloy took over the position, the State Department presented him a "Directive on Germany," which outlined basic policy. It was the duty of the high commissioner to support the development of the Federal Republic toward political independence, to establish the Bonn Republic as a "responsible" and "equal" member of a free Western Europe, to strengthen democratic government, and to encourage the Germans "to take an increasingly active part in the political and economic organization of a free Europe."[10] During 1950 a more detailed approach was developed within the High Commission that became the overall concept for Germany. Since German reunification could not be achieved within the foreseeable future or only by force against the Soviet Union, which would have led to World War III and was thus clearly unacceptable, or through the acceptance of Soviet proposals for Germany, which in the end could only lead to a Soviet-controlled Germany or a neutralized country–both horrifying concepts for most U.S. decision makers – the primary goal remained the strengthening of West Germany. For McCloy the Federal Republic played an important role in a policy designed to block future Soviet expansion. This concept also implied that the control of developments in West Germany would lead to something like "peaceful coexistence" with the Soviet bloc. An integrated West Germany might further have a magnetic impact upon the GDR, would strengthen the prestige of West German democracy and would thus in the long run become an equal and sovereign partner of the West, a country that would reject any seductive approaches from the Soviet Union.

---

10 *FRUS 1950*, vol. 3, *Western Europe* (Washington, D.C., 1977), 590–6 (Feb. 9, 1950).

For McCloy and the State Department, European integration was unmistakably more important than German unity. In fact European integration would solve most American security problems and lead to the establishment of peace in Europe. On the other hand, for political and psychological reasons a close relationship between the goal of European integration and German unity had to be established in order to gain the unwavering allegiance of the German population. McCloy formulated these goals in a letter to Washington in February 1950:

a) Convert West Germany into the positive pole of attraction in respect of German unification, b) enlist the psychological support of the German people against Soviet objectives, c) convince them of the advantages of association with the West, and d) dissuade them that integration with the West connotes a writing–off of the East.

In order to gain full support from the Germans, he even considered it necessary at the beginning of 1950 to play upon German national feeling:

The portion of Germany now held or controlled by the Soviets (including the Polish-administered territories) should be converted into an "irredenta" through the association of the Western powers and the West Germans with the deep-seated desire of the German people to unite their country and ultimately to enjoy the perquisites of an independent power.[11]

Thus one of the structural devices of U.S. planning was to attempt to use both the prospect of integration *and* the possibility of unity to advance American policy. It was quite clear to Washington and the High Commission that without a convincing concept it would hardly be possible to gain the support of these forces in German society such as the Social Democratic Party (SPD), the Protestant church, and other opponents or skeptics of "integration first" who argued that integration and unity were antiethical concepts. In this difficult situation, Adenauer became Washington's biggest asset. His loyal support for the policy of Western integration was the German pillar of U.S. policy. Unlike any other German politician, Adenauer identified his political future with integration, rapprochement with France, and the leading role of the United States in Europe. The chancellor never left any doubt that European integration was an unrenounceable political demand in order to strengthen Europe, to en-

---

11 SecState, "Attainment of United States Objectives in Germany by Denial of those of USSR," NA, RG 59, 611.62/1-2050 HICOG 196.

force a permanent linkage between the Germans and the west, and thus to prevent Soviet domination of all of Europe. As early as the end of September 1951, he informed the Allied High Commission:

We wish Ger[many] unified and integrated in West. Sov[iets] know full well integration of Europe is impossible without Germany. Sov[iets] wish to frustrate integration of Europe and will pay a good price for it. Is the integration of Europe necessary in the long run – if one accepts this it is necessary to turn down any Sov[iet] proposal whether favorable or otherwise.[12]

Since the integration of the Federal Republic into the Western alliance was necessary from the point of view of both European and American security, the importance of German economic and demographic potential grew even more after the outbreak of the Korean War.[13] Developments in Korea proved to be a watershed for the military integration of the Federal Republic into the West and laid the basis for a West German defense contribution. On the other hand, these changes significantly influenced Soviet political strategy toward Germany. After the horrible costs of Hitler's attack on the Soviet Union, Moscow was especially appalled at the prospect of German rearmament. On November 3, 1950, the Soviet government sent notes to the Western powers demanding a Four-Power Conference to deal with German demilitarization and the Potsdam Agreement.[14]

This attempt to reduce global tension to the tangled German question and rearmament was a simplification of East–West problems that was immediately rejected by the United States and the other Western powers. After all, the Soviet Union had created a paramilitary force in the GDR in May 1950, the Volkspolizeibereitschaften, as the nucleus for an army, despite Western protests. Furthermore, the wars in Korea and in Indochina, the Formosa conflict, and the unsolved Austrian problem showed that other areas of tension existed as well. From an American point of view, a conference thus made sense only if it analyzed all causes of global tension. After the entry of regular Chinese troops into the Korean War, the U.S. government rejected any attempt to discuss Germany separately from

12 Notes taken by General Hayes at a meeting of the High Commission with the Federal Chancellor at Schloss Ernich, Sept. 9, 1951, NA, RG 466, HICOG, box E0 (51) 73.
13 *Anfänge westdeutscher Sicherheitspolitik 1945–1956*, ed. Militärgeschichtliches Forschungsamt, vol. 1, *Von der Kapitulation bis zum Pleven-Plan* (Munich and Vienna, 1982).
14 *FRUS 1950*, vol. 4, *Central and Eastern Europe: The Soviet Union* (Washington, D.C., 1980), 902–3.

global problems.[15] On the other hand, it was understood that Germany would be a major topic at any Four-Power Conference. This aspect certainly played a role when Acheson suggested four topics in preparation for a meeting of the Council of Foreign Ministers at the end of December 1950: (1) German reunification and all-German elections, (2) examination of a peace treaty, (3) withdrawal of occupation troops, and (4) demilitarization of Germany.[16] On January 18, 1951, the State Department's Bureau of German Affairs submitted a German program that was accepted the same day by the Steering Group on the German Question. On January 21, the Joint Chiefs of Staff accepted it from a military perspective.[17]

The program not only was a general survey but also illuminated the goals of the State Department. First, the solution of the German question would not eliminate the causes of global tension. These could be found in worldwide Soviet activities. Second, any acceptable solution of the German problem would have to be (a) supported by public opinion in the west, (b) carried out with the support of Britain and France, (c) acceptable to the Germans, and (d) not damaging to U.S. national security interests. Third, any weakening of the American position in Europe had to be prevented so long as no East–West agreement existed on basic security questions. This meant that the United States would not accept the inclusion of the Federal Republic or a united Germany in a system of collective security that accepted the neutralization or demilitarization of any part or all of Germany. Equally unacceptable were demands for a withdrawal of U.S. troops from Europe and a Soviet proposal that threatened West German participation in the Coal and Steel Community or the planned European Defense Community.[18]

Besides this general framework that stressed the connection between Germany and Western Europe and tied the United States to the old continent, more specific ideas emerged concerning demilitarization, reunification, a peace treaty, withdrawal of occupation troops, and lifting restrictions upon the German peace economy. These concepts served a double purpose: to counter Soviet moves and to prove that the United States supported a *reasonable* solution of

15 Ibid., 904–26.
16 Tel. 3185, State Dept.–London, NA, RG 59, 762A.00/12-2850.
17 NA, RG 319, Records of the Army Staff G-3, 091 Germany TS (Sect. II D) (Book I) (Case 38 Only) (Sub. No. 1-15), RPTS D-4/5a, Jan. 20, 1951.
18 "Policy Review for Possible Talks with the Soviets–German Unity," ibid., RPTS D-4/3b, Jan. 25, 1951.

the German question. Because the Soviet Union had broken the Potsdam Agreement by creating paramilitary units in the GDR, and because it was necessary to improve Western defense "against aggression in Soviet mobilization and imperialism," demilitarization could be dealt with only in the context of a Soviet offer to reunify Germany. In order to achieve German unity, a constitutional assembly could be formed after free elections in the GDR under United Nations or Four-Power control. These contingency plans for a meeting with the Soviets also demanded the dissolution of the Volkspolizeibereitschaften, the ratification of a new German constitution by two-thirds of the German states (if the constitution was not rejected by a unanimous vote of the four powers), and the establishment of an all-German government. In addition, these proposals were based upon a termination of reparation payments, the return of Soviet-controlled companies in the GDR, and the introduction of an Allied Control Council based upon majority decisions, demands clearly indigestible to the Soviets or at least most difficult. Furthermore, until the signing of a peace treaty, Germany would not be allowed an army, with the exception of a small police force to maintain internal security. After the peace treaty had been signed, Germany would have the right to join a collective security pact. However, any German army would be limited in size and equipment. In order to reduce tension between East and West, Soviet troops in Germany had to be reduced under international control to one-third of all occupation troops, the argument being that the Soviet Union was only one of four occupation powers and that from a security point of view the Soviets did not need more troops in the GDR, which had a smaller population than West Germany. After ratification of the new German constitution a redeployment of troops would take place. Soviet troops were to be withdrawn behind the Oder-Neisse line while Western troops would fall back behind a line comprising the Weser, Fulda, Main, and Danube rivers. The proposal was also based upon the premise that an agreement on Austria was possible and Soviet troops would be withdrawn from Rumania, Hungary, and Czechoslovakia.

At this time, fairly concrete ideas were developed for the process of reunification. Three months after the constitution of an all-German government, a peace conference would take place, at which the German government would be consulted. In order to prevent endless negotiations as in the case of Austria, the participating powers had to submit a peace treaty within three months. This conference should also deal with border questions, the withdrawal of occupation troops, and provisions for the creation of a German army. From the American point of view, a formula had to be found in the meantime which would secure German admission to a Western defense organization (NATO).

Such proposals were also part of the two-track system that characterized U.S. policy at the time. For a number of reasons, such as security, Soviet prestige, and loss of influence upon developments in Germany and Eastern Europe, the proposals were clearly unacceptable to the Soviet Union, while they appeared to be reasonable from a Western point of view. Considering possible Soviet reactions, such deliberation could only be rejected by Moscow. Did this mean that these proposals had been developed to block German unity? The answer to this question is not easy. Washington rejected a compromise on Germany, since this would destroy all plans for European unity and a Western defense alliance. Not only was the Federal Republic assigned the role of economic locomotive for Europe, but a German military contribution made Western conventional defense credible. Thus the United States was not prepared to give up the part of Germany controlled by the West. This did not mean that Washington was satisfied with the division of Germany, although the position implied division for an unforeseeable future if the Soviets rejected the U.S. approach. However, at this time a number of high-ranking members of the State Department did not consider reunification on American terms totally impossible. This surprising interpretation was based upon an analysis of Soviet and American strength. At the end of December 1950, long after the famous National Security Council paper NSC 68 with its threatening perception of Soviet capacities became accepted policy, Philipp C. Jessup described the position of the West in a memorandum for Acheson in the following terms:

Actually, the Western position, in terms of basic Soviet estimates, is one of strength. The Soviets are fully cognizant of the productive power of the United States and admire it. They are impressed by the results of our effort in World War II and have not forgotten the recovery we made after Pearl Harbor. If they do not launch World War III now it may be because they realize better than we admit the basic strength of our position and because they believe our allies can be split and our position softened by the war of nerves.

Jessup was convinced that no reason existed for Western concessions to the Soviet Union.[19]

H. Freeman Matthews, deputy undersecretary of state, and members of the PPS shared this opinion. Even Acheson agreed with the analysis and favored negotiation from a position of strength.[20] The American chargé d'affaires in Moscow, Walworth Barbour, did not consider it totally unlikely that the Soviet Union might offer an agreement on Austria, the "nonneutralization of Germany" and a peace treaty in exchange for a limitation of NATO troops.[21] Negotiations from a position of strength implied that the Western powers could wait for an agreeable Soviet offer until after the Brussels Conference and only then rearm Germany. The State Department planning paper for a Four-Power Conference states:

We should approach the exploratory talks and, if it eventuates, a CFM with the belief that their value lies in a) gaining time, b) propaganda advantage, and c) convincing the Soviet that we are determined and confident. We should not be sanguine of reaching any real settlements although we should always seek them.[22]

During the discussions in preparation for a conference, the question was also posed what influence a redeployment of troops would have on the reduction of tensions in Europe. Interestingly enough, it was Acheson himself who approached the difficult issue. Already in February 1950 Acheson had stimulated discussions about withdrawal of troops from Germany, and apparently he was still interested in a reduction of occupation troops in early 1951.

The Secretary said he had wondered about the possibility of withdrawal of troops in Germany. He recalled that the Military had been against this sometime back and he wondered if there was any change in their attitude at this time. "The horse-back opinion" of Mr. Thompson and Mr. Rusk was that there was no change but Mr. Rusk said he would look into it.[23]

Even after the outbreak of the Korean War, and even more important after a decision had been made about a West German defense contribution, Acheson was still interested in a redeployment of troops

19 *FRUS 1950*, 4:922–3 (Mar. 2, 1950); *FRUS 1951*, vol. 3, *European Security and the German Question* (Washington, D.C., 1981), 1038–41.
20 *FRUS 1950*, 4:922, and passim.
21 Tel. 1457, Moscow–State Dept. NA, RG 59, 762A.5/2-451.
22 *FRUS 1951*, 3:1051 (Dec. 28, 1950).
23 NA, RG 59, Records of the Office of the Executive Secretariat, Minutes of the Secretary's Daily Meetings 1949–1952, box 4, folder: 1949–50, Feb. 27, 1950.

and a reduction of tension. A redeployment of troops would have had the advantage that the Soviet rejection would have shown that the Soviets were not willing to give up control over the satellite states.[24] Consequently Acheson submitted to the Secretary of Defense George Marshall a draft that was a modified version of the Byrnes proposals to Soviet Foreign Minister Molotov at the end of 1946 and in 1947: "Secretary Acheson wondered if there was any point in reviving such a proposal or whether the whole thing belonged to a past era."[25]

For Acheson, who was apparently also trying to come to terms with the problem of how to make clear to the Soviets that West German units did not create an offensive potential against the Soviet Union, troop reductions seem to have served a double purpose. On the one hand reductions could be described as a contribution to detente; on the other hand the suggestion could be seen as a contribution to security for Europe and from Germany: "Secretary said that, while accepting a limitation of this sort might make Eisenhower's task more difficult, if there were some natural limitation – such as the German's not raising more than 150,000 to 200,000 troops, we might be willing to take some modifications."[26] However, by the time that negotiations between the high commissioners and the Adenauer government took place at the Petersberg hotel in preparation for a German army while similar discussions were held in Paris between the Federal Republic and the other European powers, such initiatives were outdated. Both the NSC and Marshall rejected serious discussions of Acheson's deliberations.[27]

The Soviet note of March 10, 1952, confronted the United States and the Western powers suddenly with an initiative to prevent the military integration of the Federal Republic into the Western alliance. The note revealed the options of the Federal Republic: a Western defense contribution and consequently a prolongation of the division of Germany or neutralization under rather vague conditions. Any answer would have to be carefully drafted. After the first analysis,

---

24 L. D. Battle to Jessup, Feb. 7, 1951, NA, RG 59, PPS Records, box 28.
25 Memo of conversation, Feb. 13, 1951, TL, Dean Acheson Papers, Memorandum of Conversations 1951, box 66, folder: Feb. 1951.
26 Ibid.
27 NSC, Memorandum for General Marshall, March 23, 1951, NA, RG 330, Secretary of Defense, Assistant Secretary of Defense, Office of Foreign Military Affairs, Western European Section, Subject File 1951–53, folder: CD 092 (Germany).

Acheson was convinced that the main goal of the note was the prevention of a West German contribution to the European Defense Community (EDC), although it could not be excluded that the Soviets were submitting a serious offer. The test for the seriousness of Soviet intentions was free elections. Any answer to the note had to be based upon the belief that free elections were not acceptable to the Soviets as a first step toward reunification. Equally important, the West had to prove to the German people that reunification played an important role in U.S. policy while neutralization or an Austrian solution was ruled out. The Policy Planning Staff developed options in order to test Soviet intentions, but already on March 18 Acheson left no doubt "that our main purpose sh[ou]ld be to drive ahead with the signature and ratification of the EDC and the contractual relations with Ger[many] and that we sh[ou]ld not permit the Russians to accomplish their obvious purpose of frustrating both by delay."[28] This meant that European integration and the creation of the EDC clearly had priority over the German question. During the exchange of notes in the summer of 1952, discussions at the State Department were based mainly upon the hypothesis that it was both necessary and possible to show world public opinion the insincerity of Soviet proposals while at the same time the Germans had to be convinced that integration *and* unity were both possible. However, Acheson himself had considerable doubts about the justification of this argument. He informed McCloy on April 21, 1952:

> To Germany we cannot honestly or realistically predict or promise that unification will follow automatically in wake of integration. But we may point out that without integration of Federal Republic with West, Germans cannot count on ever attaining (and maintaining) German unity under conditions of freedom and equality.[29]

Although the State Department had stressed the importance of a peace treaty in the exchange of notes as the last step to overcome the stalemate in Europe, no definite guidelines existed beyond those

28 *FRUS 1952–1954*, vol. 8, *Eastern Europe; Soviet Union; Eastern Mediterranean* (Washington, D.C., 1988), 185 (March 18, 1952). For the controversial Stalin note, see Rolf Steininger, *Eine Chance zur Wiedervereinigung? Die Stalinnote vom 10. März 1952* (Bonn, 1985). On the concept of neutralization, see Andreas Hillgruber, *Alliierte Pläne für eine "Neutralisierung" Deutschlands 1945–1955*, Rheinische-Westfälische Akademie der Wissenschaften, Vorträge G 286 (Opladen, 1987).
29 See Hermann-Josef Rupieper, "Deutsche Frage und europäische Sicherheit: Politisch-strategische Ueberlegungen 1953/1955," in Bruno Thoss and Hans-Erich Volkmann, eds., *Zwischen Kaltem Krieg und Entspannung: Sicherheits- und Deutschlandpolitik der Bundesrepublik im Mächtesystem der Jahre 1953–1956* (Boppard, 1988), 179ff., esp. 183–4.

discussed earlier. The submittal of a Soviet peace treaty proposal on March 10, 1952, and discussions with the European allies convinced Washington that more concrete and detailed preparations for a peace conference could not be postponed any longer. From August to November 1952, several meetings took place in the Bureau of German Affairs. Although these first tentative attempts to formulate plans for a peace treaty were never transformed into an official draft, and although discussions were limited to a small circle and could not be completed because of the interruption of the exchange of notes by the Soviet Union, it is enlightening to explore the basic ideas. These concepts played an important role in preparation for the Berlin Foreign Ministers' Conference in early 1954 and underlined the fundamental willingness of the Bureau of German Affairs to strive for a peace treaty after free elections and the creation of an all-German government. Interestingly enough, officials reached the conclusion that neither the General Treaty, nor the European Coal and Steel Community or EDC were obstacles to reunification. On the other hand, difficult legal and political problems would have to be solved considering the differing interpretations of Article 7.3 of the General Treaty. Would a united Germany have to accept the provisions of the treaty binding Germany to the West?[30] Whatever the results of negotiations with a German government, the State Department did not intend to grant full sovereignty allowing a united Germany to choose between east and west, perhaps even declaring its neutrality.

Coburn D. Kidd, director of Government and Administrative Affairs in the Bureau of German Affairs and one of the most prolific minds concerning German affairs, submitted a draft for a peace treaty on October 2, 1952, based upon the Soviet note of March 10, 1952. Kidd feared that the United States was losing the contest with the Soviets over Germany. In order to gain continued German support, he argued that the United States should attempt to work for a peace treaty. Kidd admitted to his colleagues that when discussing Germany's future, Washington had been more interested in U.S. national interests than in German unity. The Truman administration had dealt with the German question only half-heartedly: "I am afraid

---

30 Tel. A 374, State Dept.–Bonn, NA, RG 59, 662A.00/9-1952.

that what this can lead to is suspicion as to our motives, whence it is only a step to the question whether we are acting primarily in our own interest rather than that of the Germans, desirous of unity, and the Europeans, apprehensive about peace."

Kidd further argued that the United States had avoided serious negotiations, given that neither Washington had been prepared for them nor did a clear policy outline exist. Thus the Western powers had doggedly stuck to the concept of free elections "for which there is not a ghost of a chance of Soviet acceptance."[31] Against this defensive and in the long run most dangerous attitude Kidd emphasized the advantage of his proposal. Peace treaty negotiations would prove to the Germans that the West could always submit a better proposal for unity than the Soviet Union. He also stressed negative German attitudes toward Moscow and was convinced that the German population would be more attracted by Western democracy than Soviet Communism. Because of previous experiences with the Soviet Union and the still pending negotiations over EDC, other members of the Bureau of German Affairs rejected this concept.

Apparently three different approaches existed within the State Department concerning a peace treaty at this time. These arguments are so important for understanding U.S. policy that they are quoted now at length.

1. Many people feel that however necessary it is to talk about a "peace treaty" and "unity" for the record, a unified Germany is in itself an undesirable thing and the longer the division can be continued the better. The argument is that a divided Germany is a manageable Germany; whereas a reunited Germany would be of a size and strength and disposition that there would be no holding her, but instead she would be seeking to dominate the other European nations, politically, economically, and military, as she had in the past, and that this would create havoc with our efforts at European integration, such as the CSC, EDC, and the EPC.

2. The second argument is not so much against a reunited Germany in itself, or a treaty which would bring this about, as against unification *before* means have been found of binding Germany securely in the Western camp. If a formula could be found for accomplishing this, there would be no objection to subscribing a treaty, but until such formula has been found, or other means (such as free all-German elections) have accom-

31 Memo, Kidd to Laukhuff, NA, RG 59, 662.001/10-2552.

plished the result, little value is perceived in discussing a treaty, which would be merely a repetition of the endless discussions of the CFM and Palais Rose.

3. The third argument runs that a divided Germany is necessary as a means to accomplish vital ulterior objectives. E.g., that it is necessary that American troops be stationed in Germany for the defense of Western Europe, and that if there is no way of guaranteeing this from a united Germany, there is no alternative, in the existing situation, to keeping the present division. Or that it is necessary, for the purpose of the "cold war", to maintain the present restrictions on East-West trade, and if there is no way of guaranteeing this from a united independent Germany, it is better to continue to deal with the Federal Republic.[32]

Negotiations with the Soviet Union had shown that the second line of argument prevailed among planners in the State Department. For Kidd, however, all arguments were hardly convincing in the long run: (1) the German nation could not be divided forever; (2) if the Germans were allowed to choose they would vote for the West; and (3) current military advantages of the EDC might well be nullified within a few years. In addition U.S. policy had to take into account that the Germans would request unification regardless. Even though any solution of the tangled German question was like squaring the circle, the opinion grew more and more among planners that "German disunity was an intolerable anomaly." A disunited Germany, a member of the PPS argued, was despite obvious dangers for peace in Europe "a time bomb imbedded in any peace structure." Without ending the division of Germany the division of Europe could not be overcome. Although necessary changes could only take place over a long period of time:

It must still be admitted that a united Germany should be a goal of Western policy because its absence in the long run, would create intolerable dangers and because German unity lies in the logic of history.[33]

The new Republican administration of Eisenhower continued the prevailing policy of integrating West Germany into the West while simultaneously keeping the "German question" open. Dwight D. Eisenhower and Secretary of State John Foster Dulles were perhaps

---

32 Memo, "German Peace Treaty," Kidd to Laukhuff and Morris, NA, RG 59, 662.001/11-2052. Compare similar analysis in memo by Fuller, "Squaring the Circle of German Unity," Oct. 21, 1952, NA, RG 59, PPS Records, box 16.

33 "Squaring the Circle of German Unity," Oct. 21, 1952, NA, RG 59, PPS Records, box 16.

even more committed to the priority of European unity and to consolidating the defense of the West than Truman and Acheson, although Dulles for reasons of domestic policy rejected the policy of containment and stressed the more aggressive concepts of "roll back" and "liberation." For Eisenhower, the presence of U.S. troops in Europe had always been a temporary emergency measure in order to stabilize the Old World and prevent further Soviet expansion. During his presidency, the political, economic, and military integration of the Federal Republic into a Western defensive alliance played a central role in a strategic concept designed to protect U.S. security interests. Eisenhower formulated this strategy on numerous occasions, but perhaps never as straightforwardly as in his personal correspondence with his intimate friend and successor to the NATO supreme command in Europe, General Alfred Gruenther. In autumn 1953 Eisenhower defined five reasons for the presence of the United States in Europe: (1) to support Europe economically, (2) to assist in providing the necessary military equipment, (3) to strengthen Europe through the presence of U.S. troops, help "local morale," and supply forces while the Europeans could build up indigenous forces, (4) to assure Europe that the United States would in time of trouble "instantly rush reinforcements to the affected area," and (5) to assist in greater cooperation and unification.

From the very beginning, some of our troop dispositions were visualized as temporary emergency measures. I think that none of us have ever believed for an instant that the United States could over the long term (several decades) build a sort of Roman wall with its own troops and so protect the world. Not only would the ultimate cost be excessive, equally important is the adverse reaction that eventually springs up in any country where foreign troops are stationed. . . . In addition, we have our own political situation at home. . . . You and I have long known all of this; and the considerations I have outlined are not dependent on advent or effectiveness of new weapons.

Eisenhower was not willing to say this in public, but he assured Gruenther that the Europeans would have to be educated about U.S. intentions. "However, in all honesty, we cannot allow anyone to get up and protest that we are going to keep troops in Europe forever."[34]

From this perspective, the creation of a West German army within EDC (the only concept that seemed acceptable to France) became so

---

34 Eisenhower to Gruenther, Oct. 27, 1953, EL, Ann Whitman File, Administrative Series, box 16, folder: Gruenther; see NSC, 132nd Meeting, Feb. 18, 1953, EL, Ann Whitman File, NSC Series, box 4.

important to Eisenhower that he asked Dulles repeatedly to use all pressure necessary to convince the hesitant French government and to make sure a German defense contribution would materialize within the shortest possible time. Only under this condition would it be possible to harmonize different aspects of U.S. policy: security, budgetary relief, and European integration.[35] For Dulles it was likewise obvious that integration was the only possible course to the stabilization of Western Europe and to prevent a repetition of the events of the interwar years. Like hardly any other American politician, Dulles was influenced by his personal experience with the Versailles Treaty and its failure to secure a lasting peace. He further believed that only a policy of strength and the creation of EDC would guarantee that both goals of U.S. policy – integration and German unity – could be achieved: "If an attempt were made to create German unity by some other vehicle than EDC then certainly the EDC would be finished."[36] Although Dulles as early as autumn 1953 initiated the development of options in case EDC failed, he never stood fully behind them, believing that any concept other than EDC would be dangerous and might lead to German withdrawal from the west. He feared that the Soviets might offer tempting terms concerning Germany's eastern borders or markets for German industries.[37] He strongly objected to neutralization, which he considered would be a "disaster."[38]

Although Dulles always kept trace of the goal of integration, the State Department continued its planning for a final peace treaty with Germany. As before, all plans were based upon "Eden-rock," that is, free elections as a first step on the road to unification. Although Soviet agreement was most unlikely, it could not be excluded with certainty. For example, the State Department learned from Soviet diplomats in Washington that free elections might be possible if the West would agree to neutralization.[39] And even after West German

35 NSC, 150th Meeting, June 18, 1953, EL, Ann Whitman File, NSC Series, box 4.
36 NSC, 136th Meeting, March 12, 1953, EL, Ann Whitman File, NSC Series, box 4.
37 NSC, 215th Meeting, September 27, 1954, EL, Ann Whitman File, NSC Series, box 4.
38 NSC, 216th Meeting, Oct. 1, 1954, EL, Ann Whitman File, NSC Series, box 4.
39 Telephone Conversation with James Reston, Dec. 30, 1953, EL, John Foster Dulles Papers, Telephone Call Series, box 2, folder: Memoranda (Except to and from White House) Nov. 1, 1953–Dec. 31, 1953. Reston had been asked by Konstantin G. Fedoseev and Smirnowsky to meet them in order to talk about negative reports in U.S. newspapers about the upcoming meeting. Apparently the meeting had been demanded by Soviet Foreign Minister Molotov.

admission to NATO, the Soviet ambassador to Paris, Sergei A. Vinogrodov, informed U.S. Ambassador C. Douglas Dillon on June 22, 1955 "that the USSR was prepared to accept free all-German elections under strict international control provided only that foreign troops were withdrawn from Germany in advance."[40] These were obviously trial balloons. But it was evident that Washington was not interested in negotiations with the Soviet Union about the future of Germany before the Federal Republic had been definitely bound to the West. Only from that point could four-power talks receive serious consideration. Since the Soviet Union had always warned that West German entry into any Western military alliance would block reunification, this could be interpreted as an attempt to show that the United States favored unification on reasonable terms while Soviet obstructionism destroyed any agreement. The obvious propaganda advantage of such an approach should not be dismissed entirely, because opinion polls in Germany that were known before the Geneva summit meeting and were discussed in the NSC showed that a clear majority existed in favor of unity over integration. But Dulles especially, who had always been highly critical of Soviet policy and skeptical about chances for an agreement, at least for several weeks during the summer of 1955, seems to have believed that German unity was still possible. From hindsight, but also considering the contemporary political constellation, this was a rather surprising evaluation. However, Dulles argued that since the death of Stalin, Soviet foreign policy had shifted from a hard line without concessions to one of détente and flexibility. Furthermore, the struggle over the succession of Stalin, economic difficulties, the rise of China, differences within the East bloc, as well as the sudden willingness to sign a peace treaty with Austria, the reconciliation with Tito, and the submission of concrete disarmament proposals seemed to indicate that the new leaders in Moscow might be interested in an improvement of relations with the West.[41] Consequently Dulles suggested in a letter to Adenauer: "If we stay strong and resolute it will be possible to accomplish the unification of Germany, the peaceful liberation

40 "Probable Soviet Treatment of the German Problem in the Forthcoming Conference," July 2, 1955, p. 1, NA, RG 84, HICOG/Be 2183/37, Summit Meeting Geneva, SUM D-2/4.
41 See NSC, 249th Meeting, May 19, 1955, and 253rd Meeting, July 1, 1955, EL, Ann Whitman File, NSC Records; memo of conversation, June 13, 1955, in *FRUS 1955–1957*, vol. 4, *Western European Security and Integration* (Washington, D.C., 1986), 224–8.

of the satellites and thereafter accomplish something substantial in the limitation of armaments."[42]

Dulles also interpreted the Western European Union (WEU) and NATO as defensive alliances that from a security point of view not only protected Western Europe against future German aggression but also prevented Germany from an aggressive policy of changing existing borders in the east. Soviet politicians had always argued that the German question was above all a security problem; thus, Dulles was willing to sign a security pact to remove their anxieties.[43] He went even further. Although he had always been opposed to demilitarized zones as part of such a pact, Dulles was nevertheless flexible enough not to reject them out of hand if such zones would make German unity acceptable to the Soviets. This is at least what he told the British ambassador to Washington, Sir Roger M. Makins, on July 9, 1955: "If some combination of the ideas we had been discussing would allow us to achieve the unification of Germany, the United States would be inclined to accept it, overriding objections about demilitarized strips and elements of the package."[44]

Dulles apparently based his convictions upon his belief that perhaps over a longer period of negotiations (at least once he mentioned two years) the Western solution to the German question – free elections, a constitutional assembly, the signing of a nonaggression treaty and security pact, limitation of forces and armament in Europe, inspection and fixation of troop levels as well as other means creating confidence – might have a chance. However, he also feared that the Geneva summit meeting would turn out to be a complete failure if the British and French fell into Soviet traps. But he felt even greater concern for President Eisenhower: "He is so inclined to be humanly generous, to accept a superficial tactical smile as evidence of inner warmth, that he might in a personal moment with the Russians accept a promise or a proposition at face value and upset the apple cart." Dulles feared that a policy of appeasement would make it impossible for him to stay as secretary of state.[45] Considering his conviction that he was the only person able to handle U.S. policy, this may be doubted. However, Dulles was uncomfortable about the

42 *FRUS 1955–1957*, vol. 5, *Austrian State Treaty; Summit and Foreign Ministers' Meetings, 1955* (Washington, D.C., 1988), 227 (June 13, 1955).
43 Ibid., 313–14 (July 9, 1955) and 319ff. (July 15, 1955).
44 Tel., Makins-London, July 9, 1955, PRO, FO 371/118 228 WG 1071/890.
45 C. D. Jackson Log Entry, July 11, 1955, *FRUS 1955–1957*, 5:301ff.

new situation while he at the same time warned against an inflexible approach, attacking Eisenhower's special advisor for disarmament questions, Harold E. Stassen, in a meeting of the NSC on July 7, 1955, after Stassen had warned against extending the security provisions of the WEU-Treaty to Eastern Europe.

Secretary Dulles replied with feeling that we would never succeed in our objective of a united Germany, if we insisted upon limitation of the level of German armament, which level was wholly controlled by the Western powers – that is, the unification of Germany would be impossible unless it was achieved under some sort of international control in which the Soviet Union would have a choice. The Soviets would never simply throw East Germany into the pot to be added to West Germany and the united Germany to be further armed against the Soviet Union itself.[46]

State Department planning for a peace treaty was based upon the assumption that only the Federal Republic, the GDR, and Greater Berlin would be included in a reunited Germany. This position had not changed at all since 1947. At best some correction of the Oder-Neisse line based upon historical and economic lines was possible. These considerations were, however, always based upon the premise that Poland and Germany could reach a peaceful solution at the negotiation table. The Allied High Commission had never left any doubt about Western attitudes in its talks with Adenauer, and the chancellor had accepted this position in a meeting with the three foreign ministers in November 1951. He promised: "That he would not press for any change in the present position of our three Governments as regards Germany's eastern territories."[47] It is true that Adenauer, under the burden of refugees and expellees, an important voting potential for the CDU, argued that no German government could renounce Germany's claim for the territories east of the Oder-Neisse. But he always promised a negotiated settlement based upon a new spirit of cooperation.[48] Under certain conditions, Adenauer was even willing to accept the loss of these territories. In a conversation with U.S. High Commissioner James B. Conant before the summit meeting, Adenauer stressed: "there were two phases of the reunification problem which could *not* be discussed publicly. The first was the Oder-Neisse line which he could neither agree to as the

46 Ibid., 276.
47 Landesarchiv Berlin, RG 84, HICOG, Be 2183/37, p. 1, Summit Meeting Geneva, SUM D-2/2, July 1, 1955; *FRUS 1951*, 3:1609–11.
48 *FRUS 1952–1954*, vol. 7, *Germany and Austria* (Washington, D.C., 1986), 460ff., 468–9 (May 29, 1953; June 4, 1953).

boundary of Germany nor could he refuse reunification if that were made the condition. . . ."[49] Again the chancellor proved to be a pragmatic politician who accepted the realities of international politics and thus again fulfilled American expectations. Did such a statement in Dulles's interpretation not indicate that Germany's Eastern border could be guaranteed in a final security agreement with the Soviet Union?

Dulles indeed believed even after the end of the Geneva summit meeting that chances for a solution of the German question still existed. This expectation may even have gained momentum because of the Geneva experience that from a security perspective Western and Soviet views regarding Germany were not too far apart. Although the chances for an adjustment were probably nil, he argued his case with both Eisenhower and Adenauer.[50] On the other hand, Dulles always warned that the process of reunification would take some time.[51]

Adenauer's visit to Moscow, sharply criticized by U.S. Ambassador Charles E. Bohlen because the establishment of diplomatic relations legalized the division of Germany, seems to have reduced Dulles's expectations concerning first steps toward overcoming the division of Germany.[52] Although Dulles still argued that Soviet leadership was uncertain about the next moves, he confirmed Adenauer's experience that after West German entry into NATO Moscow was no longer interested in reunification.[53] This was at least the line of argument he presented to the NSC a few days before leaving for the Geneva foreign ministers' meeting October 20, 1955. According to Dulles, the real problem was not Soviet security but the abolition of Soviet controls in the GDR in case of unity, which would have serious repercussions in the satellite states.[54] Even though the Western powers tried again to establish a nexus between the German question and European security, the main purpose of the meeting

49 *FRUS 1955–1957*, 5:188 (Apr. 4, 1955). The second point dealt with Soviet-controlled uranium mines in the GDR.
50 See notes 2 and 3. Memorandum of Conversation with Sir Robert Scott, Sept. 17, 1955, EL, John Foster Dulles Papers, Subject Series, box 1, folder: General Correspondence; Dulles to Adenauer, Aug. 15, 1955, EL, John Foster Dulles Papers, Letters.
51 Memo of conversation (with Ambassador Krekeler), Aug. 28, 1955, in *FRUS 1955–1957*, 5:554–8.
52 Tels., Bohlen to State Dept., Sept. 13 and 14, 1955, ibid., 579–80 and 583 ("Soviets have achieved probably their greatest diplomatic victory in post-war period."); ibid., 584ff. (Sept. 15, 1955).
53 Dulles to Adenauer, Oct. 3, 1955, ibid., 610ff.
54 Ibid., 618.

was to prove once and for all to Western public opinion that it was the Soviet intransigence that prevented a policy of détente. The creation of German unity through the integration of the Federal Republic into the Atlantic Alliance had failed. The policy of strength had not forced the Soviet Union to offer concessions. When Dulles returned from Geneva, he explained to the American people in a radio and television address that the conference had shown beyond doubt that Soviet leaders were only interested in improving the security of the USSR but were unwilling to pay a price: reunification.[55]

Because both sides were unprepared to grant significant concessions, there was no chance for unification during the 1950s. However, there is no doubt that the Bonn government and the majority of the West German population preferred the status quo, which granted freedom, security, and prosperity. With the failure of the Geneva foreign ministers' conference, the structures created by the aftermath of World War II were strengthened for an unforeseeable future. Only the most recent revolutionary changes in Eastern Europe and in the GDR have finally led to a reopening of the "German question," which has now been solved under totally different circumstances than politicians had expected, hoped, or feared during the first decade after World War II.

55 Speech, Dulles, Nov. 18, 1955, *Department of State Bulletin* 33 (1955):867ff.

4

Marshall Plan and Currency Reform

CHRISTOPH BUCHHEIM

This essay describes the double relationship between the Marshall Plan and the West German currency and economic reform of June 1948. Conventional wisdom still maintains that the Marshall Plan was an important condition for the success of the currency reform, which in itself was the starting point of the West German growth story. Even before the currency reform was implemented, the German public viewed foreign credits as an indispensable prerequisite. Therefore all parties placed very high hopes in the Marshall Plan, hopes that almost necessarily were disappointed in part. Arguing from the evidence of such disappointment, Werner Abelshauser has recently repeated his opinion that the direct contribution of the Marshall Plan to economic development in West Germany was relatively insignificant.[1] Moreover, he also questions the importance of the currency and economic reform for the economic recovery.[2] This essay, however, advances a contrary view.

There apparently existed no single, unidirectional causal relationship between the Marshall Plan and the success of the currency and economic reform as well as the high growth rates of the West German economy after the middle of 1948. Rather, one can detect a causality the other way round, between the currency and economic reform and the success of the Marshall Plan in creating the framework for multilateral trade and payments. To show this, one must take into account the proper role of West German production and

1 Werner Abelshauser, "Hilfe und Selbsthife: Zur Funktion des Marshallplans beim westdeutschen Wiederaufbau," *VfZG* 37 (1989):85–113; see also idem, "Wiederaufbau vor dem Marshall-Plan: Westeuropas Wachstumschancen und die Wirtschaftsordnungspolitik in der zweiten Hälfte der vierziger Jahre," *VfZG* 29 (1981):567–9.
2 Werner Abelshauser, *Wirtschaft in Westdeutschland 1945–1948: Rekonstruktion und Wachstumsbedingungen in der amerikanischen und britischen Zone* (Stuttgart, 1975), 62–3, 168–70.

trade in its international context. To do exactly that is the second purpose of this essay.

Originally the opinion was widely held among German experts and the German public interested in these matters that a currency reform should not be undertaken before production had reached a certain level.[3] The occupation powers, however, obviously did not share this opinion. An increase in the level of production did not play a role in the Allies' discussions on a currency reform, and even the British proposals regarding the subject, much softer and more Keynesian when compared to the American approach, did not include it as a precondition.[4] The Colm-Dodge-Goldsmith Plan explicitly argued against waiting for a general improvement of the economic situation in West Germany, because this would possibly reduce even further confidence in the Reichsmark (RM) and with it the stimulus to work and sell.[5]

When time passed without any sign of forceful economic recovery, when compensation trade and the black market undermined the official rationing and price control system even more, and the incentive to produce seemed to weaken rather than to strengthen, the dominant German view about the relationship of the currency reform and an increase of production also changed. More and more the former was considered a prerequisite for the latter rather than the other way around.[6] Thus the so-called *Mindener Gutachten* for the German economic administration of July 1947 clearly declared: "A currency reform is indispensable for a rise in production."[7] Leonhard Miksch, later a close collaborator of Ludwig Erhard, bluntly stated in February 1948: "The currency reform depends on nothing, but everything else is dependent on it."[8] In fact, that impression was quite right. In order to explain why this was so, the reasoning, however, must be extended somewhat.

---

3 The existence of a widespread feeling to that effect was for instance diagnosed in the Colm-Dodge-Goldsmith Plan; see Hans Möller, ed., *Zur Vorgeschichte der Deutschen Mark: Die Währungsreformpläne 1945–1948* (Basel, 1961), 225, and the article: "Also doch . . . ," *Die Zeit*, May 30, 1946.
4 Christoph Buchheim, "Die Währungsreform in Westdeutschland im Jahre 1948: Einige ökonomische Aspekte," in Wolfram Fischer, ed., *Währungsreform und Soziale Marktwirtschaft: Erfahrungen und Perspektiven nach 40 Jahren* (Berlin, 1989), 391–402.
5 See note 3.
6 "Währungsgespräche," *Handelsblatt*, Aug. 7, 1947.
7 Möller, ed., *Vorgeschichte*, p. 345; see also minutes, "Sonderstelle Geld und Kredit," Nov. 6, 1947, IfZ, Depositum Hans Möller.
8 Möller, ed., *Vorgeschichte*, 379.

The basic characteristics of the West German economy at the time were repressed inflation and the continuation of a capitalist structure; that is, most firms were under private ownership. In a capitalist economy, profit constitutes the principal motive for production, investment, and growth. This motive, however, proved obsolete under conditions of repressed inflation, with its completely distorted price structure. Given the amount of money in circulation, price controls generally set official prices too low, and, even worse, price relations no longer reflected true relative scarcities. For example, tires, officially valued at 100 RM, could be exchanged in compensation for textiles with an official value of 200 to 300 RM.[9] Thus, official prices proved irrelevant for the calculation of real profits, while lack of an acceptable medium of exchange led to the disappearance of markets and to the establishment of a primitive barter system in much of the economy, which prevented the development of another, unofficial price structure. With no prices to reckon with, the desire to secure economic survival replaced profit seeking as the principal motivating force of capitalist enterprise. This outcome could have been different only if private firms had been largely expropriated and placed under direct administrative control of managers dependent on the state. In other words, only socialist planned economies, characterized by the existence of strong incentives to fulfill a prescribed plan as well as by the absence of any risk of bankruptcy, can exhibit some dynamics of growth even in a situation of repressed inflation, which in fact is a normal feature for them.

The dominance of the survival motive meant that enterprise undertook production only so far as it strengthened their substance. Therefore they produced goods for compensation deals with other firms, for payments in kind as a supplement to official money wages, required to provide an incentive to workers to stay with their firms, and for deliveries according to administrative rationing plans, if absolutely necessary in order to qualify for further official allotments of raw materials. It is clear that no dynamic growth could result from production so narrowly limited by the specific interests of capitalist firms in a situation of repressed inflation. Instead, hoarding of raw materials and half-finished products carried a high premium as a means of conserving the capital of enterprises until the expected currency reform could be implemented. This is demon-

9 "The Status of Compensation Trade," Dec. 9, 1947, IfZ, RG 260, OMGUS, 5/359–3/1.

strated by an investigation by the Hessian Statistical Office, which revealed that in 1947 the stock of materials on hand in firms was three times that of 1936 and sufficed for twelve months' production at the then current level.[10] It was much easier to justify hoarding raw materials than finished products in case of administrative investigation, because one could always allege that a complementary input was missing. And indeed, almost all of the firms investigated by the Hessian Statistical Office cited lack of raw materials as preventing a better use of their capacities. The rapid increase of industrial production in West Germany after the currency reform, increasing by 25 percent within only two months, proved that this was not true.[11] Such a quick recovery could only have been possible because firms had hoarded whole sets of raw materials. The sudden transition to growth after the currency and economic reforms, without which the price system would have remained distorted and further prevented the profit motive from fully functioning, also confirmed that these reforms were a precondition for a thorough increase of production rather than the other way round.

Another prerequisite for a successful currency reform, however, has consistently been emphasized by German scholars, namely the need to secure a continuous flow of foreign food and raw materials, partly financed by credit, to supplement insufficient indigenous production. Otherwise, it was argued, there would be no real substance for the newly created purchasing power, thus making the currency reform a failure.[12] Of course, the Allies recognized early the fact of West Germany's crucial dependence on imports of food and raw materials. From the beginning of the occupation, the Americans and British therefore spent many millions of dollars to pay for food imports into their zones in order just to keep the population alive. In addition, in 1947 they created the Joint Export Import Agency (JEIA), to use all proceeds from bizonal exports to pay for necessary imports other than basic foodstuffs, agricultural inputs,

---

10 BA, Z 1/864.
11 The production indices have been assembled for convenient reference by Albrecht Ritschl, "Die Währungsreform von 1948 und der Wiederaufstieg der westdeutschen Industrie: Zu den Thesen von Mathias Manz und Werner Abelshauser über die Produktionswirkungen der Währungsreform," *VfZG* 33 (1985):162–4.
12 See, e.g., the "Detmolder Memorandum" of the heads of the *Länder* and Provinces in the British Zone of November 1945 and the "Reichsbankleitstellen-Memorandum" of March 1948 in Möller, ed., *Vorgeschichte*, 120–1, 388.

and petroleum products, which continued to be financed with foreign credits. The French, on the other hand, bought many products from their zone, paying dollars even for goods of secondary importance for which dollars normally would not have been spent in view of their extreme scarcity in Western Europe at the time. Out of the dollar pool thus accruing to it, the French zone had been able to finance its essential imports of food and raw materials.[13]

There was even some feeling among the occupation powers that at the time of the currency reform shortages should be avoided by all means. Of course, they were also convinced of the existence of great hoards within the German economy which would be freed by the reform, thus supporting production. Nevertheless, from December 1947 onward, JEIA seems to have been put under pressure to assure that its accumulated funds were used to conclude contracts for additional imports that would arrive when they were most needed in order to secure the success of the currency reform.[14] Thus the quantity of imported raw materials doubled in the second quarter of 1948 compared to the first.[15]

Although the Military Government had in this way done quite a lot to guarantee the survival of the West German population and economy, and although it was concerned with making monetary reform a success by securing sufficient supplies of foreign goods, many Germans greeted the prospect of the European Recover Program (ERP) as if it were the first sign of help and sympathetic involvement in German affairs from abroad. Therefore it was no wonder that hopes regarding the function of the Marshall Plan in the rehabilitation of the West Germany economy ran very high. For instance, Hermann Pünder, head of the bizonal administration, described the Marshall Plan as "a turning point in our history."[16] Lorenz Bock, president of Württemberg-Hohenzollern, wrote in a letter to the Military Government that the working of the currency reform depended upon the Marshall Plan creating the material basis

13 Christoph Buchheim, *Die Wiedereingliederung Westdeutschlands in die Weltwirtschaft 1945–1958* (Munich, 1990).
14 Memo, "Preparation to Monetary Reform on the Goods Side," Bennett to Clay, Dec. 18, 1947, NA, RG 260, OMGUS, Office of the Finance Adviser, Records relating to Export-Import and Customs Policies and to Trade Agreements, box 119.
15 Christoph Buchheim, "Die Währungsreform 1948 in Westdeutschland," *VfZG* 36 (1988):224.
16 Gerd Hardach, "The Marshall Plan in Germany, 1948–1952," *Journal of European Economic History* 16 (1987):449.

for a viable monetary system.[17] For his part, Ludwig Erhard told an audience of journalists that the German people could rightly consider the beginning of the ERP as a fateful hour for its future – the postive aspects of the Marshall Plan making an absolutely compelling case.[18] Besides the additional imports financed out of it, he thought of the counterpart funds as being a most valuable element of the Marshall Plan, because they could be used for investment purposes in a time of great capital scarcity after the currency reform.[19]

The disappointment was therefore great when ERP deliveries of raw materials began only late in 1948, again in early 1949 when some internal difficulties in selling those imports occurred, and again when the counterpart funds were held back by the Americans until autumn of that year. This disappointment culminated in the following statement written in June 1950 in a journal of which Ludwig Erhard was a co-editor: "The economic uprise has been exclusively home-made." Werner Abelshauser, who quotes this phrase, thinks that this describes the effect of the material resources transferred to West Germany from abroad more or less correctly. He sees the main contribution of the Marshall Plan to West German reconstruction as stimulating self-help by solving the problem of German reparations and creating a favorable framework for the West German export drive.[20] The latter was in fact an important function of the Marshall Plan that will also be dealt with in this essay. The reparation problem, on the other hand, was certainly much less important than Abelshauser thinks.[21] And it appears to be wrong to rely too heavily on contemporary statements criticizing the defects of the Marshall Plan, born as they were out of the disappointment of overly enthusiastic expectations.

To show this, it is necessary to analyze more closely the role that ERP imports and counterpart funds played in the context of the West German currency and economic reform.[22] Important imports financed out of Marshall Plan funds, especially at its beginning, were foodstuffs, cotton, tobacco, raw hides, and leather. At the end of

---

17 "Abschrift eines Briefes von Bock an die Militärregierung, Abteilung Wirtschaft und Finanzen, in Baden-Baden und Tübingen," Apr. 17, 1948, IfZ, ED 134/12.
18 Pressekonferenz, Apr. 14, 1948, Ludwig Erhard Archiv Bonn, NE 1516.
19 Hardach, "Marshall Plan," 447–8.
20 Abelshauser, "Hilfe und Selbsthilfe," 111–13.
21 Buchheim, *Wiedereingliederung*.
22 The following is largely based on Knut Borchardt and Christoph Buchheim, "Die Wirkung der Marshallplan-Hilfe in Schlüsselbranchen der deutschen Wirtschaft," *VfZG* 35 (1987):317–47.

March 1949, for example, the volume of Marshall Plan imports into the Bizone had reached almost 200 million dollars. Of these about 60 percent consisted of food, 20 percent of cotton, 7 percent of tobacco, and 4 percent of hides and leather.[23] They all fulfilled essential functions in order to make the monetary and economic reform a success. Thus, higher food rations, which resulted from more imports of food financed with foreign funds, increased the physical ability of the population to work more and to work harder. Together with the restored incentive to work, because money wages represented real purchasing power again after the currency reform, this led to a substantial increase in working hours as well as of labor productivity, which in itself was an important condition for economic growth.[24] Imports of tobacco, however, had been judged necessary to absorb part of the newly created money in the hands of consumers, thus reducing the danger of inflation developing, and to raise additional funds for the state through the tobacco tax, in order to balance the budget and to maintain confidence in the new mark.[25] Cotton, hides, and leather, however, were essential raw materials for two important consumer goods industries that were likely to be confronted with high pressure of demand after the currency reform, namely textiles, clothing, and shoe production. ERP deliveries constituted a very large percentage of total supply of these raw materials in the Bizone, for example, two thirds in the case of cotton between November 1948 and March 1949. Without these imports, German industry could not even have thought of meeting the demand for textiles and shoes, which in fact ran so high that despite fast rising production substantial price increases occurred in the second half of 1948.

These price increases proved to be very detrimental indeed to the acceptability of the market economy. Because higher prices tended to exclude broad segments of the population from satisfying their urgent need for textiles and shoes, great social tension developed. Mass protest, boycotts, and even a general strike were the consequences. A large majority wanted reintroduction of strict price controls. Erhard's policy was heavily criticized even by members of the

23 *Das Europäische Wiederaufbauprogramm 1.1.49–31.3.49*, Gemeinsamer Bericht der Militärgouverneure der Vereinigten Statten und des Vereinigten Königreichs Nr. 3 (n.p., n.d.), 63.
24 Buchheim, "Währungsreform," 233–4.
25 "Aufbauplan 1948/49 für die Wirtschaft des Vereinigten Besatzungsgebietes," *Wirtschaftsverwaltung* 1, no. 1 (1948):18.

Christian Democrat Union (CDU). To make matters worse, the increasing prices produced a tendency on the part of tradesmen to hold back commodities, thus adding to the problem. JEIA ran out of funds and ceased entering into new import contracts for a time in the summer 1948, which meant that industry had to deplete its stocks if production were to grow further. A collapse of production, on the other hand, would certainly have totally discredited the market economy leading to its breakdown. The first steps toward direct administrative interventions into markets had already again been taken.

However, industrial production of critical textile goods continued to grow, even before ERP-financed cotton actually started to come into the country. This was the case because textile firms, knowing that such cotton would arrive and that competition over market shares then increase, did not hesitate to run down their stocks. Thus, from the side of production, preconditions for a turn of the price trend had been fulfilled. That turn did in fact occur in December 1948 after the money supply had been tightened somewhat. Textile prices began to fall again, and by the middle of 1949 they reached a level lower than before the currency reform. Critics of Erhard's liberal economic policy grew more and more silent. And in the first elections to the federal parliament, those parties that opted for a market and against a planned economy scored a victory. Marshall Plan imports, it must be said, thus played a crucial role in securing the success of the liberal economic policy that had been adopted in the Bizone at the time of the currency reform.

Although in the middle of 1948 free markets had been reestablished in a large segment of the West German economy, there nevertheless remained important branches where price control had not been abolished, such as basic industries like coal, steel, and electricity. While in industry generally self-financing of investment played the predominant role after the monetary reform – which left the capital market in a rather barren state – those branches had not been able to earn sufficient funds for the purpose because their prices were held at an unremunerative level. Instead, in coal almost a third of gross capital formation in the years 1949 to 1951 was financed out of counterpart funds; in electricity nearly a quarter.[26] In electricity, ERP

---

26 Egon Baumgart, *Investitionen und ERP-Finanzierung*, Deutsches Institut für Wirtschaftsforschung, Sonderheft 56 (Berlin, 1961), 118–25.

credits went mainly to the big power-generating companies, where they closed a very real deficit. Without these credits probably more than half of the new public power stations built in the period could not have been erected. Thus a severe bottleneck in electricity-generated capacity would have developed and damaged West German growth. On the other hand, ERP funds did not prevent a coal shortage from occurring in winter 1950–51, for overall investment in the coal industry had nevertheless remained at too low a level.[27] This produced many plans to raise the quantity of investable funds available to basic industries. The problem acquired additional urgency because the Marshall Plan, and with it the bulk of counterpart funds, was quickly coming to an end.

Finally, at the beginning of 1952, a law regulating so-called investment aid became effective. Based on a proposal by business associations, its principal purpose was to transfer almost DM 1 billion of investable funds from the whole of West German enterprises to basic industries. This alone, however, would have proved a far too restricted undertaking to alleviate the shortage of capital in the favored branches permanently. Therefore, two clauses introduced into the law mainly through the insistence of the liberal party were of much greater significance in the longer run. One of these permitted extraordinary depreciation of capital goods in basic industries for a certain time, and the other relaxed price controls.[28] In fact, shortly afterward prices were either made practically free or raised sufficiently to allow self-financing to become a major device of capital formation in basic industries. Thus the free working of market forces had more or less been introduced in those branches, which effectively solved their investment problem.

While Marshall Plan imports contributed much to save the market economy in the time of the inflationary push immediately after the currency reform, the function of the counterpart funds was rather less beneficial as has been shown. Their existence made the liberalization of markets for basic inputs a matter of reduced urgency and delayed it until 1952. If, however, the political obstacles against abolishing price controls in basic industry were considered to have been insurmountable before, then the role of the counterpart funds of

27 Werner Abelshauser, *Der Ruhrkohlenbergbau seit 1945: Wiederaufbau, Krise, Anpassung* (Munich, 1984), 65–82.
28 Heiner Adamsen, *Investitionshilfe für die Ruhr: Wiederaufbau, Verbände und Soziale Marktwirtschaft 1948–1952* (Wuppertal, 1981).

course must be judged quite differently. In that case they dampened the capital shortage in these branches and in doing so either helped to prevent a major economic crisis or forestalled greater pressure for state intervention in investment of private enterprises.

As mentioned before, the Marshall Plan was also instrumental in creating a favorable framework for West German exports.[29] Until 1949 the foreign trade of West Germany had been controlled by the so-called dollar clause. This meant that imports were strictly limited to purchases of the most essential goods from the cheapest sources and that exports had to be paid for by the receiving countries principally in dollars. The resulting situation was characterized by the following elements:

1. Western European countries could not sell much of their produce in Germany, because either it was not considered essential by the Military Government or it was, calculated in dollars on the basis of the official exchange rates, too expensive, as most European currencies were greatly overvalued compared to the dollar.
2. The need to buy from West Germany, on the other hand, was quite urgent, for West Germany was an important source of relatively cheap coal as well as a potential supplier of much wanted investment goods.
3. Both factors together could easily lead to a large trade deficit of many Western European countries vis-à-vis West Germany, which then – as a result of the dollar clause – made necessary dollar payments to West Germany. However, dollars were very scarce in Europe in the postwar period. Therefore, in order to save dollars, there existed a great incentive on the part of Germany's European trading partners to discriminate severely against German exports and not to buy anything that was not considered to be absolutely necessary. This discrimination affected the West German export of many finished products harshly, and such exports remained quite small.

The Marshall Plan solved these difficulties. Surely, the Marshall Plan, too, aimed at the establishment of a multilateral order of global trade and payments, for this had been the principal target of American international economic policy since before the war. Originally,

---

29 For the rest of this paper in more detail, see Buchheim, *Wiedereingliederung*.

the United States had tried to reach that aim directly. Therefore, for example, the United States made its big loan to Great Britain in 1946 conditional on the early adoption of free convertibility for the pound sterling. For this reason as well the United States clung so long to the dollar clause in West German foreign trade. This policy, however, was doomed to fail, as has been shown by the impossibility of keeping the pound convertible and by discrimination against West German exports in the context of European bilateralism. Reacting to this failure, U.S. policymakers conceived of the Marshall Plan, which favored an indirect path to a nondiscriminatory world economic order. Its goal was to attain a closer economic integration of Western Europe by limiting liberalization of trade and transferability of currencies to this region alone, while for the time being permitting the continuation of discrimination against the dollar area. By this method, it was hoped that the competitiveness of European industries would be greatly enhanced, dependence on dollar imports reduced, and the transition to global liberalization and convertibility eventually achieved.

Implementation of the Marshall Plan was therefore made dependent upon the creation of a common organization of all participating countries. Thus the Organization for European Economic Cooperation (OEEC) came into being. In 1948 the first intra-European clearing agreement of the previous year was greatly enlarged by the provision of Marshall Plan dollars to finance drawing rights, which were used to balance bilateral payments among the OEEC countries. In the following year, however, the United States was prepared to continue this financing of drawing rights only if they were at least partly multilateralized. Against strong British resistance, the United States succeeded in that a quarter of the drawing rights allotted were made transferable and thereby could be used to cover a deficit with other countries than the bilateral partner originally foreseen. Also a first practical step toward liberalization of trade, the abolition of quantitative import restrictions, was undertaken. One year later, the United States again withheld $600 million of ERP funds, in order to support a more far-reaching scheme of liberalization and currency transferability. Put under such pressures, the Western European countries finally agreed on a further nondiscriminatory liberalization of imports from one another and on the creation of the European Payments Union (EPU). The EPU provided a mechanism for wholesale clearing of intra-European trade deficits and surpluses and for the financing of resulting net balances partly by credits of the countries in surplus and partly by gold and dollar payments of the debtor countries.

Thus Marshall Plan dollars were systematically and successfully used by the United States to achieve its intermediate aim of making Western Europe a region with free internal trade and payments. In doing this, dollar payments within Europe had to be minimized, however, because otherwise each country had an incentive not to liberalize in order to secure its scarce dollar funds. The West German dollar clause therefore could no longer be defended, for it produced contrary results. It was lifted in 1949. So the principal cause for discrimination against West German exports had been removed. In consequence, that discrimination quickly disappeared, especially since West German imports from Western Europe surged after liberalization. In this way West Germany could be fully integrated into the OEEC area of liberalized trade and payments. And that proved to be a very important precondition for the phenomenal growth of West German exports during the 1950s, with its healthy effects on the overall dynamics of the West German economy.

What, however, did West Germany export? Whereas in 1948 the share of manufactures in total West German exports had still amounted to less than 40 percent, by 1952 it had risen to over 80 percent. About nine tenths of the fivefold increase of exports between the two dates was accounted for by manufactures. It can therefore be said that the very low level of West German exports before 1948 primarily reflected the failure of exports of manufactures to grow sufficiently. Within the group of manufactures, metals, machinery, and transport equipment were especially significant. Together this sector represented more than 60 percent of the exports of all manufactures to the OEEC metropolitan countries in 1952. In that year West Germany had again become one of the principal suppliers of capital goods to Western Europe, a function that the German Reich had already fulfilled in the prewar period.

But in the first years after the war, Western European countries primarily turned to the United States to buy the capital goods urgently needed for reconstruction, because Germany proved unable to deliver them. As late as 1948, Austria, Denmark, France, Great Britain, Italy, Norway, and Switzerland obtained 39 percent of their imports of machinery and transport equipment from the United

States and only 4 percent from West Germany. In 1952, however, the American share of these imports had fallen to 26 percent, the West German had risen to 24 percent. And in 1955 the percentages were 20 percent and 32 percent respectively. Whereas American export of capital goods to the OEEC metropolitan area rose only by $100 million to $1 billion between 1952 and 1958, the German grew from $1.2 to $2.6 billion.

The necessity for Western European countries to replace their traditional imports of capital goods from Germany with those from the United States had been the most important single cause of the yawning dollar gap in the immediate postwar period. Almost 60 percent of the rise of American exports to Western Europe between 1938 and 1947 can be accounted for by capital goods.[30] It is therefore quite plausible that with Germany regaining her ability to export such goods in large quantities, the dollar shortage shrank greatly. In the course of this development, it is true that West Germany after 1951 regularly showed quite substantial surpluses on current account with EPU countries, with other EPU members correspondingly displaying deficits. Although these deficits had to be at least partly financed by dollars, too, the overall dollar requirement was nevertheless much lower than it would have been had the OEEC capital goods imports from West Germany been from America instead. This was so because the West German propensity to buy in Western Europe was far higher than the American. Thus, in the course of the 1950s, regular dollar earnings of most OEEC countries through trade in goods and services, private remittance, and private capital transfers sufficed not only to finance their respective dollar expense but also to build up a certain stock of currency reserves. Therefore the discrimination against the dollar area could also be abolished step by step and global multilateralism of trade and payments adopted. Finally, in 1958, formal convertibility of most West European currencies was reintroduced.

So the United States indeed reached its aim regarding the international economic system, with the Marshall Plan providing the most important leverage. The two visions around which the Marshall Plan crystallized proved to be decisive. The first of these visions was the need to integrate Western Europe in order to create a more competitive and economically viable market with reduced dependence on

30 Alan Milward, *The Reconstruction of Western Europe, 1945–51* (London, 1984), 36–7.

the dollar area. And the second considered West Germany to be an essential part of such an integrated Western Europe without which its viability could not be achieved.[31] But there were some preconditions for West Germany to fulfill its role in the context of European reconstruction and growth. As has been shown, that role mainly consisted of supplying needed capital goods to neighboring countries. One of these prerequisites had been the removal of the dollar clause as the principal regulating support for German foreign trade, in order to free West Germany to import from Western European countries and thereby to give them the financial means to buy its exports. This has been dealt with already. The other condition, which had not yet been met in the first half of 1948, was to provide an incentive to the German capitalist enterprises to produce and export the goods that were so much in demand abroad.

As we have seen, it was the currency and economic reform that reinstituted the possibility of real profit calculation. This interested capitalist firms once again in maximizing profitable production for regular markets. Before the reform, however, they had produced only to the extent that it improved their chances for survival. This meant that production remained quite low and that it displayed no dynamics, because hoarding of inputs carried a higher premium. The stimulus to export was even lower, for an important motive for production, namely to use the goods produced in compensation trade, did not work with exports. Rather the firms were paid for the exported goods according to the official price in marks. The only hope in this situation to increase exports of manufactures above a trickle was for the economic administration to replace all materials used in the production of exportables. This, however, proved impossible because of the lack of overall planning and the uncertainty of availabilities of raw materials. Only after the introduction in autumn 1947 of a 5 percent foreign exchange bonus for export earnings, which firms could use to import relatively freely products they needed, did things get a little better. But as late as the first half of 1948 the shares of manufactures in total bizonal exports lay below 30 percent. There still was a definite, rather low limit to such exports, as long as industrial production itself remained grossly inadequate.

31 Michael J. Hogan, *The Marshall Plan: America, Britain, and the Reconstruction of Western Europe, 1947–1952* (Cambridge, 1987), 35, passim.

The currency and economic reform remedied this unpleasant situation. For with the reestablishment of money as a medium of real purchasing power and a means that again permitted calculation, the incentive to increase production and sales was reinstituted, too. Exports also benefited, because shortly before the currency reform a single exchange rate for the mark had been fixed, which freed market forces in the foreign trade sector, at least so far as the German side was concerned. Thus bizonal exports of manufactures, given the great foreign demand for them, leaped forward. They grew 65 percent in the third and another 40 percent in the fourth quarter of 1948. After a retardation in 1949, because of the effects of the dollar clause, they resumed their vigorous growth in the first half of 1950, when the dollar clause was abolished.

Insofar as West German exports of manufactures and especially of capital goods to Western Europe replaced American and were instrumental in reducing the dollar gap, the currency and economic reform was a precondition for achieving the ultimate aim of the Marshall Plan. For without this reform, a strong stimulus for the capitalist West German enterprises to export would have been lacking. Exports of manufactures would therefore have remained far too low to satisfy the high Western European demand for them. The dependence of Western Europe on American supplies of those goods would have diminished much more slowly if at all, and the dollar shortage would not have disappeared quickly. The Marshall Plan could have achieved its intermediate aim of integrating Western Europe economically. Without closing the dollar gap, however, this would not have led automatically to global multilateralism. In this way, therefore, there also existed a reverse relationship between the Marshall Plan and the currency reform, with causality running from the latter to the former.

5

American Policy toward Germany and the Integration of Europe, 1945–1955

GUNTHER MAI

Autonomy and integration are the conflicting elements that, in vary-ing combinations, determine the foreign policy of modern indus-trialized nations. The imperialism of the late nineteenth century indicated that none of the major European nations was prepared to accept the interdependence that integration into a world trade com-munity and international division of labor entail. Germany in par-ticular revolted against the supposed disadvantages of its geopolitical situation in the middle of Europe and its history as a "belated na-tion," and tried radically to evade these consequences of progressing industrialization. This nonacceptance ranged from the rejection of Chancellor Caprivi's trade agreements to the "debate on the agrarian or industrial state" around 1900 and to the fight against Bethmann Hollweg's plans for a German hegemony in *Mitteleuropa*. If there was any "continuity from Bismarck to Hitler," it was this increasing in-sistence, intensified by the experience of World War I, on a broadly defined national autonomy and autarchy, which asked for a direct, territorial control of food, raw materials, and labor in Eastern Eu-rope. Stresemann's efforts toward an industrial integration into Western Europe, which took these changed circumstances into ac-count, fell victim to this antimodernistic nostalgia, which found its most radical and perverted expression in Hitler's *Lebensraum* ideas and war aims.

The United States took the opposite position. Woodrow Wilson's vision of a global free trade system was not simply the expression of the selfish interests of the world's leading industrial and financial power. It aimed, in the tradition of pacifist ideas, at the prevention of national autarchy as the basis of war-making capabilities and aggres-

The archival research for this paper was funded by the Volkswagen Foundation.

85

sion. However, this approach failed, because in the United States, economic pacifism went together with political isolationism, which rated national autonomy higher than collective security. The Atlantic Charter, the structure of the United Nations, and Cordell Hull's free trade philosophy indicated that this discrepancy still existed at the end of World War II. In 1945 military victory offered the United States the chance to enforce structural reform in Germany and Japan and to destroy the autarchy of those nations as the most important element of an economic peace making. Therefore, the United States tried to thwart Soviet intentions to build up a similar position of strategic independence: by means of Lend-Lease, German reparations, empire building in Eastern Europe, and expansion into the oil regions of the Near East. But the Soviet Union refused to cooperate, and the United States – which itself had lost its self-sufficiency and become dependent on foreign export markets and on the importation of raw materials, especially crude oil – saw itself confronted with the question of how to safeguard its own global autonomy, once it had lost its nuclear monopoly. The choice lay between an isolationist retreat into the Western Hemisphere, a hegemonical policy of "empire building," or a cooperative network of regional security systems.

Only in the light of this secular learning process and the corresponding changes in the structure of the international system can the definition of the aims and means of American policy toward Germany and its role in the integration of Europe be understood. This policy was characterized by three features:

1. The influence of the United States on the development of the institutional aspects of European integration was negligible.
2. The preponderance of the German question determined American policy toward Europe in the beginning but proved a liability in the course of events.
3. American policy toward European integration, influenced by isolationist sentiments, aimed at a possible disengagement in Europe without prejudicing the leadership of the United States in the Atlantic Alliance.

REPARATIONS AND RECONSTRUCTION, 1944–1947

In the first phase, U.S. policy toward Germany followed a pragmatic, mainly economic approach, which tried to avoid a repetition of the mistakes made after World War I. The reconstruction needs of Europe, as well as the economic and military disarmament of Germany, had to be combined in a way that would encourage a maximum of European self-help and require a maximum of American commitment and material aid. According to a State Department planning paper of April 1944,

reparation payments and deliveries shall be related, though not narrowly confined to, the process of European reconstruction. This Government envisages a reparation program which is not primarily either an instrument of punishment or a means of enforcing security measures on Germany . . . , but which is a positive series of acts on the part of Germany to assist in rebuilding the foundations of stable and prosperous economic life in the countries injured by her. . . . The economic policy of this Government with respect to Germany as a whole . . . should be so directed as to open up new possibilities for an improvement of the organization of the European economy as a whole and the development of comprehensive international institutions in the economic field. [1]

From the early stages of its postwar planning, the U.S. government tried to avoid a policy of *"repayment or revenge."* In the interest of *"security"* for the world and *"reconstruction* for the areas devastated by the Germans," German reparations had to serve the organization of a liberal postwar world economy "as envisaged in the Atlantic Charter." To prevent Germany's reemergence as a hegemonical power in Europe, its war-making potential had to be reduced by the control of strategic imports, its economic self-sufficiency destroyed "by the integration . . . into the world market." Thus, Edwin Pauley could rightly speak of a "world reparation policy of Germany."[2]

The basic idea of combining reparations and the economic disarmament of Germany was undisputed within the U.S. government, but two questions had to be answered: First, how to make German reparations deliveries a "substantial contribution to the reconstruction in Europe in a short period of years" and, second, which role the United States was to play in this process. The *isolationists,* such as Henry Morgenthau and Bernard Baruch, recommended a purely

---

1 NA, RG 107, McCloy, box 26 (WSC-54c).
2 NA, RG 59, Records of the European Advisory Commission (Philip E. Moseley), 1943–1946, box 16, folder: General Correspondence (Apr. 29, 1945). NA, RG 59, Records of the U.S. Delegation to the Allied Reparations Commission (Edwin W. Pauley Reparations Mission) 1945–1948, box 19 (Sept. 11, 1945). *FRUS 1944*, vol. 1, *General* (Washington, D.C., 1966), 278–99. *FRUS 1945*, vol. 3, *European Advisory Commission; Austria; Germany* (Washington, D.C., 1968), 1182–4, 1208.

European solution, without any direct engagement or permanent commitment of the United States. In Morgenthau's opinion, Europe did not need the Ruhr: The destruction of the Ruhr industries would automatically force the neighboring countries to develop their own resources to replace the delivery of Ruhr coal and steel.[3] The Baruch Plan of June 1945 favored a more organized approach. Baruch also demanded the destruction of Germany's heavy industry, but all plants useful to European reconstruction should be dismantled and shifted "east and west to friendly nations." In addition, the plan called for the creation of a "Supreme European Reconstruction Council to coordinate aspects of European reconstruction with German settlement of reparations and other problems." This encouraged Assistant Secretary of State William Clayton to hope as late as October 1945, that "in [the] long run reparation removals will not bring about substantial reduction in European capacity as a whole but will bring about a shift in relative strength of Germany and of rest of Europe."[4]

In the eyes of the *internationalists,* this scheme would not solve the real problem. Only a united and "prosperous," though economically disarmed, Germany would be able to prevent "the division of Europe into definite and possibly antagonistic economic spheres of influence" or "blocs." A drastic "deindustrialization" of Germany or its exclusion from export markets would only lead to a "serious new rivalry" in Europe, because it would necessarily force Germany back into a policy of autarchic "self-sufficiency." It was mainly the secretary of war, Henry Stimson, who, in opposition to Morgenthau, held the opinion that Europe would not be viable without Germany and without the maintenance of the traditional prewar trade patterns and economic relations.[5] But if, under this premise, reparations would have to "take the form of transfers of existing German capital equipment, rather than of current production," and if "the total volume of reparation deliveries would be comparatively small," German reparations could only reduce "the necessity of the extension of foreign credit or other means of providing additional imports for

3 *Das Morgenthau Tagebuch: Dokumente des Anti-Germanismus,* ed. Hermann Schild (Leoni, 1970), 199–205.
4 NA, RG 59, Pauley Reparations Mission, box 11 (June 23, 1945). *FRUS 1945,* 3:1343 (Clayton, Oct. 12, 1945). *FRUS 1944,* 1:275. NA, RG 59, Records of the European Advisory Commission, 1943–1946, folder: USGCC (June 3, 1945).
5 *Morgenthau Tagebuch,* 171–3, 209–10 (1944).

which such European countries are unable to pay."[6] Without American financial support, European reconstruction would fail. At Potsdam, Stimson already had proposed to channel these loans "through one man and one agency"; all contributing countries would constitute an "Economic Council for Europe." The duty of its American chairman, subject to the authority of the president and pursuant to the directives of an American central agency, would be, "to assist the governments of Europe *to help themselves* in the restoration of stable conditions."[7] Thus, the pattern of the Marshall Plan was set: Help for self-help, under American control, though still including Europe as a whole and only shifting or redistributing instead of enlarging the German industrial potential.

At first, though, the Baruch approach seemed to prevail. The "Plan for Reparations and the Level of Post-War German Industry," passed by the Control Council in March 1946, was a compromise between German self-support, Allied control, and European reconstruction. On the European level, the Inter-Allied Reparations Agency (IARA) distributed German reparations among the Western European creditor nations; the United Nations Economic Commission for Europe (ECE) allocated raw materials, coal, and transportation throughout Europe as a whole. Owing to its reservation toward long-term overseas commitments, the United States, in early 1947, still hesitated to coordinate its own foreign economic policy with that of Europe through the ECE. Nevertheless, it regarded the ECE as a useful instrument to induce the "economic integration of Germany and an integration of Germany into the whole European economy," especially since, as an occupation power, the United States could not afford to remain aloof. The Office of Military Government for Germany (OMGUS) was ordered to cooperate with the ECE, because the limitations on German production had repercussions on the reconstruction plans of the neighboring countries as well as on the reparation deliveries handled by the IARA. This coordination seemed to offer a chance "to favor the reestablishment of economic intercourse between all European countries and to oppose economic as well as political autarchy either of countries or blocs."[8]

6 NA, RG 84, POLAD, TS/34/1-3 (Kitteredge, Nov. 25, 1944; Murphy, Dec. 21, 1944, and Jan. 16, 1945). *FRUS 1944*, 1:288. *FRUS 1945*, 3:1320. TL, Harry S Truman Papers, Confidential File, box 2, folder: Allied Reparations Commission (Pauley, May 28, 1945).
7 *FRUS: The Conference of Berlin (Potsdam) 1945*, 2 vols., (Washington, D.C., 1960), 2:808–9.
8 NA, RG 59, 740.00119 Control (Germany)/11–646. NA, RG 165, Civil Affairs Division, 014 (Germany)/18–646 and 23–147 (Marshall).

However, this approach collapsed with General Clay's suspension of reparation deliveries in May 1946, which hit the Western European creditor nations in the same way as the Soviet Union and delayed the envisaged shifting of German production capacities. The reparations stop was only partially the result of the incipient estrangement of Western Allies from the Soviet Union; rather the United States realized that "the planned permanent depression in Germany which we are creating" by its deindustrialization stood "at cross purposes" with the needs of European reconstruction. Provided the Ruhr and the Saar were treated as "resources for the continent rather than as potential weapons for its domination," the expansion of German production deserved priority. According to Paul A. Porter, then chief of the Office of Price Administration, there was "no solution to the German problem except within the framework of an integrated European economy. The level-of-industry plan, modeled to meet the requirements of Potsdam, lays the conditions for a new autarchy." "Any dismantling of industrial facilities adaptable to peace-time uses," as Porter contended, "will strengthen the Russian position . . . ; in the critical years ahead production should have priority over re-location."[9]

The United States did not interpret the "new trends toward economic autarchy," as evinced in the French Monnet Plan, as an expression of renewed nationalist tendencies, but saw them, first of all, as a consequence of missing or reduced international trade and exchange. Thus, the Americans felt that "the current low volume of Germany's external trade is one of the major factors in the revival of autarchic tendencies throughout Europe today. A significant expansion of German exports requires, of course, a greatly increased industrial production."[10] Only if the "full use of German resources [could] . . . be reconciled with security" within the framework of a unified Europe and only if France's supply with German coal were guaranteed was there any possibility to induce the French to "modify" the Monnet Plan away from an uneconomic self-sufficiency and toward a more integrated *European* economy." Porter was therefore convinced

---

9 "The German Problem in the Light of Soviet Policy," Aug. 22, 1946, and "Notes on some economic consequences of Allied occupation policy in Germany," undated, TL, Paul A. Porter Papers, box 1, folder: Criticism.

10 Thomas C. Blaisdell to Will Clayton, NA, RG 59, 740.00119 Control (Germany)/10-146.

that a German settlement which establishes an international management of German steel and coal, and perhaps of basic chemicals and electric power, will not in itself accomplish an economically unified Europe. But it would be the most powerful lever to move Europe in that direction. It could be the economic complement of the 25-year treaty to ensure German disarmament which Mr. Byrnes had proposed. . . . A new and more stable pattern of power relationships could be brought into being.[11]

Indeed, some advisors already proposed to promote these aims by dividing Germany and by incorporating the Ruhr into a Western European customs union. However, Secretary Byrnes was not yet willing "to accept the consequences of such an irrevocable step as the formation of a Western European bloc. Among these consequences would be the renunciation of any American right to concern itself with any part of the world outside the Western hemisphere."[12]

Nevertheless, the illusion of an autonomous process of European integration had been shattered, and the unsolved German question was considered the main reason for this failure. If Germany could not fulfill the expectations because of internal and international difficulties, the United States had to move toward a more active and direct engagement by submitting its occupation policies in Germany to the interests of European reconstruction. Any "economic federation" would, in the tradition of Stimson's ideas, only be viable with American loans "as a pump-primer." But these loans were to be given not to national governments, but rather to an "Economic Council for Europe" within the United Nations.[13] The failure of the Moscow Conference of Foreign Ministers in the spring of 1947 helped to connect both the German and European approaches in the American policy, which previously had been handled separately without much coordination.[14]

In June 1947, when the American government discussed the implementation of Secretary of State George C. Marshall's Harvard speech, the conviction hardened that current American occupation policies in Germany were detrimental to the European reconstruction efforts: "United States policy in Germany cannot ignore or run counter to United States policy in Europe as a whole." In order to

11 Porter to Robert Murphy, Jan. 14, 1947, TL, Paul A. Porter Papers, box 1, folder: Criticism.
12 NA, RG 59, 740.00119 Control(Germany)/9-2046.   13 Cf. note 11.
14 NA, RG 59, Records of the Central European Division, 1944–1953, box 2 (Kindleberger, June 18, 1947).

secure maximum dollar proceeds, German exports went to the American, not the European markets; German imports were aimed at saving dollars rather than at expanding trade. The reparations stop proved detrimental to the European national economies, which could not afford substitute imports from the dollar area. To protect themselves from becoming dependent on American loans, the Europeans pressed for either a resumption of German reparation deliveries, regardless of the consequences for the German standard of living, or indirect American subsidies by making the United States pay a larger share of the occupation costs.[15] The United States was slow to accept the European view that reparations in the form of capital goods and equipment had proved a failure. In the end, however, the Americans decided against the demand of the Europeans for reparations from current production, because this would further delay the return to normal trading practices.[16] Instead, the United States proposed "to reduce the European requirement for aid from the United States" as much as possible through controlled contributions from the Bizone, even if this meant temporary increase of American occupation costs.[17] Thus, the occupation policy of the American military, aimed solely at the reduction of costs, was increasingly considered as "anti-European."[18]

This transition from reparations to trade entailed the most important reorientation in American thinking about the German contribution to the reconstruction of Europe. Though the revised level-of-industry plan of August 1947 was designed to make the rapid resumption and completion of reparation deliveries possible, its real intention was to utilize fully the still existing industrial capacities. In

15 Hilldring to Marshall, June 18, 1947, and annexes, NA, RG 59, Records of the Assistant SecState for Occupied Areas, 1946–1949, box 1, folder: Germany-Place; "Questions concerning . . . ," July 1947, ibid., box 2, folder: memoranda and despatches.
16 "Notes on some economic consequences of Allied occupation policy in Germany," undated, TL, Paul A. Porter Papers, box 1, folder: Criticism. Edelstein to Saltzman, NA, RG 59, 740.00119 Control (Germany)/8-2247. *FRUS 1947*, vol. 2, *Council of Foreign Ministers; Germany and Austria* (Washington, D.C., 1972), 216–7, 391–6, 977–82, 1055, 1118–33. NA, RG 59, Records of the Central European Division, 1944–1953, box 2, folder: Reparations (Hilldring, undated; memo, Oct. 3, 1947); NA, RG 59, Records of the Assistant SecState for Occupied Areas, 1946–1949, box 6, folder: 386.3, vol. 3 (Hilldring, July 25, 1947). Report, State Dept., Sept. 21, 1948, NA, RG 335, box 42, folder: 091.3 Germany/Rehabilitation.
17 Thorp to SecState, July 1, 1947, NA, RG 59, Records of the Assistant SecState for Occupied Areas, 1946–1949, box 1. *FRUS 1947*, vol. 3, *The British Commonwealth; Europe* (Washington, D.C., 1972), 383–8.
18 NA, RG 59, Records of the Assistant SecState for Occupied Areas, 1946–1949, box 1, folder: Germany-Place (June 18, and July 1, 1947). *FRUS 1947*, 2:1109ff.

September 1947, the United States decided definitely to stop all reparation deliveries to the Soviet Union and de facto to the IARA countries as well.[19] The stalemate in German and European reconstruction could only be broken by a revision of the Potsdam protocol. If the Soviet Union refused to agree, the United States would have to take this step regardless of Soviet opposition or lack of approval and was prepared, in the last resort, to sacrifice German unity.[20]

"GRADUALISM AND AN AD HOC APPROACH," 1948–1950

In the beginning of 1948, the United States decided, first, to end the four-power cooperation in the Allied Control Council as a prerequisite to a currency reform and the formation of a West German state;[21] second, to include the Bizone and the French zone in the Marshall Plan organization; and, third, to ask France to keep the Treaty of Dunkirk (officially directed against Germany) open for "the eventual participation of Western Germany."[22]

However, these decisions in no way moved the Western European countries to accept an extension of German industrial production to its maximum capacity; they demanded instead that their own reconstruction efforts precede those of Germany. Moreover, they had so far failed to secure the future control of the German economic potential after the end of Allied occupation, for instance by an internationalization of the Ruhr. Integration increasingly appeared to the Western Europeans to be the best means to ward off any infringement of their autonomy that was threatened by German resurgence, American financial aid and economic penetration, and Communist Cold War tactics.

---

19 *FRUS 1947,* 2:1055, 1118, 1123–44. *FRUS 1948,* vol. 3, *Western Europe* (Washington, D.C., 1974), 309.
20 *FRUS 1947,* 2:1104–44; 3:216–9, 347–55.
21 Gunther Mai, "Der Alliierte Kontrollrat 1945–1948: Von der geteilten Kontrolle zur kontrollierten Teilung," *Aus Politik und Zeitgeschichte* B 23 (1988):3.
22 *FRUS 1948,* 3:3–12. Achilles's conversation with Berard, Feb. 13, 1948, NA, RG 59, Records of the Assistant SecState for Occupied Areas, 1946–1949, box 5, folder: 8031, vol. 2. During this conversation there was open talk about "some German armed forces . . . which his Government would definitely not favor"; but the problem would be "less serious" in an "arrangement" like the Western European Union with British participation. In November 1949, Acheson denied to Truman "that there was somewhere in the Government a plan for the rearming of Germany." Memo, Nov. 17, 1949, TL, Dean Acheson Papers, box 64, folder: Memos of Conversation, Nov. 1949; memo, Dec. 1, 1949, The Dean Acheson Papers, box 64, folder: Memos of Conversation, Dec. 1949.

After the foundation of the Federal Republic in September 1949, its incorporation into the various schemes of European cooperation became more urgent, "primarily to prevent the reemergence of Western Germany as an independent, aggressive and highly nationalist threat to Western Europe." The concept of "Europe" seemed to offer that new idea and ideal that might catch the imagination of European peoples and help to "regain the initiative" in the Cold War from the Soviet Union. If the partition of Germany became inevitable, it might offer a substitute for German nationalism and a means to counter (as in France and Italy) all neutralist "third force" tendencies: "Without federation there is no adequate framework within which adequately to handle the German problem."[23]

The challenge by the German Democratic Republic increased this pressure for integration. But even though the Communist threat became more prominent in American thinking, the policy of the United States toward the integration of Europe still put more emphasis on the control of Germany than on the protection against Soviet aggression. German resources had to be maximized, without giving Germany the chance for a new domination of Europe. Only the establishment of a "common market," which included an economically strong Germany, would safeguard the "viability" of Europe without any additional or new American commitment once the Marshall Plan aid had tapered off.[24]

Neither the OEEC nor, later on, NATO was able to allay the apprehensions of the Europeans or to realize American hopes. The main question was how to interconnect the Atlantic, European, and German policy levels. Since the United States had no ideas to offer on how to achieve this, it had to wait for initiatives by the Europeans or to hope for a sort of institutional entanglement that would "somehow" develop on different levels and in differing molds. On the other hand, the United States could not allow "too firm a crystalli-

---

23 Williams to Micocci, Nov. 8, 1949, and Moore, Nov. 21, 1949, NA, RG 59, Records of the Office of European Regional Affairs (Miriam Camp), 1949–1953 [hereafter: Camp Records], box 1, folder: Miscellaneous; Thomson, Oct. 19, 1949, and Moore, March 7, 1950, Camp Records, box 1, folder: Continental Integration; *FRUS 1950*, vol. 3, *Western Europe* (Washington, D.C., 1977), 620, 638–42.

24 Minutes of meeting, Jan. 6, 1950, NA, RG 59, Minutes of the Undersecretary's Meetings, 1949–1952. NA, RG 59, Camp Records, box 1, folder: Continental Integration (Moore, March 7, 1950).

zation," in case it proved possible to melt "the many embryonic regional groups" into one. This approach became known later as the policy of "gradualism."[25]

The United States concentrated its hopes increasingly on the Benelux countries and Great Britain, whose participation in an international Ruhr authority had long been discussed, especially with a view to the formation of a "Western bloc" or "Western union." The real problem, however, seemed to be that none of the Western European nations was able or willing to accept the responsibility of leadership. The Benelux countries were too weak; the British would not join any form of closer integration; France was considered unable to exert any leadership in its "present state of apparent demoralization"; Germany was obviously out of the question. Should the United States itself therefore take the initiative by giving "from time to time . . . 'friendly aid' in the form of virtual ultimata"? Or should it "dictate on a day-to-day basis the steps which we felt should be taken"? Or would the Americans themselves have to provide an "Atlantic" framework for a grouping of continental states, including Germany and under French leadership, because "the framework would clearly have to be larger than continental if Germany were not to dominate it"?

The latter course seemed the most promising, as Special Assistant Jackson advised Hickerson:

It avoids the appearance of fact of direct U.S. intervention and yet avoids the present situation where we are very much on the sidelines and are not even coaching the players. It could be developed into an active program of collaboration and, if properly handled, would encourage European initiative and leadership, while at the same time giving us a method for putting vigor in the European movement. It would give us a chance to develop our own specific ideas in conjunction with and subject to the contributions of the Europeans.[26]

---

25 *FRUS 1949*, vol. 4, *Western Europe* (Washington, D.C., 1975), 469–94. *FRUS 1950*, 3:629, 679. Williams to Micocci, Nov 8, 1949, NA, RG 59, Camp Records, box 1, folder: Miscellaneous; NA, RG 59, Camp Records, box 1, folder: Continental integration (Moore, March 7, 1950).

26 Jackson to Hickerson, Oct. 18, 1948, NA, RG 59, Camp Records, box 2, folder: Integration; memo of conversation, Oct. 25, 1948, and Nitze, March 18, 1949, NA, RG 59, Camp Records, box 2, folder: Miscellaneous. *FRUS 1948*, 3:222–3, 301–10. Acheson, memos of conversation, Nov. 3, 1949, and Dec. 5, 1949, TL, Acheson Papers, box 64, folder: Memos of Conversation, Nov. 1949.

However, in the middle of 1949, an answer to these questions was still not in sight. In the autumn of the same year, the internal debate became more and more intensive and increasingly futile, especially since the State Department had set itself a deadline of January 1950. The department discussed two different models, which advanced no new ideas but tried to build upon existing arrangements: the European Council and the European Payments Union. The first approach favored a supranational solution from the top by creating a "political union" to bring about economic integration. The latter proposal favored the reverse, a functional approach "from the bottom up," by establishing a "common market" which, in its early stages, would ask for only small sacrifices of national sovereignty.

This continued perplexity and indecision were mainly the result of the State Department's illusion that Great Britain would take the lead in the process of European integration,[27] although it had become rather obvious that it was France which held the key to the integration of Europe and to the German question. The United States could not accept being maneuvered into a position "in which French failure will be defeat for U.S. policy." It considered a French "lead in developing a pattern of organization" vital "if Russian or German, or perhaps Russian-German domination, is to be avoided."[28] The United States was not (yet) prepared to blackmail France into accepting that leadership by threatening to cut off the Marshall Plan aid. Although the Americans realized the danger "of using terms such as 'unification' without being specific as to meaning," Acheson and his undersecretary, Webb, were forced in early 1950 to advise ECA Administrator Paul Hoffman to keep his remarks on integration vague. The United States, they argued, need "flexibility to determine these issues" until American views, intentions, and integration schemes had become more developed. "With the lack of a clear objective on our part, and on the part of the Europeans themselves, gradualism and an ad hoc approach are, at this stage, inevitable." In spite of its "current inability to foresee in more detail where 'integration' will or should lead," Ben T. Moore of the Bureau of European Affairs

27 *FRUS 1948*, 3:483–9. *FRUS 1950*, 3:617–22, 627–33, 805–10, 869–83, 955–74. NA, RG 59, Camp Records, box 1, folder: Continental Integration (Moore, March 7, 1950).
28 *FRUS 1948*, 3:306–8, 401–4. *FRUS 1949*, 4:469–72, 483–94. NA, RG 59, Minutes of the Secretary's Daily Meetings, 1949–1952, box 1 (July 1, Oct. 13, 27, and 28, 1949, and Apr. 25, 1950). NA, RG 59, Camp Records, box 2, folder: Miscellaneous (Moore, Nov. 21, 1949).

feared the United States might "by a series of ad hoc decisions, rather than by a conscious weighing of alternatives, determine the future political organization of Europe."[29]

This deadlock encouraged those critics within the foreign service who had maintained for some time that a "self-cure" of the Europeans was improbable, mainly because "the Russians are too near and the British too distant," and because France, Italy, and Germany had only feeble "caretaker governments." In the face of the British "disassociation," the fears of the French that they would be "left alone" with the Germans on the continent[30] would prevent any progress toward broader integration and fail to stop the trend toward a neutralist Third Force. These critics, therefore, demanded that the United States itself should seek the "leadership" that could not be expected from the Europeans. "Western Europe has not demonstrated a capacity to organize itself in such a way as to enlist Western Germany's resources and to ensure its Western ties. If there is to be an effective organization of Europe, it will have to be set in a framework which assures continuous and responsible leadership by the United States."[31] In this view, integration was no longer an aim in itself to make Western Europe economically "viable" and "self-supporting"; it increasingly became an instrument of American influence and control.

This debate was temporarily silenced by the French proposal of the Schuman Plan in May 1950. But even those who had been looking for French leadership viewed the Schuman Plan with some skepticism. Considering the American reservations toward a purely continental solution of a "Europe of Six," this skepticism was not a total surprise. It was fed by the apprehension that the proposed European Coal and Steel Community (ECSC), despite its obvious political advantages, might develop into a European cartel discriminating against the United States, which, for political reasons, would have to finance its future competitor; it also might be "perverted"

---

29 Thomson to SecState, Oct. 19, 1949, NA, RG 59, Camp Records, box 1, folder: Continental Integration, and ibid. (Moore, March 7, 1950).
30 *FRUS 1949*, 4:490–4. Vincent Auriol, *Journal du septennat*, vol. 3, *1949* (Paris, 1977), 49, 72. Thomson to SecState, Oct. 19, 1949, NA, RG 59, Camp Records, box 1, folder: Continental Integration.
31 *FRUS 1950*, 3:613–14, 641, 674–82, 859 (Policy Planning Staff, Apr. 14, 1950). Cleveland, March 30, 1950, NA, RG 59, Camp Records, box 1, folder: Continental Integration. Gunther Mai, "Dominanz oder Kooperation im Bündis? Die Sicherheitspolitik der USA und der Verteidigungsbeitrag Europas 1945–1956," *Historische Zeitschrift* 246 (1988):352–8.

into a neutralist Third Force movement.[32] Until the early months of 1948, the State Department, under the influence of Marshall and Kennan, had favored the idea of a global "balance of power" and the self-organization of Europe as a Third Force between the United States and the Soviet Union – free from American help, though not free from American influence.[33] Now that Europe was about to be integrated only on a continental basis, under French leadership and without British participation, the United States government was anxious to prevent any "self-neutralization" of this Europe of Six, although the idea of a Third Force had long lost its attraction, even in France, because of the Communist seizure of power in Prague and the Berlin Blockade. The project, in Acheson's sober initial reaction, had "interesting possibilities and some extremely controversial aspects. Therefore, we might express interest to the French, but no judgment."[34]

This hesitation, even if it lasted only a few days, reflected a significant change in American relations with Europe: The United States no longer was the driving force behind the integration movement, if ever it had been. On the contrary, the developing union of Western Europe seemed to limit the range of American political leadership and economic domination. Despite its strong support of the Schuman Plan, the United States sought to maintain political control of the integration process in order to protect its economic interests. In the end, the American government followed the recommendation of Ambassadors Bruce and Harriman to support the Schuman Plan publicly without reservation, but to make its economic interests felt during the negotiations about the "ultimate operation of scheme."[35]

AMERICAN ADVANCE COMMITMENTS, 1950–1952

The outbreak of the Korean War, only a few weeks after the announcement of the Schuman Plan, made all these apprehensions and

32 *FRUS 1950*, 3:722. NA, RG 59, Camp Records, box 1, folders: Briefing Papers (July 11, 1951); European Integration (Aug. 17, 1951); and European Political Community (Sept. 17 and Nov. 14, 1952). *FRUS 1952–1954*, vol. 6, *Western Europe and Canada* (Washington, D.C., 1986), 65ff., 652. Although it was mentioned very often, the question of a Third Force had received only "little consideration"; ibid., 655.
33 Minutes of meeting, May 10, 1950, NA, RG 59, Minutes of the Undersecretary's Meetings, 1949–1952. *FRUS 1950*, 3:692, 695, 722, 1047.
34 *FRUS 1950*, 3:702–4, 714–17. Cf. *FRUS 1952–1954*, 6:657–8. This resulted in articles 60 to 67 of the ECSC treaty on cartels, unfair competition, etc.
35 Mai, "Dominanz," 331ff.

reserve options obsolete. When as a result, the United States asked the Europeans to accept Germany's unlimited military and economic contribution to the Western rearmament efforts, the request aroused suspicions and objections on the part of Germany's neighbors. It became evident that the integration of Europe could not be achieved by U.S. financial aid alone, even if Germany was divided. But when the United States insisted on quick decisions, it was forced to offer advance commitments, because France would not compromise on the question of German rearmament "unless the Americans were prepared to give far more solid assurances than they have so far offered."[36]

The U.S. policy of advance commitments had started in late 1945 with the Byrnes Plan for the demilitarization of Germany. Marshall had repeated this offer of a security guarantee against future German aggression at the Moscow Conference of Foreign Ministers in 1947, an offer that France and Great Britain had correctly appraised "as a break with the tradition of 'no entangling alliances.'" [37] The Byrnes Plan, which had aimed at an all-European solution for Germany, and the Marshall Plan were each originally intended to be "an instrument of reconciliation."[38] Byrnes and Marshall regarded an American withdrawal from international responsibilities as a repetition of the mistakes made after the First World War. In their opinion, the United States would not be able to realize its global plans for a new economic and political order without a permanent overseas engagement. Initially, NATO had been a cautious compromise between this internationalist approach and isolationist tendencies in Congress. In American eyes, it did not include an automatic commitment for military intervention in Europe. On the contrary, it had been devised to prevent a direct engagement on the European continent by strengthening Western Europe's ability of military and economic self-defense. But the Korean War forced the United States to shift its

36 PRO, FO 800/460/App/Eur/50/2 (Sept. 19, 1950).
37 John Gimbel, "Die Vereinigten Staaten, Frankreich und der amerikanische Vertragsentwurf zur Entmilitarisierung Deutschlands." *VfZG* 22 (1974):258–86. *FRUS 1945*, 3:424ff., 528ff. Washington Embassy to Foreign Office, May 2, 1946, PRO, FO 371/55842/C4800. According to British sources, the plan was developed by Senator Vandenberg "as the basis for a positive foreign policy." MdAE, Y 356, Bl. 409 (Ambassade Washington, May 4, 1946). Archives Nationales, 457(Bidault)AP7 (March 14, 1947).
38 Rostow to Acheson, Feb. 20, 1948, TL, Acheson Papers, box 27, folder: State Department, General, 1948. In Kindleberger's judgment, the offer was more than just a tactical move. At least for himself the offer was "genuine." TL, Oral History Collection, Kindleberger Interview, p. 82. NA, RG 59, Records of the Central European Division, 1944–1953, box 2 (Kindleberger, June 18, 1947).

emphasis from the economic to the military aspects of the Atlantic alliance. The aim of gaining maximum political-military efficiency with a minimum American contribution could only be achieved if at least initially, the United States itself increased its political, economic, and military advance commitments. The precedence of the Atlantic and military solution over the European and economic one required a redefinition of the status of Germany, of the function of European integration, and of the American role in the Atlantic alliance.

As a result of this change in outlook and policy, the Americans now hailed the Schuman Plan as going "further than anything hitherto contemplated in tying Ger[many] economically." The United States had hoped for some time that the final solution would go beyond the merely cooperative and collaborative structure of OEEC and NATO, preferably in the form of "supranational" organizations operating "on less than an unanimity basis."[39] The American had not dared to demand from the Europeans at the same time a curtailment of their national sovereignty and the resurrection of Germany. Thus, publicly, the United States had promoted only the lowering of trade barriers and the establishment of a payments union, which corresponded to its own traditional ideas of free trade. This cautious approach had been part of the policy of "gradualism," but it was soon to be abandoned or modified when the Korean War gave the Schuman Plan a new meaning and importance.

One of the most fundamental decisions to be taken during the early stages of the Schuman Plan negotiations was to give up all hope for British participation in the integration process.[40] As a substitute for British leadership and control, the United States sought to establish a number of structural ties and institutional controls, since it had only little faith in the internal stability and pro-Western orientation of three of the participating countries (Germany, France, and Italy). The Europe of Six should be open to other European countries, at least on the levels of consultation and cooperation; it should not be allowed to be perverted into a huge cartel, discriminating against European and American business interests; and it should be prevented from breaking away into a Gaullist, Communist, or neutral Third Force.[41]

39 *FRUS 1950*, 3:696, 722, 1003.
40 Ibid., 414, 715–26, 740, 809. *FRUS 1952–1954*, 6:102–3.
41 *FRUS 1950*, 3:757–9, 764. *FRUS 1952–1954*, 6:73–4, 106–7, 127–8, 224ff.

NATO was to be the main instrument to preclude the "possibility of Eur[opean] Union becoming [a] third force or opposing force."[42] This aspect was an additional reason why the United States could not resist the temptation of trying to integrate the Schuman Plan with the economic defense measures. Even before the start of the Schuman Plan negotiations, the American efforts endangered the whole scheme, because all European states, and especially France, were not yet prepared to accept the simultaneous economic *and* military resurgence of the Federal Republic.[43] The Americans considered the demands of France to gain a lead in its military and economic buildup over Germany as so "unrealistic" that, for the first time they resorted to the open threat to "review our entire policy toward def[ense] of Western Europe."[44] But the Americans soon realized that they had to restore the flexibility of French policy by a military security guarantee against German (not Soviet) aggression, if they wanted to solve the German question and to expedite the integration of Europe. "Arrangements in [the] Atlantic area" should encourage "a framework of solidarity" in Europe for the following reasons: "(1) to meet urgent current situation of common security; (2) because of Eur[opean] reluctance to move towards greater unity in absence of full and active U[nited] K[ingdom] participation; (3) to provide a framework of leadership which [would] encourage Eur[o-pean] nations to obtain closer association among themselves and with Ger[many]."[45]

The integration process, however, seemed to bog down once it had been transferred to the technical level of the negotiations over the Schuman and Pleven plans. The United States had very limited means to push these talks ahead. Its disappointment and impatience drove it to reproach the Europeans with "apathy and uneasiness";[46] neither did they accept the American analysis of the imminence of the Soviet threat, nor did they subordinate their national anxieties vis-à-vis Germany to the collective effort against the Communist menace.

This development revived those critics within the Truman administration who expected effective and successful leadership from the

---

42 *FRUS 1951*, vol. 3, *European Security and the German Question* (Washington, D.C., 1981), 850, 871. *FRUS 1952–1954*, vol. 5, *Western European Security* (Washington, D.C., 1983), 53, 324–7. Mai, "Dominanz," 356–8.
43 *FRUS 1950*, 3:696, 744–53, 760–1. 44 Ibid., 423–4, 428–9. 45 Ibid., 450.
46 *FRUS 1951*, vol. 4, *Europe: Political and Economic Developments* (Washington, D.C., 1985), 44ff. passim.

United States alone. However, under the influence of Acheson, the American government decided on a realistic definition of American demands and European potentialities and against the transition from hegemony to "direct rule." While the Europeans accepted American "leadership" as "a necessary fact of life," Acheson accepted Deputy Assistant Secretary of State for European Affairs Bonbright's arguments that "outward signs of American influence and pressure" would meet with considerable resistance.[47] It seemed more promising for the United States to confine itself to facilitating the parliamentary passage of the Schuman and Pleven plans by financing the Payments Union and the Schuman Plan or by making the Federal Republic compromise on the Saar.[48] Only by self-restraint would the United States be able to use its "leadership" to strengthen its political (and economic) position in Western Europe and to prevent selfish national interests from obstructing palpable progress toward integration. Against its better judgment (and that of most European nations), the Truman administration accepted for what it hoped would be only a limited transitional period the European Defense Community (EDC), the precedence of the "Atlantic" over the "European" solution, and increasing military commitments in continental Europe.[49] With this decision, the United States had definitely come around to the French idea of combining a "closer" federation of continental Europe with and within a cooperative and "wider" confederation of the Atlantic nations. Tacitly, this arrangement constituted a rudimentary version of what would later develop into the so-called two-pillar structure of NATO, which offered France a special veto position and which reduced Britain to a peripheral status in Europe, both geographically and politically.

These American advance commitments, however, seemed only to encourage in Europe a "postponement of decisions until U.S. aid has been committed."[50] The Europeans, facing the alternative of pros-

47 *FRUS 1952–1954*, 5:299.
48 EL, John Foster Dulles Papers, Subject Series, box 8 (Dulles, Nov. 20, 1953). *FRUS 1952–1954*, 5:825–51. *FRUS 1952–1954*, vol. 7, *Germany and Austria* (Washington, D.C., 1986), 1403ff.
49 It was for this reason that the Truman government had insisted on the possibility of revising the NATO treaty after ten years. *FRUS 1949*, 4:33–4, 104, 242. *FRUS 1951*, 3:802, 816–17, 822, 835. For the Eisenhower administration, cf. *FRUS 1952–1954*, vol. 2, *National Security Affairs* (Washington, D.C., 1984), 454, 456, 527; *FRUS 1955–1957*, vol. 4, *Western European Security and Integration* (Washington, D.C., 1986), 99–100. EL, Eisenhower Papers, NSC-Series, box 7 (Feb. 27, 1956).
50 *FRUS 1951*, 3:5.

perity or security, seemingly balked at endorsing the speed and the range of American armament efforts.[51] Even before the Korean War, the rearmament of the Federal Republic had become the test for the willingness of the Europeans to make corresponding sacrifices of wealth and national prejudice. Their hesitation again increased in the American government the desire to influence European developments directly, especially when the Europeans answered the American demand for "burden sharing" with the demand for an "equality of sacrifice" – by developing NATO into a full-fledged military, political, and economic alliance.

Although in Europe the extension of the integration process was widely discussed (the agrarian "Green Poll" or the European Political Community), the United States concentrated solely on the EDC as a "single but key element." Its assessment, that European integration was "on the very verge of complete disaster,"[52] was partly due to the fact that the United States regarded a possible failure of the EDC as a "defeat" for American prestige. Because even the Schuman Plan seemed to be threatened, the United States feared the collapse of its entire European policy since the Marshall Plan. As early as 1951, American helplessness and, correspondingly, American pressure increased and finally resulted in the threat "to re-examine, fundamentally, . . . the whole basis of our current foreign policy objectives in Europe."[53] But, as before, this warning reflected only the considerable uncertainty whether the United States should induce the Europeans to continue and accelerate the integration process by restraint or by pressure.[54] Again, the Cold War became an important instrument in safeguarding American "leadership" within the alliance. The huge armaments program, which the Truman administration urged upon the Europeans in 1952 and which went even beyond the economic potential of the United States itself, was devised to force the Europeans by its sheer costs to give up their resistance to the

---

51 *FRUS 1950*, vol. 1, *National Security Affairs; Foreign Economic Policy* (Washington, D.C., 1977), 216–17. *FRUS 1951*, 3:30, 646–50, 748ff. *FRUS 1952–1954*, 2:191, 219, 407–8; 6:142.

52 *FRUS 1952–1954*, 6:254, 260–1.

53 NA, RG 59, Camp Records, box 1, folder: European Political Community (Nov. 14, 1952). The last part of the sentence quoted was cancelled in the manuscript and is missing in the version of December 4, 1952 (folder: Chronological File 1953) but is maintained in a qualified form in the version of January 9, 1953. *FRUS 1950*, 1:217. *FRUS 1952–1954:* 224ff., 262ff. Minutes of meetings, Dec. 13, 1951, and Dec. 5, 1952, NA, RG 59, Minutes of the Secretary's Daily Meetings, 1949–1952.

54 *FRUS 1952–1954*, 6:125–31, 142–6, 198, 224–8, 261–4.

economic and military resurgence of West Germany. Because of its analysis of the character and imminence of the Soviet threat, the United States could not and would not understand why the Europeans resisted this step so tenaciously, although they obviously knew that it could not be delayed forever. Acheson's "policy of strength" was not only designed to create the collective potential for the deterrence of the Soviet Union, but also to back up the supposedly weak and nervous European governments; only their confidence in American defense commitments would make acceptable the resurgence of Germany and encourage the European statesmen to resist Soviet pressure from without and neutralist or pacifist tendencies from within.[55]

YEARS OF ESTRANGEMENT, 1953–1956

The potential contradiction in American policy, first to strengthen Europe by advance commitments and then to (re)gain global unilateral freedom of action by disengagement, was aggravated during the Eisenhower era by an increased consideration of isolationist tendencies within the administration and in Congress. The president himself developed the formula that all informal ties had to be used "to find the economical way to make these European nations perform effectively as our allies," so that the United States could think "of developing in Western Europe a third great power bloc, after which development the United States would be permitted to sit back and relax somewhat."[56] But the Eisenhower administration did not want to provoke the danger of a Third Force, especially after de Gaulle had returned to power: "The idea of organic unity through common institutions was designed to deal with the danger of nationalist challenge or an attempt to 'reverse alliances' in either Germany or France."[57]

The United States considered the EDC the most effective instrument to realize these aims. Should the EDC fail, the Soviet Union would have realized its goal, "initially to split Germany and France and subsequently to gain control of a unified Germany."[58] Because

55 *FRUS 1950*, 1:158, 171, 217, 284, 288; *FRUS 1951*, 1:366.
56 *FRUS 1952–1954*, 2:278. *FRUS 1955–1957*, 4:349, 355, 363.
57 *FRUS 1955–1957*, 4:409. Mai, "Dominanz," 334–5. EL, Eisenhower Papers, White House Central Files, box 76, folder: MacMillan Talks (2) (June 1958).
58 EL, Eisenhower Papers, NSC-Series, box 5 (July 15, 1954).

"no satisfactory substitute for this solution [EDC] has yet been found," American aid should induce the European government to proceed with the integration process.[59] In order to make the French and Germans realize what was at stake, John Foster Dulles in late 1953 aired a first rudimentary version of the formula of "agonizing reappraisal":

We have reached a decisive moment in history. The foundation of our present European policy is that real strength and stability and effective defense in Europe depend on the development of an organic unity which includes France and Germany. . . . We cannot, of course, force either of these countries to join with the other, but if they cannot do so we will have to reassess our own interests and policies in the light of those circumstances.[60]

As early as 1951, the Truman administration had warned the Europeans unmistakably that "Germany was not a negotiable item at the present time. It could not be bartered for an easing in tensions."[61] When, in September 1953, Dulles thought of making "a spectacular effort to relax world tensions," he defined European integration and "the cementing of Germany firmly to Europe and the West" as the most important preconditions for such a policy of détente.[62] NATO was to be the controlling framework for an integrated Europe; European integration, and especially the EDC, was to assume the same function with regard to the Federal Republic, in order to prevent any seesaw policy in the period after Adenauer. Dulles argued that "the best means of doing this . . . is to so tie Germany into the whole complex of Western institutions – military, political and economic – and to so command her loyalties that neutralism or orientation to the East will be commonly accepted as unthinkable," even to "catch the imagination of the West Germans and forestall a dangerous possibility of a German movement towards reunification in opposition to what might be the broad interest of the West."[63] This policy included the final decision to partition

59 *FRUS 1952–1954*, 7:515 (NSC 160/1, Aug. 17, 1953). NA, RG 59, 740.00/2-1154, 4-2854, 8-2454; 740.05/3-2754; 840.00/4-1654. *FRUS 1952–1954*, 6:311–402 passim. *FRUS 1955–1957*, 4:261ff.
60 Dulles to Conant, Nov. 20, 1953, EL, Dulles Papers, Subject Series, box 8. *FRUS 1952–1954*, 7:1474–7. The threat was missing in the annexed letter to Adenauer. *FRUS 1952–1954*, 6:341.
61 *FRUS 1951*, 4:160.
62 *FRUS 1952–1954*, 2:458–60; 7:510–20 (NSC-160/1). NA, RG 59, 740.5/2-154.
63 *FRUS 1955–1957*, 4:363 (Dulles, Dec. 10, 1955), 370, 388, 392 (Jan. 26, 1956), 399.

Germany (which Dulles had favored as early as 1947[64]) in the interest of the integration of Europe, of détente, and of American disengagement.

When France delayed the ratification of the EDC, disengagement, disarmament, and détente were further postponed. The time factor gained "crucial importance," not only with regard to possible German attempts to revise the EDC treaty, but because any renegotiation would "seriously prejudice attainment [of] our objectives."[65] To prevent any "decline in U.S. prestige and leadership" by an early détente,[66] to force the Europeans to bring the continental integration process and the Atlantic bloc-building to a close, this impasse had to be broken by Dulles's public and diplomatic threat of an "agonizing reappraisal."[67]

Despite all warnings that the Europeans might interpret the "New Look" as an expression of "isolationism,"[68] and that "greater progress toward European unity and cohesion can now be best achieved by relaxation of direct and overt U.S. pressure to that end,"[69] the United States claimed a unilateral freedom of action for itself, even, if necessary, against the interest of its allies. It was not willing to decrease its influence in the same manner as its commitments, but instead tried to extend the entangling effects of the Atlantic alliance for the European countries, though not for itself. Again the United States was tempted to force the "closer" integration of the EDC (and the European Political Community) on the Europeans. Increased "self-help" was the price the allies in Dulles's eyes had to pay for a policy of détente: "We ought not seriously to seek discussions with the Soviets until decisions have been taken on EDC."[70]

The Cold War had become more necessary than ever. Dulles obviously did not realize that his attempts "to create in France an awareness in high quarters of the extent to which they were depen-

---

64 Charles P. Kindleberger, *The German Economy 1945–1947: Charles P. Kindleberger's Letters from the Field* (Westport, Conn., 1989), 149, 167.
65 NA, RG 59, 740.5/2-454 (W. B. Smith).
66 *FRUS 1952–1954*, 2:401 (Project Solarium, Task Force A, July 1953), 555–8. *FRUS 1952–1954*, vol. 1, *General Economic and Political Matters* (Washington, D.C., 1983), 1465–1506.
67 NA, RG 59, 740.5/4-254.
68 Report of Special Representative in Europe (Draper), "Certain European Issues Affecting the United States," May 15, 1953, pp. 1–5, EL, Eisenhower Papers, White House Central Files, Subject Series, box 99. NA, RG 59, Records of the Central European Division, 1944–53, box 1; NA, RG 59, 740.5/2-554, 2-1054, and 3-854.
69 *FRUS 1952–1954*, 2:408 (Project Solarium, Task Force A, July 1953).
70 Ibid., 720–1, 744, 748–49, 1234 (Dulles, Oct. 23, 1953).

dent on the U.S."[71] encouraged the French and other Europeans (including Adenauer) to look for "autonomy and independence" by collective self-organization and to build "in Western Europe a new power center as a long-term alternative to the American commitment, and at the same time as a counter-weight against the leading power."[72] Disenchantment, mutual suspicion, and even a feeling of crisis began to reign on both sides of the Atlantic for some years.[73]

When the EDC, as had been foreseeable for quite a time, failed in 1954, the United States faced the debris of its European policy. A combination of helplessness and insight induced the Eisenhower administration to decide on a "policy of lying low on European integration and saying and doing nothing except as asked"; had the Europeans asked for more precise advice, "we would not have known what to do."[74] Such a restraint could not last long. On the one hand, the United States saw itself confronted immediately with the protectionist tendencies and the competition of the EDC and the developing "common market."[75] On the other hand, the unsolved German question had become even more urgent since the failure of the EDC. This called for an active role of the United States, in order to eliminate the danger that the Germans might use the opportunity to discard the European in favor of the national solution. Like the preceding administration, the Eisenhower government learned from the failure of its European policy that it could only maintain and lead the alliance if it refrained from the use of "direct rule" and if it accepted integration as an autonomous European process, despite its sometimes hesitant progress and despite its encroachments of American interests. "We must recognize the fact," Dulles reflected on this experience, "that we can no longer run the free world."[76]

---

71 Dulles to Stassen, Aug. 9, 1954, EL, Dulles Papers, General Correspondence and Memoranda Series, box 1, folder: S(3); Conversation with Adenauer, Sept. 16, 1954, EL, Dulles Papers, Subject Series, box 8.
72 Konrad Adenauer, *Erinnerungen 1955–1959* (Stuttgart, 1967), 13–19. Hans-Peter Schwarz, "Adenauer und Europa," *VfZG* 27 (1979):475, 483ff., rightly maintains that "gaullist" elements in Adenauer's thinking were more than an "aberration" in his late years.
73 *FRUS 1952–1954*, 2:450. *FRUS 1955–1957*, 4:72–81. Adenauer, *Erinnerungen 1955–1959*, 3, 114, 213, 215.
74 *FRUS 1955–1957*, 4:347, 356.
75 Ibid., 261ff. passim. On the conflict between integration and competition in the case of Euratom see ibid., 294, 301–11, 361 ("We would be making the Europeans independent of us and giving up our monopoly on marketable enriched uranium . . . "), 394. The mistrust toward the Federal Republic and West German industry, respectively, made the "effective control over weapons-quality material" seem advisable; ibid., 332–8, 344–6, 348, 400, 414.
76 *FRUS 1952–1954*, 2:695.

In the meantime, the integration movement, not least in repudiation of American pressure, had gained new momentum with the "reliance européenne" and found its manifestation in the conference of Messina in 1955 and the European Economic Community. Since 1952, the height of the Cold War, the Europeans – with growing apprehension – came to acknowledge their lasting dependence on the United States and the American nuclear shield. For them, détente seemed to be the only opportunity to preserve their economic autonomy and political freedom of action, not as a Third Force between the blocs but as a "second pillar" within the Atlantic Alliance.[77]

The cause of the differences in outlook and interests were the structural asymmetries of economic power and overseas commitments, of military strength and geostrategic vulnerability. These asymmetries led to repeated attempts by the United States to over-extend its generally undisputed hegemonical leadership (based on its nuclear shield); but the American government each time consciously, though against internal resistance, decided against the temptation to pursue a European policy based upon open domination and "direct rule." To prevent any national separation (*Sonderweg*) of the Federal Republic (or France and Italy), the United States tried to force supranational integration on the Europeans, contrary to their national sentiments and resentments, and sometimes even by interfering insensitively with the sovereignty of its allies. Initially, the United States had considered the functional integration of Europe as insufficient, although it proved to be the ideal solution from the European point of view: It combined national sovereignty in Europe with collective autonomy of Europe within the alliance. Adenauer's conviction that the United States and Europe had common "fundamental interests" but that not all their "vital interests" were in accord led him to the following conclusion: "We had to avoid being taken in tow by the United States and had to find the openings for an autonomous European policy." As an alternative to the unilateralism of the Eisenhower administration, he stipulated the collective unilateralism of Western Europe: "Difference in political conceptions" (and inter-

77 Gunther Mai, "Osthandel und Westintegration 1947–1957: Die USA, Europa und die Entstehung einer hegemonialen Partnerschaft," in Ludolf Herbst, Werner Bührer, and Hanno Sowade, eds., *Vom Marshallplan zur EWG: Die Eingliederung der Bundesrepublik Deutschland in die westliche Welt* (Munich, 1990), 222–5.

ests, he should have added) would "in certain situations necessarily lead to separate political action."[78]

The emergence of the Atlantic community, although based on the consonance of cultural values and convictions, was nevertheless a complicated and novel arrangement between victors and vanquished, between sovereign states with very different interests, commitments, and power potentials. This imbalance required a process of mutual acceptance and compromise, of learning and adaption, which could not advance without friction and sometimes even crisis. It demanded a responsible wielding of global power by self-restraint, on the one hand, and the acceptance of a secular loss of power and the surmounting of national pride and prejudice by collective self-organization, on the other. In the end, it was just the precariousness of this reluctant compromise, based on a balance of interests and aimed at a balance of power, which opened the way to the stability of a hegemonical partnership and gave the Atlantic alliance that internal strength and collective efficiency which made possible its survival even beyond the Cold War.

78 Adenauer, *Erinnerungen 1955–1959*, 17ff., 223.

6

From Morgenthau Plan to Schuman Plan: America and the Organization of Europe

JOHN GILLINGHAM

To travel from the Morgenthau Plan to the Schuman Plan is to move from an American proposal to destroy Ruhr industry to the actual organization of Europe around it only five years later and to cross from the threshold of the short, unhappy period of postwar reconstruction into the far longer and better era of sustained growth and improved public welfare that continues uninterrupted into the present. This transformation required the maturation of American foreign policy. The United States wanted to withdraw from Europe after the defeat of Hitler. Roosevelt's Grand Design for the postwar world did not break cleanly with traditional isolationism. Based on the supposition that a framework of peace could be built upon the two principles of self-determination and free trade, it limited U.S. interventions to policing actions conducted jointly with the other Allied nations, especially the Soviet Union. As a reconstruction strategy, the Grand Design was worthless and as a guide to action meaningless; it would indeed remain only a big sketch.

United States policy-making after World War II developed in response to successive international crises, cropping up as a result of economic and political dislocation, shifts in the strategic balance, mutual hostility, miscalculation, and incompetence. Unguided by overall strategy, America's reconstruction policy in Europe, particularly as it affected the occupied former Reich, became the plaything of domestic factions. The Allied Control Council (ACC), through which the victor powers tried to govern Germany, was thus immobilized not only by disagreement among the Allies, but also by

The Truman Library Institute, through bestowal of its Senior Scholar's Award, provided the release time from teaching used to write this essay. For a more detailed account of the events described in this article, see John Gillingham, *Coal, Steel, and the Rebirth of Europe, 1945–1955: The Germans and French from Ruhr Conflict to Economic Community* (New York, 1990).

111

conflict within the Office of Military Government for Germany (OMGUS) itself over whether Germany should be reformed or restored. The choice at hand was a difficult one. Were the Allies to force Europe to starve until German industry had been reorganized to their satisfaction? Or was German industrial operation to resume immediately, with the result of possibly contributing to the rise of a Fourth Reich?

Only after the Marshall Plan was the dilemma resolved. Initially, no one knew what would develop from the secretary of state's proposal, and no one could define its specific objectives. Yet it contained the gist of a fundamental policy shift. A break from the Grand Design's emphasis on disengagement and globalism, it committed the United States to promoting German recovery in the context of European reconstruction. In other words, the United States would promote the economic restoration of the former enemy to the extent that it improved the welfare, and therefore increased the security, of neighboring nations. The proposal of June 5, 1947, nonetheless left two issues of critical importance unresolved. One was Britain's role in Europe: Was it to be first among equals, merely one among equals, or left out altogether? The second issue was institutional in nature. As a political entity, "Europe" existed mainly in the minds of American diplomats; the inadequate post–World War I peace settlement, depression, war, as well as weakness, poverty, and hardship arising from them had eroded the basis of international cooperation. The Schuman Plan restored it, thereby bringing the Marshall Plan to fruition and achieving the diplomatic breakthrough that has led to the phenomenon that most clearly distinguishes the past generation of European history from the one preceding it – integration.

I

President Roosevelt cannot escape responsibility for the problems of American policy in occupied Germany. Intent upon deferring all discussion of postwar problems until after the conclusion of hostilities, he rejected the sensible recommendations of the Allied planning group set up after the October 1943 Teheran meeting, the European Advisory Commission (EAC), in favor of the criminally lighthearted, vengeful proposals of his Hyde Park neighbor, Secretary of the Treasury Henry Morgenthau, to raze Ruhr industry, flood the region's mines, and return Germany to the economic conditions of circa 1850. Secretary of War Henry Stimson mercifully managed to block this criminal scheme, but its eventual substitute, the compromise policy contained in the directive JCS 1067, was still inadequate.[1] Under its terms, Germany would make little progress toward either revival or reform.

EAC's recommendations were set out in the memorandum entitled "General Objectives of United States Policy with Respect to Germany," which called for reform followed by reintegration into an economically liberalized Europe. Germany was to be required to make restitution and reparation, its war industry would be destroyed, and its economic domination of the continent brought to an end by unspecified means. The conquered people were not, however, to be forcibly impoverished, since this would create unacceptable political as well as economic problems for the rest of Europe; instead, they were eventually to be somehow "integrated" into the continent.[2] Morgenthau's scheme consigned such enlightened planning efforts to the files, and although JCS 1067 represented an improvement upon the treasury secretary's design for a soup-kitchen Europe, it too was a poor basis for policy-making. This de facto charter of OMGUS did not specify deindustrialization as an objective but was otherwise both vague and punitive. While it held the conquered population morally responsible for having inflicted misery upon itself and considered it in need of reform through denazification, economic disarmament, and forcible democratization, it concluded that the U.S. occupation government was to limit its powers to the prevention of "disease and unrest." Harsher in tone than either its British or Soviet counterparts, as well as ill-considered, narrow, and generally unenforcible, JCS 1067 turned policy-making in Germany into an American political football.[3]

Harry S Truman had served a total of eighty-one days as vice president before taking the oath of office on April 12, 1945. The Man from Missouri lacked experience in foreign affairs, and there were few to whom he could turn for help. Harry Hopkins, Roosevelt's

1 John Morton Blum, ed., *From the Morgenthau Diaries*, vol. 3, *Years of War, 1941–1945* (Boston, 1967), 343–69; see also Henry L. Stimson and McGeorge Bundy, *On Active Service in Peace and War* (New York, 1947), 576–7.
2 "General Objectives of United States Economic Policy with Respect to Germany," Aug. 14, 1944, *FRUS 1944*, vol. 1, *General* (Washington, D.C., 1966), 278–9.
3 John H. Backer, *Priming the German Economy: American Occupational Policies, 1945–1948* (Durham, N.C., 1971), 17–18; see also Nicholas Balabkins, *Germany under Direct Controls: Economic Aspects of Industrial Disarmament, 1945–1948* (New Brunswick, N.J., 1964), 13–14.

leading foreign policy adviser, was terminally ill. Secretary of State
Edward Stettinius performed a largely decorative role. The State
Department, though rapidly growing, was still small and lacked
expertise in economic planning. Furthermore, the wartime consensus that had given Roosevelt great freedom of action was eroding,
and deep conflicts held in check by the external threat had resurfaced
in the public, Congress, the cabinet, and the administration.[4] The
American left, grouped around Secretary of Commerce (and former
Vice President) Henry Wallace, considered the war a unique opportunity to fulfill the long-deferred promise of the New Deal to create
a brave new world of law, freedom, and economic justice on the basis of the Grand Design and in cooperation with the Soviet Union.
On the right, Truman had to contend with the upswelling of prim-
itivism later embodied in the person of Senator Joseph McCarthy,
who, with many less memorable like-minded colleagues, entered
Congress in 1947.[5]

Germany and its industrial heartland were but small parts of the
vast world with whose immense problems the ill-equipped American president now had to contend. The highest U.S. priority was to
maintain the wartime alliance, its urgency underscored by the atomic
bomb. Unable to discern any alternative to the Grand Design other
than chaos, the United States clung to Roosevelt's policy. Its failure
in Germany is conventionally, but misleadingly, described as the
breakdown of Four-Power cooperation, something that never existed. The United States was the only occupation power that tried to
make quadripartite rule effective; it finally gave up on the attempt
only after repeated failures to resolve reparations disputes with the
Soviet Union within the Allied Control Council. Reparations were
the drive wheel of Allied economic policy in Germany: Not until it
had been decided who would get what could a discussion of other
issues even begin.[6] The U.S. break stemmed from something more
fundamental, however, than disagreements about how to slice the
German pie. Behind it was the need to create a bipartite consensus in
Congress to endorse the break with American tradition that eventu-

---

4 John Lewis Gaddis, *The United States and the Origins of the Cold War, 1941–1947* (New York
and London, 1972), passim.
5 Herbert Feis, *From Trust to Terror: The Onset of the Cold War, 1945–1950* (New York, 1970),
16–17; see also TL, "Interview with Willard Thorpe," July 10, 1971.
6 Alec Cairncross, *The Price of War: British Policy on German Reparations, 1941–1949* (Oxford
and New York, 1986), passim.

ally occurred with the adoption of the Marshall Plan. This required a purge of the American left.

The reparations dispute was caused by the United States reneging on an agreement reached with the Soviets at the Yalta Conference to set Germany's total bill at $20 billion, to be taken in either capital removals or deliveries from current production. The Soviets were to receive one-half the total amount. The overall figure was based upon assumptions about Germany's ability to pay, in the belief that approximately this amount could be removed without driving standards of living below an undefined "modest and decent European level." Although the economic presuppositions of the conferees were wildly incorrect, the net amount available for reparations roughly coincided with Germany's costs of waging World War II.[7] Provision of this tribute was the first imperative of economic policy toward the enemy Reich; reconstruction, revival, "a return to normalcy," and so on would be out of the question until Germany had in fact paid out the equivalent of financing another five years of hostilities.[8]

The question of whose ox would be gored – that is, from whose Zone of Occupation reparations would be removed – was broached but by no means resolved at the Potsdam Conference of July and August 1945. The only provision of the protocol dealing strictly with reparations called upon the United States and Britain to deliver 10 percent of Russia's total requirements. For the rest, what emerged from the meeting was an agreed-upon framework within which the occupation powers could disagree about policy. The three main propositions of the protocols stipulated that Germany be treated as a single economic unit, not be deprived of goods necessary to make her self-supporting, and be required to run export surpluses to avoid becoming a drain on the finances of the occupation powers. Tucked away within the document, however, were articles that made a mockery of the principle that the former enemy should be treated as a single unit. One of these articles empowered each occupation authority to seize and remove goods independently and was thus a license to conduct separate policies.[9]

The so-called Level of Industry Agreement of March 1946, which the British more accurately called the Reparations Plan, represented

7 Ibid., 70.   8 Ibid., 71.
9 Charles L. Mee, Jr., *Meeting at Potsdam* (New York, 1975), 188–9.

the single most important attempt by the Allies to arrive at a common economic policy for Germany. It was an exercise in futility and madness, because the United States and Britain disagreed with the USSR about what could be considered an acceptable German standard of living. After months of contention, the Allies nonetheless arrived at a scheme. But, because of its inherent flaws, this plan would have been as bad economically as anything the USSR might have worked out on its own.

The Reparations Plan divided German industry into three groups: armaments production (to be prohibited), unrestricted production (of which the document made no further mention), and branches subject to restrictions. For the latter, the plan set output targets, as well as those for imports and exports, by sector. Working against a deadline of January 1946, the divided negotiators found themselves forced to conclude an arrangement that did not take into account the effect of cutbacks in one sector on outputs in another sector, failed to consider the relationship between allowed levels of importation and exportation on the one hand and production on the other, overlooked the effects of such dislocations on employment and consumption patterns, and did not even touch upon the structural adjustments required by drastic changes in the aggregates and components of production.[10]

Any attempt to implement the Reparations Plan would surely have resulted in a reciprocal gearing down of production caused by sectoral shortages, aggravated by attempts to favor exports over domestic consumption. It would have resulted in drastic declines in living standards, massive unemployment, and administrative chaos. The agreement of February 1946 brought Big Three planning to a moral dead end. One cannot blame Clay (who, in any case, should have received direction from above) for having cut off reparations deliveries to the Soviet zone in May 1946. The drift toward Cold War had already become irreversible, as indicated, for instance, by the fate of the Acheson–Clayton proposal developed in April 1946. Its formulators, Walt Rostow and Charles Kindleberger, two bright young men attached to the State Department, believed that a combination of dollars and federalism would entice the Soviets back into cooperating in efforts to solve the problems of both German reconstruction and European integration. Undersecretary of State Dean

10 Cairncross, *Price of War*, 130–46.

Acheson supported the proposal, as did the assistant secretary for economic affairs, Will Clayton. They persuaded Secretary of State James Byrnes to put it on the agenda at the Paris Peace Conference then engaged in drafting treaties with the former enemies. New "hardballers" in the State Department, such as George Kennan, opposed the initiative, but the real cause of its demise was lack of support at the top.[11]

Behind the scenes in Washington, conflicts between left, right, and center were coming to a head in disputes about how to administer the former Reich. On September 6, 1946, Secretary of State Byrnes delivered his famous Stuttgart Speech, which publicly justified the decision to "go it alone" made by Clay some four months earlier. The United States, Byrnes declared, had found the Potsdam agreement unworkable and was not prepared to promote the economic reconstruction of its zone of occupation as rapidly as feasible. "Maximum possible unification" was still an objective, he added, but priority would go to European economic recovery. Officials of the Central European Section of the State Department wrote Byrnes's speech. The extent to which it met with Truman's approval is difficult to ascertain.[12] Secretary of Commerce Wallace considered the initiative an attempt to force the president's hand. To prevent this development, Wallace delivered his memorable speech in Madison Square Garden in September 1946, which called for frank American acknowledgment of Soviet predominance in eastern Europe and proposed a "healthy competition" between the different economic and political systems of the two superpowers. Byrnes immediately tendered his resignation, which Truman refused to accept, demanding and receiving instead that of the secretary of commerce.[13]

Wallace was the only remaining cabinet member seriously disturbed by the growing rift with the Soviet Union and willing to hazard the fate of the Western democracies by attempting to maintain the wartime alliance. His departure was soon followed by an abrupt lurch to the right, as manifest in the results of the 1946 congressional elections. The discovery that Communists in Canada had passed atomic secrets to the Soviets was by then triggering the first of the great postwar spy scares. The dreaded House Un-American Activ-

---

11 Walt W. Rostow, *The Division of Europe after World War II* (Austin, 1981), passim; see also Charles P. Kindleberger, *Marshall Plan Days* (Boston and London, 1987), 108, 156.
12 Feis, *From Trust to Terror*, 195; see also Gaddis, *Origins of the Cold War*, 338–9.
13 James F. Byrnes, *Speaking Frankly* (New York and London, 1947), 188–9.

ities Committee would soon be back in session. The founding of a progressive but militantly anticommunist association within the Democratic Party, the Americans for Democratic Action, badly split the already demoralized left. Fellow travelers from the 1930s, Wallaceites, and other assorted malcontents would henceforth lack defenders even in liberal political institutions. Finally, to contain the rising anticommunist hysteria, Truman authorized the FBI to investigate the loyalty of all federal employees, a gigantic task which, by 1951, had resulted in the resignation of 2,000 persons with suspect, unorthodox, crank, or unpopular views.[14]

The revolt of the primitives had the most significant and lasting effect on China policy, but it was felt in occupied Germany as well. There it wrecked the program to decentralize and reform German industry. Under James S. Martin, who took over as head of the Decartelization Branch of OMGUS on December 31, 1945, the campaign to break up the organizational structure of German big business, initially a kind of second line of defense of the Morgenthau Plan, became a determined attempt to apply the Jeffersonian ideals of Thurman Arnold's Antitrust Division in the Justice Department to the trusts and syndicates believed responsible for Hitler's rise to power and the support of his nefarious policies. To the zealous Martin, the real source of enemy strength had not been "the hobnailed Nazi with tanks and guns," but a web of secret international agreements spun by monopolists of all countries but originating in Germany. The trustbuster also detected in it reflections of a larger pattern of political and economic subversion by capitalist interests unfolding in the United States.[15]

These views met with the disapproval of the head of the Economics Division, General William Draper, a Wall Street investment banker in civilian life. Although he was officially committed to implementing decartelization, Draper's main responsibility was to promote German economic recovery, and he considered Martin an untrustworthy fanatic. While the general worked behind the scenes to undercut his deputy's authority, the decartelization chief went public with his accusations. Martin's patron, Senator Kilgore, lambasted OMGUS as protector of war criminals, and his influential allies in the press subjected the apoplectic Draper and the increas-

14 Arthur S. Link, *American Epoch: A History of the United States since the 1890's*, vol. 3, *1938–1966*, 3rd ed. (New York, 1967), 665–6.
15 James Stewart Martin, *All Honorable Men* (Boston, 1950), p. vii.

ingly irritable Clay to a constant drumfire of criticism. The effort was for naught. Disagreement within OMGUS gridlocked the effort to reform the trusts and cartels. Although OMGUS had set the process in motion as early as 1945, it had accomplished little apart from the reorganization of I.G. Farben by the time Martin was forced to resign in May 1947. He and his colleagues would soon fall victim to loyalty investigations which, as in many similar cases, drove them and the unfashionable views they represented out of politics. As winter 1946–47 turned into spring, the United States found itself proposing industrial revival without reform in occupied Germany.[16]

II

The Marshall Plan originated in the winter of 1946–47, the harshest in a century. From December to the end of March, chilling winds, hard freezes, and heavy snowfalls brought rail and barge traffic to a standstill and production to a halt for whole weeks at a time throughout much of northern and western Europe. World War II, it seemed, had left more lasting damage than previously realized; recovery was perilously fragile, living standards in jeopardy, and the possibility imminent that Europe would plunge into revolutionary chaos. The winter made no distinctions between victor and vanquished. In Britain, a collapse of the transport system resulted in shutdowns throughout industry, causing a sharp decline in exports and precipitating a payments crisis so severe that the nation could no longer support the Greek government's campaign to suppress insurrectionaries from the wartime resistance who were suspected to have fallen under the influence of Moscow. Washington's response was the Truman Doctrine, whereby the United States made a blanket commitment to providing military assistance to any nation threatened by communism. By painting a lurid picture of the red bogeyman, the American president managed to entice out of the tightfisted, withdrawal-minded, Republican-dominated Congress what for the time was the enormous sum of $350 million. The Truman Doctrine, which could have seriously overstrained U.S. resources and did in fact set an ugly precedent, can only be defended as an expedient.[17] The importance of blind anticommunism in U.S.

16 Ibid., passim.
17 Feis, *From Trust to Terror*, 191–206; Gaddis, *Origins of the Cold War*, 348–9; Robert A. Pollard, *Economic Security and the Origins of the Cold War* (New York, 1985), 126–7.

policy toward Europe was soon overshadowed, however, by the Marshall Plan's emphasis on economic cooperation.

No single individual can claim credit for devising the Marshall Plan. It began as a program of economic assistance. The United States had been providing foreign aid on a large scale since the end of World War II. The Americans had loaned $3.75 billion to the British in January 1946 and $1.75 billion to the French a month later, had donated another $3 billion in aid through the United Nations Relief and Rehabilitation Administration (UNRRA), and still another several hundred million to occupied Germany through the Government and Relief in Occupied Areas (GARIOA) program.[18] In early April 1947, top-level planning for a comprehensive assistance program of unprecedented size began under the auspices of the State–War–Navy Coordinating Committee. On May 8, 1947, Undersecretary of State for Political Affairs Dean Acheson announced in the unlikely venue of Cleveland, Mississippi, that, without $8 billion in American aid, Europe would descend into bankruptcy. An alarming, even terrifying, memorandum of May 27 from Undersecretary for Economic Affairs Will Clayton prompted the announcement of June 5, 1947, by Secretary of State George C. Marshall at the Harvard commencement. "It is now obvious," Clayton wrote, "that we grossly underestimated the destruction to the European economy by the war," which included, he added, not only physical damages, but the effects of economic dislocations – nationalization, land reform, loss of capital, and the severance of commercial ties.[19] Europe, as depicted by the rich former cotton broker from Houston, faced shortages of dollars, coal, grain, and ships and was in need of an immediate infusion of $5 billion to stave off starvation. The American people, he insisted, had to be prepared to tighten their belts in order to provide the $6 to $7 billion required annually over the next

18 Feis, *From Trust to Terror*, 227, 230; Michel Margairaz, "Autour des Accords Blum–Byrnes: Jean Monnet entre le consensus national et le consensus atlantique," *Histoire, économie, société* 1 (1982):440–70; Irwin Wall, "Les Accords Blum–Byrnes: La modernisation de la France et la Guerre froide," *Vingtième siècle* 13 (1978):40–62; Werner Abelshauser, "Wiederaufbau vor dem Marshall-Plan: Westeuropas Wachstumschancen und die Wirtschaftsordnungspolitik in der zweiten Hälfte der vierziger Jahre," *VfZG* 29 (1981):546–62.
19 Memo by Under SecState for Economic Affairs [Clayton], May 27, 1947, *FRUS 1947*, vol. 3, *The British Commonwealth; Europe* (Washington, D.C., 1972), 230–1; see also Michael J. Hogan, *The Marshall Plan: America, Britain, and the Reconstruction of Western Europe, 1947–1952* (Cambridge, 1987), 40–1; Stanley Hoffmann and Charles Maier, eds., *The Marshall Plan: A Retrospective* (Boulder, Colo., and London, 1984), 7–8, 19–20; Joseph M. Jones, *The Fifteen Weeks: An Inside Account of the Genesis of the Marshall Plan* (New York, 1953), passim.

three years; but they should be assured that, instead of allocating relief through an international agency such as the United Nations, "the United States [would] run this show."[20]

The transformation of an aid program into a new policy for Europe occurred under the auspices of the Policy Planning Staff (PPS) headed by George Kennan. While the work of this new State Department think-tank reflected ideas in general circulation at Foggy Bottom, the PPS brought a new coherence to the policy-making process. For the first time, the United States would be able to proceed on the basis of a well-defined, sensible, and flexible long-term strategy. Even before the PPS had begun to work on the proposed aid program, Kennan had defined certain essential elements of a new approach. First, Western Europe was to receive priority over other trouble spots. This emphasis on a specific region constituted a clear-cut break with Roosevelt's globalism. Second, the region in question was to include both Britain and the U.S. Zone of Occupation in Germany, as well as the nations of the continent. In other words, the United States would no longer base its policy on fundamental distinctions between former enemies and allies; in economic affairs, it would treat Britain like any other European nation. Finally, Kennan diagnosed Europe's political problems as being internal and economic in origin rather than foreign and military. Thus, the security of the United States was to rest no longer on self-regulating mechanisms, nor, as after 1950, on military alliances, but on the health of agriculture and industry and the welfare of the public in Europe.[21] On May 16, 1947, Kennan drafted a tentative list of principles for turning the aid program into a vehicle of integration. American assistance was to be predicated upon intra-European cooperation, serve as a means of weaning Europe from dependence, and aim at the federation of the non-Communist nations of Europe.[22]

The Marshall Plan as conceived and presented was like a flying saucer: No one could have known what it really looked like, how big it was, or which way it was moving; nor could anyone even be altogether sure that the thing was real.[23] Yet something strange and

20 *FRUS 1947*, 3:230–1.
21 George F. Kennan, *Memoirs, 1925–1950* (Boston, 1967), pp. 335–6; see also Kennan to Acheson, May 23, 1947, *FRUS 1947*, 3:223–4.
22 Memo by the Director of the Policy Planning Staff [Kennan], May 16, 1947, *FRUS 1947*, 3:220–1.
23 Moore to Wilcox, June 23, 1947, ibid., 239.

wonderful had appeared on the horizon of American policy-making in the late spring of 1947. In the three years between the Harvard commencement address and the announcement of the Schuman Plan, it would come down to earth. The descent was less gentle than one might have wished. Though the pilots tried to steer with steady hand, updrafts, downdrafts, side winds, and other unexpected currents frequently buffeted the craft. A safe landing was assured only after it had actually touched ground.

Almost instinctively, the United States first turned to Britain for help in transforming the aid package from pledge to operational program. This was a bad choice. The British had no intention of joining Europe and objected strenuously to trade liberalization. But being weak and overextended, they were too dependent on the United States to express their objections openly. When ultimately it became clear that Britain would never take a leading role in integrating Europe, American policy seemed to have reached a dead end. It was saved by France.

A basic incompatibility in American–British economic relations had been apparent since the war. The British wanted nothing less than access to the brave new technology-propelled American world of open markets and productivity gains; they wanted nothing more than to direct the vast energies of the postwar world into maintaining their customary way of life and upholding their traditional status as a world power. The profound gulf between Yanks and Brits first became evident in the discussions of postwar economic policy that began in early 1944 in London, in which the British sought to convince their powerful ally to maintain the wartime system of combined boards set up to conduct international trade.[24] In collateral discussions, spokesmen like Lord Keynes mustered their full powers of analysis and eloquence to argue that the United States owed it to Britain to keep her payments in balance by preserving export markets for British manufactures and providing bridging loans on a more or less permanent basis. The refusal of the United States to consider such preferential measures and the abrupt decision taken in September 1945 to terminate Lend-Lease and abolish the combined

24 Informal and Exploratory Discussions regarding Postwar Economic Policy, *FRUS 1944*, vol. 2, *General: Economic and Social Matters* (Washington, D.C., 1967), 7–105; see also D. Cameron Watt, *Succeeding John Bull: America in Britain's Place, 1900–1975* (Cambridge and New York, 1975), 90–1.

board dealt a fatal blow to joint American–British economic policy-making; in this respect, the "special relationship" had ceased to exist.[25]

This was not, however, true in political matters. Alan Bullock, the official biographer of Ernest Bevin, foreign secretary in the Labour cabinet, is correct to speak of an increasing "parallelism" in this field.[26] Bevin succeeded, first of all, in drawing the United States into military engagement in Europe, as indicated by the declaration of the Truman Doctrine and the American decision to join NATO. Tormented by the costs of the occupation and its drain on payments, the British had lobbied hard and early for the formation of Bizonia; its creation fulfilled another objective of Bevin's policy. The difference between wealth and poverty made this an unequal partnership. The Labour government dropped demands for the nationalization of industry in return for U.S. agreement to pay the costs of occupation. Negotiations for these new arrangements coincided roughly with the months in which the United States tried to organize the European machinery of the Marshall Plan and thus incidentally gave hope to ERP planners who hoped Britain would help run it.[27]

The Paris deliberations, convoked to set up the Conference on European Economic Cooperation (CEEC), brought about the turning point in American–British relations on the question of Europe. CEEC faced two tasks: to devise an overall aid program and establish a permanent organization to coordinate national economic policies. The CEEC deliberations gave Britain a unique opportunity to take the lead in integrating Europe. The United States both lacked a clear idea of the scope and nature of the Marshall Plan and looked to the recipients to provide it. For their part, the continental nations were not only prepared to accept British guidance, but eager that it be offered. The British nonetheless deliberately sabotaged the machinery of the Organization for European Economic Cooperation (OEEC) built by the CEEC conferees. The designers of the Marshall Plan's international organization would have to go back to the drawing board.[28]

25 Alan Bullock, *Ernest Bevin: Foreign Secretary, 1945–1951* (London and New York, 1983), p. 124; see also Alan S. Milward, *The Reconstruction of Western Europe, 1945–51* (London, 1984), 62.
26 Bullock, *Bevin*, 314.
27 "Report on the Anglo-American Talks on Ruhr Coal Production," Sept. 17, 1947, NA, RG 260, AG47/178/1–2.
28 Milward, *Reconstruction*, 56–90; Imanual Wexler, *The Marshall Plan Revisited: The European Recovery Program in Economic Perspective* (Westport, Conn., 1983), 13–14; Hogan, *Marshall Plan*, 61–2; George Ball, *The Past Has Another Pattern* (New York and London, 1982), 77–8.

Bevin understood immediately that Marshall's speech of June 5 presented Britain with an extraordinary opportunity. Within four days, he persuaded the French Foreign Minister, Bidault, to adopt common policies with regard to the proposed aid program. The Labour statesman did not, as intimated to the State Department, mean to facilitate joint Anglo–French economic planning, but rather intended to block the Soviets (who had not yet refused to participate), contain France, keep the minor nations from outpointing the big ones, and present a solid front to the United States. As a result of this agreement, Sir Oliver Franks was named to head the Conference Executive and, in effect, direct the proceedings. The United States hoped that, in this powerful position, Franks could ease Britain's transition from imperial to European power.

Evidence that the process would not be painless soon mounted. By the end of June, Clayton protested that Britain expected to be treated as an equal with the rest of Europe rather than merely as one of its member-nations.[29] In September, the CEEC negotiations encountered severe difficulty. The United States expected the Europeans to formulate plans for attaining self-sufficiency within three to four years by means of self-help, mutual assistance, and unspecified cooperative measures. Instead, they presented a laundry list of aid requirements far in excess of anything Congress would have been prepared to fund. Franks refused to impose discipline out of respect for the principle of national sovereignty. On September 17, the ERP, the Marshall Plan body shadowing the CEEC, simply decreed a maximum of $22 million (later whittled down to $17 million). This move at least made it possible to pass a funding bill for the aid program, the European Cooperation Act of April 1948.[30]

Negotiations resumed in Paris the same month. The objective of the United States now was to turn CEEC into a permanent organization that could act as counterpart to the Economic Cooperation Administration. Failure in this round finally disillusioned the Americans. Other storm signals also loomed. The negotiations of the General Agreement on Tariffs and Trade (GATT), which Clayton had been conducting with indifferent success since 1946 in Geneva, nearly failed due to persistent British opposition to trade liberalization. They were finally concluded with a compromise, in which

29 Cited in Bullock, *Bevin*, 413f.   30 Wexler, *Marshall Plan Revisited*, 19–20.

Britain sacrificed a privileged relationship on the Canadian export market in order to retain the substance of imperial preference.[31] Britain also disappointed the United States by refusing to deny CEEC jurisdiction for bizonal economic policy.

Disagreement over the structure and powers of what would eventually become the Organization for European Economic Cooperation was the issue that ultimately disillusioned Foggy Bottom. The United States wanted the OEEC to be built around a strong secretariat – something "new, dynamic . . . and with specified functions" – but Britain refused to grant it any real power. Vigorously and persuasively defending this position, spokesmen like Franks argued on grounds of history, diplomatic tradition, and practicality that more could be accomplished informally than through centralized institutions like those dreamed of in Washington. The skillful rhetoric worked for a time,[32] but by early April 1948, the United States had placed blame for the failure of the negotiations on the British. On April 12, the American Ambassador to France, Jefferson Caffery, complained that, while France and Italy were moving toward a more liberal economy and decontrol, "in the absence of British participation and leadership it [was] unlikely that enough . . . European countries could be brought together to create a unit of efficient economic dimensions."[33]

On April 16, 1948, the Conference of European Economic Cooperation created the OEEC. It made provision for a body headed by a Council of Ministers to supervise a seven-member executive committee with its own secretariat, which was staffed by international civil servants empowered to prepare European production and import-export programs. The impressive mandate fooled no one. Without the cooperation of Britain, the OEEC could not work. The Americans therefore reacted furiously when the British seconded less than top-level officials to staff the secretariat.[34]

More consequential disagreements would soon arise between the two nations. One of them concerned payments, more specifically the American attempt to restore convertibility through the OEEC.

31 Bullock, *Bevin*, 461–2.
32 SecState to Murphy, Aug. 6, 1948, *FRUS 1948*, vol. 3, *Western Europe* (Washington, D.C., 1974), 389; see also memo, William T. Phillips to Assistant SecState for Economic Affairs [Nitze], March 4, 1948, ibid., 387.
33 Caffery to SecState, March 28, 1848, ibid., 407.
34 Acting SecState to Embassy in France, Apr. 4, 1948, ibid., 417.

Britain went along with these plans so long as their effect was to place sterling in the hands of importers of goods manufactured in the United Kingdom. It could not, however, accept an arrangement that facilitated convertibility of the chronically weak pound to the then supreme dollar, since, in the short run, this would increase pressure on the pound, while, in the long run, enable importers to purchase outside the sterling bloc. Yet is was precisely this unacceptable step that the United States insisted the British had to take. Though the United States, Britain, and their trading partners worked tirelessly in good faith to solve the difficult technical problems standing in the way of a solution to Europe's "money muddle," the two Anglo-Saxon powers were divided by a vast gulf of mutual incomprehension: What to the one was self-evidently fair trade policy was to the other a hypocritical attempt to profit from short-term advantages. Dispute over financial policy was chronic.[35] In April 1950, the head of the Marshall Plan, Paul Hoffman, threatened to cut Britain out of the aid program unless the British agreed to join the European Payments Union (EPU); after another painful compromise, this most permanent and successful of ERP-sponsored institutions came into being.[36]

The EPU was less important at the time than the disagreement between the United States and Britain over the OEEC. In a desperate attempt to breathe life into the organization, the Americans began lobbying intently in late 1949 for the appointment of the internationalist-minded, right-wing Belgian socialist Paul-Henri Spaak as the first secretary-general of the new organization. Bevin's response was an angry and spontaneous refusal to consider Spaak or any other continental for any such position. Amplifying his remarks a few days later, the foreign minister underscored his continued opposition to "politicizing" the OEEC or in fact allowing it to develop into anything more formidable than a standing committee. The United States not only dropped Spaak, but gave up on the OEEC. By spring 1950, the Marshall Plan's integration policy was dead in the water.[37]

35 Robert Triffin, *Europe and the Money Muddle: From Bilateralism to Near-Convertibility, 1947–1956* (New Haven, Conn., and London, 1957), passim.
36 TL, "Interview with Paul Hoffman," Oct. 25, 1964.
37 "Minutes of Conference of 1 July 1949 at Residence of Ambassador Bruce," NA, RG 466, DC49/1.

There was reason to doubt that France would be able to rescue it. The French were weak, frankly afraid of Germany, and no less protectionist-minded than Britain. Yet France had certain hidden, or at least not obvious, assets. During the occupation, small but well-placed elites had rejected the collective attitude stigmatized as Malthusianism, and a more generalized movement was afoot to break out of the confining molds into which France had been cast a hundred years earlier. The nation also had at its disposal an enormously effective catalyst of change, Jean Monnet.

An international financier and civil servant with expertise in managing war economies acquired in 1914–18, Monnet was a supersalesman for economic modernization and international cooperation. During World War II, serving as a *British* representative on the combined boards that administered international trade, he became a powerful behind-the-scenes influence in Washington and developed friendships with many of the men who, after 1945, would find themselves making policy not only for the United States but the world. Monnet shared their belief in reform, modernization, and international government.[38] At a time when America's international responsibilities were increasing with explosive force but during which its contacts were limited largely to the English-speaking world, Monnet was uniquely well positioned to speak on behalf of France and Europe. No foreigner has ever exercised an influence on American policy comparable to that of this former vendor of cognac. American support – given in the form of money – made Monnet an independent force in France and Europe and gave him extraordinary leverage in his dealings. General De Gaulle appointed him commissioner of the French Reequipment and Modernization Plan, with plenipotentiary powers, on the strength of his promise to secure American aid during the difficult transitional period following the occupation. The 1946 United States loan to France, which Monnet actually negotiated, rather than the revered socialist dignitary Léon Blum, gave Monnet and his staff the wherewithal to begin operations on an autonomous basis. The Plan was meant to serve not only as motor of French modernization but as model for Europe.[39]

Another French asset was *Ruhrpolitik*, something still too often described as a policy of crude anti-Germanism akin to the war aims

---

38 Jean Monnet, *Memoirs* (London, 1978), 158–9.
39 Richard Kuisel, *Capitalism and the State in Modern France: Renovation and Economic Management in the Twentieth Century* (Cambridge and London, 1981), 219–20.

exercises conducted in the Reich between 1914 and 1918. Yet, even during the years prior to the occupation of the Ruhr in 1923, French statesmen had sought some form of ultimate reconciliation with Germany, and the attempt had continued through prosperity, war, and depression. Both within the occupied country and among exiles in London and elsewhere, this determination increased after the collapse of May 1940. In discussions conducted during midsummer of 1943 in Algiers, for instance, Monnet and several colleagues later prominent in the unification movement broached plans reminiscent of the Schuman Plan of 1950. These were theoretical exercises more relevant to future than present policy-making.

In 1945, France was in no position to be generous to the Germans. The country was in fact a second-rate power, forced by defeat and occupation to return to respectability on her knees and in need of a protracted period of recuperation in order to overcome the economic and political effects of the war. The first priority of French policy toward the former Reich was to be included among the other so-called Big nations; the second was to keep Germany weak and under occupation until France's own recovery was assured. Only then would it be possible to embark upon a policy of reconciliation. The process of accommodation began as a response to the Marshall Plan, but the decision to enter a trans-Rhénanian partnership, which dates from early 1948, was France's alone. The Schuman Plan initiative was the idea of one man, Jean Monnet.[40]

France's German policy after 1945 seldom meets with praise, and no doubt was, in many respects, pusillanimous and niggardly. The occupation administration of the French zone wallowed in corruption and viceregal luxury. The French element made a pest of itself at the Allied Control Council. The men of the Quai bogged down the already tedious agendas of successive meetings of the Council of Foreign Ministers (CFM) with unworkable and even criminally irresponsible political and economic reorganization plans. Yet a note of judgmental caution is in order. French behavior in the zone, though hardly praiseworthy, weighs little in the balance of evil by comparison to what France had recently suffered at the hands of the Germans. The ACC failed for reasons far greater than any that had to do specifically with France. The "Ruhr–Rhénanie" schemes of 1946, the succession of draft proposals for internationalizing the Ruhr, and the

40 Monnet, *Memoirs*, 289.

Alphand Plan were conceived as thought-fodder for the CFM, rather than as plans of action; none of them had even a faint chance of actually being realized. Furthermore, it can be said in defense of the French that at no time did they adopt a policy as damnable as that of the Morgenthau Plan. They ruled out even as a contingency measure the possibility of another Ruhr occupation like the one in 1923. Never, in fact, did they aim at eliminating the mighty coal–steel complex as a center of economic power. France accepted the necessity of coexistence with a modern industrial Germany; at issue were always the terms of the relationship.[41]

Even prior to the Marshall Plan, French *Ruhrpolitik* – the cutting edge of policy with regard to the overall German question – was more flexible than is sometimes realized. From November 1945 to February 1946, France put out several feelers to both the Americans and the British for placing the Ruhr under international control.[42] Such initiatives had little chance for success as long as the Americans and British lacked workable reform plans for industry, since any process of territorial consolidation or institutional restoration conjured up fears of revanchism. While refusing to join the Bizone – which reduced French influence in the Ruhr to zero – Foreign Minister Georges Bidault often intimated that his nation would gladly drop its Ruhr reorganization schemes if a satisfactory basis could be found for three-power cooperation. By effectively eliminating the Soviet Union's voice in the reconstruction of Western Europe, the Marshall Plan set the stage for the London tripartite talks of 1948, from which emerged the International Authority for the Ruhr.[43]

France's reaction to the Marshall Plan announcement was more genuinely enthusisatic than that of the British, and French policy response to it more constructive. Neither Bidault nor Monnet imagined that the Germans could be kept out of the aid program; nor did they consider it desirable. Critical from their point of view was that France receive a disproportionate share of aid relative to the former Reich, thereby fulfilling the Monnet Plan and protecting national

---

41 John Gillingham, "Die französische Ruhrpolitik und die Ursprünge des Schuman-Plans," *VfZG* 35 (1987):1–24.
42 "Résumé of a Conversation between Mr. Monnet and Mr. Clayton," Sept. 24, 1945, JM, AMF 4/3/5; Monnet to McCloy, Sept. 24, 1945, JM, AMF 4/3/10; Monnet to McCloy, JM, AMF 4/3/12; "Conversations Franco-Americaines au sujet de la Ruhr et de la Rhénanie," Nov. 15, 1945, AN, 457 AP (562/prov.).
43 Milward, *Reconstruction*, 144–5.

security.[44] They thus took a cooperative stance at the CEEC negotiations, forcing the British to take the blame for failure whenever possible.

Though unfair, this policy was tactically adept. The Gallic economy was even more protectionist than Britain's – a foot of at least nine gouty toes. Monnet's attempt at steel reorganization made him the single man most detested by French big business interests; he could never have imposed liberalization upon either them or the mass of similarly inclined small producers. Yet Monnet knew from long experience with international organizations that a congress of states lacking strong executive authority, such as the CEEC, would be doomed to inaction. While Marshall Plan cables between Washington, London, and Paris were filled with mumblings and grumblings, Monnet whistled the tune Washington loved to hear, confident that convertibility and trade liberalization amounted to *Zukunftsmusik*.[45]

The most decisive change in French policy came at the beginning of 1948. Shocked to learn that, after months of discussing the issue of socialization versus detrustification (industrial deconcentration), the bizonal partners had, without so much as consulting France, decided on their own to let the Germans determine the future property settlement in Ruhr industry, the French concluded that they had no choice but to begin building bridges across the Rhine. The first phase of the occupation was over, wrote French Military Governor Pierre Koenig, and "our main concern is no longer to right past wrongs but to prepare for the future." He added that "German recovery in the cadre of Europe should take its place as rapidly as possible."[46] Emphasizing that the zone "should no longer be exploited for our own profit," Bidault ordered Koenig to stop all seizures, forced sales, and demonstrations of conspicuous consumption. "Everything must be done," he concluded, "to develop useful contacts with Germans . . . and [show] that we [do] not intend to dominate but merely play an honorable role in a united and cooperative Europe."[47] The new note in French foreign policy soon sounded at

---

44 "Memorandum pour M. Georges Bidault," July 27, 1947, AN, 457 AP622. Monnet to Bidault, July 28, 1947, JM, AMG 20/1/7; Monnet to Bidault, July 22, 1947, JM, AMF 14/1/4; "Memorandum rémis à M. G. Bidault par M. J. Monnet," July 24, 1947, JM, AMF 14/1/6.
45 Ball, *Past Has Another Pattern*, 80–2.
46 "Instructions adressées à M. Schneiter," Jan. 7, 1948, AN, 457 AP [Allemagne 15/prov.].
47 "Le Ministère des affaires étrangères à M. le Général d'Armée Koenig," Jan. 4, 1948, ibid.

the Quai, where experts from the German desk began drafting increasingly ambitious proposals for political and economic reconciliation. Within months, both politicians and businessmen had begun to take important initiatives of their own.[48]

Yet the normalization process was agonizingly slow. Only after a year of conferring in London were the tripartite powers able to arrive at an acceptable political framework for a West German state and a suitable organization for Ruhr industry. In 1949, American frustration mounted. Military Governor Clay's patience with French and British obstructionism at the ACC had come to an end, and, by January – after years of disappointing progress in putting Germany back on its feet and ending the occupation – he was ready to resign.[49] State Department and ERP dissatisfaction with the Western Allies was also growing. In addition to the debilitating differences with the British over integration policy, Washington objected vehemently to the dismantlement campaign underway in the Ruhr since November 1947, which it had allowed to continue only from fear that its curtailment would undermine military cooperation with Britain.[50] Washington was frustrated rather than angered by the failure of France to make headway in improving relations with the Federal Republic, doubly so because Foreign Minister Robert Schuman, who took office in July 1948, was an outspoken advocate of reconciliation. Yet his inaugural visit to Bonn in January 1950, during which he demanded a fifty-year lease on that perennial bone of contention, the Saar, was a major diplomatic blunder, one compounded by Adenauer's interview with the American journalist Kingsbury Smith, which put the Federal Republic in the awkward position of the over-eager, hot-breathed suitor. Marianne predictably reacted with shuddering distaste.[51]

The nagging sense that the European policies of the Big Three were at an impasse prompted Monnet to conceive, design, and launch the proposal for a coal–steel community known as the Schu-

48 Note [Fabré] Direction d'Europe, Sous-direction d'Europe Centrale, June 12, 1948, MdAE, Serie Y, 1944–9; Roger Fabré, "Note sur les aspects économiques du problème allemand," Apr. 1, 1948, ibid.; John Gillingham, "Solving the Ruhr Problem: German Heavy Industry and the Origins of the Schuman Plan," in Klaus Schwabe, ed., *Die Anfänge des Schuman-Plans 1950/51* (Baden-Baden, 1988), 499–500.
49 Clay to Army Dept., Jan. 23, 1949, *FRUS 1949*, vol. 3, *Council of Foreign Ministers; Germany and Austria* (Washington, D.C., 1974), 85.
50 "Note of Sept. 1978 by Hendricks," James P. Hendrick Papers, box 4, file: ECA-Reparations, TL.
51 Raymond Poidevin, *Robert Schuman: Homme d'Etat, 1886–1963* (Paris, 1986), 215–16.

man Plan.[52] Announced to the world in the French foreign minister's memorable radio address of May 9, 1950, the proposal called for establishing a single common authority to administer the heavy industries of France and Germany as well as any other nations (including Britain) that might choose to join it. In simple but eloquent language, Schuman presented the coal–steel plan not merely as a means of raising living standards, but as a proposal that would eliminate the causes of war and make its recurrence impossible. The appeal he made went deeper than the pocketbook; it kindled the hope of Europeans for a break with traditions that had turned the twentieth century into a living nightmare.

Sprung on an unsuspecting world, the Schuman Plan was an immediate triumph. It not only broke through a diplomatic logjam, but immediately became a force for change in its own right. Adenauer praised it as the expression of a policy which he had waited a generation to hear from a Frenchman. Once the German chancellor had made known his enthusiastic support for the initiative, the other continental nations could ill afford to reject participation. To no one's surprise, only the British were unenthusiastic about the proposition of May 9, 1950, but even they went through the motions of bestowing approval on it.[53] The support of the United States was no less critical for the success of the Schuman Plan than that of the nations who would eventually participate in it. Without American backing, the coal–steel negotiations would not have gotten off the ground; and, in fact, major U.S. intervention would subsequently save them from utter collapse.[54]

The Americans' decision to endorse the Schuman Plan was not automatic. From President Truman on down, initial American reaction to the proposal was an apprehension that it would restore the old international cartels.[55] Yet Secretary of State Dean Acheson, who made the decision to support the French initiative, and the many others whose agreement was essential to an effective policy-making consensus, had enough confidence in Monnet to swallow such doubts and effectively delegate to him the enormous task of designing and

---

52 Monnet, *Memoirs*, 228.
53 Roger Bullen, "The British Government and the Schuman Plan May 1950–March 1951," in Schwabe, ed., *Anfänge des Schuman-Plans*, 199–210.
54 Gillingham, "German Industry," 422–3.
55 Dean Acheson, *Present at the Creation* (New York, 1969), 500–1.

operating the institutions that could transform American integration from a pious wish into an operational reality.

The development of a constructive American policy toward Europe was a wrenching process. The United States, whose distinctiveness from and superiority to Europe were enshrined in national myth, had never asked to serve as world leader, but was thrust into the role ill prepared, while longing only to return to things as they had been prior to World War II. The Grand Design supposed to shape the contours of the postwar world was long on noble aims and short on everything else; and its replacement would come only after years of adjustments on the domestic scene. The well-intentioned but inexperienced president, so weak after the 1946 elections that a prominent Democratic foreign policy spokesman named William J. Fulbright recommended from the floor of the House that he resign, was responsible to a public whose ideas on foreign policy were notable unenlightened. Witch hunts and purges were the accompaniment of America's sudden emergence as a global power. A crude anticommunism was needed to appease populist demands that the nation be cleansed of persons, communists and their dupes, suspected of introducing evil foreign doctrines into American life. The Truman Doctrine, with its irresponsible promise of aid to anyone, anywhere itching from Marxist rash, was the sad but indispensable political prelude to the Marshall Plan, an essential sop to the primitives. Something more than the most unsordid act in history, the recovery program constituted a break with both globalism and isolationism and was an acknowledgment that stabilization required the United States to become a regional power with a long-term commitment in Europe. The decision to support the Schuman Plan, which would be put to the test in the year of negotiations leading to the conclusion of the Treaty of Paris creating the coal–steel pool, provides convincing proof that the United States was faithful to the profession made in the Marshall Plan to restore Europe to self-determination and independence. If nothing else, it betokened recognition that America could not and should not be solely responsible for establishing a just and sensible world order; this rather simple truth may well have been only the beginning of wisdom, but it has enabled Europeans gradually to resume control of their own destiny.

7

Return to Normality: The United States and Ruhr Industry, 1949–1955

WERNER BÜHRER

Perhaps it was his poor health alone that saved Gustav Krupp von Bohlen und Halbach from being accused and sentenced to death together with Hermann Göring, Joachim von Ribbentrop, Wilhelm Keitel, Rudolf Hess, Julius Streicher, and other leading Nazis at the first and most famous of the Nuremberg trials in 1945 and 1946. On the Allied side, hardly anyone questioned the complicity of big business with Hitler. Some even looked upon the industrialists as the driving force within that alliance. From this point of view, it was quite natural to punish Krupp severely as the supposed symbol of the powerful armorers of the Ruhr.

By 1947–48, however, when Gustav Krupp's son Alfried and several leading managers of the firm stood trial (there were prosecutions against I.G. Farben and the Flick concern at the same time), the political atmosphere had changed dramatically. The increasing gravity of the Cold War had turned former enemies into new allies. Alfried Krupp and his colleagues were treated with leniency compared to the defendants of the first trials. One of the main reasons for this mildness was that in the meantime West German industrialists were once again urgently needed to build a common Western dam against the red tide from the East. An essential prerequisite to achieve this goal was the success of the European Recovery Program (ERP). Effective economic restoration of Western Europe, however, required a substantial degree of economic rehabilitation in the Western zones of Germany. But without private industry cooperation in this effort, U.S. Military Government and State Department officials had little confidence that they could win the battle. This did not mean that the Nazi past of many of the German entrepreneurs suddenly had vanished into obscurity. Yet the "brown" stain had slowly faded, helping to create a more "sophisticated" attitude,

135

which Sir Percy Mills of the British Control Commission in Germany crystallized into the famous dictum: "They were not Nazis; they are businessmen."[1]

This pragmatic point of view won the support of an increasing number of American officials. Even the deconcentration and decartelization program developed out of American free enterprise convictions became suspected of being a communist inspired campaign of revenge against German big business. But what was the proper way to treat these powerful industrial complexes, especially those of the Ruhr region? How could the reconstruction of the industry of the Ruhr, advocated so strongly by leaders in the Military Government and in business circles of the United States, be reconciled with the political goals and claims of France and the United Kingdom? Basically, as a member of the Office of the Military Government for Germany (OMGUS) characterized the dilemma, "the problem of the Ruhr is one of assuring (a) that a future Germany will not use this industrial potential for rearmament and war, and (b) that other countries in need of these resources will have access to them."[2]

Nowadays "the Ruhr" is no longer an entity of mythic proportions. In Europe, it is a coal and steel producing region just like any other one, afflicted with similar problems of unemployment and competition from cheaper producers. In the United States, a completely new image may be in the making. "The Ruhr – Cultural Profile of a Region" was the title of a series of exhibitions and performances that took place in New York from September 1989 to January 1990. "Ruhr Works," as the even more concise short title ran, was conceived to demonstrate the area's postindustrial change "from coal to culture."[3]

The present essay is an attempt to recapitulate the first stages of the Ruhr's development from a mythical area to a place like many others in modern industrial societies all around the world. It seeks to show how American perceptions of the heavy industry along the Rhine and the Ruhr rivers and American relations to Ruhr industrialists changed during the five years from the foundation of the Federal Republic of Germany in autumn 1949 to its return to the community of sovereign nations in 1955. This process of depolitici-

1 Quoted from James Stewart Martin, *All Honorable Men* (Boston, 1950), 91.
2 Haraldson to Murphy, Jan. 10, 1948, IfZ, RG 260, OMGUS, POLAD 820–052.
3 See " 'The Ruhr': Kulturauftritt in New York," *Frankfurter Allgemeine Zeitung,* July 11, 1989; " 'Ruhr Works' in der Neuen Welt," *Süddeutsche Zeitung,* Dec. 9–10, 1989.

zation, which had already begun in 1947–48, came to an end during this period. "Depoliticization" as it is used here means that the attitudes of the American political and economic elite toward German industry became less and less determined by memories of its behavior during the Third Reich and thus more and more businesslike. The example of Krupp clearly demonstrated how quickly an unscrupulous profiteer, who had been despised only a short time before, could turn into a respected businessman. Certainly the emergence of new perceptions and relations did not occur without setbacks and obstacles. The general trend toward normalization of the relationship between the United States and the Federal Republic, however, also played a role in this regard. Some essential steps and elements of this depoliticizing process shall be outlined subsequently.

DISMANTLING AND DECONCENTRATION AS AN IMPETUS TO GERMAN–AMERICAN COOPERATION

Shortly after the Second World War, the Ruhr magnates, widely blamed for their support of the Nazi regime's outrageous and expansionist policy, were far from being accepted as junior partners in the reconstruction of Western Europe. Although Military Government experts were interested in learning about the "secrets" of Germany's wartime economic success, these conversations were a far cry from an exchange of views among partners; they were interrogations.

The Allies' dismantling measures taken to meet reparation claims provided American officials and industrialists the opportunity to establish more businesslike contacts with German heavy industry. They also provided a chance to revise opinions and perceptions determined by the experiences during the Nazi period. The prospects for revision were quite favorable, since there was considerable criticism of the dismantling efforts for both sides. In both American government and business circles, the economic utility of this program had been controversial from the beginning. After the announcement of the Marshall Plan, these doubts continued to increase. In 1947 and 1948, several commissions visited the Western zones of Germany to collect firsthand information on the possibilities of reconstruction and the most effective use of American aid.[4]

---

4 Werner Link, *Deutsche und amerikanische Gewerkschaften und Geschäftsleute 1945–1975: Eine Studie über transnationale Beziehungen* (Düsseldorf, 1978), 100–2.

A committee of businessmen headed by George M. Wolf, president of U.S. Steel Export Corp., proved to be particularly important to Ruhr industry. The Wolf Committee spent several weeks in the Ruhr area in the summer of 1948. Wolf's frank rejection of the dismantling program was not the only reason that he and his attendants cooperated so well with their German colleagues;[5] as early as September 1947, he had revealed himself to be a friend of Ruhr industry, when he had used his influence on James Forrestal, secretary of the navy, on behalf of the former chairman of the powerful Vereinigte Stahlwerke, Ernst Poensgen: "He is held in the highest regard in international steel trade circles, and is in no way the Nazi type. . . . Dr. Poensgen is one of the few men who could contribute much to restoring German – especially the Ruhr – productivity to our advantage."[6]

The final report of the Wolf Commission met the Ruhr industrialists' expectations fairly well. Franz Josef Muser of the Bochumer Verein established similarly helpful connections. Assisted by the American National Council for Prevention of War, he succeeded in organizing a massive antidismantling campaign in the United States.[7] And when in the summer of 1949 Hans-Günther Sohl of the August Thyssen Hütte and two of his colleagues proposed to give the Western powers shares equivalent to those parts of the plants that were earmarked for dismantling, Edwin Hartrich, then correspondent of the New York *Herald Tribune* in Western Germany and later an active lobbyist for Krupp, promoted their proposal in the United States.[8]

---

5 Hans-Günther Sohl, *Notizen* (Private publication: Bochum, 1985), 111–12. As to the Wolf Commission, see Werner Bührer, *Ruhrstahl und Europa: Die Wirtschaftsvereinigung Eisen und Stahl und die Anfänge der europäischen Integration 1945–1952* (Munich, 1986), 97–8.
6 Wolf to Forrestal, Sept. 3, 1947, NA, RG 59, 740.00119 Control (Germany)/9-847. Poensgen lived in Switzerland at the time. The Swiss government threatened him with expulsion, which was also pursued by the Americans. Under Secretary of State Robert A. Lovett contrasted Wolf's "Persilschein" (slang for a document that whitewashes someone's background – named after a soap powder) with the following information: Poensgen "held a number of positions of governmental importance. . . . He held the title of *Wehrwirtschaftsführer*, which was granted to key men in Nazi economy who stood well in the party. In 1941 the *Adlerschild* [one of the highest and seldom awarded decorations, W. B.] was bestowed upon him by Hitler." Ibid.
7 Cf. Hanns D. Ahrens, *Demontage: Nachkriegspolitik der Alliierten* (Munich, 1982). Note the critical comments by Volker Berghahn, *Unternehmer und Politik in der Bundesrepublik* (Frankfurt am Main, 1985), 79–83.
8 Sohl, *Notizen*, 119. Cf. Edwin Hartrich, *The Fourth and Richest Reich: How the Germans Conquered the Postwar World* (New York and London, 1980), 214–15; Bührer, *Ruhrstahl*, 109–10.

It would be inappropriate to conclude from these examples of German–American collaboration that the Ruhr industry once again enjoyed unanimous sympathy in the United States. Paradoxically it was an organization whose name hardly differed from the antidismantling lobby just mentioned that vehemently attacked the plans of misusing the Marshall Plan in order to avert dismantling. In a letter to Secretary of State George C. Marshall, the Society for the Prevention of World War III complained that the German steel magnates tried to prevent the execution of the dismantling program by arguing that dismantling and reparations were not in the interest of the ERP. The author of this letter regarded this as a "deliberate perversion of the basic aims and principles of the ERP" and concluded that "the arrogant challenge of the German steel magnates demands prompt counter-action by our Government."[9]

From the State Department's point of view, organizations such as the latter were probably not very important. Therefore their claims might easily have been ignored. Yet the American consulates in the Western zones also repeatedly sent critical reports to Washington. The U.S. Consulate in Bremen, for example, sent a pamphlet by August Heinrichsbauer[10] on German heavy industry and politics, commenting rather bluntly that it "is in effect an apology on the part of the leading western German industrialists for the help rendered by them to the Hitler Regime." Since the author, who was a well-known and active intermediary between the coal industry and the political scene during the final years of the Weimar Republic, had re-established his contacts with Ruhr industry circles, Maurice W. Altaffer, the American consul general, held Hermann Reusch, director general of the Gutehoffnungshütte and some of his colleagues responsible for the publication of the booklet.[11] Reusch, certainly one of the most important men from the Ruhr, had a rather bad reputation among American officials at that time because of his intransigent political views. Other prominent industrialists, however, showed more sensibility and hence were able to establish contact with members of the occupying authorities. In December 1948, Altaffer reported to the State Department that he had met with Hugo Stinnes, Jr.[12] As early as June, Robert Murphy, political ad-

9 Gilpin to Marshall, Aug. 12, 1948, NA, RG 59, 862.60/8-1248.
10 August Heinrichsbauer, *Schwerindustrie und Politik* (Essen-Kettwig, 1948).
11 Altaffer to SecState, Sept. 24, 1948, NA, RG 59, 862.60/9-2448.
12 Altaffer to SecState, Dec. 6, 1948, IfZ, RG 260, OMGUS, POLAD 820–52.

viser to Military Governor Clay, had transmitted to the secretary of state a lengthy memorandum by Stinnes on the relationship between Ruhr coal and the Marshall Plan.[13] Robert Pferdmenges, a banker from Cologne and a close friend of Konrad Adenauer, and also Richard Merton from the Metallgesellschaft in Frankfurt obviously had good connections to the United States. Although both of them did not rank among the Ruhr industrialists, they had close contacts to the Ruhr region. Therefore occasional statements or memoranda on their part had certainly been coordinated beforehand with the spokesmen from Oberhausen, Essen, or Dortmund.[14]

A similar coalition of interests, and thereby another possibility to collaborate, developed as well around the problem of deconcentration, which the British called "Operation Severance." Most Ruhr industrialists felt that the Allies' deconcentration and decartelization policy was one of the most serious attempts to weaken West German competitive strength. Based on Article 12 of the economic principles of the Potsdam Agreement of August 1945, this policy aimed at the elimination of "excessive concentrations of economic power." In practice, this meant breaking up the Ruhr *Verbundwirtschaft,* the integrated vertical complexes, especially the separation of coal mines and steel plants.

The Americans were rather sympathetic to the German protests. "The attitude of U.S. Military Government toward 'Operation Severance' was not one of approval," the official historian of the U.S. High Commission commented laconically in a contemporary report; "American authorities believed that some degree of vertical integration was necessary if German steel could compete on world markets."[15] German and American experts, however, differed in their opinions as to the necessary extent of vertical integration. The campaign, first started by the spokesmen of the so-called *Altkonzerne,* tried to show that deconcentration and Marshall Plan were incompatible and to free the *Verbundwirtschaft* from the suspicion that

---

13 Murphy to SecState, June 17, 1948, NA, RG 59, 840.50 Recovery/6-1748.
14 A copy of Merton's memorandum "About the Ruhr-Problem" is deposited in IfZ, RG 260, OMGUS, POLAD 820–52.
15 Hubert G. Schmidt, "Reorganization of the West German Coal and Iron and Steel Industries under the Allied High Commission for Germany," Historical Division, Office of the U.S. High Commissioner for Germany, Research Project No. 129, mimeographed manuscript, Sept. 1952, p. 17. See also Berghahn, *Unternehmer,* 84–111; Isabel Warner, "Allied-German Negotiations on the Deconcentration of the West German Steel Industry," in Ian D. Turner, ed., *Reconstruction in Post-War Germany: British Occupation Policy and the Western Zones, 1945–55* (Oxford, New York, and Munich, 1989), 155–85.

it would strive for economic or even political power. With the promulgation of Law No. 27 in May 1950, which replaced the bizonal regulation, the Allied High Commission made clear that it took seriously the liquidation of the combines.

When the Steel Trustee Association, a German advisory board for the reorganization of the steel industry, was founded in August 1949, the Bipartite Control Office had already taken care that experts as "neutral" and cooperative as possible were appointed. Hans-Günther Sohl, a member of the executive board of the Vereinigte Stahlwerke, was the most prominent person to fall prey to this Allied intention when they blocked his nomination.[16] His contacts with U.S. High Commissioner McCloy and the American control officers, however, did not seem to suffer from this discord. Sohl's candidacy proved to them that they had sought close contacts from the beginning, making no secret of their critical views on the deconcentration program, and that they had been cooperative and helpful.[17] On the issue of structural changes in the West German coal and steel industry, however, the United States had to consider French interests to an even higher degree than in the case of dismantling. And French policy at that time aimed at taking adequate precautions against the restoration of the former powerful position of Ruhr industry.

Therefore U.S. policy on the Ruhr depended upon a consensus among the Western Allies. McCloy actually expressed this point during a meeting with leading representatives of the West German coal and steel industry on June 16, 1950, a few days after the announcement of the Schuman Plan. For some people, he said, the Ruhr was still a symbol of aggressive industrial power. For that reason, reconstruction of the steel plants would make them worry about their security. The events of the past, McCloy continued, would confront them with the question of whether these combines would from now on contribute to peace or aggression, whether leading industrialists from the Ruhr, with all their influence, would support a liberal, democratic German state or try to subjugate the progressive forces and encourage the advocates of that very policy that once before had ruined Germany. Ruhr industry, the U.S. high commissioner concluded, would have to win back the confidence of

---

16 "Stahltreuhänder ernannt," *Deutsche Zeitung und Wirtschaftszeitung*, Sept. 3, 1949; Sohl, *Notizen*, 114–15.
17 Sohl, *Notizen*, 116.

the German people and of the whole world.[18] Similarly he answered
two letters Günter Henle of Klöckner had written during the final
stage of the Schuman Plan negotiations, when the quarrels about the
Verbundwirtschaft almost threatened to thwart those negotiations.[19]

The public activities and statements of Ruhr industrialists with regard to the dismantling and deconcentration policies undoubtedly
determined the attitudes of the American officials. There was indeed
a difference, depending upon whether industrialists responded flexibly to the security requests and the fear of competition in neighboring West European countries or whether they, like Hermann Reusch,
attacked the "economic nonsense" planned by the "decartelization
fanatics" privately, while publicly voicing his annoyance by refusing
to participate in the German–Allied negotiations on dismantling and
deconcentration.[20] And when such "hard-liners" also vehemently
intervened in favor of the industrialists imprisoned at Landsberg
prison, many American observers, even in the early 1950s, recalled
the "brown" past of many of the Ruhr magnates. When Reusch
called upon his listeners at a meeting of steel industrialists in April
1950 to continue to write letters to Landsberg prison, the "labor at-
taché" of the Frankfurt ERP Mission concluded

> that the Ruhr steel barons still identify themselves with those of their num-
> ber which were convicted as Nazi offenders and . . . are still making an ef-
> fort to keep the convicted Nazis within the innermost circle of the limited
> group which controls the powerful iron and steel industry.[21]

ECONOMIC FUTURE AND POLITICAL
PAST OF RUHR INDUSTRY

There were several obvious reasons why Western public opinion and
some West European governments reacted far more sensitively toward the "revival" of Ruhr industry in the early 1950s: In 1950 the
steel production of the Federal Republic exceeded that of France for
the first time after the Second World War. In February 1951, Alfried
Krupp and other arrested industrialists were pardoned by the U.S.

---

18 "Aussprache mit Mr. John McCloy," in *Informationsdienst des Studienausschusses für deutsch-
    französische Wirtschaftsbeziehungen,* June 26, 1950, BA, NL Pünder, 276, Bl. 140.
19 Henle to McCloy, Dec. 20, 1950, and Feb. 1, 1951; McCloy to Henle, Jan. 27, 1951,
    Klöckner-Archiv, NL Henle, EG/Schuman-Plan/Korrespondenz I-Z.
20 Cf., for example, Reusch to Beutler, March 8, 1951, Haniel-Archiv, NL Hermann Reusch,
    40010146/660.
21 White to State Dept., July 26, 1950, NA, RG 59, 862A.33/7-2650.

high commissioner and most of them were released. When the negotiations on the European Coal and Steel Community were successfully concluded in April, Ruhr industry became integrated into the "family" of West European heavy industry on at least formally equal terms. In the same month the Allied High Commission to a certain extent approved the exchange of shares of the new "unit companies" for shares of the *Altkonzerne*. And finally, in July 1952 the imposed annual steel production limit, which had been de facto surpassed for the first time in 1950, was also formally removed.

All these decisions and developments nourished in Western Europe particularly, but to a certain degree in the United States as well, an increasing fear of the restoration of the Ruhr companies' traditional powerful position. The American Consulate General at Düsseldorf therefore justified a thirty-six page report of September 1951 on the political background of leading personalities of the Ruhr iron and steel industry by stating that "in certain American publications considerable mention was being made of the 'Nazis getting back into power in German industry'."[22]

About eighty persons, members of the boards of directors and boards of management of the *Altkonzerne* as well as of the so-called Severance Companies and of the Steel Trustee Association, were involved in this investigation. As was expected, the new unit companies, on whose boards trade union members were also represented, showed the best results: 15 persons were considered to be former "active Nazis" and 10 "nominal Nazis," compared to 25 "non-Nazis" and 12 "anti-Nazis." The authors of the report modified this picture, which seemed by no means alarming at first sight, by pointing out that "a good number of the 'bigger Nazis' are still about and have by no means abandoned their interests in the industry." Although some of these former active and nominal Nazis seemed to be "not very suitable persons in the steel industry from a political point of view," the report admitted that "in certain instances, from a technical point of view, their presence in the steel industry may be an asset of sorts." The findings on the Steel Trustee Association did not differ very much. Although the authors attributed to Heinrich Dinkelbach, the leading member of this body, "the worst record as regards his background during the Nazi period,"

---

22 AMCONGEN Düsseldorf to State Dept., Sept. 18, 1951, NA, RG 59, 862A.33/9-1851; following quotations ibid.

they gave him credit because "he does not appear either to have been an active party member or to have played a significant role in the wartime economic agencies."

It is not surprising that the examination of the *Altkonzerne* showed the worst results: "It is here that the most objectionable people will be found today." Information was available on 26 of the members of the leading prewar companies:

Of this number, nine must be considered as having been more than nominal Nazis; the remaining 18 are divided as follows: 8 were nominal Nazis, 6 were non-Nazis and 4 were anti-Nazis.

The most prominent names from the first group were those of Wilhelm Zangen of Mannesmann and Hans-Günther Sohl and Walter Schwede of Vereinigte Stahlwerke. As far as the latter was concerned, the report noted that "a further objection to Schwede is that he is an inveterate cartelist." As mentioned before, these two traits taken together were, from the American point of view, highly unfavorable: "The American Element of the Combined Steel Group feels that this is a cogent reason for excluding him, if possible, from a position on one of the final 'unit' companies." It is also quite remarkable that Sohl was characterized as an "extremely undesirable individual" who had behind him "an unsavory career as a Nazi industrialist." Only some years later he presided over the management board of the Thyssen concern and became president of the Federation of German Industry and thus one of the outstanding personalities in West German economic history. Nevertheless, the report could make out even in this group of industrialists a number of persons with a clean record – for example Robert Pferdmenges, Günter Henle, Hermann Reusch, Karl Jarres.

The purpose of this analysis, the authors concluded, was "more than a mere dredging up of old sins." They hoped to have shown "what the reactions of the present leaders of the German iron and steel industry were to an authoritarian regime." These reactions – support, adjustment, and opposition – seemed to be not without significance for the economic and political life of the Federal Republic:

The worst offenders under the Nazis have been removed from positions where they could exert an overt influence on the industry, but many of the accommodation variety remain, and in their potential acquiescence to a new authoritarianism, whatever its political complexion, perhaps lies the greatest danger.

The authors of the report believed this threat to lie with the right as well as the left side of the political spectrum, a fact that clearly shows the change of attitude from 1945 to 1951. From this point of view, it was only consistent that the "investigators" spied not only on old Nazis but also on old and new Communists and detected some of them among the trade union representatives at the directors' and the management boards of the deconcentrated companies.

Against the background of U.S. Ruhr policy of that period, this diligent report already seemed slightly anachronistic. This did not mean, of course, that the past had been forgotten and had ceased to play its role as an instrument to discipline the Germans; what counted most was the willingness to collaborate under the conditions of the Cold War and in the reconstruction of Western Europe. McCloy's lack of understanding of the indignant reaction of Western public opinion to his clemency decision in favor of the Landsberg prisoners certainly did not result from a clandestine sympathy with the "old Nazis," but mainly from his conviction that this past now had become "history."[23] To adhere to deconcentration policy, which was certainly also to a great extent the outcome of French pressure, was not a punitive action against the "old offenders" but bore out America's liberal-capitalist mission. The integration of Ruhr industry into that of Europe, supported and sometimes even pushed by the United States, did not result from a fear of the return of the "brown Ruhr barons." It was rather a consequence of the U.S. government's new concept that aimed at preventing individual reconstruction efforts in Europe as far as possible. Integration also meant control.[24] Nevertheless all signs concerning the relationship to Ruhr industry indicated a return to normality.

RUHR INDUSTRY AND U.S. COAL EXPORTS

The economic growth of Ruhr coal mining was also carefully observed in the United States during the 1950s; but in the meantime

23 Cf. William Manchester, *Krupp: Zwölf Generationen* (Munich, 1968), 647–54.
24 The American efforts toward integration of German heavy industry into the European Coal and Steel Community nevertheless represented an important part of U.S.–German relations. Since several authors have already dealt with this problem, it seems justifiable to omit this subject here. See, for example, Klaus Schwabe, " 'Ein Akt konstruktiver Staatskunst': Die USA und die Anfänge des Schuman-Plans," in idem, ed., *Die Anfänge des Schuman-Plans 1950/51* (Baden-Baden, 1988), pp. 211–39; and Volker R. Berghahn, *The Americanization of West German Industry, 1945–1973* (Leamington Spa and New York, 1986), 132–54.

economic interests had come to the fore. American experts, for example, discussed chances for investment in the West German coal and steel industry, which could be financed by the Mutual Security Agency, the successor organization to the Economic Cooperation Administration.[25] Another problem was the dissolution of the Gemeinschaftsorganisation Ruhrkohle, the central German coal sales agency, which had been established in 1953 as a substitute for the former coal cartels, but which had soon become, in the opinion of Allied critics at least, a new cartel.[26] The most important question, however, was the export of American coal to the Federal Republic.

During the 1950s, provoked by the "Korea boom," the European Coal and Steel Community (ECSC) became the most important foreign market for American coal, although prices were below the ECSC level only in 1953 and 1954. For the U.S. mining industry, which was exposed to severe competition on the part of the oil industry, the European market was so important that producers and export firms tried to put the deliveries on a longer-term basis.[27] The Federal Republic of Germany soon turned out to be the most important customer in Europe:

Coal Imports from the United States (in metric tons)[28]

1950	1951	1952	1953	1954	1955
8,800	5,804,987	7,351,000	3,425,000	1,831,842	7,022,278

Although the steel industry in the Rhine and Ruhr region depended on U.S. coal to reach its production targets, these imports did not meet with approval because of the higher prices as compared to Ruhr coal. It was particularly annoying that from the steel industry's point of view the compulsory coal exports carried out by the International Ruhr Authority since 1950 were undertaken at prices

25 Cf., for example, AMCONGEN Düsseldorf to State Dept., Dec. 5, 1952, NA, RG 59, 862A.2552/12-552.
26 Cf., for example, AMCONGEN Düsseldorf to State Dept., March 30, 1955, NA, RG 59, 862A.2552/3-3055; U.S. Representative/ECSC to Boochever, June 15, 1955 (with appendix), NA, RG 59, 862A.2552/6-1555.
27 Cf. William Diebold, Jr., *The Schuman Plan: A Study in Economic Cooperation, 1950–1959* (New York, 1959), 534–7.
28 Figures according to *Statistische Jahrbücher der Bundesrepublik Deutschland;* AMCONGEN Düsseldorf to State Dept., Apr. 9, 1954, NA, RG 59, 862A.2552/4-954.

clearly below the world market level.[29] "The fact that American coal was imported at prices far higher than German prices," a report of the Munich consul general quoted from a statement of the Federation of German Industry's general secretary, "proves that the coal question is a critical one for German industry."[30]

When stocks grew because of declining demand during the second half of 1953, opposition against U.S. imports, which were in part "illegally" channeled into Northern Germany via the Netherlands, increased even more. Since American coal was about $2.00 per metric ton cheaper than Ruhr coal and of a better quality, North German wholesalers preferred this supply, much to the Ruhr industry's dissatisfaction.[31] Leading spokesmen of the Ruhr district therefore told American officials quite plainly that

> no further imports of American coal are either necessary or desirable even though consumers in the Hamburg-Bremen area prefer this cheaper coal. . . . Further such imports at a time when more than three and one-quarter million tons of coke were piled up at Ruhr mines would seriously affect the coal industry, which was not yet fully on its feet in spite of the great progress made since the end of the war.[32]

As was expected, this attitude and the measures taken by the government in Bonn to cut down imports provoked American protest. Representatives of the coal export firms talked of "discrimination against American commerce" and were particularly indignant because "the American coal industry made a special effort to assist Europe and Germany during a period of coal shortage several years ago." The State Department assured the critics that it would intervene with the government of the Federal Republic of Germany to decrease or even to abolish the import restrictions completely. In case this intervention should fail, "the possibility of pursuing the matter under the GATT Agreement" was even taken into consideration. The State Department rejected further steps, however: "It is of course true that except for the port area of Hamburg Germany is not

---

29 Cf. in general Carsten Lüders, *Das Ruhrkontrollsystem: Entstehung und Entwicklung im Rahmen der Westintegration Westdeutschlands 1947–1953* (Frankfurt am Main and New York, 1988), 234–67.
30 AMCONGEN Munich to State Dept., June 13, 1951, NA, RG 59, 862A.2552/6-1351.
31 Cf. AMCONGEN Düsseldorf to State Dept., Dec. 7, 1953, NA, RG 59, 862A.2552/12-753.
32 AMCONGEN Düsseldorf to State Dept., Feb. 11, 1954, NA, RG 59, 862A.2552/2-1154.

a natural market for U.S. Coal and we do not contemplate nor should the Germans fear that we plan any major volume of exports to Germany of this commodity."[33]

Because of the more favorable development of the West German steel industry, the situation on the coal market gradually eased after the middle of 1954, without leading to an immediate modification of the German attitude toward import restrictions. It was not until the first months of 1955 that a fundamental change took place, forcing the steel industry to increase imports of American coal. German producers even began to urge the U.S. government to release ships for transportation of coal to the Federal Republic so that freight rates would decline. In the meantime, the consul general at Düsseldorf considered American concessions no longer to be necessary: "It is very apparent however, that considerable American coal will be sold to Germany regardless of price considerations in view of the great demand for coal and the continued favorable state of the iron and steel business."[34] His prophecy proved right; during the following years import figures grew: from 11,557,141 metric tons in 1956 to 15,973,975 in 1957.[35] Moreover, as a consequence of the rapid fall of ocean freight rates, U.S. coking coal in 1958 was more than DM 8 per metric ton cheaper than the coking coal from the Ruhr area.[36] The government in Bonn, supported by associations of the coal mining industry, therefore once more resorted to restrictive measures to ease the crisis in the German coal industry by reducing imports. These measures, however, and the reactions from the United States, stemmed mainly from economic considerations as in the midfifties. Political concerns that had prevailed at the end of the 1940s no longer played a decisive role.

THE KRUPP CASE

It was the Krupp Case that first seemed to be an exception to the general tendency toward depoliticization. Alfried Krupp, Gustav's son, together with most of his managers, was pardoned by U.S. High Commissioner McCloy and released in 1951; he even got back his property. In the so-called Mehlem Agreement of March 4, 1953,

33 Office memo, May 10, 1954, NA, RG 59, 862A.2552/5-1054.
34 AMCONGEN Düsseldorf to State Dept., Feb.7, 1955, NA, RG 59, 862A.2552/2-755.
35 Figures according to *Statistische Jahrbücher der Bundesrepublik Deutschland.*
36 Cf. Werner Abelshauser, *Der Ruhrkohlenbergbau seit 1945: Wiederaufbau, Krise, Anpassung* (Munich, 1984), pp. 89–90.

however, Krupp had to commit himself to dispose of his coal and steel properties and to renounce any further involvement in the production of coal and basic steel. Undoubtedly this renunciation, forced by the three Western powers, was insisted upon for purely political reasons; it could not have been justified with economic or even legal arguments.[37] Although the U.S. high commissioner had signed this agreement together with his colleagues, he had not been the driving force behind the arrangement. On the American part, the desire to normalize relations with Ruhr industry did not stop even with Krupp.

As early as May 1951, Krupp representatives contacted McCloy to ask for advice regarding the future activities of the Essen firm. The U.S. high commissioner made the following suggestions: "Change the name of Krupp; contact NATO and ECA; improve their public relations; decartelization is unavoidable; think of the future and not of the past; try to make co-determination workable."[38] The Krupp delegates were especially interested in possibilities of obtaining orders in connection with Western rearmament, because there seemed to be some American demand. For example, Colonel Robert Daniels, an official at the Pentagon, asked "if Krupp had made cartridge cases of all sizes during the last war and presses for cartridges" and if so, "could they make them again?"[39] In this regard, however, Krupp management operated very carefully. Because of the "events of the past," they felt "in a special way inhibited." Of course they would never deny their "commitments to the West," as was stated in a draft of a letter, but someone else should "bear the responsibility for their collaboration."[40] The Krupp officials nevertheless tried to follow McCloy's advice. But for the time being, they left the initiative to the Americans. In July 1954, representatives of an American firm that planned to buy, for $15 million, a 51 percent interest in certain Krupp properties subject to the Allied deconcentration provi-

37 Cf. Manchester, *Krupp,* esp. pp. 662–73; Thomas Alan Schwartz, "Die Begnadigung deutscher Kriegsverbrecher. John J. McCloy und die Häftlinge von Landsberg," *VfZ* 38(1990):375–414. For a contemporary view, see the book by Gustav Krupp's brother-in-law, Thilo Frhr. von Wilmowsky, *Warum wurde Krupp verurteilt? Legende und Justizirrtum* (Stuttgart, 1950). A critical history of the trial against Krupp has yet to be written.
38 "Excerpts from Notes of Meeting with McCloy," May 4, 1951, Historisches Archiv Friedrich Krupp, WA 66 v 74.
39 Meeting Lynch/Stinnes with Daniels, Report of June 29, 1951, Historisches Archiv Friedrich Krupp, WA 66 v 74.
40 Draft of letter (handwritten note: to Kallen), Sept. 8, 1951, Historisches Archiv Friedrich Krupp, WA 66 v 74.

sion approached the State Department. Of course, Robert Murphy pointed out "that there might be some repercussions in this country to any agreement of this sort in view of the 'warmonger' reputation Krupp enjoyed among certain elements of our people," and he also remarked "that the Communists would probably make propaganda capital of an alliance between Germany and the United States." However, he thought that these considerations did not form "a basis for any objection from a foreign policy point of view."[41]

In 1955 the Essen combine itself took the initiative and made an effort to establish direct contacts with the State Department. First and foremost, a new image had to be found that would erase troublesome memories of the *Kanonenkönig* days. "We should publicize the newsworthy fact," Edwin Hartwich, who participated in this brainstorming, remembered, "that Krupp was now devoting its time and energies to the industrial development of the backward areas of the world so that their peoples would have a better way of life and be able to support themselves." The fact that Krupp and his advisers decided to choose the term "Point 4 1/2" for their program, in imitation of President Truman's "Point 4" Program, not only proved a clever flair for publicity but a good dose of self-confidence. In March 1955, Krupp officials announced their program at a press conference.[42]

To promote Krupp's proposal in the United States, several lobbyists of the Essen firm visited Washington. Edwin Hartrich was the first. He left Daniel F. Margolies of the State Department in no doubt about the purpose of his visit and of the whole "Point 4 1/2" program, as the title of Margolies's memorandum of conversation shows: "Plans of Mr. Krupp to set aside Prohibiton on his Right to Manufacture Steel."[43] Hartrich justified the timing of his visit by pointing out that the State Department had recently approached Alfried Krupp "and had urged him in the strongest terms to get back into rearmament. . . . Mr. Krupp felt that if the United States Government wished to obtain his cooperation in this regard he was then justified in raising the question of his right to engage in steel

41 State Dept., memo of conversation, July 14, 1954, NA, RG 59, 862A.2552/7-1454.
42 Hartrich, *Fourth and Richest Reich*, 255–9, quotation pp. 258–9; as to Truman's "Point Four Program" cf. *FRUS 1949*, vol. 1, *National Security Affairs, Foreign Economic Policy* (Washington D.C., 1976), 757–88.
43 Memo of conversation, Nov. 3, 1955, NA, RG 59, 862A.331/11-355; the following quotations ibid.

production."[44] The "Krupp case," Hartrich continued, was a topic that was constantly discussed in German industrial centers. "If this policy were reversed it would give a tremendous psychological boost to big business groups in Germany and would affect their entire attitude toward the rearmament program." Margolies responded cautiously to these exhaustive and quite frank representations, referring to the fact that a revision of the Mehlem Agreement would be a matter to be solved between the three Western Powers and the Federal Republic of Germany and declined to give any further comments requested by Hartrich. The visit of the new chief executive of the firm, Berthold Beitz, in early December turned out to be, from Krupp's point of view, even more disappointing. Meanwhile the American government had decided not even to reopen the Krupp case.[45]

Alfried Krupp and his collaborators, however, did not give up. In February 1956 Struve Hensel, another American-trained lobbyist, tried to change the U.S. government's position. He particularly attacked American decartelization policy but failed to gain the State Department's approval for Krupp's program. When he even indicated that Krupp might sell part of the properties "at a low price to the Russians" one of his negotiating partners sharply replied "that an expression of willingness to sell to the Russians would certainly not improve the chances of a favorable action here to Mr. Krupp's case."[46] After these setbacks it was almost surprising that an inquiry as to a proposed cooperation with Krupp undertaken by the Blaw-Knox Company, an American firm involved in the construction of steel plants, received a positive response.[47] The reason, however, seems to be quite obvious: In the latter case a limited cooperation was at stake, whereas any revision of the Mehlem Agreement and deconcentration affected not only the interests of the Three Powers but also those of the government of the Federal Republic and the *Altkonzerne*. It was true that the American government in the meantime lacked any enthusiasm in dealing with Law No. 27, but it wanted to avoid discussion of that attitude in public.

In an interim statement, the American Embassy at Bonn evaluated the prevailing activities of Krupp very realistically and almost sym-

44 Hartrich specifically mentioned the production of a new type of jet fighter engine for the Northrop Aviation Company at Krupp's plant Weser AG in Bremen.
45 Cf. Reinstein to Merchant, Dec. 5, 1955, NA, RG 59, 862A.331/12-555.
46 State Dept., memo of conversation, Feb. 17, 1956, NA, RG 59, 862A.331/2-1756.
47 Blaw-Knox Company to Robert Murphy, March 16, 1956, and State Dept., memo of conversation, March 13, 1956, NA, RG 59, 862A.33/3-1656.

pathetically: "Krupp campaign for retention properties is considered by Embassy only part of general attempt Krupp to rehabilitate his good name and in process give boost to Krupp's Point Four and a half program and Alfred (sic!) Krupp's strong personal desire for U.S. visa."[48] Alfried Krupp, the Embassy official predicted, would in any case continue his efforts. This proved to be true. Despite initial disappointments, the Essen industrialist did "invest" with his "development aid" program, for it soon became apparent that such a step advanced German–American cooperation and thus also the realization of his private ambitions very well. Stuve Hensel, one of Krupp's men in the United States and deeply involved in the preparation of the program, came to the same conclusion: "I am, nevertheless, convinced that the principle of Point IV 1/2 was a brilliant inspiration and contains promise of advantage and profit to your company from an economic standpoint, and with respect to Law 27 problems, from a political and judicial standpoint."[49] After a period of depoliticization a process of repoliticization emerged below the surface of businesslike relations with Ruhr industry.

CONCLUSION

"Did you ever think what it would be like to spend your whole life in Oberhausen?" By asking this rhetorical question, a German entrepreneur who was not involved in heavy industry tried to explain the mentality of the Ruhr industrialists to an American social scientist who in the midfifties analyzed the attitudes of West German industrial elites toward foreign policy. Businessmen from other industrial branches characterized their colleagues from the Ruhr area as politically rather indifferent or even nonpolitical; they attributed these characteristics mainly to the fact that, because of the dissolution of the big coal and steel companies, the old esprit de corps had been destroyed. According to them, a new style of political behavior and thinking had not developed yet.[50] In other words, even the "Americanization of West German Industry," as described by Volker Berghahn, was at that time not progressing very well, at least in Ruhr industry.

48 Bonn Embassy to SecState, March 28, 1956, NA, RG 59, 862A.054/3-2856.
49 Hensel to Lück, June 15, 1956, Historisches Archiv Friedrich Krupp, WA 42/573.
50 Gabriel A. Almond, "The Politics of German Business," in Hans Speier and W. Phillips Davison, eds., *West German Leadership and Foreign Policy* (Evanston, Ill., and White Plains, N.Y., 1957), 195–214, 220.

One may ask whether the depoliticization of the relationship between the United States and Ruhr industry corresponded with a similar process among the Ruhr industrialists themselves or if the latter was even a precondition of the first. To be sure, the political discretion prudently maintained by Ruhr industry fostered the normalization of the relations to the United States. More important, however, was the fact that the Cold War very quickly superseded all differences. It was thanks to those who kept remembrance alive and defended it against economic, political, and military pressures that the rehabilitation of Ruhr heavy industry, nevertheless, did not take place at a brisk pace.

8

West German Agriculture and the European Recovery Program, 1948–1952

ULRICH KLUGE

Agriculture and the agricultural policies of West Germany have been the focus of criticism for over forty years.[1] Overproduction, typified by seas of excess milk and mountains of excess butter, leads to the question of whether the opportunity to build a "healthy" agricultural development policy was not missed. Moreover, the new beginnings of postwar agricultural policy during the founding stage of the Federal Republic of Germany between the currency reform and the first legislative period (1948–53) leaves the impression of the restoration of the old German peasantry and of agricultural protectionism and a general failure to attain the goal of a free market economy.[2]

This argument overlooks three fundamental developments in the process of making agricultural policy:

1. the peculiarities of agricultural production in comparison to industrial production;
2. the structural agricultural inheritance in the Western zones as a result of the division of Germany; and
3. the limited negotiating room and the weak means of intervention on the part of state agricultural policies.

I would like to thank especially Michael T. Szeibert, as well as Dr. Folkert Krieger and Joachim Nebe, M.A., for their many troubles on behalf of this contribution. I would also like to include in my thanks the staff of the Bundesarchiv in Koblenz and the Bundesministerium für Ernährung, Landwirtschaft und Forsten in Bonn.
1 Cf. Hermann Priebe, *Die subventionierte Unvernunft: Landwirtschaft und Naturhaushalt* (Berlin, 1985), 51–3. Albrecht Funk, "Agrarentwicklung und Agrarpolitik," in Wolf-Dieter Narr and Dietrich Thränhardt, eds., *Die Bundesrepublik Deutschland: Entstehung, Entwicklung, Struktur* (Königstein/Taunus, 1979), 230–1.
2 See Günther Schmitt and Stefan Tangermann, "Regulierte Märkte in extremer Fehlentwicklung," in Wolfram Fischer, ed., *Währungsreform und Soziale Marktwirtschaft: Erfahrungen und Perspektiven nach 40 Jahren* (Berlin, 1989), 347–60.

The long-term view of growth and change in agriculture of the Federal Republic of Germany[3] leads to the conclusion that this former orthodoxy of continuity was mistaken. Even before the creation of a joint agricultural market by the European Economic Community (after 1957) the German agricultural system distinguished itself fundamentally from the agricultural systems of the Weimar Republic and the Third Reich. Innovation rather than restoration determined all aspects of the character of agriculture: land, capital, labor. But what role did the European Recovery Program (ERP) play in this change? Was it the decisive prelude to change or merely an accompaniment to a reconstructive process coming from German initiative? In other words, should one speak of an "Americanization" or a "Germanization" of West German agriculture in the years between 1948 and 1952? At the time, the former was clearly associated with fundamental modernization and freedom in trade policy, whereas the latter could hardly avoid the reproach of archaic protectionism.

THE PECULIARITIES OF AGRICULTURAL PRODUCTION AND
WEST GERMAN BASIC FUNCTIONAL REQUIREMENTS, 1945

Agricultural production is extremely different from industrial production for many reasons.[4] Agricultural products are highly perishable commodities and are highly dependent upon climate, soil, and biological processes. Technological improvements are of assistance only within limits, and the turnover of capital is slow. Finally, increasing consumer incomes do not automatically translate into sales increases for producers. It is a commonplace but indisputable fact with far-reaching consequences that "bread" and "coal" appear on the market in different fashions and are accepted differently from trade partners. The road to the market must be paved differently for agriculture than for industry. The peculiar character of agriculture allowed it to achieve an exceptional regulatory position between free competition and planned economy after 1945. Postwar agricultural protection resulted from the very "nature" of agriculture and from the immediate post-1945 history of agriculture rather than from regulatory concession on the part of the occupation forces.

3 Cf. Ulrich Kluge, *Vierzig Jahre Agrarpolitik in der Bundesrepublik Deutschland*, 2 vols. (Hamburg, 1989), vol. 2.
4 H. Strich and Georg Weippert, "Die Eingliederung der Landwirtschaft in die Marktwirtschaft," *Berichte über Landwirtschaft* 34 (1956): 371.

The division of Germany after 1945 posed grave problems for the people in the Western zones. West Germany had lost 7.1 million hectares, or 25 percent, of the arable land of the former German empire. Here small farmers dominated, with 1.978 million farms, a third of which had less than two hectares suitable for cultivation.[5] The German population found itself on the brink of catastrophic famine of preindustrial proportions. The Allies set the daily necessary per capita food ration at 2,800 calories, but actual consumption averaged merely 1,550 calories between 1945 and 1947. Liberation from National Socialism thus did not automatically bring with it more bread. The new beginning in 1945 meant hunger and even led to collective protest.[6] The protesting population failed to see, however, that hunger was the inheritance of National Socialism rather than a political tool of domination by the Allies. In the Soviet Zone of Occupation, the circumstances were somewhat different.

Self-help was not an available avenue to reestablish public provision of daily needed foodstuffs (flour, potatoes, sugar, milk, meat). Sixty-four thousand farms lay in rubble, and more than 41 million Germans depended solely on the market. There was simply insufficient arable land to supply adequate food to this market (for example, almost a half million hectares less for bread-grains in comparison to 1937–38). In addition, harvests were smaller (for example, the potato harvest was 28.4 percent of the average in the years 1935–39 in comparison). There was an acute shortage of all production inputs such as seed-grain, machines, and breeding-stock.[7]

The 1946 harvest fell far below normal. Because of drought in 1947, the public food supply system threatened to fall apart. In the U.S. zone, agriculture could produce only 1,100 calories per person per day; this was barely half of the prescribed total consumption, and the second half flowed from the "Hoover Aid Program." This was the popular name for the "Famine Emergency Committee" headed by former U.S. President Herbert Hoover. Later, the U.S. government provided additional resources through the Government and Relief in Occupied Areas (GARIOA) program. The resources of

5 Cf. Länderrat des amerikanischen Besatzungsgebietes, ed., *Statistisches Handbuch von Deutschland 1928–1944* (Munich, 1949), 90–8. Constantin von Dietze, *Grundzüge der Agrarpolitik* (Hamburg, 1967), 203.
6 Details in Christoph Klessmann and Peter Friedemann, *Streiks und Hungermärsche im Ruhrgebiet 1946–1948* (Frankfurt am Main, 1977), and Hans Schlange-Schöningen, *Im Schatten des Hungers* (Hamburg, 1955).
7 Details in Wilhelm Niklas, *Sorge um das tägliche Brot* (Bonn, 1951).

GARIOA and the British equivalent organization, U.K. Contributions, covered the costs of the import of food until the summer of 1948. The cost rose from $275 million (1945–46) to $700 million (1947–48). By the end of 1949, the young Federal Republic of Germany owed the United States the exchange value of DM 385 million.[8] The American farmer, not the German farmer, was in the best position to save vast parts of the population in the Western zones from starvation.

AMERICAN AGRICULTURAL FINANCIAL CREDIT: ORIGINS, SCOPE, AND EMPHASIS

Leading personalities of the bizonal VELF, Verwaltungsrat für Ernährung, Landwirtschaft und Forsten (Administrative Council for Nutrition, Agriculture, and Forests), among them the future first Federal Minister of Nutrition, Wilhelm Niklas (CSU), received surprising news on August 11, 1948. General Clay had urged the Bipartite Control Office (BICO) to design a plan for the advancement of agriculture.[9] Clay had thereby reacted to a VELF request for a financial promotional package of DM 700 million. The German money market was unable to supply the necessary resources shortly before the introduction of the currency reform. Without larger investments to increase agricultural production and to build up the socioeconomic basic functional requirements for modern agriculture, the goal of modernizing agriculture was unattainable. Clay did not offer Niklas any money directly, but Niklas learned nevertheless "that significant resources of capital which were generated and would continue to be generated from exports and imports were at the disposal of the military government." He proposed a line of credit of DM 296,710 million and a grant of DM 446,310 million. Niklas focused agricultural policy more on increasing production than on changing the social and economic structure of bizonal agriculture.

The dilemma of the unstable food supply system was reflected in the distribution of funding. The top two priorities, then, were to provide an incentive for farmers in order to supply a greater diversity of goods (DM 300 million) and to preserve the current supply of

---

8 Cf. Christoph Weisz, "Versuch zur Standortbestimmung der Landwirtschaft," in Ludolf Herbst, ed., *Westdeutschland 1945–1955* (Munich, 1986), 117–26, and Christoph Buchheim, *Die Wiedereingliederung Westdeutschlands in die Weltwirtschaft 1945–1948* (Munich, 1990), 71–7.
9 Remark by Dr. Steding, Aug. 11, 1948, BA, B 116/926.

grain (DM 105 million). The plan contained significantly lower sums to consolidate farmland (DM 70 million) and to build housing settlements (DM 67 million). The rest of the money was distributed among other projects such as fishing and water management.[10] Niklas responded to the current desperate situation with this plan, which lacked a structural perspective on agriculture and the stability of food supply management.

How did BICO react? Would the United States finance the VELF agricultural concept, or would VELF or the Federal Ministry for Nutrition and Agriculture (after September 1949) adapt itself to the American financial figures? In other words, would German agriculture be "Americanized" with the help of the dollar, would it be restored to its traditional basic structure, or would it be modernized with an eye toward a future West European cooperation? The history of ERP agricultural credits is rich in details and problems. It need not be recounted comprehensively here. An overview of the principal outcomes alone gives the first answers to the three possibilities for German agricultural development: "Americanization," "Germanization," or "Europeanization."

Food Shortage and Hindrances in Production, 1948

Food production did not immediately improve after the currency reform of 1948. To an overwhelming degree, consumers were not receiving the food to which they were entitled according to the rationing scheme. The situation eased only slowly and sectorally. Organized agriculture (farmer unions) demanded "just" prices and the end of rationing. These were two untimely demands. They reflected, however, the desperate situation of agriculture. To grant these demands would nevertheless have led to a breakdown of social peace. The primary goal of agricultural policy in 1948 was to provide food. Whether sufficient production resources existed remained for the time being an open question.

"Just" prices meant subsidizing broader strata of millions of consumers. Moreover, state means were insufficient by far.[11] BICO did not appear inclined to follow the suggestions to lift rationing and allow the market to shape prices.[12] But this question was decided less

10 Niklas to BICO, Food and Agriculture Group, Aug. 10, 1948, BA, B 116/926.
11 Report on various agrarian questions, Sept. 15, 1948, BA, B 102/3153, Heft 1.
12 Military Government to President of the Administrative Council, Oct. 29, 1948, BA, B 102/3153, Heft 2.

in West Germany than in West Berlin, where the population was being supplied with food from the air after the Soviet blockade. The daily requirement of food amounted to 390,000 tons, of which a part had to be raised by West German production. The liberalization of the agricultural sector failed in 1948 because of unsolved social problems in combination with the first great East–West conflict in postwar German history.

No fundamental improvement of food supply could be expected from German sources, as a 20 percent gap arose in food supply. Only 15 to 20 percent of West German farmers produced efficiently, while 50 to 70 percent posted straight average production figures.[13] Labor was available, but all other means of production were lacking, especially tractors. Only some 67,000 functioning tractors were available in the Bizone, whereas over 300,000 were needed.[14] German agricultural machinery factories had either been dismantled or suffered from a lack of capital and materials. All the material requirements for a reform in agricultural policy were absent. The pressure on West German agriculture to produce precluded any grandiose systemic restructuring. VELF refrained from suggesting systemic changes not for politically or ideologically grounded reasons but rather for pragmatic considerations. Contemporaries in 1948 could not imagine that the state agricultural administration would later be suspected of continuing National Socialist production policies without interruption. Among farmers there was great interest in Western methods of production, especially in American ones.

By the end of 1948 a group of German agriculture experts prepared a study tour of the United States. Modern methods of production were supposed to be tested for their possible adoption in Europe. But no one at this point thought about transposing American mechanical methods, not even BICO. In this regard, the administration of agriculture and food supply were based on the success of traditional methods of production, which reflected German circumstances. American heavy agricultural machinery should not be employed, but rather lightweight tractors produced in Germany, especially for small family farms.[15]

13 Hugo Berger, *Produktion und Rentabilität der westdeutschen Landwirtschaft nach der Währungsreform* (Hanover, 1949), 36.
14 VELF, "Maschinenprogramm für die Landwirtschaft," July 6, 1949, BA, B 102/3156, Heft 1.
15 "Bericht über Pressekonferenz Schlange-Schöningen," Oct. 4, 1948, BA, B 102/3151, Heft 2.

Mass Food Supply and Agricultural Reconstruction

Only in 1949 did precise data become available about the damage to agriculture that the war had either directly or indirectly left behind. Such figures promised a longer time of transition to economic normality. Agriculture was DM 2.1 billion in debt.[16] The drift of workers away from agriculture continued: By 1949 30 percent of the total 4.54 million persons employed in the agricultural sector had left their jobs voluntarily, especially agricultural laborers, who could earn two-thirds more in industry.[17] Costs for fertilizer, seed-grain, and technology rose dramatically; the total index for these production inputs reached 183 percent of prewar levels in 1947–48.[18]

The demand for all types of agricultural investment in 1949 was estimated at DM 28.1 billion, DM 19.4 billion for buildings, DM 4.8 billion for agricultural machinery and tractors, and DM 3.9 billion for new housing settlements.[19] Crop yields rose again for the first time sine 1948; the cattle stock (not including beef cattle) also seemed to be stabilizing. The price index for agricultural products in the year 1948–49 reached 161 compared to the prewar period (1938–39 = 100). Nevertheless, net proceeds in 1947–48 amounted to still only 1.1 percent of the value of 1938–39 (1946–47: 35 percent).[20] Agriculture fell into a crisis of profitability.

West Germany remained as before dependent on the world market. In 1949 2.5 million tons of wheat, 800,000 tons of rye, 1.1 million tons of corn, 1.4 million tons of feed-grain, 410,000 tons of lard, and 600,000 tons of sugar had to be imported. State agricultural policy still dedicated itself in 1949 primarily to food supply policy, and the concerns of the urban consumer stood more in the center of policy than those of the farmer. But at the same time, plans emerged for reconstruction in land, labor, and capital.

The credit plan of VELF for investments allocated a total of DM 785 million for the period from 1949 to 1952, with DM 270.1 million for 1949–50 alone. By the time Marshall Plan aid ended, German agriculture wanted to stand on its own two feet. All political parties agreed on this issue. Of course, no one ever spoke of self-sufficiency.

16 *Württembergisches Wochenblatt für Landwirtschaft* 116, no. 26 (1949): 487, in BA, B 116/1167.
17 *Deutsche Bauernkorrespondenz* 2, no. 20 (1949): 4; "Bericht an die ECA," Dec. 29, 1949, p. 42, BA, B 116/1840.
18 VELF, "Ertragslage der Landwirtschaft," Jan. 24, 1949, BA, B 102/3151, Heft 2.
19 *Deutsche Bauernkorrespondenz* 2, no. 3 (1949): 6.
20 VELF, "Ertragslage der Landwirtschaft," Jan. 24, 1949, BA, B 102/3151, Heft 2.

All of the democratic parties and unions (farmers' unions and trade unions) saw the German agricultural market as part of the world market again. Everybody wanted to be prepared for the hard competition.

Some time would still have to pass before reaching that stage, because domestic demand, especially for food, rose far faster than domestic production. No doubt remained in West German public opinion that social peace would be in danger, especially in the context of the Berlin Blockade, if the shortage continued. Democracy and the social market economy had to be legitimated by bread. In fiscal year 1948–49 alone, the bizonal administration expended DM 955 million for agricultural imports.[21] Over 70 percent of aid received in dollars served to purchase food and feed supplies.[22] After May 1, 1949, the exporting countries demanded world market prices. State administration of agriculture fell into a conflict in 1949 that appeared unsolvable: High world market prices, the OEEC order to liberalize (October 1949),[23] and the high dependency on imports from the world agricultural market severely burdened the young state economy. Only with great effort in its first weeks in office was the West German federal government able to preserve the Law of Import Compensation (*Importausgleichsgesetz*) for the protection of domestic producers and consumers against BICO until the end of 1949.

With this background the German development plan from 1949 to 1951 (Three Year Plan), which was supposed to be financed with ERP funds, came into being. The state agricultural administration included a promotional plan parallel to ERP, funded from German resources, in the first federal budget in 1949. To this end DM 207.82 million were needed, of which only DM 46.74 million came from the regular budget.[24]

Funds to support consumer prices (food subsidies) had the highest priority in the promotional plan, amounting to DM 65.88 million; funds to reduce the price of chemical fertilizers followed (DM 55.20 million); then came funds for rural housing construction (DM 40 million); to modernize water management (DM 23.30 million); for agricultural research (DM 9.3 million); for plant protection and vet-

---

21 *Deutsche Bauernkorrespondenz* 2, no. 20 (1949): 1.
22 ECA, Special Mission to Germany, Robert M. Hanes, Dec. 22, 1949, BA, B 102/3153, Heft 2.
23 Kluge, *Vierzig Jahre Agrarpolitik*, 1:145–7.
24 "Einzelplan X," BA, B 116/1027.

erinary matters (DM 4.70 million); to modernize the dairy industry (DM 4 million); for land reform (the *Flurbereinigung* program amounting to DM 994,000); for land technology and agricultural buildings (DM 600,000); and finally to expand sugar-beet production (DM 75,000). The agricultural budget for 1949 took into account three fundamental conditions which came out of the political situation of postwar Germany: the socially conscious organization of mass consumption, the stimulation of and increase in production, and the modernization of unproductive structures.

The promotion of West German agriculture by ERP funds still did not possess any solid foundation in 1949. Originally VELF demanded DM 785.0 million over three years, of which DM 270.1 million were to be used for the year 1949.[25] By the end of 1949 only DM 128 million had been granted. Half of this sum flowed into the area of investments; the other half was used in the area of consumption. In addition, contributions with no returns (grants) came about for structural reform of all kinds.[26]

The Complicated Process of Credit Policy Decision Making – the Continuation of Food Supply Policy Regionalism

Within a few months after the ECA Treaty of December 15, 1949, became effective on January 30, 1950, the Germans developed a complex decision-making process and distribution system for the approved ERP credit. Accordingly, funds could be used until June 30, 1952. The central aim of the allocation of funds was the "development of production capacity." The Federal Ministry of Agriculture (BML, for Bundesministerium für Landwirtschaft) administered this long-term credit for the reconstruction of buildings, for the utilization of land, for housing settlements, and for reforestation.[27]

The distribution of funds turned out to be complicated, because the various provincial ministries emphatically demanded their right of codetermination. Federalism in matters of credit indeed may have represented the democratic ideals of provincial politicians, but it endangered the defining of which projects had central significance for

---

25 VELF, "Dreijahresplan," July 1, 1949, BA, B 102/3153, Heft 1.
26 ECA, Special Mission to Germany, Robert M. Hanes, Dec. 22, 1949, BA, B 102/3153, Heft 2.
27 F. Steding and F. Timmermann, "Die Kredite aus Marshallplanmitteln an die Agrarwirtschaft," *Berichte über Landwirtschaft* 32 (1954): 268–9, 280.

the whole federal territory, such as the food supply industry. The BML was forced to try to operate against these centrifugal forces.

As the discussions over ERP distribution continued, grants began to be handed out. The ECA paid out most of the total of DM 55 million for the following purposes:[28]

land consolidation	DM 11.0 million
improvements in the fertility of meadows and pastureland	DM 10.5 million
agricultural research	DM 7.0 million
combatting tuberculosis among cows	DM 5.0 million
agricultural counseling service	DM 4.8 million

The ECA Food and Agriculture Division planned to test the projects submitted by the BML. Cooperation between the ECA and the BML suffered particularly because of the uncertainty of whether sufficient credit would flow before 1952. There were contradictory announcements: Originally the grant for July 1, 1950, to January 31, 1951, was to be DM 330 million; in the autumn of 1950, however, the Germans expected not more than DM 225 million and perhaps as little as DM 200 million.[29] Pressure was strong to harmonize the structure of the food industry and of agriculture, which varied so widely from region to region. But there was no ideal, material, or structural basis to accomplish this. The state governments increased their regional influence through the credit institutions. Therefore, the development aims of the states did not follow the categories of those of the central government. There was no mutual rebuilding of a standard market and supply territory. The BML relied upon supraregional food industry organizations, especially those of the sugar industry, to compensate for this trend toward regionalization. The BML behaved hostilely toward other organized branches of the economy, such as the fertilizer industry, which had sought significant credits for its products.

There were still other examples of ministerial opposition to the interests of the private sector: The BML successfully thwarted the milling industry in its attempt to restore old capacity structures. Of a total of thirty-four credit applications, fourteen were perempto-

---

28 Omar B. Pancoast, Jr., to Dr. Albrecht, Nov. 2, 1950, BA, B 116/1062.
29 *Deutsche Bauernkorrespondenz* 3, no. 19 (1950): 10.

rily turned down because they did not offer a "substantial rationalization of the process of fabrication or a considerable improvement in quality."

The formula for the regional distribution of ERP funds foreordained to failure attempts to rationalize West German agriculture. For example, from the first partial loan allocation, ERP divided funds based primarily on traditional differences between the various agricultural districts (capacity of production). The fact that current conditions (the degree of destruction caused by the war) were taken into account did not shift the focus onto attempts to standardize the structures and capacities of production. In other words, the dollar did not abolish increasing differences among the old agricultural districts.

The Growing Emancipation of German Agricultural Policy, 1951–1952

Food imports remained a prerequisite for reconstruction of the German agricultural and social order in the period of 1951–52, though not to the extent that they had been one or two years before. Breadgrain imports declined from $1.3 million (for 1950–51) to $400,000. Feed-grain, for which $500,000 were still necessary for 1950–51, was no longer purchased on the world market by the Federal Republic of Germany.[30]

In the middle of 1950, the GARIOA program expired after being phased out, thanks to ECA funds, between January and June of 1950. West German agriculture faced the world market with an uncertain outcome in 1951–52. Relations between the ECA authorities and the BML became strained, because the Germans believed that the allocation of the last ERP credit installment took too much time. Almost a whole planting season passed between American acceptance of the German program (October 1, 1951) and approval (May 28, 1952). As if that were not enough, it took another half year before the individual projects contained in this program were approved.[31]

Where and how did the BML use the credit funds? In fiscal year 1951–52, the technical modernization of West German agriculture

---

30 Günther Thiede, "Die Ernährungshilfe für Westdeutschland von 1945/46 bis 1952/53," *Berichte über Landwirtschaft* 32 (1954): 237–64.
31 Steding and Timmermann, "Die Kredite aus Marshallplanmitteln," 272.

began in earnest. Funds from the second partial loan allocation
flowed overwhelmingly into mechanization. The agricultural sector
purchased farm machinery of all kinds to the extent of DM 1,050
billion in 1951–52.[32] During this time the BML specified its promotional criteria according to regional points of view: According to the
"watering-can" principle (*Giesskannen-Prinzip*), funds from the second partial loan allocation should not have been distributed. The
amount of the distributed funds depended upon two factors: agricultural acreage and the number of farming enterprises with over two
hectares of land.[33] In other words, promotional funds were received
in the first place by agricultural regions that were traditionally structurally sound, not by problem regions.

Agriculture Minister Niklas stressed the rapid increase in production in those regions with strong performance potentials. Foremost
in state agricultural policy was the goal of attaining as much self-
sufficiency as possible, in view of the uncertainties of the East–West
conflict and of the world market. "A production of food in the immediate vicinity of our places of industrial production and of our areas of mass consumption is a great factor of assurance and security,"
he wrote in 1951. "Even the cancellation of some barges carrying
food can lead to difficulties. It must be in all cases secured and
achieved that German agriculture produces so much food that it is in
the position, at least temporarily, to carry out an emergency supply
program for consumers." In this way old experiences from the Second World War and new experiences from the Berlin blockade and
the Korean War shaped food supply and agricultural policies during
the founding period of the Federal Republic of Germany.[34]

The main share of financial support for agriculture went to medium and large farms (Table 8.1). The Emsland Plan of 1950 also had
this focus. It envisioned an increase of 500,000 hectares of land under
cultivation. Most of the federal states (*Bundesländer*) began to develop
regional programs in the early 1950s, such as the plan of 1951 in
Hesse. These plans continued to pursue the goal of putting more and
more land "under the plow" and of rebuilding or modernizing the
infrastructure of neglected regions.[35]

West German agricultural production gradually emerged from its
deep deficit of previous years. Decreased food imports proved that

32 Ibid., 280–1.   33 Ibid., 286.   34 Kluge, *Vierzig Jahre Agrarpolitik*, 1:87.
35 Kluge, *Vierzig Jahre Agrarpolitik*, 1:102.

Table 8.1. *Distribution of medium term ERP credit according to individual class size*
of farming enterprises in the credit sector of the agricultural annuity bank
(Landwirtschaftliche Rentenbank)

Class size (ha)	Portion of total loans on Dec. 31, 1952 in %	Avg. amount of loan per farm in DM
Under 10	37	2,825
10–20	25	3,704
25–50	17	5,123
50–100	11	7,433
Over 100	10	12,219
All classes together	100	3,937

Source: F. Steding and F. Timmermann, "Die Kredite aus Marshallplanmitteln an die Agrarwirtschaft," *Berichte über Landwirtschaft* 32 (1954): 298.

domestic production was increasing. The $221 million of food relief shipments received in 1950–51 amounted to only 18 percent of the value of the total food supply imports. Before this period it had amounted to still 43 percent; in 1951–52 it stood at 6 percent and in 1952–53 at only 2 percent.[36]

Structural reforms accompanied the increase in food production. The agricultural authorities of the various *Bundesländer* started programs to step up the pace of success, specifically programs to increase the amount of arable land. The degree of success varied. By 1950, 1,140 refugee farming operations already existed in Lower Saxony, which had expanded its arable land by a total of 2,500 hectares. Smaller farms previously incapable of surviving increased their size by an average of two hectares each and thereby became competitive in the market. In North Rhine-Westphalia, to name yet another example, 6,859 new settlement vacancies existed until the end of 1952, the majority of them being full-employment operations.[37]

The Complicated Last Round: Controversial Distribution of the Third ECA Partial Loan Allocation

The debate over distribution of the final grant of ERP funds dragged on for almost two years. It began on February 28, 1951, when the agricultural sector received a promise of DM 135 million from the

36 Thiede, "Ernährungshilfe für Westdeutschland," 261.
37 Kluge, *Vierzig Jahre Agrarpolitik*, 1:101.

third ECA partial loan allocation (DM 1.350 billion). Ninety-five million marks were in the form of credit and DM 40 million in the form of grants. Negotiations between the BML and the ECA Food and Agriculture Division lasted until late September 1951. The Americans often declined to reveal exact information about their intentions, causing confusion in the BML. The key figure on the German side in this exceedingly contradictory policy-making process was not the minister of agriculture, Niklas, but rather the minister of finance, Fritz Schäffer (CSU). Schäffer set the financial goals for the promotion of agriculture; the Division followed his advice promptly, at times against the will of the BML.[38]

The ECA approved the second suggestion of the BML, which called for a production credit program in the amount of 50 million marks by September 26, 1951, but only for regions with desolated production structures. The Division (Michael S. Harris and Gordon A. Fraser) criticized the previous agricultural policy of the German federal government in this regard. Instead of using public investment programs, the agricultural sector was to be helped solely by means of price increases and duty protection. The Americans clearly expressed their displeasure over the real or imagined return of the Germans to the earlier times of agricultural protectionism. "If it were left up solely to the government (of Adenauer), only very little, if any at all, of the ERP funds would have gone to the benefit of agriculture . . . ," read another accusation.[39] This type of criticism, however, in reality could be applied more to the German ministers Blücher (Marshall Plan), Schäffer (Finance), and Erhard (Economics) than to the BML.

Thirty-seven million of the total of 50 million marks flowed into the so-called Red Zone, a region whose agriculture had been destroyed by the war, and into the Green Zone, a structurally disadvantaged agricultural region. Generally, these regions tended to be either along the French-Luxembourg-Belgian border, in the Bavarian Forest along the Czech border, or in various parts of the Eifel.[40] No agreement could be reached between the Germans and the Americans about what should be done with the remaining 13 million marks.

The BML submitted to the Division two lists with development projects that could be financed with the remaining sum, but without

38 Maier to Bode, June 7, 1951, BA, B 116/1063.
39 Harris to Fraser, Sept. 29, 1951, BA, B 116/1027.
40 *Agrarpolitische Pressekorrespondenz* 42, no. 15 (1951): 732.

result. A third list was finally approved on May 28, 1952. The question of how the suggestions by the Germans corresponded to those by the Americans will not be discussed here. Beyond various differences of opinion, no fundamentally contrary development models separated the two. The main difference lay in the financial details. By the end of June 1952, the Mutual Security Agency (MSA) took over the completion of the tasks of the ERP support program. This included settling the matter of the excess DM 13 million. This money was not applied to projects in the Blue Zone. The Blue Zone was an emergency area that suffered both from overpopulation caused by refugees and from unemployment. Schleswig-Holstein received DM 6 million, Lower Saxony DM 5 million, and Hesse and Bavaria DM 1 million each.[41]

While the support programs in the Red, Green, and Blue Zones alleviated acute emergencies, the credit program of the third partial loan allocation hindered the goal of modernizing agriculture. This program promoted mechanization by providing 16 million marks, to go primarily to promote communal use of machinery. For many farmers this was a strange type of village cooperative that did not evoke much sympathy. Machinery cooperatives were a trademark of eastern Germany. Farmers often asked whether the free farmer was to be threatened by collectivization just like the farmers in the German Democratic Republic. But this worry was totally unfounded. Communal use of machinery was merely an attempt to dampen the rapid rate of individual mechanization of farming operations.[42]

Even after ERP credit resources officially came to an end on June 30, 1953, special funds still flowed into agriculture. These resulted mainly from rising interest and repayment returns, which amounted to DM 25 million for 1954. Seventeen million marks from this fund were spent on gaining new cropland, for example Emsland, and 8 million marks on the rebuilding of farms.[43] German agricultural policy at this time prepared itself for a great expansion of production. Attention was paid to every square meter of land. The Law of Land Consolidation (*Flurbereinigungsgesetz*) of July 14, 1953, provided the legal basis for the effective restructuring of unprofitable land.[44] It distributed scattered pieces of property in a long-term process, according to the principles of modern management. Agricultural pol-

41 *VELF-Sonderdienst*, July 9, 1952, p. 7.
42 Steding and Timmermann, "Die Kredite aus Marshallplanmitteln," 281.
43 Ibid., 266.   44 *Ministerialblatt* 5, no. 14 (July 22, 1953): 158–79.

icy became a piece of German national policy (*Deutschlandpolitik*) when it was employed to create a food reserve for the refugees who streamed in daily from the other part of Germany and to offer a new basis of subsistence to the farmers among them.

CONCLUSION: "AMERICANIZATION" OR
"GERMANIZATION" OF GERMAN AGRICULTURE?

Historical analysis of the effects of the Marshall Plan upon agricultural policy will not provide any fundamentally new insights into the academic debate.[45] However, one must credit this analysis for expanding the debate over an important and substantial area of politics that had not previously stood in the center of attention. How did the final balance sheet turn out? Without doubt, as far as agriculture was concerned, the Marshall Plan achieved the goal highest in the minds of its proponents and beneficiaries, namely "obtaining the highest degree of reconstruction" and of "developing production on a healthy economical foundation." In addition, financial resources brought action rather quickly, often in contravention of complex bureaucratic procedures.

More concretely, by June 30, 1953, the agricultural economy had received DM 404.056 million in the following ways:[46]

First ECA Investment Program	DM 128.500 million
Second ECA Investment Program	DM 113.506 million
Third ECA Investment Program	DM 140.000 million
Returns from the year 1952	DM 22.050 million

Of the total value of Marshall Plan aid, the agricultural economy received DM 524.256 million, or 11.9 percent.[47] In addition to the funds from the three investment programs, there were DM 117.2 million in the form of grants. Besides this, American fiduciary resources were linked to capital of the German Settlement Bank (*Deutsche Siedlungsbank*) in the amount of DM 3.0 million.[48]

The significance of American money becomes quite clear if a comparison is made to German investment funds. Between the currency

---

45 Hans-Jürgen Schröder, ed., *Marshallplan und westdeutscher Wiederaufstieg: Positionen-Kontroversen* (Stuttgart, 1990).
46 Steding and Timmermann, "Die Kredite aus Marshallplanmitteln," 266.
47 Ibid.   48 Ibid., 265.

reform of 1948 and the middle of 1953, DM 9.840 billion were invested in the agricultural economy (including the food supply industry) of the Federal Republic of Germany; of this sum, foreign resources were delivered in the amount of DM 3.94 million. Half of these foreign funds came from public sources of the Federal Republic of Germany. The share of ERP credit in total investment stood at 4 percent, in total foreign funds at 10 percent, and in public investment funds at 21 percent.[49] Arranged according to its applied purpose, the distribution of total credits as of 1953 is shown in Table 8.2.

Whether ERP funds caused the successes in agricultural production cannot be proven with certainty. Without American money, however, the balance sheet of the rebuilding of the agricultural and food supply industry would not have been so positive. Modernization and reconstruction would have, in all probability, lasted to the end of the 1950s. As it turned out, German agriculture was rather stabilized when the Federal Republic entered the European Economic Community in 1957 with the signing of the Treaties of Rome.

Regional concentration of agricultural production emerged fully independent of ERP funds. The two main criteria for the distribution of credit – production potential and advantages of location – were not questioned by any political party. As a result, the individual *Bundesländer* participated in the credit funds in varying proportions: Lower Saxony 20.2 percent, Bavaria 19 percent, North Rhine-Westphalia 16.6 percent, Schleswig-Holstein 12.8 percent, Baden-Württemberg 11.7 percent, Rhineland-Palatinate 10.2 percent, Hesse 6.8 percent, Hamburg 1.5 percent, and Bremen 1.2 percent.[50]

German and American authorities could influence agricultural development only to a limited degree. Where there were private investments, for example in motorization, influence from "above" was imperceptible. It cannot be proven whether bigger farming enterprises were supported at the cost of smaller and midsized operations. The bigger enterprises, however, used their advantage in modernization to gain access quickly and without friction to the sources of credit. They received funding commitments because they had a better chance to increase production without delay. Only later did financing from the third partial loan allocation chiefly benefit small and midsized farms. Finally, after 1955 small and midsized family farms enjoyed a quasi-constitutional recognition and thereby special

49 Ibid., 299.   50 Ibid., 288.

Table 8.2. *Overview of the distribution of DM 404.056 million of credit according to purpose*

Purpose	Long term: Over 10 yrs. × DM 1000	Middle term: Under 10 yrs. × DM 1000	%
Credit for Buildings			
Reconstruction of buildings destroyed by war	47,810.0		19.6
Remodeling and building improvements		31,377.750	
Rural Improvement Credit			
Water management improvements	27,885.1	7,500.000	
Rural drinking water supply	19,100.0		18.1
Land consolidation	6,819.7		
Reforestation incl. forest tree nurseries	11,400.0		
Housing for Refugees	41,744.0		10.3
Procurement of Agricultural Inventory and Technical Installations			
Machinery, tractors, etc.		85,508.108	25.1
Cattle		14,217.482	
Green fodder and potato drying facilities		1,817.000	
Biogas systems		450.000	
Fruit, Vegetable, and Wine Growing			
Investment for all types of growers		7,894.010	4.0
Fruit and vegetable storage and selling facilities		5,800.000	
Nurseries		2,275.950	
Potato Storage Rooms		1,542.000	0.4
Marketing of Different Products		2,280.000	0.6
Dairy Industry			
Construction and expansion of new dairies		21,930.450	5.6
Combatting tuberculosis in Oldenburg		551.800	

Table 8.2. *(cont.)*

Purpose	Long term: Over 10 yrs. × DM 1000	Middle term: Under 10 yrs. × DM 1000	%
Sugar Industry			
Construction of two new sugar factories	21,000	4,000.000	8.5
Expansion of existing sugar factories		9,400.000	
Misc. Food Industry		19,426.000	4.8
Fish Industry			
Building new trawlers	5,000		1.8
Fish marketing and processing		2,405.000	
Misc. Purposes		641.650	0.1
Agriculture, Forest, and Food Supply Industry for West Berlin		4,280.000	1.1
	180,758.8 = 45%	223,297.200 = 55%	100
		DM 404.056 million	

Source: F. Steding and F. Timmermann, "Die Kredite aus Marshallplanmitteln an die Agrarwirtschaft," *Berichte über Landwirtschaft* 32 (1954): 282.

state protection under the Law of Agriculture (*Landwirtschaftsgesetz*), which was supported by all political parties in the Bundestag.

When the ERP financial sources were exhausted it became clear that no fundamental differences existed between the "American way" and the "German way" of handling agricultural matters. The emphasis of state support for agriculture, set in 1949, continued to be the same: increasing production, protecting domestic production, modernizing the basis of production, securing the public food supply, and integrating refugees. Only one point remained controversial between the German and American authorities: the protection of German production against American competition on the world market. West German agricultural performance was nevertheless so strong that the country had become self-sufficient in feed-grain and sugar. The share of relief aid in bread-grain imports amounted to only 10 percent (1951–52: 24 percent). In connection with this, the BML announced "U.S. agricultural policy for the years 1952 and 1953 was determined more and more strongly by the concern over the sale of gigantic agricultural surpluses" (G. Thiede). All of the plans for a European agricultural union that were discussed in Bonn, Paris, the Hague, Brussels, Luxembourg, and Rome were given an important, if not the decisive impulse as a result. The United States expected some appreciation from the Europeans for their great developmental assistance financed by the ERP. Whether the European farmer in general or the German farmer in particular came to see a common interest with his counterpart oversees was uncertain in 1953–54.

It remains to be said in view of the dilemma of current agricultural overproduction that the ERP impulse may fall suspect to earlier authorship. High-ranking BML officials who often had come into conflict with the stances of the ECA came acknowledgingly to the conclusion, "One should also not underestimate the psychological effect of this aid which came at a point of time when the confident and investment-happy attitude of agricultural economics also . . . was in no way generally widespread to this extent."[51] The role of American financial resources remains decisive as the *initial charge of the production boom* of the 1950s. With the help of the dollar, modern agriculture in the western part of Germany was perhaps not initiated for the first time, but the dollar set a new course in a phase of prosperity that was unique in the agricultural development of the industrial age.

51 Ibid.

9

Science, Technology, and Reparations in Postwar Germany

JOHN GIMBEL

In their war with Germany, the British and the Americans created a number of special scientific and technical intelligence units. These included both the T-Forces, military teams whose primary duty was to secure and to guard intelligence targets, and the Combined Intelligence Objectives Subcommittee (CIOS), whose duty was to recommend targets to the T-Forces and to exploit them once they were secured.

To staff its exploitation teams, CIOS drew upon the armed services for engineers, chemists, and other experts who were transferred to CIOS. In addition, it tapped government agencies such as the U.S. Department of Commerce and the Foreign Economic Administration for civilian specialists who could be put on temporary assignment with CIOS. Finally, CIOS asked universities, private industries, and professional, trade, and industrial associations to contribute or recommend people who might serve as CIOS consultants and investigators.[1]

Whether they had served with CIOS in military uniform or as civilian consultants, hundreds of experts returned to the United States after the war to champion a postwar scientific and industrial exploitation program and to promote the transfer of German person-

This chapter is drawn from my *Science, Technology, and Reparations: Exploitation and Plunder in Postwar Germany* (Stanford, Calif., 1990), a study supported by a generous grant from the Volkswagen Stiftung and the Lehrstuhl für Wirtschaftsgeschichte of Düsseldorf University, as well as by grants and assistance from the Fulbright Commission for Germany, the National Endowment for the Humanities, the American Council of Learned Societies, and the Humboldt State University Foundation.

1 Final After Action Report, T Force and T Branch, 12th Army Group, July 1, 1945, NA, RG 332, ETO, USFET G-2 Section, Operations Branch, box 27, folder: Correspondence, 1945; SHAEF, G-2, Intelligence Directive No. 17, July 27, 1944, NA, RG 165, ABC 334.8 CIO Subcmte (30 Jul 44), Sec. 1-A; CIOS, Statement of Purpose of Grey List, CIOS (GLP-4 Revised), [Feb. 2, 1945], NA, RG 84, box 37, folder: 820.02a Safehaven; Report of CIOS for 1944, CIC 63/9, Feb. 7, 1945, NA, RG 218, box 133, folder: CCS 319.1 (11-7-44), Sec. 2.

nel to the United States to facilitate that program. For example, they reported that they found wind tunnels "far superior" to anything in use in the United States, a tacking agent for synthetic rubber judged to be "superior to any . . . so far known in allied circles," textiles and yarns "with no commercial counterpart in this country," tape recorders that promised to revolutionize the industry, and "an ingenious German machine" that promised to "revolutionize the manufacture of condensers for radio, radar, and other electric and electronic equipment."[2] Recommendations for the transfer of German personnel came from John R. Townsend of Bell Telephone Laboratories, Richard H. Ranger of Rangertone, R. H. McCarthy of Western Electric, J. D. Hanawalt of Dow Chemical, and others who returned to Washington with the names of people whom they thought should be brought to the United States for the benefit of American industry. Many feared that the British, the French, or the Russians would get to the experts first.[3] Just three days after V-J Day, an American official observed that "American industry, which has furnished most of the investigators and technical personnel for this 'intelligence' effort, is already asking for industrial information . . . secured by these investigators."[4]

THE POSTWAR COMMERCIAL-INDUSTRIAL
EXPLOITATION PROGRAM

Responding to the wishes of wartime investigators and their firms, to requests from agencies in the private sector, and to advice from his

2 Donald R. Heath, USGCC, Memorandum of Conversation with Colonel Boyd and Colonel Scharff on Oct. 6, 1945, NA, RG 84, box 726, folder: 400a Reparations; Dept. of Commerce, Release OPB-60, March 6, 1946, NA, RG 40, box 108; "German Fibers," *Business Week* (Oct. 23, 1945): 63–4; CIOS Evaluation Report 348, Mahle Werk GmbH, Fellbach, Aug. 28, 1945, NA, RG 218, box 136, folder: CCS 319.1 (11-7-44), Sec. 13; J. R. Townsend to G. D. Edwards, TIIC, Aug. 21, 1945, NA, RG 40, box 115; USGCC, FIAT, CC-13704, to 1st French Army, July 21, 1945, NA, RG 260, 7771st Document Center, box 12, folder: GBI/Tech/45 (CNE); OMGUS, ODDI, FIAT, to USFET, G-2, Nov. 19, 1945, NA, RG 338, box 27, USFET, G-2 Section, Operations Branch, Correspondence, 1945–46; TIID, Progress Report No. 11, Dec. 10, 1946, and William C. Speed to Edwin Y. Webb, Jr., TIID, Year End Review, both NA, RG 40, box 99.
3 G. D. Edwards to Roy S. Glasgow, Aug. 24, 1945, NA, RG 40, box 115; McCarthy to J. K. Libby, TIIC, Sept. 22, 1945, NA, RG 40, box 116; Karl Olsen to Donald R. Heath, Oct. 19, 1945, NA, RG 84, box 738; Hanawalt to J. K. Libby, TIIC, Sept. 22, 1945, NA, RG 40, box 147; Guellich to TIIC, Sept. 23, 1945, NA, RG 330, JIOA General Correspondence, box 4. A JIOA minute (JIOA Advisory Board Minutes, Oct. 25, 1945, NA, RG 40, box 79) notes that the agency had the names of more than one hundred German scientists and technicians whom returning investigators wanted brought to the United States.
4 Memo for Communications Subcommittee, TIIC, Aug. 18, 1945, attached to TIIC/C Agenda #11, NA, RG 40, box 123.

own government officials, President Harry S Truman authorized the postwar commercial-industrial exploitation program late in August 1945. Recommendations from the private sector came from the American Chemical Society, the American Petroleum Institute, the Scientific Apparatus Makers of America, and a host of others. Advice and suggestions of government officials came especially from Fred M. Vinson, director of War Mobilization and Reconversion, but also from Vannevar Bush, director of the Office of Scientific Research and Development, Harold Ickes, U.S. petroleum administrator for war, Edwin W. Pauley, U.S. representative on the Allied Commission on Reparations, William L. Clayton, under secretary of state for economic affairs, and Henry A. Wallace, secretary of commerce.[5] On August 25, 1945, Truman issued Executive Order 9604, which provided for "the release and dissemination of certain scientific and industrial information heretofore *or hereafter* obtained from the enemy." It defined "enemy scientific and industrial information" to include "all information concerning scientific, industrial and technological processes, inventions, methods, devices, improvements and advances heretofore *or hereafter* obtained by any department or agency of this Government in enemy countries regardless of its origin, or in liberated areas, if such information is of enemy origin or has been acquired or appropriated by the enemy" [emphasis added].[6]

Thus armed with presidential authority, the War and Commerce departments collaborated in a postwar commercial-industrial exploitation program in Germany. In Washington, the Commerce Department's Office of Technical Services (OTS) – with its advisory

5 T. M. Mints to Albert M. Orme, Dec. 1, 1945, NA, RG 40, box 123; W. C. Schroeder, "Investigation by the U.S. Government Technical Oil Mission," *American Petroleum Institute Proceedings* 25, No. 3 (1945): 24–9; Warren F. Faragher, "Collecting German Industrial Information," *Chemical and Engineering News* 26 (1948): 3816–20; "Widening Horizons" [editorial], *National Petroleum News* 37 (Nov. 7, 1945): R936; Bradley Dewey, President, American Chemical Society, to Wallace and others, Oct. 23, 1945; Dewey to Byrnes, Oct. 24, 1945; Byrnes to Dewey, Nov. 19, 1945, NA, RG 59, 862.542/10-2455; *FRUS: The Conference of Berlin (Potsdam) 1945,* 2 vols. (Washington, D.C., 1960), 1:510–11; Pauley speech quoted in Charles Fahy to FIAT, Nov. 3, 1945, NA, RG 260, box 11/2-2; "Addendum to the Statement of Arthur Paul . . . before the Senate Appropriations Committee," Oct. 30, 1945, NA, RG 40, box 153; U.S. Congress, 79th Congress, Senate, *Hearings before a Subcommittee of the Committee on Military Affairs* (Clayton testimony), June 25, 1945, p. 60; Wallace to SecWar Patterson and others, Nov. 9, 1945, NA, RG 40, box 79; Vinson to A. J. McFarland, JCS, May 14, 1945; Leahy to Vinson, June 8, 1945, NA, RG 165, box 204; Donald Keyes, TIIC, to D. P. Morgan, June 5, 1945, NA, RG 40, box 154.
6 Executive Order 9604, Providing for the Release of Scientific Information (Extension and Amendment of Executive Order No. 9568), Aug. 25, 1945, in *Code of Federal Regulations, Title 3, 1943–1948 Compilation* (Washington, D.C., 1957), 422 (emphasis added).

boards drawn from the armed services, government agencies, and the private sector – recruited technically qualified people and sent them to Europe as individuals and as teams to "screen, select, index, and microfilm documents of value to science and industry" and report their findings to the OTS. The latter collected the reports and made them available to the public through the Publication Board. In Europe, the Field Information Agency, Technical (FIAT), which had been created in May 1945 to unify the numerous agencies gathering scientific, industrial, and technical information, provided billets, work space, office equipment, supplies, communication facilities, and transportation for the OTS personnel. Further, it secured German support personnel for the operation, maintained a library, and took such other action as was necessary to accomplish the OTS mission.[7] The two agencies functioned until June 30, 1947, when General Lucius D. Clay, the American military governor, succeeded in having the operation shut down in the interests of German economic recovery.[8]

FIAT AND OTS FUNCTIONS AND OPERATIONS

To carry out their mission, FIAT and OTS concentrated on two interrelated functions: a records and documents filming project and a program to send technical consultants and technical missions to Germany on behalf of government agencies, trade and industrial associations, and private industries.

7 U.S. Congress, 79th Congress, House, *Hearings before the Subcommittee of the Committee on Appropriations,* June 26, 1946, p. 77; U.S. Congress, 80th Congress, House, *Hearings before the Subcommittee of the Committee on Appropriations,* Feb. 26, 1947, pp. 92ff; JIOA, Minutes, Advisory Board, Oct. 8, 1945; John C. Green to Gruhn, JIOA, Oct. 17, 1945, NA, RG 40, box 79; Green to Wallace, Sept. 26, 1945, NA, RG 40, box 85; Edward L. Bowles to Clay, Sept. 27, 1945; AGWAR to USFET, W-59946, Sept. 5, 1945, NA, RG 260, OMGUS Decimal Files, box 41; USFET to War Dept., S-22720, Sept. 11, 1945, NA, RG 165, ABC 334.8 CIO Subcmte (July 30, 44), Sec. 1-C; JIC 220/6, Oct. 12, 1945, NA, RG 40, box 138; Report on German Documents Conference, Oct. 22–25, 1945, NA, RG 260, box 17/19; AGWAR to USFET, W-87832, Dec. 10, 1945, copy in MSS History of FIAT, vol. 1, app. 24, p. 130, NA, RG 319, Office of the Chief of Military History, Historical Manuscript file; OMGUS, Economics Division, to FIAT, March 11, 1946, NA, RG 260, box 11/2-2; OMGUS, FIAT, Enemy Documents Branch, Daily Journal, Jan. 22, 1946, NA, RG 260, box 17/8; OMGUS, FIAT, Circular 26, July 12, 1946, NA, RG 260, OMGUS Decimal Files, box 64; John C. Green, interview, July 14, 1982, Washington, D.C.
8 OMGUS, General Orders, No. 54, June 23, 1947; FIAT, "Final Summary Report, Field Information Agency, Technical (FIAT)," July 1, 1947, 10 pp., with enclosures, NA, RG 260, OMGUS Decimal Files, box 120.

The Documents Filming Project

The "documents program," as it was called at FIAT, began ambitiously in autumn 1945. Using the wartime CIOS and T-Forces reports that it had inherited as successor to those organizations, FIAT identified some 20,000 targets as potential locations of documents for filming. Beginning in mid-January 1946, it sent reconnaissance teams to these and other targets to inventory the availability, type, condition, volume, and physical location of documents that might be copied. Document screeners and microfilm teams later visited targets that the reconnaissance teams found to be promising.[9] The document screeners were normally German-speaking, scientifically trained individuals whom the OTS recruited from universities, industrial firms, and government agencies. FIAT, which had a broad mandate to collect technical information, freeze "any and all targets," control the "disposition of personnel, documents, equipment and installations," and to arrest and intern individual Germans in the interests of its mission,[10] instructed document screeners to look for secret patent applications and information on processes, formulas, and techniques not generally known in the United States, as well as minutes, reference materials, and policy determinations of highly placed research and planning committees.[11] The microfilm teams, which sometimes spent weeks at a given location, copied the chosen records and turned them over to FIAT, which developed the films, prepared abstracts, and annotated index cards of their contents, and then sent everything to the OTS for eventual release to the public under its Publication Board program – at nominal cost of reproduction.[12]

FIAT daily journals and periodic reports show document screeners and microfilm teams working in hundreds of firms and research centers, including such prominent ones as the Ernst Leitz camera

9 Fred S. Thornhill to me, Sept. 28, 1981, in my possession.
10 W. B. Smith, Chief of Staff, SHAEF, to CG USGCC, July 11, 1945, NA, RG 218, CCS 334 FIAT (6-1-45); USGCC, INT/FIAT/312.01-1, July 14, 1945, NA, RG 260, USGCC Records, box 10.
11 FIAT, Circular No. 15, March 8, 1946, app. 30 to draft history of FIAT, Period 1 July 1946 . . . , NA, RG 260, box 20-3/5. A former investigator recalled years later that "any piece the Germans had stamped 'Geheim' was photographed, even laundry bills or love letters." Thornhill to author, Sept. 28, 1981.
12 OTS, TIID, "Collection of Technical Industrial Intelligence in Germany," Dec. 10, 1946, NA, RG 40, box 26.

works in Wetzlar, BMW in Munich, the Merck pharmaceutical works in Darmstadt, Degussa in Frankfurt, the Kerckhoff Institute in Bad Nauheim, Krupp in Essen, Bosch in Stuttgart, I.G. Farben in Höchst, and the universities in Marburg, Erlangen, Freiburg, Hamburg, Munich, and Düsseldorf.[13] A FIAT report of December 10, 1946, for example, listed eighty-seven current targets, showing in each instance the number of pages of documentary material selected for microfilming. At Leitz it was 198,000 pages, at Merck 4,000, at Düsseldorf University 18,000, at Degussa in Constance 14,000, at I.G. Farben in Höchst 311,000, at Krupp in Essen 60,000, and at other targets the quantities ranged from 1,000 to 500,000 pages (the latter representing the total for the German patent office).[14]

Available records of selected German targets help to flesh out the details of the program. Chemische Werke Hüls, I.G. Leverkusen, and Gutehoffnungshütte, Oberhausen, all reported on the presence and work of American commissions and microfilm teams in the fall of 1946.[15] The Gesellschaft für Linde's Eismaschinen A.G. reported to the Munich *Industrie- und Handelskammer* in September 1947 that it had been visited by numerous American, British, French, Norwegian, Dutch, and Belgian experts and teams. It singled out an American commission that brought along a complete microfilm unit with which it copied the plans for the foundation and structure of the buildings; documents detailing the specifications, construction, and uses of the various plant installations, and approximately 1,000 drawings, including those of the production facility. "This commission," the report observed, "operated with a mandate from the American government, apparently under a plan to acquire an archive of recent German industrial advances." However, the information taken would surely be used by private firms, the report concluded, and thus competitors from abroad would have "effortlessly come into possession of the very technology and know-how upon which

13 For examples, see K. H. Weberg to Neal D. Crane, Nov. 1, 1946, NA, RG 40, box 87; FIAT, Bi-Weekly Progress Report–FIAT, Nov. 1–15, 1946, NA, RG 260, OMGUS Decimal Files, box 64; FIAT, Daily Journal, Nov. 29, 1946, NA, RG 260, Decimal Files, box 17/9; and FIAT, Bi-Weekly Progress Report–FIAT, Nov. 16–30, 1946, NA, RG 260, OMGUS Decimal Files, box 64.
14 OTS, TIID, "Collection of Technical Industrial Intelligence in Germany," Dec. 10, 1946, NA, RG 40, box 26. See also "Scientific Cleanup," *Business Week,* May 18, 1946, pp. 19–20.
15 Dr. Baumann to Akademiker der Gruppe I, Wissenschaftliche Berichte, Chemische Werke Hüls, July 31, 1946, copy in my possession; Dr. Werkmeister, Zentralamt für Wirtschaft in der Britischen Zone, to Dr. Agartz, Nov. 26, 1946, BA, B 102/3768; Gutehoffnungshütte to Wirtschaftsministerium, NRW, Nov. 15, 1946, HSTA Düsseldorf, NW 99, Nr. 61.

our former comparative advantage was based."[16] The Dr. Alexander
Wacker Gesellschaft für Elektrochemische Industrie, GmbH, reporting on visits of ninety-four commissions from Britain, France, Norway, Czechoslovakia, Australia, the Netherlands, India, and the
United States, noted that the Americans, who had sent just over half
of the commissions, brought along a microfilm team that copied all
the important drawings and plans at the firm's Burghausen facility
(near Munich) and "the entire collection of research reports, totaling
about 20,350 pages," in the firm's Munich offices. In this fashion,
the report concluded after lengthy discussion, foreign interests had
acquired the firm's entire records collection on research, experimentation, and tests. These were obviously more important to them
than simply having the patents, which as a rule did not reveal the
processes and techniques used in production.[17] Finally, American
records show the following involvement with Degussa (Deutsche
Gold- und Silber-Scheideanstalt) in Frankfurt: Anthony Hass, the
document screener assigned to the firm, visited the central offices
and two of the firm's production facilities in Frankfurt, as well as the
firm's branch office in Constance, to which Degussa had evacuated
research laboratories and company records during the war. At each
location, Hass interviewed key personnel and determined the type
and quantity of materials to be microfilmed. In Frankfurt, he estimated the quantity to be about 100,000 pages for the central office
and another 8,000 pages for the two production facilities combined.
At Constance, he concluded that "the collection of documents is
probably one of the most interesting in the French Zone," for it included "the complete research and patent records . . . fully in-
dexed." A report filed on the completion of the microfilm work at
Constance shows the take to have been 12,310 frames on thirteen
rolls of microfilm, and other American records show that a microfilm team went to Frankfurt in March 1947 and worked under the
supervision of Hass, who remained at the target company during the
microfilming.[18] "This team," a contemporary Degussa letter shows,
occupied the firm's technical file rooms for several weeks and copied
"hundreds of reports, operating directives, and other things," during
which time it was virtually impossible to retrieve files and docu-

16 Linde's Eismaschinen AG to IHK Munich, Sept. 11, 1947, BA, B 102/3767.
17 Wacker to IHK Munich, Sept. 15, 1947, BA, B 102/3767.
18 Documents Evaluation Report No. 51, NA, RG 260, box 17/17; Dr. Schulenberg, Notiz
   betr. amerikanischen Besuch, Feb. 27, 1947, Degussa Archives.

ments when they needed them for their own purposes. About two weeks after the team left, files were in such a state of disorder that, despite the efforts of two file clerks working full-time over eight days, they had not yet been "restored to a usable condition."[19]

Technical Consultants and Missions

As part of their plan to "use vacuum cleaner methods to acquire all the technical scientific information the Germans have,"[20] the Americans sent missions to Germany at the same time that they went forward with the "documents program." In March 1946, OTS Director John C. Green wrote to the editors of all principal trade papers asking for nominations and volunteers for FIAT's documents project. He also invited private firms to tell the OTS what they wanted from Germany and to nominate or furnish investigators who could go and get it, either as individual technical consultants or as members of special missions that the Commerce Department proposed to organize on behalf of industrial or scientific groups.[21] "We intend to make it widely known in industry," Green wrote to FIAT, "that firms may send their technical men to Germany to make investigations, the expense to be borne by industry and the results to be reported to the Department of Commerce for publication."[22] Using press releases, telephone calls to industrial leaders, visits to trade associations and technical societies, and a variety of other means, OTS officials invited firms to participate. For example, an OTS official spent a day visiting engineering societies in New York City; another went to New York, Chicago, and Cincinnati to discuss with various firms "the desirability of making additional intelligence investigations in Germany." Still others attended meetings and conventions of the American Chemical Society, the National Metal Congress and Exposition, and the National Association of Manufacturers, where Green himself gave an address.[23]

Responding to the OTS recruitment campaign, a staff editor of *Food Industries* wrote: "Your government is offering you a chance

19 Degussa to Hessisches Staatsministerium, May 29, 1947, Degussa Archives.
20 Proposed press release, March 11, 1946, NA, RG 218, box 95, folder: CCS 471.9, Sec. 5.
21 Green to Editors of all Principal Trade Papers, March 27, 1946, NA, RG 40, box 99.
22 Green to Haertel, Apr. 10, 1946, NA, RG 40, box 26.
23 Reiss to Green, Progress report, Apr. 12, 1946, NA, RG 40; TIID Progress Report No. 10, Nov. 1, 1946; TIID Progress Report No. 11, Dec. 10, 1946, NA, RG 40, box 99; Webb to George C. Richert, Dec. 23, 1946, NA, RG 40, box 102.

to share in the war's reparations – reparations in the form of technological information . . . in all fields of industry and research," including such things as "testing methods, chemical research, new products, new materials, production methods and plant development."[24] In a similar story, *Science News Letter* listed chemicals, aeronautics, machine tools, industrial equipment, fuels and lubricants, metals and minerals, communications equipment, scientific instruments, shipbuilding, and textiles as fields in which OTS sought competent people. "If any industry or scientific group wishes to investigate German industrial methods," the story advised, "Uncle Sam will make the necessary arrangements for a mission to go to Germany."[25]

Throughout 1946 and the first half of 1947, the OTS sponsored hundreds of such missions for industry groups or trade associations. For example, the textile and petroleum industries each sent two missions to enlarge upon the findings of wartime investigators, and the motion picture industry sent a mission to investigate the German color-film industry.[26] Often, however, a "mission" consisted of no more than one person in search of specific information useful to his or her firm. For example, Sosthenes Behn, the president of ITT, agreed to donate the services of an ITT employee with the "understanding that [he] will be allowed to obtain for us information in which we alone are interested because of our affiliated companies."[27] Further, W. H. Reynolds, a scientific consultant from the American Instrument Company, which he claimed was the only American company that "builds high pressure, high temperature apparatus for catalytic chemical reactions," went to Germany under OTS auspices and visited the only two German firms that did the same thing. Upon his return, he expressed doubts about the general value of his investigations, "but in my own case, it was of great value to my

24 Priscilla A. Deutsch, "What Do We Want from Germany?" *Food Industries* 18 (June 1946): 81–2.
25 "Industries Asked to Probe German Technology," *Science News Letter* 49 (May 4, 1946): 279.
26 "Scientific Cleanup," *Business Week,* May 18, 1946, pp. 19–20; Gruhn, JIOA, to SecState Byrnes, Nov. 23, 1945, NA, RG 40, box 26; TIID, Electronics and Communications Unit, Review, Jan. 1, 1947, NA, RG 40, box 99; "German Technical Developments," *Federal Science Progress* 1 (Feb. 1, 1947): 18; Warren F. Faragher, "Collecting German Industrial Information," *Chemical and Engineering News* 26 (Dec. 27, 1948): 3816–20; Albert E. Miller, Chairman, API Technical Oil Mission Study, to John C. Green, Jan. 24, 1951, NA, RG 330, JIOA General Correspondence, box 33.
27 Edwin Y. Webb to Behn, Mar. 21, 1946; Behn to Webb, Apr. 8, 1946; Webb to Behn, Apr. 9, 1946, NA, RG 40, box 116.

company and we made use of it just as soon as it was released to the public."[28] An unpublished official history of FIAT shows that between July 1, 1946, and June 30, 1947, FIAT cleared and processed a total of 4,994 U.S. and Allied investigators for 2,922 field trips in Germany.[29]

Experts selected to go to Germany normally went to Washington, where they did the necessary paperwork to become technical consultants for OTS, bought uniforms, got shots, and received travel orders to FIAT. At FIAT they were briefed by division chiefs, and while they waited for military clearances and travel orders to the targets of their choice they gained access to the FIAT library and the FIAT target evaluation and assessment reports as well as those collected by CIOS and T-Forces during the war.[30] Finally, FIAT issued them travel orders and passes authorizing them to visit German plants to examine processes and products, to take photographs and samples, to demand drawings, plans, and blueprints, to interview plant personnel and, according to John C. Green, to "take all other measures appropriate to the full extraction of the information" they were after.[31]

Available American records show that investigators took Germans from their homes and workplaces to "Dustbin," a detention and in-

28 Reynolds to Reiss, Sept. 5, 1946, NA, RG 40, box 123.
29 "History of Field Information Agency, Technical (FIAT), Period 1 July 1946–30 June 1947," MSS in NA, RG 260, box 20-3/5. A tabulation prepared by FIAT on the eve of its dissolution (N. G. Gillis, Statistical Information on Material and Investigations, FIAT, June 13, 1947, NA, RG 260, 7748th Unit, box 3) shows that, in the year ending May 31, 1947, FIAT had processed and cleared 1398 American investigators and another 1075 document screeners for 969 and 640 field trips respectively; moreover, the *New York Times* reported on May 26, 1947 – when the economy-minded 80th Congress appeared to be on the verge of shutting down the OTS's German exploitation project – that "the German 'brain-picking' project is the joint venture of business and Government," adding that "to help Commerce [Department] employees dig out the documents, United States industry sent 6,000 experts of its own to Germany." (*New York Times*, May 26, 1947, p. 35). I have been unable to find official or reliable figures for the period before July 1, 1946, and I do not know where the *New York Times* got the 6,000 figure, but it probably came from OTS, which obviously inspired the story.
30 OMGUS, FIAT, Daily Journal, June 29, 1946, NA, RG 260, box 17/8, says the FIAT library had 23,381 reports on file on that date. T. G. Haertel, FIAT, to Green, Progress Report No. 52, Dec. 5, 1946, NA, RG 40, box 98, says the FIAT library had over 30,000 technical, evaluation, or assessment reports available for use by investigators.
31 Green, To Whom It May Concern, May 20, 1949, NA, RG 40, box 107; Reiss to Unit Chiefs, July 16, 1946, NA, RG 40, box 147; Worden to Reiss, Apr. 23, 1947, NA, RG 40, box 88. The directive establishing FIAT gave investigators authority to remove, arrest, and intern individual Germans, and the FIAT handbook for field teams instructed them to refer difficult cases to the nearest military intelligence officer and then file an incident report with FIAT headquarters. See USGCC, INT/FIAT/321.01-1, July 14, 1945, NA, RG 260, box 10, and FIAT, Handbook, Sept. 6, 1945, NA, RG 260, 7771st Document Center, box 14.

terrogation center for scientists and industrialists, where they could be held indefinitely for exploitation.[32] They show that an American investigator took documents from the home of Dr. H. Küppenbender, a Zeiss Optical Company official, "during his temporary absence from Heidenheim," leaving a brief receipt with the local military government detachment, recording that he had removed "various notes . . . pertaining to the development of a new type of camera shutter."[33] After officials at Brown-Boveri et Cie AG refused to give out information to investigators, claiming that the firm was partially owned by foreign interests and therefore exempt, the U.S. Military Government headquarters in Frankfurt advised FIAT that Brown-Boveri officials must answer "all questions of authorized Allied investigating teams," that foreign ownership was not an acceptable excuse for noncompliance, and that all FIAT agents operating in the field should be advised accordingly. Furthermore, the advice continued, "it is suggested that [investigators] inform persons under interrogation that any failure by them to answer properly concerning the activities of [their firm] will subject that individual to punishment under Military Government Ordnance No. 1."[34] When investigators learned that German firms had often stored important papers and documents for safekeeping from air raids, it reportedly became "standard practice" for FIAT investigators "to interrogate plant directors on this subject." In one instance, when an I.G. Farben official in Offenbach admitted that he had stored documents in a safe deposit box in a nearby bank, but claimed that the keys had been lost, FIAT "arranged to have the boxes blown open."[35] Finally, at the Ernst Leitz plant in Wetzlar, investigators who "had had considerable difficulty with the officials . . . in ascertaining the extent of the technical records . . . resorted to high pressure methods and consequently gained access to all of their material."[36]

German records are replete with accounts of similar incidents. They are also rich in references to unsuccessful attempts to refuse access to records, facilities, and unpatented know-how, to fruitless re-

32 "Dustbin" detainees could also be held briefly without exploitation. See FIAT, "Subj: Qualifications of new DUSTBIN Detainees," Jan. 7, 1946, NA, RG 332, box 103, which states: "If exploitation on the new arrival is not started within four weeks, procedures for his release will be started automatically."
33 USFET, G-2, Letter of Clearance, Dec. 12, 1945; Major Myron W. Warren, OMG Württemberg-Baden to OMG Heidenheim, Dec. 19, 1945, NA, RG 260, box 12/197-2.
34 OMG, U.S. Zone, to FIAT, Jan. 3, 1946, NA, RG 40, box 126.
35 FIAT, Industry Branch, Weekly Progress Report, May 15, 1946, NA, RG 40, box 99.
36 Reiss to Green, Progress Report No. 6, June 28, 1946, NA, RG 40, box 26.

quests for receipts, and to vain efforts to receive compensation for what they delivered in scientific and technical know-how. Furthermore, they sometimes contain pathetic comments from which it is easy to detect the implied duress under which they complied. One comment complained that, soon after Germany's capitulation, all firms with any kind of standing in their field were swarmed over by French, British, and American commissions. The commissions demanded information on technical experiences, on methods of production, and on industrial know-how of all kinds. It was nearly impossible to withhold such information, because the commissions, through various maneuvers and techniques, were usually able to surprise the Germans by using information derived from other sources to demand ever greater detail.[37] According to another German source, the visits were not just for the purpose of inspecting factories and equipment but were the occasion for gathering information of all types, for taking photographs, sample products, recipes and formulas, drawings and plans, and documents relating to the entire enterprise. On occasion, when investigators came without FIAT passes or with passes that appeared to be unclear or improper, there were unpleasant confrontations which the Germans tried to resolve by contacting units of the American occupation forces. In those cases, investigators usually returned with proper passes to do what they had wanted to do in the first place.[38] Finally, another German source notes that investigators came with reports that they had apparently bought in bookstores in the United States or Great Britain. To supplement these reports, they demanded information on production processes and internal directives. They wanted complete and detailed information on equipment, formulas, pressures, temperatures, and times, as well as specifications and drawings for buildings, laboratories, and equipment. In this fashion, the Germans complained, German industry was deprived of its most valuable capital, without control of any kind and thus without credit to Germany's reparations account.[39]

Selected cases, the details of which can only be sketched in this essay, illustrate the dimensions of the program and its apparent long-term effects. For example, the U.S. Bureau of Mines, the American

37 Ernst Rogowski to Eberhardt, Feb. 12, 1947, HStA Stuttgart, EA 1/11, 16.
38 Degussa to Grosshessisches Staatsministerium, Oct. 8, 1946, Degussa Archives.
39 "Auszug aus Aktenvermerk über die 8. Sitzung 'Forschungskontrolle' im Länderrat," March 25, 1947, HSTA Stuttgart, 6/3, 321.

Petroleum Institute, and others in the industry sent Warren F. Faragher of the Houdry Process Corporation on a follow-up mission to Germany early in January 1947 to generate written reports on some fifteen topics, including the Fischer-Tropsch synthesis and synthetic lubricating oils, to fill in gaps left by the wartime U.S. Technical Oil Mission. Four years later, the U.S. government sent Faragher on a second mission, this time to obtain those reports, which its author and his firm had refused to release without adequate payment.[40] In May 1946, "interested American cosmetic firms" sponsored Dr. Stephen A. Karas, a former chief chemist for Helena Rubinstein, Inc., on a one-man mission to investigate "trade secrets of the German cosmetic industry" and to "study the manufacture of food flavorings, a closely related field." Six months later, a Commerce Department news release noted that "one of the purposes of Dr. Karas's study was to obtain formulas for the base waxes which American manufacturers imported from Germany before the war" and reported that he had just returned "with complete details of German processes and original formulas for making synthetic glyco waxes, for extracting cholesterol from wool fat, and for making many perfumes, toilet soaps, creams, and other cosmetic products based on those materials."[41] Other selected cases included:

1. Rangertone's use of a model of a German tape recorder (Magnetophone) to produce and market a magnetic recorder by working under the "guiding inspiration of knowing . . . quite completely what the Germans had done."[42]
2. Western Electric's replication of a Bosch machine for making condensers that were smaller and cheaper than those previously manufactured in the United States, and Good-All Electric's replication of the same machine to produce millions of condensers for proximity fuses under military contract.[43]

40 Faragher, "Collecting German Industrial Information," *Chemical and Engineering News* 26 (1948): 3818; Albert E. Miller to Green, Jan. 1, 1951, NA, RG 330, JIOA General Correspondence, box 33.
41 Press Release, May 29, 1946, NA, RG 40, box 98; Press Release, OTS-450, Oct. 30, 1946, NA, RG 40, box 146. Although OTS always described its mission as the collection of *wartime* technology and know-how, it will be noted that in this instance the search was for information on materials that "American manufacturers imported from Germany *before the war*" (emphasis added).
42 Ranger to Reiss, May 2, 1947, NA, RG 40, box 153.
43 Webb to Reiss, March 26, 1948, NA, RG 40, box 102; Goodall to Webb, May 4, 1948, NA, RG 40, box 124.

3. The American Lava Company's exploitation of two German machines, one a mechanical press that automatically "stamped dry ceramics parts rather than wet [ones] as had been previously done," the other a machine for spot welding and riveting metallic lugs, pins, and other parts to ceramics. Hans Thurnauer, the firm's vice president and Director of Research had shipped the machines back to the United States while serving as a scientific consultant for FIAT, an experience he later described as "just like going out on a hunting trip into unexplored territory."[44]

TERMINATING THE PROGRAM AND EVALUATING THE TAKE

German firms, sometimes in collaboration with sympathetic American military government officials on the scene, tried from time to time to have the program modified. For example, Degussa officials, working through various channels including the *Industrie- und Handelskammer* in Frankfurt, the Hessian ministry of economics, and the American-appointed Minister President of Greater Hesse (Dr. Karl Geiler), marshaled evidence and presented arguments in the spring of 1946 to show that FIAT investigations impinged on patent rights and patent agreements (in this case between Degussa and DuPont), exposed unpatented firm secrets, interfered with current, approved production activities, restricted German efforts to rebuild German production under the Allied Control Council's level-of-industry plan, and ultimately threatened to render impossible the German economic self-sufficiency desired and encouraged by the Americans.[45] Although the American industry officer in the Office of Military Government for Greater Hesse responded by issuing written "information in regard to investigators visiting German industrial plants," little appears to have changed. Degussa officials reported several months later that the number and frequency of allied visita-

44 Press Release, NA, RG 40, box 114; Webb to Reiss, March 26, 1948, NA, RG 40, box 102; Thurnauer to Webb, May 9, 1947, NA, RG 40, box 114; Shipping instructions, FEA for JIOA, n.d., NA, RG 260, FIAT Records, box 17/18.
45 Dipl.-Ing. Anderson, "Betriebsforschungen durch alliierte Wehrmachtsangehörige," May 17, 1946; Degussa to Minister für Wirtschaft und Verkehr, Apr. 25, 1946; Degussa to IHK, Frankfurt, May 24, 1946; Dr. F. Scheller, Notiz, June 17, 1946; Anderson, "Unterredung mit Ministerpräsident Prof. Dr. Geiler am 19.6.46 wegen Betriebserkundungen durch alliierte Wehrmachtsangehörige," June 24, 1946, Degussa Archives.

tions were still unusually high and that their nature had not changed as a result.[46]

Meanwhile, Robert Bosch GmbH, apparently working in collaboration with Colonel Gerald B. O'Grady, the chief of the Industry Branch, Office of Military Government for Württemberg-Baden, proposed certain restrictions on what FIAT investigators could demand.[47] Colonel O'Grady, who once told a FIAT investigator that he "totally disapproved of such robbery," and whose office was known at FIAT for having made difficulties for FIAT investigators "on various occasions," sent the Bosch proposal to higher headquarters, only to be dressed down sharply by Colonel Ralph M. Osborne, the chief of FIAT, who wrote bitingly that FIAT operated under policies developed and approved by the president of the United States, the Joint Chiefs of Staff, the Congress, and General Lucius D. Clay, the deputy military governor for Germany.[48] The latter eventually succeeded in having the program shut down in the interests of German economic recovery.

On October 20, 1946, Clay cabled the War Department that FIAT teams had "secured valuable information for the US, which perhaps will represent our only return in reparations." However, he continued, "the work has been going on now since our entry into Germany and most of the information which existed in Germany at the time of surrender should be available by now." Furthermore, he concluded, "it is doubtful if German industrial development in peacetime industry and research . . . can be pushed vigorously until some industrial security is provided for trade processes which are developed in those industries."[49] In November 1946, during the British–American discussions in Washington on the merger and economic recovery of their two occupation zones, Clay supported a British suggestion that FIAT investigations be terminated on March 31, 1947.[50] Late in Jan-

---

46 OMG Hesse, Economics Division, to Minister for Economics and Transportation, June 24, 1946, NA, RG 260, FIAT 7748th Unit, box 1; Degussa to Grosshessisches Staatsministerium, Oct. 9, 1946, Degussa Archives.
47 Steins, Gen. Mgr. Robert Bosch, to O'Grady, March 20, 1946, NA, RG 260, box 11/2-2.
48 O'Grady to OMGUS, Economics Division, March 28, 1946; Osborne, FIAT, to Chief, Industry Branch, Economics Division, OMG Württemberg-Baden, Apr. 17, 1946, both NA, RG 260, box 11/2-2.
49 Clay to Echols, CC-5929, Oct. 20, 1946, NA, RG 84, box 760.
50 Memorandum of conversation between Todd and Rudlin (U.S.) and Albert Frost (U.K.), Feb. 7, 1947, NA, RG 59, Records of the Office of the Assistant SecState for Occupied Areas, 1946–49, box 1.

uary 1947, he cabled Washington his desire and that of his British counterpart to announce the cut-off date well in advance.[51] But there were problems in Washington, where John C. Green, the OTS director, argued that it would "be a national tragedy . . . if we allow the doors to shut before we have added all of the best of Germany's technical knowledge to our own."[52] Eventually, after considerable bureaucratic conflict and compromise, the War Department authorized an announcement in Berlin that no new investigations would be permitted after May 15, 1947, and that all investigations would end by June 30, 1947.[53]

Evaluating the Take

As early as March 13, 1946, Clay told a visitor from Washington "that scientific and technical information was being taken from German firms and individuals without any provision being made to evaluate . . . its monetary value as a . . . reparations credit."[54] Early in September 1946, he raised the issue informally with Major General H. S. Aurand, the War Department's director of research and development, asserting that the United States "must assess the values involved for inclusion in reparations accounts."[55] Less than a month later – this time in a personal letter to General Oliver P. Echols, who had been his deputy in Berlin before returning to Washington to become director of the War Department's Civil Affairs Division – Clay repeated with considerably less restraint what he had written to General Aurand. Claiming not to know what Washington's policy was, he said that the United States was taking, through FIAT, all possible information with respect to trade processes and advanced scientific thought. Observing that when the United States stopped gathering information needed to prosecute the war with Japan it entered "squarely into the commercial field," he concluded that "we

51 Clay to Noce, CC-7866, Jan. 30, 1947, copy in NA, RG 260, box 20-3/5, app. 8 to draft history of FIAT, period 1 July 1946 . . .
52 Green, "Last Call for Germany," *Federal Science Progress* 1 (Feb. 1947): 24.
53 War Dept. to Clay, Feb. 18, 1947, NA, RG 165, box 354, folder: WDSCA 387.6, Sec. IX; Clay to AGWAR, CC-8116, Feb. 21, 1947, copy in "History of the Field Information Agency, Technical (FIAT)," vol. 2, app. 10, NA, RG 319, Office of the Chief of Military History, Historical Manuscript File; War Dept. to OMGUS, Feb. 25, 1947, NA, RG 165, box 354, WDSCA 387.6, Sec. IX.
54 Routheau to Deputy Chief of Staff, War Dept., New Developments Division, Apr. 1, 1946, NA, RG 165, New Developments Division Decimal Files, box 136.
55 Clay to Aurand, Sept. 9, 1946, NA, RG 260, OMGUS Decimal Filed, box 120.

are perhaps doing the same thing that Russia is doing in taking current production from Germany without accounting, and that France is doing in removing capital equipment from Germany without accounting."[56] Finally, responding to a request by Echols's successor for a formal proposal on the matter, Clay responded on January 22, 1947, by quoting his letter to Echols: "I believe that the work accomplished by FIAT will prove to be mainly reparations to the United States from Germany," and that "steps should be taken to evaluate the information in sufficient detail to permit an accounting under reparations with our Allies and also in the final accounting with the German government."[57]

Despite Clay's recommendations, despite a great deal of internal discussion about what to do, and despite the existence of hundreds of public and private statements and estimates of the immense value of the FIAT removals, no evaluation ever took place. Virtually no one in Washington wanted to do the evaluations, and the Commerce, Navy, State, and War departments resisted actively, albeit for different reasons. On August 29, 1947, Charles E. Saltzman, the State Department's designated assistant secretary for occupied areas, informed the War Department that Clay's suggestion that the FIAT removals be valued for reparation accounting had "been discussed at considerable length in the State Department," and that "the conclusion is that the disadvantages very definitely outweigh the advantages" of doing so. Although Clay had implied that evaluation would distinguish American conduct "from improper Soviet and French" reparations removals, Saltzman continued, State Department officials believe it to be "far safer . . . for the United States . . . to continue to assert that it has derived no special advantage from the FIAT material" because it "has been put in the public domain." Clearly reflecting fears that an American statement of reparations receipts released in March 1947 during the Moscow meeting of the Council of Foreign Ministers would be exposed as fraudulent, Saltzman wrote:

To admit liability for a charge to the United States on reparation account and to attempt valuation of the information would leave the United States open to Soviet propaganda that our reparation recovery from Germany was

56 Clay to Echols, Oct. 4, 1946, NA, RG 165, box 351, folder: WDSCA 387.6, Sec. IV.
57 Jean Edward Smith, ed., *The Papers of General Lucius D. Clay: Germany, 1945–1949*, 2 vols. (Bloomington, Ind., 1974), 1:305–6.

in reality far greater than we reported. The Soviet *ad hominem* attack at the Council of Foreign Ministers, Moscow, 1947, that the United States had derived enormous reparations from the use of German patents point to the danger of recognizing a charge against the reparation account for the FIAT materials.[58]

Regarding Clay's argument that the higher level of American industrial development made the FIAT material more valuable to the United States than to other nations, Saltzman countered that "the [State] Department cannot agree." Since the information was available to all countries at nominal cost, "it could be as well argued that the more backward countries industrially derive proportionately greater benefit than the United States."

Furthermore, Saltzman's letter continued, charging the FIAT removals against the U.S. share of reparations raised two major practical problems, one domestic, the other international. Domestically, evaluation of the FIAT removals would give rise to "serious internal accounting problems," because the agencies benefiting from the German know-how "do not wish to have their appropriations charged to the full value at which" it would be "carried in the United States reparation account." Internationally, State Department officials believed that "it would not be possible" to get other nations to charge the FIAT information against their reparation accounts. Even if they agreed in principle, however, "the task of making equitable allocations among the various countries would be insuperable."[59]

CONCLUSIONS AND OBSERVATIONS

On American Reparations Receipts

Although neither the Americans nor the Germans (who tried without success) established a precise value of the FIAT removals, the popular and enduring myth that the United States took few, if any, reparations from Germany after the Second World War – a myth that I heard the U.S. ambassador to the Federal Republic of Germany repeat in Nuremberg as late as May 23, 1986 – obviously needs to be

---

58 Press Release, March 26, 1947, *Department of State Bulletin* 16 (1947): 609.
59 Saltzman to Noce, Aug. 29, 1947, NA, RG 165, box 357, folder: WDSCA 387.6, Sec. XV.

dispelled.[60] The actions and reactions of the American takers and the German givers, as well as the various statements and informal evaluations on the part of the American and German principals, show that the amount and the value were by no means insignificant. In fact, the figures bandied about by the Russians and their friends and dismissed by State Department officials as "fantastic" are probably not far from the mark.[61]

On the Question of Legality

Germans and Americans sometimes questioned the propriety of the FIAT program under existing international law, but the Americans went ahead, thinking up arguments as they went along. For example, Under Secretary of State William L. Clayton told a committee of the Congress in June 1945 that the United States had a "claim against all German inventions made during the war," because the "main reason" for German research and development was to overthrow the United States and its allies by military force.[62] Other arguments could be cited, but none was as clear and direct as the one used by John C. Green, the OTS director, in testimony before the committee of the Congress early in 1947: "The fundamental justification of this activity is that we won the war and the Germans did not. If the Germans had won the war, they would be over here in Schenectady and Chicago and Detroit and Pittsburgh, doing the same things."[63]

On the Resumption of German Research

The FIAT program had profound effect on the postwar resumption of German research and thus on the rate of German economic recov-

60 Richard R. Burt, "Beyond the Zero Hour: The Creation of a Civic Culture in Postwar Germany," speech given at the German-American Institute, Amerika-Haus, Nürnberg, May 23, 1986, p. 40; copy in my possession. For an earlier, similar statement that the Americans made no reparations demands, see Harry S Truman, *Memoirs*, vol. 2, *Years of Trial and Hope, 1946–1952* (Garden City, N.Y., 1956), 238.

61 See *FRUS 1947*, vol. 2, *Council of Foreign Ministers; Germany and Austria* (Washington, D.C., 1972), 259–60, for Molotov's reference to a figure of $10 billion at the Moscow Council of Foreign Ministers, and SWNCC 328/3, May 19, 1947, NA, RG 218, JCS Central Decimal Files, CCS 007, (3-13-45), Sec. 7, for State Department reference to Molotov's "fantastic" figures and "unsupported charges."

62 U.S. Congress, 79th Congress, Senate, *Hearings before a Subcommittee of the Committee on Military Affairs*, June 25, 1945, p. 60.

63 U.S. Congress, 80th Congress, House, *Hearings before the Subcommittee of the Committee on Appropriations*, Feb. 26, 1947, p. 120.

ery. Although they were permitted to resume peaceful research under Allied Control Council Law No. 25 and encouraged to do so by American policy and public statements, such as Secretary of State James F. Byrnes's speech in Stuttgart in September 1946, German research agencies and firms reportedly held back for fear that investigators would have access to their laboratories, research facilities, and findings. Germans discussed among themselves the "sensitive question of the intellectual plunder of German industry by representatives of foreign firms" ("die heikle Frage der geistigen Ausraubung der deutschen Industrie durch ausländische Firmenvertreter").[64] The Hessian Economics Ministry official (Dr. Friedrich Frowein) who had undertaken to develop a bizonal industrial research plan at the request of the British/American Bizonal Bipartite Economic Control Group, reported informally after meetings with industry representatives in Stuttgart, Mannheim, Munich, Frankfurt, Düsseldorf, and Hannover that in every meeting the question of the FIAT investigations came up. A number of firms were apparently inclined to hold back on their research, he concluded in his final report, observing in fact that problems had increased of late because the Americans had insisted on more and more details in the quarterly research control reports that Germans had to submit in accord with Allied Control Council Law No. 25.[65] A report of May 1, 1949, prepared for the German Office of Peace Questions by an institute under the directorship of Gustav von Schmoller, the world-famous German economist, stated that "many entrepreneurs," fearing that "newly developed knowledge will fall into the hands of unauthorized persons; yes, into the hands of foreign competitors, prefer to forgo scientific research and development as long as the current regulations are in effect."[66] Finally, a published account of a meeting in Göttingen of representatives of German research control agencies on May

---

64 "Auszug aus Aktenvermerk über die 8. Sitzung 'Forschungskontrolle' im Länderrat," March 25, 1947, HSTA Stuttgart, EA 6/3, 321.
65 Wirtschaftsministerium Württemberg-Baden, Forschungsüberwachung, "Aktenvermerk zur 12. Sitzung Länderrat Arbeitsausschuss Forschungsüberwachung," Aug. 28, 1947, BA, Z 1/424, pp. 182ff.; "Industrie-Forschungsplan für die Bizone," Apr. 4, 1948, BA, A 1/424, pp. 15ff.
66 Institut für Besatzungsfragen Tübingen, "Einwirkungen der Besatzungsmächte auf die westdeutsche Wirtschaft. Dargestellt im Auftrag des Deutschen Büros für Friedensfragen mit Unterstützung des Büros der Ministerpräsidenten" (Nur für den Dienstgebrauch), May 1, 1949, esp. pp. 37–8.

25, 1949, refers to their discussion of the implementing regulations for Law No. 25, which some believed to be the means by which the victors continued to engage in industrial espionage.[67]

On the FIAT Program and the Marshall Plan

In defending his program against those who would have terminated it in the interests of German economic recovery, John C. Green once wrote that FIAT operations had made German technology known to American industry as never before. "In fact," he asserted, "the very publicity which has been given to German industry by our program should react as an advertisement."[68] Although this is not the place to develop the theme, once the Americans decided to sponsor and underwrite a general European economic recovery program under the Marshall Plan, there appears to have been almost universal agreement in the United States that the program could not succeed without major industrial input from Germany. While the reasons given varied, and they included political, ideological, humanitarian, and economic elements as well as considerations of American power and position in the Cold War, unquestionably they also included American conceptions of the vitality and past performance of German science and industry. Those conceptions, which did not originate with the FIAT program, were in fact verified and strengthened by what the postwar scientific and technical investigators brought home with them in their baggage.

On FIAT as a Conveyor Belt for Future Business Connections

The FIAT handbook for investigators warned early on that "investigators may . . . be approached by German nationals with a view to establishing commercial contacts."[69] But there was obviously no way to control what went on in the field between investigators and their "targets" in the presence of nothing more than four walls – or

67 Thomas Stamm, *Zwischen Staat and Selbstverwaltung: Die deutsche Forschung im Wiederaufbau, 1945–1965* (Cologne, 1981), 56.
68 Green to Draper [draft, not sent], Jan. 22, 1947, NA, RG 40, box 156.
69 FIAT, Handbook, Sept. 6, 1945, NA, RG 260, box 17/14. For references to problems in controlling the investigators, see Green to Haertel, March 14, 1946, NA, RG 40, box 156; Reiss to Green, Progress Report No. 6, June 28, 1946, NA, RG 40, box 26; and Reiss to Unit Chiefs, July 16, 1946, NA, RG 40, box 99.

what was left of them in postwar Germany. Available records show that investigators, particularly those with previous German business connections, were "very hard to handle," that they sometimes "used their FIAT investigations merely as a pretext to get into Germany," that they were often more interested in their own private affairs than in completing their FIAT missions, and that there was no way to stop them from visiting their properties or their former representatives once they were in Germany. Even those who faithfully carried out and completed their FIAT missions could, as a matter of policy, ask for extensions "to conduct private affairs" before they returned to the United States.[70] A particularly revealing illustration of the conveyor-belt function of FIAT may be found in the autobiography of Karl Winnacker, a former I.G. Farben director whom the Americans removed in 1945, who then gardened for two years before he returned to Farbwerke Höchst, A.G., eventually to serve as chairman of the board. In commenting on the immediate postwar visits of chemists and industrialists who "all wanted to profit as much as possible from our technical knowledge," Winnacker named R. Lindley Murray, the president of American Hooker Company of Niagara Falls as an exception. "He took from his briefcase a whole batch of drawings, spread them across my table and asked me to agree to a detailed exchange of knowledge about the electrolysis cells of Hooker and Höchst." "In fact," Winnacker noted without giving further details, "we did come to a friendly arrangement about this," adding that "Murray's company eventually operated an electrolysis plant constructed . . . and based on our principle."[71]

70 Green to Haertel, March 14, 1946, NA, RG 40, box 156.
71 Karl Winnacker, *Challenging Years: My Life in Chemistry,* trans. David Goodman (London, 1972), 116–17.

10

American Deconcentration Policy in the Ruhr Coal Industry

ALBERT DIEGMANN

After the Second World War, the coal, iron, and steel industries indisputably represented the leading sectors of the German economy. Coal was the most important source of energy for steel making as well as for generation of electricity; iron and steel were the decisive basic ingredients not only of war production but also of peace time economy.

The heavy industries of the Ruhr were highly concentrated and cartelized. Beginning at the turn of the century, this trend had increased during the Weimar Republic and had reached it speak under National Socialism. In particular, coal and steel had been strongly integrated into the so-called *Verbundwirtschaft*. The motive for this process was the desire of the combines to secure the source of basic production inputs, raw materials and energy. In 1945, 55 percent of coal mining was combined with the iron industry technically, economically, and now by ownership: technically through the exchange of fuels and energy, economically through the harmonization of investments and of profits and losses, organically through the combination of mines and iron factories into integrated business concerns. The *Verbundwirtschaft* represented a vertical organization structure of the production from the raw material to the finished product.[1] This connection was especially marked in the concern of the Vereinigte Stahlwerke (United Steel Works). Founded in 1926, this company, through its subsidiary Gelsenkirchener Bergwerks-A.G., extracted 19 percent of the total hard coal output, which amounted to about 35 percent of *Verbundkohle* (bound coal).[2]

---

1 *Die Neuordnung der Eisen- und Stahlindustrie im Gebiet der Bundesrepublik Deutschland: Ein Bericht der Stahltreuhändervereinigung* (Munich and Berlin, 1954), 9–15.
2 Volker Berghahn, *Unternehmer und Politik in der Bundesrepublik* (Frankfurt am Main, 1985), 95.

One of the principles of Allied Occupation policy was the deconcentration of the German economy – that is, the liquidation of conglomerations of economic power that yielded political influence or power. The Allies were convinced that the Ruhr combines were not only guilty of having supported the rise of National Socialism, but also of having provided the basis for German war production and for nearly six years of warfare. When the fighting ceased, the policy of the occupying powers, understandably, was vigorously directed against cartels and concerns. The Allies pursued two objectives that seemed contradictory but really were complementary: first, the negative objective of breaking the German potential for aggression; and second, the positive objective of the reconstruction of a competitive economy.

Moreover, in the case of German heavy industry, not only domestic consumers were affected by the banked prices but also – and this was especially true for coal – foreign buyers who depended upon supplies of German coal. The predominant role of Ruhr coal in the economic reconstruction of the European nations was emphasized immediately after the end of the war. Thus deconcentration policy always had an international dimension. Deconcentration and decartelization not only were problems of the German economic structure but also had European implications. This aspect delivered a grave argument for the enforcement of deconcentration measures.

The subject of this essay is the question how far the occupying powers had implemented their policy before the provisional settlement in the spring of 1951. This account will take into consideration the development and the changes of position on the issue, especially by the Americans. An interesting question is why the Allied powers, and here again particularly the Americans, insisted upon deconcentration even at a time when discussions were under way to mitigate or lift political and economic restrictions, such as those detailed in the Occupation Statute. Why did the Allies retain their reserved rights just in the field of deconcentration?

EARLY DECONCENTRATION PLANNING

On December 22, 1945, the British Military Government seized the Ruhr coal mines and placed them under the supervision of an agency called the North German Coal Control (NGCC).[3] Management

---

3 Werner Abelshauser, *Der Ruhrkohlenbergbau seit 1945: Wiederaufbau, Krise, Anpassung* (Munich, 1984), 20ff., explains the reasons for the taking over of the coal mines.

remained in the hands of Germans; no encroachments upon the structure of the companies took place, and the terms of ownership were not touched. Even the centralized sales agencies of the coal syndicates kept operating, under British control[4] – in a time of acute coal need they were simply indispensable. Although the Rheinisch–Westfälisches Kohlensyndikat had been dissolved formally in September 1945, the British continued to use its machinery. In October 1946, the North German Coal Distribution Office (NGCDO) was set up as the central sales agency of North German Coal Control.

The reorganization of heavy industry through the dissolution of cartels and concerns was first envisaged in a plan of the Metallurgy Branch, Trade and Industry Division of the British Military Government dated July 6, 1946.[5] As a transition measure, it provided for the partition of the concerns through the separation of iron and steel works. Such newly formed companies should be confined to only one stage of the production process; that means that the vertical structure of organization of *Verbundwirtschaft* should be disbanded. Responsible for the implementation of this plan was the North German Iron and Steel Control (NGISC). "Operation Severance" began in January 1947. By April 1948, the NGISC had set up twenty-five leasing companies, so-called Severance Companies (Betriebsführungsgesellschaften), to which single iron and steel firms were handed over in trust, but without transferring ownership titles. The shares of these companies were held by a German Trustees Administration (Treuhandverwaltung) established for this purpose.[6]

In contrast, the deconcentration plan for the coal industry was never executed. "Plan Segregation" had earmarked all coal mines for separation from steel works and provided for their separate reorganization. The plan failed because the U.S. Military Government (OMGUS) opposed it, pleading for reasons of economy that mines should remain with steel enterprises, and thus for the retention of the integration, at least to a certain degree.[7]

---

4 Werner Mielert, "Die verschenkte Kontrolle: Bestimmungsgründe und Grundsätze der britischen Kohlenpolitik im Ruhrbergbau 1945–1948," in Dietmar Petzina and Walter Euchner, eds., *Wirtschaftspolitik im britischen Besatzungsgebiet 1945–1949* (Düsseldorf, 1984), 105–19, esp. 108.
5 *Neuordnung der Eisen- und Stahlindustrie*, 59.   6 Ibid., 63–4.
7 Hubert G. Schmidt, "Reorganization of the West German Coal and Iron and Steel Industries under the Allied High Commission for Germany, 1949–1952," Historical Division, Office of the U.S. High Commissioner for Germany, Research Project No. 129, mimeographed manuscript, Sept. 1952, p. 15.

American decartelization policy did not occur in the Ruhr until late 1948. In the Potsdam Protocol of August 2, 1945, the "Big Three," Truman, Stalin, and Attlee (who had succeeded Churchill as British prime minister during the Berlin Conference), had reached agreement on the deconcentration of the German economy. Article 12 of the economic principles read: "At the earliest practicable date, the German economy shall be decentralized for the purpose of eliminating the present excessive concentration of economic power as exemplified in particular by cartels, syndicates, trusts and other monopolistic arrangements."[8] The directive of the Joint Chiefs of Staff for the U.S. Military Governor, JCS 1067, provided in Article 3 (c) that "[the] German economic structure shall also be decentralized."[9] Article 36 prohibited generally cartels that eliminated market conditions through the regulation of production and pricing, exclusive exchange of technical information, and allocation of sales areas. Article 37 declared the dispersion of ownership and the control of the German economy to be official government policy.

In February 1947, the British and American military governments simultaneously enacted laws for the prohibition of excessive concentration of the German economy: Ordinance 78 in the British Zone of Occupation, Law 56 in the U.S. zone.[10] Cartels were outlawed generally because their very purpose was to restrict trade through devices such as price fixing, allocation of markets or quotas, and supervision of technology. The provisions of JCS 1067 were thus translated into enforceable law. The British version, however, explicitly exempted the Ruhr industries from the ordinance.[11]

In July 1947, a new directive for the U.S. Military Governor, JCS 1779, superseded JCS 1067. Article 21, section a, called for the following:

Pending agreement among the occupying powers you will in your zone prohibit all cartels and cartel-like organizations, and effect a dispersion of ownership and control of German industry through the dissolution of such combines, mergers, holding companies and interlocking directorates which represent an actual or potential restraint of trade or may dominate or substantially influence the policies of governmental agencies. You will not, however, prohibit governmental regulation of prices or monopolies subject

---

8 *FRUS: The Conference of Berlin (Potsdam) 1945,* 2 vols. (Washington, D.C., 1960), 2:1504.
9 U.S. Department of State, ed., *Germany 1947–1949: The Story in Documents* (Washington, D.C., 1950), 22–33.
10 Ibid., 344–8.
11 Lucius D. Clay, *Decision in Germany* (Garden City, N.Y., 1950), 326–7.

to governmental regulation, in fields where competition is impracticable. Insofar as possible, you will coordinate your action in this field with the commanders of other zones of occupation.[12]

Section (c) of the same article emphasized the advantages of free enterprise. Consequently, eventual socialization was ruled out; the decision to expand public ownership was left to a freely elected German government, which at that time was, of course, not foreseeable at all.

The U.S. military governor, General Lucius D. Clay, even favored a long postponement of such a vote in order to avoid a political controversy, which in his opinion would only serve the purposes of the Communists. In the summer of 1947, Clay advocated public trusteeship for the Ruhr industries.[13]

Before fall 1947, however, OMGUS had no direct grip in the Ruhr area because of the autonomy of the military governors in their respective zones. The Americans possessed only limited rights in other zones by means of the Allied Control Council, which was competent in all matters affecting more than one zone or Germany as a whole. Through the seizure of the coal mines in December 1945, followed by the taking over of the iron and steel industry in August 1946, the British had successfully rejected French and Soviet claims; since 1945, the French had sought to separate the Rhineland from Germany and international control of the Ruhr; meanwhile, the Soviets constantly reiterated their demand for participation in control of the Ruhr, stating their case emphatically during the sessions of the Council of Foreign Ministers.

The picture changed in the fall of 1947. With the establishment of the Bizone at the beginning of the year, the Americans had secured for themselves decisive influence in the British zone. Financial reasons were the prime factor leading to this thorough change in power relations. However, OMGUS obtained an institutionalized right of codetermination in the Ruhr industry only after the coal conference at Washington.[14]

The bilateral, Anglo–American conversations on Ruhr coal took place in the U.S. capital between August 12 and September 10, 1947. First priority was the search for means of increasing coal production.

---

12 *Germany 1947–1949*, 34–41.   13 Clay, *Decision in Germany*, 321.
14 For documentation of the Coal Conference, see *FRUS 1947*, vol. 2, *Council of Foreign Ministers; Germany and Austria* (Washington, D.C., 1972), 909–77. This is only a small selection; the complete documentation can be found in NA, RG 59, 862.6363, box 6843.

The Americans also embraced the opportunity to discuss the ownership question, which in their view was equally important to the task of raising output as the problem of housing or food.[15] Uncertainty of ownership, the Americans argued, hampered to a considerable degree efforts to raise urgently required investment capital for the industry.[16]

The results of the conference were twofold: first, the formation of a joint control organization for the Ruhr coal mine industry, the U.K./U.S. Coal Control Group (U.K./U.S. CCG);[17] and second, the formation of a trusteeship administration, the German Coal Mines Management (Deutsche Kohlenbergbauleitung, DKBL).[18] This German agency was given wide authority for the administration of the mines; it was supposed to supervise the management and was made responsible for an efficient, economic operation of the enterprises. The DKBL was to work under the superintendence of the U.K./U.S. CCG. It was believed that German direction would effect an increase in coal mining.

On the other hand, in the conference the Americans succeeded in postponing the decision on the ownership of heavy industry companies for five years. Thus for the time being, the British plans for socialization in the Rhine and Ruhr area had been wrecked.

At the London session of the Council of Foreign Ministers on December 11, 1947, Marshall, Bevin, and Bidault (as well as Molotov) approved Supplementary Principles to Govern the Treatment of Germany, which had already been proposed by Bevin at Moscow, in the spring of 1947.[19] According to these directions, the competent German agencies were charged with working out recommendations for the deconcentration of the corresponding industries and were asked to submit their findings to the Allied Control Council. Secretary of State Marshall insisted on an addition in the pertinent paragraph:

26. . . . Proposals for the public ownership of certain industries shall be regarded as one method of carrying out this provision *provided* such proposals represent the free choice of the German people [emphasis added].[20]

---

15 Tel. 1452, Murphy to SecState, June 17, 1947, *FRUS 1947*, 2:924; tel. 3638, Lovett to Douglas and Clay, Aug. 22, 1947, ibid., 950.
16 To Clay, this argument was valid still in 1948, after the issuance of Law 75. Clay, *Decision in Germany*, 196.
17 Agreed Papers by the Bipartite Board: BIB/P(47)79 and BIB/P(47)80, *FRUS 1947*, 2:940–4.
18 Memo by K. C. Bolton, "Report – Anglo American Conversations regarding German Coal Production," Sept. 22, 1947, *FRUS 1947*, 2:962–6.
19 *Neuordnung der Eisen- und Stahlindustrie*, 34.   20 Ibid., 35.

With this qualifying condition, Marshall once more rejected the British plans for the socialization of the heavy industries. The same reservation had been frequently emphasized by the U.S. Zone commander, Clay. Moreover, Clay was convinced that the longer one could delay the discussion of the subject, the less the Germans themselves would be inclined to vote for socialization, once they were acquainted with and appreciated the advantages of a competitive economy with free enterprise.[21] Clay also favored a slower pace of decartelization. He advocated his view that the enhancement of production had priority and that interference with the structure of concerns could only hinder this aim.[22]

LAW 75 AND ITS CONSEQUENCES

The conflict of the American and British occupying powers over the question of ownership was not settled before the end of 1948. Negotiations on a joint regulation of the deconcentration and decartelization of the coal, iron, and steel industries had commenced in the summer of 1948. Great Britain pleaded for the appointment of a single custodian in order to keep the pretension to socialization alive. The United States on the other hand intended to delegate the administration of heavy industry to German agencies.[23]

A compromise was reached in November, which essentially meant a success for the American objectives, but which was nevertheless acceptable to the British without their losing face.[24] On November 10, 1948, the British and U.S. military governments issued Law No. 75 simultaneously and with very similar wording.[25]

21 See, for instance, Horst Lademacher, "Die britische Sozialisierungspolitik im Rhein-Ruhr-Raum 1945–1948," in Claus Scharf and Hans-Jürgen Schröder, eds., *Die Deutschlandpolitik Grossbritanniens und die britische Zone 1945–1949* (Wiesbaden, 1979), 51–92, 83.
22 Tel. 1536, Murphy to SecState, June 24, 1947, *FRUS 1947*, 2:929; Edward N. Peterson, *The American Occupation of Germany: Retreat to Victory* (Detroit, 1978), 129–30; here Peterson renders the statement of the chief of the OMGUS Denazification Division, Bronson, of March 1948: "Clay stated to me that he had a responsibility for getting Germany economically on her feet and off the back of American taxpayers, that . . . the rule of reason would not permit the deconcentration measures at this time. . . . all hell broke loose. . . . I saw General Clay and he suggested that I meet with my staff again and tell them it wasn't a change of policy, it was a change of emphasis, a change of timing. . . ."
23 Schmidt, "Reorganization," 14.
24 Rudzio has pointed to the double-tracked British industry policy that was aimed at both socialization and decartelization. Wolfgang Rudzio, "Die ausgebliebene Sozialisierung an Rhein und Ruhr: Zur Sozialisierungspolitik von Labour-Regierung und SPD 1945–1948," *Archiv für Sozialgeschichte* 18 (1978):10.
25 Text of the laws in *Neuordnung der Eisen-und Stahlindustrie*, 319–25.

Law 75 represented the regulation of deconcentration and decartelization by making the coal, iron, and steel industries subject to reorganization. The ownership question was postponed again until a freely elected German government reached a decision. The DKBL remained the trustee for coal, now organized as a joint-stock company with the German Coal Sales Agency (Deutscher Kohlenverkauf, DKV)[26] and the Bergbaubedarf-Beschaffungszentrale (Coal Mines Procurement Agency) as subsidiary companies, supervised by the U.K./U.S. CCG, to which was assigned complete responsibility for the reorganization. Shortly afterward the DKBL was charged with the elaboration of deconcentration plans that were to be put forward to the Coal Control Group for approval.

These provisions are reminiscent of the results of the Washington coal talks. However, there existed some momentous differences: The decisions of the Washington conference had been aimed at the increase of coal output; those regarding control and management were but a few out of a catalog of measures to this end, whereas Law 75 was limited in its scope to reorganization by massive interventions in the structure of the Ruhr industry. Furthermore, in 1947 both occupying powers had just agreed upon a common policy which was now transformed into an effective law – at least in theory (we shall look at the reality shortly).

The objectives of Law 75 were stated in its preamble:[27] The first objective was the decentralization of the coal, iron, and steel industries to eliminate excessive concentrations of economic power, thus preventing the genesis of a new German war potential; here we find expressed the security aspect. The second but equally important objective was the recovery and reconstruction of the German economy, especially in the interest of Europe. Since 1947, in the context of the Marshall Plan, the vital significance of the Ruhr resources for the rehabilitation of the European economy had been stressed repeatedly, recognizing that they were indispensable for the reconstruction. The political motive of stabilizing a democratic development also played a part in the considerations.

---

26 The German Coal Sales Agency DKV had been established as successor organization to the North German Coal Distribution Office on February 4, 1948. It represented an exemption from the prohibition of cartels in order to regulate the coal trade centrally in view of the permanent coal shortage. Berghahn, *Unternehmer und Politik*, 105.
27 *Neuordnung der Eisen- und Stahlindustrie*, 89–90.

Law 75 was designed as a general framework, without specified provisions for implementation, which was left to regulations.[28] The British and the Americans, however, were not able to take joint steps, thus leaving Law 75 in the stage of mere intention.

Prior deconcentration policy was sharply criticized by the Ferguson Committee, set up by the U.S. Department of the Army. The Ferguson Report,[29] submitted in April 1949, is particularly revealing because it pointed out the principles of American deconcentration policy. OMGUS was reproached for deviating from these principles; the committee demanded a return to those aims. The report named as objectives of the decartelization program:

1. elimination of German war potential;
2. termination of the dominance of a few powerful entrepreneurs and financiers in industry;
3. restoration of a sound and democratic economy characterized by competition;
4. fostering of economic and political democracy; and
5. assistance in the economic restoration of Germany, which was also essential for the rest of (Western) Europe.

In contrast to the Military Government, the authors of the Ferguson Report held the view that consistent enforcement of decartelization would not hamper production but on the contrary increase productivity and consequently strengthen the German economy. The example of IG Farben was considered to be a clear-cut proof.

The Ferguson Committee strictly opposed socialization of the Ruhr industries, because this could mean the danger of a new concentration of power in the hands of the state, and with that an opportunity for the renewal of a potential of aggression. The criticism was directed at the provision of Law 75 leaving the decision on ownership to a German government.

Another finding one gains from the report is that neither OMGUS nor the U.S. government was unanimously agreed about the action in the decartelization policy.[30] Clearly recognizable was the conflict between hard-liners, who were determined to carry out deconcen-

---

28 Ibid.
29 Report of the Committee Appointed to Review the Decartelization Program in Germany to Secretary of the Army, NA, RG 59, 862.202/5-649, box 6705. This report referred in the first place to the implementation of Law 56.
30 See also Berghahn, *Unternehmer und Politik*, 88ff., 98–9.

tration as originally projected and without any cuts,[31] and those who advocated modification or even abandonment of the program.

The Ferguson Report had no great effect on American decartelization policy; its recommendations remained disregarded.[32] This indicates a change in attitude or at least priorities by the Truman administration. General Clay's view had largely prevailed in Washington. Nevertheless, this did not mean that the Americans were ready to relinquish the reorganization of the Ruhr industries, which was absolutely compatible with the economic and political aims.

In the occupation statute[33] the three Western powers reserved to themselves, besides demilitarization, Ruhr control, and foreign representation of the Federal Republic, rights in the fields of deconcentration and decartelization. Yet no substantial decisions concerning the structure of the heavy industries had been made; Law 75 had not been carried out.[34] Therefore the Americans began to consider a revision of the law. The reasons were manifold:

–inactivity of the Allied control organizations with respect to decartelization;
–unwillingness of the German trustee administration to put forward reorganization plans; understandably the Germans were not in a hurry as long as the occupying powers themselves did not take action;
–disagreement among the Allies on fundamental questions; the Americans and British were unable to come to an understanding on the implementation of the law.[35] Unsettled problems included

31 Clay even went so far to characterize some members of the OMGUS Decartelization Group as "extremists" who wanted to dismember the concerns into small units regardless of their economic viability. Clay, *Decision in Germany*, 331.
32 Peterson, *American Occupation*, 130.   33 *Germany 1947–1949*, 89ff.
34 Cf. tel. 386, Altaffer to State Dept., Oct. 18, 1949, NA, RG 59, 862.6362/10-1849, box 6816; Record of Meeting: Future Plans for the Decartelization–Deconcentration Program in Germany, Oct. 26, 1949, NA, RG 59, 862.602/10-2649, box 6810; memo, Baker, "Military Government Law 75 – Reorganization of the Ruhr Iron, Steel and Coal Industries," Nov. 3, 1949, NA, RG 466, HICOG, McCloy Papers, Top Secret General Records, box 1. Further proof is the instruction of the foreign ministers to the high commissioners of November 10, 1949 – suggested by Acheson – to press for the enforcement of Law 75; the foreign ministers of the three Western powers met in Paris, November 9–10, 1949. See Minutes of the Third Meeting of the Foreign Ministers (USDel/P(49)3 M'g), NA, RG 466, HICOG, McCloy Papers, Classified General Records, box 4. See also Schmidt, "Reorganization," 36.
35 In a preparatory memorandum for a meeting between Acheson and Franks, the British ambassador to Washington, Perkins, listed contested items in Anglo-American relations, with decartelization as one of the urgent problems. Perkins reproached the British with a lack of motivation. Memo, Perkins to SecState, Jan. 24, 1950, NA, RG 59, 611.41/1-2450, box 2768.

the degree of integration of coal and steel and the question of socialization[36] – the British had not yet abandoned this notion; and

–resolution in principle both of the U.S. government and the Allied High Commission to push forward the deconcentration.[37]

Two formal reasons made a new formulation necessary: the transition from Military Government to the civil administration of the Allied High Commission (AHC) and the admission of the French to the control groups, renamed Combined Coal Control Group (CCCG) and Combined Steel Group (CSG). These developments demanded the trizonal harmonization of the two laws 75,[38] which were so far only valid in their respective zones, and which now had to be made effective in the entire territory of the Federal Republic.

A new State Department directive of November 11, 1949, to the U.S. High Commissioner John J. McCloy[39] confirmed the known principles of deconcentration and decartelization and urged the speedy conclusion of current measures (which could only refer to the U.S. Zone of Occupation). The new intention was to hand responsibility over to the government of the Federal Republic of Germany as soon as possible and to reduce Allied intervention to a minimum. In the long run laws of the Federal Republic were supposed to replace laws of the Military Government. The directive left a wide scope of action to the high commissioner, since it did not comment on any of the contested points of conflict.[40]

During the course of the difficult and protracted negotiations on the revision of Law 75, especially representatives of the U.S. Element of the High Commission (HICOG) submitted numerous proposals and drafts. They recommended retention of the integration of coal and steel in order to create economically sound and competitive units in the iron and steel industry, but only to a degree that pre-

---

36 Tel. 3085, Acheson to McCloy, Dec. 1, 1949, NA, RG 466, HICOG, McCloy Papers, Classified General Records, box 5. Tel. 74, McCloy to HICOG Frankfurt, Dec. 17, 1949, ibid.

37 Memo, Byroade to McCloy, "Discussions in Washington," Feb. 1, 1950, ibid., box 7. Tel. 1097, Acheson to HICOG Frankfurt, Feb. 17, 1950, ibid., box 9. Minutes of 4th HICOG Staff Conference, Jan. 31, 1950, ibid., Staff Conference Meetings, box 1.

38 Tel. 3517, McCloy to SecState, Dec. 28, 1949 (session of the AHC), ibid., Classified General Records, box 3.

39 "Policy Directive for the U.S. High Commissioner for Germany," Nov. 17, 1949, *FRUS 1949*, vol. 3, *Council of Foreign Ministers; Germany and Austria* (Washington, D.C., 1974), 319–40; provisions regarding decartelization in articles 37 to 39, ibid., 328–9.

40 Schmidt, "Reorganization," 36–7.

cluded trade restrictions.[41] In a memorandum of November 22, 1949, a staff member of the Industry Division of HICOG called for the prevention of monopolistic practices of the DKV and its early dissolution.[42] The centralized sale of coal should soon prove to be one of the most aggravating issues not only for the drafting of the new law but also for its application.

Another conflict in the AHC arose over the preamble of the draft submitted by the Law Committee in mid-March 1950.[43] French High Commissioner François-Poncet protested against the declaration of intent to leave the solution of the ownership question to the Federal Republic's government.[44] Appealing to his government, he delayed the proclamation of the law for thirty days.[45] The State Department tried through the ambassador in Paris, David Bruce, to exert pressure on the French and to induce them to accept the law – and they succeeded: The French government took no further steps to postpone the project.[46] On May 16, 1950, AHC Law 27 became effective.[47]

LAW 27 AND DECARTELIZATION

Law 27 did not differ substantially from its predecessors. It created two distinct procedures for the reorganization of the coal, iron, and steel industry:[48]

1. Liquidation of concerns that represented excessive concentrations of economic power. Trustees were to be appointed to dissolve and

41 Report of the U.S. representative in CSG, Feb. 6, 1950, ibid., 38–9.
42 Memo, Griffin, Fuel and Power Branch, Industry Division, to Hanes, Director, Office of Economic Affairs, ibid., 41–2.
43 Tel. 1786, Webb to HICOG Frankfurt, Mar. 18, 1950, NA, RG 466, HICOG, McCloy Papers, Classified General Records, box 11. Tel. 119, McCloy to SecState, March 31, 1950, ibid. Tels. 1492, 1450, and 2245, Acheson to Douglas; Bruce; and McCloy, Apr. 3, 1950, ibid., box 12. Tels. 1579, 1534, and 2392, Acheson to Douglas; Bruce; and McCloy, Apr. 8, 1950, ibid. In an AHC session in January 1950, François-Poncet had proposed to enact the law as soon as possible without a preamble. Tel. 1, McCloy to SecState, Jan. 5, 1950, NA, RG 59, 762.0221/1-550, box 3835.
44 The French government had demanded a long-term retention of Allied control mechanisms, such as the International Authority for the Ruhr; see *aide mémoire*, March 1, 1950, encl. to office memo, Margolies to Jacobs, March 9, 1950, NA RG 59, 72.0221/5-950, box 3835.
45 Tel. 163, McCloy to SecState, Apr. 14, 1950, NA, RG 466, HICOG, McCloy Papers, Classified General Records, box 12.
46 Schmidt, "Reorganization," 56–7.
47 Text in *Neuordnung der Eisen- und Stahlindustrie*,341–57.   48 Ibid., 95.

capitalize the remainders of the assets left after the formation of unit companies.

2. Reorganization through the formation of unit companies. The assets of the old concerns were made subject to seizure and transfer to new independent companies.

Responsibility for the implementation of the reorganization was placed in the hand of the control groups, CSG and CCCG.

A number of questions, however, remained undecided. It was not clear whether Law 27 should be interpreted chiefly as a means for the elimination of economic concentration and prevention of the re-emergence of a war potential, or rather as reorganization for the purpose of economic recovery. In other words, which of the objectives outlined in the preamble should have priority? The law contained no information as to how far the reorganization should go, nor as to the permissible degree of vertical integration of coal and steel. The question of whether to end the trusteeship in case the Germans decided against public ownership remained unanswered. Again the solution of these problems had to be reserved for regulations that had to be negotiated among the Allies. The State Department did not share McCloy's inclination to settle these matters before publication; Washington was anxious to enact a harmonized law as quickly as possible.[49]

Thus foundations were laid for future conflicts, not only with the Germans but also among the Allies. This was even more true since at that time only the Americans seriously advocated the far-reaching breakup of the big combines. Yet the announcement of the Schuman Plan on May 9, 1950, promoted the readiness of the French to carry out deconcentration measures quickly, in order to secure German participation in the European Coal and Steel Pool. It is in this light that one has to look at some drastic changes of the French positions.

In September 1950, the U.S. member of the CSG, Clark, proposed an outline of characteristic features of the reorganization.[50] He recommended establishment of a large number of independent, economically sound, and competitive unit companies in the iron and steel industry. They should only be allowed to dispose of or to control colliery property in exceptional cases; integration should be per-

---

49 Schmidt, "Reorganization," 60–1.
50 Tel. 9, Hays to HICOG Frankfurt, Sept. 13, 1950, NA, RG 466, HICOG, McCloy Papers, Classified General Records, box 19.

mitted only when economic production could not be achieved otherwise, and if the capacity of the mines did not exceed the iron and steel works' consumption of coking coal.

Since August, a discussion had gone on in the Economics Committee of AHC concerning the DKBL and DKV. The U.S. representative pointed out that the functions of both DKBL and DKV were incompatible with the Allied decartelization policy. He demanded that the powers of the DKBL be restricted to cooperation in reorganizing the Ruhr coal mining industry; moreover, he called for the dissolution of the DKV, which he called a cartel, within six months.[51] The British and French, for the time being, favored retention of the DKV.[52] The French argued that a central coal sales agency was necessary to carry out the decisions of the International Authority for the Ruhr regarding the allocation of Ruhr coal for domestic consumption and export. The performance of the DKV supervised by the CCCG was said to protect German as well as foreign customers from secret arrangements.[53] The British representative saw no reason at all for the liquidation of an organization that worked well. The American representative insisted upon the independent sale of coal. On the basis of a memorandum of the CCCG, the controversy was finally settled. Early in October, the British and French agreed to a compromise to the effect that

1. central sales agencies with compulsory membership ran counter to the intentions of Law 27 and consequently were impermissible;
2. single coal mines were allowed to sell their own production separately but also to join collective marketing organizations unless the share in the total sale reached excessive proportions; and
3. for technical and economic reasons, integration of coal and steel should be maintained.[54]

Now the occupying powers appeared to have found a common purpose.

The first regulations pursuant to Law 27, issued in September 1950,[55] aroused vehement German protests. These arose in the first

---

51 Schmidt, "Reorganization," 86. *Chronological Record: Reorganization of the West German Coal and Iron and Steel Industries under Allied High Commission Law No. 27*, comp. Francis H. Baldy, ed. Historical Division, HICOG (n.p., 1952), 7–8, 10.
52 Tel. 2615, McCloy to SecState, Sept. 27, 1950, NA, RG 59, 850.33/9-2750, box 4945.
53 Schmidt, "Reorganization," 87.   54 Ibid., 89; *Chronological Record*, 14–15.
55 Regulations (Durchführungsverordnungen, DVO) Nos. 1, 2, and 3, Sept. 14, 1950, in Hubert G. Schmidt, ed., *Documents on the Reorganization of the West German Coal and Iron and*

place from the order to liquidate the six largest steel concerns before the completion of the corresponding reorganization plans.[56] In the subsequent exchange of notes and letters between the Federal Republic's government and Allied High Commission,[57] the following chief points were at stake:[58]

—size and number of the unit companies;
—coal–steel integration (*Verbundwirtschaft*); and
—dissolution of the DKV.

Regarding centralized coal sale, the French had altered their attitude radically. Meanwhile, impressed by arguments of the French Schuman Plan delegation led by Monnet, they regarded the continued existence of the German sales monopoly as an obstacle to the removal of the central buying agency of the French steel industry. Therefore they pleaded for the dissolution of the DKV, as the Americans did.[59] The present constellation of a largely cartelized economy would make dubious the success of the Schuman Plan, which designed a large common market with competition as one of its main features. The Americans took the High Authority of the Schuman Plan to be the proper body to regulate market problems and to avert renewed concentration processes in the heavy industries provided that it was vested with adequate powers. The U.S. government therefore insisted on the supranational organization of the community.[60]

As far as *Verbundwirtschaft* was concerned, the Americans were willing to permit a partial integration of the Ruhr industries. Steel

Steel Industries under the Allied High Commission for Germany, 1949–1952, Historical Division, HICOG (n.p., 1952), 32–7. Regulation No. 1 ordered the liquidation of the first six concerns on September 30: Vereinigte Stahlwerke AG; Fried. Krupp; Mannesmannröhren-Werke; Kloeckner-Werke AG; Hoesch AG, Gutehoffnungshütte Aktienverein für Bergbau und Hüttenbetrieb, Gutehoffnungshütte AG Oberhausen.

56 Tel. 165, McCloy to State Dept., Sept. 24, 1950, NA, RG 466, HICOG, McCloy Papers, Classified General Records, box 19. See also Schmidt, "Reorganization," 72.

57 For a selected but nevertheless detailed documentation, see *Neuordnung der Eisen- und Stahlindustrie*, 413–55.

58 Briefing Paper, Office of the U.S. High Commissioner for Germany: Nato Problems, Schuman Plan, German Participation, Feb. 2, 1951, *FRUS 1951*, vol. 4, *Europe: Political and Economic Developments* (Washington, D.C., 1985), 86–90.

59 A HICOG [?] memorandum informed about Monnet's suggestions for the dissolution of the DKV: "Monnet Views on Settlement under Law 27," Jan. 15, 1950 [sic, 1951], NA, RG 466, HICOG, McCloy Papers, Classified General Records, box 6.

60 See, for example, the joint comment by the State Department and the ECA on developments in the Schuman Plan negotiations: tel. 1717, Webb to Bruce, Oct. 3, 1950, *FRUS 1950*, 3:754–8.

plants should, in the interest of efficient production, be allowed to cover their requirements of energy from mines that they controlled, but without enjoying unsuitable advantages vis–à–vis their competitors in times of coal shortages.[61] Precisely this fear turned the French into opponents of a too close integration of coal and steel.[62]

The objectives of HICOG can be characterized, to use a short formula, as consistent decartelization and moderate deconcentration. McCloy and his staff – here should be mentioned especially the general counsel, Robert Bowie – defended the U.S. point of view in numerous meetings with representatives of the government of the Federal Republic, the trade unions, and Ruhr industrialists.[63] They exerted considerable pressure on the Germans,[64] telling them unmistakably that progress with respect to the revision of the occupation statute was contingent upon their willingness to cooperate in the field of decartelization. First of all, the HICOG people stressed the connection between decartelization and the Schuman Plan. The Federal Republic's government and the managers supposed that with the Schuman Plan they had found an instrument to lift Allied controls and restrictions like deconcentration. The Americans, no doubt, had a very strong interest in German participation in the Schuman Plan, but they were not willing as a price to sacrifice de-

---

61 Tel. 6850, McCloy to SecState, Feb. 19, 1951, *FRUS 1951*, 4:91; Minutes of 63rd HICOG Staff Conference, Feb. 27, 1951, NA, RG 466, HICOG, McCloy Papers, Staff Conference Meetings, box 2.

62 In December 1950, during the Paris Schuman Plan negotiations, the French advanced the same arguments in relation to *Verbundwirtschaft:* As long as the coal–steel integration in the Ruhr industries was not largely dissolved, the resistance of French governmental and industrial circles (especially of the steel cartel) against the anticartel provisions of the Schuman Plan treaty could not be overcome. Tel. 3484, Bruce to State Dept. (tel. 413, HICOG Frankfurt for Bowie), Dec. 18, 1950, NA, RG 466, HICOG, McCloy Papers, Classified General Records, box 13.

63 As early as September 1949, regular AHC meetings with Federal Chancellor Adenauer were taking place. Some of McCloy's reports on these meetings to the State Department can be found in *FRUS,* but not all are printed completely. The first meeting after the issuance of the regulations took place on September 23, 1950: Minutes of 20th Meeting of AHC with Adenauer, HICOM/FED/M(50)11, Sept. 23, 1950, NA, RG 466, HICOG, McCloy Papers, Classified General Records, box 19.

64 See, e.g., McCloy's report on a meeting with Adenauer after an AHC session: tel. 211, McCloy to SecState, Oct. 13, 1950, ibid., box 20. Robert Bowie, as General Counsel of HICOG competent in decartelization matters, reported in an interview with Klaus Schwabe on October 4, 1988, at which I was present, about several meetings with German industrialists. Bowie characterized the managers as the main obstacle to a quick agreement. He said he had clearly explained to them that the Americans were determined to go ahead with the decartelization policy, preferably with German consent; in case of protracted opposition, the Americans would proceed without or even against them.

cartelization policy.[65] Consequently these hopes of the Germans were not fulfilled.[66]

At a conference of French and U.S. representatives of AHC with Jean Monnet at Paris in December 1950, all participants declared general agreement as to the valuation of Law 27.[67] Adherence to the decartelization program would be a precondition for attaining the aims of the Schuman Plan; Law 27 and the anticartel provisions of the coal and steel community were said to be consistent and complementary to each other. Fears of the French government that the Americans would diminish their efforts were, if not removed, at least considerably eased after this meeting.

Bilateral, German–American negotiations on the application of Law 27 had been taking place at the Petersberg since January 1951.[68] François-Poncet left it to the Americans, since French interests coincided largely with those of the United States. British High Commissioner Kirkpatrick kept himself in the background because British positions had hardly taken effect. Yet Kirkpatrick refrained from any action that could have disturbed the course of the negotiations.[69]

Conversations between McCloy and Federal Minister of Economics Ludwig Erhard were held informally and confidentially. McCloy contested the future of the DKV, repeatedly indicating that, as a coal sales monopoly, it was incompatible with Law 27. He also agreed with the French position that emphasized the DKV's incompatibility with the principles of the Schuman Plan. According to Monnet, the German sales monopoly would cause unsurmountable difficulties in breaking up the French steel cartel, which would furthermore, in case of the continued existence of the DKV, insist on maintaining a central import agency for coal. There was a danger that the coal and

65 Memo, Thorp to SecState, "Current Status of the Schuman Plan Negotiations," Dec. 14, 1950, *FRUS 1950*, 3:765. Tel. 4213, Bruce to SecState, Jan. 20, 1951, NA, RG 59, 850.33/1-2051, box 4947.
66 Klaus Schwabe, " 'Ein Akt konstruktiver Staatskunst': Die USA und die Anfänge des Schuman-Plans," in idem, ed., *Die Anfänge des Schuman-Plans 1950/51* (Baden-Baden, 1988), 211–39, 235ff.
67 "Memo of Meeting held 19 December on Coal and Steel Problems," Dec. 29, 1950, NA, RG 466, HICOG, McCloy Papers, Classified General Records, box 23. See Schmidt, "Reorganization," 97–8.
68 Schmidt, "Reorganization," 111–15.
69 On January 30, 1951, Bowie reported in the HICOG Staff Conference on the conversations and on the attitude of the French and British toward these developments. Minutes of 61st HICOG Staff Conference, Jan. 30, 1951, NA, RG 466, HICOG, McCloy Papers, Staff Conference Meetings, box 2.

steel community would become a European supercartel, which was not in the French and much less in the American interest. Consequently, McCloy was not ready to compromise with regard to the liquidation of the DKV, although he acknowledged the necessity of a transition period for the establishment of a decentralized sales organization.[70] Deliberations went on for more than two months. On February 12, 1951, the first decisive breakthrough came when McCloy and Erhard achieved a formula acceptable to both sides.[71] Certain steel firms were permitted to receive up to 75 percent of their coal supplies from mines that they owned or controlled. The parties agreed to liquidate the DKV after a period of transition. Now all was set for a successful settlement of the negotiations.

Finally on March 14, 1951, Adenauer produced a compromise proposal set forth in a letter to the High Commission.[72] For publicity reasons, it had been suggested that the proposal should emanate from the chancellor. Adenauer summarized the attitude of the Federal Republic toward decartelization Law 27. He agreed to the establishment of twenty-four unit companies in the iron and steel industry – in this point slightly deviating from a draft of the CSG; he made concrete recommendations for the allocation of coal mines to iron works, thereby reducing their quota in the total output to about 16 percent;[73] and he presented a plan for the gradual liquidation of the DKV.[74] Adenauer made effectiveness of the Schuman Plan a precondition for implementing these measures, since the High Authority was supposed to assume decisive functions of market regulation.[75]

The Allied High Commission accepted Adenauer's proposals on March 30, 1951.[76] On the political level the negotiations were thereby terminated, even though the Allied–German exchange of notes continued. Indeed in the future, massive conflicts about de-

70 "McCloy Negotiations," Dec. 14, 1950, *FRUS 1950*, vol. 3, *Western Europe* (Washington, D.C., 1977), 765. Tel. 4213, Bruce to SecState, Jan. 20, 1951, NA, RG 59, 850.33/1-2051, box 4947.
71 McCloy to Adenauer, Feb. 12, 1951, NA, RG 466, HICOG, McCloy Papers, Eyes Only General Records (1 box).
72 *Neuordnung der Eisen- und Stahlindustrie*, p. 455ff.
73 Schmidt, "Reorganization," 118. *Neuordnung der Eisen- und Stahlindustrie*, 190, figures the quota at less than 15 percent.
74 The DKV was liquidated in April 1953 and replaced by six sales agencies coordinated by the Gemeinschaftsorganisation Ruhrkohle (GEORG, Ruhr Joint Services Organization), which, in turn, was dissolved in 1956 upon the insistence of the High Authority of the European Coal and Steel community.
75 Tel. 7411, McCloy to SecState, Mar. 15, 1951, *FRUS 1951*, 4:102–3.
76 Cf. *Chronological Record*, 40ff.; *Neuordnung der Eisen- und Stahlindustrie*, 457–8.

cartelization and reorganization were to occur, but the center of the discussions shifted from political to economic questions. As a final observation[77] with regard to future developments, it should be mentioned that in November 1951 the formation of coal unit companies began,[78] and that Regulation No. 17, issued under Law 27 on May 17, 1952, ordered the liquidation of the DKV.

CONCLUSION

American adherence to the decartelization policy was based on the following considerations:

1. The interest in the Schuman Plan, which realized two fundamental objectives of American policy toward Germany: (a) the integration of the Federal Republic in the West and with that a containment of the "German menace," that is, the resurgence of German nationalism and hegemony in Europe; (b) the Franco–German rapprochement; the conflict of these former rivals had often enough led to war; and
2. a general interest by the United States in a competitive economy in the framework of liberal (world) trade; the reestablishment of the principles of competition could, on the one hand, guarantee the elimination of the German war potential, and it could on the other hand, attain a sound and efficient structure of the German economy.

American deconcentration policy went through some amazing changes: from a policy of severe punishment (1945–47), to a period of temporary relaxation (1947–49), back to a determined attitude with the intention to translate the modified concept of deconcentration consistently into action (1950–51).

77 Because of space limitations, the analysis of American decartelization policy has to end at this point. I plan to write my doctoral dissertation on the United States and the decartelization of the Ruhr coal industry, 1947–1954, and discuss further developments there.
78 See Regulation No. 9 of November 9, 1951, in *Neuordnung der Eisen- und Stahlindustrie*, 377–82.

11

Technology Transfer and the Emergence of the West German Petrochemical Industry, 1945–1955

RAYMOND G. STOKES

Fundamental changes in U.S. occupation objectives in Germany between 1945 and 1955 exerted an enormous effect on one of the country's most successful industries, chemicals. Early policies stressing control, elimination of excessive economic concentration, and exploitation altered the industry's traditional structure and hampered its recovery. Later attempts to stimulate economic growth in and give political sovereignty to the nascent Federal Republic provided the framework within which West German chemical producers regained much of their former predominance. This essay examines the connection between American policy and resurgence of the West German chemical industry.

I focus on technology transfer,[1] which both indicated and helped effect changing U.S. policy in the ten years after 1945: It at first hindered, and then spurred technological change. By the early 1950s, key chemical firms began replacing coal-based with petroleum-based processes. Establishment of domestic petrochemicals production enhanced the competitiveness of West German firms, in the process strengthening the Federal Republic's political and economic fortunes and accomplishing altered U.S. policy objectives. I concentrate on the most significant players in the technological transforma-

---

1 There is no generally accepted definition of technology transfer. See, for instance, Ole Börnsen, Hans H. Glismann, and Ernst-Jürgen Horn, *Der Technologietransfer zwischen den USA und der Bundesrepublik* (Tübingen, 1985), 1–3. I use a commonsense definition of the concept here, i.e., "adoption by a firm or firms in one country of production techniques developed by a firm or firms in another country." Useful overviews of international technology transfer include: Thomas Ilgen and T. J. Pempel, *Trading Technology: Europe and Japan in the Middle East* (New York, 1987), 1–25; essays in John R. McIntyre and Daniel S. Papp, eds., *The Political Economy of International Technology Transfer* (New York, 1986); and Nathan Rosenberg and Claudio Frischtak, eds., *International Technology Transfer: Concepts, Methods, and Comparisons* (New York, 1985), 3–23.

217

tion of the German chemical industry, the successor firms to I.G.
Farbenindustrie A.G.

We are all familiar with a wide variety of products of the modern
chemicals industry. Synthetic dyes and pharmaceuticals, which entered large-scale production in the late nineteenth century, are two
important examples. In the first third of this century, chemical producers added synthetic ammonia, chemical weapons, synthetic fuels,
and synthetic rubber to their palette. Especially since the 1930s, a
broad range of plastics have substituted for natural materials. Because such products have, besides allowing increased standards of
living for larger numbers of people, often posed hazards to the
environment (and sometimes offended our aesthetic sensibilities),
their profound impact upon everyday life in the modern world is
incontestable.

Virtually all of the products I mentioned are "organic chemicals,"
that is, substances manufactured from carbon and hydrogen compounds.[2] The primary source of the hydrocarbon starting products,
or feedstocks, for organic chemical manufacture has changed through
time. Components of coal tar, a by-product of coking coal, provided
the first organic chemical feedstocks and included benzene, xylene,
and toluene. Later, acetylene, also produced initially from coal,
proved a key material in production of synthetic rubber and plastics.
Since the 1920s, petroleum and natural gas have begun to rival coal in
providing chemical feedstocks. These hydrocarbons eventually provided ethylene, benzene, propylene – and even acetylene – at prices
lower and quantities higher than dreamt of previously.

The United States first mass-produced automobiles; it also
boasted the first large-scale petroleum industry. As a result of these
interrelated developments, U.S. chemical manufacturers had the first
opportunity to produce organic chemicals on a large scale using by-
products of petroleum refining. Beginning in the 1920s, and increasingly in the 1930s and 1940s, U.S. firms surged to world leadership
in this new area.

2 "Organic Chemistry," in *Encyclopedia of Chemistry,* 4th ed. (New York, 1984), 656–67. Organic chemistry is generally the chemistry of carbon compounds, although there are exceptions. One is synthetic ammonia, the only nonorganic chemical mentioned in the paragraph
  above.

German firms, until 1914 world leaders in organic chemicals production and even in the 1930s a major force to be reckoned with,
lagged behind their American rivals in switching from coal to petroleum feedstocks. This applied especially to those companies that
in 1925 formed the I.G. Farbenindustrie A.G., which from its creation was the largest German firm and a leading world chemical
producer. In the Weimar period, limited availability of oil and prior
success with coal prevented I.G. managers from seriously considering alternative feedstocks. Nazi policies of autarky, or self-
sufficiency, and continued success with coal-based technologies
ensured continuity through 1945. By the end of World War II, German coal-based chemistry – especially as represented in the products
and processes of I.G. Farben – was extremely sophisticated and manufactured many modern products. At the same time, costs were high,
and the I.G.'s multistage processes were less complicated chemi-
cally, but also less amenable to economies of scale, than those of
American firms. Even before 1945, German chemical industrialists
realized that they would have to adopt American-style petrochemical
technology to compete effectively in the postwar international
marketplace.[3]

Feedstock selection and technologies associated with a particular
feedstock thus played a critical role in the history of organic chemicals manufacturing. Two additional factors shaped the industry:
First, it has always been research intensive; second, especially in
Germany, it has traditionally depended upon export.[4] Together,
these characteristics have made technology transfer a key feature of
the business of producing and selling organic chemicals. In the
decade after 1945, such transfers played a pivotal role in allowing
West German chemical firms to change the primary source of their
feedstocks.

3 Carl Krauch of I.G. Farben recognized the possibilities of petrochemicals in the 1930s. See
Peter Spitz, *Petrochemicals: The Rise of an Industry* (New York, 1988), 514. After the war, interest was immediate, as shown, for example, in Dr. Reitz's presentation to BASF researchers on December 11, 1946, on "Neuere amerikanische Arbeiten uber Erdolchemie," BASF
Unternehmensarchiv, Ludwigshafen, [hereafter: BASF-Archiv] F9/66. Interest only intensified with time. See, for instance, W. A. Menne, "Internationaler Erfahrungsaustausch,"
Chemische Industrie 4 (1952):1. My thanks to Dr. Peter Morris for his helpful comments on
the preceding paragraph and on other technical portions of this paper.
4 L. F. Haber, *The Chemical Industry in the Nineteenth Century* (Oxford, 1958); Haber, *The
Chemical Industry, 1900–1930* (Oxford, 1971); Spitz, *Petrochemicals,* 106–15; Peter F. Hayes,
"Carl Bosch and Carl Krauch: Chemistry and the Political Economy of Germany, 1925–
1945," *Journal of Economic History* 47 (1987):353–63.

TECHNOLOGY TRANSFERS AND THE WEST GERMAN
CHEMICAL INDUSTRY

Between 1945 and 1955, changes in the modes of technology transfer between West Germany and other countries, most notably the United States, both reflected and helped implement changes in occupation policy. I divide my treatment of the postwar decade into three major periods (1945–48, 1948–51, and 1951–55), reflecting key technological and political changes affecting the chemical industry. Let us examine each in more detail.

1945–1948

The chemical industry provided the German war machine with such key goods as synthetic gasoline, synthetic rubber, and other substitute materials; its control therefore formed an important objective for occupation officials. Hampering technological change was central to the Allied control effort, with limitations on production and control of research key policy elements. Even the Allied breakup of I.G. Farben affected the industry technologically by ending traditional production and research relationships among individual factories.[5] Forced transfers of technology from Germany to Allied countries formed a critical element in the control program and occurred on a massive scale; still, such transfers proved a rather blunt instrument for realizing initial Allied intentions.

Although most severe in the Soviet zone of occupation,[6] physical removal of industrial plant and equipment also occurred in the Western zones and was one aspect of technology transfer from Germany to countries victimized by German aggression. Chemical plants represented a key policy objective. As the occupation began, well over half of the industry's plant was slated for removal; even the more generous revised level of industry plan issued in August 1947 for the combined U.S.–U.K. zones stated that "between 40 and 50 percent

5 Joint Chiefs of Staff directive 1067 states U.S. policy in these areas. The April 1945 version (made public in October of the same year) is in U.S. Department of State, ed., *Germany 1947–1949: The Story in Documents* (Washington, D.C., 1950), 22–33.
6 Dismantling in the Soviet zone reached a scale unknown in the other zones: e.g., Sachsen-Anhalt, an industrial province, lost about 40 percent of its total industrial substance; and Leuna, the largest I.G. Farben plant, lost half its capacity remaining after bombing. See "Demontage in der Ostzone," *Angewandte Chemie* B 20 (1948):148–9.

of the total chemical capacity . . . will . . . be removed as reparations or destroyed."[7]

Still, this figure undoubtedly overstated the extent of dismantling: Over three fourths of the total capacity slated for removal represented war-related explosives plants; and actual dismantling never reached even these revised targets. A more reasonable estimate compiled in late 1949 by the Bremen Committee for Economic Research at the behest of the German Office for Peace Questions pegged average loss of postwar capacity for the chemical and chemical-technical industry at 6 percent.[8] This figure had distinct advantages over many other estimates: It eliminated from consideration removal of purely war-related plants, while at the same time including measures of the effects of wartime destruction and of reconstruction in the immediate postwar period. It thus reflected the scale of dismantling of physical plant as a form of technology transfer, although the broad range of firms and countries involved and differing methods of valuation of seized assets continue to impede a more precise assessment.[9]

The fact that something on the order of 94 percent of the 1936 western German chemical capacity was available in November 1949, however, tells us remarkably little about the quality of intact capacity. In fact, it varied tremendously. Bombing affected only 5 percent of Hoechst's main production facilities; they were little affected by reparations or dismantling, as was the case with most factories in the U.S. zone. Hoechst's physical plant was, however, relatively old and worn out. BASF's main factories at Ludwigshafen and Oppau rep-

---

7 "Revised Plan for Level of Industry in the Combined U.S.–U.K. Zones of Germany: Joint Statement by State and War Departments," Aug. 29, 1947, in *Germany 1947–1949*, 361–2.
8 Bremer Ausschuss für Wirtschaftsforschung, "Gesamtumfang der Demontagen" [end of Nov. 1949], B1. 22, BA, Z35/317. "Postwar capacity" is all intact capacity in 1945 plus machinery repaired or rehabilitated as of 1947–48 (about an additional 10 percent of 1945 capacity). Postwar Western German chemical and chemical-technical capacity was approximately that of the equivalent area in 1936. "Demontagen in Westdeutschland," *Chemie-Ingenieur-Technik* 23 (1951):593–4, provides a critical review of the report.
9 Critiquing estimates of dismantling and reparations, Werner Abelshauser states bluntly that "an exact reckoning of the actual extent of reparations and their capacity-reducing effect on the fixed assets of West German industry is not possible." See "Neuanfang oder Wiederaufbau? Zu den wirtschaftlichen und sozialen Ausgangsbedingungen der westlichen Industrie nach dem Zweiten Weltkrieg," *Technikgeschichte* 53 (1986):264–6, quote p. 265. To illustrate the complexity of formulating such figures: BASF reported differences of about DM 25 million between Allied and German estimates of the present-day value of assets seized from its factories. BASF, "Meldung an Landesregierung Rheinland-Pfalz, Wirtschaftsministerium Ref. IX," Dec. 7, 1950, p. 1, BASF-Archiv, B4/659.

resented the other end of the spectrum, with relatively modern plant that was both more heavily bombed and more affected by dismantling.[10] Other major chemical factories lay between the extremes.

Variations in the Allies' dismantling policies and practices determined the differing experiences of chemical factories. American occupiers, finding little equipment worth carting away and charged with seeing that the German economy did not become a major burden for the U.S. taxpayer, chose other means of realizing policy objectives: Information, not hardware, was the preferred means of transfer. The Russians found much equipment that seemed worth removing, and the French and British ranked themselves between the two superpowers.

Given such variability, how is one to sum up the experience of West German chemical firms with regard to dismantling? For one thing, for the factories involved, losing some plant represented an unpleasant experience, but also had positive points: It provided some impetus for technological improvement. On the other hand, one must not ascribe too much weight to this point. Few factories lost more than a fraction of their capacity. Most used prewar and wartime equipment to reenter domestic and export markets.[11]

In sum, despite dismantling, the overwhelming majority of capacity remained intact in West Germany. And, as Allied policies changed, all – including the latest – equipment fell from dismantling lists. Even the worst affected emerged with something to be happy about. BASF, for instance, reported in the early 1950s:

Measured against the original dismantling program, . . . it has to be seen . . . as a success that the proportion of the factory that fell victim to dismantling was not much larger. It was particularly fortunate that it was possible to retain the especially endangered facilities for large-scale synthesis on the basis of acetylene. This furnished promising preconditions for further development, especially in the plastics area.[12]

The picture was even less gloomy than BASF indicated: Already in mid-1948, despite dismantling, chemical plants in the French zone,

10 Production Control Agency, SHAEF, "Industrial Investigation Report 16: I.G. Farbenindustrie A.G., Werk Hoechst," 1945, p. 2, HStA Wiesbaden, 649, OMG Hesse, Bipartite Liaison Division ED, 17/164-1/12; Herbert Moulton, "Subject: The Höchst Plant of I.G. Farbenindustrie A.G.," July 30, 1945, Hoechst Firmenarchiv, Frankfurt-Höchst; BASF, "BASF schreibt Geschichte," Chemische Industrie 4 (1952):A580.
11 Raymond G. Stokes, "Technology and the West German Wirtschaftswunder," Technology and Culture 32 (1991):1–22.
12 BASF, Bericht über die Neugründung 1952–1953, 28–9. A brief summary of the end of the dismantling effort is in "Demontagen in Westdeutschland," 593–4.

led by BASF, produced at 91 percent of their 1936 level. Factories in the Bizone lagged behind, but still produced at more than half the 1936 rate despite bombing damages, reparations, transportation outages, and fuel and raw material shortages. Inadequate transportation, fuel, and raw materials – *not* insufficient production capacity – were the most important bottlenecks in the reconstruction of the industry.[13]

Physical removal of machinery represented only a minor form of technology transfer; much more substantial was the massive effort to seize *"geistige Reparationen,"* or intellectual reparations, from the defeated country. Allied teams gathered information on German wartime scientific and technological developments by investigating plant and interrogating personnel, all for the purpose of exploiting German achievements in the service of Allied military and industrial needs. Information transfer also occurred when German scientists and technicians emigrated to work in Allied countries, although this form of technology transfer appears to have been relatively unimportant for the chemical industry.[14]

Chemical and Engineering News (CEN) reported in late 1946 on the scale and objectives of one important American group of "more than 200 civilian technicians [who] have been sent to Germany to seek out scientific and technical information of value to United States industry." Sponsored by private firms, the men became nominal employees of the U.S. Department of Commerce and wore the uniforms of army officers with shoulder patches identifying them as "Scientific Consultants."[15]

---

13 For zonal figures, see Werner Abelshauser, *Wirtschaftsgeschichte der Bundesrepublik Deutschland 1945–1980* (Frankfurt am Main, 1983), 38; for BASF performance and factors impeding recovery of the chemical industry immediately after the war, see Raymond G. Stokes, *Divide and Prosper: The Heirs of I.G. Farben under Allied Authority, 1945–1951* (Berkeley, 1988), 95–6, 109–51.

14 Allied organizations conducting the "exploitation" effort (as internal documents termed it) included the British Intelligence Objectives Subcommittee (BIOS), the Field Information Agency, Technical (FIAT), and a number of others. For a general account of such efforts, see John Gimbel, "U.S. Policy and German Scientists: The Early Cold War," *Political Science Quarterly* 101 (1986):433–51. An earlier, still useful, work on American use of German scientists is Clarence Lasby, *Project Paperclip: German Scientists and the Cold War* (New York, 1971), esp. 18–26, 129–30, and 163–4. On technical investigations see, e.g., Leslie E. Simon, *German Research in World War II* (New York, 1947); Arnold Krammer, "Technology Transfer as War Booty: The U.S. Technical Oil Mission to Europe, 1945," *Technology and Culture* 22 (1981):68–103; and for chemical industry investigations Spitz, *Petrochemicals*, 2–17, 48–52, 113–14, 303–4, 346.

15 "Civilian Scientists Sent to Germany," *Chemical and Engineering News* 24 (1946):2637–8, quote p. 2637.

What did the investigators concentrate on? Chemical technology constituted a primary target. Of the more than two hundred technicians described by CEN, some seventy were in the chemicals unit. In addition, several other units, including fuels and lubricants, metals and minerals, pharmaceuticals and medical, rubber, and textiles, engaged in investigations of interest to the chemical industry. Of course, the Department of Commerce–sponsored group was only one of many sent (not only by the Americans, but also by other Allies) to investigate the state of German technology. Were its interests representative of the investigative effort as a whole? The subjects of publications describing the state of German technology in specialized areas, the primary products of these and other investigatory groups, provide additional evidence of the extent of interest in chemical technology and, especially, in developments at I.G. Farben during the war: Reports by the investigators concentrated heavily on developments in the areas of synthetic fuels, synthetic rubber, and acetylene chemistry in general.[16]

What the investigations brought to firms based in the Allied countries is unclear. Peter Spitz, a participant in and student of the history of the petrochemicals industry, contends that Vladimir Haensel's experience in Germany as a member of a technical team was helpful to his work in the United States on catalytic processes for hydrocarbon conversions, while Spitz himself used the reports as aids in designing chemical plants.[17] Still, Spitz and others often encountered the pitfalls of relying exclusively on the written reports. Almost invariably, they turned to German chemists and German firms for the know-how to make their information usable.[18]

For the purposes of this essay, though, the effects on German companies are most important. Evidence is mixed. On the one hand, estimates of the value of Allied seizures of patents from German industry, which the technological investigation effort only enhanced, appeared damning to the competitive prospects of German firms. In February 1947, for instance, a German patent attorney claimed the

16 Ibid., pp. 2637–8. I base my remarks on the subjects the Allies investigated and on an evaluation of the "Alphabetical Subject Index of CIOS, BIOS, FIAT, and JIOA Final Reports," n.d., PRO, FO 1005/1602.
17 Peter Spitz, *Petrochemicals*, 176, 329–31.
18 For instance, BASF LK-Abteilung, "Aktennotiz: Betr. Besuch der Herren von der Mitsubishi Chemical Industries Limited," July 27, 1953, BASF-Archiv, F9/79; Spitz, *Petrochemicals*, 329–31. This experience is not surprising in light of recent research. See Keith Pavitt, "Technology Transfer among the Industrially Advanced Countries: An Overview," in Rosenberg and Frischtak, eds., *International Technology Transfer*, 3–23.

"American experts estimate the worth of confiscated German patents abroad to be several million dollars."[19] The Munich-based economic think-tank Ifo-Institut pegged losses of patents and trademarks for the chemical industry alone at $10 billion, including 200,000 foreign patents, 24,000 internationally registered trademarks, and about 200,000 foreign-registered trade names.[20]

On the other hand, I have already mentioned that printed technical information is only useful insofar as know-how is also available. Eventually, German patent-holders sold or bartered their know-how to minimize the effects of patent seizures. What is more, rapid changes within the industry meant that in a relatively short time newly developed and patentable products made up an increasing portion of a firm's revenue. In 1963 Gilbert Burck wrote in *Fortune* that "today probably more than half the [European chemical] industry's revenues come from products that did not exist twenty-five years ago." For Bayer A.G. in particular, "nearly 60 percent of . . . world sales . . . now come from products that did not exist fifteen years ago."[21] The same was true for other major West German chemical producers.

All in all, the dismantling and exploitation efforts illuminate crucial aspects of occupation policy in the immediate postwar period. For one thing, their consequences differed significantly by zone; such zonal variation in policy and practice was typical of the early occupation period.[22] Only later did U.S. aims take the upper hand in West German occupation policy. For the American zone in particular (and this was to some extent true in the other zones as well), the effects of occupation practices mirrored vagueness and ambiguity in policies. If the primary policy objective – to curb future German war potential – seemed clear enough, the means to accomplish it were not. Was elimination of the defeated country's war-related facilities the best way to prevent future German aggression? Or was undermining German competitiveness through transfer of equipment and information to the country's competitors the best means to this end? By answering, "all of the above," the Americans meant to signal their determination to root out German aggressive potential.

19 Werner Colrausz, "Vorschläge für das Patentgesetz," *Angewandte Chemie* 19, Teil B (1947):50.
20 Ifo-Institut, ed., *Chemie einschliesslich Kunststoffe* (Munich, 1952), N5.
21 Gilbert Burck, "Chemicals: The Reluctant Competitors," *Fortune* 68 (1963):148, 152.
22 For a similar point, see John Gimbel, *The Origins of the Marshall Plan* (Stanford, Calif., 1976), 143–6.

But it was far from clear how undermining competitiveness would accomplish the objective of curbing German war potential. Unless the policy were carried out ruthlessly and to its logical conclusions – something that was not the case – German disaffection was a likely outcome. What is more, intact industrial capacity had the potential of making that disaffection dangerous. In any case, one effect of concentrating so heavily on transfer of information from German to American industry was to undermine U.S. credibility as being interested primarily, and unselfishly, in future peace.

There were even more basic problems in occupation policy. What, for instance, constituted a war-related, as opposed to a peacetime, industry? Explosives manufacturing seemed a cut-and-dried candidate for removal as purely war-related. Even in this extreme case, though, ambiguities were rife: Explosives were needed for clearing away war damages, for mining, and for road building, all peacetime pursuits. Of course, explosives were available from foreign suppliers, but that would require foreign exchange, and the Americans were the only ones who could supply that. They were generally unwilling to do so when domestic sources of supply were available. In other words, the goal of curbing war potential often conflicted with other fundamental objectives, such as keeping the occupation as short and as inexpensive as possible. The same sort of conflicts emerged in the exploitation efforts, since curbing war potential and constraining future German industrial competition – objectives themselves not fully compatible with one another – contradicted the desire to limit the costs and length of the occupation.

In any case, dismantling and exploitation soon fell victim to other considerations. Perceptive occupation officials recognized within weeks of beginning their task that their main problem was not how to contain the German economy, but rather how to keep it from collapsing completely; within a fairly short time, this reality became clear to key policymakers.[23] Spiraling occupation costs soon took their toll; British officials in particular began to doubt whether they could afford the spoils of victory. Added to this was growing tension

23 An indication of the policy change was U.S. Secretary of State James F. Byrnes's Stuttgart speech in September 1946, printed in Beate Ruhm von Oppen, ed., *Documents on Germany under Occupation, 1945–1954* (London, 1955), 152–60. A concrete expression of the change was the founding of the combined British and American Zone of Occupation, or the Bizone, on January 1, 1947. For the text of the agreement of December 2, 1946, creating the Bizone, see ibid., 195–9.

between East and West, which contributed gradually to a belief that western Germany might serve as an indispensable ally and as an engine for western European economic growth. One important result of this combination of developments was the official end to technical investigations in the combined British and American zone in June 1947.[24] Dismantling stopped and production prohibitions were slowly lifted between April 1949 and April 1951.[25]

1948–1951

By 1948 the seriousness of the impasse between East and West had become obvious, as had the growing economic differences between the Soviet zone and the three Western zones of occupation. The Marshall Plan and other aid programs, directly or indirectly, began to supply raw materials and capital for the reconstruction of Western German industry.[26] For the chemical industry, the end to intelligence-gathering efforts marked an important stage in its effort to stave off further siphoning off of technical information to competitors while increasing cooperation among the three Western Allies eased contacts and trade among chemical companies in the Western zones. Nineteen forty-eight also saw the gradual reestablishment of traditional, more equal contacts between German and Allied firms: A major petrochemical producer, Shell, and a German firm, BASF, began to discuss a joint production venture based on petroleum feedstocks. The fact that Shell sought out BASF's cooperation indicated that German producers had something to offer in the international trade in ideas.[27]

All the same, the period from 1948 to 1951 was a transitional one. Despite clear economic growth and increasing recognition of Ger-

---

24 OMGUS, Public Relations Office, "Press release," March 27, 1947 [Abschrift], BASF-Archiv, B4/1543. General Clay opposed aspects of the program from at least October 1946 onward; he believed it represented concealed reparations and benefited the United States more than other countries. See Clay (personal) for Daniel Noce, Jan. 22, 1947, in Jean Edward Smith, ed., *The Papers of General Lucius D. Clay: Germany 1945–1949*, 2 vols. (Bloomington, Ind., 1974), 1:305–6. A file on discontinuing the Allied investigations is in PRO, FO 371/65032.

25 Stokes, *Divide and Prosper*, pp. 170–3; "*Demontagen in Westdeutschland*," 593–4.

26 Stokes, *Divide and Prosper*, 150–1, 185–6. For a somewhat different view of the indirect effects of aid, see Werner Abelshauser, "Hilfe und Selbsthilfe: Zur Funktion des Marshallplans beim westdeutschen Wiederaufbau," *VfZG* 37 (1989):85–113.

27 Interview with Bernhard Timm, BASF Ludwigshafen, Aug. 10, 1988.

man political sovereignty by 1948, the West German state began to function only in autumn 1949. Official establishment of successors to I.G. Farben occurred only in late 1951 and early 1952. Allied discussions of, and actions on dismantling, level of industry, and production prohibitions followed a zigzag course until mid-1951: It appeared that negotiators could not decide whether to grant full sovereignty in this regard or to take advantage of the last remaining chance to reform and chasten the German economy.[28] Indecision on these crucial issues hindered movement on the technological transfer front: Unilateral transfers from defeated Germany largely stopped; transfers to aid in retooling western German firms for the rigors of the world market had not yet started in earnest.

1951–1955

Nineteen fifty-five witnessed the official end of the Allies' political control over the Federal Republic of Germany, thus completing the gradual transfer of sovereignty to the Germans that started in the late 1940s and accelerated in the early 1950s. In a parallel set of developments, the period 1951 to 1955 saw the establishment of the successors to I.G. Farben and their return to a more traditional role within the international chemical industry.[29] The symbol of their new status was the establishment of the first West German petrochemicals plant, the Rheinische Olefinwerke (ROW). Instead of largely passive objects of international technological exploitation, West German companies began to trade technical information on a more equal basis. The extent to which they could help foreign firms in developing new or existing technologies became the currency with which I.G. Farben successors bought their way into modern organic chemistry; such a transaction could only occur in the context of the U.S.-dominated economic order, an expression of evolving American policy on Germany.

By 1951 West German chemical industrialists saw their premier task as twofold: recapturing foreign markets and catching up with new standards of excellence in chemical technology. Sales and study

---

28 Hanns D. Ahrens, *Demontage: Nachkriegspolitik der Alliierten* (Munich, 1982), 69–70, argues that inclusion of Western Germany in the Marshall Plan spurred Britain to press for more dismantling. Whether or not this is so, there was a renewed spurt of dismantling in 1949 and 1950.

29 Stokes, *Divide and Prosper*, ch. 7.

visits were one way to accomplish both. Thus, as soon as their legal position allowed, and insofar as foreign exchange was available, a steady stream of representatives from major firms reestablished contacts with their counterparts abroad and inspected foreign factories. The United States proved a favorite destination.[30]

I have already noted that Germans were well aware that the establishment of a U.S. petrochemical industry represented a major challenge to future German competitiveness. On-site inspection of plants only strengthened this impression. In a presentation to top BASF officials in March 1954, two company engineers reported their sense of awe during a 1953 visit to a new Shell Chemical catalytic cracking plant in Houston: "Although we had, in the course of our other visits, already digested a few impressions of petrochemistry and had seen a few things from the highways as we drove by, I have to say this: as I now stood here before one of the most modern cat crackers, I first had to take a deep breath."[31]

Although they worked for one of the most technologically advanced German firms, the BASF engineers witnessed something entirely new to them: Indeed, the *scale* of production in U.S. petrochemical factories constituted a qualitative change in chemical technology, especially since it necessitated considerable automation.[32] German companies had just begun to make real progress in this area. Other aspects of petrochemical production differentiated it from coal-chemical technology, although many Germans persisted in believing that the new processes did not differ substantially from those familiar to their own chemical technologists. In fact, American (and also British) petroleum and chemical firms developed new methods – such as catalytic cracking using first fixed-bed and then fluidized-bed processes – to produce the feedstocks needed for petrochemical production. Subsequently, they also applied such processes to chemical production, as, for instance, in the use of fluidized-bed technology to synthesize acrylonitrile from propylene. Other areas

30 W. A. Menne, head of the chemical industry trade association and by 1952 a member of the Hoechst managing board, reported on two such visits to the United States in 1951 in "Internationaler Erfahrungsaustausch," 1–2. See also the visits noted below; and, Stokes, *Divide and Prosper*, 195–6, 204.
31 BASF LK-Abteilung, Dr. Günther Daumiller and Dr. Rudolf Keller, "Eindrücke einer Reise in den Vereinigten von Nordamerika im Herbst 1953. Referat im Hauptlaboratorium am 1. März 1954 und Besuchsberichte," 17, BASF-Archiv, F9/39.
32 Menne, "Internationaler Erfahrungsaustausch," p. 1. More generally, see B. Sturm, "Betriebskontrolltechnik in den USA und in Deutschland: Eine vergleichende Betrachtung über den Stand der Automatisierung," *Chemische Industrie* 7 (1955):17–19.

of American petrochemical technology had also moved forward substantially during the war, even as German progress in this area
ground to a halt: For example, "by the early 1950s, U.S. polymer
technology [crucial for modern thermoplastic production] was well
ahead of German research."[33]

The need for German firms to catch up, already plain in the early
occupation, became even more pressing when their representatives
saw the progress made in the United States. Cooperation with
American and British firms seemed a shortcut to this end, but the
challenge for German companies was to entice the Anglo-Saxons to
aid them at the lowest possible cost. Fortunately for them, they could
offer something substantial in return.[34]

Given wartime developments in petrochemical technology (especially in the United States and Britain) and the large-scale effort to
collect technical intelligence on German industry, it seems surprising how attractive German expertise was to Anglo-Saxon firms.
That it was, though, is indisputable. I have mentioned some of the
limits to application of written intelligence reports. In addition,
American petrochemical producers showed considerable interest in
German acetylene chemistry. Walter Reppe and other researchers at
I.G. Farben's Ludwigshafen plant (BASF) had developed techniques
for handling volatile acetylene at high pressures and for using it
to manufacture a wide variety of products, including butadiene
(needed for synthetic rubber production) and plastics intermediates.
At first, a number of products of Reppe chemistry proved impossible to reproduce via chemistry based on cheaper petrochemical
starting products. Representatives of U.S. chemical companies,
hoping to use natural gas rather than coal to produce acetylene,
were therefore extremely interested in Reppe chemistry. In addition,
U.S. firms, which had automated chemical production extensively
in their large-scale factories, used centralized laboratories for product analysis; they were interested in the complementary plant-

33 On the basis of a study visit, H. Miessner, of FF Bayer, reported that American process
technology (whether the processes themselves or the apparatus) with few exceptions "were
not substantially different from the German." H. Miessner, "Interessante Entwicklungen
aus der Verfahrenstechnik in USA," *Chemie-Ingenieur-Technik* 23 (1951):231. For U.S. technical superiority see Spitz, *Petrochemicals,* esp. ch. 3, 4, and pp. 135–8, 346–7, quote p. 346.
An interesting mixture of both points of view is in a study-visit report by BASF's Dr. Rudolf Gäth, "Vortrag am 30.5.52 vor der Werksleitung bzw. der Direktionspostsitzung über
meine Amerika-Reise," June 10, 1952, BASF-Archiv, F9/134/4.
34 E.g., Spitz, *Petrochemicals,* 305, and the cases below.

stream analyzers pioneered by the Germans to allow on-the-spot analysis of product.[35]

As a result of such proven technological capabilities, beginning in the early 1950s companies such as BASF attracted a steady stream of visitors from the American chemical industry who complemented German contingents to the United States. American interests varied widely, demonstrating the widespread appeal of German technology despite war and occupation. High-ranking representatives of the chemical engineering firm M. W. Kellogg arrived in Ludwigshafen in March 1951 to negotiate for rights to a BASF process for the cracking of methane in the presence of steam and oxygen in order to produce hydrogen and carbon monoxide. Kellogg was also interested in BASF's process for producing acetylene from methane "without using an electric arc." Shortly thereafter, Monsanto negotiated an option on BASF's butine diol-related acetylene processes (part of Reppe chemistry). Sidney Caldwell from U.S. Rubber Company arrived in Ludwigshafen later in 1951 to begin talks on purchasing know-how in the plastics area.[36]

Such expressions of interest in BASF's technical prowess were undoubtedly flattering, but in the short term brought little financial remuneration. That changed by 1953 when the Pittsburgh-based Koppers Company purchased technical information from BASF for the design of a commercial plant for production of polyethylene. Besides bringing in very useful dollars, the agreement also implicitly recognized BASF's technological capabilities in a petrochemical process.

35 M. H. Bigelow (Plaskon Division of Libby-Owen-Ford Glass Co.), one of the technical investigators, conveys American excitement in "Reppe's Acetylene Chemistry," *Chemical and Engineering News* 25 (1947):1038–42. Some firms later acted in this regard. Monsanto was one; material on their negotiations with BASF is in BASF-Archiv, B4/1395 and F9/248. On acetylene chemistry's potential to produce goods that petrochemical technology at first could not, see Walter Reppe, "Die Bedeutung der Acetylenchemie für die Industrie der Kunststoffe im Vergleich mit anderen Grundstoffindustrien," *Chemische Industrie* 3 (1951):602; BASF Patentabteilung, "Bericht über den Besuch der Herren Wilson und Menke der Monsanto Chemical Co. vom 15., 16. und 19. März 1951," March 29, 1951, p. 6, BASF-Archiv, B4/1395. On plant stream analysis, see B. Sturm, "Betriebskontrolltechnik," 19

36 "Besuch der Herren Warren L. Smith, Präsident von The M. W. Kellogg Company, New York, und Z. A. Toula, Vizepräsident von Kellogg, Paris, in Ludwigshafen am 5. März 1951," March 5, 1951, BASF-Archiv, B4/1815; "Entwurf of Monsanto-BASF agreement," Apr. 13, 1951, and letter BASF (Walter Reppe and Hans Freiensehner) to Monsanto (W. K. Menke), "Subject: Reppe Chemistry," Apr. 19, 1951, BASF-Archiv, B4/1395; BASF Patentabteilung (Kleber), Aktennotiz, "Betr. Besuch von Dr. Sidney Caldwell am 1.8.1951," Aug. 2, 1951, BASF-Archiv, B4/1813.

On the other hand, Koppers was just entering this production area; an agreement by early 1954 to provide Monsanto, a more established chemical producer, with similar information signaled to other companies that BASF was a force to be reckoned with in the petrochemical area.[37]

The attractiveness of German technology per se was one reason foreign companies were interested in German firms; prewar contacts and a long-standing reputation for high-quality chemical research and production were another. At the beginning of their lengthy visit to more than forty firms in late 1953, two BASF engineers reported feeling especially nervous about how they would be received. Still, "we soon perceived that the 'Badische' has a good name and has, even over there, friends who are happy to stand helpfully at our side." One key contact was Frank Howard, former vice president of Standard Oil of New Jersey and a long-time associate of the Ludwigshafen leadership. Howard arranged visits to several firms, including Union Carbide and Carbon; Pittsburgh Consolidation Coal; Humble Oil in Houston; the Ethyl Corporation in New York; and American Viscose Company. He also facilitated visits of representatives of interested American firms to BASF.[38]

Continued respect for their technology and reestablishment of prewar contacts paid off for West German firms by bolstering their prestige in international chemical diplomacy and by providing them with much-needed hard currency. The combination also proved an important means to starting a domestic West German petrochemicals industry. The founding of the Rheinische Olefinwerke GmbH (ROW) as a 50:50 subsidiary of Shell and BASF was a case in point.

Shell was, of course, not an American firm, but the Anglo-Dutch oil giant had important holdings in the United States and its pioneering efforts in petrochemicals drew heavily on technical developments by its American subsidiaries.[39] According to Bernhard Timm, BASF's chief negotiator on the deal and later chairman of the company's managing board, Standard Oil of New Jersey would, under other conditions, have been the more probable choice for the joint venture

37 Agreement [Koppers and BASF], Apr. 6, 1953, BASF-Archiv, F9/31/1; correspondence from April and May 1954 on exchanges of technical information between Monsanto and BASF, BASF-Archiv, F9/248.
38 Frank Howard, *Buna Rubber: The Birth of an Industry* (New York, 1947); Daumiller and Keller, "Eindrücke einer Reise," 3–4, 67, quote p. 3; Aktennotiz, "Betr. Besuch von Caldwell."
39 "Erdölkonzern Shell – Pionier der Petrochemie," *Chemische Industrie* 7 (1955):385–9.

because of long-standing cooperation between the two. But BASF's leaders did not want to compromise Esso's managers, who were under suspicion of having aided BASF and I.G. Farben to the detriment of U.S. national security before the outbreak of the war. In addition, two representatives of Shell, one from the Shell Group in London and one from Deutsche Shell in Hamburg, appeared in Ludwigshafen in 1948 to explore the possibility of supplying BASF with feedstocks for a wax-cracking venture. Timm immediately seized the opportunity to begin talks on a much larger, more cooperative venture. More specific discussions followed and continued during the coming years.[40]

Limitations of space prevent a detailed discussion of the most important negotiations during 1952.[41] What emerges clearly from them, though, is that they were not at all one-sided; instead, they featured tough bargaining between firms that perceived one another as equally sophisticated technologically. Timm, for instance, pushed Shell (and some of his own associates) to agree to purchase a larger site than originally planned for the plant, despite much higher costs. In fact, he saw the higher costs themselves as a means of tying Shell and BASF more closely to each other in this crucial area. As he wrote to one associate, "the additional cost does not frighten me if it can be seen as a down-payment on an even closer and more comprehensive cooperation between Shell and us. And I believe petroleum chemistry [*Oelchemie*] offers such chances." He pointed out, too, that a smaller site would demonstrate only too clearly to potential competitors the limits of expansion, whereas BASF could always threaten to build on a larger site, thus keeping potential competitors at bay longer.[42]

BASF also took the lead in convincing Shell to take a more active role than simply providing ethylene feedstocks (through its partner Union Kraftstoff GmbH) to the ROW. BASF provided most personnel to run the plant as well as the patents and know-how for production in the facilities. Still, both parties placed product and process improvements at the disposal of the firm and could use improvements gained in the joint-venture operation. In later negotiations, Shell committed technical personnel to ROW.[43] Construction

40 Timm interview.
41 Most material on the negotiations is in BASF-Archiv, F9/165.
42 Timm to Dr. Hans Freiensehner, Aug. 4, 1952, BASF-Archiv, F9/165.
43 Aktenvermerk, "Betr.: Krackolefine, Besuch bei Shell, London, am 23.6.1952," June 25, 1952, pp. 9–10, BASF-Archiv, F9/165; BASF Rechstabt., Dr. Dribbusch, Aktennotiz,

began in 1953; in 1955 the ROW started producing LUPOLEN (BASF's trademark for polyethylene) using German technology.

ROW's production of polyethylene exclusively from petrochemical feedstocks in Wesseling in 1955 marked the beginning of an era. Other major chemical firms, including Hüls, Bayer, and Hoechst, followed suit. In each case, the details differed. Hüls, for instance, decided in the early 1950s to abandon its synthetic rubber process (which yielded less satisfactory product at higher cost) in favor of American cold-rubber technology. Representatives of the firm enlisted the support of their government to accomplish this objective, and the Bunawerke Hüls GmbH – a subsidiary of Hüls and the three major I.G. successors – came on line in July 1958.[44] Bayer entered the petrochemicals field in earnest later that same year. The firm's major breakthrough had come in 1957 with the formation of Erdölchemie GmbH (EC), a 50:50 subsidiary of Bayer and BP Germany. With EC, Bayer loosely followed the model established by BASF in the ROW. EC's cracking facility entered production at the end of 1958.[45] Hoechst's experience in petrochemicals differed initially from that of all other successors: the company entered the field with little outside help. This was apparently not entirely voluntary. When BASF and Shell formed the ROW, Hoechst lost its most attractive foreign partner for petrochemical development. Despite pride in internally developed technology, Hoechst gradually adopted many foreign processes, and, in 1961, entered into long-term cooperation (mainly in supply of feedstocks) with Caltex Oil (Germany) GmbH.[46]

The common thread to these stories is that the German firms put their technological background to good use in entering into cooperative and licensing agreements with American companies. By the mid-1950s most major West German chemical producers had entered the petrochemicals field; by 1961 West German firms produced over

"Betr.: Polyäthylenanlage Wesseling, Besprechung in Ludwigshafen am 8. und 9. September 1952," p. 2, BASF-Archiv, F9/165.

44 Peter Morris, "Buna S versus GR-S: A Comparative Study of Industrial Research in Germany and the United States," unpublished paper; Chemische Werke Hüls A.G., *Bericht über das Geschäftsjahr* (1955), 10; idem, *Bericht über das Geschäftsjahr* (1958), 9, 15; for documentation on the negotiations to obtain American cold-rubber technology (1952–55), see BA, B102/9576, Hefte 1 and 2.

45 Bayer, *Geschäftsbericht für das Jahr* (1957), 15; idem, *Geschäftsbericht für das Jahr* (1959), 22.

46 Hoechst A.G., "Petrochemie Hoechst 1957," n.d., Hoechst Firmenarchiv, (no record group); Farbwerke Hoechst AG, *Geschäftsbericht* (1955), p. 12; idem, *Geschäftsbericht* (1961), 18–19; Spitz, *Petrochemicals*, 443.

50 percent of organic chemicals from petroleum or gas feedstocks, up from just 15 percent in 1950. In 1964 the figure rose to 69 percent.[47] Making this transition enabled West German companies to continue to compete successfully on world markets, thus fulfilling altered American policies of strengthening the German economy and integrating it into the postwar western economic order.

CONCLUDING REMARKS

Changes in modes of technology transfer influenced the postwar Western German chemical industry. They also both mirrored and helped effect changing occupation policy. Immediately after the war, transfers flowed away from Germany and toward Allied and neutral countries; investigations of German factories, interrogations of managers, scientists, and engineers, and, to a lesser extent, seizure of machinery formed their mechanisms. The transfers themselves expressed policies seeking to curb German war potential and to force the defeated country to pay some sort of restitution to its enemies.

By the late 1940s, unilateral transfer of technology stopped, and during the final four years of Allied control, chemical firms established more equal relationships with companies abroad. They offered their experience, research results, know-how, and patents to the highest bidder on the international market; they used the proceeds – or sometimes bartered with their own expertise – to obtain technologies and feedstock-supply agreements. Through this, the companies began large-scale petrochemical production during the 1950s and 1960s, an opportune time: The Western World economy began a pronounced and prolonged period of growth; in the chemical industry, information on the latest technologies became more generally available than before 1945.[48] Several West German firms secured a competitive position in international markets that has lasted to the present. Since the early 1970s, Hoechst, Bayer, and BASF all have ranked among the world's top five chemical firms in terms of sales turnover.[49]

47 Klaus Schworm, *Die chemische Industrie* (Berlin, 1967), 54, 56–7.
48 On the last point, see Spitz, *Petrochemicals*, 313ff. One factor may be that publication of reports on technical investigations released American scientists and engineers from secrecy agreements that had previously prohibited them from passing information from one firm to another; see ibid., 316.
49 Thomas F. O'Boyle, "Germany Beats World in Chemical Sales," *Wall Street Journal*, May 3, 1988, p. 26.

The technological transition of the chemical industry conformed well to changed American economic and security policy objectives in Germany. Improved competitiveness allowed West Germany to serve as an economic motor for Western Europe. At the same time, dependence on overseas sources not just for markets but also for raw materials fundamentally changed the outlook of the industry. Loyalties divided between fostering international trade and developing German self-sufficiency gave way to single-minded allegiance to the Western world economic order. In effect, despite initial policy, the Americans ultimately aided the Germans in fostering their industrial competitiveness; ironically, by tying the firms to overseas sources of raw materials *and* markets, they also achieved more effectively their objective of curbing German war potential.[50]

At the same time, technology transfer formed only part of the reason for the success of German chemical firms after the war and the ways they went about achieving it. Transfers shaped some similarities between these producers and other internationally oriented, competitive chemical firms. West German companies differed from their foreign counterparts, however, in traditions of labor relations and technological change, and in a number of other areas. German traditions in turn formed a prerequisite to allowing the chemical industry to accept and make use of technological transfers from abroad. This study thus confirms findings of others that successful transfer of technology presupposed extensive native technological capability.[51] Far from being "Americanized," West German chemical firms successfully turned their history to their advantage to meet the technological challenges of the postwar period.[52]

50 Raymond G. Stokes, "German Energy in the Postwar U.S. Economic Order, 1945–1951," *Journal of European Economic History* 17 (1988):621–39.
51 Rosenberg and Frischtak, eds., *International Technology Transfer*, pp. vii–viii; Pavitt, "Technology Transfer," 13–15.
52 Thomas P. Hughes, *Networks of Power* (Baltimore, 1983), ch. 14, esp. pp. 405–7; on "Americanization", see Volker Berghahn, *The Americanization of West German Industry, 1945–1973* (Leamington Spa and New York, 1986), although Berghahn's conclusion itself casts doubt on the concept; Stokes, "Technology and the Wirtschaftswunder."

12

The Free University of Berlin: A German Experiment in Higher Education, 1948–1961

JAMES F. TENT

The Free University of Berlin was a product of divided Berlin and the Cold War, a fact that should surprise no one. However, the new institution of higher learning that emerged in the autumn of 1948 – in the midst of the blockade and airlift – was a reform institution, one intended by its founders not only to provide an alternative to the Soviet zone's universities but also to influence German universities in what soon became the Federal Republic of Germany. While certain of the Free University's novel features proved enduring and influential, on the whole the reform institution of 1948 did not long survive the building of the Berlin Wall in 1961. Given the fact that the Free University was perhaps the most ambitious experiment ever undertaken in German higher education, it is instructive to examine the conditions that led to its creation and to trace the fate of its reform characteristics down to the watershed event of August 13, 1961.[1] To be sure, the situation that gave rise to divided Berlin and to a division in higher education in Berlin assumes new immediacy now that the status of the former capital and its universities has once again come under intense discussion.

Although a wartime Allied commission had already agreed in mid-1944 to divide Berlin into three, later four sectors, the fundamental factor that affected all Berlin institutions, including higher education, was exclusive Soviet control of the former capital from late April to early July 1945. The Soviets alone had conquered the city at the cost of a hundred thousand of their soldiers, and consciously or unconsciously they adopted the attitude that it was their

---

1 For a lengthier treatment of the history of the Free University, see James F. Tent, *The Free University of Berlin: A Political History* (Bloomington, Ind., 1988). This work also appeared in translation as *Die Freie Universität Berlin, 1948–1988: Eine deutsche Hochschule im Zeitgeschehen* (Berlin, 1988).

city. The Western Allies were interlopers who would soon face reality and simply go away. Most Berliners adopted a fatalistic attitude,
and the dominant Soviet presence – along with their German ideological allies, the KPD, later the SED – continued to hold sway at
least until the first citywide elections of October 20, 1946.

In this context, it is scarcely surprising that control of higher education including control of the famed, but now defunct Friedrich-
Wilhelms-Universität, reverted to the Soviet authorities in Karls-
horst and to their newly erected Zentralverwaltung für Volksbil-
dung. The latter institution served as a cultural ministry and was a
Soviet-SED–dominated bureaucracy created in the summer of 1945.
Its president was Paul Wandel, a KPD loyalist who had joined the
German Communist emigration to Moscow in 1933 and had been a
personal assistant to Wilhelm Pieck.

From the start, American, British, and French educational representatives on the Allied Kommandatura's Education Committee
(AKEC) demanded four-power control of the old university in the
Soviet sector, but by September 6, 1945, the Soviet representative,
Colonel Pjartley, disabused them of their illusions. Claiming it to be
a university of Brandenburg Province, that is, a Prussian university,
he announced exclusive Soviet control. The matter was never resolved. The Western Allies refused to acquiesce, and the Soviets unilaterally reopened the battered institution on January 29, 1946,
calling it Berlin University. It was also frequently referred to as Universität unter den Linden. American authorities adopted a thinly dis-
guised suspicion of anyone and anything connected to Berlin
University thereafter.[2]

An irony enters the postwar history of Berlin higher education at
this point. From the summer of 1945 to approximately April 1948, it
was chiefly Soviet and SED initiatives that unwittingly set in motion the train of events that led to the creation of the Free University.

First, the Soviet-SED authorities were exclusively responsible for
admitting the first postwar students. Selecting anti-Fascists and so-
called Victims of Fascism as priority groups, they matriculated in the
first semester approximately 3,000 students, most of whom had had
their higher education blocked or interrupted by the Nazis until
1945. At most only 4 percent of the new students were from
working-class backgrounds. They were four or five years older than

2 Minutes of AKEC meeting, Sept. 6, 1945, NA, RG 260, OMGUS, 4/16-1, box 145.

was normal for newly matriculated students. Significantly, the great majority had had their fill of extreme ideology whether from the Right or from the Left. The social, political, and age composition of this initial student population goes far in explaining the split in Berlin higher education three years later. The assembling of a mature, politically cautious, independent student body had increased the potential for tensions between the occupation authorities and their student selectees.

The Soviet-SED authorities, however, compounded their problems. They actively encouraged the students to form their own student volunteer association: the Studentische Arbeitsgemeinschaft zur Bekämpfung von Faschismus und Militarismus (St.A.). Wandel and his liaison officials such as ex-soldier and veteran of the Nationalkomitee Freies Deutschland, Rudi Boehm, deliberately made the St.A. politically nonaligned. They even installed medical student and CDU member Georg Wrazidlo as its first chairman. Therefore, the volunteer organization took on a nonpolitical tenor. Its members learned democracy through practical experience. They started by organizing discussion groups to combat fascism and militarism but rapidly expanded their mandate. In short order they became the de facto student government, organizing work gangs to clear rubble and repair university buildings, securing social welfare benefits for students such as a student medical clinic, aiding admissions procedures, and helping with the day-to-day business of running a university. In the process they achieved legitimacy in the eyes of their fellow students and ultimately enlisted 20 percent of the student population in their organization, a significant achievement given the extreme lethargy and political caution of the postwar generation.[3]

A time of tranquility followed, one that accurately reflected the Soviet authorities' willingness to commit scarce resources to the reopening of higher education. This was in sharp contrast to the confused and ambivalent attitudes of American, British, or French authorities in Berlin. However, the honeymoon between students and Soviet zone authorities ended abruptly on May 1, 1946. On that traditional Labor Day, some students and authorities celebrated the recent founding of the SED by hanging out symbols and slogans of

3 Rudi Boehm prepared a succinct description of the goals of the Studentische Arbeitsgemeinschaft zur Bekämpfung von Faschismus und Militarismus. A copy of his memo "Arbeitsgemeinschaft demokratischer Studenten," dated May 22, 1946, survives in NA, RG 260, OMGUS, 5/297-3.

the new Communist unity party on the walls of the university. Dismayed by practices reminiscent of the totalitarian past, thirty members of the St.A., officially recognized Victims of Fascism, protested what they felt was a politicization of the university. The Western press duly noted this slap in the face of the Eastern authorities – and with good reason.[4] It proved to be nothing less than the start of a student dissident movement that was to result in the creation of the Free University three years later. The university authorities immediately replaced St.A. chairman Wrazidlo with an SED student, a move that the other student volunteers blocked. In democratic fashion they promptly elected their own replacement, Otto Hess.

In rapid succession the falling out produced other major points of confrontation: admissions criteria, obligatory lectures, the status of student government, and even the physical safety of students.

As the first semester drew to a close necessitating the admission of more students, numerous students and even a few faculty members claimed that an overt bias in favor of SED-oriented candidates had materialized. Biologist Else Knake, who served as acting dean of the medical faculty, prepared a widely circulated report on the subject. Its critical findings soon reached the West-sector press, which promptly launched a series of attacks upon Wandel and his Zentralverwaltung.[5] Edwin Redslob, an American-approved licensee for the West-sector *Tagesspiegel* now took up the student cause and demanded the creation of a university outside Soviet-SED control.

The winter of 1946–47 saw a steady escalation of tensions. The admissions issue continued to simmer, and Wandel in a rare public press conference stated that his Zentralverwaltung would continue to favor admission of students from working-class and peasant backgrounds, a priority the Western critics labeled as a subterfuge with which to install SED-oriented candidates. The Soviet authorities tried other tactics to quell the nascent dissident groups. They announced the creation of a student journal, the handsomely appointed *Forum*, which was strongly sympathetic to the SED point of view. They dissolved the St.A. at the end of 1946 in favor of a more orthodox *Studentenrat* and set the elections for February 1947. Undeterred, the

---

4 It took some time for news of this event and its significance to reach the public. See *Tagesspiegel*, May 9, 1946.
5 Eighteen-page report by Else Knake, "Material über die Zulassung der Studenten zum Wintersemester 46–47 an der Universität Berlin," Oct. 22, 1947, NA, RG 260, OMGUS, 5/297-3. See also *Tagesspiegel*, Oct. 17 and 22, 1947.

St. A. veterans entered the contest en masse and promptly won a landslide victory. The following month, the Soviet-SED authorities demonstrated that they meant business in controlling the student body. In March 1947, they arrested six students, including dissident leader Wrazidlo, tried them secretly, and sentenced them to long prison terms. Word of their fate emerged only slowly, actions that reminded the students of Nazi-style Night and Fog terror tactics.[6]

Reactions by dissident students to this stark intimidation was not what the Soviet and SED authorities expected. The dissidents refused to be cowed. In May 1947, students Otto Hess and Joachim Schwarz started a student journal of their own, *Colloquium,* American licensed with a middle-of-the-road political position. For most of the first year of its existence *Colloquium* omitted any overt criticisms of the SED authorities, but its potential as an organ of dissent was apparent. Other irritations surfaced. Obligatory political lectures provoked boycotts by medical students, who dismissed them as blatant Marxist-Leninist propaganda. A second *Studentenrat* election in December 1947 witnessed yet another lopsided dissident victory. However, electoral candidates had had to campaign amid riotous conditions and frequently found themselves threatened by SED students during tense political gatherings.[7]

The editors of *Colloquium* finally threw down the gauntlet in January 1948. Hess and Schwarz, along with a talented contributor, Otto Stolz, published several articles strongly critical of SED practices in higher education. Stolz was especially effective in goading the Eastern authorities with his satirical lampooning of a ceremony making the change in the rectorship at Berlin University.[8] This journalistic broadside was a bold move. What had made the hitherto cautious dissidents take on the SED authorities in such a provocative way?

The answer lies with the dissident students' behind-the-scenes activities of 1947. In essence, they successfully courted West Berlin publicists, journalists, and politicians and convinced them that politically independent students were experiencing deteriorating political

6 The West sector press duly noted the student disappearances. See *Telegraf,* March 23, 1947. Concerned by such intimidating tactics, American and British intelligence-gathering units also took note of the incident. See "Excerpts from paper on 'Developments in the Soviet Zone of Germany, 1945–1948,' " p. 2, NA, RG 59, Lot 55D 374, Records of the Central European Division, G 801.4, Berlin II. See also Berlin PIR no. 56 (weekly report ending Apr. 3, 1947), p. 12, PRO, FO 1005/1729.
7 See *Colloquium* 1, no. 8 (Dec. 1947):13.
8 See *Colloquium* 2, no. 1 (Jan. 1948), esp. 13–15 and 24.

conditions at Berlin University. These newly won allies included prominent Berlin personalities such as Ernst Reuter, the future governing mayor of West Berlin, and *Tagesspiegel* editor Edwin Redslob among others. Just as important, the students established effective contacts with U.S. Military Government authorities in Berlin and convinced them that the students were serious about their confrontation with Wandel, the SED, and by implication, the Soviet authorities. This was no easy task. Following the Soviets' unilateral takeover of Berlin University in the autumn of 1945, Colonel Frank Howley, America's senior official for the American Sector in Berlin, had reacted with open suspicion toward all students. He denied residence permits and ration cards to incoming students by 1946, and at his command education officials shut down all Berlin University institutes and departments in the American Sector even though this move worked hardships on many. After the wave of student arrests in early 1947, dissident leaders Otto Hess, Horst Roegner-Francke and others quickly determined that British and French authorities were either indifferent to the students' fate or else felt helpless about intervening in their behalf. For a time they appeared to have no allies, the Americans included.[9]

Yet, their isolation did not last. Key dissidents like Hess overcame American hostility through an oblique approach. They started by initiating contacts with a prominent German-American historian, Fritz Epstein and his wife, Herta Epstein. Having fled Germany in 1933, Epstein returned to postwar Berlin as an American official to gather German foreign policy documents for the State Department. He was intrigued by the dissident students, who were so unlike the extremists who had forced him abroad after the Nazi seizure of power. A kind of "Salon Epstein" developed in Dahlem in 1947, and through the Epsteins' many contacts, the students achieved high visibility among prominent American officials whom they would not have met otherwise. The dissidents now had allies if a confrontation with the Soviets ensued.[10]

That event took place on April 16, 1948, when President Wandel dismissed the three student leaders Hess, Stolz, and Schwarz from

9 Interviews, author with Otto Hess, Sept. 24, 1985, and with Horst Roegner-Franke, Feb. 26, 1986.

10 Epstein had been pleasantly surprised by the postwar generation of German students who espoused humanitarian and democratic ideals in contrast to the bulk of the generation of students that had helped Hitler to power in 1933. See Epstein to Fisher, Dec. 19, 1947, Epstein Papers, file 9, BA.

Berlin University, claiming that they had acted contrary to the good manners and dignity of a student. In reality, their campaign of words in *Colloquium* led the Soviet-backed authorities to make the move despite the clear danger of a strong student reaction.[11] That reaction did not take long to materialize. A week later, 2,000 students gathered at the Hotel Esplanade to protest the dismissals and to call for the creation of a new "free" university in the Western sectors of Berlin. It was at this time that the students' careful preparations paid off. Press and film crews were on hand to turn the protest into what a later generation would call a "media event." A coalition of well-placed Berlin citizens including Reuter rallied to the cause.

The chain reaction continued. An internal university appeal process for the dismissed students was rapidly exposed as a sham, and at the end of May, the *Studentenrat* resigned en masse and moved west under the temporary protection of the students of the British-sponsored Technical University. Berlin University students by the hundreds began signing petitions calling for a new university in the West. By June 19, 1948, an all-German Preparatory Committee met in a clubhouse in Dahlem and declared its intention of creating a new university.

Only now did American authorities commit their first significant act of support, and even then it was done in secret. Although Military Governor Lucius D. Clay and his advisers had held a heated internal debate about the wisdom of helping the students – detractors felt the protests of April and May were a mere flash in the pan – enough crucial support developed among the Americans to tip Clay's hand. The general's respected cultural adviser, Herman B. Wells, gave his assent as did another Clay intimate, Professor Carl Joachim Friedrich from Harvard University. A visiting journalist, Kendall Foss, also played a central role, providing liaison between students and Military Government officials. Clay and Wells respected his acumen, energy, and enthusiasm and appointed him to chair a committee to study ways for Americans to aid the students' cause. Despite a sometimes bitter internal dispute, Foss's committee prevailed, and it became obvious over the summer of 1948 that

11 Interviews, author with Paul Wandel, July 15 and Dec. 5, 1986. Wandel was prepared to move more slowly in creating a Marxist-Leninist oriented university, because he could see that student resistance among the immediate postwar semesters was stiffening. By the spring of 1948, however, ideological lines were rapidly hardening in the Cold War and in Stalin's growing breach with Tito. SED hard-liners gave him no choice but to press harder in making the university students in Berlin conform to the party's expectations.

support for a new university would be forthcoming from the Americans in Berlin. Following the Preparatory Committee's first meeting, Clay secretly juggled Military Government's books and deposited DM 2 million in an account in anticipation of further German initiatives in creating their proposed university.[12]

This was a vital factor in the project's success. The German participants had taken the first initiative. Now, the Americans decided to act in a supporting role, an indispensable need in Berlin in the summer of 1948. No sooner had the Preparatory Committee met than in rapid succession currency reform, a Soviet land and water blockade, and an Anglo–American airlift directed the eyes of the world upon Berlin. While most watched in fascination as the fate of the city hung in the balance, some noted with equal amazement how the founding members of the new university overcame all legal, organizational, and financial obstacles and created their own university only eight months after the students' declaration of intent at the Hotel Esplanade. On December 4, 1948, the founding members, prominently represented by students, formally opened the doors of the Free University. Was it to be a university in the same tradition of established institutions like Göttingen? What, in the final analysis, was to be its function?

The founders of the Free University, prominent among them the students, had hoped to found a university that was a haven from ideological strife. This was obviously a reaction against growing Marxist-Leninist influences at the old university (which formally changed its name to Humboldt University in the autumn of 1948). They created an institution that was insulated as far as possible from the direct influence of the state. A *Kuratorium* or board of trustees with university, city, and private representatives as well as at least one student would obtain an overall budget from the state (in this case West Berlin) and apportion it as it saw fit. This feature was a reaction against the heavy-handed methods of Wandel's *Zentralverwaltung*.

However, the student founders on the Preparatory Committee and on all-student committees had their own agenda. They wanted to create a new kind of university. They wanted strong student participation in its governance. Besides student representation on the pow-

12 For the extensive debate within U.S. Military Government about support for the Free University, see James F. Tent, *Mission on the Rhine: Reeducation and Denazification in American-Occupied Germany* (Chicago, 1983), 286–99.

erful *Kuratorium,* they installed two student representatives in the university senate, a right that entitled them to review the appointment of professors, a student prerogative unheard of up to that time. Students were represented on the committees of each of the faculties or schools as well. These unusual rights were a direct result of the students' central role in founding the Free University. Their self-confidence was also a result of extensive experience in self-government gained at the old Berlin University. It was their hope to create a more democratic university although they did not try to define the term precisely. They wanted an institution of higher learning where students were actively engaged in the political and social issues of the day – that is, not cut off in an ivory tower – but without politicizing or polarizing their university as had happened in the East.

As a direct result of previous experience, the founders agreed that students would serve on all admissions committees, and they assigned a high priority to admitting students from working-class and poor rural families, a priority they adopted from their former SED associates. While respecting their professors, they sought to create a more democratic working relationship with them. The founding students, many of them officially recognized Victims of Fascism, wanted to create a university with a more liberal and democratic atmosphere than had typically been the case in the traditional German university. In this, the postwar students were reacting to the reactionary political climate that had permeated the universities before and after 1933 and had seen them acquiesce altogether too easily in the Nazi takeover. For that reason, the founding students banned dueling fraternities because of their reactionary, militaristic, and anti-Semitic associations. Together, founding students like Otto Hess, political leaders like Ernst Reuter, academicians like the first rector, Friedrich Meinecke, and university administrators like the able visiting chancellor from Kiel University, August Wilhelm Fehling, the founders assembled a reform university, one that proudly proclaimed itself to be based on a new model, the "Berlin Model." It would serve, they hoped, to influence the other universities in the West.[13]

13 The goals, ideals, and discussions about the new institution they were creating can be found in the minutes of the prepatory committees. See Hochschularchiv der Freien Universität Berlin (HSA FUB), Kurator, persönliche Akte ohne Nummer, Gründungsvorgänge: Vorbereitender Ausschuss . . . Sitzungsprotokolle; see also ibid., Rektor, persönliche Akte ohne Nummer, Gründung, Sitzungen des vorbereitenden Ausschusses. Numerous eyewitnesses recounted their motives to me as well.

Given its experimental features, the Free University began its existence as a unique institution, one that was effectively cut off from the Soviet zone universities but that was also greeted coolly by universities in the West. The West German Rectors Conference (WRK) refused to take a position with respect to the Free University because its members, led by Walter Hallstein, hoped not to deepen the split in the German academic world at the moment when all other German institutions were being split by the Cold War.[14] Given the environment in which it existed, the brave little enterprise in Dahlem scarcely looked like the opening wedge in a reform movement. Despite the idealism displayed by its founders, the Free University gave more the appearance of impoverished orphan than the beginning of a university reform movement.

The founders received a prompt reminder of the precariousness of their enterprise when, in the summer of 1949, the university experienced a major budgetary crisis. The newly constituted government of West Berlin claimed not to have the financial resources to keep it afloat, and U.S. High Commissioner John J. McCloy contemplated, as an economy measure, a forced merger of the Free University with the Technical University. To the last man and woman, the founders balked at such a proposal, one that inadvertantly put the lie to any assumption about alleged American grand designs in creating the Free University as a weapon in the Cold War. If anything, the financial debacle of 1949 and McCloy's ill-considered proposal demonstrated American officialdom's profound lack of understanding of, or goals for, the university they had helped to create.

The crisis was short-lived. Somehow Governing Mayor Ernst Reuter provided enough funding to demonstrate that West Berlin was committed to its university. In October 1949, McCloy visited the Free University one day after his controversial decision and was instantly transformed from critic into ardent supporter. That transformation speaks volumes about the special spirit that permeated the new institution and its founders. From 1949 to 1955, McCloy and succeeding high commissioners allocated on average $2 million in public funding annually to the Free University. Eventually, this largess caused grumbling among other German universities at the disproportionate amount accorded to the Free University at their

---

14 Archives of the Westdeutsche Rektoren-Konferenz (WRK), minutes of meetings in Braunschweig, July 27, 1948, p. 10, and in Würzburg, Nov. 6–7, 1948, pp. 49–52.

expense.[15] McCloy went further, arousing interest by the Ford Foundation, which also donated millions in private aid to the fledging university. About the time American aid scaled back in the late 1950s, the economically prospering Federal Republic and a revived West Berlin were able to assume the Free University's financial obligations.[16]

For thirteen years after its founding, the Free University put its reform features to the test in an unwalled city. It was a frankly experimental period in which the unique features either proved themselves or did not. This consolidation period was hardly as dramatic as the founding phase or the later testing by the student protest generation of the 1960s. Yet, it is instructive as to how the reform ideals for this university functioned at a time when it was not an integral part of the university system in the West.

It should come as no surprise that some of the ideals embodied in Germany's newest university did not survive long. The first casualty was the word "free" in the university's title. The attempt to create an institution outside the ideological strife of divided Berlin proved to be hopeless from the start. Inevitably, a militant anticommunism arose among the founding students. Those who came from Soviet zone or East Berlin universities were inclined to be hostile to communism anyway, and many were bitter at their treatment by Soviet-SED authorities. The Free University's students handled admissions procedures virtually on their own. Reacting to years of Soviet-SED interference, they drastically simplified application forms, pointedly refrained from asking the current political affiliations of would-be students, and assigned a high priority to admission of Communist-persecuted students from the East.[17] In the process they also demonstrated unequivocally that they were anything but neutral with respect to Marxism-Leninism as espoused by Josef Stalin. Founding FU students like Dietrich Spangenberg created a special office in West Berlin to monitor the status of East zone students. Although not formally an FU institution, this student bureau was closely associated with the Free University and reinforced its militantly anti-Communist image.

15 Memo, Maynard to Conant, Dec. 17, 1953, NA, RG 84, HICOG, Lot 59A, 543, box 2175.
16 McCloy outlined his plans in discussions with other officials of the High Commission. See minutes of HICOG Staff Conference, Oct. 11, 1949, NA, RG 466, McCloy Papers, D(49)265.
17 See *Neue Zeitung,* July 27, 1948. See also Helmut Coper, "Boltzmannstr. 4," in *Colloquium* 2, no. 8 (Aug. 1948):12.

One result of the stridently anti-Communist atmosphere was that the study of Marx and Marxism was severely limited at the Free University at least until the mid-1960s. Since the institution eagerly sought to become a center for research and studies in the social sciences, this was no minor handicap. It was well known among students in the 1950s and early 1960s that virtually the only instructor with whom they could confront the theories of Marx was a sociology assistant, Hans-Joachim Lieber, later to become a professor and then rector of the Free University. In at least one instance, an FU student in the early 1950s dared to criticize the anti-Communist militancy in a West German newspaper. This prompted the chairman of the Allgemeiner Studentenausschuss (AStA) to request the name of the student author preparatory to his expulsion from the Free University. The editor of the newspaper promptly turned down the request.[18]

Another early casualty among the FU reform features was the right of students to participate in faculty appointments. The justification for this feature was grounded in the social and political conditions of post-Hitlerian Germany. The students, many of them officially recognized Victims of Fascism, were intensely interested in the political credentials of faculty applicants. They did not want former National Socialists to enter the teaching ranks of the Free University. Yet, the total exclusion of anyone with any kind of connection to the Nazis was an impossibility in the postwar years. The Nazis had ordained that all professionals join their ranks after May 1, 1937, or suffer dismissal. Usually, such individuals were ranked as "followers" after the war, and if no one else was qualified, they would receive a teaching post with the consent of the vigilant, anti-Fascist student representatives. At the Free University, this meant that out of an original group of thirty-one professors (associate or above), seven had been party members. All universities made compromises with respect to denazification including the Soviet zone universities and the neighboring Humboldt University.[19]

In 1950 student representatives objected vociferously to the proposed appointment of one Gunther Brandt to become a professor of

18 Interview, author with Kurt Nevermann, March 2, 1987. The AStA chairman's correspondence with the newspaper editor is in HSA FUB, AStA, Akte ohne Nummer, Juristische Fakultät . . . bis 11.11.51, correspondence for March/Apr. 1950.
19 I investigated the files available on FU instructors at the Berlin Document Center and found that the seven ranked as professors were assigned to the "follower" category. See Tent, *Free University*, 233–8.

law at the Free University. Far from being a Nazi, Brandt was an SPD loyalist, but it transpired that he had served on a disciplinary committee of the old Berlin University and had ruled with the majority that President Wandel had been within his rights to expel students Hess, Schwarz, and Stolz in April 1948. Now, two years later and in trouble with the SED, he wanted to follow the expelled students to Dahlem, a move they decried. FU law professor Wilhelm Wengler objected just as vehemently to what he considered to be student meddling in faculty appointments and wanted Brandt to be appointed anyway. The aggrieved parties reached a compromise, and Brandt entered the faculty as an adjunct professor rather than as a full professor. No one was satisfied, but students and faculty avoided an open breach. It also marked a turning point whereby student participation in faculty appointments fell into abeyance.[20]

The Brandt–Wengler affair was exceptional in that students scarcely ever confronted professors. The core of the Berlin Model was a special working relationship between students and instructors in Dahlem. Each group needed the other's cooperation in order to allow the new institution to function despite every conceivable shortage including libraries, laboratory equipment, and building space. The students proved to be diligent and shared unstintingly in the burdens of administration. They took on responsibilities that no student body today would accept. The professors accommodated these demands on students' time. Indicative of this new spirit, an imaginative tutorial program emerged within a semester or two whereby assistants, aided by professors, organized student support groups. Older, more experienced students took incoming students under their wings and helped orient them to their studies and to university life.[21]

Another index of the founding students' desire to create a reform institution was their campaign to ban dueling fraternities from university life. The great majority of early students felt that such organizations had helped bring the Nazis to power and were now thoroughly discredited. Matriculating students were required to pledge not to join such organizations. Membership, the founding

20 Interview, author with Wilhelm Wengler, March 5, 1987. See also HSA FUB, Akte ohne Nummer, Juristische Fakultät . . . bis 11.11.51, which contains various memoranda and petitions by students on the Brandt appointment.
21 See Brigitte Berendt, "Studenten helfen Studenten: Elf Jahre Tutorenarbeit an der Freien Universität," in *Fünfzehn Jahre Freie Universität Berlin, 1948–1963* (Berlin, 1963), 40–1.

students told them, was incompatible with the goals of the Free University. Ultimately, in 1958, a supreme court ruling in the Federal Republic nullified that and similar rules elsewhere. Even so, it was a rare FU student who joined such organizations thereafter. This commitment impressed influential outside observers such as Columbia University political scientist Franz L. Neumann and convinced him that the postwar FU students were a breed apart.[22]

German emigrés played an appreciable role in building the Free University as a reform institution. Its key political patron, Governing Mayor Ernst Reuter, had returned from a twelve-year exile in Turkey. A compatriot from the Turkish exile, Ernst Hirsch, returned to teach law, and as rector in 1954–55, upgraded the pay and status of FU faculty to levels comparable to West German universities. Two other German emigrés, Sigmund Neumann from Wesleyan University and Franz L. Neumann from Columbia University, sought successfully to reinvigorate the social sciences, comparative studies, and international studies at the Free University. Along with such luminaries as Otto Suhr, who had just opened his Hochschule für Politik, several FU political scientists like O. H. von der Gablentz and Otto Stammer created an active political science department that, following the death of Suhr in 1957, became the Free University's Otto-Suhr-Institut. It received considerable American public support in the early and mid-1950s as well as Ford Foundation aid. Simultaneously, early key academicians like Max Vasmer and Werner Philipp put the Free University on the map as a center for learning in Slavic studies. The FU's Osteuropa Institut quickly attained fame and respect.[23] Later, former emigré Ernst Fraenkel developed an active American Studies program that eventually emerged as the John F. Kennedy Institute for North American Studies. Among the historians, Karl Dietrich Bracher produced his great opus, *Die deutsche Diktatur,* thus helping to build a respectable German historical literature on the origins and nature of National Socialism.

---

22 For a description of the struggle against Korporationen, see Dietrich Schmidt-Hackenberg, "Freie Universität und Korporationen," ibid., 32–4. For Franz L. Neumann's initial impressions of the Free University, see his "Preliminary Report . . . ," Feb. 10, 1950, NA, RG 260, OMGUS, 5/300-1, box 69, folder 4.
23 Report, Sigmund Neumann, "Status and Progress of Social Sciences in German Universities," Aug. 22, 1949, NA, RG 260, OMGUS, 5/300-1, box 69. Franz L. Neumann produced several reports. See the preceding note. See also report, Franz L. Neumann, Sept. 19, 1952, Ford Foundation Archives, roll 489, PA 54-41. See also Klaus Dieter Seemann, "Die Slavistik an der Freien Universität Berlin," in Herbert Braeuner et al., eds., *Materialien zur Geschichte der Slavistik in Deutschland* (Berlin, 1982), 19–44.

There were other features about the Free University that set it apart in its first decade. An imaginative evening division offered courses to adults who were working toward the *Abitur* but who had to hold down full-time jobs. A *Funkuniversität* or university of the air waves offered coursework for thousands of other would-be students. Such programs reflected the founders' commitment to providing academic preparation to citizens who had been unable to acquire a higher education because of the war and its aftermath. These experimental programs were a mixed success, partly because the Free University was plying uncharted waters. No German university had engaged in such programs before, leaving them to *Volkshochschulen* and other nonuniversity institutions instead. Other innovative features included an unprecedented international affairs program that brought scores and later even hundreds of visiting faculty and students to the Free University from all parts of the world. In divided Berlin, that policy made good sense, and it paid valuable dividends.[24]

Perhaps the most intriguing aspect of the Free University's first decade was that it functioned – unofficially to be sure – as a "State University of the GDR." Between 1948 and 1961, as much as one-third of the student body came from the Soviet zone or the GDR and from East Berlin. In fact, many of them were commuter students, traveling daily from their homes in East Berlin, Potsdam, Oranienburg, Staaken, Teltow, and other bordering towns and villages to West Berlin. The Free University's faculty and students, with West Berlin city support, placed a high priority on admitting GDR-based applicants, and thousands attended the university at any one time. The reason for this was simple. The impoverished GDR simply did not have enough university space to accommodate its students. Moreover, the SED continued to prefer applicants from worker and peasant origins at the expense of middle-class families. To be sure, this class distinction was artificial given the extreme postwar impoverishment of the entire GDR population. Families whose university-age children did not receive the right to study felt strong resentment over this reverse discrimination. Many simply moved west. Others chose the less drastic option of applying to the Free University. Until 1955 the percentage crept up to one third. Then, as scholarships and incentives for West German youth increased, the number of students from the Federal Republic rose commensurately and caused the

24 See Tent, *Free University*, 244–9.

percentage of GDR students at the Free University to decline. In absolute terms, however, several thousand were attending the Free University at any given time in the late 1950s. This situation changed overnight when, on August 13, 1961, Khrushchev and Ulbricht "solved" the Berlin crisis. Although unforeseen at that time, the Wall was to have considerable impact upon the political attitudes and composition of the students at the Free University.[25]

Although several of its reform features functioned well in the 1950s, this should not alter one overriding fact about the Free University. With time it adapted to trends in West German higher education rather than imposing its reform features upon that system. In a number of significant ways, the special student–professor relationship that most observers professed to see in Dahlem and that formed the core of the Berlin Model changed over time. The evidence for this return to a more orthodox German university is convincing. First, the student body grew younger as the decade progressed. This was inevitable as the backlog of applicants from the era of National Socialism and war made way for *Abiturienten* from the more typical age brackets. Founding students like Otto Hess, Ernst Benda, or Eva Heilmann were mature men and women in their late twenties and thirties. They took their administrative duties seriously, and conscientiously fulfilled their obligations. Student participation in elections to the *Konvent* and AStA was high at first; 80 percent of the student body voted in early elections. Participation still exceeded 50 percent until approximately 1954. Thereafter voting trends dropped dramatically. Other evidence of changing student attitudes accumulated. Whereas student representatives had carried on conscientiously with admissions procedures in the first years, by middecade irate university officials and even fellow students were forcing the resignation of student admissions representatives for neglect or for incompetence. A distinguished outsider observer, George Shuster, gained the impression by 1956 that student administrators were simply going through the motions in performing their duties. The significance of those institutional features that had emerged from the events of 1948 had grown dim.[26]

There were also new voices of discontent as the decade of the 1950s waned. The assistants, that is, untenured teaching assistants, lectur-

25 Ibid., 265–9.
26 George N. Shuster, "Report on the Free University of Berlin," Apr. 11, 1956, HSA FUB, Rektorat, Akademisches Aussenamt, Akte Ford Foundation . . . ca. 1952–1966.

ers, and other junior staff, were a small group at first, but their numbers grew as the university consolidated itself. However, no provision existed for them in the FU constitution, one that had been written by the founding students, faculty, and public officials. Periodically, groups of assistants petitioned faculties, the university senate, and other FU administrative echelons for a regularization of their status vis-à-vis the professors and with respect to representation in the various university councils – but to no avail. The status of the rapidly expanding ranks of the assistants at the Free University was still an open question as the 1950s ended. Quiescent for a time, it ultimately proved to be an explosive issue as the decade of the 1960s unfolded.[27]

The core of the Berlin Model, the special professor–student relationship in the late 1940s, also relied unwittingly upon a small student elite. Demands upon students had been high and expectations of academic excellence no less so. Barely 2,140 students matriculated in the first semester, and until the mid-1950s at least, enrollment was limited to about 5,000 students. Despite exceptions such as the Brandt–Wengler affair, they enjoyed the respect and confidence of the professors. The professors bent the rules as the situation demanded, and both groups helped to make their modestly appointed university function. Unfortunately no one found a mechanism with which to institutionalize this mutual respect in the university constitution. No one thought at that time of triple-parity voting schemes or other power-sharing relationships. Mutual cooperation remained an unwritten but central feature of this reform university, one where most of the community knew each other and met frequently at the small, hastily erected *Mensa* or student cafeteria.

With time the attitudes of students and professors changed. The FU students one decade later had become indistinguishable from students at West German universities. The professors, too, were showing unmistakable signs of seeking the same status and perquisites of academicans elsewhere in the West. Ever fewer of the pre-1945 and postwar faculty were to be found. Ever fewer exiles like Ernst Hirsch settled at the Free University. Larger budgets and civil service status

27 Memo, Asmuss, Schmidt, and Lieber to Redslob, Jan 7, 1949; memo, Margass and Frygang to Goethert, Jan. 27, 1949; report by Leisegang, May 30, 1949; all HSA FUB, Philosophische Fakultät, Dekanat, Akte Assistenten (vor 1959). See also report, "Zur Situation der wissenschaftlichen Assistenten der Freien Universität," n.d. [1957], HSA FUB, Philosophische Fakultät, Dekanat, Akte Allgemeine Assistenten-Angelegenheiten.

for professors meant that it could compete successfully with other universities for qualified academicians. The sense of sacrifice and idealism faded as the institution consolidated itself. The trend toward conforming to the higher educational system of the Federal Republic had eroded the goals that originally had inspired the founding generation. FU students were not supposed to be mere technicians. Outside the university they were supposed to be politically aware and politically engaged, yet free of ideological rigidity. In reality the engaged ones tended to dedicate themselves to combatting communism in any form. The divergence between practical realities and ideals began to be painfully obvious by the late 1950s, and another special feature about the Free University became manifest. Founded with media support and with a worldwide spotlight on its activities, the Free University had by its nature become an irresistible focus of media attention. If significant or long-term differences of opinion arose within the FU community, it was unlikely that the public media would ignore them. In all likelihood, such media attention would exacerbate internal tensions.

This is precisely what began to take place as the 1950s waned. Student spokesmen began to take stands on world issues, such as the Soviet invasion of Hungary in 1956, the Algerian civil war, German rearmament, nuclear disarmament or any number of other issues of national and international importance. This caused intense discussions among students and professors alike and led to hitherto unheard-of tensions in the FU community. A left-leaning journalist, Erich Kuby, announced in 1958 in a public address at the Free University that its very title "free" indicated that it was an unfree institution; that is, it was reacting to political conditions in the East. This caused an outburst of criticism, and the rector banned Kuby from ever speaking at the Free University again. Sensing discord, the media began canvassing the many diverse opinions of the increasingly vocal university community. The conservative press, not surprisingly, condemned what it felt were irrational positions by a few students with no real mandate. For a brief time it appeared that a showdown might be brewing between students determined to take controversial political stands, and professors determined to exclude the Free University from the politicization process. By 1958 sufficient dissension had emerged that it became – in retrospect – a foreshadowing of the events of 1965 to 1968. However, a dramatic development halted this incipient crisis. Soviet Premier Nikita

Khrushchev announced on Thanksgiving Day, 1958, that the Allies had just six months to leave Berlin. The ensuing crisis that led to the building of the Wall swept this student–faculty tiff aside.[28]

Yet, the Wall, too, was to have its effect. Overnight the Free University ceased to function as a "State University of the GDR." Formerly the largest identifiable single group among students, the GDR contingent dwindled into insignificance within a few years and was replaced by a vastly increased stream of students arriving from the Federal Republic. It arrived with the active support, financial and otherwise, of the authorities in Bonn, in West Berlin, and at the Free University. This was a generation that had not known war or occupation or want. It had other concerns and would soon make its presence felt. The officials of the Free University were delighted at the prospect of acquiring a new pool of students. It would aid the young university in becoming an institution of national importance, they reasoned.

The institution that emerged from the Cold War and the special conditions of divided Berlin had carried on in its original form for little more than a decade. Many factors besides students–faculty tensions accounted for the demise of the institution as originally conceived. Its student population had expanded to nearly 13,000 by 1961, and contemporaries complained that heavy enrollment increases were swamping such institutional innovations as the tutorial program. The tutorial concept suffered another blow in the period 1959–61. An American-aided attempt to build a *Studentendorf* (student village) that would function like a college in Oxford, Cambridge, or one of the Ivy League universities failed utterly. True, student lodgers fully occupied the *Studentendorf*, but the experiment foundered on one vital oversight. No one had anticipated the difficulties in transferring the special student–tutor relationship to a German university, even a self-proclaimed reform institution like the Free University. Bricks, mortar, and student lodgers were all that came of the enterprise.[29]

The Free University had grown out of the unique conditions of divided, postwar Berlin and had developed unique institutional

28 For representative documents that depict the growing estrangement between students and faculty, see Tilman Fichter and Siegwart Loennendonker, eds., *Freie Universität Berlin 1948–1973: Hochschule im Umbruch,* 5 vols. (Berlin, 1973–83), esp. vol. 3, items 253–63.

29 Report, John H. Stibbs, Tulane University, to Ralph Brown, American Mission, re Studentendorf, July 7, 1964, HSA FUB, Rektorat, Akademisches Aussenamt, Akte Ford Foundation Spende, vol. 2.

features as a result. With time society changed, and the individuals who composed the Free University community found themselves conforming to the features of West German universities rather than the other way round. Some welcomed this trend toward orthodoxy while others deplored it. Nevertheless, the trend continued unabated, with the result that most if not all of the reform features of the Free University had atrophied by 1961. The crisis surrounding the Wall brought a halt to incipient confrontations in the academic community and temporarily restored a common purpose. Yet, that consensus, the heart of the Berlin Model, disintegrated for good with the emergence of the student protest movement in 1965. Students, claiming to recapture the rights of students from the founding generation, were joined by a vastly increased body of assistants who were dissatisfied with their uncertain status. The professors became one of their primary targets, and the ensuing confrontations shattered the Berlin Model, a model predicated upon the assumption of mutual trust and respect between students and faculty. The Berlin University Law of 1969 formally ended the original constitution of 1948. An experiment in German higher education also ended, and the Free University embarked on a period of dramatic expansion and equally dramatic clashes among political factions that submerged its identity. It emerged in the 1980s as a mammoth university little different from its sister institutions in the Federal Republic.

The dramatic events of 1989 that set in motion the merging of the two Germanies has reopened the issue of higher education in Berlin. For forty years the Free University and the Humboldt University had virtually no contact with each other, even after the former had established institutional ties with Leningrad University and other universities in Eastern Europe. The emergence of a reunited city reopens the issue of higher education in Berlin. In some respects the situation reverts to the one obtaining in 1945 when the Allies failed to agree on how to rebuild higher education. Until then a "call" to Berlin for a university professor meant achieving the pinnacle of professional success. Berlin was his or her *Endstation*. How the Germans in general and the Berliners in particular resolve the status of higher education may decide whether or not Berlin, the Free University and the Humboldt University will become the *Endstation* for future German academicians.

13

HICOG and the Unions in West Germany

A Study of HICOG's Labor Policy toward the Deutscher Gewerkschaftsbund, 1949–1952

MICHAEL FICHTER

In a speech before the delegates to the founding congress of the German Trade Union Federation (Deutscher Gewerkschaftsbund, DGB) in October 1949, Harvey W. Brown, prominent American Federation of Labor (AFL) leader and newly named director of the Office of Labor Affairs of the U.S. High Commissioner for Germany (HICOG), attributed to the unions a twofold responsibility in securing democracy in Germany. A democratic way of life, he stated, depended above all on how successful the unions proved to be in their struggle for social justice. At the same time, he reminded his audience that the chance for democratic growth hinged greatly upon the means employed by union leaders in pursuit of their goals.[1]

This chapter explains how HICOG sought to ensure that organized labor in Germany, represented by the DGB, would live up to the standards set by Brown. The discussion is limited to the period from the middle of 1949 to early 1952. Overall, this was a decisive time for the formation of the Federal Republic, during which crucial decisions were made affecting labor's programmatic visions of the future. It was during this period, too, that HICOG exerted considerable effort to impress upon organized labor in Germany just what Americans regarded to be the role of trade unions in a democratic society.

During the years of military occupation from 1945 to 1949, American policy toward the reestablishment and development of unions gradually matured into a finely tuned instrument combining elements of control, persuasion, advice, and support.[2] Under occupation control, the unions and the military government were not equal

---

1 Harvey W. Brown, Address to the Delegates, Protokoll, Gründungskongress des Deutschen Gewerkschaftsbundes, München, 12.–14. Oktober 1949, p. 27.
2 See my study, *Besatzungsmacht und Gewerkschaften: Zur Entwicklung und Anwendung der US-Gewerkschaftspolitik in Deutschland 1944–1948* (Opladen, 1982).

partners. Union leaders repeatedly acquiesced to American policy decisions that ran counter to their own programmatic goals. Although they complied with American demands often only reluctantly, they were generally able to justify their submission on the grounds that they still had something to show for it or that they had no other choice.

According to the Occupation Statute, HICOG was to exercise reserved powers over labor affairs "only insofar as foreign affairs, displaced persons and refugees, and respect for the Basic Law of the new West German Federal Republic and the Land constitutions were concerned."[3] Thus, early plans for the creation of HICOG relegated labor affairs to a subordinate position within the division handling economic matters. Immediately, the director of the Manpower Division of the Office of Military Government for Germany (OMGUS), Leo R. Werts, raised objections and insisted that HICOG needed an independent office for labor affairs, in much the same way as a government had a ministry of labor. Furthermore, he argued, the high commissioner should have the benefit of direct and top-level contact with labor specialists, who could provide pertinent information on union activities and probable reactions to decisions taken by HICOG; a high organizational ranking would, moreover, provide such specialists with the authority necessary to make German labor leaders attentive to the overall policy goals pursued by HICOG and, in turn, the German government. Similarly, Werts pointed out, the organization of HICOG to reflect the importance of labor in building a strong and stable democracy in Germany would secure the continued support of labor organizations in the United States as well as bolster international liaison activities essential to the HICOG mission.[4]

Decisive support for a stronger organizational position for labor within HICOG came from the chairman of the Free Trade Union Committee (FTUC) of the AFL, Matthew Woll. At the request of German union leaders,[5] Woll implored John J. McCloy, designated high commissioner, to consider the establishment of HICOG as an appropriate impetus for giving a labor division "more authority and facilities for developing its work." Indeed, Woll continued, the AFL

3 J. F. J. Gillen, *Labor Problems in West Germany*, (Bad Godesberg-Mehlem, 1952), 1; Occupation Statute, April 8, 1949, in U.S. Department of State, ed., *Germany 1947–1949: The Story in Documents* (Washington, D.C., 1950), 89ff.
4 See Gillen, *Labor Problems*, 2.
5 Fritz Tarnow an die Bundesvorstände, June 11, 1949, in Hans-Böckler-Stiftung Düsseldorf (hereafter: HBS, Bestand 10/19 (Gewerkschaftsrat).

regarded the expansion of the labor division and the position of labor advisor as so important that it was willing to place the president of its largest member union at McCloy's disposal.[6] This offer seems to have ensured McCloy's decision to include an Office of Labor Affairs (OLA) at the headquarters level of HICOG as one of its eight major functional divisions. And he readily took up the offer Woll had made on behalf of the AFL, naming Harvey W. Brown, president of the International Association of Machinists (IAM), to be his labor advisor and the director of OLA.[7]

The general functions of OLA covered activities related to industrial relations, management associations, wages, employment and unemployment, housing, social insurance, cost of living problems, and labor productivity. OLA advised the U.S. Occupation Forces regarding their employment of Germans and represented HICOG on the Labor Affairs Committee of the Allied High Commission after it had been established in April 1950. Finally, OLA maintained an office in Düsseldorf to report directly on developments in the Ruhr and to serve as liaison to the Deutscher Gewerkschaftsbund.

The OLA staff never included more than twenty Americans and thirty-eight Germans, making it by far the smallest of the functional offices at HICOG headquarters in Frankfurt. The next largest office had almost four times the personnel of OLA. Each of the land commissioners in Bremen, Hesse, and Württemberg-Baden employed only one labor officer, while Bavaria and Berlin stood out as exceptions with two staff members assigned to labor affairs.[8]

But despite its small size and lack of any direct authority to rule on German labor matters, OLA has been described as one of the most active units within all of HICOG, devoting a great deal of time to work in the field "when certain other HICOG officials sat most of the time in their offices pushing papers."[9] Since OLA's assignment demanded that it deal with mass membership labor organizations, this comparison may be a bit unfair to the other functional offices. In

---

6 Matthew Woll to John J. McCloy, June 29, 1949, NA, RG 260, OMGUS, 7/43–1/14. All OMGUS records cited in this essay are from the collection "US-Besatzungsakten," Freie Universität Berlin, Zentralinstitute für sozialswissenchaftliche Forschung [hereafter: FU-ZI SOWIFO]. Regarding the intervention on behalf of an independent labor office by the Labor Department, see Werts to Arnold Zempel, July 20, 1949, NA, RG 260, OMGUS, 7/43–1/59.

7 McCloy to Woll, July 18, 1949, NA, RG 260, OMGUS 7/43–1/14.

8 Ibid., pp. 3–7. Harold Zink, *The United States in Germany, 1944–1955* (Princeton, Toronto, London, and New York, 1957), 53.

9 Zink, *The United States in Germany*, 289.

any case, there is no lack of evidence for the wide range of OLA involvement and activity regarding union matters.

As stated in the official U.S. Policy Directive for the High Commissioner issued in November 1949, the goal of the United States in the field of labor and industrial relations was "to encourage the development of free, democratic trade unions and the negotiation of agreements and cooperative settlement of problems between them and employer organizations. Your Government is also interested in promoting the re-establishment of relations between such German unions and democratic union movements in other countries."[10]

American labor officials regarded their mission as ensuring the democratic reorientation of German labor. Officially, they had no direct powers to exercise, and HICOG and OLA insisted continuously that interference and pressure were not instruments of their policy toward trade unions. From the outset, the OLA staff claimed that its purpose was to furnish information, offer assistance, and "otherwise help but never to attempt to force or indeed seek to persuade the German labor leaders to follow American ideas."[11] Realistically however, the line between assistance and direct involvement blurred in a relationship between parties of differing and largely unequal political and economic strength. For example, OLA based its requests for more personnel at the field level on the need to preach to German trade unionists "the American way of life" or to "sell American concepts to labor leaders at the local level."[12] If OLA's efforts fell short of the mark, or if proposals put forward by the German unions did not receive adequate recognition, this was not because the labor officers had not tried. In at least one instance, OLA labor officers invested considerable time and effort in justifying their work and placing the blame for dissatisfactory results on the German unions.[13]

From the outset, OLA operated a sizable array of projects and programs in support of its reorientation objectives. According to available figures, which are presumably incomplete, OLA's budget in this field grew from $500,000 and DM 500,000 in 1950 to almost

10 Office of the U.S. High Commissioner for Germany, Policy Directive for the U.S. High Commissioner for Germany, Nov. 29, 1949, FU–ZI SOWIFO, 6/124–1/20.
11 Zink, *United States in Germany*, 289.
12 Brown to Tobin, March 31, 1950, NA, RG 466, HICOG, box 90, folder: 560 Labor Affairs March 50; Bertram to Parker, Oct. 26, 1951, NA, RG 466, HICOG, box 93, folder: 560 Labor Affairs Oct. 1951.
13 W. L. White, Difficulty of Liasion with West German Trade Unions, Oct. 2, 1950, NA, RG 59, 862a.062/10-250; H. F. Kern to Hans Böckler, Oct. 2, 1950, HBS, Ordner DGB-Bundesvorstand, Abt. Vors. (H. Böckler), Oktober 1949 bis 16.2.1951.

$900,000 and DM 2.1 million in 1952. Such figures do not include donations of books and journals or payments budgeted with other agencies (such as the European Cooperation Administration) and channeled through OLA.[14] OLA pursued several different goals with the funds and personnel it provided for educational and training purposes. The Americans wanted to help the DGB recruit new members, train a new generation of leaders, and in general propagate the "American way of life." A third consideration was to show the German unions the advantages of working together with government and employers for the good of all. Indeed, OLA directed its activities not only toward the unions, but toward management as well. A few examples will serve to illustrate this policy.

Having impact overall was the program that sent German trade unionists, government labor officials, as well as managers and representatives of employer associations to the United States. OLA Director Harvey W. Brown called this exchange program the most important part of the labor reorientation effort.[15] In 1950, the first year of the program, OLA sponsored travel for some 140 Germans to the United States. Their length of stay ranged from thirty to ninety days. For the following fiscal year, the labor staff set a goal of sending 250 Germans, including 100 young trade unionists who were to study for a full year at American universities with recognized programs in labor–management relations. However, this projection proved to be too ambitious. HICOG cut the university studies part of the exchange by 50 percent, and only 156 Germans actually participated in the program that year. After OLA received substantial budget increases for fiscal year 1952, the labor staff made plans to send a total of 325 Germans to the United States and an additional 40 to various European countries.[16]

The question, of course, is just what effect this program had on the trade union participants. Only very few of them found much to criticize; others noted that many practices peculiar to the American system of industrial relations were not necessarily suitable in the German context. But judging from most reports and speeches the German trade

14 Georg Reuter, Aktennotiz für Kollegen Böckler, Nov. 25, 1949, HBS, Ordner DGB-Bundesvorstand, Abt. Vors. (H. Böckler), Okt. 1949 bis 16.2.1951; Brown to Werts, Feb. 24, 1950, NA, RG 466, HICOG, box 90, folder: 560 Labor Affairs Feb. 1950; Bertram to Parker, Oct. 26, 1951, NA, RG, 466, HICOG, box 93, folder: 560 Labor Affairs Oct. 1951.
15 See Gillen, *Labor Problems,* 66.
16 Bertram to Parker, Oct. 26, 1951, NA, RG 466, HICOG, box 93, folder: 560 Labor Affairs Oct. 1951.

unionists made upon their return, the program left an overwhelmingly positive impression on the vast majority of them.[17] August Scholle, president of the Michigan State Council of the Congress of Industrial Organizations (CIO) who reviewed the program in the United States and in Germany for HICOG, concluded that the program served to show German labor leaders "how democracy works":

The visits have been the best form of visual education. Visitor after visitor told me that he could not understand what Americans were talking about in telling of democratic institutions and processes until he made his trip to America. No amount of telling would convince them of many things in American life until they actually saw them. Most of the trade union leaders who visited America did change their attitudes to a perceptible degree, according to statements from their friends and acquaintances who have known them for a long time. Germans have gained through their visits to America a marked degree of appreciation of the higher wages and consequent higher standard of living of American workers. This has resulted in a greater respect for the democratic form of government. The visits have helped answer affirmatively for the exchangees the question of whether democracy can fulfill the needs and aspirations of working people.[18]

A second example of OLA's educational activities is the Training-Within-Industry (TWI) Program. As with the exchange program, TWI had been set up under the OMGUS Manpower Division. The labor officers viewed shop-level relationships in Germany as being often authoritarian or paternalistic and believed that the American experience, upon which TWI rested, could and should be shared with the Germans. To be sure, TWI was directed primarily toward management and shop foremen, but its success depended on the support of the unions as well.[19]

Under the auspices of HICOG, OLA expanded this program and, by 1952, it had set up TWI committees of representatives from management, labor, government, and the chambers of industry, commerce, and handicrafts in many major cities. Unlike its practice with the exchange program, however, OLA made every effort to have German groups actually run TWI and make it work through their own efforts. The labor officers themselves concentrated on organizing staff training courses conducted by American instructors, on provid-

17 For examples see Gillen, *Labor Problems,* 68.
18 August Scholle, "Appraisal of the Cultural Exchanges Program and the HICOG Labor Affairs Program in Germany," Aug. 28, 1951, desp. 825, Frankfurt, NA, RG 59, 862a.062/9-1751, box 5201.
19 See Edwards to de Schweinitz, Aug. 31, 1951, NA, RG 466, HICOG, box 93, folder: 560 Labor Affairs Aug. 1951.

ing logistical and financial support for training programs, and on supplying the committees with appropriate literature. To this end, OLA began publishing and distributing free of charge a journal titled *Soziale Beziehungen in der Industrie,* which reprinted articles from various American labor and management journals. The fact that by August 1951, just six months after the journal had first appeared, its circulation had already reached 10,000, clearly indicates its success.

As with TWI, OLA's attempts to interest German labor in a productivity program were received less than enthusiastically. Many labor leaders argued that, based on their experience, employers would use such a program solely to their own advantage. As Harvey Brown reported, they were completely unwilling to participate unless reasonably assured that workers would share in the benefits. Since OLA deemed the cooperation of the German unions absolutely essential for the success of the program, it directed its efforts toward convincing union officials – especially the economic staffs – that OLA supported the program for the same reasons. This argument seemed to have been successful.[20] Increasingly, union leaders voiced their conviction that increased production would not only lower the cost of individual consumer goods and make them available to larger numbers of their members, it would also lead to an increase in wages. After attending an OLA-sponsored seminar on ways in which labor could help increase production, DGB executive committee member Ludwig Rosenberg appeared to be more sympathetic to the program.[21] Nonetheless, the DGB refrained from taking any concrete steps to initiate a permanent program of its own.

In addition to the TWI journal, OLA sponsored and distributed a number of other publications – books, pamphlets, and journals – and films within labor and employer circles, all of which were intended to further labor–management cooperation or improve democratic practices within the unions. *Gift of Freedom,* a publication of the U.S. Department of Labor that praised the high standard of living enjoyed by the American worker, was translated and distributed in large numbers. A weekly compilation of labor news from around the

---

20 See Kern to Stern, March 21, 1950, NA, RG 466, HICOG, box 95, folder: 560.1 Trade Unions March 50. Kern makes reference to the article "Mehr und billiger produzieren! Eine gewerkschaftliche Stellungnahme," *Welt der Arbeit,* March 17, 1950.
21 Brown to Hanes, Jan. 16, 1951, NA, RG 466, HICOG, box 96, folder: 560.1 Trade Unions Jan. 1951; "Träger betrieblicher Sozialpraxis," *Die Neue Zeitung,* May 31, 1951, p. 4. Gillen, *Labor Problems,* 75. See also Baldwin to State Dept., Nov. 14, 1952, NA, RG 466, HICOG, box 96, folder: 560.1 Trade Unions Jul.–Dec. 1952.

world, *Internationale Arbeitsmitteilungen,* provided labor circles with information they could not yet gather on their own. Moreover, films and pamphlets produced by unions in the United States on such topics as democratic procedure at union meetings or the art of speechmaking and how to conduct discussions were used by OLA as a means to "call attention of the German workers to the fact that it is possible to conduct discussions on a free basis. . . . It is one of the difficulties of all German labor organizations that in their meetings the leaders tend to speak dogmatically in order of seniority with little discussion on the part of subordinates." The Office of Labor Affairs, as Gillen has written, hoped "that this situation may be gradually changed."[22]

Soon after HICOG began operation, the Office of Labor Affairs approached the newly founded DGB with a list of projects to be implemented. OLA apparently did not consult the unions about the subject area of the projects; rather, it informed the DGB as to what projects it would sponsor and what kind of participation it expected from the unions. OLA's initial project list included seven different proposals: a study of labor courts; the study program for one hundred young trade unionists in the United States; a short-term visit to the United States by selected labor leaders to study American unions, the educational system, and youth facilities; courses on the Marshall Plan and possibilities of cooperations for the unions in Europe; publication of a handbook on the German unions; production of a recruiting film for the unions; and expansion of the union-sponsored correspondence courses *(Briefschule).*[23]

During the next three years, this list grew to include a number of other interesting activities. For example, OLA provided funds to the DGB weekly newspaper *Welt der Arbeit* for a regular propaganda section on the Marshall Plan, and, subsequently, on the Schuman Plan.[24] The HICOG Special Projects Fund and OLA's reorientation budget supported labor academies operated by the unions in Frankfurt, Dortmund, and Hamburg, as well as various union schools and adult education facilities. Together with allocations made to the women's affairs, youth, and education offices of the DGB and its mem-

22 Gillen, *Labor Problems,* 73.
23 See Georg Reuter, Aktennotiz für Kollegen Böckler, Nov. 25, 1949, HBS, Ordner DGB-Bundesvorstand, Abt. Vors. (H. Böckler), Oktober 1949 bis 16.2.1951.
24 See Siggi Neumann, Aktennotiz, June 19, 1951, Nachlass Henssler, SPD-Parteivorstand, Archiv der sozialen Demokratie, Bonn-Bad Godesberg. See also Rosenberg to Enderle, Trepte, and Dr. Potthof, "Betr.: ERP-Propaganda," June 23, 1949, HBS, Bestand 10/20.

ber unions, OLA funneled up to approximately DM 1.2 million yearly to the DGB. This sum does not include monies provided to various research projects, such as a study on unemployment and morale of the German youth and the Darmstadt and Frankfurt community surveys.[25]

In accord with HICOG's emphasis on the democratization of Germany, the Office of Labor Affairs attached great importance to the question of democracy in the unions. OLA Director Harvey Brown regularly pointed to the necessity for unions to "develop an organizational structure which will permit the rank and file members full opportunity to participate in determining union policy and to assume responsibility for such policies." In this way, unions could "strengthen the influence of organized labor in shaping the development of Germany" and, at the same time, "train the membership in their responsibilities as citizens." As Brown declared:

Local union meetings are the universities of the working people. Here they learn about the issues which affect them as workers and as citizens and here they can make the decisions which affect these issues. Such meetings must be held in union halls and not within the four walls of the employer's plant. An over centralization of the union structure will destroy this opportunity for action at the local level.[26]

From the outset of the occupation period, U.S. labor policy prevented German labor leaders from building highly centralized organizations. It supported those unionists who favored autonomous industrial or craft unions. American representatives argued that centralized power structures were susceptible to misuse; moreover, a union organization of this type would be "top heavy" and could not possibly attend to the needs of its members at the workplace. After the founding of the DGB in 1949, American labor officers viewed with trepidation the power accrued by its chairman, Hans Böckler. After his death in early 1951, they welcomed the prospect of a successor with less authority and, hence, of a weakening of centralistic tendencies.[27]

25 Gillen, *Labor Problems*, 25–7, 75–7.
26 Harvey W. Brown, "Labor's Unfinished Tasks," *Information Bulletin of the Office of the U.S. High Commissioner for Germany* (Oct. 1951):21.
27 See Brown to McCloy, Dec. 22, 1949, NA, RG 466, HICOG, box 94, folder: 560.1; Weigert to Brown, "State of Industrial Relations in Western Germany, Spring 1951," June 5, 1951, NA, RG 466, HICOG, McCloy Papers, D(51)1046. For a caustic critique of the I.G. Metall and the DGB in comparison to the United States Steel Workers of America and the CIO, see the detailed report by Meyer Bernstein, encl. to desp. 375, Düsseldorf, NA, RG 59, 862a.062/1-952.

Concomitantly, American labor officers continually stressed their concern over the fact that German unions did not reach their members on the job. To the Americans, the factory local formed the backbone of union organizational strength. Such a unit did not exist in Germany, where its place was assumed by the legal institution of works councils. American labor officers only grudgingly accepted the reconstitution of works councils and subsequently sought to limit independent works council activities and to increase union influence.[28] Within OLA as well, the belief prevailed that works councils usurped functions at the shop level that were basic to union existence. As labor officer Meyer Bernstein wrote, the local was "the source of the union's life and at the same time the point of impact. Without the local practically nothing can be done. The success of any contract depends upon the manner in which the local union officers carry it out or enforce it." In contrast, he continued, the institution of works councils in Germany resembled plans initiated by American steel companies in the 1930s "for the purpose of thwarting labor organizations in the industry."[29]

However, the American labor officers were only secondarily concerned about the dangers of employer control over works councils. More immediately, they perceived the threat posed by Communists as the primary cause for alarm. Returns from works council elections, especially in the Ruhr industries, showed that Communists were being elected by relatively large numbers of non-Communist workers. Moreover, as Harvey Brown complained, "too many unionists, including officers, still believe that a Communist can at the same time also be a good trade unionist."[30] As an obvious example of such a situation, Brown's staff pointed to a case in which the chairman of the works council at the Robert Bosch GmbH in Stuttgart, an active member of the Communist Party (KPD), was selected to join the executive committee of his union (I.G. Metall), despite a DGB recommendation that he be removed from all union offices.[31] Confirming Brown's complaint, the local labor officer attributed such Communist successes to the fact that workers voted "for the most vigorous trade unionists and the best bargainers. It

28 See Fichter, *Besatzungsmacht und Gewerkschaften*, 175–91.
29 Meyer Bernstein, encl. to desp. 375, Düsseldorf, NA, RG 59, 862a.062/1-952.
30 Brown, "Labor's Unfinished Tasks," 21.
31 Friedman to Brown, Oct. 6, 1950, NA, RG 466, HICOG, box 96, folder: 560.1 Trade Unions Oct. 1950.

seems that the Communists fulfilled these requirements better than any other group of individuals."[32]

The only immediate remedy to such a situation that HICOG labor officers could offer to the non-Communist union leadership was to follow the example of American unions and expel all Communists. In a conference with the leaders of the DGB unions in August 1950, Harvey Brown described how his own union, the International Association of Machinists, had successfully rid itself of all Communist influence. He was convinced of the German unions' sincerity in their willingness to battle "the KPD menace," but, at the same time, "he realized that they do not have a formula." Since the greatest Communist activity seemed to be at the shop level, Brown proposed "as a first step, to make it illegal for the KPD to hold office in trade unions and works councils."[33] Such exhortations did not go unheeded, although they were surely not wholly responsible for the subsequent administrative steps taken by the DGB unions against Communists. At the conference, several union leaders openly stated that they were already confronting the KPD proponents within their organizations. Within the DGB leadership, the subject of Communist activity in the unions constituted a major point of discussion; in October 1950, the DGB executive committee served notice that it would fire any union officeholder or employee who supported the politics of the KPD. It also recommended that its member unions do the same.[34]

Both the German trade union leadership and HICOG labor officers agreed that such administrative measures offered no real solution to the problem. In the long run, the only way to effectively combat Communism was to eliminate unemployment and improve the living conditions of the workers. However, substantial differences of opinion separated the German unionists and the HICOG staff as to the most desirable means of achieving these goals.

Traditionally, organized labor in Germany has always represented more than just the workers' "bread and butter" demands. This was

32 Friedman to Brown, Nov. 22, 1950, NA, RG 466, HICOG, box 96, folder: 560.1 Trade Unions Nov. 1950.
33 Brown to McCloy, "Meeting with leaders of the sixteen trade unions of Western Germany on August 14, 1950," Aug. 28, 1950, NA, RG 466, HICOG, box 94, folder: 560.1. See also Gillen, *Labor Problems*, 22–5.
34 See *Geschäftsbericht des Bundesvorstandes des Deutschen Gewerkschaftsbundes 1950–1951* (Düsseldorf, 1952), 29–30. See also the report published by the DGB in October 1950 entitled *Feinde der Gewerkschaften – Feinde der Demokratie: Tatsachen und Dokumente*.

especially true for the post-1945 Occupation period. Generally recognized as a reliable force for the democratization of Germany, labor became deeply involved in political and economic recovery, laying claim to equal recognition based on its programmatic essentials. Economic democracy, heralded as the key element, would be achieved through socialization or public ownership of basic industries or both, coupled with the creation of national, regional, and industrywide planning councils of representatives of labor, capital, and government. However, since Allied economic controls prevented an early decision on the ownership question and militant works councils in the Ruhr industries demanded union action to alleviate food shortages and to force acceptance of labor's demands for economic democracy, union leaders welcomed the opportunity offered them for instituting company-level codetermination.[35] As the prospect of socialization became less and less realistic, the concept of codetermination developed into the actual centerpiece of labor's demands for economic democracy in the course of the next few years.

For various reasons, HICOG's labor officers remained skeptical of the advantages German labor associated with codetermination. They raised the question of whether the persons chosen by labor for positions in the upper echelons of large companies would in fact be able and willing to represent labor's interests, especially in conflict situations.[36] Furthermore, the OLA staff fundamentally disagreed with the notion that the German unions were ready "to put all their eggs into one basket and to fight practically exclusively for codetermination, even at the expense of wages."[37] The Americans also disapproved of the preference of German labor for codetermination by legislation instead of using collective bargaining to achieve its goals. Through "a fuller appreciation of the effectiveness of collective bargaining," unions (and employers) would "cast off the autocratic practices which in the past have dominated both public and private life" and show a better understanding of the American objective of

---

35 See esp. Horst Thum, *Mitbestimmung in der Montanindustrie: Der Mythos vom Sieg der Gewerkschaften* (Stuttgart, 1982). Gloria Müller, *Mitbestimmung in der Nachkriegszeit: Britische Besatzungsmacht, Unternehmer, Gewerkschaften* (Düsseldorf, 1987). See Diethelm Prowe's contribution in this volume for a discussion of American opposition to institutionalized (corporatist) organs of cooperation between business and labor.

36 See, for example, the case study by Meyer Bernstein, DGB Meeting with Labor Advisers, Aug. 20, 1951, encl. to desp. 103, NA, RG 59, 862a.062/8-2051, box 5201.

37 H. F. Kern, HICOG Staff Meeting, Jan. 16, 1951, NA, RG 466, HICOG, McCloy Papers, HICOG Staff Conferences 1949–1952, D(51)53, box 2.

democratic reorientation.[38] According to Gillen, Harvey Brown "could not understand why the unions always refused to strike. He was against strikes except as a last resort, but he felt that the moment for the last resort had long since passed."[39]

In response to such criticism, DGB leaders emphasized that it had been their policy all along to strive for wage levels that would support economic reconstruction and enable German industry to regain a share of the export market. Thus, so the argument ran within the DGB, the interest of American labor officers in wage hikes camouflaged an attempt to deny German industry a competitive edge in international markets.[40] This was a serious matter for the DGB leadership. As the new DGB chairman, Christian Fette, stated in a meeting with Allied officials in August 1951, his organization realized "that under the present international and political situation it would be most unfortunate for the German economy if . . . wage negotiations should become deadlocked and force the unions to take more drastic steps. . . ."[41] Beyond this consideration, union leaders harbored the fear that the rank and file, largely without any trade union experience and without any real savings after the currency reform, would not hold out in a prolonged wage struggle.[42] And, as Otto Kirchheimer reported to the U.S. Department of State in a study of the organization and policies of the DGB, there was little inclination on the part of the unions to "fight it out with the employer" because they believed that,

in the long run, more substantial gains are likely to be derived from union pressure on the Government than from struggles with the employers. Pressure on the employer, so runs the argument, is limited largely to the wage front and, if successful, carries with it the danger of a wage–price spiral. Union pressure on the German administration and parliament would not only achieve success in any number of issues of social and labor policy, but would also enhance the union's influence on economic policy. It would allow the trade unions – and the individual worker via the exercise of

38 Harvey W. Brown, "Labor-Movement Pattern," *Information Bulletin of the Office of the U.S. High Commissioner for Germany* (Nov. 1950):83.
39 Gillen, *Labor Problems*, 20. See also Brown's follow-up memorandum to this incident, in which he tried to placate critics within HICOG. Brown to McCloy, Aug. 10, 1950, NA, RG 466, HICOG, box 94, folder: 560.1.
40 Albert Stenzel an Erich Bührig, Mar. 4, 1949, HBS, Bestand 10/13.
41 Harvey Brown, Meeting of the Labor Affairs Committee, Aug. 16, 1951, desp. 657, NA, RG 59, 862a.062/8-3151.
42 Oskar Weigert, Memo on Economic Policies in West Germany, July 27, 1950, NA, RG 59, 862a.06/7-2750, box 5191.

codetermination by the works councils – to take its full share in the remodeling of present economic institutions which are considered responsible, in part, for the worker's plight.[43]

Nevertheless, by the end of 1952, the preference of the unions for
political means had been enormously dampened by their failure to
secure adequate codetermination provisions in a newly adopted general law on works councils. Within a short time, the alternative strategy – the improvement of the workers' living standard through
collective bargaining – became widely accepted within the individual DGB unions. Not surprisingly, this shift was also personified by
the election of Walter Freitag to succeed Christian Fette as DGB
chairman. Freitag admired American production methods and attempted to convince German manufacturers that American-style
mass production represented the key to raising the German standard
of living and ensuring future prosperity and stability.[44]

Beyond the policies and programs pursued by the Office of Labor
Affairs, several issues crucial to the political and economic stability of
the fledgling Republic marked HICOG's relationship to the unions
during McCloy's tenure as high commissioner: the lifting of the suspension imposed by the Military Government on the economic codetermination provisions of works council laws in Hesse and
Württemberg-Baden; the legal continuation of codetermination provisions existing since 1947 in the iron and steel industries and their
extension to the coal industry; decartelization and the ownership of
industrial property under trusteeship; and, finally, German defense
production and rearmament. On the whole, these issues have been
well covered in several publications. But as my initial research indicates, the question of HICOG's role and its relationship to the DGB
unions in these matters needs to be looked at more closely.

By early 1947, Military Government had approved *Land* constitutions, and the first elected state governments had taken office. From
that time on, the unions directed their efforts toward securing legislation on behalf of their demands for codetermination. With the
passage of such laws in Hesse (May 1948) and Württemberg-Baden
(August 1948), providing for factory-level employee, union, and

43 Otto Kirchheimer, Organization and Policies of the German Trade Union Federation
(Deutscher Gewerkschaftsbund) in the Federal German Republic, Jan. 1950, FU-ZI
SOWIFO, 6/124-1/20.
44 See Baldwin to Donnelly, Conversation between Secretary of Commerce Sawyer and
DGB chairman Walter Freitag, Nov. 29, 1952, NA, RG 466, HICOG, box 96, folder: 560.1
Trade Unions Jul.–Dec. 1952.

works-council participation in decision making, the unions appeared to have taken a large step toward achieving their goals.

Certain provisions of both laws, however, did not meet with the approval of OMGUS. In letters to the ministers president of Hesse and Württemberg-Baden in the fall of 1948, Clay ordered the suspension of the economic codetermination provisions of both laws. Invoking his "defense of federalism" argument, he stated that he could not condone such a development on a state basis. Economic codetermination was a matter with ramifications beyond the individual state level and could only be handled by federal legislation. Since the proposed Basic Law was soon to be completed, Clay argued "that it would be a serious mistake to prejudge this basic law now by resolving separately in several states their separate economic patterns."[45] Despite numerous protests and resolutions demanding the lifting of the suspensions, OMGUS showed no signs of reconsidering its decision until after the passage of the Basic Law in May 1949. Following Clay's departure from Germany in July 1949, McCloy decided to uphold the suspension and give the first federal government time to enact proper legislation before taking final action. But after the State Department informed him in October 1949 that the constitutional reasons for the suspension advanced by OMGUS had lost their validity,[46] McCloy realized that he could no longer postpone the issue. As he told his staff on November 23, lifting the suspension "may impair the flow of investments, but I don't think I have any recourse but to take that step."[47] Nevertheless, he ignored pleas for quick action from the State Department resulting from union charges of "undemocratic behavior of United States authorities in Germany." Instead, he wished to give Adenauer, who was claiming to have already initiated action, more time.[48]

Perhaps the lack of strong pressure from the DGB leadership influenced McCloy's willingness to avoid "precipitous action." Union chairman Hans Böckler calmly accepted McCloy's arguments in

---

45 Clay to Stock, Sept. 3, 1948, quoted in Gillen, *Labor Problems*, 37. See also John Gimbel, *The American Occupation of Germany: Politics and the Military, 1945–1949* (Stanford, Calif. 1968), 233–7.

46 See Gillen, *Labor Problems*, 37–8.

47 HICOG Staff Meeting, Nov. 23, 1949, NA, RG 466, HICOG, McCloy Papers, HICOG Staff Conferences 1949–52, D(49)391, box 1.

48 See State Dept. cable, Nov. 25, 1949, NA, RG 466, HICOG, McCloy Papers, D(49)393, box 4; HICOG Staff Meeting, Nov. 30, 1949, NA, RG 466, HICOG, McCloy Papers, HICOG Staff Conferences 1949–52, D(49)408, box 1. On Adenauer's double strategy at this point, see Thum, *Mitbestimmung*, 38–9.

their first meeting on December 20, presumably, as Harvey Brown surmised, because Böckler favored centralism and was more interested in federal legislation on codetermination than in championing the *Länder* cause.[49] Nevertheless, McCloy did go on record as being opposed to indefinitely maintaining the suspension. At the AFL's insistence, he had set a deadline of April 1, 1950 for the federal government to take action. When this date passed without evidence of any substantial progress, McCloy acted swiftly. On April 7, he informed the respective ministers president that he had lifted the suspension.[50] In doing so, he placated the State Department (which had been urging him for months to take this step) and rid himself of a latent controversy with labor. To be sure, the decision had no marked effect on labor relations in either of the two *Länder,* at least in part because, at this point, interest in the codetermination issue had gravitated to the national level. Whether or not this decision put the federal government under pressure to introduce national legislation, as has been claimed, is still an open question.

Before the codetermination issue had to be decided for the whole economy, a conflict arose over this issue in the iron, steel, and coal industries of the Ruhr. Following the decision of the British Military Government in 1946 to set up twenty-five new iron and steel companies under trusteeship, the properties sought union support in protecting their investments from dismantling and further decartelization. By 1947 an agreement had been reached with the unions (and sanctioned by the British) giving labor five seats out of eleven on the board of directors (*Aufsichtsrat*) and the right to nominate the executive director for personnel. The unions heralded this arrangement as an important victory for economic democracy and a model for labor's participation in all segments of the economy. It remained virtually unchallenged throughout the amalgamation of the British and American zones and survived intact the subsequent unification of all three Western zones into the Federal Republic.[51]

49 Memorandum of Meeting between Mr. McCloy and representatives of the DGB, Frankfurt, Dec. 20, 1949; Brown to McCloy, Dec. 22, 1949, NA, RG 466, HICOG, box 94, folder: 560.1. See also Gillen, *Labor Problems,* 39.
50 Werner Link, *Deutsche und amerikanische Gewerkschaften und Geschäftsleute 1945–1975: Eine Studie über transnationale Beziehungen* (Düsseldorf, 1978), 73–4; Gillen, *Labor Problems,* 39.
51 See Müller, *Mitbestimmung;* Thum, *Mitbestimmung;* Abraham Shuchman, *Codetermination: Labor's Middle Way in Germany* (Washington, D.C., 1957), 122–6; Herbert J. Spiro, *The Politics of German Codetermination* (Cambridge, Mass., 1958), 27–36.

But by autumn 1950, the future of codetermination in the Ruhr iron and steel industry, as well as the opportunity for labor to win full recognition of its programmatic demands in this field, seemed to be in danger. The draft codetermination laws for the whole economy introduced into the Bundestag by the federal government and the CDU/CSU fell far short of union demands. Moreover, powerful interests were moving toward an open attempt to eliminate the parity model of codetermination from the iron and steel industries under trusteeship. American representatives of the Combined Steel Group questioned the necessity of union representation on the board of directors. German Law No. 27, which had been promulgated in May 1950 to succeed Allied Law No. 75 on the reorganization of certain basic industries, contained a modification promising the old owners adequate compensation for their investments. Economics Minister Ludwig Erhard's statement to the effect that, since German corporate law contained no provisions for labor representation on the board of directors, this practice could not be continued once ownership had passed from Allied trusteeship into German hands, further threatened union positions. The import of this statement was confirmed when word leaked out that Erhard's ministry was planning an administrative order for Law No. 27 that would reorganize the companies according to German law and exclude labor from its representation.[52] The DGB immediately announced its opposition to any reorganization plans that did not include the codetermination already in practice. An I.G. Metall strike vote showed almost 96 percent of the membership ready to walk out in support of union demands. Because of the planned organizational connections between the iron and steel companies, on the one hand, and the coal companies (in which no such codetermination existed), on the other, the miners union (I.G. Bergbau) decided to prepare for a strike as well.

While the State Department regarded this conflict in principle as a German issue in which McCloy should not be involved, it was deeply concerned – in light of the Korean War – about the prospective loss of production and social unrest a strike would entail. Thus,

52 Gillen, *Labor Problems*, 57; Wolfgang Hirsch-Weber, *Gewerkschaften in der Politik. Von der Massenstreikdebatte zum Kampf um das Mitbestimmungsrecht* (Cologne and Opladen, 1959), 89; Horst Thum, *Mitbestimmung*, 61–4; *Montanmitbestimmung: Das Gesetz über die Mitbestimmung der Arbeitnehmer in den Aufsichtsräten und Vorständen der Unternehmen des Bergbaus und der Eisen und Stahl erzeugenden Industrie vom 21. Mai 1951,* Quellen zur Geschichte des Parlamentarismus und der politischen Parteien, 4. Reihe, Bd. 1, ed. Gabriele Müller-List (Düsseldorf, 1984), xliii ff.

in a message dated December 9, 1950, the State Department cabled that, if HICOG thought that the positions taken by Chancellor Adenauer and the DGB were irreconcilable, it favored putting pressure on Adenauer. The message concluded hopefully: "You may be able to suggest a course of action which would favor neither side and insure industrial peace for an indefinite period until political and economic implications of management–labor row no longer are magnified by necessities of defense effort."[53] The State Department had drafted the message after talks in Washington with DGB vice chairman Georg Reuter, whose stance had impressed State Department officials. McCloy, too, had received information from his labor affairs director that there was little possibility of the unions backing down on their demands. They were not prepared, as Brown wrote, to let the German people be "sold down the river the third time" by what they termed to be "certain elements among the industrialists and bankers [who] on two occasions wrecked our country." In addition, he warned McCloy that the United States would be "bitterly condemned" if HICOG or the Combined Steel Group interfered on behalf of the employers or gave the impression that they were "picking the German Government's chestnuts out of the fire." Brown concluded that the "important thing to keep in mind now is that codetermination (right or wrong) is the basic article of faith of the German labor union movement, and if we kill that, we would not have that much-needed influence necessary in making the German labor movement a greater force for democracy."[54]

At the same time, McCloy had received a memorandum from a member of his labor staff accusing the American representatives on the Combined Steel Board of encouraging Minister Erhard to campaign against codetermination. The labor officer urged McCloy to meet with union leaders to discuss the codetermination issue and present HICOG's position. At McCloy's request, the meeting took place on December 14, during which he emphasized his intention to remain absolutely neutral and leave the final decision to the Germans. While the unions accepted this statement, they nevertheless expressed skepticism as to whether McCloy could maintain such a position for very long if the Germans could not reach an agreement. According to the German minutes of this meeting, McCloy replied

53 Byroade to McCloy, Dec. 9, 1950, NA, RG 59, 862a.062/12-950, box 5200.
54 Brown to McCloy, Dec. 6, 1950, FU-ZI SOWIFO, 17/258-1/1. Gillen, *Labor Problems,* 59–60.

that in those circumstances, even he would not take a decision which would infringe on the interests of German employees.[55]

McCloy was also aware that labor and business interests in the United States supported the positions their respective partners in the Federal Republic had taken on the issue. Thus, any form of intervention would have caused serious repercussions with one side or the other. It is not surprising, then, that in early January, McCloy informed the State Department that he and his fellow high commissioners had agreed to maintain a strict neutrality on the issue, not the least in order to provide "good offices for labor–management negotiations" if necessary.[56]

Once agreement had been tentatively reached at the end of January, McCloy reported to the State Department that his decision to remain neutral had been a "major factor" in the settlement, because it had "convinced the parties [that there was] no chance of intervention."[57] For Adenauer, the Allies' neutrality meant that his government's political future depended upon resolving the issue and avoiding a strike. To the employers, it forced Adenauer to accede to labor's demands in order to avoid a crippling strike. As for labor, neutrality on the part of the Allies was apparently more than it was ready to expect. Many of the union leaders continued to harbor suspicions of American motives, fearing that HICOG and American business interests were in fact working behind the scenes to sabotage labor's efforts on behalf of a general codetermination law for the whole economy.[58]

The conflict over codetermination in the iron, steel, and coal industries erupted at a time of intense union frustration over some very basic issues. The DGB favored the nationalization of basic industries, the limitation of far-reaching decartelization of the iron, steel, coal, and chemical industries, and the prevention of the return

55 "Aktenvermerk Deists über eine Besprechung von Gewerkschaftsvertretern mit dem Hohen Kommissar der Vereinigten Staaten von Amerika McCloy in Bad Godesberg," Dec. 14, 1950, in *Montanmitbestimmung*, doc. 54. See also Kern to Stone, Dec. 8, 1950, ibid., doc. 49.
56 Cable 457 Bonn, Jan. 11, 1951, NA, RG 466, HICOG, McCloy Papers, D(51)35, box 24. A subsequent move by the French and British high commissioners on January 25 to inform Adenauer that, in the event of a strike, the Allies intended to extend existing codetermination regulations to other steel companies as well as to the coal industry was blocked by McCloy. Apparently, this move had no direct influence on negotiations between the employers and the unions already in progress. See cable 481, HICOG Bonn to State Dept., Jan. 25, 1951, ibid., D(51)96, box 24.
57 Tel. 6202, HICOG to State Dept., Jan. 26, 1951, NA, RG 446, HICOG, McCloy Papers, D(51)100, box 24.
58 See McCloy to State Dept., Jan. 23, 1952, NA, RG 466, HICOG, box 89, folder: 560 Codetermination. See also Kern to Stone, Dec. 8, 1950, in *Montanmitbestimmung*, doc. 49.

of property rights in these industries to the former owners. For a time, the conflict over codetermination not only diverted attention from the issues of decartelization and ownership, but, in the end, it even offered the unions a respite and a possible way out of a strategically weak situation.

As mentioned earlier, the DGB worried that German Law No. 27 would be used to allow the former owners of companies under trusteeship to regain their power. At the same time, DGB leaders viewed HICOG's decartelization policy as a thinly veiled attempt to cripple the economic potential of German industry. They argued that if, in fact, American policy aimed at preventing German industry from leading Germany into war again, participation of organized labor in management would be a far more effective means to this end than a stringent decartelization program.[59] HICOG waived any legal claim to responsibility regarding the question of ownership (Law No. 27) and codetermination even as the unions attempted to enlist Allied moral support.[60] Nevertheless, the problem of the reorganization of those industries under trusteeship continued to be a bone of contention between HICOG and the unions. Indeed, Laws No. 27 and 35 (I.G. Farben) gave the Allies full responsibility for the final decision on reorganization.

OLA staff members claimed to be making every effort to involve the DGB and the individual unions directly affected in the planning process for the new firms. But as one labor official reported to the State Department in early October 1950, this liaison work had proved to be "of extreme difficulty." He continued,

The tendency has been for the trade unions to do little planning ahead of time to meet situations or problems that might arise, and therefore to be surprised when confronted with these situations and problems, too late to be able to do anything about influencing either. As a result, the trade unions often complained about not having been consulted. This process had repeated itself again and again in regard to impending problems despite the fact that the unions had been warned and urged to get busy and make their positions known in time for them to have some influence on policy.[61]

---

59 See Gillen, *Labor Problems*, 27–8. The DGB position was given full support by the AFL. See Irving Brown to Dean Acheson, July 5, 1950, NA, RG 59, 862a.062/7-550, box 5200.
60 See Böckler to Kirkpatrick, Oct. 13, 1950, HBS, Ordner DGB-Bundesvorstand, Abt. Vors. (H. Böckler), Oktober 1949 bis 16.2.1951.
61 W. L. White, "Difficulty of Liaison with West German Trade Unions," Oct. 2, 1950, NA, RG 59, 862a.062/10-250.

In a personal letter to Hans Böckler, another labor staff member voiced the same criticism and cited specific examples. For months, he wrote, he had asked for "concrete case material about the accusation that important and controlling positions in German industry were turned back to the former owners and former Nazis." Nothing was forthcoming except further promises.[62]

Without more information, it is difficult to draw any conclusions as to the intent of such statements. Whether the DGB had in fact failed to deliver material and to submit plans, as the Americans charged, is not certain. The DGB head office rejected the accusations immediately.[63] American labor officials may also have been trying to head off any criticism of their work within HICOG or in Washington. American officials were aware that criticism of U.S. policy was spreading in the unions and had even begun to receive public attention. Just a week before the OLA staff members wrote their statements, union leader Viktor Agartz spoke to a mass rally, claiming that the Americans listened only to the employers and excluded the DGB from the organization process.[64] If union criticism was valid, this was the result of decisions taken by higher American authorities. Indeed, there were instances in which HICOG had pointedly rejected attempts by the other Allies to enlist labor support for industrial deconcentration, because it wanted at all costs to avoid "showing any favoritism" to labor. Subsequent development, such as the Allies' decision in May 1951 to return stock holdings to their former owners, also showed that labor's anger was not unfounded.[65] For their part, OLA labor staffers vehemently rejected the generality of union criticism (in their eyes "anti-Americanism"). Although they may have even agreed with its basic thrust, they needed to show their superiors that the alleged shortcomings were not their fault; and as to the unions, the OLA officers might have been trying to tone down the shrillness of their accusations.

Although the question of German rearmament and participation in a Western military alliance had received public attention before the outbreak of the Korean war (AFL leader Matthew Woll had

62 Kern to Böckler, Oct. 2, 1950, HBS, Ordner Abt. Vors. (H. Böckler), October 1949 bis 16.2.1951.
63 See Stenzel to Böckler, Oct. 12, 1950, ibid.   64 See White, "Difficulty of Liaison."
65 See, for example, HICOM Council Meeting, Oct. 19, 1950, NA, RG 466, HICOG, McCloy Papers, D(50)2347a, box 20; Thum, *Mitbestimmung,* 110–19.

already made such a proposal in 1945),[66] the conflict in the Far East
catapulted the issue into the forefront of Allied, German, and European concern. At first, proponents of a possible West German defense contribution argued that the United States needed the available
West German industrial capacity to support its own military production. The so-called Korea boom resulted in increased employment
and considerably higher income for labor, and the DGB joined various government planning and advisory committees to help guide
the economy.[67]

The actual rearmament question did not become a matter of immediate importance to the DGB unions – at least in their relationships with HICOG – until many months later. During a meeting
with OLA Director Brown in August 1950, at which the Korean War
and possible contributions by the West Germans and their labor organizations in support of U.S. involvement constituted the main
topic, none of the union leaders suggested the need for a West German army. August Schmidt of the mine workers union thought that
the Federal Republic was "in danger of being overrun," but that no
one knew for certain what to do about it. None of the other participants felt called upon to pick up this line of thought, preferring
instead to talk about the problems of dealing with Communist influence in their unions.[68]

Shortly after this meeting, however, statements by Chancellor
Adenauer and French Prime Minister Pleven opened a broad political discussion of the arms issue which the DGB could not
long ignore. Apparently in preparation for the DGB executive
committee meeting on November 21, 1950 to discuss an official
union statement, DGB leaders Böckler and Reuter met with
McCloy. As reported to the State Department, the union leaders
had an "affirmative attitude toward a German contribution to
European defense." It would be "absurd," said Böckler, in view
of the overwhelming danger posed by the East, for West Germans
to do nothing while others were defending their freedom. To
make the idea of rebuilding a German army more palatable to
the workers, Böckler and Reuter called for new elections, which

66 See Link, *Deutsche und amerikanische Gewerkschaften*, p. 88.
67 See Theo Pirker, *Die blinde Macht: Die Gewerkschaftsbewegung in der Bundesrepublik*, 2 vols.
   (Berlin, 1979), 1:207–8.
68 Brown to McCloy, Meeting with leaders of the sixteen trade unions of Western Germany,
   Aug. 28, 1950, NA, RG 466, HICOG, box 94, folder: 560.1.

could result in the formation of a grand coalition that would include the SPD.[69]

Böckler's support for Adenauer's rearmament policy, which has been linked to a trade-off involving codetermination in the Montan industries,[70] found sufficient backing within the DGB executive committee, but remained highly controversial among members and lower echelon union leaders. After Böckler's death in February 1951, his successor, Christian Fette, continued to assure HICOG that the unions were in favor of West German participation in military defense. The unions, he told McCloy, would not shirk their responsibility. But a German contribution to a European army would presume that "Germany should have the same rights and chances as other free nations." Above all, the unions wished to exert their influence to prevent a German military force from being dominated by the old guard and endangering democracy.[71]

This essay has concentrated on the relationship between HICOG and the West German trade unions during McCloy's tenure as high commissioner. During this period, basic (but not necessarily final) decisions were made on issues involving organized labor that were crucial to the future of the Federal Republic: codetermination, the Schuman Plan, decartelization, and rearmament. Under McCloy's successor, HICOG labor officials did little more than report to the State Department on general union matters, and the new commissioner maintained only sporadic contact with union leaders. An example of this can be seen in the conflict in 1952 over a national works constitution law to regulate codetermination at the individual-company level. There is no evidence of HICOG involvement, nor did the issue generate any substantial internal activity within HICOG or the State Department.

Although HICOG had no specific powers to intervene directly in most labor issues, the Americans still exerted a considerable

---

69 Tel. 3851, HICOG to State Dept., Nov. 8, 1950, NA, RG 466, HICOG, McCloy Papers, Top Secret General Records, T.S.(50)146.

70 See Arnulf Baring, *Aussenpolitik in Adenauers Kanzlerdemokratie: Bonns Beitrag zur Europäischen Verteidigungsgemeinschaft* (Munich and Vienna, 1969). Baring maintains that Böckler agreed in August 1950 to support Adenauer's rearmament policy if the latter would support codetermination. McCloy, for his part, saw the connection between the two policies somewhat differently: Labor was backing the Federal government on the Schuman Plan and to a certain degree on a German army largely because of Adenauer's success in having the Bundestag approve a union-supported codetermination bill for the Ruhr. See McCloy to State Dept., Jan 23, 1952, NA, RG 466, HICOG, box 89, folder: 560 Codetermination.

71 Tel. 54, HICOG to State Dept., Oct. 6, 1951, NA, RG 466, HICOG, box 96, folder: 560.1 Trade Unions Aug.-Sept.-Oct. 1951; minutes of dinner meeting, Oct. 10, 1951, ibid.

amount of influence on union policies. In part, this influence re-sulted from programs and policies aimed directly at the unions. But to a large extent, American influence on the unions flowed more in-directly, a product of the general integration and reorientation poli-cies applied to the Federal Republic. Involvement and attempts to exert influence in the field of labor affairs took on a variety of forms. As in the case of the codetermination conflict, McCloy's steadfast neutrality even seems to have speeded agreement. Codetermination is also an issue on which American tutelage did not always lead to success. Organized labor simply refused to part with its goal of leg-islated codetermination.

In the end, "selling the American way of life" to German labor remained a pillar of American policy, but not an end in itself. Rather, it was more of an ideal and a means to a more politically and stra-tegically defined end. Of greater import to HICOG's concern for la-bor affairs and its attempts to influence the policy of the German trade unions was the goal of ensuring that organized labor would contribute to the political stability and economic growth of the Fed-eral Republic, as well as to its integration into the Western Alliance. Measured in these terms, the results indicate that success crowned American policy. But this conclusion can only be tentative as long as the extent of American influence has not been weighed against other determining factors within the German political sphere. This aspect should receive due consideration in future research.

14

U.S. Military Occupation, Grass Roots Democracy, and Local German Government

REBECCA BOEHLING

The democratization of Germany, one of the chief goals of the U.S. Military Government (MG), was to begin on the level of local government. In the early postwar period, this was the only level of German bureaucracy that remained in any way intact. Moreover, local government was the only sphere in which the local MG detachments had the authority to appoint German officials to lead the administrations. The American occupation authorities realized that "city government had been the one point where there existed a strong tradition of self-government in Germany."[1] Hence one might assume that the American occupation authorities would have welcomed and supported grass roots democratic initiatives. This was not, however, the case.

The revival of local German self-government meant an introduction of democracy only "insofar as the persons who were appointed to office were [supposed to be] democratic."[2] According to the U.S. occupation authorities, the prerequisite for a revival of "democratic political life even on the lowest level" was the democratization of local government and the formation of democratic political parties.[3] The U.S. occupying forces, however, postponed German democratic political revival until August 27, 1945, when they first permitted political activity and allowed the formation of political parties on the local level in their zone. Before then, a ban on all political activity was in effect, and U.S. MG's primary objective had been to restore public order and to revive municipal administration. "Political activity was not the need of the moment," argued the Office of the

---

1 *Civil Affairs Guide*, July 22, 1944, p. 2, NA, RG 59, Records of the Bureau of Intelligence and Research (R & A Reports), 1941–1961, 1655 15.
2 J. F. J. Gillen, *State and Local Government in West Germany, 1945–53*, Historical Division of the Office of HICOG (n.p., 1953), 5.
3 Ibid.

Political Advisor for the U.S. Zone of Occupation; instead "the need was for a period of practical emergency organization and for political stock taking."[4] Public order, a smooth-running bureaucracy, and an expedient material reconstruction took priority for most local MG detachments over any goals of democratization, even after the ban on political activity had been lifted. U.S. occupation authorities discouraged grass roots democratic initiatives either because they considered them to be political or because both German and MG officials perceived democratic initiatives as less organized and orderly, and therefore less efficient, than more authoritarian administration.[5]

The ban on political activity suppressed the potential for German grass roots democratic initiatives at a time when such initiatives would have had the strongest impact and could have provided the impetus for change. If U.S. policy inhibited grass roots initiatives at the municipal level, where democracy and self-government were to be restored first, then there was even less potential for far-reaching democratization on the *Land,* zonal, or later the national level. Once all the cogs of the bureaucratic wheel had been well greased and functioned smoothly, this propitious moment for initiating the process of reconstructing local democracy in Germany was gone.[6]

Some Germans initiated grass roots reforms from the earliest days of the occupation. The Antifa (Anti-Fascist) committees, for example, sought to redistribute housing according to need and the degree to which persons had suffered political discrimination or persecution. Because MG regarded this Antifa activity as "political," it prohibited these democratic action committees throughout the U.S. zone in the spring and summer of 1945, except temporarily in Stuttgart.

Another example of German grass roots initiative took the form of pressure that those who had not been included in the municipal administration placed upon the appointed mayors to form advisory city councils. These "outsiders" sought some level of reform-oriented in-

---

4 Encl., Perry Laukhuff to SecState, Nov. 21, 1946, p. 2, IfZ, RG 84, POLAD/746/9.
5 This argument differs considerably from that of the literature of the 1970s, which explained the development of a "Neuordnung oder Restauration?" in terms of a conscious victory of capitalism over socialism. Although this article will also emphasize the developing role of the Cold War over time in terms of high-level MG policy, it does not purport to further the thesis that this ideological conflict played a major role early on in the implementation of occupation policy. On the local detachment level, the emphasis on expediency by the U.S. Military Government detachments and their appointed officials, as well as a skepticism regarding German overt political activity, were much more instrumental in influencing German developments than any clear-cut anti-Communism or anti-Socialism.
6 Cf. Alfons Sollner, ed., *Zur Archäologie der Demokratie in Deutschland,* 2 vols. (Frankfurt am Main, 1982), 1:193.

put into municipal decision making in the crucial first months of the occupation. For its own reasons, the U.S. MG permitted its appointed mayors to form citizens' councils with exclusively advisory functions a few months after the mayors' appointments to their posts. This permission came, however, before the U.S. occupation authorities had lifted the ban on political activity and authorized the formation of political parties.[7] Since the advisory councils were not formally composed of political factions (because, technically speaking, political parties did not yet exist), MG did not consider them to violate the ban on political activity. As far as MG was concerned, their members were administrators rather than politicians. Generally Germans who, at least until that point, had been excluded from positions of municipal influence initiated the formation of the councils rather than the mayors or MG. On the other hand, the advisory councils eventually won the support of MG and the mayors as a means of competing with, or co-opting, the activist and, from their perspective, overly autonomous Antifa committees.

The MG-appointed mayors usually recruited advisory councilors from the major non-Nazi parties that had been represented in the last elected city councils of the Weimar Republic. In fact, they generally asked former leading members of those parties to suggest party lists, from which the mayors then chose advisory council members.[8] Reliance on the officially nonexistent political parties to form the supposedly apolitical advisory councils had implications not only for the refounding of the political parties but also for the potential success of any grass roots groundswell. This pattern of restoration of parties from above, even on the local level, squelched virtually all grass roots democratic initiatives. This top-down party development excluded many members of the Antifa committees who were too young to have had party affiliations before 1933 or who simply had not found their political niche prior to the inception of the Third Reich.

In the final days of the war and in the period immediately following the cessation of hostilities, spontaneous anti-Fascist activist groups sprang up in most major German cities.[9] Antifa committees were

7 Gillen, *State and Local Government*, p. 6.
8 This was the case in Frankfurt, Munich, and Stuttgart. See StA Munich, BuR 1537, StA Stuttgart, Hauptaktei 0621, and StA Frankfurt am Main, Mag 1060/1, Bd. 1.
9 Lutz Niethammer et al., eds., *Arbeiterinitiative 1945: Antifaschistische Ausschüsse und Reorganisation der Arbeiterbewegung in Deutschland* (Wuppertal, 1976), 12. See also Joseph R. Starr, *Denazification, Occupation, and Control of Germany, March-July 1945* (Salisbury, N.C., 1977), 127.

often run by Communists, because the lines of continuity among Communists that had been maintained during the period of illegality allowed for quick reemergence and organization. To a lesser extent, the same was true of Social Democrats and members of socialist splinter groups, who were also well represented in the Antifa leadership.[10] Often a coalition group of Social Democratic, Communist, and Center or Democratic party members led an Antifa group, such as the one in Höchst on the outskirts of Frankfurt.[11] In Stuttgart, the core group consisted of equal numbers of former KPD members and persons without prior political affiliation.[12] The composition of all Antifas was meant to reflect political parity and to constitute a united front of all anti-Fascists, regardless of previous political, religious, or union affiliations, in order to denazify and democratize German society, facilitate reconstruction, and contribute to a lasting peace.[13] However, since they rarely met their broad recruitment goals, the groups were vulnerable to charges of being "Communist inspired and Communist-used."[14]

The ban on political activity hurt the survival prospects of the Antifas. Partly as a way to circumvent this ban, the Antifas emphasized the practical aspects of their initiatives for the reconstruction of everyday life. Their denazification efforts included compiling lists of former Nazis and attesting to their level of complicity in order to have them committed to work details, arrested, or dismissed from employment[15]; tracking down Nazis who tried to cover up their identities; allocating furniture and housing according to a person's degree of resistance to, or complicity with, the regime;[16] searching lists of potential voters to determine who was to be excluded because

---

10 OSS report, "Action Groups in Post-Collapse Germany," p. 2, encl., POLAD report to SecState, May 29, 1945, IfZ, RG 84, POLAD TS/32/28, May 1945.
11 "Erinnerungen aus 1945," Peter Fischer Nachlass, StA Frankfurt am Main, S 1/30.
12 Lutz Niethammer, "Kampfkomitees und Arbeitsausschüsse in Stuttgart," in Lutz Niethammer et al., eds., *Arbeiterinitiative 1945*, 582.
13 Ibid. See also "Resolution zur Lage und die Aufgaben der antifaschistischen Arbeiter, Bauern, Bürger," Peter Fischer Nachlass, StA Frankfurt am Main, S 1/30. See also Starr, *Denazification*, 127.
14 Encl., Perry Laukhuff to SecState, Nov. 21, 1946, p. 2, IfZ, RG 84, POLAD/746/9. See Gillen, *State and Local Government*, 6.
15 Zentralstelle des Arbeitsausschusses Gross-Stuttgart an die württembergische Regierung, Jan. 12, 1946, and Kampfkomitee Ortsgruppe Botnang an OB Klett, May 2, 1945, StA Stuttgart, Hauptakten 0052-2. For Frankfurt, see Peter Fischer Nachlass, StA Frankfurt am Main, S 1/30, and OSS report, "Anti-Fascist Organizations and Tendencies in the Frankfurt Area," June 18, 1945, NA, RG 266, OSS, XL11911. For Munich, see OB Scharnagl an den Münchner Antifaschistischen Wirtschaftsausschuss, StA Munich, BuR 1647.
16 Chef der Stuttgarter Polizei an OB Klett, June 21, 1945, StA Stuttgart, Hauptaktei 0051-1.

of a Nazi past;[17] training of committee members in democracy, with an eye toward obtaining civil service positions;[18] and putting pressure on appointed local governments to allow democratic input into municipal decision making.[19] In addition, the groups engaged in more prosaic tasks, such as chopping and delivering wood, removing rubble, and requisitioning housing. All these roles had political implications. Denazification was a very political process because of its goal of purging former Nazis from political and socioeconomic life and restricting their activities according to their level of complicity until, and if, they became reeducated and rehabilitated. Antifa training, aimed at the creation of a new elite to fill the void left by denazification, was also political and represented the positive side of the purge policy, which was so obviously absent in other contexts. Unfortunately, this training never received the full support of the municipal administrations and was eventually stopped, ostensibly because the revival of *Volkshochschulen* made it redundant.[20] Even the more mundane tasks of collecting wood, removing rubble, and requisitioning and assigning housing had very political overtones, particularly in the early phase of the occupation. Since the Antifas called on former NSDAP *Parteigenossen* to help with these tasks and to give up or share their housing with those who had been persecuted by the Nazi regime, it was a kind of restitution of a political nature. Thus, the intentions of these Antifa actions were clearly political and, indeed, should be seen within the framework of "far-reaching measures of socialization and democratization."[21] The Antifas were committed politically to an anti-Fascist, democratic, and, for some, socialized Germany. Their activism reflected their genuine desire to accomplish this objective.

The Antifas exerted pressure on city governments to implement denazification[22] and to establish either advisory city councils, district councils, or Antifa advisory committees to help each municipal department. In the major cities in Württemberg, advisory city councils

17 OB, Bekanntmachung, July 30, 1945, StA Munich, BuR 1778.
18 OB an Zentralstelle der Arbeitsausschüsse Stuttgart, Oct. 20, 1945, StA Stuttgart, Hauptaktei 0434-1.
19 OB Klett an Dr. Könekamp et al., July 16, 1945, StA Stuttgart, Hauptaktei 0434-1.
20 Aufruf der Zentrale der Arbeitsausschüsse Gross-Stuttgart an alle Mitarbeiter, Sept. 18, 1945, StA Stuttgart, Hauptaktei 0434-1.
21 Leonard Krieger, "The Potential for Democratization in Occupied Germany: A Problem in Historical Projection," *Public Policy* 18 (1968):49.
22 In the first municipal elections of 1946, Nazi Party members were excluded from active and passive rights of citizenship.

actually replaced the Antifa committees, and for this explicit reason, the mayors encouraged the formation of councils.[23] In Stuttgart, the Antifas suggested that Mayor Klett appoint not only a thirty-two-member advisory council, but also a larger group of Antifa representatives who would participate in the various departments of the municipal administration and send a member to attend the city council meetings on a rotating basis. In this way, the Antifas argued, each area of expertise and "each direction in a democratic respect" would have their perspective represented.[24] However, the municipal authorities never granted this Antifa representation; instead they often used the advisory city councils to pull the rug out from under the Antifas' democratic initiatives and their reform potential. The Antifas were then co-opted into this broader, more traditional structure, in which the old political parties reigned from the top down, or they were replaced altogether with allegedly representative advisory councils.

An Office of Strategic Services report of May 1945 divided "action groups in postcollapse Germany" into the left-wing local Antifas and the "conservative forces which had more or less unwillingly allied themselves with Nazism," and which had been "allowed to maintain contacts and an interchange of ideas." Thus, they were now able "to exercise some sort of organized influence on the course of events."[25] Whereas the Antifas represented an impetus for change, the conservative forces focused on "the preservation of some sort of continuity in German social and economic life and the avoidance of violent changes."[26] U.S. MG ultimately banned new, autonomous organizations; local MG detachments and German municipal administrations approved and encouraged the reconstruction of more traditional structures, such as the chambers of commerce or organizations of industrialists and business people with less overtly political goals, which "were quickly revived to look out for the interests of the business community."[27]

The same OSS report did not acknowledge the political implications of encouraging such traditional conservative forces interested in restoring the status quo ante while discouraging forces of change by prohibiting the Antifas:

23 Protokoll der Sitzung der Landesverwaltung des Innern mit den Oberbürgermeistern der grösseren württembergischen Städte, July 31, 1945, StA Stuttgart, Hauptaktei 0434-1.
24 Gemeindebeiratsprotokolle, Oct. 12, 1945, p. 195, StA Stuttgart, Hauptaktei 0434-1.
25 OSS report, "Action Groups in Post-Collapse Germany," pp. 3–6, encl., May 29, 1945, POLAD report to SecState, IfZ, RG 84, POLAD TS/32/28, May 1945.
26 Ibid., 4.   27. Ibid.

With the Nazis gone, these elements [leaders of the business community] occupy the most important positions in German society; they want to remain in these positions and to use their influence to bring Germany back to something like normal as quickly as possible. . . . The Left puts the emphasis on rooting out all traces of Nazism as the prerequisite to a new start; the Right concentrates on attempting to conserve whatever is potentially valuable from the shambles left by the Hitler regime. Such opposition as exists between the two tendencies is not a reflection of a normal political struggle for power. Rather it grows out of differing approaches to the problem of reconstituting the very bases of organized existence.[28]

The Conservatives, the report continued, wanted to restore a Wilhelminian Empire or a Third Reich without war or Hitler and Nazi terror; the Leftists, on the other hand, desired a real break with the past, which even Weimar had not provided, in order to democratize and socialize "the very bases of organized existence." The fight between the two groups was not "a normal political struggle for power," because these were not normal times in terms of traditional party politics; if not a *Stunde Null,* it was at least an interregnum. The primary enemy of both groups, the Nazis, had been defeated. This common victory did not mean, however, that they now shared common goals. Their rivalry over continuity or change, as reflected in their support or lack of support of a thorough denazification campaign through the reallocation of housing and goods or the training of new elites, had considerable significance for Germany's future social, economic, and political structure. Whether forces of change, like the Antifa activists, would have been able to win broad popular support for an agenda of long-term structural change in the midst of an increasingly popular call for a return to normal times is a question open to speculation.

To be sure, the Germans did not act autonomously or in a void, but rather within the context of an unconditional surrender and a quadripartite military occupation. Those individuals who had the support of the occupying power(s) gained the advantage in implementing their porgrams, if not the exclusive opportunity to do so. Once the democratic process had been restored, this development could theoretically be altered by popular ballot. However, the occupying authorities were able to continue to influence those Germans and their political parties whose postwar vision corresponded most closely to their own. This influence, which was clearly evident in

28 Ibid.

election results, was most direct from 1945 until 1949, but it continued in less overt ways until at least 1955. For example, administrators who had belonged to an organization like the appointed municipal administration, formed by the MG, usually had an advantage in the election of 1946 and later elections.

The Marshall Plan and the currency reform of the Western Allies gave clear signals to West Germans as to whose side to support in order to achieve the most rapid material reconstruction and a return to what were perceived as normal times. Most Germans, including former Nazi party members, were more concerned with their material situation, having a warm, safe place to live, enough food to eat, and steady employment, than with sacrificing or postponing material aims in order to guarantee or even strive for a long-term structural democratization. Only a minority of Germans had risked their lives in acts of anti-Nazi resistance during the Third Reich or had made personal sacrifices in the early postwar period. These committed few had different stakes in the outcome of this interregnum; they had less to lose materially and more to gain ideally by fulfilling their twin goals of denazification and democratization. The continuation in power of most appointed officials and lower-level bureaucrats, together with the high priority given by the MG to restoring order and capitalist economic reconstruction, meant the victory of continuity over change. The democratic potential represented by the Antifas scarcely survived after their formal prohibition in the early summer of 1945, and it virtually expired after the reinstitution of democratic elections in the spring of 1946.

In Munich in early 1946, a district committee was formed primarily by former Antifa members after their organization had been dissolved. The district police, arguing that the population was uneasy over the existence and activities of a grass roots district committee, appealed to Mayor Scharnagl to suppress this group. Scharnagl responded that such committees could not be permitted to exist, because the MG had not yet vetted its members. Moreover, he continued, committees, in particular district committees, were not allowed to constitute themselves but should instead be formed through nomination by the three political parties (BVP/CSU, SPD, KPD), the churches, or the district police.[29] Ironically, the mayor used the excuse of an "uneasy" popular opinion to squelch one of the

29 StA Munich, BuR 1647.

remnants of the Antifas' grass roots activity. The banning of the Antifas was not just an MG policy, but rather one in which the MG-appointed administrations had an equal, if not greater, interest.

German municipal leaders' distrust of the Antifas can be traced to their essentially leftist character. In Stuttgart, Police Chief Weber reported to Mayor Arnulf Klett in late September 1945 that he had no general objection to the activities of the Antifas. However, Weber continued, since the majority of their members consisted of Communists, important segments of the population distrusted or totally rejected their activities.[30] Who these segments were and whether their importance was based on their numbers or their influence, Weber failed to explain. However, adamantly anti-Communist, and therefore anti-Antifa, elites used their influence to turn others against the Antifas. For example, the Roman Catholic hierarchy of Württemberg was "among the most determined opponents of the *Kampfkomitee*[s]," according to a U.S. Field Intelligence Study of July 1945. According to the vicar general and his liaison to MG in Stuttgart, the Antifas were " 'camouflaged' bodies for the propagation of Communism," and many Nazis were joining them.[31] There is no evidence of the latter claim, which was probably used to manipulate public opinion and MG against the Antifas.

High-level U.S. MG agencies were particularly concerned that the KPD was using the Antifas to maintain pressure for joint action by the Left.[32] In Frankfurt and in Munich, SPD and KPD members formed united fronts after the Antifas were banned. In Munich, a united action committee met for the first time on June 11, 1945, signed a united action agreement on August 8, and continued to meet until January 1946, when the local, more conservative SPD leadership put pressure on party members to withdraw.[33] A similar committee did not exist in Stuttgart, apparently because an Antifa organization was allowed to continue there until 1948.

The refounding of the political parties also eventually spelled the demise of the united front represented by the Antifa movement. Although SPD-KPD united action committees grew directly out of the shared Antifa experience, including the city administrations'

30 StA Stuttgart, Hauptaktei 0434-1.
31 NA, RG 266, OSS, FIS 5, July 2, 1945, pp. 4–5.
32 Ibid., FIS 43, Dec. 1, 1945, p. 15.
33 Protokolle der Aktionsgemeinschaft SPD-KPD München, Georg Fischer Nachlass, IfZ, Du 005. See also HStA Munich, RG 226, OMG Bavaria, 10/110-2/19, p. 2.

discrimination against them and the ultimate MG ban, the revived parties, with their old leadership, particularly in the case of the SPD, restored old party boundaries and rivalries.

MG eventually permitted all municipalities to have exclusively advisory citizens' councils, appointed by the mayors, because the latter were ultimately responsible to MG for all decisions and/or actions taken by any municipal organization or administrative official. Despite the fact that the Left often took the initiative in suggesting the formation of these councils,[34] the mayors and MG often used them to reduce the influence of the Left, whom they felt had an organizational advantage over the groups of the center and the non-Nazi Right.[35] Yet MG and the mayors did this less to even things out between the Right and the Left, than to help those political groups with whom they felt the most sympathy.

Stuttgart's advisory council was one of the least democratic in the U.S. zone. Formed quite late, it played at best a passive role in municipal affairs, not only because it rarely met, but also because it could meet only when convened by the mayor. Although half of the advisory council was supposed to have come from the *Arbeitsausschüsse* (Antifas), and thus predominantly from the working class, the percentage of workers dropped from 33 percent in 1932 to 14 percent in 1945.[36]

Not only was Stuttgart's council unrepresentative of the city's social composition, but it was also constrained in its democratic potential both because Mayor Klett insisted that "Politics don't belong in city hall,"[37] and, ironically enough, because the U.S. city commander Military Government Officer (MGO) Jackson reprimanded the council for not acting "democratically."[38] After the council's first meeting on October 12, 1945, when it made plans to set up committees for the council members, Klett unilaterally changed the number and composition of the standing committees and postponed their meetings. By the time of the council's second plenary session on November 30, the press had gotten wind of the council's discon-

34 Sitzung der Inneren Abteilung, Nov. 28, 1945, StA Stuttgart, Gemeindebeiratsprotokolle, and Bürgerratsprotokolle, Sept. 6, 1945, StA Frankfurt am Main.
35 U.S. POLAD Murphy to SecState, June 28, 1945, IfZ, RG 84, POLAD/730/1.
36 Ibid.
37 StA Stuttgart, Gemeindebeiratsprotokolle, Nov. 30, 1945, p. 255. Rudolf Gehring (SPD) criticized Klett for not understanding that almost every municipal activity was political and for representing the notion "Politik gehört nicht aufs Rathaus."
38 Ibid., 258.

tent with the delay; it published an anonymous member's poem that compared the way the council was being handled with Hitler's rubber stamp parliaments.[39]

The plenary session on November 30 began with demands for an explanation for the seven-week delay. Instead of a response by Mayor Klett, MGO Jackson, attempting to justify the delay, noted that Klett's heavy workload had left no time for a council meeting. Jackson's intercession took Klett off the hook; he made it clear to the councillors that the MGO was not to be contradicted or even really questioned. In practice, this further diminished the possibility of democratic exchange and also prevented the councillors from helping Klett perform tasks of government as they had hoped.[40] Yet one councillor pointed out that in a democracy it is "not only a right, but under certain circumstances also an obligation" to express public criticism. "This criticism should not be disparaging or destructive, but encouraging and constructive."[41] After the councilors applauded the speaker, MGO Jackson reprimanded the group. Recognizing, he said, "You have not had the opportunity in twelve years for such a democratic exchange; your ideas of democracy have become a little rusty." Jackson called for a meeting to convene the following week, "at which time [he] wanted to see another type of meeting," where only "constructive criticism" would be expressed.[42]

The councilors strongly resented Jackson's patronizing stance. As one councilor put it: "If we are not allowed to express our opinion really openly and say what we think is right, then the others should also not go beyond the limits that lead to real infringements." This councillor also expressed his regret that the councilors were not given the opportunity to engage in discussion with Jackson, "in order to give [him] a picture of what we understand under democracy."[43] All four parties in the council then issued a collective public statement about Jackson's deprecation of the criticisms they had expressed at the plenary session. Pointing out that all of those who had spoken at the previous session were experienced parliamentarians who rejected being treated in public as "parliamentary children, who first needed training in municipal politics," the councilors retorted that their ideas of democracy had not in any way become "rusty" in the last

39 Hermann Vietzen, *Chronik der Stadt Stuttgart 1945–1948* (Stuttgart, 1972), 154.
40 Ibid., 153–6.
41 StA Stuttgart, Gemeindebeiratsprotokolle, Nov. 30, 1945, p. 258.   42 Ibid., p. 285.
43 StA Stuttgart, Innere Abteilung, 1945–46, Dec. 4, 1945, p. 4.

twelve years.[44] They felt that MG was preaching a democracy that it did not practice. Indeed, this MG intervention did not advance democratization in Stuttgart's municipal politics. Instead, it provoked the council's resentment and strengthened Klett's tendency to ignore the council, especially now that Klett knew he had MG's backing and that MG overtly distrusted the councilors' ability.[45]

In the case of Frankfurt, Mayor Kurt Blaum's authoritarian ways caused such discontent among the left-wing parties of the advisory council that he was defeated in the 1946 mayoral election. Although the SPD and the KPD had 50 percent of the seats in the council, the Left only marginally influenced municipal politics while Blaum was mayor. Like Klett, Blaum wanted to keep politics out of city hall and paid little attention to the council. An OSS report on Frankfurt, written in late September 1945, described the political situation there as follows:

> In its simplest terms, the political problem of Frankfurt boils down to the fact that the administration is in the hands of the business men and professional administrators, while the Left parties on the outside are trying to secure not merely more positions for themselves in the government, but responsibility of the administration to the political party leadership as a first step toward the establishment of a politically-based city government. Underlying this problem is the precedence accorded by occupation policy to the restoration of administration over the revival of political life.[46]

At the first meeting of the Frankfurt city council, Mayor Blaum complained that "the tempo of denazification in the city administration had been so rapid that 'the tool of reconstruction was being knocked out of his hand.' " The SPD and KPD protested Blaum's statement, because, "deeply conscious of the strength derived by the right from the imperial professional bureaucracy retained under the Weimar republic, they fear[ed] that the slightest compromise on the purge issue [would] enable the bureaucracy which supported Nazism to survive under the guise of technical expertise."[47] Because of their lack of influence on the council, the two parties of the Left turned to the public and published in the *Frankfurter Rundschau* an editorial criticizing the mayor and a news story on the session. The only newspaper licensed in Frankfurt at the time, the *Frankfurter Rundschau* was

44 StA Stuttgart, Gemeindebeiratsprotokolle, Dec. 7, 1945, pp. 293–4.
45 Ibid., Nov. 30, 1945.
46 IfZ, RG 260, OMGUS, 15/109-2/7, p. 1; NA, RG 266, OSS FIS 23, Sept. 24, 1945, p. 29.
47 NA, RG 266, OSS, FIS 23, Sept. 24, 1945, pp. 30–1.

controlled by seven licensees, six of whom were either Communists or Social Democrats, including three members of the advisory council. Thus, the political debate extended beyond the council itself. The Left used its influence on the press to inform and shape public opinion. But Blaum's supporters on the Right, who, according to the OSS report, seemed "to include all the Liberal Democratic leaders and much of the business community," felt "that the left [was] abusing its control over the only press organ in the city."[48]

The press in Frankfurt, at least until elections in May 1946, played a more direct role in democratization than the advisory city council. If the council could exert no influence over the mayor, the press could do so, especially since Blaum had political ambitions and wished to continue in office after elections were permitted. The Americans also controlled the press, not through the MG detachment, but rather, at least at this early stage, through the much more reform-oriented District Information Services Control Command (DISCC) and Information Control Division (ICD).

The United States allowed political party organization on a district basis beginning on August 27, 1945, and on a zonal basis beginning in February 1946, so long as the parties were anti-Nazi and democratic.[49] If any of the groups that applied to the local MG for licenses were discovered to be "militaristic, undemocratic, hostile to Allied purposes, or prejudicial to military security and the maintenance of order," their authorization could be withheld, or if already granted, withdrawn.[50] In the first half of 1947, MG officers were instructed to show impartiality toward all authorized parties and party personalities and to stop any intervention in internal party disputes.[51] Impartiality was often not to be found on the local level, and there are numerous examples of MG intervention, not so much directly in interparty affairs, but certainly in intraparty ones, especially prior to these 1947 directives. Apparently, various MG officers had assumed that they could exercise personal preference and intervene in the Germans' political affairs.

During the first year of the occupation, the initial mayoral appointments to a large extent determined MG's relationship with the

48 Ibid., p. 31.
49 Werner Friedmann, *The Allied Military Government of Germany* (London, 1947), 128.
50 Gillen, *State and Local Government*, 5–8.
51 Seymour R. Bolten, "Military Government and the German Political Parties," *Annals of the American Academy of Political and Social Science* 267 (1950):57–8.

various political factions. The MG detachment tended, either consciously or not, to adopt its appointees' biases and political positions. MG, which made a distinction between experts and partisans, preferred less explicitly political administrators for local government.

An Information Control Division (ICD) policy advisor, William Hale, singled out the mayors of Cologne, Munich, and Frankfurt as examples of right-of-center German officials, whom MG had put into office, who did not have sufficient initiative to make denazification and democratic reforms work. On the other hand, he cited the mayor of Marburg as an example of MG's lack of support for appointees who tried to make those policies work. Hale described the Marburg mayor as "a very tame Social Democrat, whose influence our local MG detachment nevertheless felt it necessary to curb by surrounding him with an aggressive group of reactionary German Nationalist officials headed by the county councilor." Hale complained that Washington had not dictated such choices, but that the local MG had decided "not to upset the civic apple cart." He then noted: " 'Safe' as such preferences on the part of MG officers may be, their cost is high in terms of the growing disillusionment and discouragement of those anti-Nazi forces in Germany which had awaited our coming and had dedicated themselves to building a new democratic and peaceable Germany." Furthermore, after talking to anti-Nazi concentration camp survivors at the time of their liberation and then seeking them out several months later at their homes, Hale lamented, "that these forces, although never strong, were stronger when we came than they are now."[52] The possibility of change in the *Stunde Null* was not realized, largely because of who was and who was not appointed by MG.

The first municipal elections in two major cities, Frankfurt and Stuttgart, represent examples of direct MG intervention in the democratic process in order to prevent political parties from playing their legitimate legal role. In Frankfurt the newly elected city council with its SPD majority chose an SPD mayor and a majority of SPD department heads. MG expressed its disapproval of this left-wing majority by dismissing the elected SPD deputy mayor on the grounds of political incrimination during the Third Reich, a debatable charge, which MG had apparently known about for almost a year while the

---

52 William Harlan Hale, "Our Failure in Germany," *Harper's Magazine* 191, no. 1147 (Dec. 1945):521.

official had served in another high municipal post. The detachment also threatened to find grounds to dismiss additional SPD elected officials unless more CDU members were included among the department heads. Under this coercion, the SPD members were compelled to vote for CDU members in a new department head election.[53] The MG detachment in Frankfurt thus successfully counteracted the electoral defeat of the considerably more conservative, but officially nonaligned appointed mayor, Dr. Kurt Blaum, by reducing the political influence of the SPD in the Frankfurt city government.

In Stuttgart, a Württemberg-Baden MG officer, Charles Lincoln, forced the local SPD and CDU leadership to keep the unaffiliated Dr. Klett as mayor in May 1946.[54] After the city council had been elected in May, it had to choose a mayor. The local SPD and CDU council leadership planned to vote the unaffiliated Dr. Klett out of office, partly because both parties were interested in choosing someone whom they considered a more politically representative figure. Lincoln told them that MG would intervene if Klett were not elected mayor. Under this pressure, both parties backed down and agreed to have their municipal government representatives elect Klett. Lincoln, who had no authority to make such a threat and therefore had lied, felt he had saved the day for the continued proper functioning of the city. He bragged that "his little intrigue" had served the citizens of Stuttgart. He rationalized this intrigue with an expression of his dislike of party politics and of his feeling that Klett had proven himself to be a capable mayor.[55] Needless to say, this did not represent a very positive lesson in democracy for an MG that was supposed to be fostering democratization.

Sometimes a mayor or a department head who wanted the extra weight of MG backing in order to strengthen his own political preferences and weaken his opponents manipulated the MG detachment. Generally, local MG detachments obtained their information on political parties from the weekly mayors' reports, from the Combined Intelligence Committee (CIC) and, after the dissolution of the OSS,

---

53 Beschluss vom 6. Sept. 1946, StA Frankfurt am Main, Mag 1058; see also Mag 1050/1, Bd. 2. Personal interviews with Emil Carlebach and Rudi Menzer, who was present at the SPD meeting following the dismissal of the Zweiter Bürgermeister, Frankfurt, May 30, 1983. See also HStA Wiesbaden, Abt. 502, Nr. 975.
54 Lincoln's dislike of party politics becomes even clearer in his statement: "Er [Klett] hatte keine politische Maschinerie hinter sich, aber er hatte etwas aufzuweisen," Charles Lincoln, *Auf Befehl der Militärregierung,* trans. Hans and Elsbeth Herlin (Munich, 1965), 140–3.
55 Ibid.

from other less-skilled intelligence sources. The CIC reports were
often extremely biased against Communists and Socialists. Other intelligence reports contained blatant errors, such as designating Kurt
Schumacher as the KPD chief of the British zone.[56]

The mayors' weekly reports to MG were often extremely subjec-
tive. In Frankfurt, Mayor Blaum composed them himself without
relying directly on any departmental reports. The local MG sometimes translated them verbatim, although it did not admit it, and sent
them on as their own weekly reports to the *Land*-MG.[57] The Frankfurt MG was exceptionally ill-informed and easily influenced by its
appointees. This is especially ironic, since Frankfurt, initially the
headquarters of U.S. Military Government, was expected to set an
example for the rest of the zone. The local MG detachments submitted bimonthly political activity reports to the *Land*-MG, which sent
them on to the OMGUS zonal headquarters.[58] Because local detachments provided most of the information used by higher-level offices
to make policy decisions, the reliance of local detachments on city
administrations' portrayals of political activities for this information
gave city administrators immense influence.

The advisory councils were formed almost simultaneously with the
U.S. authorization for the formation of political parties on the local
level. It is significant, however, that the former process did actually
precede the latter. By falling back upon the officially nonexistent political parties to form the supposedly apolitical advisory councils, the
major Weimar Republic political parties were de facto restored in the
immediate postwar period, despite the existing prohibition of political activity in the U.S. zone. The old Social Democratic and Communist political parties reemerged almost immediately. Centrist and
liberal parties took a bit longer to coalesce, because they included
former splinter parties. Because this initial restoration of the four political parties, the KPD, SPD, CDU/CSU, and FDP, was based
upon the appointed mayor's reliance upon the old local party elite for
the suggestion of council members, the hierarchy of power among
the individual members of the parties was also immediately re-

56 Special Brief of Political Affairs, Dec. 2, 1946, p. 5, Walter J. Müller Nachlass, IfZ, MA
1427/2.
57 Rebecca Boehling, "Die politischen Lageberichte des Frankfurter Oberbürgermeisters
Blaum an die amerikanische Militärregierung 1945/1946," *Archiv für Frankfurts Geschichte
und Kunst* 59 (1985):494–6.
58 Gillen, *State and Local Government,* 5–7.

stored. This happened, whether consciously or unconsciously, under the auspices of the U.S. Military Government.

The early restoration of the pre-1933 political parties inhibited the formation of new political parties when parties were officially permitted to form in late August 1945. Because no new parties had representation in the advisory city councils, they lacked any opportunity to participate formally in local self-government until the first elected city councils replaced the advisory councils in May 1946. Even then, the absence of visibility during the first postwar year hurt the new groups in the elections and generally doomed new parties to a short-lived, if not obscure, existence. They were barred from entering the public arena until the mid-1946 elections. By then, they were also faced with percentage clauses as high as 15 percent in order to win seats in the city councils.[59]

After receiving instructions to prevent a return of the extremely fragmented multiparty system that was blamed for the downfall of the Weimar Republic, MG detachments also regarded new parties skeptically.[60] If new parties were not licensed, they could not run candidates for election. MG political officers actually discouraged applications from what they termed "small splinter groups," instructing new party sponsors to seek agreement with one of the "four major parties" (KPD, SPD, FDP, CDU/CSU).[61] New parties trying to get licensed had been effectively discouraged until the four major parties were firmly ensconced after the first elections. According to one of his MG colleagues, Colonel Dawson, the *Land* MG chief in Württemberg-Baden, "discourage[d] applications from small splinter groups. He advised their sponsors either to seek agreement with one of the major parties or to be content with permission to form societies rather than political parties per se."[62] From the

59 The state of Hesse introduced a 15 percent clause in 1945 for all upcoming local and state elections. But after parties like the LDP, a forerunner of the FDP, and the KPD each won over 10 percent of the votes but less than 15 percent and were denied seats in local elections, the clause was changed to 5 percent for the 1946 elections for the state constitutional convention. Until 1948, however, when the second postwar municipal elections were held, only the SPD and the CDU were represented in the municipal councils of many Hessian towns and cities.
60 "Political Analysis of the Weimar Republic," Oct. 10, 1945, NA, RG 266, OSS, XL 35658.
61 "Political Activity in North Württemberg-Baden," Dec. 1, 1945, p. 12, NA, RG 2665, OSS, FIS 43.
62 Moses Moskowitz, "The Political Re-education of the Germans: The Emergence of Parties and Politics in Württemberg-Baden (May 1945–June 1946)," *Political Science Quarterly* 61 (1946):545.

perspective of MG officers, who were accustomed to a two-party system, the KPD, SPD, FDP, and CDU/CSU, which were the first parties to be licensed, were already more than enough. The four major parties of course welcomed this MG stance.

New parties, however, did arise, although most were not licensed until after the 1946 elections, by which time the four major parties were firmly in place. With the exception of various women's political parties and the Arbeiterpartei in Frankfurt, Stuttgart, and Mannheim, which represented an alternative for discontented Social Democrats and Communists, almost all new parties were on the right of the political spectrum. As seen by the treatment of the Antifas in the first months of the U.S. occupation, the combined onslaught by the MG and appointed mayors discouraged new organizational political initiatives on the Left.

There was another reason not to license new parties. U.S. MG was particularly concerned about the possibility of complicating "the political stage to the Right of the Communists and Socialists" by licensing "small 'Splitter' groups," that might "weaken considerably the non-Communist and nonsocialist political forces." In a memorandum of November 23, 1945, on "American policy and possible prevention of too many political parties representing the Center and Right," a member of the Office of the Political Advisor for Germany lamented the clauses in the Potsdam Agreement permitting and encouraging all democratic parties, because he wanted local MG "to prevent the emergence of too many parties." Using the excuse of the negative experience of the Weimar Republic's multiparty system, the memorandum's author asked Robert Murphy, the head of the Office of the Political Advisor, if MG could "not also refuse to permit the organization of local political groups which do not seem to have any real support on a larger geographical or national basis, on the grounds that too many 'Splitter' parties should be prevented."[63] Indeed, MG managed to keep out most new parties until after the 1946 elections, which effectively eliminated them from politics until at least 1948, when the next elections were held. MG could and did shape German political developments by preventing the emergence of grass roots, local parties, even before zonal and national parties were permitted. Grass roots developments, officially encouraged by MG's written policies, were in fact actively discouraged by MG officers.

63 IfZ, RG 84, POLAD/729/37, p. 4.

These policies predestined any new progressive parties to play a minor role. This, in turn, had major implications for the continuity of the ideology and the hierarchical structure of the old parties of the Weimar Republic. The lack of competition from new sources early in the postwar era allowed the parties to sink comfortably back into their old structures, ideologies, and traditional party rivalries. This prevented a real internal spring cleaning of the parties. Thus, a serious reassessment of ideas, methods, and structures, which all the parties surely needed after the experience of their demise during the Third Reich, did not take place. Such critical self-evaluation might have stimulated new alignments and a real democratization of the parties as grass roots movements from the bottom up rather than from the top down, as it actually took place. This restoration, from the top down, of old structures and of old attitudes inhibited internal party reform.

The continuity of party leadership also prevented the channeling of new ideas into the parties from new members, who felt the effects of party discipline, even exclusion from the party, if they dared to question the party line established by the party elite.[64] Such dissenters included members of the multiparty Antifa committees and female city councilors, like those in Munich who collaborated across party lines to introduce various motions.[65] Such dissenters had little decision-making power within the party hierarchy and could generally be quelled from above. For example, Kurt Schumacher himself intervened in local politics when he forbade any Social Democrats from serving on the multiparty licensee board of the *Frankfurter Rundschau*. On orders from Schumacher, the Social Democratic chairperson for Hesse, Willi Knothe, an original *Rundschau* licensee who had since resigned, informed SPD journalists that they would be expelled from the party if they volunteered their services as licensees to ICD. Rather than fight the accusation that the *Frankfurter*

---

64 This was especially true for members who exemplified cross-party cooperation by remaining in anti-Fascist organizations, such as the Union of Persecutees of the Nazi Regime (VVN) and the SPD-KPD Arbeitsgemeinschaften. See Emil Carlebach, "Frankfurts Antifaschisten 1945," In Ulrich Schneider, ed., *Als der Krieg zu Ende war: Hessen 1945* (Frankfurt am Main, 1980), 12–15. A more general account can be found in Günther Plum, "Versuche gesellschaftspolitischer Neuordnung: Ihr Scheitern im Kräftefeld deutscher und alliierter Politik," in *Westdeuschlands Weg zur Bundesrepublik 1945–1949: Beiträge von Mitarbeitern des Instituts für Zeitgeschichte* (Munich, 1976), 97–8.

65 In 1948, 25 percent of the city councilors in Munich were women. On several occasions, they presented their own motions, to the dismay of the male members of their various parties. For examples, see protocols RP 722/9, Personalausschuss, Apr. 2, 1949; RP 722/1, Stadtrat, March 29, 1949; RP 722/2, Stadtrat, Apr. 12, 1949, all StA Munich.

Rundschau was really a Communist newspaper, the SPD hierarchy strengthened the basis of the accusation by withdrawing its licensees. The Americans in Information Control Division, however, outwitted Schumacher and company by bringing in an SPD journalist-in-exile, Karl Gerold, from Switzerland, and getting a commitment from him before he was aware of the SPD policy or subject to party discipline.[66]

The preferences and biases of the occupying power influenced the success of German political parties. Though warmth or friendliness toward any Germans was not typical of MG officers' behavior during the earliest postwar phase, a certain amount of respect was displayed toward the Communists that was noticeably absent in their behavior toward most other Germans.[67] The SPD, on the other hand, was less transparent in the eyes of the U.S. occupation authorities; its resistance record was not as uncompromising as that of the KPD. MG trusted clergy or active lay members of churches more than Social Democrats, assuming, albeit incorrectly, that the churches as institutions had resisted the Nazis. Groups that had earned anti-Nazi credentials after Nazi defeat was imminent, such as the Freiheits-Aktion-Bayern (FAB), were regarded skeptically.[68] MG officers relied most heavily on either the nonaligned or the representatives of middle-of-the-road parties, who seemed less politicized and, thus, more pragmatic; these were men like the Frankfurt, Stuttgart, and Munich mayors, Kurt Blaum, Arnulf Klett, and Karl Scharnagl. The Communists, although initially used as advisers, were not appointed to high posts except those in charge of denazification. Denazification, in turn, involved tasks that, with the qualified exception of the SPD, the other parties tended to avoid because they might make them unpopular with prospective party members and voters.

By late 1945, there had often been a turnover in MG detachment personnel; when the men trained specifically for civil affairs reached the end of their military stint and returned home, even less well-

66 IfZ, RG 260, OMG Hesse 8/190-2/9, p. 5. Cf. Cedric Belfrage (press control officer for the *Frankfurter Rundschau*), *Seeds of Destruction: The Truth about the U.S. Occupation of Germany* (New York, 1954), 213. See also Emil Carlebach, *Zensur ohne Schere: Die Gründerjahre der "Frankfurter Rundschau" 1945/47* (Frankfurt am Main, 1985), 93–5.
67 IfZ, RG 260, OMG Bavaria 10/90-1/20, p. 1. Also personal interviews with the former city councilors Dr. Ludwig Schmid (CDU), Oskar Neumann, and Adelheid Liessmann (KPD), and the journalist Georg Wulffius in Munich, and the KPD councilor and journalist, Emil Carlebach, in Frankfurt.
68 IfZ, RG 260, OMG Bavaria 10/90-1/20, p. 1.

prepared officers and enlisted men took their place. These MG officers considered SPD supporters suspect, not because they had resisted the Nazis insufficiently, but because they had joined in various action committees with the Communists.[69] By autumn 1945, the seemingly more pragmatic FDP (LDP) and CDU/CSU clearly had won MG over to their side. In the case of the CDU/CSU, the religious, middle-class traits played a role.[70] With the FDP (LDP), old-style liberalism won many MG hearts.

The trend for the rest of the occupation period was set in early 1946; by then Leftists had become completely suspect to MG policymakers. The U.S. occupiers' spirit of collective guilt and anti-Nazism had given way to anti-Communism. Anxiety about whether the SPD would go more to the Center or to the Left continued to grow. By the spring of 1947, MG intelligence reports were stressing that "Communism has gripped key offices or institutions, and the sympathy of a larger percentage of a destitute population than is generally realized. The full significance of the facts can best be appreciated when considered relative to the unknown but suspected existence of party workers incognito."[71]

In the 1950s, U.S. anti-Communism was the primary source of intervention into local German affairs. Although the KPD was legal until 1956, a year after the Allied occupation formally ended, U.S. MG, now called the High Commission for Germany, or HICOG, restricted Communist Party publications, campaign posters, and even tried and sentenced German citizens in special courts for criticizing U.S. foreign policy. For example, the HICOG Resident Officer in Stuttgart expressed his dismay to Mayor Klett on April 18, 1950, over anti-American slogans and inscriptions painted around Stuttgart. Threatening that the "American citizens, who are heavily taxed in order to support Germany" would not have a "friendly impression of the German people," the resident officer complained that "it cannot be understood why some German citizens or German officers on their own initiative fail to institute the removal of such

69 See Carlebach, "Frankfurts Antifaschisten," 12–14.
70 Personal interview with Georg Wulffius, May 3, 1982, Munich. The American Consulate General in Munich on August 20, 1945, noted that "certain SPD functionaries in Munich have stated that they now feel that American Military Government has started to pursue a policy in its supervision of political activities here in that it now favors the CSU. They state that the reason for this 'partiality' is that we now wish to build up a strong Catholic bloc against Soviet Russia." IfZ, RG 84, POLAD/746/7, p. 1.
71 Stadtkreis Stuttgart Intelligence Report, May 12, 1947, p. 1, HStA Stuttgart, RG 260, OMG Württemberg-Baden, 12/221-2/1.

objectionable advertising."[72] Newspapers were closed for propagating anti-Allied material; for example, the *Sozialistische Volkszeitung* advocated holding a plebiscite on remilitarization and a peace treaty and was shut down because of it.[73]

In Stuttgart in October 1951, a fifty-two-year-old German woman, Lily Wächter, was tried and found guilty of provoking animosity and prejudice toward the Allies in a special American court. Lily Wächter was the West German delegate to the International Democratic Women's Federation, who had been sent to North Korea to investigate charges of atrocities against civilians on the part of American and South Korean troops. Because as a member of this delegation she had signed a report stating that indeed U.S. troops had been involved in such atrocities, Wächter was also found guilty of undermining U.S. occupation troops in Germany; the American court felt that such criticism could have a negative effect on the reputation of U.S. troops elsewhere.[74] MG treated Wächter as an enemy agent for North Korea, because she dared to participate in an investigation of atrocities involving U.S. troops.

In order to appraise its success in democratization in the summer of 1949, the Military Government for Württemberg-Baden conducted a survey on local self-government and the growth of democratic attitudes. Complaining about Stuttgart citizens' lack of political awareness and involvement, the report criticized the establishment of political parties for not being "very appropriate to promote democracy." It went on to note that "party dogmatism makes cooperation and compromise, two fundamentals of the democratic process, very difficult. As the political line of the parties is usually decided by top men in higher quarters, membership has not much influence." Lamenting the fact that twenty- to thirty-five-year-olds were showing "practically no evidence of political interest and democratic attitude,"[75] the intelligence officers who authored this report obviously made no connection between this lack of democracy and the way in which MG had allowed political parties to form, how MG had discouraged grass roots democracy in the first place, and why active democratic political development was absent.

72 StA Stuttgart, Hauptaktei, 0315/II.   73 StA Frankfurt am Main, May 2110/1.
74 *Württembergische Abendzeitung,* Oct. 5, 1951, StA Stuttgart, Hauptaktei 0311-3. See also "Bericht der internationalen Frauen-Kommission für die Untersuchung der von den amerikanischen und südkoreanischen Truppen in Korea verübten Greueltaten" in the same file.
75 Stuttgart LSO Report, Aug. 1, 1949, p. 37, IfZ, RG 260, OMG Württemberg-Baden, 12/141-2/1-29.

United States occupation authorities did initiate some measures to democratize Germany. Besides the unsuccessful attempts to eliminate the *Berufsbeamtentum* and to secularize and democratize Bavarian education, U.S. MG also introduced town meetings. The town meeting idea met a fair amount of resistance from municipal administrators, who resented what they perceived to be a new level of accountability. Accustomed to reporting primarily to the mayor and secondarily to the city council, professional department heads did not like this notion of democratic involvement from the ordinary citizenry. At a town meeting (*Bürgerversammlung*) on December 7, 1949, in Herrsching, outside of Munich, the *Landrat* of Starnberg rejected the principle of citizens' committees, calling them "an American invention." He warned of the danger of a "hyperdemocracy" resulting from citizen input in committees. In response, the chairperson of this particular committee complained that the *Landrat*, as the highest-ranking governmental representative there, was destroying the work of the citizens' committees with such talk, and that one could not even talk yet of democracy in Germany, let alone of "hyperdemocracy." While the chairperson went on to explain that the citizens' committees served the function of "a safety valve against bureaucratic encroachments," another participant defended the initiative of the U.S. MG as having been necessary to awaken Germans out of their apathy and disinterest in their roles as citizens.[76]

In Frankfurt the first so-called *Bürgerforum*, took place at the MG's initiative on September 16, 1948. An MG member opened the meeting by justifying the necessity of such structures with a reference to the history of democratic organizations in Germany and the structural limits that had prevented the realization of political democracy. Thereafter, district meetings were held throughout the city, but neither the mayor (the Social Democrat, Walter Kolb), nor the department heads attended regularly. MG, on the other hand, sent regular representatives and encouraged a framework whereby the theme of a meeting would be publicized ahead of time and the appropriate city administrator would be there to answer questions. The leaders of the district meetings sent out numerous requests to have department heads attend. These administrators, however, refused, insisting instead that they would respond to written questions in writing, because they did not feel it was appropriate that they be put on the spot

---

76 *Neue Zeitung*, Dec. 8, 1949.

in such meetings. Finally, in 1954, under pressure from the SPD majority in the city council, the department heads agreed to attend. By that time, and probably not coincidentally, new procedural rules had been passed that limited the calling of meetings of citizens' assemblies to at most a few times a year and then only when "special circumstances" arose.[77]

In Munich, in the winter of 1951–52 the city council and the HICOG senior resident officer clashed over the council's decision to suspend town meetings during carnival (*Fasching*). Despite the mayor's argument that city councilors, who would normally attend these meetings, would be tied up with *Fasching* and campaigning for the spring 1952 elections, the resident officer wrote the mayor that "every effort should be made to continue this program, and that no steps should be taken to retard its progress." The city, however, did not resume the town meetings until after Lent and the election, despite a newspaper article by the resident officer that publicly criticized the city council's suspension decision and expressed the hope, "that in the future neither the city council nor government representatives should intervene in the great and very important citizens' right of assembly and freedom of expression."[78] MG's perception of the citizens' right of freedom of expression, however, did not extend to criticism of occupation or U.S. foreign policy in general.

The different forms of local democratic initiatives that Germans took during the early postwar period were not without effect, yet they did not result in major structural change or path-breaking, lasting reforms. Compared to the Third Reich, local government was democratized in the sense that political parties were eventually authorized and Germans were allowed to elect their own municipal officials. However, the restraints placed on grass roots political activity by both U.S. Military Government and its appointed German officials in 1945 and 1946 inhibited not only the development of new and renewed political parties, but also the potential for the democratic transformation of German society and the economic order.

The only real provision made by MG for German democratization was that its appointees be democratic.[79] Given the undemocratic nature of most bureaucracies, placing democrats into leading positions in nondemocratic structures, such as the appointed city administra-

77 StA Frankfurt am Main, Mag 4.389.   78 StA Munich, BuR 2023.
79 Gillen, *State and Local Government*, 5.

tions and the advisory councils, could not guarantee democracy. One must also take into account what MG officials understood to be democratic. In practice, MG officers seemed to equate a democratic German with a non-Nazi, pro-American, anti-Communist one. This differs considerably from Webster's definition of a democrat as "a person who believes in and practices the principle of equality of rights, opportunity, and treatment."[80] One grass roots democratic movement, that of the Antifas, was anti-Nazi rather than just non-Nazi, not anti-American, but also not pro-American capitalism, but instead non-Communist or sometimes even pro-Communist. The Antifas' activities, their heterogenous political composition and their plans for a thorough denazification of German society all represented trends, however, that would have further democratized postwar German society and politics. But they needed the support of the occupying authorities in order to realize their plans and continue their activities, and this they did not have.

The MG ban on political activities in the spring of 1945 did not prevent a revival of the old parties of the Weimar Republic. The mayors' reliance on the old Weimar political party leaders for the selection of the members for the advisory city councils guaranteed a revival of the old parties and the old party hierarchies. This prevented grass roots formation and democratization of the parties. Political life was revived but not revitalized. The early restoration of the old parties, in combination with the MG practice of discouraging new parties, made it very difficult for any new parties to acquire political influence and to succeed in elections.

The MG and its appointed mayors often formed advisory councils to take the wind out of the sails of the Antifas and other grass roots movements. Thus, the democratic potential that advisory councils represented, in terms of including more of the community in municipal decision making, was inhibited by the motivation behind their formation. This led to councils that were not truly representative and had minimal power. Most mayors had not wanted these councils in the first place, but managed to use them to create a facade of democracy while continuing in their own autocratic ways.

The growing political emphasis on anti-Communism and economic emphasis on capitalist reconstruction led MG and many Germans to deemphasize anti-Nazism and denazification and ultimately,

80 *Webster's New World Dictionary of the American Language,* 2nd college ed. (New York, 1970), 375.

whether consciously or not, to restrict the democratization of German society. German political groupings were dependent on MG support for any genuine success. Directly, they needed MG authorization for their continued existence, while indirectly, they needed their approval and active encouragement to gain the support of the German electorate. Most Germans, after the experience of wartime and postwar shortages and material discomfort, wanted an expeditious return to normal times and material well-being. The American and the German political parties they supported seemed to represent the best hope for this. Because long-term political reform and socioeconomic structural change were advocated predominantly by Leftists, these goals came to be associated with Communism. The growing influx of expellees from Eastern Europe and refugees from the Soviet zone of occupation added fuel to MG's anti-Communist propaganda in the U.S. zone. Material well-being seemed incompatible with Communism to most Germans. Thus, many Germans were all too willing to sacrifice the ideals of structural political and socioeconomic democratization in return for U.S. style capitalism, which most Americans equated with democracy, as long as it meant an end to the chaos, disorder, and shortages of the postwar period.

15

German Democratization as Conservative Restabilization: The Impact of American Policy

DIETHELM PROWE

When the U.S. occupation troops arrived in Germany in 1945, they were clear about one thing: World peace and stability would return only if Germany was not only demilitarized and denazified, but permanently democratized. Today West Germany stands as one of the most stable and prosperous democracies in the world. Europe, if not the world, has enjoyed a longer period of peace in the last decades than ever before. Is this the result, perhaps the proudest achievement of American foreign policy in this century?

The question of the precise role of Americans in the democratization of Germany is still far from settled. There are three classic positions, which have been refined in various combinations over the years. The orthodox view that dominated in the postwar years and the Cold War was that the United States played a positive and decisive role in bringing democracy to Germany. Revisionists on both sides of the Atlantic have maintained since the late 1960s that the reverse was true, that Americans, intent on expanding U.S. capitalism, prevented or even consciously destroyed a strong German movement for a genuinely democratic society. Finally, disgruntled Americans have mused whether their efforts were not ultimately wasted. John Gimbel quotes the U.S. Military Government's pessimistic report on the meager results of its grass-roots reorientation program, lamenting the "long uphill battle against the forces of tradition, political and social apathy, and post-war cynicism."[1] Whether the failure stemmed from the perennial staff shortages in the reeducation program, which James Tent has described,[2] or whether the dictatorial arrogance of

---

1 OMG Hesse, Historical Report 1948, p. 1, as cited in John Gimbel, *A German Community under American Occupation: Marburg, 1945–52* (Stanford, Calif., 1961), 184.
2 James F. Tent, *Mission on the Rhine: Reeducation and Denazification in American-Occupied Germany* (Chicago, 1983), esp. 121–3, 313–16.

American officials is to blame, as Edward Peterson has argued,[3] this
interpretation has judged direct American influence too weak to reeducate Germans in the American image.

The greatest weakness of all three of these interpretations is that
they have underestimated the role of traditional German political-
social forces in shaping West German democracy. After almost a
half-century of prosperity and democracy in the new Germany, it is
easy to forget that the political behavior of postwar Germans was
conditioned above all by two central, if obvious facts. First, the
whole population was deeply traumatized and insecure in the wake
of the catastrophic Nazi defeat. Second and more important here,
postwar Germans remained steeped in values and assumptions with
which they had grown up.

The persistence of the old political culture meant most evidently
that the traditional political and economic elites of Western Germany
remained very much intact and were only minimally challenged by
a politically apathetic population, even as these leaders were fearful
of revolutionary disorder. The enduring political culture also precluded any widespread commitment to democracy for its own sake.
In the eyes of the elites, the value of democracy was mainly functional. At that historical moment it seemed to be an ideal tool for
restabilization. It obviously fit the language of the triumphant West
and it agreed with specific policy goals of the U.S. occupation government, seconded by the British and the French. Within German
society, it allowed the elites to share the heavy burden of reconstruction more widely. When they spoke of "democracy" they meant a
carefully controlled opening up of the traditional networks of power
from above, in the defense against revolutionary chaos or change.

This dominance by established elites and centralized organizations
was reinforced by a political apathy of the general German population that grew out of the sense of insecurity, fear of chaos, and an
"exhaustion of individuals and apathy of a shattered society," as
Wolfgang Jacobmeyer has expressed it.[4] In extensive empirical research on labor in Stuttgart, Michael Fichter and colleagues found
that "the widespread longing in the working class for peace, order,

3 Edward N. Peterson, *The American Occupation of Germany: Retreat to Victory* (Detroit, 1978),
345–6.
4 Wolfgang Jacobmeyer, "Die Niederlage 1945," in *Westdeutschlands Weg zur Bundesrepublik
1945–1949: Beiträge von Mitarbeitern des Instituts für Zeitgeschichte* (Munich, 1976), 23.

and 'normality' generated a dominant will for cooperation, consensus, and integration."[5] Despite determined American efforts to promote democratization from below, democracy could thus come only "from above" in war-torn, largely apathetic Germany. It was introduced through elites and old centralized organizations, which had dominated German political culture for a century and beyond.

In order to penetrate German society, this process of building democracy had to go well beyond the establishment of formal democratic institutions. The foundation of democracy lies rather in the broad acceptance of democratic *Umgangsformen,* or modes of political interaction, in all spheres of public life. The critical difference between the Weimar and Bonn republics was not the technical perfection of formal democratic institutions, but the breadth of acceptance of democracy in the larger population and, perhaps most important, among the established political, economic, social, and cultural elites.

It was most vital, therefore, that the population become accustomed to democratic forms of discourse and action in those areas of life that were closest to the essential experiences of postwar Germans. These were not in parliaments, elections, or political parties, but primarily in two areas: in local issues and in the economy, which, in the words of one Bavarian deputy, "nowadays simply means life itself."[6] This is not to devalue the role of intellectuals, including journalists, which contrasted markedly with the part played by Weimar intellectuals. It is simply to concentrate on democratization efforts closest to everyday life of postwar Germans in local administration and economic organization. It is here, rather than in the distant and, from the citizen's perspective, artificial reeducation, reorientation, and press programs, that the American role in the democratization of German political culture is best tested. In fact, this was precisely the level where Americans hoped to begin the reorientation of Germans toward democracy but which usually eluded them in the reeducation and reorientation programs: at the grass roots of everyday citizen activity.

The areas of local administration and economic regulation shared a number of similarities. Obviously, both were centrally concerned

5 Michael Fichter, "The Labor Movement in Stuttgart, 1945–1949," manuscript of paper presented at the Annual Meeting of the German Studies Association, 1987, p. 2.
6 Bayerischer Landtag, 17. Sitzung, 29. Mai 1947, p. 491.

with the most pressing issues of everyday life, such as food, lodging, production, and labor. This reality gave rise to two apparently opposite phenomena. On the one hand, the need for experts and centralized organizations with the skills necessary to organize production, distribution, and labor, favored a growing presence and influence of traditional elites. Yet on the other hand, the gargantuan task of reconstruction and the potentially explosive social situation indicated by the famed hunger marches also forced the leadership to search for ways to share responsibility and thus inevitably power.

The typical protodemocratic institution that emerged from this attempt to broaden the political base both in the local context and the economic administrations was the *Beirat* or advisory council. Such councils had a long tradition in German society as channels to allow a broader educated "public" some access to the authoritarian state institutions. In this period they were organized to gain expert advice for dealing with the most urgent issues, mainly economic. More important, under the intense pressures of the postwar years, the new *Beiräte* served as vehicles to open political networks beyond traditional power sharing both locally and in economic administration. The structure of these councils was often along corporatist lines, as I have argued elsewhere.[7]

When local communities began to dig out from under the rubble of Hitler's war in the spring and summer of 1945, old local elites began to reemerge, too. At first the leading men from industry and politics trod softly, mindful of the lessons of the Nazi period either because they had been in danger under the Nazis, or because they feared that their collaboration with that regime would endanger them under the new political conditions. These men were therefore often less visible in the first months than the "anti-Fascist" (Antifa) or similar action committees, which typically operated under the guidance of experienced organizers from the local Socialist and especially Communist parties.[8] But with the need for the kind of expertise that could identify and mobilize the local resources necessary for reconstruction, traditional networks of power reemerged. Leading businessmen and especially officials from the central institution

---

7 Diethelm Prowe, "Economic Democracy in Post-World War II Germany: Corporatist Crisis Response, 1945–1948," *Journal of Modern History* 57 (1985):451–82.

8 Hartmut Pietsch, *Militärregierung, Bürokratie und Sozialisierung: Zur Entwicklung des politischen Systems des Ruhrgebietes 1945 bis 1948* (Duisburg, 1978), 68–70; cf. Lutz Niethammer, Ulrich Borsdorf, and Peter Brandt, eds., *Arbeiterinitiative 1945: Antifaschistische Ausschüsse und Reorganisation der Arbeiterbewegung in Deutschland* (Wuppertal, 1976).

in each regional economy, the chamber of industry and commerce,[9] tended to play a key role in the small circles of "leading citizens" which advised both the military government and the newly appointed German mayors. In Stuttgart, for instance, executives from the local industrial giants of Bosch and Daimler-Benz and former chamber president Gustav Kilpper met in the days after the surrender to found a local committee to organize economic and political reconstruction.[10] When Kilpper was put in charge of economic affairs by Mayor Ernst Klett, he relied heavily on his chamber colleagues.[11] In Frankfurt, the U.S. city commander was advised behind the scenes by a "Council," dominated by leading clergy, managers from I.G. Farben and Metallgesellschaft, and the executive director of the chamber of industry and commerce.[12] Konrad Adenauer's well-known return to the mayor's office in Cologne was perhaps the most striking restoration of the old city elite. It was accompanied by a supporting network of top businessmen, administrators, and most prominently the manager of the chamber, Bernhard Hilgermann.[13] The latter, a man of great resourcefulness and wit, later described his close relationship with banker Robert Pferdmenges and lawyer Robert Ellscheid, as they adjusted to the managed economy by building on old Cologne connections.[14] Rebecca Boehling, Hartmut Pietsch, and others have described many similar situations all over the American and British zones.

In this early stage, American influence appeared in two ways. First, the appointment of mayors and their cabinets tended to favor traditional elites because the arriving troops usually had to rely on

---

9 Cf. Diethelm Prowe, "Im Sturmzentrum: Die Industrie- und Handelskammern in den Nachkriegsjahren 1945–1949," *Zeitschrift für Unternehmensgeschichte*, Beiheft 53 (1987): 91–122.

10 3. Sitzung, vorläufiger württembergischer Wirtschaftsrat, May 8, 1945, HStA Stuttgart, EA 6/3/2006.

11 Harald Winkel, *Geschichte der württembergischen Industrie- und Handelskammern Heilbronn, Reutlingen, Stuttgart/Mittlerer Neckar und Ulm 1933–1980* (Stuttgart, 1981), 185–6.

12 Rebecca Boehling, "German Municipal Self-government and the Personnel Policies of the Local U.S. Military Government in Three Major Cities of the U.S. Zone of Occupation: Frankfurt, Munich, and Stuttgart," *Archiv für Sozialgeschichte* 25 (1985):344–5.

13 Cf. Gerhard Brunn, "Köln in den Jahren 1945 und 1946: Die Rahmenbedingungen des gesellschaftlichen Lebens," in Otto Dann, ed., *Köln nach dem Nationalsozialismus: Der Beginn des gesellschaftlichen und politischen Lebens in den Jahren 1945/46* (Wuppertal, 1981), 66–71, and Heribert Treiss, "Britische Besatzungspolitik in Köln," ibid., 73–81.

14 Bernhard Hilgermann, *Der grosse Wandel: Erinnerungen aus den ersten Nachkriegsjahren. Kölns Wirtschaft unter amerikanischer und britischer Militärregierung* (Cologne, 1961), and Hilgermann, *Auf dem Wege aus dem Chaos zum Wirtschaftswunder: Dr. Agartz, der erste Leiter des Zentralamts für Wirtschaft in der britischen Zone* (Cologne, 1979).

Diethelm Prowe

advice from the only continuing institutions they knew, the churches. Alternatively, they established informal advisory groups consisting of "leading citizens," as Boehling has shown in the case of Frankfurt.[15] Second, an Allied ban on all political activities hampered political organization primarily on the left. The prohibition hit precisely where the left's greatest strength lay, namely in the mobilization of masses. Moreover, "nonpolitical" organizations, above all the chambers of commerce and industry, were exempted from the ban.[16] Thus it clearly favored and reassured the traditional leadership. Americans could not change the direction of local political development so fundamentally by these steps as to "force capitalism" on a Germany ready for revolution, as authors of the "New Left" asserted in the early seventies.[17] Given the generally acknowledged apathy of the population, the Antifas were not likely to succeed in any case;[18] and the traditional elites could depend on old networks of power, which would have been difficult to overcome. Yet, it is clear that the American military government reinforced existing tendencies toward a reassertion of traditional elites in local governments.

Significantly, however, the process did not stop with the restoration of traditional dominance in local government. Just as striking was the determination of local leaders to broaden the power base beyond what it had been before 1933. This process began quietly and informally as soon as the victorious Allied troops entered the towns and the local Nazi administration collapsed. Already in the last months of the Nazi dictatorship, individual leaders from business, labor, the old civil service, and a few intellectuals and professionals had intensified their private discussions about Germany after Nazism. These underground contacts had forged closer personal links especially between business and labor leaders as well as former officials from the moderate left and right, spurred on by Hitler's betrayal of the nation and army at Stalingrad and the foreboding of defeat. The executive director of the Cologne chamber of commerce and industry, Hilgermann, who maintained personal contacts with a number

15 Boehling, "German Municipal Self-government," 344–5.
16 Cf. Michael Fichter, "Non-State Organizations and the Problems of Redemocratization," in John H. Herz, ed., *From Dictatorship to Democracy: Coping with the Legacies of Authoritarianism and Totalitarianism* (Westport, Conn., 1982), 63.
17 Cf. Ute Schmidt and Tilman Fichter, *Der erzwungene Kapitalismus: Klassenkämpfe in den Westzonen 1945–48* (Berlin, 1971), 7.
18 Fichter, "Labor Movement in Stuttgart," 5; Niethammer, Borsdorf, and Brandt, eds., *Arbeiterinitiative 1945*, 690–1, 709–11.

of key labor activists, including the later Social Democratic head of the Zentralamt für Wirtschaft in the British zone, Viktor Agartz, later spoke of this phenomenon as the "20th of July Complex" because of the parallelism to the circle of conservatives and labor leaders behind the attempted July 1944 coup.[19]

Thus when the appointed mayors began to establish advisory councils (*Beiräte*), they represented both old and new social groups remarkably broadly. Typically, the advisory councils included representatives from the main local industries, labor unions, the churches, refugee, and consumer groups. For example, Cologne's council included representatives from nine vocational groups, labor, industry, women, the Jewish congregation, and former concentration camp prisoners.[20] In Duisburg, eighteen labor delegates sat with twelve representatives from small business and large industry.[21] This was, of course, not democratization in the sense of expansion of direct power of citizens, because power was not extended to a broader general populace. Instead, it was a carefully controlled power sharing in which political networks were extended to representatives of existing, usually centralized organizations that had not been in the inner circle previously. In this sense postwar Germans followed corporatist, rather than popular democratic traditions. Yet this was not simply restoration. It was restabilization with a conscious and significant opening of the old system.

The American military government's interference on the local level was never systematic enough to influence this process in a basic or lasting way. Rather, the often arbitrary actions were generally occasioned by particular personalities on both the German and American sides. Only in one way did the U.S. occupation clearly promote democratization on the local level: through its decree that the powerful *Landrat,* or district president, be elected rather than appointed as previously. On balance, Americans mainly reinforced the continued development of traditional patterns of local government.

The American role in the other area of everyday politics, economic administration, was quite different. Here German political culture spawned rather remarkable efforts at democratization designed to broaden participation in decision making in the economy. As soon as the new economic agencies began to tackle the most urgent tasks of

19 "Aktenvermerk" Hilgermann, Nov. 19, 1946, Rheinisch-Westfälisches Wirtschaftsarchive, Cologne, 1/186/3.
20 Treiss, "Britische Besatzungspolitik," 81–2.   21 Pietsch, *Militärregierung,* 62–3.

allocating raw materials, labor, and consumer goods, such efforts surfaced. They quickly went beyond advisory councils that could build on old political habits. Prominent individuals from both the right and the left of the political spectrum presented a number of elaborate proposals for more permanent, broadly based institutions to plan and manage economic policy and reconstruction. As political and economic structures restabilized, business and labor organizations as well as political parties began to champion similar schemes.

Such initiatives flourished earliest in the most heavily industrial British Zone of Occupation. A November 1945 draft by the Christian labor leader and later North Rhine-Westphalian minister president Karl Arnold, in cooperation with the executive director of the most important chamber of industry and commerce in the region, proposed a Provincial Economic Chamber and a series of local chambers with equal business–labor representation to plan and manage the entire regional production, labor allocation, and transportation, in place of the traditional business chambers.[22] Similarly, when the British military government asked a former president of the international chamber of commerce, Abraham Frowein, to form a German Economic Advisory Board in the fall of 1945 and to provide "expert advice and assistance on economic and technical matters,"[23] he turned this council into a device to broaden the leadership in the only area partly available for Germans at this time, economic policy and regulation, by drawing on representatives from labor, consumer, and professional groups.[24] As in the case of all subsequent proposals for economic councils, Frowein and his successors consciously translated the British Military Government's mandate for an advisory council to conform with previous German corporatist democratic tradition, specifically the Reichswirtschaftsrat of the Weimar years, which had brought together representatives from business, labor, and other social groups in an advisory economic parliament on the national level during the Weimar Republic.[25]

All major political and economic organizations in the British and French zones presented similar corporate-democratic schemes. The

---

22 HStA Düsseldorf, RWN 116, and Archiv beim DGB Bundesvorstand [hereafter: DGB-Archiv], Böckler 5.
23 MG/Econ 2/43513, Technical Instruction No. 8 (Minden, Oct. 20, 1945), BA, Z8/1965.
24 *Deutscher Wirtschaftsrat*, Apr. 30, 1946, BA, Z8/1965.
25 Frowein to Dr. Hegemann, March 28, 1946: "It is my goal to build it [the council] up gradually in such a way that it can function like the former provisional *Reichswirtschaftsrat*." BA, Z8/4.

most elaborate was the labor union's draft for a law on economic chambers with equal management and labor representation, which were to administer all levels of the managed economy.[26] The chambers of industry and commerce, mainly in defense against such assaults upon their traditional role as representative institutions of businessmen, countered with a number of proposals for economic parliaments with equal business–labor representation to advise, supervise, or even make economic policy.[27]

The three main non-Communist parties of the British zone followed suit. The CDU called for economic councils or chambers with equal representation from business, labor, and consumers to plan and manage the economy in its Ahlen Program of February 1947[28] and submitted a bill to the parliament of North Rhine-Westphalia based on the Arnold Proposal.[29] The SPD sponsored labor union drafts for business–labor economic chambers in Lower Saxony and North Rhine-Westphalia.[30] Even the neoliberal FDP floated a number of proposals for economic councils. It is telling for the postwar political atmosphere that the most elaborate of these corporatist democratization schemes were drawn up by men from the top industrial elite, namely the executive director of the powerful Iron and Steel Manufacturers Association, Wilhelm Salewski, and the later manager of the West German Manufacturers Association (BDI), H. Wilhelm Beutler.[31]

In the British and French zones, these efforts for a democratization of the economy did, in fact, bear some modest fruits. Most remarkable were the Wuppertal Agreement in the British zone and the establishment of advisory economic councils in the French zone. The

26 *Wirtschaftskammergesetz: Entwurf eines Gesetzes über die Errichtung und Aufgaben von Wirtschaftskammern* (Bielefeld, 1947).
27 Cf. Woldmar Liebernickel, "Bestimmungen über Aufbau, Aufgaben, und Arbeitsweise von Gebietswirtschaftsräten," Sept. 11, 1946, Stiftung Westfälisches Wirtschaftsarchiv [hereafter: WWA], K5-100/2/21; Oelkrug Resolution of July 18, 1946, WWA, K5-100/2/4; Franz Greiss, "Vorschlag zur Bildung eines Landeswirtschaftsrates," 1947, DGB-Archiv, "Wirtschaftskammergesetz."
28 Ossip K. Flechtheim, ed., *Dokumente zur parteipolitischen Entwicklung in Deutschland seit 1945*, 2 vols. (Berlin, 1963), 2:53–8.
29 Landtag Nordrhein-Westfalen, LDI/112 (March 1947).
30 Landtag Niedersachsen, 7. Sitzung (Feb. 12, 1947); 10. Sitzung (March 25, 1947); 11. Sitzung (March 26, 1947); Landtag Nordrhein-Westfalen, LDII/364 (Apr. 1, 1948).
31 Wilhelm Salewski, "Skizze zur Reform der wirtschaftlichen Selbstverwaltung," June 16, 1947, HStA Düsseldorf, RWN 96/37; Heinz Wilhelm Beutler, intraparty circular, June 26, 1946, p. 22, Friedrich Naumann Stiftung-Politisches Archiv; cf. also Franz Blücher, "Wirtschaftsgrundsätze: Aufsatz für die erste Nummer der *Hannoverschen Neuesten Nachrichten*," July 1, 1947, BA, Nachlass Blücher, 154.

Wuppertal Agreement, concluded by the central organizations of the chambers of industry and commerce and the labor union, in the British zone in February 1947, established regional business–labor commissions, which met fairly regularly in all but one of the chamber districts in the following two years to deal with problems of the managed economy.[32] In all three *Länder* of the small French zone, economic councils with representatives of business, labor, agriculture, the handicrafts, and the professions advised the governments and later parliaments.[33] They were clearly favored by the French corporatist heritage, which had blended with its democratic traditions for over a century. The best known of these councils, the Hauptwirtschaftskammer of Rhineland-Palatinate was anchored in that state's constitution and functioned until 1962.[34]

Further efforts to institutionalize this broadening of economic management through formal legislation failed. But the fact that legislative initiatives were taken in almost all West German states and that laws for power-sharing economic chambers were actually passed by overwhelming majorities in Germany's key political and economic centers, Berlin and North Rhine-Westphalia, indicates the centrality of this form of democratization. It was at the intersection of German political traditions and the insistent demands of the catastrophic postwar situation. In their search to overcome an apparently desperate economic and moral crisis, established groups on the left and right naturally sought cooperation through an opening of the system by broadening corporatist-type representation. They did this notably without direction or even encouragement by the military governments. In contrast to the building of parliamentary democratic institutions, this process was therefore clearly and exclusively an indigenous German effort that grew from an important strand of German political culture.

One way to assess the long-term American impact on German democratization is therefore to ask how the U.S. Military Govern-

---

32 Wuppertal meeting of Feb. 18, 1947; text of the agreement in WWA, K5-115/2/7.

33 *Amtsblatt des Staatssekretariats für das französisch besetzte Gebiet Württembergs und Hohenzollerns*, no. 10, July 1, 1946, HStA Stuttgart, EA 6/3/2006; meeting of Badischer Industrie- und Handelstag, Apr. 4, 1946, Stiftung Wirtschaftsarchiv Baden-Württemberg [hereafter: WAB-W], A4/11; Landesversammlung Rheinland-Pfalz, Drucksache 13, "Verfassung für Rheinland-Pfalz," March 5, 1947, articles 71–3, and *Gesetz- und Verordnungsblatt Rheinland-Pfalz*, 1949, 141ff.

34 Anton Felix Napp-Zinn, "Wirtschaftsräte und überbetriebliche Mitbestimmung in Deutschland," in Walter Weddigen, ed., *Zur Theorie und Praxis der Mitbestimmung*, 2 vols. (Berlin, 1964), 2:119–32.

ment interacted with these characteristically German efforts toward "economic democracy," as they were generally called at the time. This German–American interaction began naturally in the U.S. zone, but later extended to the British and ultimately all Western zones. German efforts to create economic councils in the U.S. zone basically followed the pattern in the other zones, and in the spring and summer of 1946 there were highly promising initiatives to establish permanent economic councils in all three South German *Länder*.

Under the pressure of labor demands for membership in the chambers of industry and commerce as a way to gain a voice in regional economic administration, the Hessian chambers began to discuss the idea of a regional business–labor council as early as October 1945.[35] After heated internal debates, the chambers were ready for limited power sharing with the labor unions by the spring of 1946, because, in the words of the leading chamber representative, the old antagonism between bourgeois and socialist factions was outdated and had been replaced by an attitude of cooperation, "which is in keeping with the needs and the critical situation of the present time."[36] On May 18, 1946, the central organizations of the chambers of industry and commerce, the handicraft chambers, and the labor unions signed an agreement to establish a Hessian Economic Council (*Landeswirtschaftsrat*) with a membership of fifteen business and labor representatives each.[37]

Interestingly, this Hessian initiative had been enthusiastically endorsed by the director of the U.S. Manpower Division, General McSherry, and his civilian advisor, labor unionist Joseph P. Keenan.[38] It thus came as a considerable shock when the U.S. Military Government promptly vetoed the *Landeswirtschaftsrat*. The Economic Division had protested sharply against the formal institutionalization of a representative body, which would permit business and labor organizations to play a formal role in the political process.[39]

35 Meeting of Arbeitsgemeinschaft der hessischen Industrie- und Handelskammern [hereafter: AIHK Hess.], 6. Sitzung, Oct. 16, 1945, p. 6, Archiv der Industrie- und Handelskammer Frankfurt am Main [hereafter: IHK Frankfurt], AIHK Hess.
36 Erich Köhler in AIHK Hess., 15. Sitzung, Mar. 12, 1946, p. 4, IHK Frankfurt, AIHK Hess.
37 Sozialpolitischer Ausschuss; Military Government, IHK Frankfurt.
38 AIHK Hess., 21. Sitzung, May 28, 1946, and 22. Sitzung, June 11, 1946, p. 3, IHK Frankfurt, AIHK Hess.
39 Dr. Alfred Petersen, "Aktennotiz über meine Besprechung mit Mr. Keenan im Carlton-Hotel am 9. Juni 1946," IHK Frankfurt, Wirtschaftsministerium 1946; Petersen to Kloepfer, June 13, 1947, IHK Frankfurt, Korrespondenz Petersen.

The corporatist conception of democratization that stood behind the *Landeswirtschaftsrat* ran clearly counter to the American ideal of a representative democracy based on direct elections and a separation of politics and economic organizations. The German Organizations Branch of the Economic Sub-Division under Otto W. Brodnitz had left no doubt about the vehement American opposition to any governmental role for economic organizations.[40] For Americans, the kind of power sharing represented by the economic councils was fundamentally undemocratic and quasi-Fascist. Whatever hopes Joseph Keenan and the Manpower Division may have had of opening communications between business and labor, this fundamental aversion to corporatist democratization would guide American policy throughout the occupation years.

Initiatives for economic councils in Württemberg-Baden and Bavaria quickly succumbed to the same opposition. A proposed article in the Bavarian constitution for a *Landeswirtschaftsrat* to hear all laws relating to economic matters was withdrawn due to American objections even after Minister President Wilhelm Hoegner had taken steps to establish a council composed of twenty-two labor and twenty-two business representatives.[41] In Württemberg-Baden, plans for a similar body stalled in direct response to the veto in Hesse.[42] Renewed efforts of the Economics Ministry to draft legislation for a *Landeswirtschaftsrat* ran into a further veto by the American Military Government in spring 1948.[43]

The kinds of pressures for grass-roots labor–business councils that led to the Arnold Proposal and the Wuppertal Agreement in the British zone quickly became irrelevant in the American zone. This was because the councils were built around the traditional German chambers of industry and commerce, which, as officially sanctioned regional organizations of all industrial and commercial enterprises, played a central role in the allocation of raw materials and labor in the postwar years.

40 Otto W. Brodnitz, "Travel Notes," Feb.. 19, 1946, NA, RG 260, 11/1–3/5.
41 Wirtschaftsbeirat beim Bayerischen Staatsministerium für Wirtschaft, "Vorschlag für den III. Hauptteil einer bayerischen Verfassung," Aug. 20, 1946, Konrad-Adenauer-Stiftung, St. Augustin, I-109/AO:002; Hoegner to Bayerische Gewerkschaften, Sept. 9, 1946, HStA Munich, MA/114283.
42 Minutes, June 17, 1946, p. 10, WAB-W, Arbeitsgemeinschaft der nordwürttembergischen und nordbadischen Industrie- und Handelskammern.
43 "Gesetz zum Aufbau der wirtschaftlichen Selbstverwaltung," Jan. 1948, HStA Stuttgart, EA 6/10 (Bü 2503/1); Aktennotiz Dr. Breucha, March 17, 1948, HStA Stuttgart, EA 6/10/2503/1.

Their hostility to corporatist traditions, however, led Americans quite logically to attack the institution of the existing chamber of industry and commerce itself. The idea of a nongovernmental institution legally representing all business firms in a region was repugnant to the American conception of democracy. Americans saw the German chambers as nothing more than special-interest organizations with compulsory membership and fees. Worse, they regarded any delegation of governmental functions to such institutions as fundamentally undemocratic. Over the tenacious resistance of German authorities and experts from government, labor, chambers, and the legal establishment,[44] the U.S. Military Government therefore mounted a determined campaign to turn the chambers into American-style voluntary organizations. From the start of the occupation, military authorities repeatedly issued decrees prohibiting "compulsory membership" and the delegation of government functions to private economic organizations.[45] They kept close watch over individual chambers and issued frequent warnings that regulations must be followed to the letter.[46] In early 1946, Economic Sub-Division Controller Brodnitz personally visited most chambers of the zone. He criticized them severely for gross noncompliance and recommended further field investigations.[47] The last major offensive, launched in September 1947 with extensive hearings and explanatory sessions in all of the *Länder*,[48] finally pushed through the transition.[49] It was not until 1956 that the West German Bundestag reinstated the traditional chambers under the influence of chamber officials from the former British and French zones.

44 Cf. German expert opinions in NA, RG 260, 15/99-3/10.
45 A.G. 014.1 GEC-AGO of Aug. 14, 1945, MGR 4-6 of Apr. 1, 1946, and MGR 13-120 of Mar. 19, 1947, NA, RG 260, 3/122-3/7 and 15/99-3/10.
46 Cf. OMGUS Letter (CA), "Relationship between Military and Civil Government," Sept. 30, 1946; AG 091.3 MGBE/D, Oct. 24, 1947; OMGUS statement to Director, OMG Bavaria, "Policy Regarding Vocational Self-Administration," Oct. 1947; AG 080 (CA), "Policy Regarding Non-Governmental Business and Professional Associations," March 19, 1948, NA, RG 260, 15/99-3/10, 11/1-3/3 & 4.
47 Otto Brodnitz, "Travel Notes," Feb. 19, 1946, and Apr. 9, 1946, NA, RG 260, 11/1-3/5.
48 OMG Bavaria, "Report on Investigation of Trade Associations and Chambers of Commerce in Bavaria, 9, 10, and 12 September 1947," NA, RG 260, 11/2-3/8; cf. also memo announcing an information meeting in the Bavarian Ministry of Economics, Sept. 9, 1947; Lt. Col. T. B. Blocker, Deputy Chief, Economic Division, OMG Bavaria, to Bavarian Ministry of Economics (Aug. 26, 1947) for meeting on Sept. 15, 1947, both NA, RG 260, 13/77-1/2; Col. S. Y. McGiffert, Director, Economic Division, OMG Bavaria, Oct. 23, 1947, NA, RG 260, 13/77-1/3; Memo, John B. Holt, Sept. 4, 1947, NA, RG 260, 15/99-3/10; memo, Edward M. Mueller, Sept. 16, 1947, NA, RG 260, 13/116-2/2.
49 Brodnitz, Staff Report, Dec. 16, 1947, NA, RG 260, 4/138-3/20.

With the abolition of public-law chambers with compulsory membership and control over regional economic administration, the basis for power sharing with labor also faded away. While labor unions still advocated institutions of economic self-government based on a broad power sharing among business, labor, and others, they had no interest in entering purely private business chambers.[50] Both for the traditional elites who had dominated the chambers and for the labor unions, the corporatist democratization of the business–labor councils on the local level was destroyed with the institutions on which it was built in the British and French zones. It robbed old elites of the necessity to open up their power networks. Naturally, the U.S. opposition to the new business–labor chambers desired by labor was at least as fierce as to the old chambers. This effectively cut off one form of grass-roots democratization.

Yet American opposition to grass-roots cooperation through local interest organizations was not total. U.S. authorities were strikingly tolerant of purely advisory councils linked to and controlled by the administrative agencies. Here Bavaria developed an even more elaborate system of councils than the economic administrations of the British zone. Launched by Bavaria's first postwar economics minister, Ludwig Erhard, primarily to gain expert advice from business managers, these committees evolved under his Social Democratic successor, Rudolf Zorn, into full-blown *Beiräte* on *Land*, regional, and local levels with representatives from chambers of industry and commerce and labor unions as well as refugee, war-injured, and housewives' organizations.[51] Hesse and Württemberg-Baden developed similar, if somewhat less complete *Beirat* systems.[52] There can be little question that these councils made a contribution to grass-roots democratization, which the reorientation program so fervently tried to achieve with meager success. As one Bavarian official testified during extensive evaluations of the system in 1947–48: "Such

50 "Die Stellung der Gewerkschaften zu den Industrie- und Handelskammern," Apr. 1947: "2. Nachdem die Zwangsmitgliedschaft zu den Kammern aufgehoben worden ist, . . . erheben [die Gewerkschaften] ebensowenig Anspruch, in diesen Organisationen mitzuwirken, wie sie den Unternehmern das Recht einräumen, in den Gewerkschaften mitzuwirken." NA, RG 260, 13/77-1/2.
51 Bavarian Economics Ministry decree of Apr. 15, 1947 (Nr. W/121/12845), HStA Munich, MWi/10339.
52 Erlass des Wirtschaftsministers von Grosshessen, June 27, 1946, HStA Wiesbaden, 507/6205; memo, July 17, 1946, HStA Stuttgart, EA6/3/2006 (Bü 259); Wirtschaftsbeirat, meeting, March 24, 1947, HStA Stuttgart, EA6/3/2006; Ministry of Economics, internal memo (n.d., ca. 1948), HStA Stuttgart, EA6/10/2503/1.

committees are undoubtedly valuable for the democratization of the administration and for the democratic education of the people in accustoming them to participation in public affairs."[53]

This independent German development was tolerated by the U.S. Military Government with surprisingly little notice. The main studies of the occupation never mention it. This is quite understandable, since the Military Government generally overlooked these bodies as well, while it worked hard to organize "grass-roots" discussions in the reorientation program. While the *Beiräte,* in typical German tradition, remained linked to centralized organizations and thus offered few individual citizens direct participation, they had one obvious advantage over the reorientation program: They did not operate in a vacuum, but dealt with concrete needs and concerns of the day and offered at least small chances for solutions.

With the unification of the Western zones, U.S. influence began to extend to all of West Germany. American opposition against formalized institutions in the corporatist democratic tradition came to overwhelm the ambivalent attitude of the British and the sympathetic posture of the French. The most important laws establishing corporatist democratic institutions, which were passed by overwhelming majorities by the Berlin and North Rhine-Westphalian legislatures, were ultimately vetoed at the insistence of the United States.

The Berlin Economic Chamber Law (*Wirtschaftskammergesetz*), passed in June 1948 with the votes of the two large parties, CDU and SPD, was the most elaborate attempt to broaden the power structure in the entire economy from industry to handicrafts and from economic planning, price control, oversight of wages and working conditions to industrial research, arbitration of labor and business disputes, and promotion of exports.[54] In a typically corporatist manner, it proposed to do this by giving an equal voice to representatives of management, labor, and the general public in one comprehensive institution that would serve as an umbrella organization, with subdivisions for individual branches of industry, commerce, and handicrafts.

American opposition to this corporatist democratization scheme was determined and fierce. "From the U.S. viewpoint this proposed

---

53 Regierungsdirektor Dr. Zehler for Oberbayern, June 14, 1947, and Nov. 2, 1948, HStA Munich, MWi/9737 and 9730, respectively.
54 Stadtverordnetenversammlung Berlin, 1. Wahlperiode, Drucksache 108, Vorlage 777 (Apr. 27, 1948), 1–10.

law is extremely vicious in that it violates practically all of the U.S. basic principles with respect to conduct of business on democratic lines," the deputy director of the U.S. Office of Military Government for Germany in Berlin wrote to his director.[55] He proceeded to list U.S. prohibitions against the delegation of governmental functions to nongovernmental bodies, compulsory membership, and the creation of economic organizations by decree from above. One OMGUS advisor pointed to structural similarities to Nazi chambers and judged the law "dictatorial and undemocratic,"[56] while another speculated "that the totalitarian spirit of the Law reflects the minority Communist influence."[57] The Berlin Allied Kommandatura consequently vetoed the law.[58]

Even the considerably more benign North Rhine-Westphalian *Wirtschaftskammergesetz,* passed by a large CDU/SPD majority in July 1949,[59] ultimately fell victim to the same staunch U.S. opposition. The North Rhine-Westphalian law was basically an attempt to institutionalize the business–labor committees established by the Wuppertal Agreement of 1947 and to provide them with an official mandate to supervise regional economic administration. Local economic chambers, composed of equal numbers of representatives from the traditional chambers and the labor unions, would have become legally sanctioned institutions of economic self-government, supervised and financed by the state. A Main Economic Chamber was to serve as an advisory body on the state level.

Despite the initial assumption that the law would be approved by the British military government,[60] a veto arrived three months later.[61] Appeals by the North Rhine-Westphalian union

55 A. W. Moran, OMG Berlin Sector, May 24, 1948, NA, RG 260, 4/134-3/5.
56 Harry L. Franklin to Col. Glaser, Chief of Civil Administration Branch, OMG Berlin Sector, May 28, 1948, NA, RG 260, 4/127-2/27.
57 J. W. Darling, Deputy Chief, Economics Branch, OMG Berlin Sector, to Civil Administration Branch, Mar. 14, 1949, NA, RG 260, 4/137-1/10.
58 Allied Kommandatura Berlin to Oberbürgermeister, City of Berlin, May 18, 1949, BK/0(49)99, NA, RG 260, 4/127-2/27.
59 Landtag Nordrhein-Westfalen, 100. Sitzung, July 12, 1949; LDII-1135 and LDII-1142.
60 Küster in Präsidialkonferenz der Vereinigung der Industrie- und Handelskammern Nordrhein-Westfalen, Archiv der Vereinigung der Industrie- und Handelskammern des Landes Nordrhein-Westfalen, Düsseldorf, July 29, 1949; Deutscher Gewerkschaftsbund Bezirk Nordrhein-Westfalen, "Tätigkeitsbericht," Sept. 1949, p. 1, and Oct. 1949, p. 1, DGB-Archiv, Landebezirk Nordrhein-Westfalen, Sitzungen, Tätigkeitsberichte . . . 1949; letter Werner Hansen to Dr. Erich Potthoff, Oct. 4, 1949.
61 General Bishop to Gockeln, Oct. 4, 1949, as announced in Landtag Nordrhein-Westfalen, 1. Wahlperiode, 107. Sitzung, Oct. 10, 1949, pp. 2929–30, and 112. Sitzung, Nov. 7, 1949, pp. 3315–16.

chief[62] found a sympathetic response from the British commissioner, but he was overruled by Berlin Command[63] "after consultation among the Allies,"[64] strongly suggesting the influence of the American authorities. Ultimately this action affected more than North Rhine-Westphalia. It immediately discouraged similar initiatives in Hamburg and Schleswig-Holstein. The chamber elites no longer felt it necessary to open up their power networks except to offer membership to labor in the vocational training committees.

In the final months before the creation of the first successful German republic, U.S. and British authorities tipped the scales once more decisively against corporatist power sharing in the tenuously evolving democracy. In June 1948, the two occupation powers had in fact taken a remarkable step in conceding the legitimacy of a part of the German corporatist tradition when they permitted the delegation of most of the remaining raw material allocation to "industry groups" staffed by trade associations.[65] But when the bizonal parliament voted to open the "Functional Economic Agencies" (*Fachstellen*), established in response to this Allied invitation, to equal labor and business representation,[66] the action ran directly into a veto of the military governments.[67] In part this was an antisocialist move against "a compromise unsatisfactory to business at large,"[68] but the opposition was more basic. While both Britons and Americans encouraged government consultation of business and labor, they opposed any structures that competed with the institutions of classical parliamentary democracy. If administrative tasks were to be delegated to any nongovernment organizations, this should be based only on "practical business consideration" and never "purely on political" principles.[69]

62 Werner Hansen to General Bishop, Oct. 10, 1949, and "Akten-Notiz. Betr. Besuch bei General Bishop am 4. November 1949," Nov. 5, 1949, DGB-Archiv, "Wirtschaftskammergesetz."
63 Ibid., and Bishop to Hansen, Oct. 24, 1949, DGB-Archiv, "Wirtschaftskammergesetz."
64 Minutes of DIHT-Kammerrechtskommission, Nov. 17, 1949, p. 3, WWA, K5-100/1/1.
65 BICO/Memo(48)46, June 9, 1948, NA, RG 260, 15/99-3/10; cf. Eberhard Bömcke, "Die wirtschaftliche Selbstverwaltung: Ihr Anteil an den staatlichen Aufgaben," *Wirtschaftsverwaltung* 1 (Aug. 1948):11–12.
66 Wirtschaftsrat des Vereinigten Wirtschaftsgebietes, *Wörtliche Berichte*, 21. Vollversammlung, Aug. 31, 1948, pp. 858–68.
67 Governmental Advisers Standing Committee Meeting, Aug. 26, 1948, BICO/GL(48)85, Sept. 6, 1948; Bipartite Board, 38th meeting, Oct. 29, 1948; 40th meeting, Nov. 29, 1948, all in NA, RG 260, 11/129-3/9.
68 BIPC&I/Sec/060, Oct. 6, 1948, NA, RG 260, 11/129-3/9.   69 Ibid.

Even the well-known American opposition to postwar German initiatives to socialize basic industry can be viewed from this perspective. German socialization efforts never aimed at nationalization or state ownership, nor were they ever "revolutionary" in the sense of an overthrow of the old order. Postwar socialization plans instead followed a variety of corporatist democratic schemes of cooperation among as many major interest groups as possible. The initiatives generally came from socialists and labor unions, but they enjoyed broad, if sometimes reluctant support from the political center – from CDU support of socialization in the Hessian constitution and in the Ahlen Program of 1947 to the FDP's proposal of limited socialization of the Ruhr coal industry. There can be no doubt that the determined U.S. opposition to the various socialization attempts sprang from antisocialism. Yet in effect U.S. opposition to socialization did not work to prevent a full blown socialist economy or state in Germany, because Social Democratic and Christian Socialist initiatives never sought this. In actuality, American rejection of socialization proposals prevented what were only the most far-reaching, "socialist" of the postwar German efforts toward corporatist democratization in the economy.

The question of the U.S. impact on German democratization can thus be answered in a new light. Peter Merkl and others demonstrated many years ago the ways in which American officials modified the form of West German democracy in the constitutional deliberations, especially regarding the issue of federalism.[70] The foundations of that democracy grew out of Germany's own democratic tradition, but American influence significantly reshaped certain parts of it. These conclusions can now be extended. Americans also did not create the grass-roots foundations of West German democracy. Without underestimating the importance of American reeducation, reorientation, and press efforts, scholars generally agree that the impact of these formal programs was limited.

The critical impact of Americans was rather that they significantly modified German grass-roots democratization. Americans both suppressed and reinforced important German political traditions in this process. They suppressed incipient corporatist democratic institutions

70 Peter Merkl, _The Origins of the West German Republic_ (New York, 1963), esp. 119ff.; Elise Foelz-Schröter, _Föderalistische Politik und nationale Repräsentation 1945–1947_ (Stuttgart, 1974).

with remarkable consistency and success. Important remnants certainly survived in the British and French zones. Traditional public-law chambers reasserted themselves with some minor labor participation; codetermination survived in the coal and iron industries and was expanded in 1974; social councils (*Sozialräte*) in public insurance are reminiscent of such patterns. But in the end, it is remarkable how little of that tradition has survived in West German democracy – far less than in the Weimar Republic. There has been no Bundeswirtschaftsrat to parallel the Reichswirtschaftsrat of the first German democracy. No lower-level economic chambers were created or even mandated in the constitution as they had been in Weimar. Even the most successful economic parliament, the Hauptwirtschaftskammer of Rhineland-Palatinate ceased to exist by 1962.

On the other hand, Americans served to reinforce the established elites in local administration through the early political prohibitions and in the economy by opposing all new "political" institutions of power sharing. In spite of the initial wholesale condemnation of German political traditions implied by U.S. denazification and reeducation programs, the occupation in fact reconsolidated the dominant role of established conservative groups on the most basic levels of German society, both generally and to a lesser degree within the labor movement. Democratization therefore had to come from those groups that remained as elites of the rump Germany in the west, primarily industrial and administrative leadership.

Yet within this context, continued pressures of reconstruction and the threat of radicalization continuously forced the elites to seek cooperation with groups outside traditional networks of power, most importantly with labor, but also with other new groups such as refugees,[71] women, and consumer groups. The option that the elites had ultimately used in the crisis of 1929–33, namely the repression of the Left, was obviously not available after 1945. Both the lessons of the Nazi years and the specific demands of the Western Allies precluded the option of dictatorship. Moreover, conservative elites found a more willing partner than ever before in the Social Democrats and labor unions, which feared antidemocratic Communism and regarded reconstruction as their first priority in order to provide the

---

71 Cf. Uwe Kleinert, *Flüchtlinge und Wirtschaft in Nordrhein-Westfalen 1945–1961* (Düsseldorf, 1988), 75ff.

goods their followers desperately needed. A labor movement that proclaimed itself as a "force for order" (*Ordnungsmacht*) was clearly ready for cooperation in a basically conservative order.

Even though Americans opposed corporatist power sharing, they reinforced this kind of opening of the system, as they claimed in the basic policy statement to labor unions and employer organizations regarding codetermination: "It has been the policy of Military Government since the beginning of the Occupation to encourage consultation between the German governments, trade unions, employers, and farmers."[72] Even when they clearly aided in the consolidation of established elites, Americans never sought simple restoration as disillusioned reformers have claimed. Instead they increasingly aimed at restabilization on the basis of an established leadership which was ready to open its power networks to labor, new citizens, and new entrepreneurs. Both Britons and Americans thus promoted informal business–labor interaction. Officials from the American as well as the British Manpower Divisions repeatedly called meetings of business and labor leaders to instill a spirit of cooperation and a new civility of interaction that may in the end have promoted democratization.

The most remarkable of these informal forums sponsored by Americans was the Gemeinschaftsausschuss für Wirtschaft und Arbeit or Joint Management–Labor Committee. It illustrates both the kind of broader cooperation Americans sought, based on their own experience during the New Deal, and the care U.S. authorities exercised to prevent such cooperation from ever hardening into formal corporatist institutions.

When U.S. Manpower Advisor Joseph Keenan returned to Germany in the spring of 1947, he almost immediately pressed business and labor leaders to meet in a regular bizonal discussion forum to advise the bizonal military governments. Keenan's primary aim was to overcome what was by now generally regarded as poor business–labor relations in the American zone.[73] U.S. opposition to corporatist democratization and to compulsory chambers had lifted from business organizations the pressure to open up its power networks and had left labor in a confrontational opposition.[74] In this situation, Economics and Manpower Division advisors Brodnitz and Keenan

---

72 BISEC/Memo(49)9, March 1, 1949, NA, RG 260, 4/29-1/31.
73 Vorstandssitzung der Vereinigung der Industrie- und Handelskammern in der Britischen Besatzungszone, WWA, K5-100/2/4, July 23, 1947.
74 Kloepfer to Petersen, June 16, 1947, IHK Frankfurt, Korrespondenz Petersen.

united to force the reluctant antagonists to the table.[75] The labor union leadership of the British zone, lacking such pressure from its Military Government, opted not to participate, because it saw the zonal body as a step backward from the business–labor committees of the Wuppertal Agreement and away from full-blown labor–business chambers.

Even in this rump form, the Joint Management–Labor Committee met almost monthly from July through December 1947, alternately under the chairmanship of business representative Dr. Rudolf Müller and Labor leader Fritz Tarnow.[76] Discussion topics ranged from immediate concerns such as dismantlement, currency, and the black market to broader issues such as the market versus the planned economy. A number of subcommittees presented findings on specific issues. On the pressing concern of dismantlement, the most natural area of agreement between management and labor, the commission presented a forceful resolution to the military government. The co-chair from labor, Tarnow, captured the new spirit of cautious cooperation when he wrote to the head of the union in the British Zone, Hans Böckler, that the discussions in the committee were

generally on a high level. . . . On the business side there is certainly not just a "reactionary mass." . . . For many years to come there is only the alternative between a state-bureaucratic command economy and a mixed system of state planning and direction together with self-administration of the economy. It should be self-evident that this self-administration cannot be run by labor alone, but requires cooperation with management.[77]

Tarnow's ideas went well beyond the American intent. He saw in this bizonal commission once again the germ of a corporatist democratic council like the Reichswirtschaftsrat, of which he had been a member. Predictably, American enthusiasm quickly waned in response to such ideas and apparent actions. Once again a body established to provide a forum of informal discussion threatened to harden into a corporatist institution controlled by centralized organizations. American authorities thus became increasingly cautious. United States representatives met only irregularly with the committee, while the British did not come at all, leaving the

75 Petersen to Kloepfer, June 13, 1947, IHK Frankfurt, Korrespondenz Peterson.
76 Meetings July 17, Aug. 11, Sept. 13, Oct. 17, and Dec. 5, 1947, DGB-Archiv, Britische Besatzungszone/Wirtschaftspolitik.
77 Tarnow to Böckler, March 11, 1948, DGB-Archiv, Britische Besatzungszone/Wirtschaftspolitik.

Gemeinschaftsausschuss isolated and ineffective until it suspended its meetings without dissolving officially.[78] Ultimately it did not fit with the American concept of democratization.

In noting this particular American role in the German democratization process, we must not make the error of the disillusioned reformers and the radical enthusiasts of the sixties. It is not likely that the United States prevented a perfect democracy in Germany by blocking indigenous corporatist democratic institutions. It is not at all clear whether local radical reform committees, economic councils, or socialization of basic industries would have brought more freedom or prosperity or even real participation for the average worker or consumer, just as it is not certain that they would have failed. Even though democratization could not have been successful without building to a significant extent on the partly corporatist traditions of German political culture, and even if the American military government never clearly understood the potential of these traditions, their partial destruction did not necessarily work against genuine democracy; it was just shaped differently.

Once Americans began to retreat from direct control, once their primary goal became *restabilization* rather than reform in Germany, the confrontation between German and American democratic conceptions eased. Americans began to use and trust traditional German structures and their political culture. Thus the Working Party on Trade Associations reported in May 1948: "Hitherto the main emphasis has lain on securing our requirements by direct methods with perhaps too little regard for traditional German practices (not always harmful and dangerous). . . ."[79] Much of this rethinking coincided with the Marshall Plan. As Michael Hogan has argued so effectively, Marshall Planners hoped to achieve restabilization in Germany and Europe by exporting the "New Deal Synthesis," that is, "by organizing national and transnational networks of power sharing between private groups and between these groups and government authorities," thereby overcoming stagnation and preventing "the dual dangers of bureaucratic statism and class conflict," that is, socialist overthrow from either above or below.[80] The Joint Management–Labor Committee was clearly a step in that direction, coinciding with the preparations for the Marshall Plan in the second part of 1947.

---

78 Ibid.   79 BICO/P(48)135, May 12, 1948, NA, RG 260, 15/147-2/29.
80 Michael J. Hogan, *The Marshall Plan: America, Britain, And the Reconstruction of Western Europe, 1947–1952* (Cambridge, 1987), 428.

General Lucius D. Clay summarized this gradual American adjustment to the fact that German democratization would not follow the specific pattern envisioned by U.S. reeducators and reformers. In response to his Civil Affairs Division chief Edward H. Litchfield, who reported disillusionment among his officers that German democratization was lagging because Germans tended to rely on parties and organizations, Clay mused:

> Somehow we have to find out what is the true essence of democracy rather than what is the true essence of what Americans would like. We have a tendency to criticize everything in Germany that doesn't follow the American pattern. Yet I think the most of us will agree that France, over a great many years, has basically been as democratic and probably a more democratic country than we have. . . . I think that your own people in studying this thing have got to distinguish between reforms that we would like to have because we say we do them at home or the Continental practice. . . .[81]

Germans similarly became comfortable with American prohibitions. Strikingly, very few corporate democratic initiatives of the postwar years resurfaced and succeeded even after Germans became masters of their own house. Neither the economic council laws of Berlin and North Rhine-Westphalia nor the socialization mandate of the Hessian constitution were enacted after 1949. The new West German democracy emerged as a mixed system. It had been significantly Americanized and yet continued to build on German traditions of old elites, powerful comprehensive organizations, state administrations, and political parties, and even remnants of economic democracy in the codetermination system. The mixture seems to be successful.

81 OMGUS Staff Conference, March 27, 1948, pp. 16–17, NA, microfilm.

16

America and the Rebuilding of Urban Germany

JEFFRY M. DIEFENDORF

American policy toward the rebuilding of the bombed German cities was far less dramatic than the policies that dealt with the political rehabilitation of West Germany, its rearmament and integration into NATO, or even its economic recovery. There was no consistent, high-level American policy on what, if anything, to do about helping the Germans repair the damage left by the war. In the end the Americans developed only what amounted to a relatively modest position on housing construction, though at moments the Americans seemed to be reaching for something grander, such as an attempt to connect urban reconstruction with democratization. Certainly the Germans themselves expected something far greater in the way of American leadership and help than what the Americans finally offered.

Moreover, the modesty of American policy on urban reconstruction is interesting because it clearly contradicts so much popular wisdom. American aid is part of the founding myth of West Germany. Whether one asks Germans or Americans today, it is a common belief that American aid was enormously important in physical reconstruction, just as CARE packages were important for providing food and clothing. There is great symbolic worth in the image of rebuilding what one has destroyed, and there was at least one attempt, unsuccessful at that, to galvanize private support in the United States to aid reconstruction.[1] And if American aid was in fact

---

1 The guiding spirit was one Siegfried Goetze, who acted as the spokesman for an organization variously called "The National Committee to Rebuild German Cities, Inc." and "American Aid to Rebuild German Cities, Inc." On the one hand, between May 1949 and July 1950, Goetze and his group sought to obtain the approval of Dean Acheson and President Truman for their efforts. On the other hand, Goetze traveled to Germany in November 1949 to try to establish the legitimacy of his committee with German officials. Goetze's efforts were brushed aside in Washington. It took a few months for the Germans to realize

not as important in rebuilding as is often thought, it is nonetheless interesting to consider how important it might have been. Would the German Economic Miracle have taken a different pace and shape if Marshall aid had primarily been channeled into physical reconstruction of the bombed cities, rather than going into other areas of the economy?

Through the period under consideration here, we can identify central themes and a central, if often removed, personality. The Americans obviously recognized the great need for massive housing construction, both to replace the housing damaged in the war and to provide housing for refugees and displaced persons, and they consistently urged the Germans to build modern, mass-produced, inexpensive housing units. There was also sporadic American interest in modernizing, streamlining, and democratizing German town planning. The central personality whose influence was felt in the areas of planning and housing was Walter Gropius, the founder and former head of the Bauhaus and, since 1937, a professor at Harvard. Gropius on occasion served as an advisor to American authorities, and he was seen by many Germans as representing American policy toward German cities. When Americans spoke of modern housing and town planning, what was meant was the kind of modernization advocated by Gropius.

During the period of military occupation, an American program to assist the Germans in the rebuilding of their cities would have been a major commitment to help raise the German standard of living above what it was at the war's end. Such a commitment would thus have come into conflict with the guidelines present in the now infamous Joint Chiefs of Staff directive 1067, which instructed General Eisenhower to prevent the occupation forces from taking any "steps (a) looking toward the economic rehabilitation of Germany, or (b) designed to maintain or strengthen the German economy."[2] The tone of JCS 1067 was clearly punitive, but it also reflected the absence of much positive planning in wartime Washington on what should happen in a defeated Germany. Thus on June 5, 1944, Secretary of War Henry Stimson wrote to Secretary of State Cordell Hull

that Goetze in fact had nothing to offer them. See NA, RG 59, 862.502/5-549 and 7-1449; StA Munich, Bauamt und Wiederaufbau: 1104, contains correspondence between Goetze and the lord mayor and chief reconstruction official of Munich.

2 This directive is reprinted in many places. I have used U.S. Department of State, ed., *United States Economic Policy toward Germany*, Publication 2630 (Washington, D.C., 1946), 63.

to inquire what was being planned for occupied or liberated parts of Europe, noting that "our military civil affairs agencies have confined themselves to the relatively restricted field of relief and rehabilitation and, in the absence of any definition of national policy of economic reconstruction, have obviously been unable to point their activities toward any such program." Hull replied that a "policy pertaining to rehabilitation and reconstruction" was being considered, but that for now any relief effort would be limited to that "which perhaps would prevent suffering and unrest among the civilian population."[3]

Whatever policy was being considered, it had little to do with physical reconstruction. A policy planning committee for Germany had already recommended that there be "minimal interference with established administrative mechanisms and procedures" and that "municipal services [and] municipal enterprises" should continue under local German control.[4] In July 1944 it was proposed that the Nazi heavy construction program known as the Organisation Todt be continued after the war, but with new supervision and with forced foreign labor replaced by voluntary or "semivoluntary" German labor. This organization, highly experienced in large-scale engineering and construction, could be used for major reconstruction projects both in Germany and in areas that had been occupied by Germany.[5]

Nothing came of this idea, and the U.S. Military Government in Germany began working without any clear-cut program that might have led to aid in physical reconstruction. The wartime activities of the American Commission for the Protection and Salvage of Artistic and Historic Monuments did not lead to any general program to rebuild damaged buildings of historic value, though there were isolated instances of American help in this regard.[6] German municipal administrations were the first to be reinstituted, and the Americans viewed rebuilding as the responsibility of municipal housing and construction offices. Moreover, already by autumn 1945, cost cutting forced the reduction of military government staffs, and physical reconstruction was just the sort of thing that could be turned over to

---

3 NA, RG 165, Civil Affairs Division, 380, box 134, letters of June 5 and July 5, 1944.
4 Records of Harley A. Notter, LC, Microfilm Division, film T 1221, reel 1, CAC report 32, Dec. 17, 1943.
5 Ibid., reel 4, report 247, July 6, 1944.
6 Among other things, this commission prepared lists of important buildings throughout Europe to help the bomber forces try to avoid unnecessary damage to cultural artifacts.

the Germans. Military government officers did not always like the way city officials pursued reconstruction, but the Americans seldom intervened in local decisions on rebuilding priorities, town planning, or architecture.[7] The Military Government was concerned about stimulating the production of building materials and controlling black market trading in such materials, but their allocation was normally left to the Germans – apart from whatever materials were needed for the construction of facilities for the occupying forces. In the early postwar years, this was considerable. For example, in Bavaria in the first quarter of 1947, the U.S. army requisitioned 83 percent of the production of new bricks, nearly 90 percent of the cement, and 50 percent of the roofing paper.[8]

General Clay certainly wanted to help alleviate the housing crisis, but he felt duty bound by JCS 1067 not to take any steps to improve the German standard of living. In time he became comfortable using the escape clause that allowed measures to prevent "disease and unrest" in order to take steps to get crucial segments of the economy functioning again, but housing construction he considered a task for the Germans. His staff did assist Herbert Hoover in February 1947 in preparing a report on the awful housing situation, and he recognized that housing was a major, long-term capital problem, but in Clay's opinion, "it was an entirely German problem."[9] As tension between the United States and the Soviet Union grew and as policymakers in Washington adopted an increasingly Cold War mentality, it became clear to General Clay that he could not expect to proceed indefinitely in the American Zone on the basis of JCS 1067, even loosely interpreted, nor could he realistically expect to be able to coordinate

7 For example, in early 1948, Colonel James Kelly told Munich officials that, while the Americans sympathized with the desire to rebuild in a traditional style, "it would not hurt if also a newer style were used." Indeed, "reconstruction should be undertaken in a modern sense," and it should not be obstructed in the "musty offices of the bureaucracy." Such exhortations, however, did not translate into actions by the military government in Bavaria. StA Munich, BuR, 1969, meeting of Jan. 29, 1948, with the lord mayor, and Ratsitzungsprotokolle, 721/12, Besprechung über Stadtplanung, Feb. 24, 1948.
8 "Survey of allotment of building material," prepared by Bayerisches Staatsministerium für Arbeit und soziale Fürsorge, May 9, 1947, in NA, RG 260, OMG Bavaria, Manpower, Labor Relations and Standards B1, Statistical Reports 30 3/13 and 31 1/13, box 52. In that year, a U.S. officer estimated that "approximately 60% of all construction was done with material secured through other than regular channels." Memo, Herman Stern, Field Operations Supervisor for Franken, to Chief, Executive and Field Operations Branch, "The Use and Misuses of Building Materials," Oct. 14, 1947, p. 5, NA, RG 260, OMG Bavaria, Manpower 1051/13, box 85, file 11.
9 NA, RG 260, OMGUS, Shiplist 13 1/10, cont. 5911, Information Service Division, Motion Picture Branch, Minutes of Bipartite Board of April 30, 1949. See also John H. Backer, *The Winds of History: The German Years of Lucius DuBignon Clay* (New York, 1983), 52ff., 158.

American policy in Germany with Soviet policy. One result of this changing situation was Clay's invitation to Walter Gropius to come to Germany as a visiting consultant on housing and city planning. Gropius arrived in August 1947 in Berlin, where he toured the city, gave public lectures, and met privately with German planners and architects.[10] From Berlin he went on to Hanover, Frankfurt, Stuttgart, and Munich. There was widespread interest in his visit, both because of the high prestige Gropius enjoyed as a founder of architectural modernism and because he was thought to speak for American policymakers.

There was good reason to think so. In his lectures and subsequent reports, Gropius placed his recommendations in a very wide context that appeared to fit well with overall American policy on democratizing Germany. He argued that "there is a political corpse buried in Germany's rubble and it is the job of the reconstruction planners to insure that it isn't revived." Just as the Nazis had been able to connect "building and politics" in their "superhuman," monumental building program, so "sound planning – planning that is healthy for the development of democracy – considers the individual human being first and foremost. It is scaled to his needs and it provides him with the physical plant to house democratic institutions." Healthy planning, Gropius thought, meant breaking up big cities "into small communities of self-contained neighborhood units, in which the essential importance of the individual can be realized, his needs met and his voice heard." Urban reconstruction, in other words, should also be political reconstruction. The model Gropius referred to here was the New England town with its town meeting, but the idea that proper urban design and democracy were related was not something that he had first conceived during his exile in the United States. At

10 Harry Wann, Director of Education and Religious Affairs Division of the American Military Government in Hesse, had already invited Gropius in June 1947 to attend an international conference for engineering in Darmstadt, noting that Gropius's presence would be "in the interest of Military Government." Gropius apparently had little interest in this conference. Gropius Papers, Houghton Library, Harvard University, bMS Ger 208, no. 769. Gropius's report to Clay on his trip was published as "Reconstruction: Germany," *Task* 7–8 (1948):35–6. He discussed the conclusions reached in "Will Europe Build Cities or Shanty Towns?" *Weekend*, the magazine of *Stars and Stripes*, Jan. 3, 1948, pp. 5 and 15. German planners and architects commented widely on the visit, for example: "Gropius und das künftige Frankfurt," *Die neue Stadt* 1, no. 3 (Dec. 1947):128–9. The trip has been discussed in Jeffry M. Diefendorf, "Berlin on the Charles, Cambridge on the Spree: Walter Gropius, Martin Wagner, and the Rebuilding of Germany," in Helmut F. Pfanner, ed., *Kulturelle Wechselbeziehungen im Exil – Exile across Cultures* (Bonn, 1986), 348–9, and Friedhelm Fischer, "German Reconstruction as an International Activity," in Jeffry M. Diefendorf, ed., *Rebuilding Europe's Bombed Cities* (London and New York, 1989), 140–1.

the time of the German revolution of 1918–19 and during the Weimar Republic, Gropius and other modernist architects and planners had published polemics calling for modern cities and modern housing for a modern, democratic Germany.[11]

To put such a program of town planning into practice in the Germany after 1945, Gropius called for new planning and building laws that would facilitate massive realignment of property lines, the creation of a new research institution to investigate all aspects of urban life, and a strong central ministry of reconstruction to oversee the process. Personnel should be drawn from the ranks of "the best technical experts . . . to be chosen for their ability rather than for party membership."[12] In the same way that Clay still persisted in working for U.S.–Soviet cooperation on Germany, Gropius suggested that an "Institute for Planning and Building Integration" might be created under the auspices of the Institut für Bauwesen der Deutschen Akademie für Wissenschaft – located in the Soviet Sector of Berlin – if the military governments could support such an organization. Further gains in specialized knowledge could be obtained from more visits to Germany by appropriate foreign experts as well as from the visit of "well-chosen Germans" to America. Gropius also observed that the existing "shortage of manpower and materials" implied "a rationalization of building methods." He cautioned against the excessive emphasis on standardization that had appeared in the Nazi years, and he doubted that prefabrication could solve all of Germany's reconstruction needs, but steps in the direction of standardization and prefabrication would help overcome Germany's traditional and outmoded building designs and construction techniques.[13]

11 Gropius, "Will Europe Build Cities or Shanty Towns?" 5. In fact, many German planners in the 1920s and even under the Nazis advocated the breakup of the big city into such small units, and this idea was everywhere part of the discussion of how to rebuild. For example, see Johannes Göderitz, Roland Rainer, and Hubert Hoffmann, *Die gegliederte und aufgelockerte Stadt* (Tübingen, 1957), an essay written during the war, though only published ten years later. Gropius's ideas on town planning in America had taken shape in a series of essays he wrote during the war with Martin Wagner, a former chief town planner of Berlin, for whom Gropius secured a position at Harvard in the late 1930s. An example is Gropius and Wagner, "The New City Pattern for the People and by the People," in *The problem of the Cities and the Towns: Conference on Urbanism* (n.p. [Cambridge, Mass.?], 1942), 95–116. For the Weimar years, see Barbara Miller Lane, *Architecture and Politics in Germany, 1918–1945* (Cambridge, Mass., 1968), and Joachim Petsch, "Neues Bauen und konservative Architektur der 20er und 30er Jahre," *Der Architekt*, no. 4 (1983):188–93.
12 Gropius, "Reconstruction: Germany," 35. This naturally appealed to those who considered themselves to have been apolitical technocrats while working for the Nazis.
13 Ibid., 36.

The German response to Gropius's recommendations was mixed. In Berlin his ideas on breaking up the metropolis and his praise for his friend Hans Scharoun was interpreted as a criticism of the new city planner, Karl Bonatz. Bonatz replied that Gropius knew too little about conditions in Berlin to criticize the efforts of the hard-pressed planning office.[14] Other Germans, on the other hand, felt that Gropius's ideas ran parallel to their own proposals for bizonal legislation on reconstruction.[15] The greatest sensation, however, was caused by another part of his trip to Germany. While in Frankfurt, Gropius led planners and journalists to think that he intended to make Frankfurt's reconstruction a project for some of his Harvard students, which raised hopes that Gropius was going to become permanently engaged with German reconstruction. In fact Clay apparently had asked Gropius to write a highly confidential report on planning for a reconstructed Frankfurt as a capital city for a future West German state. The press did not find out about this until shortly after the collapse of the London Foreign Ministers' Conference in December, well after Gropius had returned to the United States. His friends and admirers in Germany of course anxiously inquired about the Frankfurt project, something that they expected to be of great importance for that city, for reconstruction planning elsewhere, and for the political future of Germany. Gropius, however, denied that he had ever intended to develop such plans for Frankfurt; he admitted only to having prepared a general sketch: actual planning "would have to be done by the Germans."[16]

Gropius never did in fact develop plans for Frankfurt as a capital city, and this episode became no more than another piece of evidence for early American thinking leaning toward the division of Germany. (Clay's interest in Frankfurt as a capital city came a year before the currency reform and Berlin Blockade and two years before the creation of the two new German states.) Gropius's recommendations for a national minister for reconstruction and for the national research institute also came to naught. Other recommendations,

---

14 Karl Bonatz, "Anmerkungen zu den Presseinterviews mit Professor Gropius und zu seinem Vortrag im Titania-Palast am 22. August 1947," *Neue Bauwelt* 2 (1947):550–1.
15 Frau P. Schäfer, General Secretary of the Deutscher Verband für Wohnungswesen, Städtebau und Landesplanung, to Gropius, Feb. 9, 1948, Gropius Papers, no. 640.
16 Gropius to Frau P. Schäfer, Jan. 9, 1948, Gropius Papers, no. 640. On this affair, see Diefendorf, "Berlin on the Charles, Cambridge on the Spree," 349, and Fischer, "German Reconstruction," 140–1.

however, found an echo in subsequent American policy, particularly in the area of housing and in the visit of other planning experts.

Let us examine first the visit of two other planners to Germany. This visit seems to have reinforced some of the recommendations made by Gropius. In July 1949, Samuel Zisman, who headed a citizens' planning organization in Philadelphia, was invited by the U.S. Military Government to travel to Germany to advise on city planning. He brought along Hans Blumenfeld, then a town planner for Philadelphia.[17] Between July 19 and November 3, they spoke to fourteen German audiences totaling some 975 persons and made one radio address in Nuremberg. The subject of the talks was city planning and housing policy in the United States. Most of the Germans Zisman and Blumenfeld met were planners, architects, local officials, and students. Upon their return home, they submitted a set of recommendations about American policy to the State Department that merit detailed consideration.

Some of what they said was an implicit criticism of existing policy on German economic recovery and on denazification. They felt that German reconstruction was suffering from a lack of coherent, centrally directed, long-range planning. Obviously there could be no central planning until a central government had been formed, but Blumenfeld also noted that:

the emphasis on the rights of the individual versus the state, healthy and natural as a reaction against the totalitarian tyranny of the Nazi Regime, has been frequently turned, in the dogmatic way characteristic of much German thinking, into opposition to any restriction of private activities, even where such restrictions are clearly in the interest of the great majority of the people.[18]

17 Born in Hamburg, Blumenfeld had studied in Germany and then worked there as an architect during the 1920s. He was a member of the German Communist Party, and, from 1930 to 1937, he had worked in the USSR, after which he emigrated to the United States. He resigned his job in Philadelphia in 1951 in protest over the need to take a loyalty oath, though he did take the oath. In 1955 he went to Canada, where he spent most of the rest of his life. He died in 1988, having just published a new volume of memoirs, *Life Begins at 65: The Not Entirely Candid Autobiography of a Drifter* (Montreal, 1987). I have been unable to find further information about Zisman. It is likely that this visit was part of the OMGUS exchange program, which was taken over by the High Commissioner for Germany after mid-1949. Considerable hunting in the State Department, OMGUS, and HICOG records revealed little about the origins of this trip or the fate of its recommendations. Archivists at the National Archives report that many records from the transition period from OMGUS to HICOG were misplaced or are virtually impossible to track down. The following discussion is based upon a report submitted by Blumenfeld on December 8, 1949, to Fernando Eugen Ropshaw, who had been an OMGUS officer up to 1949 and who then moved to the State Department: "City Planning in Germany," NA, RG 59, 862.502/12-849.
18 Blumenfeld report, "City Planning in Germany," 1.

In fact, "with the current aversion of German public opinion against officialdom, there is a tendency to consider *any* kind of private agency . . . as more democratic than any public agency."[19] This was potentially dangerous: German government agencies had been denazified, but some towns seemed to turn to private, voluntary planning organizations "as vehicles to bring back into positions of power persons who are ineligible for public office because of their political pasts."[20] Moreover,

the carrying out of the currency reform without a simultaneous "Lastenausgleich" [equalization of burdens] shifted economic power from the states, municipalities, cooperatives, and building societies to the owners of real estate and commodities. This has made condemnation for public purposes extremely difficult. In addition it has led to a misdirection of resources into nonessential building. . . .[21]

Even the requirement of balanced budgets on all levels of government, because it restricted the judicious use of credit, acted to undermine long-range planning.

Blumenfeld and Zisman urged the high commissioner "to encourage the establishment and continued effective activity" of a strong, federal planning agency along the lines of state planning agencies in Northrhine-Westphalia and Lower Saxony, and they felt that the High Commission itself should have its own high-level planning committee to help coordinate regional and town planning activities. Here they pointed with approval to the Conseil Franco-Allemand d'Urbanisme functioning in the French zone. Such central planning offices would deal with broad problems; actual construction should remain in the hands of local city planners. They also recognized that German cities, such as Hamburg and Frankfurt in the 1920s, had had strong local planning offices, and they recommended against trying to transplant American urban planning practices, which they thought were comparatively weak.

A federal planning agency should, in turn, have at its disposal a strong federal city planning law.[22] Such a law should remove the central obstacles to new planning and reconstruction: inadequate

19 Ibid., 5.   20 Ibid., 6.   21 Ibid., 2.
22 The English displayed far greater energy than the Americans in encouraging town planning in their zone of occupation. They sent a steady stream of speakers to Germany, set up exhibitions, and invited German planners to visit Britain. They also encouraged passage of comprehensive town planning and building laws. See Fischer, "German Reconstruction," and Jeffry M. Diefendorf, "Reconstruction Law and Building Law in Post-War Germany," *Planning Perspectives* 1 (1986):114–15.

financing and legal barriers hindering the redistribution or consolidation of parcels of land for new building under modern conditions. The historic division of building lots in older cities had to be overcome if wider streets and better public amenities were to be built during reconstruction. Existing legal procedures and requirements for compensation for land confiscated for public use had to be changed because they enabled individual property owners to use the courts to obstruct progressive changes. Moreover, the currency reform of 1948 weakened the financial position of the towns, depriving them of the resources needed to compensate adequately all property owners who would be required to give up parts of their land for new streets or for the consolidation of building lots. For this reason both a law equalizing the burdens of reconstruction and a law providing additional sources of financing for reconstruction were needed.

The two visiting planners also contended that the Americans needed to address the housing problem. The war damage, the lack of an extensive housing construction program under the Nazis, and the influx of people expelled from the former German lands in the East had created "intolerable overcrowding and unsanitary conditions" that posed "serious moral, social, and political dangers." "The seriousness of the situation," they argued, "makes it impossible to treat this problem as a matter of no concern to the High Commission."[23] Part of the solution had to come through long-term planning of new housing projects, part had to come through creating new legal and fiscal tools to enable impoverished property owners to rebuild damaged buildings, and part had to come through basic changes in the design of housing units and the techniques of construction. Here it was necessary to replace outmoded conservative German construction, which sought to build houses that would last indefinitely, with more modern forms, particularly prefabrication. The Germans should learn the concept of "functional obsolescence" and accept the idea that housing should be replaced regularly.[24] The financing of a massive program of housing construction could come through deficit financing (currently prohibited by the Allies) or through foreign assistance. The latter would of course include Marshall Plan counterpart funds, which Blumenfeld and Zisman felt would be "one of the most productive uses to which these funds could be put."[25]

23 Blumenfeld report, "City Planning in Germany," 12.   24 Ibid., 14.   25 Ibid.

To shape public opinion in favor of stronger urban planning and changes in the methods of housing construction, Zisman and Blumenfeld suggested that the High Commission support the German Association for Housing, Town and Regional Planning and that this association be rehabilitated as a full-fledged member of the International Federation for Housing and Town Planning. They also strongly encouraged American support for cultural exchanges, preferably run by private organizations rather than government and by German agencies rather than the American government.[26] Zisman and Blumenfeld laid the groundwork for a three-month-long visit to the United States of ten German officials, architects, university teachers, and economists in the field of planning and a two-semester stay at an American university for a dozen or more German students in fields relating to urban reconstruction. In addition, they argued that the American government should support the visit of groups of German officials from all levels of government as well as visits by architects and individuals involved in social housing projects in order to familiarize the Germans with American approaches to housing construction. Zisman and Blumenfeld also recommended that the United States arrange for lecture tours by German-speaking American experts in the fields of town planning and housing construction. Finally, they encouraged an exchange of professional periodicals in the relevant fields between American and German publishers and professional associations.

It has not been possible to determine whether these recommendations, like those of Gropius earlier, had any direct and immediate impact on American policy. When a German planner wrote Gropius in 1951 for a copy of his 1947 report to Clay, Gropius observed that "it was moldering, like so much else, in the archives of the occupation army."[27] That may well have been the case with the recommendations of Blumenfeld and Zisman. The American government opposed, in fact, the kind of strong building and planning law suggested by all of its visiting experts, from Gropius to Blumenfeld.

26 For such programs generally, see Henry P. Pilgert, *The Exchange of Persons Program in Western Germany*, Historical Division, Office of the U.S. High Commissioner for Germany (Washington, D.C., 1951), and Henry J. Kellermann, *Cultural Relations as an Instrument of U.S. Foreign Policy: The Educational Exchange Program between the United States and Germany, 1945–1954*, Cultural Relations Programs of the U.S. Department of State, Historical Studies, No. 3 (Washington, D.C., 1978). These official histories cover the programs of OMGUS and HICOG.
27 Gropius to Eugen Blanck, Jan. 1, 1951, Gropius Papers, no. 470.

However, an examination of the policy eventually adopted by the Americans on housing construction suggests that the recommendations of those planners who visited Germany did indeed have some influence in this area.

American policy regarding housing construction in Germany derived from several sources. As we have already seen in the reports filed by Gropius, Blumenfeld, and Zisman, there was a steady American interest in prefabricated housing. The debate over the usefulness of prefabrication was an old one, both in Germany and America. Gropius, for example, had been part of a group set up by Martin Wagner in Berlin in 1931 to develop designs for prefabricated, modular housing. Wagner was then Berlin's chief planner, and, like Gropius, he had strongly believed that a democratic society required modern (and by definition democratic) housing and planning.[28] Their interest in this subject continued after the two men migrated to America and in the 1930s. In 1941 Wagner and Gropius presented a joint paper to a U.S. House Select Committee investigating population migrations derived from the war effort in the United States; the paper advocated industrialized housing construction.[29] If prefabricated housing was touted as a solution to America's housing problem, surely it would work for Germany. Moreover, it quickly occurred to members of the U.S. Military Government that Germans might be able to export simple prefabricated housing to other devastated countries and thereby improve her foreign trade balance, and with American encouragement some effort was made in this direction.[30]

It was only with the advent of the Marshall Plan, however, that the Americans became actively involved in influencing housing construction in a major way. They feared that the lack of good housing for lower-income groups – workers and refugees – might under-

28 See Martin Wagner, *Das neue Berlin* (1932), unpublished book manuscript in Bibliothek des Senators für Bau- und Wohnungswesen, Berlin.
29 The paper was entitled "How to Bring Forth an Ideal Solution of the Defense Housing Problem." See Gilbert Herbert, *The Dream of the Factory-Made House: Walter Gropius and Konrad Wachsmann* (Cambridge, Mass., 1984), 138ff., 234ff.
30 Robert Murphy, U.S. Political Advisor for Germany, to SecState, Apr. 22, 1946, with OMGUS Press Release of Apr. 18, 1946, NA, RG 59, 862.502/4-2246; report on housing signed by Luther H. Hodges, Chief, Industry Division, Office of Economic Affairs, but in fact written by James W. Butler, head of the housing division, ECA mission to Germany, p. 7, NA, RG 466, HICOG, box 69, file 504.21. Butler received a commendation for the report, dated April 5, 1951, which stated: "This is the first comprehensive, intelligent and constructive report on the German housing situation that has reached the Department [of German economic affairs] in the course of five years."

mine their policy of democratization, and one official observed that "the potential danger of several million people housed under deplorable conditions is difficult to exaggerate."[31] The Americans felt that rents for existing housing were currently too low; taxes, interest rates, and building costs for new housing were too high. New sources of funding for housing were desperately needed in the new West German state, and the Germans looked to the Americans for help. The First Federal Housing Law of April 24, 1950, which made available a variety of governmental subsidies and tax credits, provided the framework for funding most of the new construction, but counterpart funds under the Marshall Plan also made an important contribution and provided an opening for the Americans to influence the shape of reconstruction. Under an agreement with the Federal Housing Ministry, European Recovery Program (ERP) funds were to be allocated in keeping with the provisions of the Federal Housing Law. That meant that ERP-financed housing had to be social housing: dwellings built "at the lowest possible costs at such places where the demands . . . is [sic] considered most urgent. . . ." Rents were to be kept low, and persons assigned to the housing should be working in an area essential to economic recovery (such as mining, industry, or export trades) or else belong to categories of especially needy persons, such as refugees from the East or those disabled by the war.[32] Before any ERP funds could be used for housing, however, the proposed expenditures had to win the approval of the American mission for the Marshall Plan.

The Americans pursued several goals here. In keeping with the overall aim of the Marshall Plan and as suggested by the agreement with the federal housing minister, they wanted most of all to help stimulate the German economy. When individual Germans sought the assistance of the High Commission in obtaining financial aid for housing, they were told: "Housing is allocated with the view to increasing the general productivity of the German economy by

---

31 U.S. Political Advisor for Germany, "The Problems of Housing in the Bizonal Area," memo of May 6, 1949, in Vertical Files, Loeb Library, Harvard University. It is interesting that, during the Nazi years, German authorities pursued programs of slum clearance in part because they felt that bad, unhygienic housing conditions bred communism. See Ursula von Petz, *Stadtsanierung im Dritten Reich,* Dortmunder Beiträge zur Raumplanung, vol. 45 (Dortmund, 1987).

32 Official translation of letter from the Federal Minister for Housing Wildermuth to the ministers (Senators) of the *Länder* in charge of housing, June 19, 1950: Directives concerning the utilization of the ERP funds for the Social Housing Construction, scheme 1950, NA, RG 466, HICOG, box 69, file 504.21.

bringing workers closer to their work, by relieving labor shortages and inefficiencies. This policy does not permit us to direct our aid to those persons who perhaps have a greater claim to our friendship, appreciation and generosity."[33] In other words, economic growth was more important than rewarding political loyalty.[34]

The Americans were extremely frustrated by the unwillingness of the Germans to build or to live in temporary housing structures made of wood: German authorities always insisted on solid masonry construction that would last decades, and they placed obstacles in the way of prefabricated dwellings.[35] Even where architects were inclined toward new construction methods and designs, local bureaucrats stifled innovation by insisting that builders conform to all petty regulations or that the design of individual buildings harmonize with traditional local styles. The Americans hoped to use ERP funds to pressure the German *Beamten* into giving up their traditional thinking.[36] Productivity should be raised in the housing industry through greater efficiency. The Americans also wanted to help house the large number of refugees in West Germany. The allocation of funds and the assignment of completed housing units should reflect some measure of social equity. All of these goals were pursued simultaneously.

The first extensive housing construction program sponsored by the Americans was the building of small residential settlements in

---

33 Sam Gillstrap to Erich Groeppler, Dec. 28, 1950, NA, RG 466, HICOG, box 69, file 504.21. This was a standard reply.

34 This is typical of the American retreat from earlier denazification and democratization policies. To take another example, the High Commission was asked in 1950 by several citizens to intervene when a group of houses in Zuffenhausen, near Stuttgart, were to be turned over to their previous owners, former SS and Nazi Party members. The housing settlement had been built in 1939 for politically reliable persons, taken over by UNRRA for displaced persons in 1945, then turned over to the military government in 1947 but immediately seized by the city and given to victims of Nazism. The original owners sued to regain their homes, and the German courts ruled in their favor. The High Commission felt this was unjust, and there was concern about having a settlement with a high concentration of former Nazis, but the Americans felt it was too late to do anything without causing other problems. Report on Rotweg Housing Settlement by H. W. Weigert, March 14, 1950, NA, RG 466, HICOG, box 69, file 504,21.

35 Office memo, James W. Butler to F. L. Mayer, Sept. 27, 1951, NA, RG 466, HICOG, box 69, file 504.21. In July 1949, at the moment of transition from OMGUS to the High Commission, the Americans considered making a documentary film that would encourage prefabricated housing construction by making "the 'reactionary builder type' the butt of comic ridicule in the film." Harold J. Hurwitz, OMGUS Information Services Division, to Mr. Stuart Schulberg, July 6, 1949, NA, RG 260, OMGUS, Shiplist 13 1/10, cont. 5911, box 264.

36 Report on housing signed by Luther H. Hodges, Chief, Industry Division, Office of Economic Affairs, written by James W. Butler, p. 5, NA, RG 466, HICOG, box 69, file 504.21.

fifteen German cities.[37] The Americans wanted to use their control of funding "to break traditional building methods" by releasing Economic Cooperation Administration (ECA) funds only if construction costs were held down through the use of standardized building techniques.[38] Cities wishing to participate had to provide suitable land near important industries and to assume the costs of improving the land. To obtain widespread German participation in developing progressive designs and construction methods, a nationwide competition was announced in the summer of 1951. Some 3,300 dwellings were to be built in developments of from 200 to 300 units with DM 37.5 million in ERP funds. All were to be social housing projects in keeping with the provisions of the Federal Housing Act, but the Americans also wanted most of the housing units to become the private property of the residents.

The goal of stimulating interest in the program was clearly fulfilled. Seven hundred twenty-five entries, an extraordinarily large number, were submitted by individual architects or architectural teams. To judge the competition, an international committee was appointed. Entries were evaluated on the basis of the quality of planning, arrangement of the housing units, building cost and efficiency, construction techniques, and appearance. The State Department asked Gropius to serve as the American cochairman. He declined but sent in his stead Professor Walter Bogner, a Harvard colleague who concurred with Gropius's ideas about town planning, modern design, and standardized construction techniques. The German cochairman was Professor E. H. Bartning, president of the Association of German Architects and, like Gropius and Martin Wagner, part of the 1931 Berlin group that had worked on prefabricated housing. Moreover, Bernard Wagner, the son of Martin Wagner and also an architect, served on the committee as an ECA housing consultant.[39]

---

37 For this program see Ulrich Höhns, " 'Neuaufbau' als Hoffnung, 'Wiederaufbau' als Festschreibung der Misere: Marshallplan und Wohnungsbau in der Bundesrepublik nach dem Kriege," in Bernhard Schulz, ed., *Grauzonen – Farbwelten: Kunst und Zeitbilder 1945– 1955* (Berlin, 1983), 85–102.

38 Memo by Luther H. Hodges, Chief, Industry Division, Office of Economic Affairs, "Housing and City, Town, and Country Planning. Cost," March 1, 1951, NA, RG 466, HICOG, box 69, file 504.21.

39 Gropius to Otto Bartning, the president of the Bund Deutscher Architekten and the German cochairman of the committee, Oct. 6, 1951, Gropius Papers, no. 416. Other American members of the committee were Mack Arnold, a manufacturer of building materials from Greensboro, North Carolina; Charles M. LaFolette, former director of the military government in Baden-Württemberg; Donald Monson, a former Detroit planner; William Wittausch, an official in the Washington housing administration; and James W. Butler, the

In an essay describing the ECA program, Bernard Wagner stated that it was intended to help German architects "pick up where Poelzig, van der Rohe, Gropius and Martin Wagner left off" because the "Nazi regime systematically strangled any new ideas in architecture, thoroughly eradicated the earlier modern spirit and saw to it that German architectural schools produced nothing but obedient servants in the National Socialist conception of art and architecture."[40] We can see here again the ideology of modernism that moved from Germany in the 1920s to America in the late 1930s and, now sponsored by the United States, was to return to Germany after the war in the ECA competition.

The prize committee spent forty days traveling around Germany examining entries and prospective building sites. Many of Germany's best known architects had entered the competition. The decisions of the prize committee are interesting; the wartime activities of ideology of the participating architects obviously played no role at all. Among the winners were architects who had prospered during the Nazi regime, such as Konstanty Gutschow and Hans Bernhard Reichow, and architects who had suffered, such as Werner Hebebrand. Losers included famous modernists like Hans Scharoun and conservatives like Hermann Rimpl.[41] Almost all of the 725 entries featured small row or terrace houses with small gardens according to the prevailing theory of ideal residential planning and house design.[42] As it turned out, only one of the thirteen winning entries – in Bremen – was located in an urban area destroyed by bombing; the

author of the program and head of the housing division of the ECA mission to Germany. Bernard Wagner came to the United States in 1938, finished his studies in architecture at Harvard, served in the American army, and after the war worked for the National Housing Agency.

40 Bernard Wagner, "More Homes for Germans," *Information Bulletin of the Office of the U.S. High Commissioner for Germany* (Dec. 1951), clipping in Vertical Files, Loeb Library, Harvard University, and also idem, "German Architecture Looks Up: E.C.A. Housing Development Program Helps German Architects and Contractors to Introduce Modern Methods in Housing," *Journal of the American Institute of Architecture* 17 (1952):10–17.

41 The full list of entries, along with twenty-two essays on the competition, is to be found in Herman Wandersleb and Hans Schoszberger, eds., *Neuer Wohnbau*, vol. 1, *Bauplanung* (Ravensburg, 1952). Gutschow's winning entry was in Hanover, Reichow's in Lübeck, and Hebebrand's in Bremen.

42 See Johannes Göderitz, Roland Rainer, and Hubert Hoffmann, *Die gegliederte und aufgelokkerte Stadt* (Tübingen, 1957). In fact written during the war, the ideas in this book had been widely disseminated in articles before the volume was published. I have discussed this work at some length in "Cities of Rubble to Cities in Germany: Postwar Reconstruction Planning in Germany," *Planning History* 12 (1990):19–20.

others were on the outskirts of the towns, a result that received some sharp criticism. Costs were indeed kept down, but there was much criticism of the small size of the dwellings, the paucity of imagination in site planning, and the poor quality of construction.[43]

In spite of these criticisms, or perhaps through them, this ECA-funded competition was clearly important. Another ECA-sponsored housing program, this time for miners, was organized by James Butler, head of the housing division of the ECA mission to Germany. Since the days of the Occupation, everyone was aware that the low level of coal production was hurting all areas of the German economy and preventing a rapid rise in productivity. Part of the problem was the lack of suitable housing for miners in the Ruhr coal fields. Butler suggested using ERP funds both to support "standardized and efficient construction" in terms of the external shell and the interior amenities and fixtures, and to establish "an incentive plan to distribute a greater share of the housing built to mines showing highest relative increase in coal production."

We suggest building distinctive ECA housing projects, clearly identifiable as such and properly publicized at the outset, so that we can move immediately towards our prime objective, namely increased production through improved morale. We can do this by impressing the miners with the fact that they can expect to get good, inexpensive housing soon, housing which will be built within properly planned communities, not under the control of individual mines, but under their own control as members of a community and as private owners of individual houses contained therein.[44]

To guarantee that the design quality would be progressive (and not left in the hands of local officials), once again an international committee was appointed to approve the designs for the miners' housing projects. The United States was represented by Mack Arnold, who

43 See "Kritik aus USA" by the American members of the prize committee, in Wandersleb and Schoszberger, eds., *Neuer Wohnbau*, 1:127ff. In noting that construction costs for the winning projects were 20 percent less than comparable German housing projects, Walter Bogner claimed that "a reduction of this magnitude, if applied to the 40 billion Deutsche Marks that will have to be spent for housing by the West Germans during the next 15 years, would result in vast savings. However, of greater significance at this time of world tension is the fact that methods seem to have been found whereby more housing can be built in a country where it is so desperately needed to keep workers contented and productive." "A Housing Development Program for Western Germany," *The Record* 8 (March/April 1952):10.

44 "Special Miners' Housing Program from 1950/51 Reserve," Oct. 30, 1951, NA, RG 466, HICOG, box 69, file 504.21.

had served on the ECA prize committee, and Martin Wagner, now retired from Harvard and making his first trip back to Germany since fleeing in the 1930s.[45]

The nine miners' housing settlements, which were to contain some 5,000 dwellings, were supported with an infusion of DM 100 million in counterpart funds. In contrast to the earlier ECA competition, more time was spent on planning, and entries were solicited from the prize winners in the ECA program to ensure that mistakes made in 1951 were not repeated. Planners also surveyed residents in the ECA projects and prospective residents in the miners' housing. Surveys taken a few years after completion indicated that the miners' projects were largely successful.[46]

The impact of the American-sponsored housing programs was greater than the total of 8,000 new dwellings might suggest. In 1958 Hermann Wandersleb of the Federal Housing Ministry claimed that housing construction and town planning had received "strong stimulation and experienced further development through the ECA competition. Repeatedly winners of large planning competitions have stated that the prize-winning entries were based on the ECA planning."[47] Freed of American control, German planners and architects designed larger, more substantial housing units than the Americans had thought necessary, but the ECA settlements, now viewed as model projects and objects of research, stimulated new thinking among Germans in the field.

How important, however, was the overall contribution of the Marshall Plan to housing construction in Germany's bombed cities? About 25 percent of Germany's 1939 housing stock of 16 million units had been destroyed or badly damaged, and in cities with pre-war populations greater than 250,000, an average of 45 percent of the housing stock had been destroyed. Of the DM 1.187 billion in counterpart funds made available in the first year of the Marshall Plan, DM 81.5 million went into housing construction.[48] This included, for example, 779 units in Bavaria, 280 of which were in badly

45 Report, Dec. 13, 1952, NA, RG 466, HICOG, box 68, file 504.21. This was a truly international committee, with representatives from six countries in addition to those from West Germany and the United States.
46 Lotte Tiedemann and Emmy Bonhöffer, "ECA Entwicklungsbauten – von ihren Bewohnern und von Frauen gesehen," in Hermann Wandersleb and Georg Günthert, eds., *Neuer Wohbau*, vol. 2, *Durchführung von Versuchssiedlungen. Ergebnisse und Erkenntnisse für heute und morgen. Von ECA bis Interbau* (Ravensburg, 1958), 18ff.
47 Wandersleb and Günthert, eds., *Neuer Wohnbau*, 2:9.
48 Höhns, " 'Neuaufbau' als Hoffnung," 102, n. 2.

bombed Munich. In Baden-Württemberg, 3,155 units were built, including 741 in Stuttgart. In a report prepared in September 1951, James Butler noted that nearly DM 450 million in ECA counterpart funds had gone into housing and that the 100,000 housing units which the ECA had thus helped finance amounted to about "one out of every five constructed since the initiation of ECA aid to housing," but he estimated that at least 40 billion marks would be needed to reach the prewar level of housing in West Germany.[49] In fact, the Marshall Plan provided only 5 percent of the financing for housing in 1950 and by 1952 contributed almost nothing. Only 1.63 percent of the total of DM 31.6 billion invested in housing between 1950 and 1954 came from Marshall aid.[50] That sum is not insignificant, but it fell far short of the high expectations of many Germans that American aid would rebuild the cities bombed in the war.

In fact, neither the initial ECA competition nor the miners' housing program had been conceived in terms of the reconstruction of the ruined cities. There was, however, one bombed city that received a wide range of American financial support in rebuilding. Berlin was a unique political symbol and thus had special need for American aid. Because of its isolation and because of the blockade, the former capital had been slower to begin rebuilding than West German cities. It was necessary to stimulate the city's economy in order for it to resist the pressures placed on it by the Soviet Union, but it was also important that the city *appear* healthy. Democratic Berlin had to

49 K. Fredericks to George Godfrey, Dec. 4, 1950, and "Master List of ECA Financed Housing Projects in Bavaria," Nov. 3, 1950, NA, RG 466, HICOG, box 26, Bavarian Land Commissioner, file 504.21; Simonson to Garrett, "List of Württemberg-Baden ECA Financed Housing (Revised)," Nov. 30, 1950, and Butler to Frank Miller, "Facts about German Housing," Sept. 8, 1951, NA, RG 466, HICOG, box 69, file 504.21. Butler broke down the ECA allocations to date (in DM) as:

At Once Aid Program	81.3 million
Special Refugee Program	105.3
General Housing Program	108.0
1950 Ruhr Miners' Housing (through mine companies)	23.3
1951 Ruhr Miners' Housing	45.0
Berlin Housing	50.0
Development Projects Housing	37.0
Total	449.9 million

50 Arthur Brünisch, "Der Wohnungsbau in der Bundesrepublik Deutschland 1945–1955," *Der Architekt* 4 (1955):255. The bulk of the money came from private individuals, private lenders, cooperative housing associations, and local and federal government agencies.

look good too. By 1958 the total value of the counterpart funds in Germany, when converted into credit in a revolving fund, had reached a level of DM 13 billion. Of this, about DM 4.5 billion went to Berlin alone.[51] Most of the ERP aid to Berlin during this period went into four areas: an investment program that channeled funds into the rebuilding of factories, office buildings, retail stores, and hotels; a program to help underwrite orders for goods produced in the city; support for the city's operating budget; and a reconstruction program that by 1960 had spent 208 million marks on such things as clearing rubble, 233 million on housing, 43 million on schools and other buildings for social services, 466 million on new utilities, subways, streets, and bridges, and 120 million on the repair of green areas like the Tiergarten.[52] In addition to this infusion of Marshall aid, the Americans also contributed to specific building projects, such as the Kongresshalle.[53] The American effort in this one city dwarfed anything done to help any other West German city. The irony is that this massive American support for Berlin was not the result of a policy to aid urban recovery but rather the result of political sympathy for this particularly beleaguered city.

Why did the Americans not have a stronger policy on helping the Germans rebuild their other cities? The policymakers of the New Deal were obviously aware that massive public works projects had helped pull America out of the Great Depression, and some of them may have been aware of the fact that a Nazi-sponsored construction boom had been the real engine of German recovery from her own depression.[54] Perhaps the Americans did not, or psychologically could not, really admit that they had made war on cities and civilians? Perhaps the Americans, like many Germans, chose to view the destruction of the cities as some form of natural catastrophe for which they bore no responsibility, and thus a sense of responsibility to help rebuild was wanting? Perhaps they believed – rightly or wrongly – that physical reconstruction was something that would follow from, rather than be something that would itself help create,

51 *ERP und die Stadt Berlin* (Vienna, 1961), 16.   52 Ibid., 26–30, 39–44.
53 The Kongresshalle was the American contribution to Interbau, the 1955–57 international building exhibition. The building was designed by Hugh Stubbins, who as a young man had been Gropius's assistant when the latter first came to Harvard. See Barbara Miller Lane, "The Berlin Congress Hall, 1955–57," *Perspectives in American History*, new series, 1 (1984):131–85.
54 See W. S. Allen, *The Nazi Seizure of Power: The Experience of a Single German Town, 1922–1945*, rev. ed. (New York, 1984), 271–2.

economic recovery?[55] In any event, though American urban policy was consistent in its modernism from the Occupation through the Marshall Plan, it was never a central concern of the Americans. The power of the bureaucracies in the German building offices were not broken by the intermittent American pressure for democratization of decision making in urban affairs. Economic recovery, the development of a democratic constitution and democratic political parties, and the international rehabilitation of the Federal Republic enjoyed higher priority than the rebuilding of Germany's bombed cities.

55 Thus, in a letter to the author on May 25, 1989, Charles Kindleberger, who helped formulate the Marshall Plan, said that his "interest 43 years ago was in money, trade, food, investment in productive activities, plus property questions, and not in the German standard of living in housing."

17

U.S. Policy toward German Veterans, 1945–1950

JAMES M. DIEHL

The Occupation policy of the victorious Allies[1] was guided by a variety of "D's": denazification, demilitarization, decartelization, decentralization, and democratization.[2] Of these policies, demilitarization was the one that was initially most pressing and the one that found the most consistent support of the Allies – and of the Germans.[3] Because of this, demilitarization was achieved more unequivocally than any of the other D's, a fact that was to cause some embarrassment and difficulty in the 1950s, when the Allies changed their minds and began to push for German rearmament.

Demilitarization as an Allied goal was first stated in the Atlantic Charter, was reiterated in numerous wartime and postwar statements, including those following the Yalta and Potsdam conferences, and was embodied in Joint Chiefs of Staff directive 1067, which laid down U.S. and Allied occupation guidelines.[4] Allied proclamations invariably spoke of the need to rid Germany of Nazism and militarism. In the mind of the Allies the two were inextricably linked, and the latter was the cause of the former.[5] Germany's enemies accepted fully the contention of Nazi propagandists that the Third Reich was

1 Although the focus of this chapter is U.S. policy, I have placed it in the larger context of Allied policy, in order to provide comparisons and contrasts where useful.
2 On this, see, for example, Edwin Hartrich, *The Fourth and Richest Reich: How the Germans Conquered the Postwar World* (New York and London, 1980), 55ff.
3 According to Edward N. Peterson, "Demilitarization was welcomed by most, resisted by none." Edward N. Peterson, *The American Occupation of Germany: Retreat to Victory* (Detroit, 1978), 138.
4 Gerhard Wettig, *Entmilitarisierung und Wiederbewaffnung in Deutschland 1943–1955: Internationale Auseinandersetzungen um die Rolle der Deutschen in Europa* (Munich, 1967), ch. 1; Beate Ruhm von Oppen, ed., *Documents on Germany under Occupation, 1945–1954* (London, 1955), 13ff.
5 Wettig, *Entmilitarisierung*, 23–4; Kurt Tauber, *Beyond Eagle and Swastika: German Nationalism since 1945* (Middletown, Conn., 1967), 255; Eugene Davidson, *The Trial of the Germans: An Account of the Twenty-Two Defendants before the International Military Tribunal at Nuremberg* (New York, 1966), 22.

the logical culmination of the Prussian military tradition, albeit with different conclusions.[6] If the immediate cause of the Second World War was Hitler and the Nazis, the long-term cause was German militarism. The failure to stamp out German militarism after the First World War had led to the Second.

To eradicate German militarism, the Allies set out to destroy everything that helped to preserve or promote military values and traditions. They tore down monuments, ransacked libraries for materials that celebrated the nation's military past, and they prohibited veterans' organizations. Former soldiers returning from prisoner-of-war camps found that the wearing of military insignia was forbidden and that persons clad in the field-gray uniforms of the Wehrmacht could be shot. Since the only clothes most veterans had were their uniforms, this meant a booming business for dye shops, a phenomenon that prompted the wry remark of a British journalist that it was a question of "dye or die."[7] The question of uniforms was only the beginning, however. As German veterans and their families were to learn, Allied demilitarization measures extended far beyond disarmament, with unexpected and often unintended consequences.

For purposes of analysis, veterans can be divided into three groups: prisoners of war, the war-disabled, and former professional soldiers. Of the three groups, the first was the largest. The combined dictates of total war and unconditional surrender assured that virtually every member of the German fighting forces became, at least nominally, a prisoner of war (POW). As the flood tide of Nazi expansion receded, growing numbers of German POWs were caught up and interned. The Allies transported hundreds of thousands of them to Great Britain and the United States. As the Allies systematically conquered Germany, they brought the remaining forces of the Third Reich under their control, disarmed them, and interned them. At the time of Germany's capitulation, over eleven million German troops were in the custody of the victors. Of these, some eight million were held by the Western powers, the vast majority of these by the United States.[8]

6 Wettig, *Entmilitarisierung,* 23.
7 Ibid., p. 106; the phrase was equally euphonious in German: "Es heisst färben oder sterben."
8 Arthur L. Smith, *Heimkehr aus dem Zweiten Weltkrieg: Die Entlassung der deutschen Kriegsgefangenen* (Stuttgart, 1985), 11; Earl F. Ziemke, *The U.S. Army in the Occupation of Germany* (Washington, D.C., 1985), 291ff.; see also Peterson, *American Occupation,* 114–16, and *Freiheit ohne Furcht: Zehn Jahre Heimkehrerverband,* ed. Verband der Heimkehrer, Kriegsgefangenen und Vermisstenangehörigen Deutschlands (Berlin, n.d.), 41.

The Allies designated newly captured German military personnel either as Disarmed Enemy Forces (DEF) or Surrendered Enemy Personnel (SEP), a maneuver that permitted their captors to circumvent the formalized rules for treatment of POWs laid down in the Geneva Convention of 1929.[9] For U.S. authorities, the main advantage of the new designation was that it permitted a quick recycling of captured German forces back into civilian life and allowed the removal of a massive economic and administrative burden. For the European powers, the German prisoners' labor represented a form of reparation for the damage done to their countries by German armed forces.[10] The British and French utilized the ambiguous status of the German prisoners to exploit them as much-needed sources of labor, both in their occupation zones and at home. German soldiers captured by the Soviets disappeared into the Gulag.

By early 1947, nearly two years after the cessation of hostilities, the United States had repatriated nearly all of its POWs, but the British still held nearly a half million German prisoners (350,000 in England alone), while 640,000 remained in French custody. The USSR officially claimed to have 890,000, though the actual number was much higher.[11] While U.S. officials deplored the misuse of German POWs by their allies, they remained deeply suspicious of the former POWs in the American zone. Well aware of the disruptive role of German veterans after World War I and fearful of the emergence of armed resistance groups, they banned veterans' organizations of all types, and both U.S. and German officials treated warily the isolated POW self-help organizations that began to spring up on the local level in 1946.[12]

9 Smith, *Heimkehr*, 11, 24–5.
10 Hartrich, *Fourth and Richest Reich*, 30; on the different treatment of German POWs by the Allied powers, see Smith, *Heimkehr*, ch. 4.
11 Smith, *Heimkehr*, 62–3, 83, 91.
12 Since all veterans, including former POWs and the war-disabled, were organized in Nazi affiliate organizations, the banning of Nazi organizations and the arrest and internment of many of their functionaries deprived veterans of existing organizations and potential leaders, and the implementation of JCS 1067, which ordered "the total dissolution of all military and paramilitary organizations . . . together with all associations which might serve to keep alive the military tradition in Germany," prohibited the formation of new ones. This process was sealed with the issuance of Control Council Law No. 34, which dissolved the Wehrmacht and, in addition, "disbanded, completely dissolved and declared illegal" the general staff, officers corps, reserve corps, military schools, along with "war veteran organizations, and all other military and quasi-military organizations, together with all clubs and associations which serve to keep alive the military tradition in Germany." For the relevant documents, see Ruhm von Oppen, ed., *Documents on Germany*. On the fears of resistance groups composed of veterans, especially former officers, see below.

By the middle years of the Occupation, this negative attitude began to weaken. The military threat of veterans that the occupiers had feared failed to materialize, and, in the context of the emerging Cold War, the harsh treatment of German prisoners by the Soviets helped to promote a more humane policy on the part of the Western Allies. As former POWs streamed back in increasing numbers from Western camps, organized forms of assistance began to crystalize and soon found the support of the Anglo-American occupation authorities. In 1947 the U.S. Military Government permitted the formation of a committee for POW affairs that soon became a part of the *Länderrat*. A similar committee formed in the British zone, and networks of organizations dedicated to assisting the reintegration of POWs spread throughout the Western zones. Attempts at organizational consolidation following the creation of Bizonia failed, however, and it was only after the foundation of the Federal Republic that a central office for POW affairs was created.[13]

In the war-ravaged conditions of 1945, life was hard for all Germans, but especially hard for the war-disabled. War disability legislation (*Kriegsopferversorgung*) during the Occupation was governed by Allied attempts to reform the existing benefit system, which they believed was undemocratic and promilitarist. JCS 1067 prohibited the payment of "all military pensions, or other emoluments or benefits, except compensation for physical disability limiting the recipient's ability to work, at rates which are no higher than the lowest of those for comparable physical disability arising from non-military causes."[14] In a series of decrees culminating in Control Law Number 34 (August 20, 1946), the Allies systematically dismantled the German system of war-disability benefits.[15]

The laws enacted during the occupation subordinated the care of war victims to civilian disability programs and scaled down benefits. The victors believed that, in the past, the separate (*gehoben*) treatment of war victims in Germany had served to encourage pro-military

---

13 Smith, *Heimkehr*, 35–6, 42–4, 65–8, 170ff.
14 James K. Pollock et al., eds., *Germany under Occupation: Illustrative Materials and Documents* (Ann Arbor, Mich., 1947), 113. On the genesis of JCS 1067 and its implementation, see John Gimbel, *The American Occupation of Germany: Politics and the Military, 1945–1949* (Stanford, Calif., 1968), and Ziemke, *U.S. Army*, 104ff.
15 For the text of Control Council Law Number 34, see Ruhm von Oppen, ed., *Documents on Germany*, 151–2.

sentiment and to shield Germans from the horrible consequences of war. In their view, the treatment of the war-disabled as a favored group only worked to perpetuate the German tradition of glorifying the military and war, a practice that had allowed the military to retain its position as a privileged caste. As a report of the U.S. Military Government put it: "The objective of abolishing war pensions is to discredit the military class in Germany, to reduce their influence in society and to impress upon the public that a military career bears neither honor, profit or [sic] security."[16] In addition to this political and unmistakably punitive goal, the occupiers were also motivated by the desire to rationalize and cut the costs of German social services, which, in a period of social dislocation and economic stagnation, presented a tremendous fiscal burden.[17]

While the Allies' unanimous desire to stamp out militarism ensured that the treatment of German war victims would be harsh, their disunity prevented them from imposing a common policy. The Soviets, not surprisingly, adopted the hardest line, followed closely by the British and Americans. The French, contrary to the standard view of their occupation policies, pursued the most lenient course. Yet no matter which zone they were in, the war victims were worse off than they had been before 1945.[18]

Impelled by the dual imperatives of ideological conviction and financial necessity, Allied policies had a devastating effect. Hundreds of thousands of disabled veterans, their families, and survivors of soldiers killed in the war were reduced to poverty and made dependent on the already overburdened general welfare services. The material desperation of the war victims was matched by an equally great sense of injustice and degradation. German officials, charged with implementing the unpopular policies and aware of the general support for the war victims' case, urged the military governments to

16 "War Pensions in Connection with Demilitarization," AC 019 (MD), Jan. 8, 1947, NA, RG 260, OMGUS, box 56, folder 10.

17 According to one estimate, between 25 and 30 percent of the population in the three Western zones needed monetary assistance. Fritz Blücher, "Financial Situation and Currency Reform in Germany," *The Annals* 260 (Nov. 1948):64.

18 For overviews of the treatment of war victims in the Western zones, see *Die Versorgung der Kriegsopfer in der Bundesrepublik Deutschland: Stand 30.9.1952*, ed. Presse- und Informationsamt der Bundesregierung (Bonn, 1952), 18–19, and Helmut Rühland, "Entwicklung, heutige Gestaltung und Problematik der Kriegsopferversorgung in der Bundesrepublik Deutschland," Diss. phil., Cologne University, 1957, 88–98, 103–19. On the development of *Kriegsopferversorgung* in the French zone, see Rainer Hudemann, *Sozialpolitik im deutschen Südwesten zwischen Tradition und Neuordnung: Sozialversicherung und Kriegsopferversorgung im Rahmen französischer Besatzungspolitik* (Mainz, 1988).

change their policies.[19] Progress was slow, however. When, for example, German officials in the fall of 1946 considered plans to set aside 12 percent of work force places for seriously disabled workers, U.S. authorities reacted in alarm, fearing that the measure would lead to a "flood of militarists" streaming into German factories and public administration.[20]

Gradually, Military Government officials responsible for the formulation of social policy began to realize that their policies had produced genuine hardship for a class of citizens that was innocent, and that, in their zeal to root out militarism, they had created conditions that were producing political consequences exactly the opposite of those intended. Whereas the old system of war-disability pensions had been scrapped out of fear of fostering a pro-military (and, thus, by definition, antidemocratic) group within German society, concern now began to grow that the new policies might create a large, bitter, and resentful social group that would become a significant obstacle to the growth of democracy. This change of viewpoint was summed up in a January 1947 report of the Office of Military Government for Germany (OMGUS):

The objective of abolishing war pensions is to discredit the military class in Germany. . . . At the same time to leave a large category of disabled, aged, and survivors without any means to care for their needs [other] than public relief, especially when large numbers were unwilling draftees, would run the danger of creating a revengeful, self-conscious, underprivileged class detrimental to successful democratic development in Germany. The problem is therefore to cut off all privileges heretofore accorded for military service without creating a resentful class dangerous to democracy and without promoting obvious injustice.[21]

19 German authorities were aware of the need to cut the levels of benefits, especially for some groups, e.g., dependent parents, but they were generally opposed to the Allied schemes to subordinate *Kriegsopferversorgung* to other social programs. The dialogue between German and U.S. Military Government officials can be traced in the protocols of the *Länderrat* subcommittee on Social Insurance, NA, RG 260, OMGUS, boxes 102 and 107, and the OMGUS Manpower Division policy papers, NA, RG 260, OMGUS, boxes 51, 52, and 56. Polls of German public opinion in 1946 placed war victims at the head of those that were felt to deserve public assistance. Information Control Intelligence Summary No. 45, June 8, 1946, NA, RG 319, OMGUS, box 699, and Anna J. and Richard L. Merritt, *Public Opinion in Occupied Germany: The OMGUS Surveys 1945–1949* (Urbana, Ill., 1970), 121.
20 Länderrat, Sozialpolitischer Ausschuss, Sept. 17, 1946, NA, RG 260, OMGUS, box 102, folder 7.
21 "War Pensions in Connection with Demilitarization," AC 019(MD), Jan. 8, 1947, NA, RG 260, OMGUS, box 56, folder 10.

With such considerations in mind, military governments began to introduce systems of war-disability benefits that conformed to their principles of reform. In 1946 the British instituted a system of war-disability payments that was administered under the old-age disability insurance program. In early 1947, after nearly a year of negotiations with German officials, the U.S. Military Government approved a war-disability system subordinate to the industrial-accident disability insurance program.[22]

While the introduction of the new programs helped to ease the uncertainty and destitution that had plagued German war victims in the early stages of the occupation, benefits, especially the pensions for survivors (widows, children, and dependent parents), were substantially less than they had been under the old system. The discontent of the war victims remained high. Moved by sympathy and concerned about the potentially explosive consequences of further inaction, German officials continued to urge military government authorities to liberalize their policies and struggled to improve and unify the war-disability programs.

The Bizone experienced some progress in the immediate aftermath of its creation, but, thereafter, efforts became stalled, and the American and British systems were never completely integrated. The first and most significant move to create a uniform system of benefits came in May 1947, when the British reorganized their zonal system according to the principles employed in the U.S. zone, transferring the care of the war-disabled from the old-age disability program to the industrial-accident disability program, which experience had shown was better suited to the needs of the war-disabled.[23] A number of differences remained in the calculation and payment of benefits in the two zones. A bizonal committee convened to iron out these differences. In early 1949, it presented a bill to the Wirtschaftsrat, but the bill languished.[24] In May a new bill for the standardization and improvement of benefits was introduced, but it foundered on fiscal and legal considerations. In July 1949, the Wirtschaftsrat finally worked out and passed a compromise, only to

22 Rühland, "Kriegsopferversorgung," pp. 88–95; Hudemann, *Sozialpolitik*, 444–50; *Versorgung der Kriegsopfer*, 18–19.
23 Rühland, "Kriegsopferversorgung," 91, 94–5.
24 Ibid., 92–3; *Akten zur Vorgeschichte der Bundesrepublik Deutschland, 1945–1949*, ed. Bundesarchiv and Institut für Zeitgeschichte, vol. 5 (Munich, 1981), 604.

see it rejected by Military Government officials on the grounds that legislation relating to war victims should be drafted and implemented by the soon-to-be-formed Federal Republic.[25]

While the POWs and the war victims were more or less unintended victims of Allied demilitarization efforts, those efforts consciously targeted former professional soldiers for punitive action. In the Allies' view, the prime carriers of the virus of militarism were the German General Staff and the German Officer Corps. The way in which the Allies grappled with the problem of the treatment of the German Officer Corps provides one of the most interesting examples of how the victors of the Second World War tried to learn the lessons of the past and sought to avoid repeating the mistakes that had been made following the First World War.

In late June 1945, American intelligence experts drew up a report "To analyze the potentialities of the German Officer Corps as a whole in relationship to the demilitarization of Germany and to present appropriate recommendations."[26] Noting that the German General Staff had been adequately dealt with by JCS 1067, which provided for the immediate arrest of its members, the authors centered their discussion on the German Officer Corps as a whole. The purpose of the report, they pointed out, "was *not* to minimize the importance of the General Staff . . . but rather to emphasize that the General Staff is only part of the problem." A seven-page enclosure traced the history of the German Officer Corps since the defeat of 1918. In the Empire, it noted, officers had enjoyed high prestige and social status and "were accorded privileges ordinarily denied to civilians." After the war, this ended. Not only were officers deprived of their privileges, but:

Defeat had hurt their military pride. They were humiliated and embittered. All around them they saw rising elements dangerous to their considered interests. A large number of them were dispersed and were forced to find their way in pursuits that did not carry with them the dignity to which these men, as officers, were accustomed. The members of the old Officer's Corps under the guidance of the General Staff quickly concentrated all their efforts on one aim: the re-establishment of the Army in a State that would bring back to them their position of power and respect.

25 Rühland, "Kriegsopferversorgung," p. 92; *Akten zur Vorgeschichte der Bundesrepublik Deutschland*, 5:604, p. 652.
26 USGCC, Joint Intelligence Staff, "German Officer Corps," June 25, 1945, NA, RG 260, OMGUS, box 123, folder 34.

Many former officers, "unable or unwilling to adjust themselves to civilian pursuits," had joined the Free Corps. The report then traced the illegal, aggressive, and antidemocratic activities of the Free Corps and concluded that "it must be reemphasized here that the activities of the Free Corps would hardly have been possible had they not been organized by trained and experienced officers of the German Officer's Corps." Thereafter, these officers had worked for the overthrow of the Republic, and "their activities in helping to bring the Nazis to power were later openly admitted and applauded by the Nazis themselves." In the Third Reich, the Officer Corps had been fully nazified. Reserve Officers were less of a threat, since they would be better able to adapt themselves to peacetime conditions; but, the report noted, "it must be realized that many Reserve Officers were strong in their Nazi sympathies and that a considerable number of reserve commissions were given to young men who had not had time to learn any civilian pursuits."

The significance of all this for the present was clear in the light of the aftermath of the First World War. "These officers know only the art of war. Their prestige will be broken and they can only become a dissatisfied and potentially dangerous element in German society." The humiliation of defeat and occupation, coupled with harsh living conditions and the fact that the German people were "still sufficiently immature in their political thought to follow any demagogue or movement that promises to better their lot," offered "a most fertile field for a Free Corps, indeed for subversive activity of any kind." Moreover, among the German people, "great repentance for their deeds has not been made manifest, and the alternative to repentance is bitterness. Bitterness breeds resistance." Officers, a large number of whom would be "unable to fit themselves into civilian society . . . would be not only willing but quite capable of leading resistance groups."[27]

The report concluded that all officers were a potential threat, and it recommended that their indiscriminate demobilization was to be avoided at all costs. By August, the Allies had identified two aspects of the problem: the need to determine which individuals might be dangerous among the approximately 350,000 officers scheduled for

---

27 Although the report conceded that there had not been any signs of resistance, it cited events in Aachen, as well as the resistance to Nazi occupation, as reasons to fear German resistance to Allied occupation. USGCC, Joint Intelligence Staff, "German Officer Corps," June 25, 1945, pp. 6–7, NA, RG 260, OMGUS, box 123, folder 23.

release from detention, and the manner of their future disposition.[28]
They debated three possible modes of distribution once the potentially dangerous officers had been identified. The first was "banish-
ment or exile of the 'St. Helena' nature." The second was the
"dispersal, individually or in small groups, throughout the world to
places under control of the Allied governments, who would assume
responsibility for their domicile and maintenance and for enforcing
restrictive measures and exercising surveillance." The third was "retention in Germany under severe restrictive measures prescribed by
the Control council and closely supervised by the appropriate Zone
Commander." Ultimately, the Allies determined that, of the 345,000
officers to be demobilized, some 58,000 would be "potentially
dangerous."[29] An analysis of the advantages and disadvantages of the
three modes of disposition of these officers concluded that exile,
while advantageous in some regards, was on balance impracticable
for a number of reasons.[30] For one thing, "the removal of the outstanding figures of German militarism from Germany might be
urged [sic] by isolationists as an argument for the too-rapid reduction, or untimely withdrawal of the Allied armies of occupation,
since it could be claimed that we had thus rendered Germany militarily innocuous." Moreover, the effect on the German population
was likely to be counterproductive. "Just as Napoleon at St. Helena
came to be, for France, a symbol of her vanished glory and the focal
point of hopes for future greatness," the report observed, "so might
the hope of all Germany be turned to these men 'suffering martyr-
dom for their loyal service to the Reich.' "

The dispersal of dangerous officers to remote areas under the control of the Allies only differed in degree from the "St. Helena" so-

28 "Disposition of Potentially Dangerous Officers of German Armed Forces," Aug. 9, 1945,
NA, RG 260, OMGUS, box 135.
29 "Specifications for Determining Those Officers of the German Armed Forces Who Should
Be Subject to Restrictive Measures," "Disposition of Potentially Dangerous Officers of
German Armed Forces," Aug. 9, 1945, Tab A, NA, RG 260, OMGUS, box 135. Exactly
how this figure was arrived at is unclear. Group I, the officers who were considered to be
"the most potentially dangerous," were drawn from three categories, officers of "Flag
rank," i.e., Major General and above, General Staff Officers, and "Other Officers of
Marked Potential Danger." While the criteria for determining the first two catagories were
fairly precise, those for the third were considerably vaguer and included, e.g., early indoc-
trination in German military tradition as a result of birth and position, formal military
training, prewar military activity, and wartime military record.
30 "Analysis of Proposed Plans for Disposal of German Officers Who Must Be Subject to
Restrictive Measures," "Disposition of Potentially Dangerous Officers of German Armed
Forces," Aug. 9, 1945, Tab B, NA, RG 260 OMGUS, box 135.

lution, and the report rejected it for the same reasons. This left only the third alternative, retention in Germany under close surveillance. There were many advantages to this solution: first, while quadripartite unity on the issue was desirable, it would not be necessary – one could act unilaterally; second, it was considered likely that public opinion outside Germany would be favorable "to the idea of solving German problems in Germany rather than to distributing them all over the world"; third, the effect of this solution on the German population would be beneficial, "since it integrates the other purposes of the occupation with this purpose, and provides a fitting disposition of these persons before the eyes of other Germans"; finally, the third policy offered the best prospect of weathering possible future changes of government in the Allied countries and would have "the best chance of the three solutions discussed of withstanding assault by proponents of a softer policy, both because it will not be as much before the public eye, and also because it does not lend itself to attack on moral and social grounds." The Allies agreed to keep officers considered to be potentially dangerous in confinement as POWs until conditions had materially improved and then, after their release, to keep them closely controlled and watched.[31]

Officers fortunate enough to be released soon found that freedom was a mixed blessing. Jobs were not easy to find, and those who had counted on pensions to ease their plight were bitterly disappointed. Allied efforts to economize and to demilitarize German society neatly intersected in the question of military pensions.[32] Convinced that military pensions in the past had glorified and helped to maintain militarism in Germany, the Allied powers abolished them.

The deliberations of a British Military Government Working Party to study pension policy clearly reflected the attitude of the Anglo-American forces on this question. Starting from the goal of lowering the prestige of the Wehrmacht in the eyes of the German people, the committee concluded that the traditional method of payment was dangerous, since Versorgungsämter were a potential tool for clandestine mobilization. As a result, the committee decided to abolish all military pensions.[33]

---

31 The extent to which this control was actually implemented is uncertain.
32 This was also true in the case of war-disability and survivor pensions.
33 Control Commission for Germany (British Element), Chief of Staff's Conference, "Payment of Pensions in Germany," July 12, 1945. Extracts from First and Second Reports of the Working Party on the Payment of Pensions in Germany, PRO, FO 944/313.

However, not all elements of the British military approved the cavalier cutoff of military pensions. Responding to the proposals of the Working Party, the Service Chiefs of Staff recommended that pensions be continued. They argued that, to begin with, the nonpayment of pensions was unlikely to discredit the Wehrmacht, since there was "nothing discreditable in being denied an earned emolument." Moreover, there was no likelihood that the Germans would be able to use their pensions machinery as a camouflaged mobilization office because of the entirely different conditions that existed in post–World War II Germany compared to those prevalent after the first World War. In fact, to discriminate against the Wehrmacht in favor of civilians might do considerable harm. As the Service Chief of Staff pointed out:

There is little to choose, ethically, between Civil Servants who worked against us and Wehrmacht who fought against us and the pensionable element of the latter is at least as reliable and influential a section of the community as the former. It behooves us, therefore, to avoid victimizing and antagonizing an element which on the one hand may produce reasonable citizens and on the other, the core of resistance and agitation against us.[34]

The Working Party decisively rejected the Service Chief of Staff's arguments. It admitted that the efficacy of withholding pensions in order to discredit the military was debatable. Still, the Working Party concluded that the withholding of pensions to the Wehrmacht would "undoubtedly show the German people that the Allies were determined to carry out the terms of the Potsdam Declarations that the German armed forces are to be utterly destroyed." While there might be a case in equity for granting pensions, "the political aspect of the matter far outweighed the legal." With regard to the second argument, the Working Party called upon the lessons of history, citing a passage from General J. H. Morgan's book, *Assize of Arms,* which showed how the Germans had used pension machinery for mobilization purposes after the First World War. As to the third argument, the Working Party agreed that there might be little to choose *ethically* between civil servants and the Wehrmacht that fought against the Allies. However, the Potsdam Declaration made clear the goal of destroying the German armed forces root and branch, whereas the civil service, once purged, was to continue. The

34 Fourth Meeting of Working Party on the Payment of Pensions in Germany, Sept. 10, 1945, PRO, FO 944/313.

Working Party categorically rejected the contention of the Service Chiefs of Staff that there were elements among the Wehrmacht who were at least as reliable as the civil service. With the argument that "It is quite clear," the Working Party maintained, "that we cannot afford to trust the pensionable element of the Wehrmacht. It has always been the evil influence which has incited the German people to aggression."[35]

A series of laws implementing these ideas culminated in Control Council Law Number 34, which, in addition to dissolving the Wehrmacht officially, also abolished veterans' organizations and military pensions.[36] A Military Government survey of about the same time noted that "the lot of ex-regular officers at present is obviously not a happy one." But, the survey concluded, "ex-officers do not so far present a separate and specific problem as a class apart from other Germans. . . . and there is little evidence of undue discrimination against ex-officers as such."[37]

Not surprisingly, the former officers saw things differently. From their ranks came countless complaints of discrimination and endless tales of woe. Former officers inundated Allied and German officials with memoranda complaining of the injustice of the cutoff of their pensions and chronicling the human misery that followed in its wake.[38]

Gottfried Hansen, a retired admiral who lived in Kiel, conducted the most energetic and persistent campaign for the restoration of military pensions. The catalogue of arguments with which the

35 Ibid. In its final report, the Working Party again refuted the arguments of the Service Chief of Staff report and stuck by its original recommendations. Third Report of the Working Party on the Payment of Pensions in Germany, PRO, FO 944/313.
36 Wettig, *Entmilitarisierung*, 102–6; Ruhm von Oppen, ed., *Documents on Germany*, 151–2.
37 Information Control Intelligence Summary, no. 55, Aug. 17, 1946, NA, RG 319, OM-GUS, box 699. The report consisted of an extensive citation from a British survey reported in July and noted that "preliminary investigation in the American Zone by ICD representatives indicate that the findings in the British study are applicable to AMZON as well."
38 Field Marshal Wilhelm von Leeb, interned in Allendorf, wrote to General McNarney in October 1946, laying out the reasons why he and his colleagues felt the cutting off of pensions was "legally as well as morally and humanely" impossible. Leeb's letter was clearly designed to appeal to a fellow military professional. Pensions, he argued, were a historical and legal right. They had been deducted from pay. With their removal, "men were placed helplessly before the void, whose only sin was to have, true to their oath, served their country in the way all soldiers of the world do." NA, RG 260, OMGUS, box 130; in letters to the *Länderrat* of the U.S. Occupation Zone and OMGUS in Berlin (Feb. and March 1947), General Lequis wrote on behalf of men like himself, who had retired before the National Socialists had come to power, describing their difficulties and arguing that members of the General Staff were not militarists or warmongers. NA, RG 260, OMGUS, box 56, folder 15. For further examples, see the materials cited in note 41 following.

indefatigable admiral bombarded officials seemed endless. Just as the governments of Weimar Germany had sought to undermine the "War Guilt Lie" in order to force an end to reparations by destroying the moral claim upon which they rested, so Hansen worked to bring to an end the "Defamation" of the Wehrmacht that was embodied in the charges brought against the military at Nuremberg which provided the moral basis for Control Council Law Number 34. He repeated and expanded the arguments employed by the defense counsel of the General Staff and Supreme Command at Nuremberg; according to Hansen, the fact that the two organizations had been acquitted provided grounds for the revocation of the Control Council's measures.[39] The officers of the German armed forces, Hansen argued, had not been political and had no decision-making powers. They had simply done their patriotic duty like soldiers the world over. Far from being a hotbed of Nazism, the officer corps had provided a refuge from the National Socialist party. Indeed, there had been more resistance to the regime within the Wehrmacht than within any other group in society. A point of special outrage to Hansen was the fact that, while civil servants, many of whom had been active Nazis, received pensions, military officers with unblemished records who had been truer and infinitely more selfless servants of the state did not. Similarly, while the authorities allowed communists to organize, they denied this fundamental right to former officers. They thus permitted to enemies of the state and Western values privileges withheld from those who supported them.

In addition to reiterating ceaselessly the illegality and injustice of the Control Council's prohibition of pensions, Hansen provided numerous examples of former officers and their families forced to endure discrimination, degradation, poverty, and even death – often by suicide – as a result of the harsh measures of the occupying forces. Presumably representatives of democratic values, those forces, the

---

39 While Hansen was quick to point out how the court had judged the General Staff and High Command not guilty, he was silent about how it had based its verdict on the technical consideration that the General Staff and High Command were, in fact, not groups or organizations as indicted. The admiral also overlooked the stinging statement that accompanied the court's finding: "Many of these men have made a mockery of the soldier's oath of obedience to military orders. When it suits their defense they say they had to obey; when confronted with Hitler's brutal crimes, which are shown to have been within their general knowledge, they say they disobeyed. The truth is that they actively participated in all these crimes, or sat silent and acquiescent, witnessing the commission of crimes on a scale larger and more shocking than the world has ever had the misfortune to know." Quoted in Davidson, *Trial of the Germans*, 563.

admiral charged, employed the same sort of unjust, collective punitive measures [*Sippenhaft*] that the National Socialists had used against their opponents. Such actions could hardly be expected to convince former officers of the virtues of democracy. The continued unfair discrimination against and degradation of former officers, whose skills and energies could be used to rebuild the country, would only harden their bitterness and turn them against the new state. It could even force them to turn to the East.[40]

Countless letters sent by former officers to officials of the Bizone echoed Hansen's arguments.[41] They described their hardships in detail and the universally condemned injustice of their treatment. If nothing else, the Allied measures appeared to have convinced this group of Germans of the desirability of equality before the law and of legal, democratic process, for the offended officers self-righteously and repeatedly stressed how their rights had been violated and how their treatment contradicted the legal and democratic principles espoused – hypocritically, they claimed – by the conquerors. They lamented how they had done less than civilians to bring the Nazis to power, and then had been made the scapegoat for Germany's problems. In many cases, pathos became bathos. The complaints frequently cited instances of suicide and joint suicide pacts of retired officers and their wives.[42] According to one correspondent, it seemed that the intent of the measures taken against former officers must be "to starve them or drive them to suicide." If this was the

---

40 For a representative collection of Hansen's arguments, see his letters to Hermann Pünder, the director of the Wirtschaftsrat, BA, Z13/338, Bd. 1; see also Sammlung Ritter von Schramm, "Materialien zu einer Geschichte der deutschen Berufssoldaten zwischen 1945 und 1955: Zwei Handakten des Admirals Hansen," BA/MA, MSg 118/5. In published form, the arguments of Hansen and his associates can be found in *Der Notweg: Wirtschaftlicher Wegweiser für versorgungsberechtige ehemalige Angehörige der Wehrmacht und deren Hinterbliebene*, first published in April 1949, passim.

41 An extensive and representative collection of these can be found in BA, Z13/338, Bd. 2; see also Sammlung Ritter von Schramm, "Einzelerlebnisse," BA/MA, MSg 118/4, and the material from the Donat Nachlass cited by Georg Meyer, "Zur Situation der deutschen militärischen Führungsschicht im Vorfeld des westdeutschen Verteidigungsbeitrages 1945–1950/51," in *Anfänge westdeutscher Sicherheitspolitik 1945–1956*, ed. Militärgeschichtliches Forschungsamt, vol. 1, *Von der Kapitulation bis zum Pleven-Plan* (Munich and Vienna, 1982), 637, n. 135.

42 Reports of such suicides, especially in the wake of the currency reform, were a standard staple of the petitions and memoranda of the former professional soldiers. An example that was repeatedly cited was the report that forty-three former officers had committed suicide in the Regierungsbezirk Lüneburg within a period of one hundred days. For this and other examples, see Sammlung Ritter von Schramm, "Schicksale Deutscher Berufssoldaten von 1945–1955," BA/MA, MSg 118/1, 60-1. Also see Meyer, "Zur Situation der deutschen militärischen Führungsschicht," 637, n. 135.

case, then "on the grounds of Christian compassion [*christlicher Menschen-, Nächsten- und Feindesliebe*] one should at least give us the necessary cyanide capsules or revolver."[43] Others complained that they were being treated as badly or worse than the Nazis had treated their victims. One former officer equated the sufferings caused him and his peers to that of the Jews in the Third Reich. He concluded that the plight of the officers was even worse, since no one was willing to help them, while "the Jews were able to count on the support of worldwide Jewry."[44]

Such hyperbole left Military Government officials unmoved. Although the French restored pensions to officers who had retired before 1933, the British and Americans continued to enforce Control Council Law Number 34 strictly.[45] German officials were generally sympathetic to the plight of the former officers, but they neither could nor would support the full restoration of officers' pensions, since economic and political constraints made it impossible.[46] The

43 Concluding sentences of a two-page memorandum on military pensions prepared by Gerhard Gieren, a retired Major from Hameln, dated June 15, 1948, BA, Z13/338, Bd. 1. For another example of this type of complaint, see Meyer, "Zur Situation der deutschen militärischen Führungsschicht," 638.

44 "Durch die Einstellung der Zahlungen nach dem Waffenstillstand . . . sind die Angehörigen dieses Berufsstandes in eine unverschuldete Notlage geraten, die grösser ist als die der Juden während der Herrschaft des Nationalsozialismus, weil diesen die Unterstützung des Weltjudentums sicher war, während für den Stand der Berufssoldaten sich erst jetzt einzelne Deutsche einzusetzen wagen." Generalmajor a. D. Gerhard Müller to the Landtagsfraktion of the SPD Rheinland-Pfalz, Nov. 16, 1948, BA, Z13/338, Bd. 2. For similar views, see the letter of Hugo Oster (July 3, 1948) and the memorandum accompanying the letter of Anita Sievert (Aug. 26, 1948), BA, Z13/338, Bd. 2.

45 On conditions in the French zone, see "Pensions – Instructions in Force in the French Zone," BA, Z40/68, and Meyer, "Zur Situation der deutschen militärischen Führungsschicht," 646. In the U.S. zone, all service pensions had been prohibited since May 1945, and, as a German memorandum noted in 1947, although limited pensions for the war-disabled had been restored, "alle Bemühungen, eine Aufhebung oder Lockerung des Zahlungsverbots für die *dienstmässig* erworbenen Versorgungen ehemaliger Militärpersonen und ihrer Hinterbliebenen zu erreichen," remained unsuccessful. Finanzministerium Württemberg-Baden to Generalsekretariat des Länderrates, May 23, 1947, BA, Z1/296.

46 Many German legislators and officials, especially those on the left, were convinced that the needs of those who had suffered physical and material damage as a result of the war (e.g., the war victims, those who had been bombed out, and the expellees) should come before those of the former professional soldiers, and that, for political and moral reasons, those who had been persecuted on political or racial grounds during the Third Reich had to be compensated before the claims of the soldiers could be considered. See, for example, "Stellungnahme des Unterausschusses Sozialversicherung zum Entwurf eines Gesetzes über die Zahlung von Unterhaltsbeträgen an berufsmässige Wehrmachtangehörige und ihre Hinterbliebenen, Anlage 2," June 24, 1948, BA, Z1/296, and "Bericht über die Sitzung des Parlamentarischen Rates in Stuttgart am 19. Juli zum Entwurf eines Gesetzes über die Zahlung von Unterhaltsbeträgen an berufsmässige Wehrmachtsangehörige und deren Hinterbliebene," July 20, 1948, BA, Z1/297. On the Entschädigungsgesetz, see Hans-Dieter Kreikamp, "Zur Entstehung des Entschädigungsgesetzes der amerikanischen Besatzungs-

distinction between acceptance of the demands of former officers in principle and unwillingness to support full restoration of their pensions was often lost on the officers, who frequently complained that German officials were as vindictive as the Allies.[47] German officials nonetheless continued to press for some form of relief and, by early 1948, were able to achieve a small success when Military Government officials gave permission for the issuance of Maintenance Grants (*Unterhaltsbeträge*) to former professional soldiers. These payments were to be modest and limited to former officers who had joined the Wehrmacht before January 1933, were two-thirds disabled, or over sixty-five years of age, and in need.[48] The drafting of the legislation providing for Maintenance Grants, which was interrupted and complicated by the currency reform of June 1948, proved to be more difficult than expected.[49] Efforts to create a uniform system of grants on either the bizonal or zonal levels failed. Individual state governments began to introduce *Unterhaltsbeträge* in the summer of 1948, but the process was slow and uneven. A year later, on the eve of the founding of the Federal Republic, the payment of Maintenance Grants to former professional soldiers was neither uniform nor universal.[50]

zone," in Ludolf Herbst and Constantin Goschler, eds., *Wiedergutmachung in der Bundesrepublik Deutschland* (Munich, 1989), 61–75. Another obstacle to the restoration of service pensions to former professional soldiers was the fear that it would trigger new demands by the war victims. On this, see point four of the memorandum prepared by the Social Insurance section of the Labor Ministry in the British Zone, Zentralamt für Arbeit in der britischen Zone, Hauptabteilung IV, Sozialversicherung IVa/821/48, June 8, 1948, BA, Z40/68.

47 See the materials cited in notes 40 and 41 for examples.

48 Regional Government Coordinating Office to Erich Rossmann, Director of the *Länderrat*. Subject: Maintenance Grants to Career Military Personnel, March 15, 1948, BA, Z1/296.

49 Following the enactment of the currency reform, for example, the majority of the Parliamentary Council in Stuttgart felt that it was impossible to act on the law under the present circumstances, since "man können [sic] nicht eine Gruppe herausgreifen und besserstellen, wo durch die Währungsreform unzählige Andere ebenfalls vor dem Nichts ständen, das würde 'vom Volke nicht verstanden werden.' " "Bericht über die Sitzung des Parlamentarischen Rates in Stuttgart am 19. Juli [1948] zum Entwurf eines Gesetzes über die Zahlung von Unterhaltsbeträgen an berufsmässige Wehrmachtsangehörige und deren Hinterbliebene," BA, Z1/297.

50 The guidelines accompanying the Military Government's permission to provide the Unterhaltsbeträge suggested that the legislation be coordinated by the states, so as to avoid substantial variations that would then necessitate strict residence requirements in order to prevent migration from one state to another by recipients seeking better payments. In the American zone, the Finance Committee of the *Länderrat* produced a draft law in late May, which then circulated through the *Länderrat*'s legislative apparatus. After much wrangling among the committees and the states, a final law, scheduled to take effect on January 1, 1949, was passed by the *Länderrat* and submitted to the Military Government in September 1948. In April 1949, the Germans were informed by the latter that a zonal law was

Meanwhile, occupation officials continued to block efforts by former officers to improve their situation through the formation of interest groups. In late 1948, American authorities dissolved self-help groups in Hesse and Bavaria, and they continued to scrutinize closely the leaders of informal efforts to help former officers.[51] British authorities were more lenient. They allowed Hansen to form an organization in Schleswig-Holstein, and his colleague, Admiral Raul Mewis, formed a similar one in Hamburg. Eventually, a network of representatives in other states, the so-called Hansen-Kreis, formed, and in April 1949, a newspaper, *Der Notweg,* began to appear.[52] The British, however, rejected Hansen's efforts to create a zonewide organization.[53]

The Allies eased their control measures following the creation of the Federal Republic. In December 1949, they lifted Control Council Law Number 34 and replaced it with a milder decree.[54] Members of the Hansen-Kreis spearheaded the formation of *Notgemeinschaften* in the *Länder* and, in April 1950, these *Länder*-based *Notgemeinschaften* met in Bonn to form the Bund versorgungsberechtigter Wehrmachts-angehöriger und Hinterbliebener, with Hansen as president. Disabled veterans and former POWs formed similar organizations and, by 1950, they were actively lobbying the new government of the Federal Republic for legislation on their behalf.[55]

Half a decade after Germany's defeat, it appeared as though the demilitarization policy of the United States and its Allies had suc-

unnecessary, and that the *Unterhaltsbeträge* were a matter for state legislation. In the meantime, a number of states, using the *Länderrat* law as a guideline, had begun to pass legislation on their own. On developments in the U.S. zone, see the materials in BA, Z1/296–97; the process in the British zone was somewhat different, but the outcome was the same. For the British zone, see the materials in BA, Z40/68.

51 Krafft Freiherr Schenk zu Schweinsberg, "Die Soldatenverbände in der Bundesrepublik," in Georg Picht, ed., *Studien zur politischen und gesellschaftlichen Situation der Bundeswehr* (Witten and Berlin, 1965), 98; Sammlung Ritter von Schramm, "Schicksale Deutscher Berufssoldaten von 1945–1955," BA/MA, MSg 118/1, 88–9; Meyer, "Zur Situation der deutschen militärischen Führungsschicht," 643–4.

52 Meyer, "Zur Situation der deutschen militärischen Führungsschicht," 642–5; "Anhang zum Verzeichnis der Akten Admiral a. D. Hansen 1945–56: Beiträge zu einer Geschichte des BvW, VdS/BvW und VdS," BA/MA, N222, Nachlass Hansen, Findleiter.

53 See Hansen to Pünder and accompanying documents, Sept. 25, 1948, BA, Z13/338, Bd. 1.

54 Allied High Commission Law No. 16, in Ruhm von Oppen, ed., *Documents on Germany,* 445–6; the new law still prohibited "oragnizations which require any of their members to be war veterans," but this restriction was circumvented by the acceptance of the next-of-kin of former professional soldiers.

55 The founding of these organizations and their role in shaping veterans' legislation in the Federal Republic is covered in a book-length study on German veterans after 1945 which I am currently completing.

ceeded. The Federal Republic had no army, and the prestige of the military profession was at an all-time low.[56] Not only had the physical manifestations of militarism been eradicated, but the long-term goal of psychological immunization against things military also appeared to have succeeded. The campaign had succeeded too well in fact; for, when the United States began to push for German rearmament in the early 1950s, these efforts met widespread opposition. To the amazement of the Americans, the supposedly incorrigibly militaristic Germans refused to respond to the siren call of rearmament. Five years after prohibiting veterans' organizations as a threat to democracy, the U.S. government found itself in the embarrassing position of not so discreetly promoting the formation of a unified veterans' organization, hoping that it would combat the pervasive *ohne mich* mood among former soldiers and potential conscripts.[57]

Was this dramatic change in German attitudes the result of Allied reeducation efforts? Had the efforts to apply the lessons learned after the First World War produced success after the Second? Not really. The main agents of reeducation had been the Third Reich and the Second World War. After the Second World War, there was no *Dolchstoss* legend to feed military fantasies. Germany's defeat was unequivocal, as were the causes for it. In 1945, unlike 1918, returning veterans were not seen as political heralds. The obliteration of the distinction between the home and the fighting fronts had destroyed the mystique of the front – as well as that of the front fighter. The barriers and myths that developed after 1918 did not reemerge in 1945. The romantic militarism that had fed Nazism after the First World War did not survive the Second. The consequences of a regime imbued with "soldierly virtues" had been experienced firsthand – with disastrous results. Civilians and soldiers alike were united in their efforts to survive in the harsh postwar environment and in the desire to rebuild their shattered country. Common membership in the *Notgemeinschaft* of postwar Germany helped to forge a consensus that war was futile.

What effect, then, if any, did the antimilitarist legislation directed against veterans during the occupation period have? In retrospect,

---

56 On this, see the relevant public opinion polls in the section on defense in Elisabeth Noelle and Erich Peter Neumann, eds., *The Germans: Public Opinion Polls, 1947–1966* (Allensbach and Bonn, 1967), 436–55, as well as the poll on occupational prestige, ibid., 345.
57 Tauber, *Beyond Eagle and Swastika*, 272, 291; this will be covered in more detail in the book mentioned in note 55.

the harsh treatment of veterans in general, and the prohibition of veterans' organizations in particular, can be seen to have had several positive consequences, though they were more often indirect than consciously planned. One consequence was to focus anger on the occupation governments for the difficulties of the postwar period, rather than on a fledgling German government, as had been the case after World War I. Material hardship and legal proscriptions also combined to force a reversal of the sequence of social integration and organizational activity that had followed the First World War, and this worked to moderate veterans' politics. In 1918 veterans returned to a relatively intact society as alienated outsiders. They joined together immediately after the war when the collective veteran consciousness was high, and in later years, veterans' organizations helped to sustain a separate veteran identity that became highly politicized. Activity as veterans (often paramilitary in nature) thus preceded social reintegration and retarded psychological demobilization. After 1945 the Allies denied German veterans political activity qua veterans, and their difficult economic circumstances forced them to form new economic and social ties – ties that worked to reintegrate them into society as individuals. Social reintegration therefore preceded activity in veterans' organizations, and this helped to foster pragmatic policies by the latter when they were again permitted.

The relatively quick and uncontested passage of legislation for war victims and former professional soldiers further aided the concentration on political, as opposed to interest group, activity following the First World War.[58] The hiatus in established war-disability and pension programs after the Second World War made it impossible to take benefits for granted and sharpened the need for pragmatic interest politics. The rank and file repeatedly reined in leaders who attempted to depart from such a policy and, while in some cases the process was slow, veterans' organizations generally came to accept the fact that they could gain more through cooperation than through confrontation.

The desire to avoid the mistakes of Weimar also played a not inconsiderable role in the different outcome of veterans' politics after

58 On post–World War I war victim legislation, see Robert W. Whalen, *Bitter Wounds: German Victims of the Great War 1914–1939* (Ithaca, N.Y., 1984), and Michael Geyer, "Ein Vorbote des Wohlfahrtsstaates: Die Kriegsopferversorgung in Frankreich, Deutschland und Grossbritannien nach dem Ersten Weltkrieg," *Geschichte und Gesellschaft* 9 (1983):230–77. For a biased but not inaccurate account of officers' pensions, see Hans Ernst Fried, *The Guilt of the German Army* (New York, 1942).

World War II. The government designed its policy consciously to appease the legitimate demands of veterans and to wean them from extremist positions, a goal that was achieved through an astute combination of threats and concessions. The parties pursued similar policies.[59] Finally, veterans and their leaders had also learned lessons.[60] Eventually, the new Republic restored much that had been taken away during the occupation, and this worked to engender loyalty to the new political order.[61] In the area of veterans' politics, therefore, Bonn definitely is not Weimar. Perhaps lessons *can* be learned from history.

59 The Social Democratic Party, for example, while opposing some aspects of the legislation providing pensions for former professional soldiers, generally approved the payment of pensions to former officers, including those of the Waffen-SS. See Udo Wengst, *Beamtentum zwischen Reform und Tradition: Beamtengesetzgebung in der Gründungsphase der Bundesrepublik Deutschland, 1948–1953* (Düsseldorf, 1988), and David C. Large, "Reckoning without the Past: The HIAG of the Waffen-SS and the Politics of Rehabilitation in the Bonn Republic," *Journal of Modern History* 59 (1987):101–2.

60 For a good example of this, see the presentation by D. Schmoeckel, "Eingliederung in das Volksganze," which was given at the first general meeting of BvW representatives, "Sitzungsprotokoll der Vertreterversammlung des B.v.W.," BA/MA, N222/228, 26–36.

61 On the role of social legislation, including pensions for former civil servants and military officers, in legitimizing the Federal Republic, see James M. Diehl, "Social Legislation and the Legitimation of the Federal Republic," in the forthcoming conference volume of papers given at the conference, "A Framework for Democracy: Forty Years of Experience with the Grundgesetz of the Federal Republic of Germany," held in Philadelphia in April 1989.

18

Grand Illusions: The United States, the Federal Republic of Germany, and the European Defense Community, 1950–1954

DAVID CLAY LARGE

On May 27, 1952, Chancellor Konrad Adenauer and the foreign ministers of the five other member states of the prospective European Defense Community (EDC) assembled in the ornate Salon d'Horloge in the Quai d'Orsay to sign the EDC treaty. Present too were Anthony Eden and Dean Acheson, the project's "godparents." The speeches accompanying the signing were as grand as the setting. Acheson declared that the ceremony was "the beginning of the realization of an ancient dream – the unity of the free peoples of Western Europe."[1] Adenauer characterized the EDC as a mighty step toward the unification of *all* Europe, east and west: "The EDC will pull toward it other European lands and thereby serve as a tool not only for the reunification of Germany, but the establishment of European unity."[2] These expostulations reflected the passion for a "united Europe" that had blossomed in the wake of World War II, which for many, especially in Europe, signaled the bankruptcy of nationalism.[3] As we know, the EDC hardly lived up to the hopeful visions of its sponsors: Indeed, it did not live at all, since France, which had conceived the scheme in the first place, thwarted its realization by rejecting the EDC treaty in August 1954. For those who had chosen to believe in it, the EDC was therefore a "grand illusion," one of the grandest of the postwar era.

I would like to thank the German Marshall Fund of the United States for financial assistance with the completion of this essay.

1 Dean Acheson, *Present at the Creation* (New York, 1969), 647.
2 Mitteilung an die Presse, May 27, 1952, Stiftung Bundeskanzler-Adenauer-Haus, Bundespresseamt-Sammlung, 1952.
3 Walter Lipgens, "Die Bedeutung des EVG-Vertrages für die politische europäische Einigungsbewegung," in Hans-Erich Volkmann and Walter Schwengler, eds., *Die Europäische Verteidigungsgemeinschaft: Stand und Probleme der Forschung* (Boppard, 1985), 9–30.

In this essay, I examine the expectations for the EDC entertained by
the two nations that became, after initial severe misgivings, its most
ardent champions: the United States and the Federal Republic of Germany (FRG). In investigating these countries' official "conversion"
to the project, I will also discuss the lingering doubts about the plan
harbored by some of the converts, as well as the continuing hostility
toward it expressed by its opponents. In conclusion, I will try to assess the significance of the EDC's failure within the broader context
of West German rearmament.

In the wake of the Communist attack in Korea, which many in the
West saw as a harbinger of similar aggression in Europe, United
States military planners insisted that the creation of regular West
German military forces was necessary to bolster the defense of Europe. Of course, they did not have in mind the recreation of an independent Wehrmacht; rather, the West Germany troops would be
thoroughly integrated into the new North Atlantic Treaty Organization (NATO), which would provide the top commanders and supply what heavy armaments the Germans might be allowed. As
Acheson said at the New York Foreign Ministers' Conference in September 1950: "The German contingents would have no existence
apart from the forces of freedom."[4] West Germany, in other words,
would be rearmed and contained at the same time.

Sound as this plan appeared to the Americans, it seemed sheer
madness to the French, who, for understandable reasons, preferred
to restrict any German "defense contribution" to monetary payments. Soon convinced, however, that, if it refused to accept German
rearmament in any form, America and Britain would simply arm the
Boche as they saw fit, France elected to offer its own alternative
scheme, the famous Pleven Plan. With this initiative, France hoped
not only to gain a voice in the German rearmament process, but also
to delay it and to ensure that, when German rearmament did happen,
it would pose no threat to French security. The French government
also hoped to make German rearmament more palatable to its people
by harnessing it to the ideal of European unity.[5] Accordingly, it fore-
saw German rearmament exclusively within the context of a "European Army" modeled on the proposed European Coal and Steel

4 *FRUS 1950*, vol. 3, *Western Europe* (Washington, D.C., 1977), 1207.
5 Alfred Grosser, *Das Bündnis: Die westeuropäischen Länder und die USA seit dem Krieg* (Munich,
1978), 178.

Community (the Schuman Plan). The Pleven Plan provided for the integration of national army units at the "lowest possible level" – namely battalions – and the creation of a common defense budget, arms procurement agency, and defense administration responsible to a European Parliament. These bureaucratic and political institutions were to be in place *before* any troops would be assembled. The plan was patently discriminatory against the Germans in a number of ways. It provided for a "transition period" of undetermined duration, during which all aspects of German rearmament would be under the control of the "European Defense Commissar." (This provision reflected Jean Monnet's promise that "the first soldier recruited in Germany will be a European soldier.")[6] The scheme allowed the other European powers to retain their existing defense ministries and keep some of their forces outside the new European Army; the FRG, on the other hand, would have no defense ministry or general staff, and *all* its troops would stand under the European command. Most significant of all, under this arrangement, the FRG would not be a direct partner in NATO, since the European Army was meant to be a separate entity linked by treaty to the Atlantic Pact.[7] Though the plan did not explicitly preclude West Germany from joining NATO sometime in the future, Premier René Pleven and Foreign Minister Robert Schuman said privately that France had no intention of allowing this to happen.[8]

Upon its announcement in October 1950, the Pleven Plan immediately encountered a storm of derision. Even some Frenchmen were critical. A member of the French Embassy staff in London told a Foreign Office official in confidence that the plan was "military nonsense." Its "real purpose" was to "meet a parliamentary emergency" and to obstruct the American effort to rearm the FRG.[9] Certainly most of the French military leaders agreed; they rejected battalion-level integration as militarily unsound and resented the partial sacrifice of military sovereignty that the scheme entailed.[10] France's European NATO allies, particularly the British, were openly hostile.

6 Jean Monnet, *Erinnerungen eines Europäers* (Munich, 1978), 441.
7 Royal Institute of International Affairs, ed., *Documents on International Affairs 1949–1950* (London, 1951), 339–44.
8 Gerhard Wettig, *Entmilitarisierung und Wiederbewaffnung in Deutschland 1945–1955: Internationale Auseinandersetzungen um die Rolle der Deutschen in Europa* (Munich, 1967), 369.
9 A. G. Gilchrist to Foreign Office, Oct. 24, 1950, PRO, FO 361, box 85089.
10 Pierre Guillen, "Die französische Generalität, die Aufrüstung der Bundesrepublik und die EVG (1950–1954)," in Volkmann and Schwengler, eds., *Die Europäische Verteidigungsgemeinschaft*, 132–3.

British Defense Minister Emanuel Shinwell insisted that it "would only excite laughter and ridicule" in the country it was supposed to intimidate: the Soviet Union.[11]

But more significant for the plan's future was the reaction of the EDC's other sponsor, the United States. Dean Acheson, who had become an apostle of German rearmament after initially opposing it, saw the Pleven Plan as a monkey wrench in the American plan to get the Germans to the front with all possible speed. It would, he said, "raise problems necessitating almost endless delay"; and since it seemed "to give Germany permanently second-class status," it "would never be accepted by the German people."[12] American officials in France and Germany reacted rather more positively to the plan. David Bruce, American ambassador to France, claimed to see in it "an approach which would do much toward bringing about a closer association among the free nations of Europe."[13] John McCloy, the U.S. high commissioner for Germany, accepted the sincerity of the French proposal, though he was skeptical of many of the plan's details and was not prepared to endorse it fully without revisions.[14] Crucial was the Pentagon's perspective, which was unambiguously negative. While the Pentagon had earlier espoused a "European Defense Force," it had in mind little more than a conventional alliance, envisaging integration of national contingents only at the top levels of command.[15] Recalling recent difficulties even with this level of command "cooperation," American generals and military officials had no use for France's much more ambitious amalgam. The Chairman of the Joint Chiefs of Staff (JCS), General Omar Bradley, said he could not believe his ears when first informed of the Pleven Plan;[16] Secretary of Defense George C. Marshall confessed that he could not penetrate the "miasma" of the thing.[17]

11 FRUS 1950, 3:420.   12 Ibid., 411–12.
13 Thomas A. Schwartz, "From Occupation to Alliance: John J. McCloy and the Allied High Commission in the Federal Republic of Germany 1949–1952," Ph.D. diss., Harvard University, 1985, 2:383.
14 Ibid., 386.
15 JCS memo, "European Defense Force and Related Matters," Aug. 30, 1950, NA, RG 330, 09107 (Europe), 1950.
16 Wilhelm Meier-Dörnberg, "Politische und militärische Faktoren bei der Planung des deutschen Verteidigungsbeitrages im Rahmen der EVG," in Entmilitarisierung und Aufrüstung in Mitteleuropa 1945–1956, ed. Militärgeschichtliches Forschungsamt (Herford and Bonn, 1983), 184.
17 The History of the Joint Chiefs of Staff, vol. 4, Walter S. Poole, The Joint Chiefs of Staff and National Policy 1950–1952 (Wilmington, Del., 1980), 212.

Adenauer also had his reservations about the Pleven Plan. In private, he was very critical of its anti-German features.[18] But he was unprepared simply to reject the initiative out of hand, for he was strongly attracted to its larger political goal of European unity. He was determined to anchor the FRG securely within the European and Atlantic West, and he saw rearmament within the European context as a possible means to this end. As for the plan's many drawbacks, he expected these could be eliminated through negotiation.[19] In the meantime, West Germany could begin to rearm as a partner in NATO.

Adenauer's various security advisers were especially concerned lest the FRG sacrifice its "national interests" on the altar of European unity. Former generals Hans Speidel and Adolf Heusinger urged the chancellor to demand military "equality" (*Gleichberechtigung*) as a "precondition" for rearmament. They insisted that the German troops be organized in armored divisions with the latest weaponry. "We cannot be expected to contribute cannon fodder," they declared.[20] The security experts who drew up the famous "Himmeroder Denkschrift" in October 1950 reinforced this view.[21] This memorandum provided the main guidelines for Adenauer's official security adviser, Theodor Blank, who took up his duties the day after the Pleven Plan was announced.

Bonn's reservations regarding the Pleven Plan were duly noted in Washington, which, of course, harbored similar doubts. But since the Truman administration was also convinced that effective European security required the cooperation of the French, the United States came forth with a modification of the Pleven Plan known as the Spofford Compromise (named after Charles Spofford, American representative to the NATO Council). This proposal called for "provisional" integration of German troops into NATO at the smallest level "consistent with military viability" – the "regimental combat team" (five to six thousand men).[22] Since the American JCS

18 Herbert Blankenhorn, *Verständnis und Verständigung: Blätter eines politischen Tagebuchs 1949 bis 1979* (Frankfurt am Main, Berlin, and Vienna, 1980), 115–16; Hans-Peter Schwarz, *Adenauer: Der Aufstieg, 1876–1952* (Stuttgart, 1986), 831.
19 Werner Weidenfeld, "Konrad Adenauer und die EVG: Eine Studie zum subjektiven Faktor in der Politik," in Volkmann and Schwengler, eds., *Die Europäische Verteidigungsgemeinschaft*, 257–63.
20 Klaus von Schubert, ed., *Sicherheitspolitik der Bundesrepublik Deutschland: Dokumentation 1945–1977*, 2 vols. (Cologne, 1978), 2:67–71.
21 For this *Denkschrift*, see ibid., 91–8.
22 *Anfänge westdeutscher Sicherheitspolitik 1945–1956*, ed. Militärgeschichtliches Forschungsamt, vol. 1, *Von der Kapitulation bis zum Pleven-Plan* (Munich and Vienna, 1982), 397–8.

believed that the regimental level-of-integration was still too low, another NATO paper stipulated that the combat teams would be increased "to the required size" as soon as Supreme Headquarters Allied Powers, Europe (SHAPE) determined that this was necessary.[23] Unlike the Pleven Plan, this proposal also allowed for the creation of a German "defensive air force of limited size" and a "naval force of light craft." German industrial production would be exploited "to the greatest extent possible" in the joint defense build-up, but the FRG would not be allowed to produce heavy military equipment. Most important, this American initiative permitted the raising of troops *before* the creation of unified European institutions.

France was by no means enthusiastic about this "compromise," but, after a bitter debate on December 6, the Council of Ministers elected to accept it as a basis for further negotiation. As one of its members put it, a blunt refusal to endorse the plan would have left France "alone to face Russia and resurgent Germany."[24] Shortly thereafter, the NATO foreign ministers formally agreed in Brussels to accept the NATO Military Council's recommendation that the Allied High Commission embark immediately on negotiations with the Federal Republic regarding a West German defense contribution to NATO. At the same time, the ministers gave France the green light to open negotiations aiming at the creation of a European Army within the context of NATO.

In the negotiations between the FRG and the High Commission, which opened on the Petersberg on January 9, 1951, the German delegation, led by Blank, set forth a rearmament plan modeled closely on the "Himmeroder Denkschrift." On the all-important question of military organization, it stressed the need for fully operational armored divisions supported by tactical air and coastal defense units. In making this argument, the Germans drew on their unique experience fighting the Russians, as well as on the *U.S. Army Field Manual*, which stated that "the only unit organized to act independently was a division."[25] Thus, the Germans were not much happier with the Spofford proposal for nationally mixed "regimental combat teams" than they had been with the original Pleven Plan. Speidel insisted

23 *FRUS 1950*, 3:518.
24 Wilfried Loth, *Sozialismus und Internationalismus: Die französischen Sozialisten und die Nachkriegsordnung Europas 1940–1950* (Stuttgart, 1977), 288.
25 *FRUS 1951*, vol. 3, *European Security and the German Question* (Washington, D.C., 1981), 999.

that these teams would not work: Coordination and communication would be impaired, and there would even be quarrels over food, as "the Bavarians would want sauerkraut and beer, the French troops white bread and red wine, the Italians spaghetti and chianti!"[26]

The German delegation's primary concern with "equality" was evident in the field of military administration. Blank insisted that the FRG would not be content with anything short of a ministry of defense. The main reason, he argued, was that only this principle was compatible with the FRG's "democratic structure" and parliamentary supervision of the army.[27] In a sense, this justification was disingenuous, for Blank's boss, Adenauer, had himself tried (and would continue to try) to circumvent the influence of parliament in the shaping of security policy.[28]

One area in which the Germans did *not* want equality was finance – in footing the bill for its military contingent. Pressed to state how much they might contribute to the costs of their rearmament, they replied that their "social situation" (i.e., refugee problems, urban reconstruction, Berlin assistance) "left no funds available for the financing of German contingents." Since West Germany's unhappy financial situation could not be allowed to prevent its rearmament, "other methods to raise revenues must be discussed, including loans."[29]

These and other technical matters presented a host of difficulties to the Allied negotiators, who could only answer that they would have to take them up with their respective governments and the NATO Council. In the meantime, they drew up an "Interim Report," whose most significant feature from the German point of view was its emphasis on retaining the NATO framework for German rearmament. This option became known as the "Petersberg Solution."[30]

However, given continued French objections to a German role in NATO and France's apparent ability to hold up such a "solution," it now seemed advisable to look for an acceptable formula under the "European Army" rubric – that is, to focus more intently on the concurrent EDC talks in Paris, which none of the powers (including France) seemed to be taking very seriously.

26 Ibid., 1024.   27 Ibid., 1032.
28 Arnulf Baring, *Aussenpolitik in Adenauers Kanzlerdemokratie: Bonns Beitrag zur Europäischen Verteidigungsgemeinschaft* (Munich and Vienna, 1969).
29 *FRUS 1951*, 3:1028.   30 Wettig, *Entmilitarisierung*, 408–9.

The United States, in particular, had not put much stock in these negotiations, to which it, like Britain and many of the smaller NATO states, had sent only an observer delegation. The American delegation's chief function, said Acheson, was to judge the conference's progress on the basis of "whether or not it serves to strengthen the North Atlantic community."[31] The conference hardly seemed to be doing this, and, by late June, after about four months of meetings, Acheson cabled Ambassador Bruce that the time had come for "energetic" American leadership to remove the "deadlock" in the negotiations.[32] The United States should pressure the French to accept an immediate commencement of German rearmament within the NATO context, pending solution of the military, political, and economic issues surrounding the EDC. Acheson reminded Bruce that the United States backed the EDC *only* as a "long term approach to the problem of European defense"; in the short run, it would be best to proceed on the basis of the Petersberg solution.[33]

Bruce did not agree, and his disagreement inaugurated what was to be the most important diplomatic development in the Paris negotiations: a switch on the part of the American government to a solid, even fervent, support for the EDC as the best solution to the problem of German rearmament. Bruce responded to Acheson's cable by warning against any interim West German rearmament outside the EDC context. Such a move, he insisted, would be a "serious blow to our objectives in Europe," for it would amount to the re-creation of a German national army, "something opposed by just about everyone, including the Germans."[34] Moreover, said Bruce, the EDC option would actually produce German troops *faster* than the Petersberg/NATO alternative, because it offered the only framework in which France "and perhaps other nations" would accept the concessions to German military equality without which the Germans would not participate. Furthermore, if the United States forced the French to accept a method of German rearmament that they felt endangered their security, they would not cooperate in achieving a rapid resolution of the political questions that also impeded German participation.[35] In short, whether America liked it or not, the EDC had become the only viable option, and the United States would do best to throw its considerable weight behind it.

---

31 *FRUS 1951*, 3:761.   32 Ibid., 801.   33 Ibid., 803.   34 Ibid., 806.   35 Ibid., 807.

At the time, Bruce could not have known how quickly his advice would be heeded. The key figure in the American realignment was not Acheson, who continued to have his doubts about the EDC, but the new Supreme Allied Commander in Europe, Dwight Eisenhower. Ike began his tenure as SACEUR with his own strong doubts about the European Army idea. He considered the Pleven Plan to be "more divisive than unifying in its effect," since it included "every kind of obstacle, difficulty and fantastic notion that misguided humans could put together in one package."[36] In early March, he told Cyrus Sulzberger of the *New York Times* that the European Army was like "putting the cart before the horse," because it "represented a political entity that did not yet exist."[37] Then, however, he began discussing the EDC with several European Army partisans, including Bruce, Jean Monnet, and McCloy (whom Monnet had converted to the idea). Under the influence of these men, Eisenhower not only dropped his objections to the EDC, but very quickly emerged as a veritable missionary for the entire concept of European unity – military, economic, and political – which he now saw as the answer to all of Europe's problems.

Ike's passionate conversion to the ideals of Europeanism was evident in a speech he delivered in London on July 3, 1951. Unity, he declared, would bring the Europeans "miracles for the common good" as well as military security. Given these advantages, the goal of a European federation should not be pursued "by slow infiltration," but "by direct and decisive assault, with all available means." As a timetable for European unification, Ike suggested six months, or perhaps a year![38]

It has been suggested that these astonishing declarations were typical of Ike's midwestern enthusiasm and political naiveté.[39] There is certainly some truth in this charge, but Ike's conversion to Europeanism was also based on a conviction that had deep roots in the American political tradition: namely, the belief that it was not in America's best interest to become "permanently entangled" in the affairs of Europe or to serve as the world's policeman. "We cannot," he declared, "be a modern Rome guarding the far frontiers with our

36 Stephen E. Ambrose, *Eisenhower*, vol. 1, *Soldier, General of the Army, President-Elect, 1890–1952* (New York, 1983), 508.
37 Schwartz, "From Occupation to Alliance," 549.
38 Robert McGeehan, *The German Rearmament Question: Diplomacy and European Defense after World War II* (Urbana, Ill., 1971), 128.
39 Ibid., 129.

legions."[40] The key point is that Ike saw European unity – and the EDC – as the most promising route along which the Europeans might become strong and secure enough to allow the United States eventually to bring its troops home. He hoped this would not take too long. "If in ten years, all American troops stationed in Europe for national defense purposes have not been returned to the United States," he observed, "then this whole project will have failed."[41]

What is notable about this perspective, aside from its touching optimism, is its unintended irony. While Eisenhower had converted to the EDC in order to allow an eventual American military exodus from Europe, many of those Europeans who favored the EDC did so largely because they saw it as a way of guaranteeing the American presence by demonstrating Europe's shared commitment to the defense of the West. Actually, this consideration was on Ike's mind, too, but only as a short-term weapon against the isolationist tendencies that had surfaced in the Republican Party and that threatened to undermine America's NATO commitment.[42] Thus, he spent much of his brief tenure as SACEUR trying to promote the Europeans' own defense build-up and their flagging interest in the EDC. Indeed, he told George Marshall that he had shifted his position on the European Army because NATO needed "some spectacular accomplishment" to convince the American public that the alliance warranted continued American support.[43] Curiously enough, then, Ike's conversion to the EDC was a function both of his short-term internationalism and his long-term nostalgia for that time-honored American insularity expressed first (and perhaps best) in George Washington's "Farewell Address."

The American about-face on the EDC caught the Germans by surprise, since they had expected full American support for the Petersberg solution. Their delegation at the Paris talks had instructions from Adenauer to work for equality, but not to push so hard that the talks foundered on German intransigence. Adenauer feared that a complete failure would both poison Franco-German relations and foster the revival of extreme nationalism at home.[44] The German delegation fully expected difficulties, for in their view, the Paris conference was primarily a French ploy to delay West German rearmament. No wonder Theodor Blank was so distressed by the American

40 Ambrose, *Eisenhower*, 1:505.   41 Ibid., 506.
42 Cf. Phil Williams, *The Senate and U.S. Troops in Europe* (London, 1985), 43–107.
43 Ambrose, *Eisenhower*, 1:508.   44 Weidenfeld, "Adenauer und die EVG," 263.

reversal. When McCloy told him on July 4 that French resistance to the Petersberg approach necessitated a reorientation in favor of the EDC, Blank replied that America might kick Adenauer around, but not *him*. The Pleven Plan was simply *indiskutabel*, and if it were up to him, the Germans would provide no military contingent at all![45]

Of course, this was really little but bluster. Once the Germans had recovered from their shock, they saw that they had no choice but to accept McCloy's advice and try to work within the framework of the EDC plan. In early July, Adenauer signaled the Germans' willingness to cooperate by sending Blank to Paris to take over the German delegation. It seemed that, if West Germany *had* to rearm within the EDC context, it was determined to play a major role in the design of the European Army. As soon as he arrived in Paris, Blank focused on precisely those issues that most clearly separated the French and German bargaining positions: discrimination against the FRG in the "transition period," questions over the size and makeup of the national contingents, and, above all, the relationship of the EDC to NATO.

On most of these issues, the Germans had the support of the Americans, who shared the German concern for military efficiency, and who quickly informed the French that their conversion to the EDC did not mean a willingness to let France impede the creation of a viable force. In effect, what the United States hoped to do was to "marry" the Petersberg and Paris approaches in a way that would win the approval of *both* the French and the Germans.[46]

Backed by the American delegation, Blank was quickly able to make progress on the question of the transition phase. He proposed that, during this period, Germany's military buildup should be controlled by the German government and parliament, but to assuage French fears, the German troops might be placed under SHAPE command as soon as they were recruited.[47] Hervé Alphand, head of the French delegation, replied that France would have to "study" the matter.[48] Eventually, the delegates reached an agreement whereby *all* EDC members would be in charge of their own recruiting and training until the supranational institutions were in place.[49]

On the knotty issue of level of integration, the Germans also successfully pressed their case. Their original demand was for nationally

45 Baring, *Aussenpolitik*, 108.   46 Spofford to Acheson, July 8, 1951, *FRUS 1951*, 3:821.
47 Ibid., 825.   48 Ibid.   49 Ibid., 843–7.

homogeneous corps – the Himmerod formulation; but, as a "concession" to prevent the talks from failing, their delegation proposed international mixing at this level, leaving the divisions national.[50] The French continued to fight on this issue into the summer, when they came under renewed pressure from the Americans to give way. Bowing to this pressure, France formally agreed to "depoliticize" the question by turning it over to SACEUR for adjudication. SACEUR quickly came up with a compromise proposal involving the creation of *groupements de combat* as the basic national building blocks in the European Army. These units would be slightly smaller than the standard division, but large enough to be militarily self-sufficient.[51] The Germans readily accepted this compromise; and so, rather less readily, did the French. Perhaps it helped that France had been invaded by German divisions, not *groupements de combat*.

Having given in on the quarrelsome level-of-integration issue, the French felt justified in asking the FRG for a formal commitment to the EDC, something it had as yet evaded. But by late August, Adenauer had decided openly to embrace the European Army. Increasingly, he had come to understand that, for many of his countrymen, rearmament was acceptable only if it was tied to the vision of a united Europe. This aspiration for the EDC was especially strong among younger people and Catholics, whose support the chancellor clearly needed in order to counter the antirearmament drive of the Social Democratic Party (SPD) and the neutralist or pacifist Protestants around Gustav Heinemann and Martin Niemöller.[52] In an interview with the United Press International on September 10, Adenauer praised the unifying qualities of the EDC, though he insisted that it must not replace NATO.[53] In a memorandum to McCloy, he formally announced his acceptance of the principle of the EDC, but added that many details needed to be clarified.[54]

50 The concession was made at the suggestion of Ulrich de Maizière. See Ulrich de Maizière, *In der Pflicht: Lebensbericht eines deutschen Soldaten im 20. Jahrhundert* (Herford and Bonn, 1989), 149.
51 Wettig, *Entmilitarisierung*, 441.
52 On the Catholics and rearmament, see Anselm Doering-Manteuffel, *Katholizismus und Wiederbewaffnung: Die Haltung der deutschen Katholiken gegenüber der Wehrfrage 1948–1955* (Mainz, 1981); on the Protestants, see Johanna Vogel, *Kirche und Wiederbewaffnung: Die Haltung der EKD in den Auseinandersetzungen um die Wiederbewaffnung der Bundesrepublik* (Göttingen, 1978).
53 Interview text in Stiftung Bundeskanzler-Adenauer-Haus, Bundespresseamt-Sammlung, 1951.
54 *FRUS 1951*, 3:869.

One of these details was EDC's relationship to NATO – or, more specifically, West Germany's expectation of becoming a member of NATO through participation in the EDC. The Americans had previously supported the Germans on this issue. But at the Paris Foreign Ministers' Conference in late November, Acheson, now afraid that a complete German victory on this point would endanger the EDC's ratification in the French chamber, urged Adenauer to show "restraint."[55] This was a difficult policy for Adenauer to pursue, if he wanted to assure ratification in his own parliament. The ensuing deadlock on this issue lasted for several months, until, at a series of talks held on the occasion of King George VI's funeral in February 1952, Anthony Eden proposed that *any* member of *either* the EDC or NATO should be able to insist upon joint consultations between the two organizations.[56] Eden's proposal was obviously designed to pacify the Germans, who would thus be guaranteed a voice in the operation of the Atlantic Alliance without actually being a member. Adenauer welcomed this proposition, but did not thereby give up West Germany's demand for membership in NATO.[57]

During the London talks, Adenauer also raised the question of German weapons production, which Blank had already addressed on the Petersberg, when he had offered to sign a declaration foregoing *all* German weapons production in order to pacify the French. This suggestion had never been a serious concession, since the Germans expected that international economic realities would soon draw them into some form of arms production.[58] They had also concluded that a complete exclusion of German arms production would make the EDC overly dependent on American supplies, which might be questionable in terms of both quantity and quality. (Blank privately told Alphand that he had recently attended some American military exercises and seen weapons in action that "would have been out-of-date in Germany in 1923."[59]) When he raised the arms issue in London, Adenauer recalled that he had earlier agreed to the prohibition of certain kinds of weapons production in West Germany on the grounds that its territory was a "strategic zone," but it remained unclear *which* arms categories would be outlawed. This was a significant issue,

55 Baring, *Aussenpolitik*, 114.   56 Anthony Eden, *Full Circle* (Boston, 1960), 46.
57 Wettig, *Entmilitarisierung*, 467.
58 Blankenhorn report, undated, BA, B 136, Bundeskanzleramt, 2160.
59 "Aufzeichnung über das Gespräch zwischen Herrn Blank und Herrn Alphand am 11.10.51," BA/MA, BW9/2048, 17.

because a number of German firms were beginning to show an interest in arms manufacture, and some forms of weapons production might complement the civilian manufacturing economy. Adenauer implied as much when he protested against the EDC draft-treaty's "vagueness and imprecision" in this area. What about gun powder manufacture, for example? This material was needed for all sorts of purposes, including mining.[60] Adenauer was eventually successful in refining the list of prohibited items, but not in substantially reducing its scope. He agreed that West Germany forgo production of warships and aircraft, as well as atomic and biological weapons. Chemical weapons for a time remained a matter of dispute – these being an old German specialty – but their production, too, was ultimately banned.[61]

In addition to working out rules for weapons production, the EDC planners were also called upon to develop a common code of conduct for the European Army. Early in the negotiations, the French presented a *discipline générale* that looked very much like the code prevailing in the French army. According to Blank, this draft embraced some practices that were "worse than anything the Nazis had tried to do," and others "that we Germans once had but do not wish to return to."[62] Thus, the German delegation set out to modify the French draft along lines approximating the elaborate and quite progressive military reform proposals being developed by Count Wolf von Baudissin in the Dienststelle Blank.[63] Hoping to create a set of regulations that were faithful to the "advanced technological requirements of modern military forces" and to the need for "individual personal development and self-expression" in a democratic society, the Germans advanced a program that minimized the traditional distinctions between military and civilian life.[64] But they quickly ran into opposition from the other powers, especially the

60 Paul Weymar, *Konrad Adenauer: Die autorisierte Biographie* (Munich, 1955), 433.
61 Baring, *Aussenpolitik,* 120.
62 Sonderausschuss zur Mitberatung des EVG-Vertrages, 4. Sitzung, Sept. 10, 1952, Parlamentsarchiv, Bonn.
63 See esp. Dietrich Genschel, *Wehrreform und Reaktion: Die Vorbereitung der Inneren Führung 1951–1956* (Hamburg, 1972); and Donald Abenheim, *Reforging the Iron Cross: The Search for Tradition in the West German Armed Forces* (Princeton, N.J., 1988), 88–120.
64 "Das Innere Gefüge der Streitkräfte," BA/MA, BW9/764.

French, who, according to one German delegate, were "very reluctant" to adopt new forms, always putting "the national before the European."[65]

In this area, the Germans got no support from the United States. The Americans understood "democracy" in military organization to mean little more than guaranteeing promotion by merit and securing the soldiers' basic constitutional rights. The American military establishment, moreover, openly admired the military "competence" of the old Wehrmacht and was in fact busy remodeling its own forces according to the "lessons" learned from the Germans in World War II.[66] Increasingly, the main worry of American military leaders was not that their new German allies might be difficult to contain, but that – as SACEUR General Alfred Gruenther put it in 1954 – "the quality of the soldiers in the new German army would not be as high as those of the Second or Third Reich."[67] No wonder Baudissin discovered, on a study trip to America in 1955, that the American officers had little use for his concept of *innere Führung*. "They simply wanted German soldiers as quickly, as numerous, and as good as possible," he reported disgustedly.[68]

While West German military planners were working to put their imprint on the proposed European Army, politicians were busy subjecting the draft EDC treaty (or what they knew of it) to critical scrutiny. This is not the place for a thorough review of the wideranging debate that culminated in German ratification of the EDC treaty in March 1953. But it is necessary to touch on a few of the key objections to the treaty raised in these discussions.

The SPD had expressed sharp misgivings from the outset about German rearmament within the context of a European Army. Kurt Schumacher, whose abiding preoccupation was German reunification, had denounced the Pleven Plan as "the death of the European idea."[69] Though the SPD eventually assisted contructively in laying the groundwork for rearmament, the party continued to have little

---

65 Kurzprotokoll, 17. Sitzung des Ausschusses Innere Führung (Dienststelle Blank), May 26, 1953, BA/MA, BW9/1291.
66 "Mit Guderians Anregungen," *Der Spiegel,* Dec. 3, 1952, p. 14.
67 "Gruenther Takes Precautions," *Foreign Report* (published by *The Economist*), Oct. 21, 1954, pp. 5–6.
68 "Bericht über die Reise in die USA vom 30.6. bis 29.8.55," BA/MA, BW9/626.
69 See Ulrich Buczylowski, *Kurt Schumacher und die deutsche Frage: Sicherheitspolitik und strategische Offensivkonzeption von August 1950 bis September 1951* (Stuttgart, 1973), 115–16.

use for the EDC. During the great *Wehrdebatte* in the Bundestag on February 7 and 8, 1952, Erich Ollenhauer questioned the security and political benefits the FRG would allegedly receive from the pact. Instead of guaranteeing the American presence, he said, the EDC and German rearmament would give the Yankees an excuse to bring their boys home. The occupation powers' offer of "sovereignty" in exchange for participation in the EDC was "blackmail," since it made the former, which in any case was only partial, contingent on the latter. At the very least, the FRG must not be forced to join the EDC before the General Treaty went into effect. Once fully sovereign, the FRG would be able to decide if it wished to join NATO. According to Ollenhauer the present EDC arrangement was no substitute for membership in NATO; on the contrary, it amounted to an elaborate ruse through which vital German interests were to be subordinated to foreign control and represented an attempt to "cover up" German political problems in "European fancy dress."[70]

The Free Democratic Party (FDP), though it ultimately supported the EDC treaty, shared some of the SPD's reservations.[71] It, too, urged *full sovereignty* as a precondition to EDC membership. It also demanded a release of German prisoners from Allied jails, along with an Allied declaration that "the past was a closed matter, that there were no longer any victors or vanquished, but only comrades in a common enterprise."[72] Such demands reflected the extent to which the FDP had taken up the banner of German national interest. The party took this line in the Bundesrat as well, where Reinhold Maier protested against an arrangement whereby "foreign generals, who remained for all practical purposes under the command of their own governments, would assume control over the German contingent." Maier dismissed as "nonsense" Adenauer's contention that EDC membership would promote German reunification.[73]

The Christian Democratic Union/Christian Social Union (CDU/CSU), as the mainstay of the government coalition, was prepared to back Adenauer's belated push for the EDC, but the Union parties resented the fact they had been kept largely in the dark about the

70 Deutscher Bundestag, *Stenographische Berichte*, 190. Sitzung, Feb. 7, 1952, pp. 1808–15.
71 The best study on this is Dieter Wagner, *FDP und Wiederbewaffnung: Die wehrpolitische Orientierung der Liberalen in der Bundesrepublik 1949–1955* (Boppard, 1978).
72 August Martin Euler speaking for the FDP. See Deutscher Bundestag, *Stenographische Berichte*, 190. Sitzung, Feb. 7, 1955, p. 8132.
73 Reinhold Maier, *Erinnerungen 1948–1953* (Tübingen, 1966), 447.

treaty negotiations. Some party figures, moreover, were not in total agreement with what they *did* know.[74] They feared that Adenauer was not demanding enough political and economic concessions from the Allies in exchange for rearmament; and that the Dienststelle Blank lacked a "new Scharnhorst" capable of pushing through necessary military reforms in the EDC.[75] Franz Josef Strauss, chairman of the Union's "Defense Policy Working Group," declared at a CSU *Fraktion* meeting that the party would have to assume responsibility for preventing the government from automatically signing the EDC treaty and thereby "rolling over" parliamentary authority.[76]

These concerns, and others as well, were echoed in the discussions of the Bundestag's Sonderausschuss zur Mitberatung des EVG-Vertrages (Special Committee for Consultation on the EDC Treaty). In this forum, members of all the main parties worried that the FRG's lack of membership in NATO would make its contingent vulnerable to manipulation by the Atlantic powers. Wilhelm Mellies of the SPD warned that, if the United States mobilized the EDC to wage a "preventative war" in Europe, West Germany could do nothing to stop it.[77] Fritz Erler, the SPD's leading military expert, fretted that no German would be in a position to "guarantee us that our 400,000 troops will be used to defend our homeland and not that of some other people."[78]

Representatives of the FDP objected to the EDC's restrictions on Germans arms production, including that of "ABC" (atomic, biological, chemical) weapons, because their development might aid the civilian economy through important technological "spin-offs."[79] Strauss, no doubt thinking of the future Bavarian arms industry, wondered how long it would be before "we will be able to build our own tanks?"[80] Questions also arose regarding the ideological viability of a European Army. Was there such a thing as a "common European feeling?" Though some, like Strauss, believed it existed, others doubted it. Carlo Schmid (SPD) thought that the "concert of

74 Innenpolitische Berichte, Jan. 8, 25, and Feb. 5, 1952, BA, B 136, Bundeskanzleramt, 2160.
75 Ibid., Feb. 7, 1952.   76 Ibid., Jan. 22, 1952.
77 Sonderausschuss zur Mitberatung des EVG-Vertrages, 5. Sitzung, Sept. 11, 1951, Parlamentsarchiv, Bonn.
78 Ibid.
79 Sonderausschuss zur Mitberatung des EVG-Vertrages, 9. Sitzung, Sept. 10, 1952, Parlamentsarchiv, Bonn.
80 Sonderausschuss zur Mitberatung des EVG-Vertrages, 11. Sitzung, Oct. 19, 1952, Parlamentsarchiv, Bonn.

Europe" had validity only among intellectuals. A Bavarian trooper
might risk his life for Hamburg, but would he be prepared to do so
for London?[81]

Such criticisms and reservations did not prevent the Adenauer
government from asserting that, all in all, the FRG had done rather
well in the EDC negotiations, had managed to turn a scheme that
was patently discriminatory into one that offered a large measure of
"equality." Blank could boast that "the superior negotiating position
of the German delegation had succeeded in overcoming most of the
original anti-German tendencies of the Pleven Plan and producing a
treaty based almost exclusively on German ideas." The Germans had
"caught the French in the logic of their own scheme" and made them
pursue it more seriously than they intended.[82]

Of course, this was precisely the problem with the German success: The more attractive the Germans were able to render this
scheme from their point of view, the less attractive it became to the
French. The Adenauer government, with the backing of its main
sponsor, the United States, had helped replace the Pleven Plan with
the EDC treaty; but while the former was not acceptable to the FRG,
the latter was not acceptable to France.[83]

The American and West German governments condemned
France's killing of the EDC with all the indignation of recent converts to the deceased's good cause. President Eisenhower's secretary
of state, John Foster Dulles, fumed that "in one country [France] nationalism, abetted by Communism, had asserted itself so as to endanger the whole of Europe."[84] Ike himself was similarly appalled
by France's action, but also anxious to pick up the pieces and look for
alternatives. "America," he announced, "has never quit in something that was good for herself and the world. We will not quit
now."[85] When he first learned of the French vote, Adenauer *was*
tempted to quit. He later insisted that this moment was "the bitterest
disappointment and the greatest defeat" he had suffered in his entire
career.[86] For this humiliation, he blamed not so much the French na-

81 Sonderausschuss zur Mitberatung des EVG-Vertrages, 38. Sitzung, July 8, 1953, Parlamentsarchiv, Bonn.
82 Innenpolitischer Bericht, Jan. 8, 1952, BA, B 136, Bundeskanzleramt, 2160.
83 Wilhelm Meier-Dörnberg, "Die Europäische Verteidigungsgemeinschaft," in Alexander
Fischer, ed., *Wiederbewaffnung in Deutschland nach 1945* (Berlin, 1986), 86.
84 Dulles's full statement is in *FRUS 1952–1954*, vol. 5, *Western European Security* (Washington, D.C., 1983), 1120–2.
85 Dwight D. Eisenhower, *Mandate for Change* (New York, 1963), 403.
86 Konrad Adenauer, *Erinnerungen 1953–1955* (Stuttgart, 1966), 298.

tion as its new prime minister, Pierre Mendès-France, whose failure to support the EDC he explained as follows: "You see, Mendès-France is after all a Jew. We have had experience with our German Jews. They all have an inferiority complex, which they try to compensate for by taking extreme nationalist positions. Mendès-France wants to be seen as a good patriot in France by holding down the Germans, and this at the expense of Europe."[87]

Outraged as the American and German governments were over the French "betrayal," indignation soon gave way almost to a sense of satisfaction in some official quarters that this ambitious scheme had not come to fruition. In November 1954, after the powers had decided to rearm West Germany in the NATO framework after all, a SHAPE report declared that senior officials in the FRG "appear in some ways to be relieved that the EDC has been torpedoed."[88] The NATO solution, of course, had been their preference all along.[89] Officials in the Dienststelle Blank were frustrated over the waste of time that had gone into planning for a European Army, but many of them preferred the NATO arrangement on the grounds of simplicity, military viability, and less "discrimination" against the FRG. Blank expressed satisfaction that the FRG would now be able to engage in independent arms production.[90] Even Baudissin, who believed strongly in the European ideal, had come to wonder whether the EDC was compatible with the Germans' reformist aspirations.[91]

Finally, we should note that Adenauer, the European politician most devastated by the EDC's collapse, did not take long to recover his equilibrium. In the wake of the defeat he reread the EDC treaty and examined the French chamber debates. To Walter Hallstein, who had played an important role in negotiating the treaty, he now said: "What the people there in the French parliament said is perhaps not so stupid after all. I've now looked carefully at the treaty that you negotiated and find that it's not nearly so good as you always insisted."[92]

87 Peter Koch, *Konrad Adenauer* (Reinbek bei Hamburg, 1985), 285.
88 "SHAPE Prepares for Germans," *Foreign Report,* Nov. 8, 1954, pp. 6–7.
89 Report by the Joint Strategic Committee to the JCS on EDC Alternative Planning, June 24, 1954, NA, JCS File 092 (Germany).
90 Ausschuss für Fragen der europäischen Sicherheit (Bundestag), 20. Sitzung, Nov. 10, 1954, Parlamentsarchiv, Bonn.
91 See Baudissin's comments in Axel Eggebrecht, ed., *Die zornigen alten Männer: Gedanken über Deutschland seit 1945* (Reinbek bei Hamburg, 1975), 217–18.
92 Koch, *Adenauer,* 283–4.

No doubt this was true enough – the treaty did have its severe deficiencies, above all its presupposition that one could *begin* the European unity process at the military level. Armed forces, after all, were rather more important to national sovereignty than coal mines and steel mills. Certainly, the history of the EEC has shown how difficult economic integration has been; effective military integration would have been much harder. No doubt, too, the EDC treaty continued to contain anti-German features, despite the Germans' successful assault on the original scheme. Blank and his planners were correct in assuming that the NATO framework would provide more flexibility, more room for the Germans to operate according to their own lights.

Nevertheless, the failure of the EDC was a significant blow to the Adenauer government's efforts to secure widespread popular backing for its security policy. For many West Germans, European unity was the sugar coating on the bitter pill of rearmament. Following the EDC collapse, the Dienststelle Blank registered a dramatic decline in West German enthusiasm for this "necessary evil," and indeed for European engagement in general.[93] In terms of popular appeal, the Paris treaties, which established the framework for rearmament, were no substitute for the EDC.

Victor Hugo once observed: "There is nothing more powerful than an idea whose time has come." For the sake of the new Bundeswehr's image and appeal, it was perhaps unfortunate that the EDC was so far ahead of its time.

---

93 See correspondence between Baudissin and Ernst-Egon Schütz in BA/MA, BW9/4026.

19

The Federal Republic of Germany as a "Battlefield" in American Nuclear Strategy, 1953–1955

KLAUS A. MAIER

THE STRATEGIC CHANGE IN THE "NEW LOOK" OF THE EISENHOWER ADMINISTRATION AND WHAT IT MEANT FOR EUROPE

Following the principle that "we must not destroy what we are attempting to defend," President Dwight D. Eisenhower was unwilling to permit American society to be transformed into a "barracks state" through inflation or government intervention in the American economy resulting from unbridled defense expenditures.[1] At the same time, he by no means dissociated himself from the portrayal of communism as the enemy in National Security Council paper NSC 68. However, whereas NSC 68 considered Communist ideology to be merely a tool but not a determinant of Soviet policy, Eisenhower and Dulles obviously believed that the objective of Soviet policy was "to extend its system throughout the world and establish its 'one world' of state socialism."[2] This interpretation of Soviet foreign policy, which emphasized its ideological premises, allowed the new American administration to concentrate more on Soviet intentions than on Soviet capabilities.[3] Concentration on Soviet intentions in turn facilitated the Eisenhower administration's search for a longer-term containment strategy accompanied by a simultaneous reduction of costs. Under this premise, the U.S. government conducted, from May 1953 onward, large-scale evaluations as part of "Project Solar-

---

1 Memo, Special Assistant to the President for National Security Affairs (Cutler), July 16, 1953, Annex to Minutes of the 155th NSC Meeting, July 16, 1953, *FRUS 1952–1954,* vol. 2, *National Security Affairs* (Washington, D.C., 1984), 397–8.
2 Dulles on July 7, 1950, quoted from John Lewis Gaddis, *Strategies of Containment: A Critical Appraisal of Postwar American National Security Policy* (New York, 1980), 137.
3 Ibid., 145.

ium" in an attempt to arrive at a concrete reformulation of the American policy of containment toward the Soviet Union.[4]

NSC 162/2, which was approved by Eisenhower in October 1953, eventually embodied the strategy of containment under the rubric "New Look."[5] At the heart of the New Look strategy was the threat of massive retaliation with strategic nuclear weapons and the planned use of battlefield nuclear weapons as part of "conventional" warfare. The nuclear arsenal had, in fact, first been included in strategic planning under Truman, but it was not until Eisenhower's presidency that its use was explicitly advocated. NSC 162/2 stated that in the event of a war with the Soviet Union or China the United States would consider nuclear weapons "to be as available for use as other munitions."

The major region for application of the policy of nuclear deterrence with massive retaliation and tactical nuclear weapons was Western Europe which, according to the findings of NSC 162/2, could not for the foreseeable future be defended by conventional means alone against a serious aggression from the East – even after the activation of West German contingents as part of the European Defense Community (EDC) – without placing an unbearable burden on the economies of the states of Western Europe. NSC 162/2 stated: "The major deterrent to aggression against Western Europe is the manifest determination of the United States to use its atomic capability and massive retaliatory striking power if the area is attacked." The directive thus emphasized the employment of the Strategic Air Command (SAC). The presence of American ground forces in Western Europe, on the other hand, was intended more to contribute "to the strength and cohesion of the free world coalition." Indeed, after nuclear weapons, reliance upon the alliance was the second most important leg of the new U.S. strategy. According to NSC 162/2, the United States was unable "to meet its defense needs, even at exorbitant cost, without the support of allies." However, to prevent the Europeans from adopting the New Look principle of "more bang for the buck" and slackening in their conventional rearmament efforts, the Americans argued to their allies that battlefield nuclear

---

4 *The History of the Joint Chiefs of Staff*, vol. 5, Robert J. Watson, *The Joint Chiefs of Staff and National Policy 1953–1954* (Wilmington, Del., 1986), 11–14. Memo for the Record, Special Assistant to the President for National Security Affairs (Cutler), Subject: Solarium Project, May 9, 1953, and Paper Prepared by the Directing Panel of Project Solarium, June 1, 1953, *FRUS 1952–1954*, 2:323–6 and 360–6.
5 See *FRUS 1952–1954*, 2:577–97; *History of the Joint Chiefs of Staff*, 5:21–6.

weapons doctrine had by no means rendered superfluous the conventional rearmament programs within the framework of NATO and the EDC, in particular the involvement of the Federal Republic of Germany. The employment of these weapons, the Americans argued, would only make sense if the aggressor were forced by sufficient conventional defensive forces to concentrate his troops, thus permitting the defender to identify in good time the intended points of main effort, which would be worthwhile targets for nuclear weapons.[6]

The New Look strategy assumed concrete forms during discussions surrounding American force planning for fiscal year 1955. When the Pentagon presented to the National Security Council a 1955 defense budget amounting to $43 billion on October 13, 1953 – which, although lower than the revised 1954 budget, was still $3 billion over the target – it attracted criticism from those members of the NSC who had hoped for a sizable reduction for 1955. The chairman of the Joint Chiefs of Staff, Admiral Radford, countered this criticism by arguing that, as things stood, he could not propose any lower force strengths. He considered a reduction possible only if the NSC were to authorize unequivocally the Joint Chiefs of Staff to assume in their plans that nuclear weapons would be used immediately at the outbreak of war.[7] As a result, Secretary of Defense Wilson requested the Joint Chiefs of Staff to submit a plan for a U.S. military strategy along the lines of NSC 162. In this context, Wilson once again recalled the essential principles of that document and, presumably with regard to Radford's demands, made the following remarks: "We have entered an era where the quantity of atomic weapons and their military application necessitates a review of their impact on our strategy. We shall assume that such weapons will be used in military operations by U.S. forces engaged whenever it is of military advantage to do so."[8] On November 30, 1953, an ad hoc committee chaired by Lieutenant General Frank F. Everest, U.S. Air

6 General Bradley on January 28, 1953: "We need enough to make them concentrated. We don't have enough atomic weapons to plaster all of Europe. Twelve German divisions would put a completely different picture on the situation. It would force them to a considerable build-up before they could attack. German participation would make it certain that we were given warning." Memo of Discussion, State-Mutual Security Agency-Joint Chiefs of Staff Meeting, Held at the Pentagon Building, Jan. 28, 1953, *FRUS 1952-1954*, vol. 5, *Western European Security* (Washington, D.C., 1983), 711–17, quote p. 714.
7 Memo of Discussion, 166th NSC Meeting, Oct. 13, 1953, *FRUS 1952-1954*, 2:534–49.
8 Memo, Secretary of Defense, to Chairman, JCS, Oct. 16, 1953, quoted from *History of the Joint Chiefs of Staff*, 5:27.

Force, submitted a plan as requested. After extensive discussions, this plan was accepted by the Joint Chiefs of Staff and, on December 16, 1953, approved by the NSC and the president together with a revised military budget for fiscal year 1955.

The plan of the Joint Chiefs of Staff envisaged, for fiscal year 1957, a total strength of U.S. forces of 2,815,000 men, which constituted a reduction of almost 600,000 men compared with the total strength in late 1933. The brunt of the reductions was to be borne by the U.S. Army, which was to lose almost one-third of its total strength, while the U.S. Navy and the Marine Corps would be cut 15 percent and 20 percent respectively. In contrast, the strength of the U.S. Air Force was to increase by 60,000 men. As prerequisites for these new force strengths for fiscal year 1957, the Joint Chiefs of Staff named the following conditions:

1. changes in the present U.S. deployment in some forward areas;
2. emphasis upon the capability of inflicting massive damage upon the USSR by retaliatory striking power as the major deterrent to aggression, and a vital element of any U.S. strategy in the event of general war;
3. an integrated and adequate continental defense system;
4. the provision of tactical atomic support for U.S. or allied military forces in general war or in a local aggression, whenever the employment of atomic weapons would be militarily advantageous;
5. the constitution, generally on U.S. territory, of a strategic reserve with a high degree of combat readiness to move rapidly to any threatened area;
6. maintenance of control over essential sea and air lines of communication;
7. maintenance of a mobilization base adequate to meet the requirements of a general war;
8. maintenance of qualitative superiority of armed forces.

The Joint Chiefs of Staff assumed that even after 1957 it would still be necessary to station U.S. ground forces in Western Europe. A maximum of seven army divisions were to be deployed outside the United States in times of peace, although the Joint Chiefs of Staff did not specify how many of them were to be stationed in Western Europe. Secretary of Defense Wilson called for "reasonably attainable action . . . in the politico-military field," in his October 16 order to the Joint Chiefs of Staff, thus supporting the proposals of the Everest

Committee "that foreign aid be allocated so as to shape allied military forces in the desired direction, that force requirements be constantly reviewed in the light of nuclear capabilities, and that the establishment of German and Japanese forces be encouraged." Any withdrawal of U.S. forces from Western Europe was to be preceded by a "program of education" with which the Allies would have to be convinced of the advantages of the new strategy.[9]

Dulles had this "program of education" proposed by the Joint Chiefs of Staff for the European allies in mind in the NSC meeting on December 10, when he warned against any American agencies raising the issue of withdrawal from Europe of sizable elements of the American formations stationed there before the State Department had prepared the European allies for this through diplomatic channels. Eisenhower too stressed "that our one great objective at the moment was to secure the ratification of EDC. Accordingly, it seemed crystal-clear to the President that we could not afford to take any steps toward redeployment, or even to talk about redeployment, until these objectives have been reached. The French have an almost hysterical fear that we and the British will one day pull out of Western Europe and leave them to face a superior German armed force."[10]

Accordingly, Dulles avoided all reference to a possible reduction of the American formations in Europe at the NATO ministerial meeting in Paris in December 1953. However, his detailed remarks on the new capabilities of nuclear arms, plus his reference to the necessity of establishing a costly "Continental Defense" to protect the United States against Soviet nuclear attack, obviously had the purpose of preparing the allies for this very eventuality.[11] Confirming the results of the Western summit meeting in Bermuda, December 4–8, 1953, the NATO Council accepted the "long haul" policy, that is, the shift from previous NATO strategy which followed the premises of NSC 68 to a strategy to counter a longer-lasting, but no longer as acute, threat.[12] At the same time, the council agreed that

9 Ibid., 31; cf. 67–9.
10 Memo of Discussion, 174th NSC Meeting, Dec. 10, 1953, *FRUS 1952–1954*, 5:449–54.
11 Notes, Assistant SecState for European Affairs (Merchant) on Restricted Session of North Atlantic Council, Dec. 16, 1953, *FRUS 1952–1954*, 5:476–9. Record of the restricted meeting of Ministers of the NATO Council, Dec. 1, 1953, PRO, PREM 11/369.
12 For the Bermuda Conference of the Heads of Government of the U.S., U.K., and France, Dec. 4–8, 1953, see *FRUS 1952–1954*, 5:1710–1848; PRO, PREM 11/619 and 11/369; Evelyn Shuckburgh, *Descent to Suez: Diaries 1951–56* (London, 1986), 110–17; J. W. Young, "Churchill, the Russians and the Western Alliance: The Three-Power Conference at Bermuda, December 1953," *English Historical Review* 101 (Oct. 1986):889–912.

the alliance's force planning should be reviewed, taking into account the new nuclear arsenal that would be available in 1957.[13] As this new strategy took shape, however, the Europeans became increasingly aware that, together with the alleged advantage of economical force planning, it also had certain drawbacks. The West Europeans' fears revolved not only around the possibility that American units might be withdrawn from Europe, but also around the question to use battlefield nuclear weapons, which in the event of war would in all probability turn Europe into an atomic battleground. In early 1954, the French and Italian delegations in the NATO Military Committee had pointed out that if the American NATO units were to be extensively armed with nuclear weapons while at the same time the conventional component of NATO forces was reduced, the latter would be too weak to repel an aggressor effectively. If this were the case, in the event of war the European members of NATO would depend solely on the United States, which would reserve the right to decide whether and when it resorted to nuclear weapons.

On May 27, the Joint Strategic Survey Committee demanded a comprehensive agreement granting all the rights necessary for the conduct of American operations "by the single decision by which each NATO government commits its armed forces to action." NATO commanders would receive preliminary authorization to take all measures envisaged in an approved NATO defense plan without having to seek permission from a higher authority. Secretary of Defense Wilson sanctioned these deliberations on June 11 but waited for the findings of the three studies commissioned by the NATO Council in December 1953, one from each of the three NATO commands: Europe, Atlantic, and Channel. These studies were published in July 1954 and formed the basis for corresponding planning activity in the NATO Standing Group, which in turn was to submit its report to the Military Representatives Committee on October 1 and to the Military Committee at the end of November. In a draft presented to the Joint Chiefs of Staff on August 13, 1954, the Standing Group assumed that the outcome of a future war would probably be decided in the first few days by an intensive exchange of nuclear blows. Thus, instead of planning for a maximum reinforcement following the outbreak of hostilities, NATO should

13 PRO, PREM 11/369, Report by the Chief of the Imperial General Staff on the NATO Meetings in Paris, Dec. 7–16, 1953, Chiefs of Staff Committee, Confidential Annex to COS (53) 144th Meeting held on Tuesday, Dec. 22, 1953.

concentrate on maintaining combat-ready formations equipped with nuclear weapons. To a very large extent, the Standing Group had followed the consideration in the Joint Chiefs of Staff Memorandum of July 11, 1954, which Wilson passed on to the State Department on August 16 with the remark that it would require considerable psychological preparation to get the NATO Allies to consent to the kind of agreements desired by the Joint Chiefs of Staff. In the course of this preparation, the State Department should use the studies of the NATO commands, which indicated "the absolute necessity for 'normalized' use of atomic weapons in the defense of Western Europe."[14] After Churchill, in reply to a question in Parliament on March 23, had publicly confirmed the rights granted to the United States two months earlier to station aircraft for strategic missions at bases in Great Britain, it was only understandable that the French government also strove to get French agencies likewise involved in the nuclear-strategic discussion. On March 30, Bidault suggested to the State Department through a representative that he, Foreign Secretary Eden, and Secretary of State Dulles discuss privately the employment of nuclear weapons in Europe in general and from French bases in North Africa and metropolitan France in particular.[15]

In the French armed forces, the nuclear-strategic reorientation leading away from supranational European military integration within the framework of the EDC was already well underway. In a draft of January 1954, a special staff chaired by Marshal Juin, NATO Commander-in-Chief Central Europe since June 1951, had reduced the EDC to "an organization existing purely for suggestion, coordination and control, without political integration and supranationality, with strict political and military dependence on NATO, with a council of ministers, a permanent international staff, national delegates for the establishment and administration of the national contingents."[16] When Marshal Juin publicly declared himself opposed to the EDC on April 19, the French government relieved him of his national command. On June 30, however, the French Army General Staff also proposed a new "European defense organization"

---

14 *History of the Joint Chiefs of Staff*, 5:304–6.
15 Memo of Conversation, Special Assistant to the Counselor of the State Dept. (Galloway), March 30, 1954, *FRUS 1952–1954*, 5:486–7.
16 Pierre Guillen, "Die französische Generalität, die Aufrüstung der Bundesrepublik und die EVG (1950–1954)," in Hans-Erich Volkmann and Walter Schwengler, eds., *Die Europäische Verteidigungsgemeinschaft: Stand und Probleme der Forschung* (Boppard, 1985), 125–57, quote p. 155.

by modifying and enlarging the Brussels Treaty. The Federal Republic of Germany would join NATO but would not become a member
of the Standing Group. As a letter dated September 11, 1954, from
the French Army General Staff to the Quai d'Orsay shows, the ultimate aim of these deliberations was a European group, including
Great Britain, within NATO. In order not to be totally dependent
on the United States, this European group would have to possess nuclear weapons. France would thus have to become a nuclear power,
but under no circumstances the Federal Republic of Germany. Since
France, however, could not alone bear both the burden of nuclear
weapons and that of maintaining conventional forces equal to those
of the Federal Republic of Germany, the French Army General Staff
recommended "the creation of an integrated European nuclear force
(with British participation if possible) within the framework of an
Atlantic nuclear pool, with the European nations providing raw materials, technicians, and funds, thereby helping to ensure that this nuclear force is established collectively in relatively secure regions
(Southern France, North Africa)."[17]

Why should France forsake nuclear weapons, which would enable
her to have her own "New Look," would give her voice in NATO
and, especially when discussing nuclear-strategic planning in the
Standing Group, a weight at least comparable to that of the British.
In addition, a French nuclear force would guarantee a balance – unattainable by means of conventional armament – with the German
defense contribution. On the basis of the few sources accessible
to date, it cannot yet be said with any certainty how far Mendès-
France personally favored a separate nuclear force, or whether he
merely yielded to pressure from the military or the Commissariat à
l'Energie atomique (CEA). What is certain, is that Mendès-France
had had in his possession since August 25, 1954, a report in which
Boegner (directeur du cabinet du ministre) examined the situation
of France within NATO and proposed the creation of a national
French nuclear force. By signing a decree on the establishment of the
"Commission supérieure des applications militaires" on October 22,
Mendès-France took the initial concrete steps toward such a force.[18]

---

17 Quoted ibid., 156–7.
18 Aline Coutrot, "La politique atomique sous le gouvernement de Mendès-France," in François Bédarida and Jean-Pierre Rioux, eds., *Pierre Mendès-France et la Mendésisme* (Paris,
1985), 310–14. Georges-Henri Soutou, "Die Nuklearpolitik der Vierten Republik," *VfZG*
37 (1989):605–10.

On December 17, 1954, the NATO Council approved the report of the Military Committee on "The most effective pattern of NATO military strength for the next few years (MC 48)" without, however, delegating the national governmental responsibility "for putting plans into action in the event of hostilities" to the NATO commands.[19] This report, which was based on assumptions for 1957, formed the new foundation for NATO's defense planning particularly with regard to nuclear weapons. MC 48 provided for NATO to reply to any aggression from the East with a massive retaliatory strike using strategic and tactical nuclear weapons. Proceeding on the logical assumption that the first aim of a serious Soviet aggressor would be in all probability to attempt to knock out NATO's nuclear weapons with its own, NATO anticipated an initial nuclear phase of the war lasting thirty days, during which it imagined itself to be at an advantage thanks to the superior American delivery systems. After a necessary reorganization of its forces, NATO would attempt in a second phase to end the war by means of conventional and nuclear operations. For this strategy, American NATO units had 125 nuclear warheads at their disposal by October 1955. Through the massive use of nuclear weapons and about thirty Western divisions, NATO believed that it would be able to fight a successful defensive battle against eighty-two Soviet divisions in the central European region. The planned forward line of defense ran along the rivers Weser, Fulda, Main, and Ludwig Canal. Forward of this line lay zones containing targets for NATO's own conduct of nuclear operations (troop concentrations and fixed installations). However, it was not planned to conduct the actual main defense before the Rhine and Ijssel rivers.[20]

WHAT THE NEW LOOK MEANT FOR THE SECURITY OF THE
FEDERAL REPUBLIC OF GERMANY

When the foreign ministers of the three Western occupying powers, meeting in New York, agreed on September 19, 1950, upon a secu-

---

19 *History of the Joint Chiefs of Staff,* 5:316–20.
20 Christian Greiner, "General Adolf Heusinger (1897–1982): Operatives Denken und Planen 1948 bis 1956," in *Operatives Denken und Handeln in deutschen Streitkräften im 19. und 20. Jahrhundert,* ed. Militärgeschichtliches Forschungsamt (Herford and Bonn, 1988), 225–61, esp. 235. Christian Greiner, "Das militärstrategische Konzept der NATO von 1952 bis 1957," in Bruno Thoss and Hans-Erich Volkmann, eds., *Zwischen Kaltem Krieg und Entspannung: Sicherheits- und Deutschlandpolitik der Bundesrepublik im Mächtesystem der Jahre 1953–1956* (Boppard, 1988), 211–45, esp. 227.

rity declaration which stated that the Western powers would regard an attack against the Federal Republic of Germany or Berlin as an attack against themselves,[21] this represented an improvement on the previous situation – in which the occupying forces but not the occupied territory enjoyed the protection of the NATO guarantees. The Federal Republic and West Berlin were henceforth included in the territory to be defended by the West. As long as there were no adequate forces in Western Europe, however, including a West German defense contribution, it would have been impossible to keep this security promise in the event of war. At the time of the New York security declaration, the commanders in chief of the Brussels Treaty forces were governed by the directive "to hold the enemy in Europe as far to the East as possible." The Western European Union Short Term Plan changed this directive, which had been expressed in general terms, to "carrying out a planned withdrawal to the line of the Rhine/Ijssel rivers and holding the enemy there." Somewhat more favorable assumptions formed the basis of the revised Medium Term Plan, which stated that the line of defense should be "as far to the East as possible (i.e., up against the Soviet Zone)."[22]

The New York security declaration was no contractually binding guarantee of security between the Federal Republic of Germany and the Western powers. It was merely a declaration of intent, unilaterally revocable by the Western powers at any time, the prime purpose of which, regardless of its internally admitted military nonredeemability, was for the time being the necessary psychological preparation for the West German defense contribution.

Without underestimating the autonomous European accent of the foreign policy of the first German federal chancellor, Konrad Adenauer, it can be said that his policy of integrating the Federal Republic of Germany into the West (putting the reunification of Germany last, at least for the time being), replacing the Occupation Statute, and rearming the Federal Republic within an international framework served the very purpose of obtaining the most realisti-

---

21 Decision of the Foreign Ministers of the U.S., UK, and France with Regard to Germany, Doc. 37 (Final), Sept. 19, 1950, *FRUS 1950*, vol. 3, *Western Europe* (Washington, D.C., 1977), 1286–99. See also NATO Council Doc. C5-D/11 (Final), Resolution on the Defense of Western Europe, Sept. 26, 1950, SecState to Acting SecState, Sept. 26, 1950, ibid., 350–2, esp. 351.

22 PRO, CAB 134/37, AOC (Atlantic Official Committee) (50)43, Agenda for the North Atlantic Council Session, Sept. 15 and 16, 1950. Note by the Joint Secretaries. Appendix "F": North Atlantic Council Agenda, Item 4: Certain strategic considerations affecting the defence of Western Europe.

cally possible guarantees for a defense of the Federal Republic along its eastern borders.

It was difficult for the responsible agencies within Germany to get a picture of the new strategy and its impact on the security of the Federal Republic. Apart from occasional contacts between former German Wehrmacht officers in the Amt Blank and from the German delegation at the EDC Interim Committee in Paris and individual figures from NATO, the Germans were not officially informed about the new strategy – not that they, disarmed and not a member of NATO, could have had even the slightest influence on the formulation of strategy.

The aspect of the new strategy that appeared to be the most positive for the security of the Federal Republic was the enhanced deterrent effect. Thus, on June 15, 1953, the chancellor of the Federal Republic, addressing the outgoing NATO Supreme Commander, General Ridgway, welcomed the stationing of American 250 millimeter guns in Europe, remarking that Europe lived safely under the shield of American nuclear weapons and that this security could be enhanced even further if a part of this shield itself were stationed in Europe.[23] On November 18, 1953, however, the chancellor conveyed to the State Department this "grave concern" that the United States would withdraw the majority of its troops from Europe as part of the modernization of its armed forces with nuclear weapons. He had great misgivings about the impact that this measure would have on the Soviets and the members of NATO.[24]

Nobody could be more interested in deterrence than the front-line state, the Federal Republic of Germany. On the other hand, however, the question also arose, more often in the Federal Republic than elsewhere, as to what would happen if deterrence failed.

What tasks did the still to be activated twelve German divisions have under the new defense strategy? In the official German comment on the New Look strategy in 1954, there is a conspicuous tendency to make light of nuclear warfare, which cannot be explained simply by a lack of information and knowledge of the facts. Rather,

23 Aufzeichnung über eine Besprechung des Bundeskanzlers mit General Ridgway, June 15, 1953, BA/MA, BW 9/2295. SecState to the Office of HICOG, July 17, 1953, *FRUS 1952–1954*, vol. 7, *Germany and Austria* (Washington, D.C., 1986), 486–7. On July 20, because of the forthcoming West German elections, the chancellor vetoed any announcement of the deployment of U.S. atomic artillery in the Federal Republic; see NA, RG 59, 5/7-2053.
24 Memo of Conversation, Acting Director of the Office of German Affairs (Lewis), Nov. 18, 1953, *FRUS 1952–1954*, 7:555–8.

it is an expression of the desire to save the "conventional" raison d'etre of the West German forces to be activated.

At the West German Foreign Ministry, officials asked themselves, after considering "the entire New Look complex," "whether the 'Dulles Doctrine,' which had been proclaimed with considerable publicity, really represented a revolutionization of warfare, or whether it was not, at least in part, designed to bring about a certain propagandistic affect." Referring to the opinion of military experts, the Foreign Ministry believed it "could describe the New Look strategy as the result of a natural process of evolution, starting with the invention of the atomic bomb and now culminating in the conception of certain empirical principles." Nor did the ministry think that Eisenhower's definition of New Look as an attempt by intelligent people to keep up with the times allowed any other conclusion.[25]

Heusinger also warned against journalistic exaggeration that could lead to "pernicious and wrong conclusions being drawn in support of a neglect of conventional arms." By means of a "superior art of command and control," Heusinger intended to master "the added difficulties of ground warfare caused by the existence of nuclear weapons."[26]

Closely connected with the conventional rationalization of the West German defense contribution through "superior art of command and control" was the problem of the defense of the territory of the Federal Republic of Germany. In the "Himmerod Memorandum" of October 9, 1950, a committee of military experts convened by the federal chancellor had demanded, as the fundamental expression of equal military rights for the Federal Republic, that Germany must "not be considered, on land, to be a *glacis* of a main defense intended to be conducted on, say, the Rhine."[27] For this very reason, the Amt Blank rejected the proposal made by Colonel von Bonin (ret.) for a rigid line of defense along the demarcation line between East and West Germany. Bonin's proposal appeared "highly dangerous" to Heusinger, for political reasons more than anything else:

25 Auswärtiges Amt to Bundeskanzleramt, Dienststelle Blank, "Betr.: Die neue amerikanische Verteidigungskonzeption (New Look)," Apr. 2, 1954, Depositum Graf Kielmansegg, BA/MA.
26 "Vortrag Heusingers vor dem EVG-Ausschuss des Deutschen Bundestages," July 12, 1954, BA/MA, BW 9/982.
27 Hans-Jürgen Rautenberg and Norbert Wiggershaus, "Die 'Himmeroder Denkschrift' vom Oktober 1950: Politische und militärische Ueberlegungen für einen Beitrag der Bundesrepublik Deutschland zur westeuropäischen Verteidigung," MGM 21 (1977):135–206, esp. 169.

"Such a defense, with formations organized merely for antitank defense, would conform exactly to the idea expressed by the French in particular. They would welcome the creation of a so-called *armée de couverture* in Germany with the task of delaying the advancing Soviet formations until the main body, consisting of French and other forces in rearward positions, had established a defensive front further to the rear. Germany would thus evidently have to be considered a *glacis* in the event of a war." According to Heusinger, the problem of defending West Germany could only be solved by close interaction between mobile defensive forces, whose combat mission was to delay and stall the enemy, and strong offensive forces held ready to mount a counterattack.[28]

In his opposition to ideas of a German protective shield "behind which the others can hide," Heusinger received public support from NATO. Although NATO had made arrangements in its defense plan for a main line of defense on the Rhine and Ijssel rivers, its Supreme Commander (since May 1953), General Gruenther, spoke of the possibility of "forward defense" as soon as the NATO forces had been reinforced by the West German divisions. However, Gruenther made it clear that the tactical nuclear weapons, "as the backbone of western defense," were just as indispensable to "forward defense" as the German defense contribution.[29]

While Heusinger, with his art of command and control and high degree of operational mobility, obviously still wanted not just to ensure the defense of the territory of the Federal Republic of Germany but also to bypass the problems of nuclear war itself, it was clear to Gruenther and NATO that if deterrence failed NATO would definitely have to fight a future war with nuclear weapons, with or without German divisions. Since Soviet nuclear countermeasures, or even a nuclear preventive strike against NATO's nuclear potential, were likely, a purely conventional concept of operations had become obsolete, both in general terms and for the German forces at the forward edge of the battle area in particular. In June 1955 at the latest, when the NATO maneuver "Carte Blanche" took place with the two NATO tactical air forces stationed in central Europe, this dilemma became clear not only to military experts but also to the public at large. Nevertheless, attempts were still made in the Federal

28 "Stellungnahme Heusingers zur Studie 'von Bonin,'" Aug. 20, 1954, BA/MA, BW 9/2403.
29 *Bulletin des Presse- und Informationsamtes der Bundesregierung*, no. 28 (Feb. 10, 1955):22.

Republic of Germany to justify the activation of German forces with conventional operational categories. According to Heusinger, the maneuvers had admittedly "shown just how hideous and terrible a future war would be, and should cause all people to do everything within their power to prevent such a war."[30] However, when informing the federal cabinet on July 11, 1955, he remained true to his conventional escapism. He now assigned conventional forces the task of achieving air supremacy as quickly as possible in order to protect their own potential. The army formations were to assume responsibility for protecting air force infrastructure and prevent the Federal Republic of Germany being invaded and overrun by Soviet armored formations.[31]

On the other hand, Franz Josef Strauss, at that time federal minister for special tasks, had no doubt that ground forces had lost their original classic function. Therefore, he argued, the West German contingent must not be a "shadow contribution" that could no longer hold its own in the face of technological reality. In view of the "apocalyptic specter of self-destruction," Strauss considered the sole purpose of German forces to be to complement and reinforce the NATO formations and thus contribute to deterrence.[32]

Since the New Look, the government of the Federal Republic of Germany had been in the dilemma of having to justify the establishment of purely conventional forces at a time when the nation's territory had become a nuclear battlefield according to NATO defense plans. At the same time, the prospects of being able to influence the modification of NATO strategy in the Alliance following the activation of twelve German divisions were dwindling because the importance of the West German defense contribution had fallen to second place below nuclear weapons, since the primarily conventional objectives of rearmament had been replaced by the New Look.

It is true that in early 1955, the U.S. army's criticism of a purely nuclear strategy, which had been expressed from the outset, and the increasing realization that the credibility of the threat of massive retaliation was diminished as a result of its self-deterrent effect, led to a partial restitution of conventional defense planning. However, the

30 Ibid., no. 120 (July 2, 1955):1002.
31 BA/MA, BW 9/2527-11. Greiner, "Heusinger," 244–5. See also the statement of Defense Minister Blank before the Bundestag, *Bulletin des Presse- und Informationsamtes,* no. 131 (July 19, 1955):1112–13.
32 Strauss in the 100th session of the Deutscher Bundestag, July 16, 1955, *Bulletin des Presse- und Informationsamtes,* no. 132 (July 20, 1955):1117.

nuclear component remained at the center of operational calculations. NSC 5501, approved by the American president on January 7, 1955, stated:

The ability to apply force selectively and flexibly will become increasingly important in maintaining the morale and will of the free world to resist aggression. As the fear of nuclear war grows, the United States and its allies must never allow themselves to get into the position where they must choose between (a) not responding to local aggression and (b) applying force in a way which our own people or our allies would consider entails undue risk of nuclear devastation. However, the United States cannot afford to preclude itself from using nuclear weapons even in a local situation, if such use will bring the aggression to a swift and positive cessation, and if, on a balance of political and military consideration, such use will best advantage U.S. security interests. In the last analysis, if confronted by the choice of (a) acquiescing in Communist aggression or (b) taking measures risking either general war or loss of allied support, the United States must be prepared to take these risks if necessary for its security.[33]

However, even as a member of NATO, Germany received very little information about the "nuclear plan" of American NATO units. During the NATO maneuver "Black Lion" in 1957, German agencies at least learned that a total of 108 tactical nuclear weapons had been released for use in the combat area of the two commands of Central Army Group (CENTAG) and Northern Army Group (NORTHAG). On the basis of the destruction assumed in the exercise, German military observers assumed that at least 100 enemy strategic nuclear weapons had been employed, with at least 20 directed at targets in the Federal Republic of Germany, "since around 30 Rhine bridges and at least 10 large cities have been *permanently* destroyed." Because the enemy's stocks of nuclear weapons were considered to be for the most part exhausted after the strategic strikes, only 25 enemy tactical nuclear weapon strikes were "ascertained" during the maneuver, fifteen of them on the territory of the Federal Republic of Germany.[34]

33 Quoted from *History of the Joint Chiefs of Staff*, 5:54, see also 321.
34 Draft, "Einsatz von Atomkörpern im Rahmen der Uebung 'Lion Noir,' " Apr. 11, 1957, BA/Zentralarchiv, BW 2/14245, BMVg IV A2, Tgb. Nr. 48/57.

20

The Presence of American Troops in Germany and German-American Relations, 1949–1956

BRUNO THOSS

When the new Eisenhower administration undertook a comprehensive review of American defense policy in the spring of 1953, Security Adviser Cutler asked the president whether the five U.S. divisions in Europe were not merely a psychological crutch for the Western Europeans' will to assert themselves. However, Eisenhower – who as SACEUR (Supreme Allied Commander, Europe) had himself actively joined in the debate on a reinforcement of the United States' direct military commitment in the Old World in 1950–51 following the shock of the Korean War – vehemently disagreed with this suggestion: "He said that he would have sent more American divisions, not fewer, if the United States had had more available, and he stressed that they were a real physical deterrent to the Soviets and not merely a psychological one."[1] Three years later, however, in the summer of 1956, it was to be his very administration that triggered the most serious German–American crisis of confidence so far with its public reflections on an extensive reduction in the number of troops (the Radford Plan). But this turnabout was by no means as surprising as the alarms in Bonn might have suggested. Despite Chancellor Adenauer's fears that it was a harbinger of a "withdrawal to 'Fortress America',"[2] it did not represent a revolutionary turning point in the European policy of the United States. In fact the Truman and Eisenhower administrations had not committed themselves to a permanent stationing of ground forces in Europe. Moreover, the conventional commitment of the United States as a whole was not an issue in summer 1956 despite the plans to slim the U.S. presence.

---

1 *FRUS 1952–1954*, vol. 2, *National Security Affairs* (Washington, D.C., 1984), 273.
2 Cf. Konrad Adenauer, *Erinnerungen 1955–1959* (Stuttgart, 1967), 204.

Adenauer's nervous reaction to the Radford Plan revealed once
again just how sensitive a yardstick of American interest in Europe
the issue of the presence of American troops was for him. Together
with the majority of Western European politicians, Adenauer concluded from his awareness of Europe's loss of power in two world
wars that it was central to Western European security to couple it to
the transatlantic potential of the superpower United States. For the
Federal Republic of Germany, the Western powers had agreed at
Potsdam to demilitarize Germany, thereby assuming responsibility
for protecting their zones of occupation. In the subsequent West German rearmament discussions of the early 1950s, the Allies had,
moreover, never left any doubt that German contingents were acceptable to them only on a limited scale and in a controlled form,
which meant that they would continue to be jointly responsible for
the security of the Federal Republic, even in the event of West German accession to the Alliance.

During the phase in which he formulated his ideas on security policy, as early as 1948–49, Adenauer came to agree with former Lieutenant General Speidel that the Western powers had to fulfill their
obligation to protect the Federal Republic by giving a security guarantee for the territory of West Germany and by stationing forces adequate for its defense.[3] The fact that his reliance from the outset fell
mainly on the personnel and material capabilities of the United States
was simply a consequence of the precarious economic and military
situation of the two other occupying powers, Great Britain and
France, with their unsolved recovery and colonial problems.

Such considerations assumed additional urgency with the outbreak
of the Korean War in the summer of 1950. West German perceptions
of threat resulting from the Federal Republic's location immediately
on the border with the Communist sphere of influence now corresponded to a stronger geostrategic feeling of affinity on the part of
the United States toward Western Europe, which it had identified as
the real target area of Soviet global strategy.[4] Adenauer therefore intensified his twin demand for an allied security guarantee for the
Federal Republic of Germany and an effective increase in the number

3 Cf. Norbert Wiggershaus, "Zur Frage der Planung für die verdeckte Aufstellung westdeutscher Verteidigungskräfte in Konrad Adenauers sicherheitspolitischer Konzeption 1950," in
  Heinz-Ludger Borgert, Walter Stürm, and Norbert Wiggershaus, *Dienstgruppen und westdeutscher Verteidigungsbeitrag* (Boppard, 1982), 19, 21–2.
4 Cf. John Lewis Gaddis, *Strategies of Containment: A Critical Appraisal of Postwar American National Security Policy* (New York, 1980), 114–15.

of occupying troops. Realizing that the Western powers alone could not be expected to move NATO's line of defense forward to the eastern border of the Federal Republic – a move that was imperative as far as West German security interests were concerned – he concretized his previous hints concerning a possible West German contribution to the Alliance.[5] Conversely, as early as September 1950, President Truman, acting on a suggestion by the Joint Chiefs of Staff, approved an increase in the number of U.S. ground troops in Western Europe from one to five divisions, most of which were to be stationed in West Germany by the spring of 1951.[6]

There was, however, considerable domestic opposition to the idea of tying the United States to Europe to such an extent in peacetime and to increasing the defense budget radically. In a policy dispute lasting several months (the "great debate"),[7] the opposition Republicans strongly warned of the economic and social costs of such a mobilization of U.S. potential in peacetime. Rather than contain the Sino-Soviet bloc at every conceivable point and thereby overstretch one's own forces, they advocated strategic concentration. The United States should keep the bulk of its mobile forces together on the American continent as a strategic reserve of the West and fulfill its Alliance commitments by means of its modern navy and air force together with its nuclear weapons, which were deemed more economical. Referring to Western Europe, this "Gibraltar of western civilization," former U.S. President Hoover put this criticism in a nutshell: Instead of making the continental battlefields the "cemetery of millions of U.S. boys," the United States should rely on its deterrent potential.[8]

In contrast, Secretary of State Dean Acheson, supported by the Supreme NATO Commander in Europe, General Eisenhower, argued that the lessons of the Korean War showed that strategic bomb-

---

5 For the security memorandum of August 8, 1950, see Klaus von Schubert, ed., *Sicherheitspolitik der Bundesrepublik Deutschland: Dokumentation 1945–1977*, 2 vols. (Cologne, 1978), 1:79–81; for an assessment of this memorandum, see Wiggershaus, "Frage der Planung," 51–74.

6 See Christian Greiner, "Die alliierten militärstrategischen Planungen zur Verteidigung Westeuropas 1947–1950," in *Anfänge westdeutscher Sicherheitspolitik 1945–1956*, ed. Militärgeschichtliches Forschungsamt, vol. 1, *Von der Kapitulation bis zum Pleven-Plan* (Munich and Vienna, 1982), 296; see also William P. Mako, *U.S. Ground Forces and the Defense of Central Europe* (Washington, D.C., 1983), 11.

7 Cf. *The History of the Joint Chiefs of Staff*, vol. 4, Walter S. Poole, *The Joint Chiefs of Staff and National Policy 1950–1952* (Wilmington, Del., 1980), 221–4; Gaddis, *Strategies of Containment*, 119–20.

8 Quoted from Gaddis, *Strategies of Containment*, 119.

ing alone would not prevent the United States' allies from being overrun by the Red Army in Europe. Therefore, if the United States wanted to counteract the growing defeatism among the Western Europeans and to activate their military powers of self-help, it would have to decide to mount an effective supporting action, military, political, and psychological, at least temporarily. At the same time, proponents of an increased U.S. commitment in Europe objected to a one-sided overemphasis on the nuclear component. Because the Soviet Union had successfully tested a nuclear weapon in August 1949, the time was now foreseeable when the deterrent potentials of the two sides would reciprocally neutralize each other and imbalances in conventional forces would assume decisive significance. To be ready for this event, the United States thus had to begin immediately to develop a more balanced force structure with an adequate conventional component.[9] In the end, Congress accepted this course in April 1951, thereby paving the way for the stationing of the four additional U.S. divisions in West Germany.[10]

With the conclusion of the great debate, the political and strategic foundations had been laid for the medium-term stationing of an adequate U.S. contingent on West German soil. Until the West German contribution to the Alliance began to take effect in the early 1960s, these U.S. forces formed, from a strategic point of view, the real backbone of conventional defense in Central Europe. Their presence directly linked the United States with NATO's Alliance planning, and these ties were additionally reinforced by Eisenhower's appointment as the first SACEUR. In terms of military policy, the U.S. force also acted intially as an impetus and later as a military shield for a reactivation of Western European self-aid, which was NATO's common rearmament goal formulated in Lisbon (1952). As far as control was concerned, the U.S. troops furthermore helped to allay the fears of Germany's former wartime enemies in Western Europe that the Federal Republic would regain preponderance after rearmament, which was first considered in September 1950. Finally, on the psychological level, the U.S. presence endowed its commitment in Europe, and in particular in West Germany, with permanence and reliability. This also touched upon its sensitive function in the field of German-American relations. Because German Chancellor Adenauer

9 See note 7.
10 Cf. Mako, *U.S. Ground Forces*, 11.

believed that the longer term interests of the United States lay in regaining the international nonalignment it had possessed prior to
1941,[11] the presence of American troops assumed, in his eyes, the
role of the real yardstick of the reliability of Washington in the sphere
of Alliance and European policy.

With the arrival of the additional U.S. divisions in the Federal Republic of Germany in the spring of 1951, the question of the permanence of the American commitment appeared to have been settled
for the time being. But this lull did not last very long. Only a year
later in the 1952 election campaign, the Republicans resumed their
attacks upon the Truman administration's defense policy. Their principal goal was to find a balance between national security and an af-
fordable defense ("solvency"). The Republicans promised if they
won the election to reduce the defense budget to a level commensu-
rate both with security and financial prudence. Their presidential
candidate, Eisenhower, wanted to find a way "so that our boys may
stay at home . . . and not go off to foreign shores to protect our
interests."[12] That this was more than just a popular election slogan
became apparent in the discussions between the newly elected president and his defense advisers during a tour to Korea in December
1952. The future chairman of the Joint Chiefs of Staff, Admiral Radford, objected more than anyone else to the unfavorable deployment
of U.S. forces around the globe and instead advocated their strategic
concentration on the American continent and a greater conventional
commitment on the periphery of the Communist sphere of influence
by the Allies located there.[13]

In Bonn, however, for the present nothing was heard of such deliberations. Adenauer followed the election campaign in the United
States closely but was merely relieved that the Republicans nomi-
nated Eisenhower, who was familiar with the circumstances in Europe, rather than the isolationist, Taft. Eisenhower's inaugural speech

11 See Lucius D. Clay, "Adenauers Verhältnis zu den Amerikanern und die deutsch-
amerikanischen Beziehungen nach 1945," in Dieter Blumenwitz, et al., eds., *Konrad Ade-
nauer und seine Zeit: Politik und Persönlichkeit des ersten Bundeskanzlers*, vol. 1., *Beitrage von
Weg- und Zeitgenossen* (Stuttgart, 1976), 466–76; Kurt Birrenbach, "Adenauer und die
Vereinigten Staaten in der Periode seiner Kanzlerschaft," ibid., 477–509; and Klaus Dohrn,
"Das Amerikabild Adenauers," ibid., 510–23.
12 Quoted from *The History of the Joint Chiefs of Staff*, vol. 5, Robert J. Watson, *The Joint
Chiefs of Staff and National Policy 1953–54* (Wilmington, Del., 1986), 4; on security issues in
the 1952 election campaign, see Gaddis, *Strategies of Containment*, 129–30.
13 Cf. Robert J. Donovan, *Eisenhower: The Inside Story* (New York, 1956), 17–19; Stephen E.
Ambrose, *Eisenhower*, vol. 2, *The President* (New York, 1984), 30–5.

in January 1953, with its rejection of any "fortress America" thinking, went a step further toward convincing the chancellor that the new administration was pursuing a course of continuity.[14] However, he believed that a dangerous situation could arise if a further stagnation of European security policy encouraged the isolationist forces in and surrounding the administration. He thus took the opportunity of the first visit by the new secretary of state, John Foster Dulles, in February 1953 to lay down a common course, the first priority of which was to accelerate the ratification of the European Defense Community (EDC) treaties in the national parliaments as the most secure bond to hold together the transatlantic links.[15] This was fully in line with Washington's intentions. The view from the American capital was that a real distribution of burdens between the United and its allies would not be possible until there had been a concentration of Western European potentials through their integration. Tacitly, however, this German-American consensus was based on different hopes for the future. For Adenauer, Western European integration was also designed to permanently tie the United States as a partner; for Eisenhower and Dulles it would help to reduce this very commitment.

As early as February, President Eisenhower set the tone with his demand in the National Security Council (NSC) "to figure out a preparedness program that will give us a respectable position without bankrupting the nation."[16] The internal struggle to achieve a balanced relation between national security interests and expenditures occupied the U.S. administration through 1953 and finally produced the basis for the "New Look" concept. However, a cutback in defense expenditure could only be achieved by redefining strategy. Concentration of American forces instead of dispersal all over the globe, modernization of the armed forces, and nuclearization of doctrine, while simultaneously reducing personnel levels and sharing the burden with United States' allies in order to be able to endure the Cold War over the "long haul" – these were the projected goals in Washington.[17]

14 Cf. Konrad Adenauer, *Erinnerungen 1945–1953* (Stuttgart, 1965), 551–2; Gaddis, *Strategies of Containment*, 129–30.
15 Cf. *FRUS 1952–1954*, vol. 5, *Western European Security* (Washington, D.C., 1983), 1569–71; Adenauer, *Erinnerungen 1945–1953*, 552–9.
16 *FRUS 1952–1954*, 2:236; profoundly analyzed in Gaddis, *Strategies of Containment*, 129–36.
17 See Glenn H. Snyder, "The 'New Look' of 1953," in Warner R. Schillings, Paul Y. Hammond, and Glenn H. Snyder, eds., *Strategy, Politics, and Defense Budgets* (New York, 1962.)

The trouble was that the Eisenhower administration inherited a legacy in Western Europe that held out little hope for the time being of quick self-help. On the contrary, the U.S. delegate to the North Atlantic Council warned in early March that the Alliance would fall far short of its planned force goals in 1953–54 and the United States would do well to start considering alternatives immediately. The politicians in Washington, meanwhile, were in a dilemma. If they reduced the American commitment in Europe in order to force U.S. allies to make more effort themselves, they might only achieve a further slackening by the allies, especially since the Western Europeans had already started to feel less threatened after Stalin's death. On the other hand, if the United States kept its defense aid at the previous level, the politicians would fail to achieve their declared objective of adjusting the budget, and at the same time they would support the Western Europeans' "boarder" mentality. At any rate, in the spring of 1953 Eisenhower and Dulles were in agreement – opposed by those advisers who pressed for a tougher course of action – that the issue of the presence of American troops should not yet be emphasized in the defense policy review, because such a focus would place an additional burden on the necessary process of Western European integration within the framework of the EDC, which was then in a difficult phase.[18] However, with a view to the future weight of a united Western Europe, the United States did not lose sight of its own medium-term reduction goals.[19]

Meanwhile, however, things had also started to happen in the field of Eastern and German policy that affected the issue of the presence of American troops in Germany. After Stalin's death in March 1953, Churchill reacted immediately by probing its consequences for détente, and one month later Eisenhower also responded with a speech ("The Chance for Peace") that was noted throughout the world.[20] In it, Eisenhower called for, among other things, Soviet agreement to a free and united Germany. To avoid entering a debate on Germany as unprepared as his predecessor in 1952, and in search of a new containment strategy, the president assembled a group of experts for

18 *History of the Joint Chiefs of Staff*, 5:284–5; *FRUS 1952–1954*, 2:278.
19 Memo, Special Assistant to the President for National Security Affairs (Cutler), July 31, 1953, *FRUS 1952–1954*, 2:440.
20 See Rolf Steininger, "Ein vereinigtes, unabhängiges Deutschland? Winston Churchill, der Kalte Krieg und die deutsche Frage im Jahre 1953," *MGM* 36 (1984):109–11; for Eisenhower's speech, see Ambrose, *Eisenhower*, 2:94–6.

Project Solarium.[21] Against the background of updated threat analyses, three working groups were to develop options for future U.S. policy toward the Soviet Union. Two of the three working groups concluded that if the United States wished to test the seriousness of the Soviet desire for détente in Central Europe, then the possibility of a disengagement of the two blocs would have to be considered.[22]

But such ideas were still a long way from becoming practical policies. Nevertheless, they still found their way into the central position paper NSC 160/1, together with all the misgivings regarding their feasibility. It was clear that the Soviet Union would immediately link any serious offer concerning Germany to the question of a withdrawal of troops and would thus force the West to react.[23] This would not, however, as Dulles reflected with the explicit agreement of his president, necessarily turn out to the disadvantage of American policies. Would it not perhaps be possible to use the policy of détente to further the United States' own requirements concerning security and Germany? Any unilateral step taken by the United States to reduce its commitment in Germany was bound to trigger an alarm among the Germans and the other West Europeans who feared a withdrawal to Fortress America. If the reduction of U.S. troops were to be included in an overall Western concept as a means of reducing Soviet preponderance in Central Europe, however, then it might be possible to realize the New Look policy with the consent of the Western Europeans.[24]

Another reason that such considerations came to the fore was that similar ideas were now being voiced in Western Europe. In the summer of 1953, the Belgian foreign minister, van Zeeland, and as yet not clearly identifiable elements in the triangle formed by the Office of the Federal Chancellor, the German Foreign Ministry, and Dienststelle Blank developed – independently of each other – related concepts regarding a partial or total withdrawal of Anglo-American and Soviet troops from Central Europe. Such conceptions were bolstered by the uprising of June 17 in East Germany. Could the overtaxed su-

---

21 For documentation, see *FRUS 1952–54*, 2:323–8, 349–54, 360–6, 387–424; see also Hermann-Josef Rupieper, "Deutsche Frage und europäische Sicherheit: Politisch-strategische Ueberlegungen 1953/1955," in Bruno Thoss and Hans-Erich Volkmann, eds., *Zwischen Kaltem Krieg und Entspannung: Sicherheits- und Deutschlandpolitik der Bundesrepublik im Mächtesystem der Jahre 1953–1956* (Boppard, 1988), 185–7.
22 *FRUS 1952–1954*, 2:406, 419.
23 Ibid., 517–18 (paragraph 13).
24 Ibid., 457–63.

perpower in the East perhaps now be interested in coexistence with the West, which would involve fewer risks and be more economical?[25] Thus, in the midst of Washington's review of its own security policy, there arose an opportunity to bundle together the American and Soviet desire to ease their burdens and the Western Europeans' hopes for détente to form an overall package to benefit everyone.

At any rate, the State Department began to review American and Western European disengagement plans in late September 1953, initially with an open mind. The advantages of a reciprocally controlled troop withdrawal were obvious. Withdrawal of Soviet troops would make the German question solvable and at the same time would reduce military pressure on Western Europe. If a withdrawal could be extended to cover Czechoslovakia and Poland, this would constitute the first sign of a peaceful "roll back" by the Soviet Union from Eastern Europe. But this course involved certain risks. Excessive détente signals before the Western bloc had completed its internal security arrangements could have caused the military integration of Western Europe to slacken. In the opinion of NATO and the Joint Chiefs of Staff, however, an impermeable defensive shield, including a West German contribution to the Alliance, was necessary to ensure that a phased thinning out of troops would not lead to the United States being driven off the continent, the Western Europeans being at the mercy of the Soviet preponderance, and the Germans being given a free hand between East and West that would be irreconcilable with the security interests of Europe as a whole.[26]

Of course, attention was now focused on precisely those risks that led to the anticipated irritations in Paris and Bonn immediately after the American ideas had leaked out informally. For the French government, there was the danger of unpredictable repercussions on the upcoming debate in the National Assembly on the ratification of the EDC treaties. If hopes were aroused here that a four-power conference would be held in the near future, a majority would quickly form in favor of postponing ratification.[27] Adenauer, too, who in the summer had himself considered a European security system as an over-

---

25 Cf. Hermann-Josef Rupieper, "Wiedervereinigung und europäische Sicherheit: Deutsch-amerikanische Ueberlegungen für eine entmilitarisierte Zone in Europa 1953," in *MGM* 39 (1986):91–7.

26 Cf. ibid., 111–23; Rupieper, "Deutsche Frage," 187–9; *History of the Joint Chiefs of Staff*, 5:293–4.

27 See Rupieper, "Wiedervereinigung," 99–100.

ture to the East,[28] was now alarmed at the concrete manner in which the United States was obviously thinking about a withdrawal of troops. He therefore let it be known in the State Department just how concerned Bonn was about map exercises that could have amounted to a withdrawal by the United States to the fringes of Western Europe. A contributory factor to this concern had apparently been that the disputes between defense and finance politicians in Washington had given the federal chancellor a first glimpse of the overall framework of "New Look" and the problems involved for the presence of U.S. troops in Europe.[29]

Thus, the first tentative feelers had shown provisionally that disengagement was an unsuitable means to prepare the Europeans psychologically for the New Look. Eisenhower and Dulles therefore made it clear that it would be inopportune to pursue such plans before the EDC treaties had been ratified.[30] This was exactly the course that the NSC now pursued. Although the financial experts insisted that clear statements on the scope and pace of a reduction of the United States' conventional overcommitment be included in position paper NSC 162/2, for the present the president and his security advisers stuck to their view "that unless this redeployment [of U.S. troops from Europe] were handled with the greatest delicacy . . . , [it] could bring about the complete collapse of our coalition in Europe."[31]

In essence, however, this merely deferred a redistribution of the Alliance's burdens, which was still considered necessary, and a reduction of the conventional U.S. commitment as part and parcel of this redistribution. In the interservice disputes about the distribution of the budget, it was already becoming apparent that the politicians would side with navy and air force in favor of a modernization of the deterrent capacity and against the army's warnings against reducing the United States' conventional defensive capability. The discussions in the NSC thus came to the conclusion that, "for the present," an immediate start to the reduction in the number of troops was out of the question in order not to endanger the incipient stabilization of NATO by means of a ratification of the EDC treaties. For the future, however, Eisenhower indicated "that the real issue was not the pros

28 *FRUS 1952–1954*, 5:1606.
29 *FRUS 1952–1954*, vol. 7, *Germany and Austria* (Washington, D.C., 1986), 549–50.
30 Ibid., 545–6, 548–9.
31 *FRUS 1952–1954*, 2:526–7.

and cons of redeployment, but rather how fast such a redeployment could be carried out."[32]

This sealed the fate of the disengagement plans for the upcoming conference of foreign ministers with the Soviet Union in Berlin in early 1954. In the discussions among the Western powers at working group level prior to this conference, the Anglo-French position that a withdrawal of troops should not yet be included in East-West negotiations because it could be misunderstood in Western Europe as a signal that the United States was turning away from Europe prevailed.[33]

Nevertheless, Bonn's uneasiness with the American ideas persisted through November and December 1953. The Chancellor Adenauer, who had consented in the summer to the stationing of new nuclear-capable U.S. guns in the Federal Republic of Germany because any strengthening of the American nuclear shield could only enhance the security of Western Europe,[34] now recognized the problematic connection between a further nuclearization of Alliance strategy and the plans of the United States to reduce its conventional forces. He thus informed the State Department, that any tampering with the presence of American troops would place a great strain on German-American relations. In reply, Undersecretary of State Bedell Smith "emphatically" reassured Ambassador Krekeler that the U.S. divisions in West Germany would be maintained "at about the present level." Smith admitted that he again made the mental reservation that it might be necessary to reconsider the matter in the future, but, he said, this would only be done in mutual consideration.[35]

This reply did nothing to allay Adenauer's fears. In order to achieve a permanent U.S. commitment, the chancellor backed the French demand for a long-term guarantee that U.S. troops would remain in Europe. He appreciated the constitutional difficulties involved in such a commitment but wondered whether Congress could perhaps be moved to consent to an addendum to the NATO treaty.[36] But this German attempt was just as unsuccessful as the French insistence at the conference of the Western heads of government in Ber-

---

32 NSC 162/2, "Basic National Security Policy," Oct. 30, 1953, ibid., 567–97; see also *History of the Joint Chiefs of Staff*, 5:21–6.
33 See Rupieper, "Wiedervereinigung," 108; *FRUS 1952–1954*, 2:1234–5.
34 *FRUS 1952–1954*, 7:486–7.
35 Ibid., 556.
36 Ibid., 683.

muda at the beginning of December 1953. Foreign Minister Bidault warned urgently against considering the future European Army as a compensation for the Anglo-American forces on the continent, since this would deal the death blow to the EDC in the French National Assembly. The American administration however, prior to the conference, had already declared its opposition to any additional constriction of its own scope of action.[37] On the contrary, the Joint Chiefs of Staff continued to pursue their force planning (until 1957) and included possible cuts of up to 40 percent of the personnel in Western Europe in their calculations. Implementation of this plan was not, however, to be contemplated until the political climate permitted. Instead, the chiefs envisioned a kind of psychological program of education for the Western Europeans, designed to convince them of the greater efficacy and economic efficiency of an Alliance strategy based primarily on nuclear weapons.[38]

In mid-December 1953, Secretary of State Dulles was actually able to win the support of the NATO Council for a first step in this direction. This involved a general review of NATO's previous force planning in light of the nuclear weapons that would be available by 1957, although there was as yet no reference to concrete American plans for troop reductions. Rather, Dulles initially confined himself to getting the Allies to think in categories of nuclear deterrence. At the same time, however, he warned against a further delay in Western European self-help through ratification of the EDC treaties with the unmistakable threat that otherwise an "agonizing reappraisal" of the U.S. policy toward Europe policy might be necessary.[39]

Dulles pursued this tactic throughout 1954. In order not to interfere with the integration of the Federal Republic of Germany into the Western Alliance, Washington would exercise the utmost restraint in the issue of troops while pressing ahead with the debate on a nuclearization of alliance strategy.[40] The threat of a general review of U.S. policy toward Europe would remain hovering over the heads of the Western Europeans merely as a lever to prevent the French from blocking West German rearmament. Because Paris had stated that a ratification of the EDC treaties would be impossible without British and American guarantees that their troops would remain on the con-

---

37 Cf. *FRUS 1952–1954*, 5:1734–6, 1800.
38 Cf. *History of the Joint Chiefs of Staff*, 5:28–9.
39 See *FRUS 1952–1954*, 5:454–6, 463, 476–8.
40 *History of the Joint Chiefs of Staff*, 5:304–6.

tinent for the long term, Eisenhower in spring of 1954 finally issued
a formal declaration confirming the earlier American promises made
to NATO. Internally, meanwhile, he made it clear that this initially
only involved a troop commitment for the next two years.[41]

Despite the American threat of an "agonizing reappraisal," the situation remained basically unchanged, even after the French National
Assembly had failed to ratify the EDC on August 30, 1954. It is true
that the United States continued to warn France that it would withdraw to a peripheral defense of Western Europe consisting of a chain
of naval and air bases if the French further delayed West German rearmament. As early as mid-September, however, the internal re-
views in the State Department and the Pentagon[42] concluded that in
the long run the price for persisting in this threat would be a total
reconception of NATO strategy as a whole. Thus, the only course
left for the autumn conferences of 1954 in London and Paris and for
the subsequent tug-of-war surrounding the ratification of the Paris
Agreements through May 1955 was to continue the "gentle shock
therapy" from EDC times. The West Europeans were to be offered
either the "stick" of a withdrawal of U.S. troops or the "carrot" of
a repetition of the presidential guarantee that these troops would remain in Europe if an acceptable alternative solution could be found
for the accession of the Federal Republic of Germany to the
Alliance.[43]

At the London Conference in late September 1954, Dulles stuck to
this tactic. To promote agreement among the Western Europeans, he
held out the prospect of a renewal of the presidential declaration of
the spring, but he was unwilling to make any further commitments
that would have restricted the right of every American president
during his term of office to decide on the nature and scope of the
employment of armed forces. Moreover, Eisenhower's declaration
was not to be repeated in public until it was certain that the Paris
Agreements would be ratified.[44] This was to prevent a resumption
of the French delaying tactics.

In Bonn, at least, the message had the desired effect, as was apparent from Adenauer's explanation of the results of the London

---

41 Cf. *FRUS 1952–1954*, 5:886–99, esp. 889.
42 See ibid., 1163–77, and JCS memo of Sept. 15, 1954, NA, RG 218, CCS 092 Germany
(5–4–49) Secto 23.
43 *FRUS 1952–1954*, 5:1261–2.
44 Cf. ibid., 1308–13, 1357–65. For the JCS view that "[there] should be no promise to maintain any specific minimum force," see *History of the Joint Chiefs of Staff*, 5:314.

Conference to the executive committee of the CDU: "The danger
[of "neoisolationism"] is all the greater because people in the Pentagon are of the opinion that the development of nuclear technology
for aircraft and, of course, submarines will, in the near future – they
talk of one or two years – mean that the United States no longer requires a country in Europe."[45] If, therefore, they wished to tie the
United States to Europe on a long-term basis, the Western Europeans had to show that they were capable of acting in the field of security policy, and this meant that the Paris Agreements of October
23, 1954, had to be ratified by the national parliaments without delay. However, this did not take into consideration the fact that the
very success of Western Europe in reaching agreement in the fall of
1954 paved the way not just for the desired strengthening of American ties with Europe but also to at least the same extent for a reduction of the U.S. commitment in Europe. After all, Washington
considered the troop level at that time a stopgap until Western European self-help began to take effect!

The Paris Agreements had scarcely cleared their first parliamentary hurdles in the French National Assembly and German Bundestag when the State Department resumed its deliberations on
Germany in early January 1955. This appeared all the more necessary
in view of the Soviet diplomatic offensive against the successful
Western Agreement, which had led the Allies since the fall of 1954 to
expect at any time an offer to the Germans similar to that of the Stalin notes of 1952. Moreover, French Prime Minister Mendès-France
had for weeks pressed for a resumption of the East-West dialogue,
which had so far been refused on the grounds that it was first necessary to ensure parliamentary approval of the Paris Agreements.[46]
It was therefore essential for the West to agree internally and in a
timely manner on a negotiating package with the Soviet Union if it
wanted to prevent individual countries from going it alone and pursuing their own Eastern policy.

In London, however, there was a feeling of unpleasant surprise at
the speed at which the State Department was acting. If the Western

45 Archiv für Christlich-Demokratische Politik, Konrad-Adenauer-Stiftung, St. Augustin,
  VII-001-003/5, 6–7.
46 See René Girault, "La France dans les rapports est-ouest au temps de la Présidence de Pierre
  Mendès-France," in François Bédarida and Jean-Pierre Rioux, eds., *Pierre Mendès-France et
  la Mendèsisme* (Paris, 1985), 251–60, esp. 257–9.

Europeans did not succeed at an early stage in getting the Americans to include Western European interests in Washington's thinking then the Americans might become set upon making internal commitments that would be very difficult to revise at a later date. One aspect that was particularly critical was that the Eisenhower administration again wanted, as in 1953, to include the issue of the withdrawal of troops from the outset of future East-West negotiations. In the opinion of American diplomats, the only way out of constantly reacting to Soviet initiatives was to test the seriousness of the Soviet Union's desire for détente by making concrete offers of their own. And the only way to force the Soviet Union to name a realistic Western price for its accommodation in the German question would be to exploit the mutual willingness to disengage the military potentials in Central Europe. The British view, however, was that this meant starting the negotiating process from the wrong end. A withdrawal of American troops should not take place until lasting détente had been achieved; otherwise the West would risk a withdrawal of the U.S. divisions back across the Atlantic while the Soviet contingents in Byelorussia remained in place and continued to pose a potential threat to Central and Western Europe.[47]

But the State Department gave the British clearly to understand "that once the West German Government endorses a Russian offer to take Russian (and Polish etc.) troops out of East Germany, pressures here for removing American troops will become so great that no American Government can be expected to withstand them. . . . In fact it looks as though the presence of Soviet troops in Germany is the unwritten but real condition of the American undertaking to keep troops there too."[48] An attractive offer by the Soviet Union concerning Germany, one that a German government would no longer be able to reject, could have been on the table sooner than the West had previously expected. After all, the Kremlin had indicated a shift in the issue of all-German elections as early as mid-January 1955, and barely a month later had substantiated this through its willingness to conclude an Austrian State Treaty. The public response to this in the West, the continuing French insistence on a rapid resumption of the East-West dialogue, and an increasingly an-

---

47 See Rupieper, "Deutsche Frage," 190–2, and PRO, FO 371/118 198/WG 1071/117.
48 Report of the British Embassy in Washington, PRO, FO 371/118 202/WG 1071/245.

imated reunification debate in the Federal Republic of Germany, which reached deep into the ranks of the coalition in Bonn, meant that the West could not afford to wait too long with internal preliminary discussions prior to a new round of four-power talks.[49]

Faced with a more and more comprehensive and flexible détente offensive by the Soviet Union in the nascent Khrushchev era, however, the Western offers for a security arrangement in Central Europe had to contain more than the proposals of the 1954 Berlin Conference, which were determined predominantly by tactical considerations.[50] Consent to the Soviet demand for neutralization of Germany as the price for her reunification was still irreconcilable with the security interests of the West. It might, however, have been possible to reduce the density of troops and arms on the territory of a future united Germany to the benefit of both sides. The only question was what reductions the West should propose in order to interest the Soviets seriously but without harming its own security requirements at the same time. The Americans attached prime importance to linking their own plans for reductions in conventional troop numbers to a disengagement in Central Europe. In contrast, the Western Europeans considered it imperative that the presence of U.S. troops be maintained as an indispensable tie for the transatlantic security community. For this reason, they were more in favor of a smaller scale of West Germany rearmament as an offer to the Soviet Union.[51]

Meanwhile, the détente offensive launched by the Soviet Union, the growing interest in it showed by the West, and the buoyant mood in the Federal Republic of Germany resulting from an international situation in which things had started to move placed Bonn in an additional dilemma. The political gains from the Federal Republic's accession to NATO were not to be sacrificed to the Western powers' overriding interest in probing opportunities for détente; on the other hand, the Federal Republic did not want to insist too rigorously on maximum positions and thereby assume the unpopular role of the party who applied a brake to the process of détente. As in the summer of 1953, Adenauer now in the spring of 1955 once again became the chief proponent of a new round of four-power talks. He made it

---

49 Cf. Bruno Thoss, "Modellfall Oesterreich? Der österreichische Staatsvertrag und die deutsche Frage 1954/55," in Thoss and Volkmann, eds., *Zwischen Kaltem Krieg und Entspannung*, 128–30.
50 Cf. Hermann-Josef Rupieper, "Die Berliner Aussenministerkonferenz von 1954," *VfZG* 34 (1986):427–53.
51 Records, American-British-French-German working party, London, Apr. 27-May 5, 1955, PRO, FO 371/118 209/WG 1071/478 to 371/118 211/WG 1071/517.

known that he had joined the discussion in the West on disengagement, although he did not allow the accession of West Germany to the Alliance to be questioned again, nor did he raise the question of the presence of troops, an issue fraught with problems.[52]

The Chancellor's insistence that his allies become active in the field of Eastern policy as domestic proof of his own initiative in German affairs was, however, taken by the State Department as an occasion to return to its own thinking of 1953. It is true that the Joint Chiefs of Staff, in April 1955, once again stressed the importance of adequate U.S. troops in the Federal Republic of Germany,[53] but this was before the conclusion of the Austrian State Treaty and the hopes it aroused for East-West relations. Was not the first dividend of Western staying power becoming tangible in Vienna, and did this not indicate a profound crisis in the Soviet system and a corresponding desire by its leaders for peace and quiet on the international front? If the West were to meet this requirement halfway with disengagement in Central Europe, this could loosen the Soviet grip on Eastern Europe for the first time since 1945 and, at the same time, make it possible for the New Look concept to be partially realized. In May 1955, therefore, new analyses by the Pentagon considered partial and total withdrawals of Allied troops from Central Europe conceivable, provided that this did not affect the German military contribution to NATO, even after reunification. In other words, a reunified Germany could not become neutral. Otherwise, to prevent a military vacuum in the center of Europe, it would be necessary to grant the Germans so many arms that this would be incompatible with the security requirements of their neighbors in Western and Eastern Europe.[54]

In Adenauer's eyes the Soviet Union had overextended its power and was looking for a reprieve. But he feared exaggerated Western hopes and did not believe in rapid results. He advocated a policy of "holding out." No premature and excessive Western concessions could be made before the other side was ready to compromise too. An increasingly widespread disengagement discussion in the U.S.

---

52 Interviews of Feb. 17 and March 5, 1955, *Bulletin des Presse- und Informationsamtes der Bundesregierung,* no. 34 (Feb. 18, 1955), and no. 49 (Dec. 12, 1955).
53 JCS to Secretary of Defense, Apr. 20, 1955, NA, RG 218, CCS 092 Germany (5–4–49) Secto 29.
54 JCS to SACEUR, June 6, 1955; SACEUR to JCS, May 25, 1955; memos, Admiral Radford, May 27 and June 8, 1955, NA, RG 218, CCS 092 Germany (5–4–49), Secto 30. Cf. Rupieper, "Deutsche Frage," 196–9.

press and a positive statement by Eisenhower on the issue of neutrality thus caused the chancellor to sound the alarm in mid-May, although Washington immediately reassured him that the American commitment in the Federal Republic of Germany would not be affected and that there was no reason to be concerned. From this time on, the impression was firmly entrenched in Adenauer's mind that his strongest ally could possibly deal directly with the Soviet Union over the heads of the Germans.[55]

For the upcoming Geneva Four-Power Conferences in the summer and fall of 1955, therefore, the chancellor sought to get away from the excitement of general expectations. He wanted the process of détente to be spread over a long period and put forward instead the problems of disarmament as a starting point for debate. At the moment, however, the Western powers were against this idea, since the difficult nature of the subject meant that hardly any progress could be expected at the upcoming conferences.[56] On the contrary, they agreed with the Soviet Union to give priority to the agenda items "European security" and "German question." In return, the Germans demanded and received from the Western powers at least an assurance that any Western compliance with the Soviet security desires would be tied to parallel concessions regarding Germany.[57]

At the same time, Bonn actively intervened, with the so-called Heusinger Plan, to terminate a Western disengagement offer to the Soviet Union. For the Germans, it was crucial that demilitarized zones in Central Europe should involve neither a guarantee of the existing borders nor a neutralization of Germany nor a total withdrawal of the Western Powers' troops.[58] The combination of the future West German divisions with an adequate number of divisions of the Western Allies had to be maintained to guarantee the transatlantic security system. However, since the Geneva Conference of Foreign Ministers in the fall of 1955 did not even discuss the issue of the pres-

---

55 Cf. Konrad Adenauer, *Erinnerungen 1953–1955* (Stuttgart, 1966), 441–6; Herbert Blankenhorn, *Verständnis und Verständigung: Blätter eines politischen Tagebuchs 1949 bis 1979* (Frankfurt am Main, Berlin, and Vienna, 1980), 216–17.

56 For Macmillan's reports on the meeting of the Western Foreign Ministers with Adenauer in New York on June 18, 1955, see PRO, FO 371/118 219/WG 1071/727, 735 to 737, and 740. See also Adenauer, *Erinnerungen 1953–1955,* 461–2.

57 On the connection between the German question and European security at the Geneva Conference, see *Die internationale Politik 1955,* ed. Arnold Bergstraesser and Wilhelm Cornides (Munich, 1958), 837–55.

58 Cf. Helga Haftendorn, *Sicherheit und Entspannung: Zur Aussenpolitik der Bundesrepublik Deutschland 1955–1982* (Baden-Baden, 1983), 81–3; Rupieper, "Deutsche Frage," 199–204.

ence of troops but foundered earlier on irreconcilable differences over Germany, the plans for disengagement were just as unsuccessful in 1955 as they had been in 1953–54.

If it was therefore not possible to achieve a reduction of the U.S. conventional burden by means of an all-Western concept of détente, Washington now wanted at least to see an acceleration of Bonn's own military efforts. However, the NATO Annual Review of fall 1955 only served to strengthen the considerable doubts as to whether the Federal Republic of Germany would be able to fulfill its own obligation to activate the Bundeswehr in a period of three years.[59] The dissatisfaction mounted at the end of 1955 when Bonn opposed an increase in the funds for the establishment of its own armed forces or at least the continued payment of stationing costs for the Allied contingents in the Federal Republic until West German rearmament began to take effect.[60] Moreover, at a conference of NATO defense ministers in October 1955, the Pentagon had learned that the British, too, were now setting about an intensified development of their nuclear component and, to this end, were considering cuts in conventional forces because of chronic budgetary problems.[61] Added to this was the substantial thinning out of French troops in southwestern Germany for the war in Algeria, all of which meant that, in the spring of 1956, the hopes for reductions that Washington had placed in the New Look concept were farther off than ever.

The American files do not, as yet, reveal how important a role this frustration at the Western Europeans' failure to comply with their Alliance commitments played in the discussion concerning a reduction of U.S. troops in Europe, which became public in the summer of 1956. Meanwhile, Adenauer felt that he had been duped in two ways. On his most recent visit to the United States in mid-June, Dulles had informed him in general terms of the necessity of adapting American defense expenditure to the changed international and military-strategic circumstances, but had left him in the dark as to the concreteness and scope of the American deliberations. Moreover, their discussion in public was carried out just when the chancellor faced difficult disputes in the Bundestag on the size of the future

---

59 See reports of U.S. diplomats in Bonn and Paris (NATO) of October and November 1955, NA, RG 59, 762.5
60 See PRO, PREM 11/1343.
61 *FRUS 1955–1957*, vol. 4, *Western European Society and Integration* (Washington, D.C., 1986), 25.

West German armed forces. Together with the simultaneous news of British plans to reduce the size of the British Army of the Rhine,[62] the prospect of reducing the U.S. forces by 800,000 men, which was attributed to Admiral Radford,[63] must have seemed like confirmation of the opposition criticism of Bonn's military planning. How was the German public to be convinced of the need for an armed forces program involving twelve divisions and eighteen months' military service if the strategic reorientation of the Federal Republic's main allies now signaled lower conventional force requirements?

For Adenauer, at any rate, the ideas circulating in Washington were fully in keeping with his distrust of the most recent motives of the leading Western power since the disengagement debates of the previous year. Whatever the reasons were for this untimely move in going public – to catch up in world public opinion with the Soviet announcement of further unilateral personnel reductions in the Red Army, as a domestic prelude to the presidential election campaign in the fall, as an effort by the U.S. services to rally public support for their budget demands, or to signal discontent with the United States Western European allies – the chancellor saw it as the start of a new phase of isolationist temptations of the United States.

In addition, the process of a public debate without warning, let alone consulting, the Allies did not bode very well for the future. Adenauer thus resorted to a wide-ranging crisis strategy that involved recalling his ambassadors from the capitals of the West, alerting the Western European Union (WEU) and NATO bodies and even going so far as to intervene directly in Washington by sending a delegation headed by General Heusinger. Furthermore, for the first time he dealt in the cabinet in detail with the dangers of a further nuclearization of Alliance strategy at the expense of conventional defensive power in Central Europe. At the same time, his minister for nuclear affairs, Strauss, saw another source of danger on the horizon. How reliable was the protection afforded by the United States, given that it was so one-sidedly focused on nuclear deterrence, if, in the near future, the Soviet Union drew level in the nuclear field and the

---

62 See William Snyder, *The Politics of British Defence Policies, 1945–1962* (London, 1964), 19, and C. J. Bartlett, *The Long Retreat: A Short History of British Defence Policy, 1945–1970* (London, 1972), 105–7.
63 On the Radford crisis see Adenauer, *Erinnerungen 1955–1959*, 193–210; Martin Geiling, *Aussenpolitik und Nuklearstrategie: Eine Analyse des konzeptionellen Wandels der amerikanischen Sicherheitspolitik gegenüber der Sowjetunion (1945–1963)* (Cologne and Vienna, 1975), 119–21; Hans-Gert Pöttering, *Adenauers Sicherheitspolitik 1955–1963* (Düsseldorf, 1975), 62–80.

Americans themselves would be vulnerable as a result of long-range weapons? Local conflicts around Berlin or along the inner-German border might then no longer be a sufficient reason to jeopardize the survival of the United States itself by threatening to go nuclear. If, however, the way to a dependence on a strategy of nuclear deterrence was irreversible, then Bonn, too, might have to reconsider its earlier renunciation of nuclear, biological, and chemical (NBC) weapons.[64]

There was a perceptive easing in the purely military discussions surrounding the Radford Plan immediately following Heusinger's return from the United States, when the NATO Standing Group made it known that the previous American targeting plans would remain valid until 1960 and that the formulation of new proposals for 1960–61 was not expected until early 1957, that is, once the waves had settled following the presidential elections. In addition, the U.S. administration sought to reassure Bonn by now only talking of "modernizing" and no longer of "reducing" its forces, and even after this modernization an adequate U.S. contingent was to remain stationed in the Federal Republic of Germany.[65] What was more important to the chancellor, however, was that this did not signify an end to the fundamental American desire for a conventional redistribution of the Alliance's burdens. In his eyes, the policy of the Federal Republic and of Western Europe as a whole had to adapt itself in a timely fashion to a future in which the American commitment in Europe would become less certain and the need for self-help would become more pressing.

Thus, in the fall of 1956, Adenauer tried through the political activation of the WEU to strengthen Western European clout in NATO in order to become less susceptible to the vagaries of American security and Alliance policy.[66] But his initiative petered out in 1956–57 and was just as unsuccessful as a series of similar attempts during the subsequent crises of confidence between the United States and Western Europe that recurred chronically thereafter. The continuing effects of special national interests, politico-economic embargoes on necessary increases in Western European defense expenditure, and, not least, the fear that greater military efforts by the

---

64 Kabinettssitzung, July 20, 1956, BA, B 136, Bundeskanzleramt, vol, 27A; for a similar hint by the German ambassador in London, Herwarth, on August 4, 1956, see NA, RG 59, 762A.5/8–456.
65 Adenauer, *Erinnerungen 1955–1959*, 207–11.
66 Cf. ibid., 219–25.

Europeans themselves would do the preliminary work for American desires to reduce their troops – all these factors proved to be more dominant at all times than the desire for independence in the Alliance. Contrary to the original intentions, the presence of U.S. troops in Europe has thus assumed the character of a provisional arrangement in perpetuity. In this way, however, their twin function for Western European security and for German-American relations has been retained up to the present day. Politically, militarily, and psychologically, they continue to act as guarantors of NATO's transatlantic ties and to safeguard Western Europe for the world power across the Atlantic; as far as the Federal Republic of Germany is concerned, they are the most visible expression of the United States' continuing responsibilities for Germany and – this should not be overlooked – they add weight to the conventional West German contingent in proportion to the other Western European military potentials. At the same time, however, any change in their nature or size remains, as in the 1950s, closely tied to their being embedded in an all-European security arrangement.

21

John J. McCloy and the Landsberg Cases

THOMAS ALAN SCHWARTZ

On January 31, 1951, the U.S. high commissioner for Germany, John J. McCloy, announced his final decisions regarding executive clemency for eighty-nine German war criminals held in Landsberg prison. McCloy affirmed five death sentences out of a total of fifteen, primarily for members of the infamous *Einsatzgruppen,* the SS men who killed thousands of Jews in eastern Europe. The high commissioner also reduced the sentences of seventy-nine inmates. These reductions, coupled with credit for pretrial detention and good conduct, allowed the immediate release of thirty-two of the prisoners.[1] Among them was the industrialist Alfried Krupp, convicted of the abuse of slave labor and plundering in German-occupied countries. McCloy also returned to Krupp his vast industrial holdings, which had been subject to a confiscation order.

McCloy's clemency decisions were the most controversial actions he took as high commissioner. Coming only a few months after the outbreak of the Korean War and the American proposal of German rearmament, McCloy's decisions were blasted by contemporary critics as the height of political expediency, an attempt to win Germany's favor in the increasingly tense Cold War. As one released industrialist put it, "Now that the Americans have Korea on their hands they are a lot more friendly."[2] Subsequent popular and historical treatments have been equally harsh. William Manchester sharply attacked the release of Krupp in his bestseller, *The Arms of Krupp,* and the historian Frank Buscher contended that McCloy's decisions played a ma-

1 John Mendelsohn, "War Crimes Trials and Clemency in Germany and Japan," in Robert Wolfe, ed., *Americans as Proconsuls: United States Military Government in Germany and Japan, 1944–1952* (Carbondale, Ill., 1984), 251–2.
2 Fritz Ter Meer, an I.G. Farben defendant, in Tom Bower, *Pledge Betrayed: America and Britain and the Nazification of Post-War Germany* (Garden City, N.Y., 1982), 350. See also William Manchester, *The Arms of Krupp* (New York, 1970), 737–70.

jor role in the overall "failure" of the war-crimes program to achieve its twin objectives of punishment for the guilty and the democratization of German society.[3]

The recent availability of the bulk of documentation from the High Commission period allows a new examination of McCloy's decisions. This essay addresses three questions: First, why did McCloy initiate a new and comprehensive review of the Nuremberg sentences? Second, why did McCloy make the final decisions that he did? And third, what significance did these decisions have for American policy in Germany and the overall process of Germany's integration into the West?

THE DECISION TO REVIEW

By July 1949, when John J. McCloy arrived in Germany to replace General Lucius Clay, the United States alone had tried almost 1,900 Germans for war crimes, imprisoned more than 700 of these, and executed 277, with 28 still on death row. These results came from three different sets of criminal proceedings. At the first and most famous of the trials, a four-power tribunal decided the fate of such infamous Nazis as Hermann Goering, Rudolf Hess, and Albert Speer. Imprisoned subsequently at Spandau in Berlin, these war criminals remained under four-power jurisdiction. After the end of this trial in October 1946, each of the major powers conducted trials in its own zone of occupation. Each country followed the new international codes adopted for the first proceeding, but with solely its own nationals as judges. Over the next three years, the United States conducted the most extensive proceedings, with twelve tribunals and 185 defendants. The targets of these trials were high ranking Germans – members of the German High Command, major government ministries, the SS *Einsatzgruppen* and Gestapo, and leading industrialists. The crimes included wholesale massacres, medical experimentation on inmates, the shooting of hostages, and the abuse of

3 Frank M. Buscher, *The U.S. War Crimes Trial Program in Germany, 1946–1955* (New York, 1989), 160–4. Gotthard Jasper argues that Western leniency toward war criminals was intended to strengthen Adenauer's policy of *Westintegration,* as the chancellor's coalition relied on conservative and nationalist political forces that rejected Nuremberg. Gotthard Jasper, "Wiedergutmachung und Westintegration: Die halbherzige justizielle Aufarbeitung der NS-Vergangenheit in der frühen Bundesrepublik," in Ludolf Herbst, ed., *Westdeutschland 1945–1955* (Munich, 1986), 183–202.

slave labor by the industrialists. Apart from these trials, the U.S. army placed 1,672 lower ranking Germans on trial before the military commissions or special courts, using the traditional rules of the Geneva Convention. Though often confused with the other Nuremberg trials, these "Dachau" cases involved both the guards at concentration camps in the American zone and Germans who killed captured American soldiers. The most famous was the Malmédy massacre case, where seventy-three SS men were convicted of killing unarmed American prisoners during the Battle of the Bulge.[4]

The atmosphere surrounding the war-crimes cases changed substantially between 1945 and 1949. Feelings of revenge and outrage over the war and the concentration camps gave way to concerns about Germany's position in the growing conflict with the new enemy, the Soviet Union. The courage of the Berlin population during the Berlin Blockade provided Americans with a positive image of the Germans. After the proclamation of the Marshall Plan and the new emphasis on German economic recovery, some conservative critics of the Truman administration focused their attention on the Nuremberg trials.[5] Senator William Langer argued that the continuing trials, coupled with the dismantling of German industry, played into Stalin's hands by "wiping out the middle classes," and slowing German reconstruction.[6] Allegations of physical brutality and other forms of coercion during the investigation of the Malmédy massacre led to charges by Senator Joseph McCarthy that the army employed "Gestapo and OGPU [Soviet secret police] tactics."[7] While a Senate committee ultimately exonerated the army from the most serious charges, the furor over the Malmédy verdicts raised doubts about the fairness of all of the Nuremberg trials, and encouraged demands for a new review. Most important, the congressional protests led the secretary of the army, Kenneth Royal, to order a temporary halt to all executions.[8] Royal's order came after Clay asked if he could carry out the remaining death sentences, "to free my successor from this thankless task," and "give him a clearer and more constructive

4 Mendelsohn, "War Crimes Trials," 226–8, 247–8.
5 William J. Bosch, *Judgement on Nuremberg* (Chapel Hill, 1970), 116.
6 Glenn H. Smith, *Langer of North Dakota* (New York, 1979), 150.
7 James J. Weingartner, *Crossroads of Death: The Story of the Malmédy Massacre and Trial* (Berkeley, 1979), 221.
8 Grey to General Huebner, June 8, 1949, NA, RG 338, Records of the Theater Judge Advocate Division (TJAD), General Administrative Records (GAR), War Crimes Branch Administrative Files (WCBAF), box 2, folder: Organization 1950.

task."[9] Clay later apologized to McCloy when he handed over these unresolved cases.

As the new high commissioner, McCloy's authority was limited to the twelve American tribunals at "Nuremberg,"amounting to some one hundred war criminals and fifteen death sentences. (General Thomas Handy, the new army commander in Germany, was responsible for the Dachau cases.) There was an irony in McCloy's new position. As assistant secretary of war, McCloy played a critical role in devising the Nuremberg system, defending it against Treasury Secretary Henry Morgenthau and the British government for the summary execution of war criminals. McCloy told a London meeting in April 1945 that such trials "might operate as an added deterrent to waging aggressive war in the future."[10] McCloy saw Nuremberg as a way to purge Germany judicially and allow the reconstruction of a liberal and democratic state. As early as Potsdam, McCloy believed that America should have as its ultimate goal "to enable the German to build himself up again morally and politically and economically to a position of stability."[11] When he became high commissioner in 1949, he saw himself as inaugurating a new phase in America's relations with Germany, one in which the United States would seek to strengthen those "liberal" and "progressive" elements in German society. A strong cold warrior, McCloy came to favor ending any restrictions on German economic recovery. Along with other American leaders of his generation, he feared a resurgence of radical German nationalism, and hoped to use his power to promote the political legitimacy of both the democratic system and the new government of Konrad Adenauer. He told Secretary of State Dean Acheson "we should avoid the mistakes that we made after Weimar where we were rather hasty to give up to the wrong government things we had long begrudged to a better one."[12]

McCloy's concern underlines the important role played by the new German government and members of the Bundestag in pushing for a renewed consideration of the war-crimes cases. With the excep-

9 Clay to Tracy Voorhees, March 3 and 29, 1949, in Jean Edward Smith, ed., *The Papers of General Lucius D. Clay: Germany 1945–1949*, 2 vols. (Bloomington, Ind., 1974), 2:1038, 1062.
10 McCloy Diary, Apr. 16, 1945, McCloy Papers, Amherst College. See also Bradley F. Smith, *The Road to Nuremberg* (New York, 1981), 92–3.
11 McCloy Diary, July 17, 1945, McCloy Papers, Amherst College.
12 *FRUS 1949*, vol. 3, *Council of Foreign Ministers; Germany and Austria* (Washington, D.C., 1974), 597.

tion of the small Communist Party and a few Social Democrats, German political leaders were united in their call for a reassessment of the Nuremberg verdicts, an end to executions, and greater leniency toward those convicted. In this effort, they faithfully reflected popular sentiment in West Germany, where resentment at notions of collective guilt mixed with a form of psychological denial to reduce support for war-crimes trials.[13] (One survey showed only 10 percent of the population expressed *any* approval of Nuremberg.[14]) Citing the Basic Law's prohibition against capital punishment, Adenauer appealed to McCloy to commute all the remaining death sentences.[15] His conservative coalition partners, the Free Democrats (FDP), and the German Party (DP) were even more vocal in their attacks on the Nuremberg trials.[16] These politicians justified their actions to critical American officials by arguing that their efforts would keep the issue from becoming the tool of right-wing nationalists opposed to the new democracy in Bonn. The war-crimes trials were a "poisonous form of bacteria" that could be used in "the political warfare" and become "grist to the mills of the radicals."[17]

Lawyers and churchmen were also prominent in the clemency campaign. Because American leaders saw both groups as important "progressive forces" in building a liberal democracy, they could not ignore their concern with the war-crimes issue. On November 30, 1949, Professor Kurt Geiler of the University of Heidelberg led a delegation of lawyers to see McCloy and plead for action on the Landsberg cases. These lawyers, who later organized themselves into the Heidelberger Juristenkreis, focused their attention on matters of sentence review and possible clemency.[18] A few days later McCloy complained to the State Department that he was getting "more and more complaints from church people" about the war-crimes cases.[19]

13 Marion Dönhoff, *Foe into Friend,* trans. Gabriele Annan (London, 1982), 22–3, and Alistaire Horne, *Return to Power* (New York, 1956), 60.
14 "Current West German Views on the War Criminals Issue," Sept. 8, 1952, NA, RG 338, TJAD, GAR, WCBAF, box 3, folder: News Clipping.
15 McCloy to Adenauer, Apr. 24, 1950, D(50)1228, NA, RG 466, McCloy Papers, Classified General Records (CGR). Adenauer's letter was dated Feb. 28, 1950, and is referred to in McCloy's reply.
16 Buscher, *War Crimes,* 115–27, provides an excellent discussion of the politics of the Landsberg issue.
17 Freiherr von Hodenberg to Col. Damon M. Gunn, May 31, 1951, NA, RG 338, TJAD, GAR, WCBAF, box 2, folder: Organization 1951.
18 McCloy to Acheson, Dec. 2, 1949, D(49)408, NA, RG 466, McCloy Papers, CGR, box 4.
19 McCloy to Henry Byroade, Dec. 9, 1949, D(49)440b, NA, RG 466, McCloy Papers, CGR, box 5.

Cardinal Joseph Frings, the chairman of the Fulda Bishops Conference and a friend of Konrad Adenauer, pleaded for commutation of the death sentences because many of the defendants' actions "do not stem from a criminal disposition."[20] Munich Auxiliary Bishop Johannes Neuhäusler also "intensively lobbied" Americans from 1948 to 1951 on behalf of the Landsberg inmates. Using his own imprisonment in a concentration camp as proof of his anti-Nazi sentiments, Neuhäusler continuously attacked the war-crimes trials, telling visiting U.S. congressmen that the prosecution relied upon "professional witnesses" who testified against the defendants in return for being well treated by American officials. He also criticized certain procedural irregularities, the coercion used in obtaining confessions, and the lack of an appellate court.[21] The efforts of Frings and Neuhäusler helped bring a Vatican letter urging mercy toward the condemned war criminals.

The Protestant church was as active in this arena as the Catholic. Two bishops, Hans Meiser of Munich and Theophil Wurm of Stuttgart, led the campaign, but they received support from Berlin's Otto Dibelius, who served as president of the German Evangelical Church Council, and such prominent opponents of Nazism as Pastor Martin Niemöller.[22] In a memorandum expressing the sentiments of the bishops of the Evangelical Church within the American zone, the bishops protested against "discrimination against the defense as compared with the prosecution, influencing of witnesses, application of a new law which is not generally binding, arbitrary choice of defendants, judging soldiers by a court which is in reality not a military court," and demanded the creation of an appeals court. After detailing all of their respective complaints, the bishops concluded that "the highest expression of justice is not necessarily sentence and punishment," and that "as servants of God we ask that in suitable cases mercy be shown."[23]

This combination of the shift in American policy toward Germany, the doubts created by American opponents of the trials, and the near-unanimity of German sentiment made some form of action on the Nuremberg cases a political necessity. McCloy responded

20 Frings to McCloy, Nov. 17, 1949, D(49)440a, NA, RG 466, McCloy Papers, CGR, box 5.
21 Neuhäusler to Francis Case et al., March 23, 1948, NA, RG 338, TJAD, Post-Trial Activities, WCBAF, box 11, folder: Bishop Neuhäusler. See also Buscher, *War Crimes*, 95–7.
22 Buscher, *War Crimes*, 97.
23 Memorandum by the Evangelical Church in Germany on the Question of War Crimes Trials, 1949, NA, RG 338, TJAD, GAR, WCBAF, box 6.

with both firmness and conciliation. He defended the Nuremberg trials to Adenauer, telling the chancellor the "defendants were guilty of deliberately torturing and killing hundreds and in certain cases thousands of helpless human beings."[24] The high commissioner rejected any notion of an amnesty, noting that such a move "would . . . be taken as an abandonment of the principles established in the trials," and might convey the idea that "those crimes have . . . been sufficiently atoned for . . . [and] . . . that the German people should now be allowed to forget them."[25] But while his words were firm, even eloquent, McCloy was seeking some way to "solve" the problem he faced. He commissioned a legal opinion which affirmed that the high commissioner had the right only to *reduce* sentences.[26] He also instituted a system of time off for good behavior, noting that the British had a similar practice.[27] But the new procedure allowed the release in August 1950 of all the industrialists in the Flick and I. G. Farben cases, and led critics to charge McCloy with "unwarranted leniency."[28]

The initiation of the good–conduct system was not McCloy's only concession. The Simpson Commission, which had investigated the army's handling of the Malmédy case, recommended that a permanent body be established to consider petitions for clemency and pardons, and in November 1949 the army created the War Crimes Modification Board to handle the Dachau cases. Only a few weeks later on December 15, 1949, McCloy told his fellow high commissioners that he was appointing a similar board to draw up a system of clemency and parole for the Nuremberg prisoners.[29] It is a revelation of McCloy's independence that he made his announcement *before* he had the approval of the State Department. Indeed

24 McCloy to Adenauer, Apr. 24, 1950, D(50)1228, NA, RG 466, McCloy Papers, CGR, box 3.
25 McCloy to Rev. A. J. Muench, Jan. 11, 1950, D(50)57, NA, RG 466, McCloy Papers, CGR, box 6.
26 Memo, General Counsel, Oct. 11, 1949, D(49)278, NA, RG 466, McCloy Papers, CGR, box 3.
27 McCloy to Acheson, Dec. 28, 1949, NA, RG 466, McCloy Papers, Office of the Executive Director (OED), 321.6 War Criminals, box 28.
28 McCloy to Manfred George, Aug. 28, 1950, D(50)2065, and Weekly Staff Conference, Aug. 29, 1950, NA, RG 466, McCloy Papers, CGR, boxes 18 and 1. The State Department was annoyed by the bad publicity surrounding the release of Friedrich Flick and asked McCloy to warn them before any further releases. Acheson to McCloy, Sept. 1, 1950, NA, RG 466, McCloy Papers, OED, 321.6 War Criminals, box 28.
29 Minutes of the 10th Meeting of the Allied High Commission, Dec. 15 and 16, 1949, D(49)447b,NA, RG 466, McCloy Papers, CGR, box 5.

Secretary of State Dean Acheson opposed McCloy's original suggestion of a review board that would consider both the Nuremberg
and Dachau cases. Acheson did not want the State Department to
take on the controversial Malmédy case and doubted that any comprehensive review was needed. He feared that a high-caliber board of
experts would "attract attention" and might create "the impression
that legal basis and procedure of Nuremberg trials [are] under review." Acheson thought McCloy should handle the matter with his
existing staff.[30]

McCloy was not deterred. He accepted that the army's cases
should be handled separately, but he told General Handy in a telephone conversation that he had "been giving this thing a lot of
thought as to how we ought to clean it up." McCloy wanted two or
three people who "might review the whole thing, not in terms of
reviewing the cases again but just taking a look at it in terms of what
has happened since those trials took place with the general thought
that there were certainly some of them that richly deserved the
full punishment but others perhaps in light of any extenuating circumstances there might be some commutation. . . ."[31] In responding to Acheson's objections, the high commissioner emphasized
that "whether clemency is warranted in a particular case must be decided after thorough and dispassionate review of all relevant factors,"
and that he needed "a board of qualified individuals who are recognized for objectivity and independence of judgment." After noting
that an extensive review would be too much for his present staff, he
stated firmly that the "mere addition of staff assistants would not
achieve review by body capable of expressing independent opinion."
Pointedly reminding Acheson of the "strong and conflicting views
expressed here, in England and in the United States concerning
proper disposition [of] war crimes sentences," McCloy emphasized
that "whatever action I take must be publicly justified as based upon
thorough and dispassionate review and advice." He concluded by
adding that "my own conscience is involved and though I am prepared to make ultimate decision and accept ultimate responsibility I
require the help of such a group." Acheson quickly replied that "in-

30 Acheson to McCloy, Feb. 8, 1950, NA, RG 466, McCloy Papers, OED, 321.6 War Criminals, box 28.
31 Telephone Conversation between General Handy and Mr. McCloy, Feb. 11, 1950, NA, RG
338, TJAD, GAR, WCBAF, box 14, folder: Miscellaneous.

asmuch as you feel so strongly necessity for forming special group to review death sentences [I] am prepared to proceed if special precautions are taken on handling publicity."[32]

THE CLEMENCY PANEL AND MCCLOY'S DECISIONS

Despite Acheson's worries, McCloy hoped that an expert and independent panel might help him "clean up" the war-crimes problem and defuse the political controversy. Both Acheson and McCloy feared adverse publicity, especially if it gave the impression that the Allies were questioning the Nuremberg verdicts. They also feared that "individual groups" might give the decision a "mistaken interpretation," a discreet reference to the Jewish organizations that would criticize any further review. To counter such attacks, McCloy emphasized that the panel was not to "review the decisions of such Tribunals on questions of law or fact," though it could consider "newly discovered evidence not available at the time of trial." Aware of the political pressures, the high commissioner told Acheson that "delay will only make task more difficult," and asked the secretary for help in recruiting the panel.[33]

The pressure of time and McCloy's approach to staffing led to confusion about whether the panel would function as an appellate court or a clemency board. The distinction was extremely important. An appellate court hears from both the prosecution and the defense, and if it considers new evidence, this evidence can be challenged by the prosecution. A clemency board is not required to be so even-handed, since it is only concerned with mitigating factors and reasons for mercy and cannot question the soundness of the verdicts. McCloy created a board that functioned as both, but with procedures that favored the German prisoners. McCloy's general counsel, Robert Bowie, emphasized the appellate court function of the panel. He noted that "since the [Nuremberg] tribunals are no longer in existence, there exists no judicial forum to which a motion

---

32 McCloy to Acheson, Feb. 17, 1950, and Acheson to McCloy, Feb. 22, 1950, D(50)472, NA, RG 466, McCloy Papers, CGR, box 9.

33 Memo, Bowie to McCloy, March 2, 1950, NA, RG 466, McCloy Papers, OED, 321.6 War Criminals, box 28. McCloy assured Robert S. Marcus of the World Jewish Congress that "such a review should not be construed in any sense to constitute a reopening of the Nuremberg proceedings, a re-examination of the validity of the decrees or a departure from the principles upon which the sentences were predicated." McCloy to Marcus, March 29, 1950, D(50)1023, NA, RG 466, McCloy Papers, CGR, box 11.

for a new trial may be addressed. Every legal system ought to provide some machinery for the presentation of evidence which would
vitiate or substantially affect the earliest decision of a court."[34] In
keeping with this view of the panel, McCloy appointed David W.
Peck, the presiding justice of the Appellate Division, First Department, of the New York Supreme Court, and Conrad Snow, an assistant legal advisor in the State Department.

McCloy's messages to the State Department emphasized only the
clemency role of the panel. Searching for men with reputations of
"integrity and objectivity," the high commissioner wanted at least
one parole board man, and appointed Frederick A. Moran. Moran
was chairman of the New York State Board of Parole, and the governor's chief advisor on all matters relating to parole and clemency.
Moran played a particularly important role in the panel's deliberations, coming to Germany well before the other panel members,
meeting with each of the Landsberg prisoners, and conducting an investigation into the personal history, background, and character of
each criminal.[35] When Moran asked the high commissioner what
"specific factors" could be grounds for clemency, McCloy gave him
wide discretion. John A. Bross, the assistant general counsel, made it
clear to Moran that McCloy was hoping the committee, "carefully
selected for their experience and demonstrated qualities of objective-
ness [sic] and judgment," would help him resolve this thorny political problem.[36]

The Advisory Board on Clemency for War Criminals, known as
the "Peck Panel," began its hearings in Munich on July 11, 1950.
Over the next six weeks the panel considered all petitions for clemency filed on behalf of the defendants. It reviewed the 3,000 pages of
judgments and considered written and oral presentations from some
50 defense counsels representing 90 of the original 104 defendants.
The panel did not review the actual evidence used in the trial –
which amounted to some 330,000 pages – nor did they hear from
any of the former prosecutors, even though one of them, Benjamin
Ferencz, was still in Germany.[37] On August 28, 1950, the panel met

34 Memo, Bowie to McCloy, March 2, 1950, NA, RG 466, McCloy Papers, OED, 321.6 War
   Criminals, box 28.
35 McCloy to Acheson, Feb. 17, 1950, D(50)472, and McCloy to Moran, Oct. 9, 1950,
   D(50)2063, NA, RG 466, McCloy Papers, CGR, boxes 9 and 18.
36 Bross to Moran, May 22, 1950, NA, RG 466, McCloy Papers, OED, 321.6 War Criminals,
   box 28.
37 Benjamin Ferencz, *Less Than Slaves* (Cambridge, Mass., 1979), 73.

with McCloy in Frankfurt and submitted its report. Citing three major reasons for clemency – sentences disproportionate to sentences imposed for similar offenses in other cases, evidence that the prisoner's responsibility for the offenses was less than appeared manifest, and mitigating circumstances, such as refusal to carry out a criminal assignment or order – the Panel recommended reductions in the sentences of 77 of the 99 defendants, including the commutation of seven of the 15 death sentences.[38]

The Peck Panel's report sought to appease all sides of the issue by combining a strong defense of the Nuremberg principles and a wide-ranging leniency. The panel reaffirmed the Nuremberg picture of a Nazi conspiracy to conduct aggressive warfare, emphasizing that all of the organizations it considered – the SS, the Wehrmacht, the concentration camps, the courts, the government, and the major industries – were parts "all integrated in a massive design which despite its madness was thoroughly worked out to incorporate every endeavor." It rejected the defense of superior orders, insisting that if "there is to be a world of law and justice, individuals in positions of some authority at least must be answerable for their acts." The advisory board also rejected the charge that Nuremberg represented ex post facto law, arguing that "murder, pillage and enslavement are against law everywhere and have been for at least the twentieth century."[39]

While the panel reaffirmed the general principles of Nuremberg, it did not do the same for the specific individual punishments. It found that many of the defendants occupied "such subordinate positions," in which they were "little more than common members of a criminal organization." In reaching this judgment, the panel decided to consider all the cases together as a single group, taking into account the "differences in authority and action among the defendants" and placing them "in proper relation to each other and the programs in which they participated." This approach had important implications for many of the lesser defendants. Compared to ideological fanatics like Otto Ohlendorf or Paul Blobel, who supervised and directed thou-

---

38 Letter of transmittal, Aug. 28, 1950, and "Report of the Advisory Board on Clemency for War Criminals to the United States High Commissioner for Germany," Aug. 28, 1950, NA, RG 84, 71A-2100, box 373 [hereafter: Advisory Panel Report].

39 Advisory Panel Report. The introduction to the Peck Panel's Report was included in the publication, *Landsberg: A Documentary Report,* and is reprinted in *Information Bulletin of the Office of the U.S. High Commissioner for Germany* (Feb. 1951).

sands of murders, many of the bureaucrats and industrialists seemed far less directly responsible for such atrocities. The panel tended to excuse these "white-collar" war criminals.[40]

The panel's report also made it clear that it considered the quality of some of the judgments that the original tribunals had made. It argued that while it "worked under a directive that it was not to review the judgments on the law or the facts," it had concluded that its authority to review the sentences "required a differentiation between specific facts found and established in the evidence and conclusions that may have been drawn therefrom. We have considered ourselves bound by the former but not by the latter." As such the panel frequently concluded "that the facts as stated in the judgments themselves are not sufficient to establish beyond a reasonable doubt the defendant's responsibility for specific crimes." The problem with this conclusion was that the panel did not examine the vast bulk of evidence that was *not* contained in the 3,000 pages of judgments and in which there was often evidence that supported the Nuremberg court's original determination.[41]

Although McCloy received the Peck Panel's report at the end of August, he did not turn his attention to it immediately. The high commissioner played an active role in the September meeting of the foreign ministers in New York, during which the United States proposed the rearmament of Germany. In the wake of the outbreak of the Korean War in June, McCloy abandoned his opposition to German rearmament. He recognized that rearmament and the need to ally Germany with the West would change her status, and advised President Truman that "certain of the things we would like to see done in Germany will not be completed."[42] The high commissioner hoped that European integration, through both the Schuman Plan and later the European Defense Community (EDC), would ensure that the addition of Germany's strength to the West would not lead to a new nationalist danger.

The rearmament decision transformed the atmosphere in Germany, and encouraged those groups seeking clemency to tie the question to a "German contribution to the defense of the West." Bishop Neuhäusler told McCloy that now that the "German Federal Republic has been called upon to form, together with Western pow-

---

40 Ferencz, *Less Than Slaves*, 74.   41 Advisory Panel Report.
42 Memorandum for the President, "The Situation in Germany," Sept. 10, 1950, TL, President's Secretary's Files, Germany, box 178, folder 2.

ers, a strong defensive block against the Bolshevism of the East," the United States should show mercy toward the Landsberg prisoners.[43] The two ex-Generals, Adolf Heusinger and Hans Speidel, who were Adenauer's chief advisors on rearmament, told the High Commission's Bonn liaison that "if the prisoners at Landsberg were hanged, Germany as an armed ally against the East was an illusion."[44] A group of Bundestag deputies from all the major parties except the Communists told McCloy that they felt it "their duty to call for modification of the death sentences," especially given the "political and psychological factors at a time when Western Germany was being called upon to make a military contribution to Western defense."[45] They also emphasized that the long periods the prisoners spent on death row were not in keeping with the German tradition of a speedy imposition of the penalty and constituted a severe psychological punishment. In a meeting with the high commissioners on November 16, 1950, Adenauer requested the "commutation of all death sentences not yet executed to sentences of confinement, since capital punishment has been abolished by Article 102 of the Basic Law," and the "widest possible clemency for persons sentenced to confinement."[46] Even the victims of Nazis joined in the chorus calling for clemency. The Social Democratic Party's leader and concentration camp survivor, Kurt Schumacher, insisted that further executions would violate German sovereignty.[47] He was joined by such figures as Inge Scholl, whose sister and brother, leaders of the "White Rose" resistance movement, had been killed by the Nazis. Observing these intense efforts for clemency, British High Commissioner Ivone Kirkpatrick told his superiors in London that "it is a regrettable fact that even moderate Germans such as the Protestant bishops and sensible SPD men who have suffered from Nazi persecution resent the war crimes trials."[48]

It was in this charged atmosphere that McCloy finally began to consider the Peck Panel's report. Though the German protests were

---

43 Neuhäusler to McCloy, Jan. 20, 1951, D(51)119, NA, RG 466, McCloy Papers, CGR, box 24.
44 Charles Thayer, *The Unquiet Germans* (New York, 1957), 234.
45 *New York Times,* Jan. 10, 1951.
46 *FRUS 1950,* vol. 4, *Central and Eastern Europe; The Soviet Union* (Washington, D.C., 1980), 782.
47 *Neue Zeitung,* Jan. 30, 1951, Friedrich-Ebert-Stiftung, Bonn, Schumacher Bestand, Interviews, Q-7. There is a heated debate about the SPD's position in the Fraktionsprotokolle, Jan. 9 and Feb. 1, 1951, Friedrich-Ebert-Stiftung, Bonn.
48 Kirkpatrick to Gainer, Feb. 3, 1951, PRO, FO 371/93536. The German campaign made very little attempt to distinguish between types of war criminals. Buscher, *War Crimes,* 127.

vocal, McCloy did hear opposing views. His general counsel and closest advisor, Robert Bowie, criticized the Peck Panel for its "excessive" leniency. Bowie told McCloy that he had "serious doubts" about twenty-four of the board's recommendations, and that in another twenty-two cases the board's reasoning was "inadequate." Bowie was particularly concerned about the failure of the Panel to investigate the full record of the various cases. "In only two or three instances," he discovered, had the Peck Panel checked all of the evidence. The Board's statement that "they have striven to be as lenient as possible," Bowie feared, could create the impression of "a repudiation of the Nuremberg trials."[49]

Bowie directed his sharpest criticism at the board's leniency toward German military men. In the cases of Hermann Reinecke, Walter Warlimont, and Georg von Kuechler, Bowie noted that "they were all directly implicated in the program which encompassed the murder of commandos, commissars and captured allied airmen as well as in the brutal mistreatment of prisoners of war." The lawyer pointed out that while the board recommended clemency because of the "alleged subordinate positions" of the men, "von Kuechler was a Field Marshall and Reinecke and Warlimont were Lt. Generals." Bowie also objected to the leniency shown to the *Einsatzgruppen* and those involved with medical experimentation on concentration camp inmates. For these cases Bowie's staff put together their own reports, frequently urging tougher sentences than the Peck Panel had recommended.[50]

The high commissioner found himself deciding between the recommendations of his expert panel and those of his staff lawyers. Despite his desire to promote German rearmament, McCloy agreed with his general counsel on the military cases, refusing any sentence reduction to von Kuechler, Reinecke, and Warlimont. He also refused to reduce the sentences of Field Marshall Wilhelm List and General Walter Kuntze because of their responsibility for the murder of hostages in the Balkans. (Though in the latter two cases he left open the possibility for medical parole on the basis of age.) For eighteen of the other defendants, particularly in the medical experimentation and *Einsatzgruppen* cases, McCloy decided on tougher

49 Bowie to McCloy, Oct. 31, 1950, NA, RG 466, McCloy Papers, OED, 321.6 War Criminals, box 28.
50 These reports can be found in "War Criminals 1949–1950," NA, RG 466, McCloy Papers, Administration of Justice Division, General Counsel, box 1.

sentences than the Peck Panel recommended, but still reduced the original sentences.[51] In this context, the Krupp case, despite its notoriety abroad, emerged as a relatively uncontroversial affair, since both the panel and the general counsel agreed that the sentence was excessive compared with that assessed against the Flick and Farben directors, and that the confiscation decree was not in accordance with the principles of American justice. McCloy also believed that the Schuman Plan, which would place Germany's heavy industry under European regulation, made Krupp's return to ownership less threatening to the West.

The capital cases caused McCloy the most difficulty. Despite a lifetime as a lawyer, McCloy had little experience with criminal matters. He told the German delegations who visited him with petitions that "of all the problems that he had confronted in Germany this was the most difficult and the one on which he had spent the most time," adding that it was also a duty which he "intensely disliked."[52] In part to ease his own conscience, McCloy followed an unorthodox procedure. The high commissioner was willing to speak with almost anyone about the cases, accept new petitions and evidence, and hear new witnesses. Acting like the governor of an American state, he even traveled personally to Landsberg to meet with some of the prisoners.

By mid-November 1950 McCloy informed Washington that he had tentatively decided on nine executions, including one prisoner, Ernst Biberstein, for whom the Peck Panel had urged clemency.[53] All but one of these were commanders of the *Einsatzgruppen,* and were personally responsible for thousands of executions. Despite the political pressure from Germany and the worsening international situation caused by China's entry into the Korean conflict, Washington officials did not try to change McCloy's decisions.[54] Acheson told McCloy that while he was aware "that there are individuals and organizations both in Germany and the U.S. which believe all death sentences in these cases should be commuted, I am impressed by the fact that these cases were carefully considered by the trial tribunals,

51 Ferencz, *Less Than Slaves,* 223.
52 "Meeting between Mr. McCloy and Delegation from the Bundestag," Jan. 9, 1951, D(51)17A, NA, RG 466, McCloy Papers, CGR, box 24.
53 Jonathan B. Rintels to Major J. J. Kapral, Dec. 22, 1950, NA, RG 466, McCloy Papers, OED, 321.6 War Criminals, box 28.
54 Manchester argues that Washington ordered McCloy's clemency decisions. Manchester, *Arms of Krupp,* 768.

448 Thomas Alan Schwartz

by Gen. Clay, by your advisory board and by yourself," and that "I concur in your proposed course of action, and leave to your discretion the time when [the executions] take place."[55] President Truman showed the same support for McCloy. When he was urged by a Missouri friend and member of his Masonic lodge to grant clemency, Truman curtly replied by sending him a copy of McCloy's decisions and saying, "I have to accept this as the situation because there is no way for me to interfere with things inside Germany."[56]

McCloy did not hold to these tentative decisions. Unwilling to carry out the executions near the Christmas holiday, McCloy decided to wait until the new year to announce his judgments. The high commissioner used the additional time to try to convince German officials that the death penalty was justified. The high commissioner justified the lengthy and time-consuming review by pointing out that without it some men would have been executed who would not now be. He disagreed with Adenauer and Schumacher that the *Grundgesetz*'s prohibition of capital punishment applied to the Nuremberg cases. The trials were conducted by international courts at a time when there was no German government in existence, and many of the crimes were committed against non-Germans. When one Bundestag deputy suggested that the excesses of the Nazis "should be cancelled out by a great gesture of clemency," McCloy replied with amazement that such an argument could be offered seriously. He reminded the Germans that these were "crimes of historical proportion" and a "spasm of criminality which had aroused world-wide indignation." McCloy was also disturbed by the German "tendency to put things under the carpet and refuse to acknowledge what actually happened." The German people, he emphasized, must "understand the enormity of what had been done."

Yet McCloy also made clear to the German leaders that he had "strained to find some grounds for clemency and had persuaded himself that he was justified in commuting certain of the sentences." He added that "when I go through these cases, I do so without hatred and I try to temper justice with mercy." However, in some cases he could find no such justification for mercy, and "could hardly believe that the men who perpetrated these crimes were human." He repeatedly insisted to the Germans that he was not "executing anybody for

55 Acheson to McCloy, Nov. 16, 1950, D(50)5230, NA, RG 466, McCloy Papers, CGR, box 21.
56 Truman to Frank Land, Feb. 1, 1951, TL, President's Secretary's Files, Germany – Nazi War Criminals, box 179.

political reasons" but reminded them that he "had to view things from an international as well as a bilateral perspective." While he intended to grant clemency in as many cases as possible, he remained "deeply disturbed" about the effect this might have outside Germany and feared a "worldwide reaction of cynicism and disillusion."[57]

In the last days before the decisions, the situation at McCloy's headquarters became increasingly tense. Death threats against Mc-Cloy and his children necessitated bodyguards and increased security. McCloy agonized over the decisions, locking "himself in his home, reading and rereading the testimony."[58] The high commissioner poured over the records of the cases late into the night, showing what one assistant called a "deep concern and scrupulous sense of obligation for the rights and privileges of a single individual."[59] Psychologically it is likely that McCloy was searching for a way to avoid ordering as many executions as he originally planned. At the last minute, he received " a little new evidence" in one capital case which could justify commutation.[60] But in changing this sentence, McCloy doubted whether death was appropriate for three others with a similar position of responsibility. As a result, McCloy spared four of the *Einsatzgruppen* leaders – Waldemar Klingelhofer, Ernst Biberstein, Adolf Ott, and Martin Sandberger – and ordered only five executions – Oswald Pohl, Paul Blobel, Otto Ohlendorf, Erich Naumann, and Werner Braune. On the same day that McCloy announced his decisions, General Handy commuted eleven death sentences, including all of the remaining Malmédy prisoners, and ordered the execution of two men convicted of atrocities in concentration camps. The seven were executed on June 7, 1951, the last legal executions in the Federal Republic.

THE REACTION TO THE LANDSBERG DECISIONS

The sharp contrast between the reaction within Germany and outside the country illustrates the central problem facing those American leaders who wanted to "integrate" Germany into the West. McCloy's

57 "Meeting between Mr. McCloy and Delegation from the Bundestag," Jan. 9, 1951, D(51)17A, NA, RG 466, McCloy Papers, CGR, box 24. See also Arthur Krock's column in the *New York Times*, Apr. 26, 1951.
58 Thayer, *Unquiet Germans,* 233.
59 Jonathan Rintels to McCloy, June 9, 1952, McCloy Scrapbooks, McCloy Papers, Amherst College.
60 McCloy to Peck, Feb. 5, 1951, D(51)126, NA, RG 466, McCloy Papers, CGR, box 24.

decisions, which appeared to most Germans as reasonable or even too harsh, struck many Europeans and Americans as unjustified leniency bordering on appeasement. The reactions underscore the political difficulties of accepting Germany within the West and the moral compromises and political expediency that were necessary to do so.

On the surface the German reaction to McCloy's decisions focused entirely on the condemned prisoners, and they remained at the center of attention until their execution in June. There were continuing appeals for clemency, especially from the FDP and some church officials. Bishop Wurm praised McCloy's commutations but asked whether in light of "reports on the warfare in Korea . . . [especially] partisan warfare . . . the sentences should not have been reduced to a greater extent."[61] But although these reactions attracted notable press coverage in the *New York Times* and other American journals, they distorted the picture of German reaction. A surprising consensus of elite opinion approved McCloy's actions. Adenauer praised McCloy's decisions for their "diligence and sincerity" and condemned the continuing propaganda in favor of the Landsberg prisoners.[62] While American surveys showed strong support for further leniency among average Germans, the new German political elite, at least as represented in the Bundestag, was supportive of McCloy's efforts.[63] The high commission's liaison in Bonn reported that the "reaction of politically-conscious Germans on whom after all the future of German policy largely depends has been considerably more satisfactory than one could have justifiably expected considering all the circumstances."[64] Despite fears to the contrary, the agitation over the condemned prisoners faded away quickly after their executions.

The reaction in Western countries was of a different quality altogether. In both Britain and France McCloy's decisions added to the resentments felt, especially by the political opposition, to the decision to rearm Germany and the increasing militarization of the Cold War. The pardon of Krupp drew intense reactions, with one English

61 Wurm to McCloy, Feb. 2, 1951, D(51)126, NA, RG 466, McCloy Papers, CGR, box 24.
62 McCloy to Acheson, March 5, 1951, D(51)285/A, NA, RG 466, McCloy Papers, CGR, box 25.
63 "West German Reactions to the Landsberg Decisions," March 6, 1951, D(51)126, NA, RG 466, McCloy Papers, CGR, box 24.
64 Liaison Bonn to McCloy, March 7, 1951, NA, RG 466, McCloy Papers, OED, 321.6 War Criminals, box 28.

newspaper running a cartoon of Hitler and Goering sitting in Valhalla, reading a newspaper with the headline, "Krupp freed." The caption depicted Hitler telling Goering, "Should we have hung on a little longer?" The Manchester *Guardian* ran a letter which noted that "there is a mercy which is weakness and even treason against the common good," and that the "happenings in Germany over the war criminals" reflected the truth of this statement.[65] To the French newspapers, the release was an indication of America's failure to understand the roots of German militarism. *Le Figaro* commented that "Mr. McCloy and his countrymen have not had such close relations with Krupp as we had by means of the famous Bertha gun." In both Britain and France the Krupp pardon served as a symbol of the American haste to rearm Germany. The leftist *Franc-Tireur* called Krupp's release " the worst thing about the war crimes trials," while the conservative *Paris Presse* said it had "practically destroyed Franco–American understanding."[66]

Reaction in America was less extreme, but still critical. The *New York Times* approved McCloy's action, noting that he had compromised between justice and expediency. If the Germans now "honestly condemned" these crimes, "there is some hope for the German future."[67] The *Washington Post* could not understand the release of Alfried Krupp, who "bears a share of responsibility for Hitler's assumption of power and the implementation of his plans."[68] In the more liberal *Nation*, Telford Taylor, the former Nuremberg prosecutor, blasted McCloy's decisions as the "embodiment of political expediency, distorted by a thoroughly unsound approach to the law and the facts, to say nothing of the realities of contemporary world politics."[69] Four resolutions were introduced in Congress calling for the investigation of American policy in Germany, particularly the "mass clemency orders in connection with Nazi War Criminals."[70]

---

65 Manchester, *Arms of Krupp*, 763–4. *New York Times*, Feb. 7 and 8, 1951. "Review of German and Foreign Press Reaction to the Clemency Decisions on Landsberg War Crime Cases," Feb. 10, 1951, D(51)126, NA, RG 466, McCloy Papers, CGR, box 24. London ordered the British high commissioner to return for consultation when he made a statement approving of McCloy's actions. Gifford to State Dept., Feb. 9, 1951, D(51)126, NA, RG 466, McCloy Papers, CGR, box 24.
66 "Review of German and Foreign Press Reaction to the Clemency Decisions on Landsberg War Crimes Cases," Feb. 10, 1951, D(51)126, NA, RG 466, McCloy Papers, CGR, box 24.
67 *New York Times*, Feb. 2, 1951.
68 *Washington Post*, Feb. 2, 1952.
69 Telford Taylor, "The Nazis Go Free," *The Nation*, Feb. 24, 1951, pp. 170–2.
70 James Webb to McCloy, Feb. 28, 1951, NA, RG 466, McCloy Papers, OED, 321.6 War Criminals, box 28.

Thomas Alan Schwartz

Although the subsequent congressional investigation offered only mild criticism of McCloy's policies, the passionate reactions and the intense controversy highlight the confused environment in which McCloy made his decisions. McCloy was at the center of a system of contradictory political pressures, attempting to make a decision that would satisfy the sense of justice among nations with very different understandings and experiences of World War II. Although McCloy insisted that "he was not executing anybody for political reasons," and that "at no moment did I consider any political or extraneous matter," his Landsberg decisions were fundamentally political ones, characteristic of his own search for some type of compromise between the concerns of the different Western nations and the Federal Republic.[71] To call the executions "political" does not imply that McCloy ordered men executed who were in any sense of the word "innocent." He reduced prison sentences and commuted death sentences of men who were, in terms of relative guilt and the extreme scale that must be applied to Nazi crimes, less responsible for atrocities than those he ordered executed. He spared them, at least in part, because of the strong protests made on their behalf by leaders of the Federal Republic.

To some extent McCloy was successful, in that the issue of the remaining imprisoned war criminals declined in importance after his decisions. The German government continued to lobby quietly on their behalf, with Adenauer frequently telling the high commissioner that the release of prisoners would have a positive effect on German public opinion. However, the controversy over the Landsberg cases lingered with McCloy until he left Germany in July 1952, and with the exception of General Reinhardt, whom he freed on medical parole, the high commissioner avoided any further clemency. After the signing of the EDC and Contractual Agreements in May 1952, McCloy rejected the FDP's call for an amnesty.[72] He also pressed Adenauer hard on the importance of a generous reparations policy toward Israel and the Jewish community, perhaps seeing in financial *Wiedergutmachung* a more politically acceptable policy than the continued stern punishment of Nazi war criminals.

71 "Meeting between Mr. McCloy and Delegation from the Bundestag," Jan. 9, 1951, D(51)17A, NA, RG 466, McCloy Papers, CGR, box 24. After the executions, McCloy wrote, "I experienced some human reactions that had never come my way before." McCloy to Frankfurter, July 11, 1951, Felix Frankfurter Papers, LC.
72 Buscher, *War Crimes*, 141.

Yet the Landsberg decisions also set in motion a process whereby all the remaining Nazi war criminals would be released. The issue was now seen purely as a political one, in which the U.S. government sought to appease German demands while not unduly aggravating its own public opinion. As one High Commission study put it in December 1952: "There is already a fundamental if unavoidable contradiction between the role of the United States as occupier and executor of occupation justice in Germany and the role of the U.S. as Germany's ally and friend."[73] In 1953 the Allies created the Interim Mixed Parole and Clemency Board, which became the Mixed Parole and Clemency Board when Germany finally regained her sovereignty in 1955. These boards consisted of representatives from the Western powers and the Federal Republic. They operated under regulations similar to those given McCloy's original advisory board, and they continuously reviewed the various cases, generously granting petitions for parole.[74] Of the 338 prisoners still in Landsberg in August 1952, by 1955 the number was down to 50. Fearing the domestic political reaction, the United States wanted to release the prisoners as "quietly and discreetly" as possible.[75] By May 1958 the United States freed the last four prisoners it held, including three of those spared at the last minute by McCloy. The French and British followed the same pattern, releasing the war criminals they held in West Germany by 1958.

McCloy's decisions in the Landsberg cases offer some important insights into American policy in Germany in the early 1950s. McCloy's willingness to review the cases came well before the rearmament issue emerged, and his subsequent judgments reflect a genuine attempt to balance justice and mercy. Unfortunately, he made decisions that proved much too lenient and opened the floodgates for wholesale releases. On the other hand, the high commissioner's determination to proceed with some executions demonstrates his resolve to uphold the basic concept of the Nuremberg trials in the face of significant opposition and the pressure of the Cold War. McCloy's decisions should be considered within the context of the Germany of 1951, in which as one study put it, "the problem of war criminals is

---

73 "The War Criminals Question," HICOG Office of Political Affairs, Dec. 22, 1952, NA, RG 466, McCloy Papers, OED, 321.6 War Criminals, box 28.
74 Adenauer stressed that a "far-reaching gesture toward solution of war-criminals problem" would impress public opinion. *FRUS 1952–1954*, vol 7., *Germany and Austria* (Washington, D.C., 1986), 392.
75 *New York Times*, March 26, 1954.

not a rational issue in German public opinion."[76] Few Germans approved of Allied handling of the war-crimes issue, and politicians from all the major political parties attacked the trials. Although many German leaders claimed they wanted punishment for "real" war criminals, their campaign for clemency rarely made any important distinctions among those convicted.

However, it is too simple to conclude, as one recent study has, that the war-crimes program was a "failure."[77] Certainly there were injustices, and some Nazi war criminals escaped punishment. The successful return of industrialists like Krupp and Flick to positions of wealth and prominence, a by-product of the *Wirtschaftswunder,* was also an ugly reminder of American expediency. But many war criminals were punished, and an extensive and incontrovertible record of Nazi crimes was established. In contrast with Japan, Nazi war criminals were removed from any significant role in Germany's public life.[78] Ironically enough, the very success of Germany's integration into the West, the degree to which Germany became a respected and "normal" member of the European community, is a major reason that this leniency now seems so tragic and shortsighted. The United States has a bad conscience for not dealing more severely with Nazi war crimes, and Germany now has a bad conscience for not having let it.

76 "The War Criminals Question," Office of Political Affairs, Dec. 22, 1952, NA, RG 466, McCloy Papers, OED, 321.6 War Criminals, box 28. Only 6 percent were certain that German soldiers could be reproached for their conduct in occupied countries. Elisabeth Noelle and Erich Peter Neumann, eds., *The Germans: Public Opinion Polls, 1947–1966* (Allensbach and Bonn, 1967), 202.
77 Buscher, *War Criminals,* 159.   78 Mendelsohn, "War Crimes Trials," 259.

22

Sources in German Archives on the History of American Policy toward Germany, 1945–1955

JOSEF HENKE

Among the German archives that hold documents pertaining to postwar U.S. policy toward Germany for the years 1945 to 1949 are the Bundesarchiv, the Archiv des Deutschen Bundestages, the archives of the primary political parties, state and local government archives, as well as corporate and personal archives from the American Zone of Occupation and the American Sector of Berlin. In addition, for the period 1949 to 1955, the Archiv des Auswärtigen Amts is of special importance. The holdings of these archives can be supplemented by materials of economic, press, and radio archives. This overview will not include the records of the U.S. Office of Military Government for Germany (OMGUS). Although most of these records were microfilmed in a joint U.S.–German venture and are available at the Institut für Zeitgeschichte in Munich and the Bundesarchiv (only the OMGUS Headquarters entities), the original records are under the custody of the National Archives and Records Administration in the United States. OMGUS records generated at the state level can be found in the Staatsarchive of Baden-Württemberg, Bavaria, Berlin, Bremen, and Hesse.[1]

The records of the legal proceedings of the war-crimes trials (the International Military Tribunal at Nuremberg and the twelve U.S. supplementary cases heard primarily at Dachau) should also be mentioned here. Reproductions of these records are available in various German archival collections.[2] The originals are kept by U.S. ar-

---

The chapter has been translated by Bryan van Sweringen and Axel Frohn.

1 Cf. Josef Henke, "Das amerikanisch-deutsch OMGUS-Projekt: Erschliessung und Verfilmung der Akten der amerikanischen Militärregierung in Deutschland," *Der Archivar* 35 (1982):149–58.

2 Cf. *Das Bundesarchiv und seine Bestände*, 3rd ed., prepared by Gerhard Granier, Josef Henke, and Klaus Oldenhage (Boppard, 1977), 707ff.

chives, however, and, therefore will not be described in this essay in
any detail.

In respect to both methodology and the evaluation of sources, it is
important to recall that the origins and the conceptualization of the
foreign policy of a given state (including alternatives that were not
implemented) as well as the realization of this policy are primarily
reflected in the documentary evidence of the decisive political institutions of *that* state. In contrast, documents of both governmental
and private origin of the country that is the subject of this foreign
policy show only certain aspects (which may indeed be varied and
broad) of the implementation of and perhaps reactions to this policy.
In short, the most important sources on the development of U.S.
policy toward Germany from 1945 to 1955 will be found in American archives, while the results of these policies are first and foremost
reflected in the records of German institutions, which are deposited
in German archives. Certainly, both German institutions and individuals were competent enough to evaluate, make observations
about, collect information on, and to write reports about U.S. plans
for Germany. In terms of the historical methodology to evaluate the
significance of sources, there is of course an important difference between these records and concept papers generated, for example, by
the White House or the State Department, which the archivist need
not explain to the historian.

The limitations of German archives for research on U.S. policy toward Germany outlined above, particularly for the first half of the
period under consideration, cannot be delineated precisely. The defeated and divided Germany did not have any centralized governmental or administrative institutions to prepare counterproposals or
reactions to American policies. There is, as a result, no body of German documentation that could serve as a counterweight to U.S. policy toward Germany as reflected in American sources for the years
between 1945 and 1949–51. Anyone who might have had the opportunity to conduct research, for instance, into Hitler's plans for England knows the enormous value of the counterpoint found in the
documents of the British Foreign Office and can readily understand
the consequences of the absence of such documentation for histori-
ography. The sources available on the immediate postwar period in
German archives are in this respect found wanting and incomplete.

Consequently, the German records of zonal, regional, and communal provenances document the broad and varied effects of U.S. policy toward Germany but are not suited to describe and analyze the underlying American concepts. Given the almost complete political dependency of the defeated Germans upon the allies, it is also understandable that the records of German offices for the years 1945–50 do not (unlike the earlier records of the Reich Chancellery and the Auswärtiges Amt) reflect foreign policy in the traditional sense, but rather as the implementation of American policies in the U.S. Zone of Occupation of the defeated, then reconstructed, Germany, as well as in the American Sector of Berlin. A significant exception are the records of the *Länderrat* of the U.S. Zone of Occupation, located in Stuttgart, which, from 1945 onward, functioned as a substitute for both German parliament and government. Its records were deposited in the Bundesarchiv[3] and the Baden–Württembergisches Hauptstaatsarchiv in Stuttgart. Reactions of the *Länder* governments, as well as the Bremen and Berlin governments to *Länderrat* decisions are documented in ministerial records, which are held in the Hauptstaatsarchive in Stuttgart, Munich, Wiesbaden, Bremen, and Berlin.[4]

The concrete results of U.S. policies can be found in the records of *Länder* agencies of Bavaria, Württemberg-Baden (Baden-Württemberg), Hesse, Bremen, and Berlin, as well as – in more vivid detail – in the records of local government organizations in Kreis-, Stadt- and Gemeindearchiven in Karlshafen, Marburg, and Kassel, Munich, Landshut, and Berchtesgaden, Berlin, Bremerhaven, and Bremen, Kaub, Viernheim, Ulm, and Neustadt an der Waldnaab.[5] The reference to these smaller archives, that is to the archives of smaller districts, is not frivolous. In an article with the somewhat daring title "Deutsche Aussenpolitik," published in the first edition of the *Weser-Kurier* at the end of September 1945, Felix von Eckardt correctly observed that

as a substitute for an official German foreign policy, every German must accept a very important personal responsibility. As a result of the complete

---

3 Cf. ibid., 388–9. Other Bundesarchiv record groups mentioned in this essay are also described in this inventory. Finding aids available only for use at the archives are not cited.

4 See *Übersicht über die Bestände des Hessischen Hauptstaatsarchivs Wiesbaden* (Wiesbaden, 1970), 310ff.; *Übersicht über die Bestände des Staatsarchivs der Freien Hansestadt Bremen* (Bremen, 1982); *Das Landesarchiv Berlin und seine Bestände*, ed. Jürgen Wetzel (Berlin, 1982).

5 See Verein deutscher Archivare, ed., *Archive und Archivare in der Bundesrepublik Deutschland, Oesterreich und der Schweiz*, 14th ed. (Munich, 1986).

occupation of Germany, every German, either privately or professionally, comes into contact with representatives of the victorious powers. The rule of the National Socialists, their crimes, their unprecedented cruelty, have brought the Germans into disrepute as a people without morals and civilizations. We have to turn every American, English, French, or Russian soldier who returns home into an ambassador of the German cause. We must do everything within our power to show them the qualities of an earlier Germany, far removed from military boasting, a mindless glorification of violence, and a petit-bourgeois arrogance, which often times inspired respect, trust, and even love. . . .[6]

This lowering of the level of German–American "foreign relations" in the immediate postwar period is also indicative of a change in the location of valuable source material from the traditional diplomatic institutions to the records of regional and community archives.

As noted above, the Bundesarchiv holds the very important record group Länderrat des amerikanischen Besatzungsgebietes (Bestand Z 1). It includes, in addition to the records of the (General-) Sekretariat, the Dienststellenverwaltung, and the Koordinierungsabteilung (particularly the minutes of meetings), records pertaining to press, law (especially civilian and criminal law, denazification and restitution, public, economic, and labor law), finance (including the banking and insurance system), economy (in particular industrial production, provision for the population, interzonal trade), registration of armaments, postal service and traffic matters, statistics, social policy (including refugees, housing, public health matters, and the administration of foreign charitable gifts), culture, and education. Integrated within this record group, which is also very informative with regard to the history of the British Zone of Occupation, are records of the representative of the *Länderrat* in Berlin.

There are, unfortunately, hardly any complementary records of the zonal level available, since there were only very few such specialized offices *(Fachbehörden)* in the U.S. Zone of Occupation. So, for example, the Bundesarchiv holds only a small number of records of the Oberpostdirektorium of the U.S. Zone, aside from records of those German post offices in service of the Allied Forces.[7]

The economic, and later political, fusion of the American and British zones into "Bizonia" effectively increased the number of relevant

6 Felix von Eckardt, *Ein unordentliches Leben: Lebenserinnerungen* (Düsseldorf and Vienna, 1987), 118–19.
7 Cf. *Das Bundesarchiv und seine Bestände,* 118ff.

record groups in the Bundesarchiv. They include the records of the Wirtschaftsrat des Vereinigten Wirtschaftsgebietes (Bestand Z 3) although the majority of these records are under the custody of the Archiv des Deutschen Bundestages; records of the Länderrat des Vereinigten Wirtschaftsgebietes (Bestand Z 4); and the Direktorialkanzlei des Verwaltungsrates des Vereinigten Wirtschaftsgebietes (Bestand Z 13). This almost complete set of records illustrates the function of the Verwaltungsrat as liaison between the occupation offices – in particular the Bipartite Control Office (BICO) – and the German administrative offices for the period 1947 to 1949–50.

In addition, there are the records of a number of special offices and courts: the almost complete records of the Rechtsamt der Verwaltung des Vereinigten Wirtschaftsgebietes (Bestand Z 22); Deutsches Obergericht für das Vereinigte Wirtschaftsgebiet (Bestand Z 37); Verwaltung für Finanzen des Vereinigten Wirtschaftsgebietes (Bestand Z 38); Sonderstelle für Geld und Kredit (Bestand Z 32); Büro für Währungsfragen (Bestand Z 26); Verwaltung für Wirtschaft des Vereinigten Wirtschaftsgebietes (Bestand Z 8) – including the records of the Berater für den Marshallplan beim Vorsitzer des Verwaltungsrates des Vereinigten Wirtschaftsgebietes (Bestand Z 14). The latter contains documents of particular importance concerning the distribution of ERP funds and the coordination of different assistance programs relating to production, consumption, foreign trade, finance, investment, refugee assistance, as well as the creation of jobs. Also included are the materials on the activities of the German representative to the Economic Cooperation Administration (ECA) in Washington and the OEEC in Paris. Finally, the records of the Verwaltung für Ernährung, Landwirtschaft und Forsten des Vereinigten Wirtschaftsgebietes (Bestand Z 6) should be mentioned, not only because they document the ERP agricultural programs but also because they incorporate some of the official and personal files of its director Schlange-Schöningen, which are of historical importance not only for this subject area but for the entire history of the immediate postwar period.

As a consequence of the economic fusion of the American and British Zones (and following the archival principle of arranging records by provenance), the records of the *Länder* of the British zone also reflect to a certain degree U.S. occupational policies and American policy toward Germany. One example is the issue of socialization in North Rhine–Westphalia.

The Bundesarchiv holds trizonal records on a comparatively smaller scale. Worth mentioning in this context are the records of the Büro der Ministerpräsidenten des amerikanischen, britischen und französischen Besatzungsgebietes (Bestand Z 12). This collection contains significant documents on the preparation of the Basic Law and the establishment of federal institutions and agencies. It also documents both the effect of the Occupation Statute and the influence of the ministers president upon the solution of political, legal, economic, and social problems resulting from the war. The records consequently illustrate the position of the higher echelons vis-à-vis certain aspects of the occupation policies of the Western Allies, including of course U.S. policy toward Germany. The majority of the records of the Parlamentarischer Rat are found in the Archiv des Deutschen Bundestages, the minority in the Bundesarchiv (Bestand Z 5). A closer examination of the minutes of the meetings of the Parlamentarischer Rat and its committees would be necessary to determine to what degree its decisions were influenced by American occupational authorities.

Those record groups that contain information generated both prior to and following the founding of the Federal Republic in 1949 include the records of the Deutsches Büro für Friedensfragen (Bestand Z 35), which contains, for example, documents on the Ruhr Statute, the dismantling of German industry, and the Saar district, and the Institut für Besatzungsfragen (Bestand B 120). The latter record group includes documents on the occupation of Germany, and the stationing of troops on the basis of the Contractual Agreements of 1955 and the Paris Accords of 1954. After 1949, federal ministries and agencies took over the records of zonal, bizonal, and trizonal special offices and, although the labels on these records indicate that they were generated after September 1949, they may contain valuable materials on the immediate postwar period of German history.

The creation of the Auswärtiges Amt in 1951 is of great significance for the nature of the sources available on the period under consideration. In the process of developing and formulating the Federal Republic's foreign policy, it is necessary for the Auswärtiges Amt to collect information on other states' policies toward Germany. In other words, the records of the Auswärtiges Amt provide the historian with a body of information on U.S. policy toward Germany that forms a counterweight to U.S. sources. Once again, it is important to recall the difference between the primary sources generated by the U.S. government and the counterpoint provided by German records. The fact that the Auswärtiges Amt was established only in 1951 is of no particular significance as far as its records are concerned: All relevant materials were taken over by the Auswärtiges Amt from the Chancellery. In addition, the personal union of chancellor and foreign minister, which lasted from 1951 to 1955, requires the examination of the records of both federal offices in foreign policy matters. The records of the Bundeskanzleramt are deposited in the Bundesarchiv (Bestand B 136). Access to the records of the Auswärtiges Amt – as to the other archival sources in Bundesarchiv, Bundestag, Bundesrat, and Stiftung Bundeskanzler-Adenauer-Haus – are governed by the rules and regulations of the Gesetz über die Sicherung und Nutzung von Archivgut des Bundes (Bundesarchivgesetz – BArchG) of January 6, 1988.[8]

In addition to the records of the Ministerbüro and the Büro des Staatssekretärs Hallstein, which unfortunately are still security classified, the records of *Abteilung 2 (Politische Abteilung) (bis 1954)* merit individual mention and description. Until 1955 the records of *Abteilung 2* were entered into a section registry. With the creation of subsections *(Referate)* in 1955, those records created before the end of 1954 were deposited in the Politisches Archiv (today: *Referat 117*). They compose a record group in themselves. Records created after 1955 were usually controlled by the subsection registries of *Abteilung 2* and are identified as such in the records of the *Referate*. *Abteilung 2* was responsible for questions pertaining to occupation rights, contact with the three powers, general preparation of a peace treaty, and international as well as supranational organizations. Table 22.1 provides a more complete overview.

The documents of *Abteilung 3 (Länderabteilung)* of the Auswärtiges Amt (Table 22.2) were entered into a divisional registry until 1955 and form a discrete holding in the Politisches Archiv. Documents since 1956 were entered into the *Referat* registry. *Referat 305* had jurisdiction over relations to the United States and Canada from 1951 to 1962.

Until 1955, the documents of *Abteilung 6 (Abteilung für auswärtige Kulturpolitik)* of the Auswärtiges Amt (Table 22.4) were entered into an *Abteilung* registry. Upon the creation of *Referate* registries in 1955,

---

8 *Bundesgesetzblatt* 1988, Teil I, p. 62. I would like to thank my colleague Dr. Pretsch for providing me with an overview of the records of the Auswärtiges Amt relevant to this topic.

Table 22.1. *Records of the Auswärtiges Amt, Abteilung 2 (Politische Abteilung) (bis 1954)*

Band-Nr.	Betreff	Laufzeit
242	Innenpolitische Angelegenheiten der USA	1951–52
262–3	Politische Beziehungen Deutschlands zu den USA	1949–54
279	Fortgeltung internationaler Verträge mit USA	1951
281	u.a.e. interamerikanische Aussenministerkonferenz Wahl Eisenhowers, Presseberichte der Botschaft Washington	1951–54
294–5	Politische Beziehungen der USA zu dritten Staaten	1950–54
328	Amerikanische Mittel für deutschen Wohnungsbau (Marhoefer-Plan)	1953–54
337	u.a. Flüchtlingsangelegenheiten-USA	1951–52
352	u.a. Zusammenführung von Ehegatten, von denen einer in die USA auswanderte; Auswanderung lungenkranker heimatloser Ausländer in die USA	1955–57
360–2	Vierer-Aussenministerkonferenzen	1950–54
363–6	Berliner Viermächtekonferenz 25.01.–18.02.1954	1953–54
(hierzu ergänzend: Handakten von Welck, Berliner Konferenz, 7 Bde.)		
367–9	Londoner Neunmächte-Konferenz	1954
550	Ordnung der Saarfrage, Haltung der USA-Presse	1950–52
940	u.a. Militärangelegenheiten der USA	1951–52
1259	Die Alliierte Hohe Kommission, Allgemeines	1949–55
1260–1	Der amerikanische Hohe Kommissar	1949–55

the documents that had been entered up to 1954 were in part given to the Politisches Archiv, in part taken over as prior records in the newly formed individual registries. The documents from the *Abteilung* registries that were given over to the Politisches Archiv were grouped as prior records to the holding of the *Grundsatzreferat* of the *Kulturabteilung*. The records of the *Abteilung* for foreign cultural policy were entered into *Referate* registries after 1955. The *Referate* of the *Kulturabteilung* are arranged by subject rather than by region, so that documents relating to German-American cultural relations are to be found in the records of all *Referate* of the *Kulturabteilung*.

Finally, the documents of *Abteilung 5 (Rechtsabteilung)* of the Auswärtiges Amt are of interest to our theme (Table 22.5). *Referat 507 (Friedensregelung):* These records, which have not been evaluated individually, may also document, among other things, American

Table 22.2. *Records of the Auswärtiges Amt, Abetilung 3 (Länderabteilung) (U.S.A.)*

Band-Nr. (Aktenzeichen)	Betreff	Laufzeit
010-03/80	Ministerien der USA, 2 Bände	1950–54
205-00/80	Innenpolitische Angelegenheiten der USA, 4 Bände	1950–55
441-02/80	Evangelische Kirche in den USA	1950–55
442-02/80	Katholische Kirche in den USA	1950–55
602-03/80	Ausländische Pressevertreter in den USA	1950–55
205-40/80	Parteien in den USA	1951–53
205-06/80	Wahlen in den USA, 5 Bände	1950–54
210-01/80	Politische Beziehungen zu den USA, 9 Bände	1950–55
210-02/80	Deutsche diplomatische und konsularische Vertretungen in den USA, 5 Bände	1950–55
210-03/80	Diplomatische und konsularische Vertretungen der USA in Deutschland, 2 Bände	1951–53
211-00/80	Politische Beziehungen zwischen den USA und dritten Staaten (auch SBZ), 14 Bände	1950–55
211-01/80	Diplomatische und konsularische Vertretungen der USA im Ausland, 6 Bände	1951–54
212-00/80	Bolschewismus und Kommunismus in den USA	1950–53
212-02/80	Faschismus, Nationalsozialismus, Neofaschismus (USA)	1952–53
212-05/80	Rassen- und Nationalitätenfragen in den USA	1952
212-14 E	Radio Free Europe, 6 Bände	1950–55
212-19	Aussenminister-Konferenzen, 13 Bände	1950–55
212-19 E	Berliner Viermächte-Konferenz	1953–54
212-19 E	Genfer Konferenz	1955
215-03/80	Staatsmänner (USA)	1951–54
215-06/80	Prominente Persönlichkeiten (USA)	1951–52
230-00/80	Militär-, Marine- und Luftfahrtangelegenheiten (USA)	1950–54
230-02/80	Heer (USA)	1951–53
231-00	Koreakrieg, 3 Bände	1950–53
240-01	Der amerikanische Hohe Kommissar	1950–53
241-14	Besatzungskosten, 2 Bände	1950–52
241-15	Besatzungsschäden	1950
245-01/80	Ehemaliges Reichs- und Staatsvermögen in den USA	1955

Table 22.2. *(cont.)*

Band-Nr. (Aktenzeichen)	Betreff	Laufzeit
245-03/80	Deutsches Vermögen in den USA	1955
245-03/80	Deutsches Vermögen in den USA, 2 Bände	1950–54
250-01-80	Beendigung des Kriegszustandes mit den USA	1950–54
300/01/80	Wirtschaftliche Beziehungen zu den USA	–1955
300-13/80	Wirtschaftliche Hilfe bei Naturkatastrophen in den USA	1951–52
305-11	Punkt-Vier-Programm der USA	–1955
304-05/80	Vorbereitung und Abschluss von Handelsverträgen mit den USA, 4 Bände	1950–54
400-03/80	Kulturelle Beziehungen zu den USA	–1955
400-06/80	Kulturelle Organisationen und Vereinigungen in den USA	–1955
413-02/80	Nachforschungen in den USA	–1955
511-04/80	Konsularrecht der USA	–1955
523-08/80	Ausweisungen aus den USA	–1955
524-00/80	Pass- und Sichtvermerksangelegenheiten der USA, Allgemeines	–1955
530-00/80	Bürgerliches Recht in den USA	–1955
533-00/80	Gewerblicher Rechtsschutz in den USA	–1955
541-00/80	Strafverfahrensrecht in den USA, Allgemeines	–1955
553-00/80	Arbeitsrecht in den USA, Allgemeines	–1955
554-00/80	Sozialrecht in den USA, Allgemeines	–1955
735-02/80	Kundgebungen bei Unglücksfällen in den USA	–1955
735-03/80	Kundgebungen beim Ableben von Staatsmännern und prominenten Persönlichkeiten in den USA	–1955
764-01/80	Verleihung ausländischer Orden, USA	–1955
420-01/80	Deutschtum und Volkstum in den USA	1950–53
461-03/80	Ausländische Institute und Gesellschaften in den USA	–1955
602-00/80	Pressevertreter in den USA	1950–53
602-02/80	Deutsche Pressevertreter in den USA	1951–55
602-03/80	Ausländische Pressevertreter in den USA	1951–53
602-04/80	Pressevertreter aus den USA in Deutschland, 5 Bände	1951–54

Table 22.2. *(cont.)*

Band-Nr. (Aktenzeichen)	Betreff	Laufzeit
750–06/80	Staatsbesuche ausländischer Staatsoberhäupter in den USA	–1955
752–07/80	Besuche amerikanischer Persönlichkeiten im Ausland	–1955
752–01/80	Reise des Bundeskanzlers in die USA	1953
752–01 E	Reise des Bundeskanzlers in die USA, 2 Bände	1954
752–05/80	Besuche, Aufenthalte, Durchreisen von Staatsmännern und prominenten Persönlichkeiten der USA in Deutschland, 5 Bände	1951–55
752–05/80	Besuch des früheren amerikanischen Präsidenten Hoover in Deutschland	1954
752–07/80	Besuche, Aufenthalte, Durchreisen von Staatsmännern und prominenten Persönlichkeiten der USA im Ausland, 3 Bände	1951–54
754–03/80	Besuche deutscher Staatsangehöriger in den USA	1954
754–04/80	Besuche amerikanischer Staatsangehöriger in Deutschland, 2 Bände	1952–54
Referat 305		
67	Politische Beziehungen zu den USA, Personal- und Verwaltungsangelegenheiten, Reisen und Besuche, USA-Reise des Bundeskanzlers 1955, Staatsbesuche, Besuche und Reisen prominenter Persönlichkeiten der USA in Deutschland, USA-Reise des Bundeskanzlers 1953	–1955
68	Staatsbesuche, Besuche und Reisen prominenter Persönlichkeiten der USA in Deutschland	–1955
69	USA-Reise des Bundeskanzlers 1953	1953

plans for a comprehensive peace in Germany and thus likely relate in part to the topics in this volume.

The records generated by Section 7 (Protocol Section), which document the preparation and execution of official visits, have not been thoroughly evaluated. For research purposes, however, the materials of the Protocol Section are only of secondary importance,

Table 22.3. *Records of the Auswärtiges Amt, Abteilung 4 (Handelspolitische Abteilung) (bis 1955), Unterabteilung 40*

Band-Nr.	Betreff	Laufzeit
121	Marshall-Plan	1951–54
122	Marshall-Plan, Durchführungsanweisungen	1951–54
125	Deutsches Marshall-Plan-Büro Paris	1952
234	Marshall-Plan: Wochenberichte der Deutschen Vertretung bei der MSA/FOA in Washington	1953
Referat 400		
23	Wirtschaftshilfe der USA, 4 Punkte-Programm	1955–56
Referat 404		
1–16	Deutsch-amerikanischer Freundschafts-, Handels- und Schiffahrtsvertrag	1953–54
Referat 410		
238	u.a. amerikanische Luftverkehrslinien	1952–54
Referat 414		
41–104	Handels- und Wirtschaftsbeziehungen zwischen der Bundesrepublik Deutschland und den USA	1951–54

since usually they do not reveal the substance of talks, negotiations, or other business conducted. Nevertheless, they give clues as to the atmosphere of meetings and the political situation in which visits took place.

As is the case with the records of the Auswärtiges Amt, the records of the German embassy in Washington and the German consular offices in the United States fall under the provisions of the *Bundesarchivgesetz*. They are accessible as long as they are not still security classified. The physical location of the documents – in the Politisches Archiv or an office of the Auswärtiges Amt in Bonn, at the embassy or a consulate in the United States – does not make a difference. In a letter dated August 10, 1989, the Auswärtiges Amt notes, however, that: "Records of the German Foreign Service Posts in the United States created between the end of the Second World War and 1955 do not exist. Apparently the records from the first few years were destroyed on location."

In addition to the materials of the Politisches Archiv that have already been mentioned, the record group *Londoner Schuldenabkommen*

Table 22.4. *Records of the Auswärtiges Amt, Abteilung 6 (Abteilung für auswärtige Kulturpolitik (U.S.A.)*

Band-Nr.	Betreff	Laufzeit
71–5	Kulturelle Beziehungen Deutschlands zu den USA	1950–53
79–85	Steg-Fonds für kulturelle Zwecke, Fulbright-Act-Abkommen	1950–53
94	Deutsche Kulturinstitute in den USA	1952–54
114	Deutsch-amerikanische Kulturgesellschaften in Deutschland	1951–53
119	Deutsch-amerikanische Kulturgesellschaften im Ausland	1952
122–4	Dankaktion für das Ausland (Dankspende des deutschen Volkes)	1950–53
142	Kulturelles, Viara, USA	1950–52
162–164	Kulturabkommen mit den USA	1950–53
400	Hochschulwesen in den USA	1951–53
474	Amerikanische Rundfunksender in Deutschland	1951–52
516	Reisen deutscher Professoren in die USA	1950–54
519	Studienreisen von Angehörigen der Bundesministerien und der öffentlichen Verwaltung in die USA	1949–50

(LSA) is of interest, which contains the records of the German delegation for foreign debts. The record group includes 124 volumes. Those containing references to the United States are LSA volumes 7, 9, 26, 37, 61, 115, 120, and 121. The records of another important German delegation, the Deutsche Delegation bei der Internationalen Ruhrbehörde (Bestand B 130), are deposited in the Bundesarchiv.

The records of the Zentrale Rechtsschultzstelle (Bestand 305), which the Bundesarchiv recently received from the Auswärtiges Amt, should also be mentioned here. This office provided legal counsel to Germans held in custody abroad or tried in foreign courts for war crimes or National Socialist atrocities. The Zentrale Rechtsschutzstelle was initially an office within the Federal Ministry of Justice; after 1953 it was incorporated into the Auswärtiges Amt. Its records are helpful in gaining an understanding of the U.S. government position on the sentencing of German war criminals, and they can fruitfully be used with the "War Crimes Trials" records mentioned previously.

Table 22.5. *Records of the Auswärtiges Amt, Abteilung 5 (Rechtsabteilung) (U.S.A.)*

Band-Nr.	Betreff	Laufzeit
Referat 500 (Völkerrecht und Staatsverträge)		
13	u.a. Politische Beziehungen Deutschlands zu den USA	1953
28	u.a. Völkerrecht-USA	1952–54
38	u.a. amerikanische Küstengewässer	1953
58–65	Handels-, Konsular- und Niederlassungsverträge mit den USA	1950–54
89	u.a. Verträge der Bundesrepublik mit den USA	1953
109	u.a. Staatsverträge der USA mit Dritten	1951–54
144	u.a. Kriegs- und Zivilgefangenenrecht, USA	1950–51
228	u.a. Kulturabkommen USA	–1955
229	u.a. Zollfreie Einfuhr von Liebesgütern, Lieferung von Überschussgütern	–1955
231	u.a. USA, gemeinsame Ausgaben für Verteidigung	–1955
267	u.a. Freundschafts-, Handels- und Schiffahrts-Vertrag mit den USA vom 29.10.1954	1955–58
448	Völkerrechtliche Angelegenheiten der USA	1951–64
675	Deutsch-amerikanisches Abkommen über Finanzierung von Austauschvorhaben zum Zwecke der Erziehung und Bildung/Fulbright-Abkommen	1952–63
Referat 501 (Konsularrecht, Verkehr und Schiffahrt, Beamtenrecht, Entschädigungsansprüche)		
228	u.a. USA: Postrecht	1951–53
406	Vorrechte und Befreiungen im Verhältnis zu den USA	1951–58
Referat 502 (Staats- und Verwaltungsrecht)		
51	USA: Polizei- und Verwaltungsrecht, Staatsangehörigkeitsrecht	1950–56
53	USA: Verfassungs-, Polizei- und Verwaltungsrecht	1951–56
54	USA: Personenstandsrecht, Wehrrecht, Pass- und Sichtvermerksrecht	1951–56
Referat 503 (Strafrecht, Steuerrechtsfragen)		
508	USA, Rechtshilfe, Auslieferung, Steuersachen	1950–60
509	USA, Steuerrecht	1953–60
510	USA, Doppelbesteuerung	1951–54
511	USA, Doppelbesteuerung	1954–60

Table 22.5 *(cont.)*

Band-Nr.	Betreff	Laufzeit
Referat 504 (Internationales Privatrecht)		
183–95	USA: Unterhalts-Musterprozess, Erbrecht, Patentrecht, Muster- und Warenzeichenrecht, Urheberrecht, Rechtshilfe, Schiffahrts- und Freundschaftsvertrag	–1955
673	USA: Zivilprozessrecht, Zwangsvollstreckung, Zustellungen	1950–66
674	USA: Rechtshilfe in Zivilsachen, Zustellungen, Hinterlegungen	1951–63
675	USA: Privatversicherungsrecht, Bergrecht, Bank- und Börsenrecht, Rechtsanwaltschaft	1950–64
763	USA: Internationales Privatrecht, Recht der Schuldverhältnisse, Sachenrecht, Familienrecht	1953–63
764	USA: Familienrecht	1953–63
765	USA: Erbrecht, Handelsrecht	1950–63
766	USA: Gewerblicher Rechtsschutz	1955–64
767	USA: Unlauterer Wettbewerb, Urheberrecht	1953–63
768	USA: Zwangsvollstreckung, Kosten- und Gebührenwesen, Armenrecht	1950–61
Referat 505 (Sozialrecht)		
33–7	USA, Sozialwesen	1954–56
406	USA, Sozialwesen	1955–60
Referat 506 (Auslandsvermögen)		
522–67	USA: Deutsches Vermögen	1951–63
890	u.a. Deutsche Ansprüches gegen die USA	1954–58
1042	USA: Deutschlandpolitik, Finanzverhandlungen, Verteidigungshilfeabkommen, Freundschafts, Handels- und Schiffahrtsvertrag, Atomenergiegesetzgebung	1953–64

Information on the foreign economic policies of the Federal Republic can be found in the Bundesarchiv record groups Bundeswirtschaftsministerium (Bestand B 102) and Bundesministerium für den Marshallplan/Bundesministerium für wirtschaftliche Zusammenarbeit (alter Art) (Bestand B 146). This also applies mutatis mutandis for all ministries, though obviously more for the Bundes-

ministerium der Finanzen (Bestand B 126) than for the Bundesministerium für Angelegenheiten des Bundesrates und der Länder.

Certainly, the parliamentary records in the Archiv des Deutschen
Bundestages, in particular those of the Auswärtiger Ausschuss, are
of special importance for the general subject. A more complete picture is gained through the inclusion of the records of the foreign affairs committee of the Bundesrat.

In comparison, information found in the records of the *Länder*
governments, including those of the U.S. zone, are of less value –
despite the fact that there were representatives of the U.S. High
Commissioner for Germany at the *Länder* level too. This observation, however, does not apply to the Western sectors of Berlin, because of the special political situation of this city. The unique
relationship between West Berlin and the United States is documented in the records of the Berlin Senate, which are found in the
Landesarchiv Berlin. This archive also holds the personal papers of
the former Lord Mayor Ernst Reuter and his successor Otto Suhr.
Other interesting materials can be found in the records of the district
administrations of the U.S. Sector of Berlin, for example in the collection Bezirksverwaltung Zehlendorf. They reflect in particularly
vivid detail the political, cultural, and social effects of the American
presence in Berlin.

Aside from government records, a large number of non-official archival sources have been deposited in the Bundesarchiv. Among the
materials from private-law institutions are the records of the Studiengesellschaft für privatrechtliche Auslandsinteressen (Bestand B
184) and the Gesellschaft zur Förderung des deutsch-amerikanischen
Handels (Bestand B 140). The records of the Studiengesellschaft,
which was founded late in 1948 in Bremen, show the efforts of the
federal government, the central economic associations (for example,
the Bundesverband der Deutschen Industrie and the Deutscher
Industrie- und Handelstag) as well as many personalities in German
public life to preserve or regain those private German assets that had
been seized or confiscated in foreign countries – including the
United States – as reparations. The records of the Gesellschaft zur
Förderung des deutsch-amerikanischen Handels, founded in June
1950 by the Bundesverband der Deutschen Industrie, the Deutscher
Industrie- und Handelstag, and the Zentralverband des Deutschen
Handwerks, reflect the activities of many West German political au-

thorities and economic organizations to promote the export of German goods to the United States. After the expiration of the Marshall Plan in 1952, these exports were supposed to reduce or eliminate the dollar gap in the trade balance of the Federal Republic. A recently completed finding aid will make this record group more accessible and may help to gain new insights into German–American trade relations.

The archival collections described above in somewhat more detail are just examples of records of political-economic relevance. While it should be noted that the accessibility of the archives of private German firms may vary, archivists at the regional German economic archives in Dortmund (Westfälisches Wirtschaftsarchiv), Cologne (Rheinisch-Westfälisches Wirtschaftsarchiv), and Hohenheim (Stiftung Wirtschaftsarchiv Baden-Württemburg at Hohenheim University) are usually most forthcoming.

The importance of private papers of individuals active in public life is evident and does not need to be explained. They are more than mere supplements of the records generated by government offices. Relevant material for the topic under consideration may be expected in the papers of all those personalities who had political or other contacts with the U.S. occupation forces or the American government. For the purpose of this essay, it is less important to identify specifically the contents and whereabouts of the papers of certain politicians than to note that the state archives already mentioned and the archives of the major political parties and foundations hold such collections. This is exemplified by the case of the papers of the Bavarian ministers president Schäffer, Hoegner, and Ehard, which have been deposited in three different archives: Schäffer's in the Bundesarchiv, Hoegner's in the archive of the Institut für Zeitgeschichte, and Ehard's in the Bayerisches Hauptstaatsarchiv in Munich. The papers of the ministers president of Württemberg-Baden (Baden-Württemberg) Reinhold Maier (1945–1953) and Gerhard Müller (from 1953) are located in the Hauptstaatsarchiv Stuttgart.[9] A smaller part of Müller's papers was deposited in the Archiv für Christlich-Demokratische Politik der Konrad-Adenauer-Stiftung in Sankt Augustin near Bonn.[10] The papers of the independent Hessian

9 See *Nachlass Reinhold Maier: Inventar des Bestandes O 1/8 im Hauptstaatsarchiv Stuttgart*, prepared by Wilfried Braunn (Stuttgart, 1980).
10 See *Dei Bestände des Archivs für Christlich-Demokratische Politik der Konrad-Adenauer-Stiftung: Kurzübersicht* (Melle, 1986).

minister president Geiler are under the custody of the Hessisches Hauptstaatsarchiv in Wiesbaden, while those of his social democratic successors Stock and Zinn are located in the Archiv der sozialen Demokratie der Friedrich-Ebert-Stiftung in Bonn-Bad Godesberg.[11] The Staatsarchiv Bremen acquired the papers of the long-time mayor of Bremen Wilhelm Kaisen, while the papers of the lord mayors Reuter and Suhr in the Landesarchiv Berlin have already been mentioned.

An example of the papers of the civil servants of the *Länderrat* or other institutions in the Western zones are the papers of General Secretary Erich Rossmann held by the Bundesarchiv. The papers of his American counterpart, the director of the Regional Government Coordinating Office James K. Pollock, are at the University of Michigan at Ann Arbor. Copies are available, however, at the Bundesarchiv.

The papers of Konrad Adenauer, held by the Stiftung Konrad-Adenauer-Haus in Rhöndorf, are obviously of utmost importance for the history of the Federal Republic. Next to the records of OMGUS, HICOG, the State Department, and the Auswärtiges Amt they are one of the central sources for the topic under consideration. Of the other papers that were deposited in the Bundesarchiv and are of particular relevance for German–American relations, the papers of Federal President Theodor Heuss should be mentioned along with those of Vice-Chancellor Blücher, Ministers Lübke, Schäffer, and Seebohm, and especially those of *Staatssekretär* Hallstein and CDU/CSU Parliamentary Party Leader von Brentano.

This list of private papers would be incomplete if it included only the papers of politicians. Depending on the research topic, the papers of historians, for instance, like Hans Rothfels, Fritz Epstein, or Arnold Brecht can be very valuable sources.

Regrettably, there is an increasing tendency among politicians and ranking officials to deposit their papers not in state archives but in archives related with political parties. For the CDU and DP, the papers of Adenauer's close advisers *Staatssekretäre* Hans Globke, Otto Lenz, and Felix von Eckardt in the Archiv für Christlich-Demokratische Politik der Konrad-Adenauer-Stiftung in Sankt Augustin should be named.[12] This archive also holds the papers of

11 A guide published in 1984 gives an overview of the holdings of this archive.
12 See note 10.

politicians Andreas Hermes, Ernst Lemmer, Hans Joachim von Merkatz, and Theodor Blank, who played a decisive role in connection with German defense arrangements and the creation of the Bundeswehr in 1954. In addition, the papers of Heinrich Krone and Kurt Georg Kiesinger, since 1954 chairman of the Bundesausschuss für Auswärtige Angelegenheiten, are worth mentioning.

Among the collections of the Archiv für Christlich-Soziale Politik der Hanns-Seidel-Stiftung in Munich are the papers of Josef Müller, which, unfortunately, are still closed to researchers, and those of CSU politicians Franz Elsen, director of the Bayerische Staatsbank and General Secretary of the Wirtschaftsbeirat der Union e.V., August Schwingenstein, a member of the committee that founded the CSU in Munich in 1945, and others.

The Konrad-Adenauer-Stiftung also holds the CDU party and parliamentary group records as does the Hanns-Seidel-Stiftung for the CSU. The *Bundesvorstandsprotokolle* of the CDU for the years 1950 to 1957 have already been published or will be published soon. The records of the CSU-Landesgruppe in Bonn at the Hanns-Seidel-Stiftung only go back to the year 1954; older records are supposedly still under the custody of the *Landesgruppe* itself.

The Archiv der sozialen Demokratie der Friedrich-Ebert-Stiftung holds the papers of former party chairmen Kurt Schumacher and Erich Ollenhauer, former speaker of the SPD executive committee Fritz Heine, and those of Willy Brandt, Fritz Erler, Gustav Heinemann, Kurt Mattick, and Carlo Schmid as well as the records of the SPD executive committee and the SPD parliamentary group from the first and second voting periods.[13]

From the materials of the Archiv des Deutschen Liberalismus der Friedrich-Naumann-Stiftung in Gummersbach (formerly called the Politisches Archiv) the following record groups should be mentioned:[14]

–*Protokolle der Bundesparteitage und des Bundesvorstandes der FDP;*
–*Akten des Bundesfachausschusses Deutschlandpolitik;*
–*Akten des Ostbüros;*
–*Protokolle der FDP-Bundestagsfraktion;*

13 The Archiv der sozialen Demokratie prepares special finding aids in mimeographed form, for instance, to the Heinemann Papers.
14 For the holdings of the Friedrich Naumann Foundation, only a mimeographed inventory is available. Unpublished finding aids exist for special record groups, e.g., the Thomas Dehler Papers.

—Nachlass Max Becker;
—Nachlass Thomas Dehler;
—Nachlass Hans Reif;
—Nachlass Franz Blücher.

Film and other audiovisual materials are increasingly recognized as valuable historical sources.[15] In the first place, weekly newsreels (*Wochenschauen*) should be mentioned. *Fox-Tönende-Wochenschau,* an American production, is available at the Bundesarchiv for 1950–51 (to the extent that copies survived) and from 1952 on (complete). The weekly newsreel *Welt im Film,* which was produced prior to the surrender and shown in Germany from May 1945 on, is also completely available at the Bundesarchiv. In addition to newsreels, beginning in 1945, the occupation authorities produced documentary films in order to inform the German people about the crimes of the National Socialist regime (an example is the film "Mills of Death") and to reeducate them in the spirit of democracy. The Bundesarchiv holds about 150 films of this kind, which clearly show the changes in both form and content of the American attempts at reeducation.

Of even greater significance are the audiovisual materials of the radio stations. Primarily those of the Radio in the American Sector of Berlin (RIAS), but also those of the Bayerischer Rundfunk, Süddeutscher Rundfunk, Hessischer Rundfunk, Radio Bremen, and Sender Freies Berlin. Access to the materials in radio archives could, however, be improved.

The importance of the archives of U.S.-licensed newspapers – in particular for the immediate postwar period – is obvious. The records of the Information Control Division of the U.S. Military Government for Germany vividly document the great importance placed by the U.S. government and occupation authorities upon the development of a democratic press in Germany. The archives of the larger newspapers in the American zone, such as the *Süddeutsche Zeitung, Stuttgarter Zeitung,* or *Frankfurter Allgemeine Zeitung* certainly reflect the implementation and effects of U.S. press policies. Felix von Eckardt's account of the licensing process of the *Weser Kurier* in Bremen[16] is not only proof of the importance attributed

15 Peter Bucher, "Der Film als Quelle: Audiovisuelle Medien in der deutschen Archiv- und Geschichtswissenschaft," *Der Archivar* 41 (1988):497–524.
16 Eckardt, *Ein unordentliches Leben,* 114ff.

to press matters by the U.S. military government but may also direct attention to the archives of middle-sized and smaller regional newspapers.

It is one of the archivist's tasks to process records, make them available for research and their existence known to prospective users, who are mostly historians. Apart from the many changes in content and methodology of historical research, a thorough examination of the sources continues to be its foundation. In this context, the present opportunity to describe – or at least to mention – sources of German archives on the history of American policy toward Germany, 1945–55, is most welcome. May it contribute to filling the archives' reading rooms to their capacity.

23

U.S. High Commissioner for Germany and Related Records

Sources for the History of the Federal Republic of Germany,
1949–1955, in the U.S. National Archives
and Records Administration

ROBERT WOLFE

With the proclamation of the Basic Law on May 23, 1949, and its
effectuation by the promulgation of the Occupation Statute on September 21, military government came to an end in Western ("Tri-
zonia") Germany. There began an interim of semisovereignty for the
Bundesrepublik Deutschland (Federal Republic of Germany, FRG)
under the Occupation Statute, supervised jointly by the Allied High
Commission (AHC) for Germany, consisting of high commissioners
for Germany from France, Great Britain, and the United States.
During the several stages between September 1, 1949, and May 5,
1955, when restrictions on sovereignty were all but lifted by proclamation of the AHC, culminating in the replacement of the high commissioners by ambassadors, by reason of its overwhelming economic
and military power the United States played a decisive role in determining the pace and limits of progress toward near emancipation.
Consequently, the records of the U.S. federal government deposited
in the National Archives and Records Administration (NARA), second only to those deposited in the Bundesarchiv in Koblenz and
Freiburg/Breisgau, and the German Foreign Office Archives in
Bonn, are a major source for the study of the history of the Federal
Republic of Germany between 1949 and 1955. It should be noted,
however, that the progressive reduction of direct Allied activity from
operations to mere observation, advice, and assistance with only an
occasional direct intervention, contributed to much reduced paperwork and thus, a smaller archival residue.

The information provided in this chapter was current as of October 1992. The author, while
assuming responsibility for its accuracy, is beholden to the following of his colleagues in the
National Archives who furnished much of the data: Judith Barnes, Richard A. Boylan, George
C. Chalou, Mary T. Donovan, Maria T. Hanna, Susan H. Karren, Sally B. Marks, Laura Mc-
Carthy, Don C. McIlwain, Mary Ronan, Amy K. Schmidt, Ronald E. Swerczek, Timothy
Willard, and especially John P. Butler, David A. Langbart, and David A. Pfeiffer.

Listed hierarchically, but not necessarily in order of their value as
sources, these American records are

–Presidents' papers and papers of their White House subordinates de-
    posited in the Truman and Eisenhower libraries (Presidential Li-
    braries are integral components of NARA);
–State Department Central, Post, and Lot Files;
–records and papers of high commissioners John J. McCloy and
    James B. Conant and their subordinate staffs, offices, and
    agencies;
–records of the *Land* commissioners and their subordinates in the
    former states of the American zone (Bavaria, Bremen, Hesse,
    Baden-Württemberg); and
–records of the occupied Western enclave of the city of Berlin, espe-
    cially the U.S. Berlin Element of the Allied Kommandatura
    whose commander was directly subordinate to the U.S. high
    commissioner.[1]

The largest (ca. 3,000 cubic feet) pertinent series of these records,
those of the Records of the U.S. High Commissioner for Germany
(HICOG), while allocated to a separate NARA Record Group of its
own (NARG 466), is not easily accessible to research. Substantial
portions of that record group still await declassification or will remain security-classified indefinitely.[2]

Many HICOG records, particularly those at the *Land* level, were
retained for use by U.S. diplomatic or consular missions, which between 1952 and 1955 gradually inherited remaining HICOG functions in Germany; such records were retired to the United States
with the Bonn, Frankfurt, Berlin, Munich, or Stuttgart Post Records

1 Although there is a HICOG filing entry entitled Bonn Element, reflecting the U.S. high
  commissioner's function in the Federal Republic of Germany from 1949 to 1955 as opposed
  to his military government function in Berlin, the distinction has not been carefully maintained by file clerks. Technically, the Allied Control Authority (ACA) for all of Germany,
  with the four military governors constituting its Allied Control Council (ACC), continued
  a dormant existence after the Soviet walkout of March 1948. The Allied Kommandatura for
  Berlin (AKB), however, continued to function as a tripartite agency under the Allied High
  Commission (although its commander reported directly to EUCOM or USAREUR in his
  purely military capacity), with the door always open to Soviet return after the walkout from
  this body in June 1948. The voluminous records of the U.S. agencies of the ACA, understandably covering mainly the OMGUS period, have not yet been accessioned by NARA
  from their temporary depository in the Berlin Document Center (BDC). Microfilm (287
  rolls) of records of U.S. elements of ACC, AKB, and the Bipartite Control Office predating
  1949 are held by NARA; the original records are still in the BDC as of October 1992.
2 A substantial portion of these, however, are records of U.S. occupation courts, mainly criminal case files for petty crimes, and court registers.

(NARG 84) at varying intervals, and have only recently been accessioned by NARA from the Department of State. It is estimated that perhaps as many as 1,000 cubic feet of these records will be transferred to HICOG NARG 466 after accessioning.[3]

Contrariwise, a considerable portion of the HICOG record group consists of Office of Military Government, U.S. (OMGUS)[4] records retained in the files of HICOG agencies after 1949 when they assumed responsibility for American diplomatic and economic – but not military – operations in Germany. While this assured continuity in actions then in progress, it now presents archival problems for archivists and researchers.

With President Truman's Executive Order No. 10062 of June 6, 1949, the U.S. High Commission was placed under the Department of State, while the U.S. military commander was to report directly to the Joint Chiefs of Staff. Nevertheless, the intertwined activities of American military forces (European Command: EUCOM, March 1948, NARG 349; U.S. Army, Europe: USAREUR, August, 1952, NARG 338) with HICOG civilian staffs in Germany recommend examination of the records of those commands and of the Civil Affairs Divisions of the Departments of Defense (NARG 330), Army (NARG 335), and Air Forces (NARG 340), as well as the records of the Joint Chiefs of Staff (NARG 218) for the study of such topics as control of German scientific activities in nuclear, space, chemical, and explosives research, as well as U.S. forces' activities in and relations with governments and citizens of the Bundesrepublik, and especially the evolution of West German participation in the defense of Western Europe and ultimately in the NATO Alliance. Paramount for the latter evolution, however, are the records of the Supreme Headquarters, Allied Powers in Europe (SHAPE), 1951–53, and the European Defense Community (EDC), 1952–54, both like EUCOM, to be found in Records of Joint Commands (NARG 349). NATO documents, to the extent they are declassified, will be found interfiled in some series of these latter record groups.

Pertinent records of the Department of State are to be found in the Central Decimal Files (NARG 59) and Lot Files, as well as in the

3 Some of these diplomatic and consular records of U.S. posts in Germany during the 1952–55 period will remain in RG 84, but are, nevertheless, listed here with their predecessor regional (*Land*) commissioner records. Unless another record group such as RG 84 is given, files listed in upper case are in RG 466.
4 The bulk of OMGUS records are deposited in RG 260, Records of U.S. Occupation Headquarters, World War II.

files of American diplomatic and consular posts in Germany (NARG 84), already mentioned as being transferred to NARG 466. Invaluable insights for many studies of U.S.–FRG relations during the 1949–55 period are obviously to be found in both Central and Post files dealing with American relations with third parties, particularly, Great Britain, France, and the Soviet Union. NARG 59 also includes Policy Planning Staff (PPS) records, and some interfiled declassified National Security Council (NSC) documents. NSC records proper, however, are assigned to NARG 273, most of them still classified.

Other NARA records potentially useful for the study of the history of the Bundesrepublik from 1949 to 1955 are deposited in NARG 469, Records of the U.S. Foreign Assistance Agencies, 1948–61: the Economic Cooperation Administration (ECA), 1948–51, which administered the European Recovery Program (Marshall Plan); the Mutual Security Agency (MSA), which provided military, economic, and technical assistance to friendly nations in the interest of international peace and security, 1951–53; and MSA's successor, the Foreign Operations Administration (FOA), 1953–55. (The records of AID proper, since its establishment in 1961, are in NARG 286.)

STATE DEPARTMENT GENERAL RECORDS (NARG 59)

The Central Decimal File of the Department of State, part of NARG 59, General Records of the Department of State, for the period 1949–55 are substantially open. Few diplomatic records dated after 1949, however, are as yet available on National Archives microfilm.

The most precise and direct access to the State Department Decimal File is through pertinent documents published in the appropriate annual volumes of the *Foreign Relations of the United States* (*FRUS*) series, which are annotated with the decimal or lot file numbers from which the printed individual documents were selected. Ideally, a researcher should approach the decimal file with a copy of the contemporary file system (known as the "classification manual") in hand. For the researcher lacking either a pertinent *FRUS* volume or classification manual, a brief explication of the main principles may be useful here.

Classification Schemes

At the outset, it must be stressed that for the General Records Decimal File of the period 1949–55 we are dealing with *two different* basic decimal classification schemes, an earlier one valid only through December 31, 1949, and a later system in effect January 1, 1950, through January 1, 1963, with slight revisions on January 1, 1955, and again on January 1, 1960. Both schemes assign a distinguishing two-digit number to each country; for the pre-1950 scheme, the U.S. country number is "11," Germany is designated "62," and Austria, for example, "63."

As of January 1, 1950, some country numbers were reassigned to conform to postwar realignments; Austria remained "63," but Germany, while retaining its previous "62," was also subdivided into "62a" and "62b" corresponding to the Federal Republic of (West) Germany and to the (East) German Democratic Republic, respectively.

The country number will sometimes precede the decimal point and sometimes follow it; in either case the file number begins with a single-digit prefix denoting a particular class of activity. For example, after 1950, Class "5" was entitled "International Informational and Educational Relations, Cultural Affairs, and Psychological Warfare." Accordingly, between 1950 and 1963 decimal "511.62a" was the file number for records of U.S. cultural activities in the FRG, and "562a.11" applied to records of West German cultural activities in the United States.

Rearrangement of classification numbers and titles, also as of January 1, 1950, has caused some confusion. For the period through 1949, the Central Decimal File was broken down into nine "classes": Class 0, Miscellaneous; Class 1, Administration; Class 2, Extradition; Class 3, Protection of Interests; Class 4, Claims; Class 5, International Conferences, League of Nations, United Nations, Multilateral Treaties; Class 6, Commercial Relations; Class 7, Political Relations of States; Class 8, Internal Affairs of States.

As of January 1, 1950, the former Class 5, "International Conferences, League of Nations, United Nations, Multilateral Treaties," was redesignated Class 3, bearing the same title minus the defunct League of Nations. The former Class 3, "Protection of Interests," was renumbered "Class 2," subsuming thereunder the former Class 2, "Extradition," and Class 4, "Claims." The pre-1950 Class 6, "Commercial Relations," became Class 4, "International Commerce." The former Class 7, "Political Relations of States," was redesignated Class 6 and renamed "International Political Relations, Other International Relations, Bilateral Treaties." The previous

Class 8, "Internal Affairs of States," was dispersed among Class 5, "Informational and Educational Relations" (full class title already given above); Class 7, "Internal Political and National Defense Affairs"; Class 8, "Internal Economic, Industrial, and Social Affairs"; and Class 9, "Other Internal Affairs, Communications, Transportation, Science."

Under each class are suffixes of one or more digits representing specified activities. For example, after 1950, "511.62a3" denoted "Exchange of Students and Professors" between the United States and the FRG. In files containing documentation of reciprocal activity between two countries, the lower country number is placed before the decimal point and the higher number after it. Where, however, records of such activity of each country toward or in the other have been filed separately, the country numbers will precede or follow the decimal point, as in this example: "511.62a5" the last 5 denoting "motion pictures," means U.S. motion pictures in West Germany, whereas in reverse sequence, "562a.115," the 5 refers to FRG motion pictures in the United States.

In Class 6 of the 1950–63 classification scheme, "International Political and Other Relations, Bilateral Treaties," the lower country number precedes the decimal point unless it is specifically stated otherwise. Accordingly, records of German political relations with Austria involving "Peace, Friendship, Alliance, Nonaggression" were filed under "662a.631," whereas records of "War, Hostilities," between Austria and Italy (country number "65") were filed under "663.652." Subjects such as "1" (Peace, etc.), "2" (War, Hostilities), or "9" (Bilateral Treaties), could be elaborated by two or more digits for more specific subheadings; for example, "611.62a91" covers extradition treaties between the United States and West Germany.

Under Class 7, "Internal Political and National Defense Affairs," the records are filed under the number of the country whose internal affairs are the subject; records pertaining to the FRG Cabinet would be "762a.13," whereas proceedings in West German courts would be "762a.32."

Class 8, "Internal Economic, Industrial, and Social Affairs," follows the same principle as Class 7, so that "862a.06" would refer to "food conditions, rationing, black markets," and "862a.03" to "labor conditions" in West Germany. The subheadings in Classes 6 through 8 are so numerous and so variegated as to require researchers to consult the State Department Decimal File Classification

Manual, a copy of which is always available from the diplomatic staff of the National Archives.

The basic file numbers for country, class, and specific activity (e.g., 611.62a1) are followed by a slant mark (/). Numbers following the slant mark complete the file number of an individual document. These numbers usually reflect the date the document was created. For example, a document on U.S.–FRG political relations dated May 5, 1952, would be filed under 611.62a1/5-552. Sometimes an outgoing document is given the same file number as its corresponding incoming document to keep them together in the files.

Central Decimal Files

In the State Department Central Decimal File for the years *1950–54*, the following files concern more or less directly U.S.–FRG relations (boxes are "archives boxes," three of which equal 1 cubic foot):

411.62a U.S.–FRG International Commerce, boxes 1849–51.
511.62a U.S.–FRG Informational and Educational Relations, boxes 2436–56.
611.62a U.S.–FRG Political Relations, boxes 2961–6.
662a.   Other FRG International Relations, Bilateral Treaties.
762a.   FRG Internal Political and National Defense Affairs, boxes 3841–3905.
862a.   FRG Internal Economic, Industrial, and Social Affairs, boxes 5179–5256.
962a.   Other FRG Internal Affairs, Communications, Transportation, Science, boxes 6016–41.

For the years *1955–59*, Central Decimal File records pertaining to West Germany:

511.62a boxes 2187–95.
611.62a boxes 2533–6.
662a.   boxes 2659–61.
762a.   boxes 3518–38, 3548–70.
862a.   boxes 4745–81.

For the [East] German Democratic Republic (then contemptuously referred to as the "Soviet zone"), there are

411.62b. box 1851.
511.62b   box 2456.
611.62b   box 2836.
662b.   box 2966.

762b.   boxes 3905–13.
862b.   boxes 5257–5264.
962b.   boxes 6041–3.

(One surmises that State Department personnel and researchers in its records welcome German unification, if for no other reason than to be rid of those pesky "a's" and "b's.")

Special (Lot) Files

Other than the decimal file, pertinent source materials in the General Records of the State Department (NARG 59) are some of the special files – so-called lot files. These files have been in large part catalogued through 1984 in Gerald K. Haines, *A Reference Guide to United States Special Files* (Greenwood Press, Westport, Conn., 1985). Lot files are usually allocated to NARG 59, but they are listed here with former lot file numbers and estimated quantity:

Secretary of State (Acheson), 1944–52, 9 cubic feet (cf)
Bureau of European Affairs
    Assistant Secretary for European Affairs, 1945–57, 6 cf
    European Defense Arrangements 1948–54, 4 cf
NATO 1950–61
    Subject Files re European Security 50–56, 2 cf
    Officer-in-Charge European Politico-Military Affairs
    (Leonard Unger) 1950–57, 1¼ cf
Office of European Regional Affairs, 1949–53, 3 cf
Public Affairs Advisor, European Regional Affairs, 1948–55, 1 cf
Records of the Legal Advisor regarding War Crimes, 1942–46, 5 cf
Western European Affairs, 1941–54; Miscellaneous German Files, 1943–54, 9 cf
Central European Division, 1944–53, 5 cf
Office of German Affairs, 1949–55, 1⅓ cf
Records of the Assistant Legal Advisor for German Affairs, 1946–56, 39 cf
Subject Files, Assistant Legal Advisor for German Affairs, 1952–5, 1 cf
Policy Planning Staff (PPS), 1947–53. 1954. 1957–61.
Records of the Policy Plans and Guidance Staff, 1947–55, 1952–62
Records of the Psychological Strategy Board relating to the National Security Council (NSC), 1947–61.
NSC numbered papers:
    70, 70/1 *May Day and Whitsuntide Youth Rallies in Berlin*, April 28 and May 3, 1950.
    71 *U.S. Policy toward Germany*, June 9, 1950.
    71/1 *The Rearmament of Western Germany*, July 3, 1950.

82 *U.S. Position regarding Strengthening the Defense of Europe and the Nature of Germany's Contribution Thereto,* Sept. 11, 1950.

89 *U.S. Policy with Respect to Berlin and Eastern Germany,* Oct. 20, 1950.

106 *The Safety of the American Civilian Population in Germany and Japan in the Event of Hostilities,* March 12, 1951.

106/1,2 *The Possibilities of Reducing the U.S. Civilian Population in Sensitive Areas Abroad,* Aug. 31 and Sept. 13, 1951.

115 *Definition of U.S. Policy on Problems of the Defense of Europe and the German Contribution,* Aug. 1, 1951.

132, 132/1 *U.S. Policy and Courses of Action to Counter Possible Soviet or Satellite Action Against Berlin,* May 29 and June 12, 1952.

160, 160/1 *U.S. Position with Respect to Germany,* Aug. 4 and 17, 1953.

160/1 *Supplement and Annex, U.S. Policy toward East Germany,* Sept. 12, 1956.

173 *U.S. Policy and Courses of Action to Counter Possible Soviet Action Against Berlin,* Dec. 1, 1953.

5404, 5404/1 *U.S. Policy on Berlin,* Jan. 13 and 25, 1954.

5435, 5435/1 *Expansion of the Labor Service Organization in Germany,* Oct. 1 and 18, 1954.

Post Records

The decimal file scheme for Post Records prior to 1948 was adapted from the pre-1950 eight-class system applied to the decimal file of the General Records. From 1949 to 1963 Post Records were filed under a simplified six-class system separating political, military, economic and social, and cultural records into Classes 3 to 6, respectively. This foreign post–decimal file scheme applies not only to records of U.S. Posts in the FRG for 1949–55 accessioned or to be accessioned into HICOG NARG 466, but to most of the HICOG records proper as well, *with the notable exception of most of the land commissioner files.*

Post Records (NARG 84) dated after 1935, specifically those for 1949–55, like HICOG NARG 466 and NARG 469, are deposited in the Archives annex housed at the Washington National Records Center in Suitland, Maryland, in the environs of Washington, DC, pending the move of most NARA twentieth-century holdings to the new National Archives building at College Park, Maryland, in 1994–95.

HICOG RECORDS

Clearly, the paramount research resource for the study of American policy toward and role in Germany from September 21, 1949, to

May 5, 1955, is the ca. 4,000 cubic feet (roughly 12,000 boxes)[5] of NARG 466, Records of the Office of the U.S. High Commissioner for Germany, accessioned and to be accessioned by NARA; unclassified, declassified, and still classified; arranged and not arranged.

The following descriptions of these records will adhere to their arrangement as of October 1992, which understandably does not conform strictly to the convoluted and transitory hierarchies shown in the contemporary organizational charts. This approach should best serve researchers and archivists for retrieval and citation. Nor will estimated quantities remain valid, since State Department records managers following guidelines approved by NARA, and NARA archivists disposing of records not appraised as having permanent historical or documentational value, may destroy considerable quantities. Such disposals are desirable lest the permanently valuable records be difficult to retrieve from an overwhelming mass of routine ephemeral paperwork. Regrettably, some questionable disposal decisions resulted in the destruction of substantial amounts of Post Records of the early 1950s that most archivists would have rated as permanent.

Description	Boxes
United States High Commissioner for Germany, John J. McCloy	
Office of the U.S. High Commissioner	
CLASSIFIED GENERAL RECORDS, 1949–52	43
TOP SECRET GENERAL RECORDS, 1949–52	6
SUPPLEMENTARY GENERAL RECORDS, JULY–OCTOBER 1949	
PRESS RELEASES, 1949	1
EYES ONLY (E.O.) GENERAL RECORDS, 1951	1
EXTRACTS FROM HICOG STAFF CONFERENCE MEETINGS, 1949–52	2
STAFF ANNOUNCEMENTS, 1949–50	1
Historical Division	
HISTORICAL ANALYSIS OF THE MCCLOY ADMINISTRATION, 1949–52	4
(a register [journal] of daily activities conducted by John J. McCloy, with references to documents in the above series)	

5 An archives box measures 40 × 13 × 27 centimeters; three archives boxes are roughly equivalent to 1 cubic foot.

Description	Boxes
Publications Relating to the U.S. Occupation of Germany, 1945–55	6

STATUS REPORT ON MILITARY GOVERNMENT OF GERMANY, March 15, 1946

Civil Administration Division
DOCUMENTS ON THE CREATION OF THE GERMAN FEDERAL CONSTITUTION SEPT–DEC 1949

Civil Administration Division, Council of Foreign Ministers (CFM), Secretariat
SUMMARY OF CFM AGREEMENTS AND DISAGREEMENTS ON GERMANY: A DETAILED BREAKDOWN OF FOUR POWER POSITIONS AT THE FOURTH SESSION OF CFM, MOSCOW, 1947
SUMMARY OF MULTIPARTITE AGREEMENTS AND DISAGREEMENTS ON GERMANY, parts I and II, 15 September 1948

Berlin Sector
SIX MONTHS REPORT, 4 JULY 1945–3 JANUARY 1946
SIX MONTHS REPORT, 4 JANUARY–3 JULY 1946
SIX MONTHS REPORT, 4 JULY 1946–1 JANUARY 1947
A FOUR YEAR REPORT, July 1, 1945–September 1, 1949

Economics Division
A YEAR OF POTSDAM: THE GERMAN ECONOMY SINCE THE SURRENDER [1946]

Political Adviser for Germany
CERTAIN INTERNATIONAL AND U.S. POLICY DOCUMENTS REGARDING GERMANY, 15 January 1949

HICOG Publications
4TH QUARTERLY REPORT ON GERMANY, July 1–Sept. 30, 1950
5TH QUARTERLY REPORT ON GERMANY, Oct. 1–December 31, 1950
6TH QUARTERLY REPORT ON GERMANY, January 1–March 31, 1951
7TH QUARTERLY REPORT ON GERMANY, April 1–June 30, 1951
8TH QUARTERLY REPORT ON GERMANY, July 1–September 30, 1951
9TH QUARTERLY REPORT ON GERMANY, Oct. 1–Dec. 31, 1951
10TH QUARTERLY REPORT ON GERMANY, January 1–March 31, 1952
REPORTS ON GERMANY, Sept. 21, 1949–July 31, 1950

Policy Reports Secretary
1950 BERLIN CONSTITUTION AND ELECTORAL LAW, January 15, 1951
SOVIET ZONE CONSTITUTION AND ELECTORAL LAW, February 1, 1951
ORGANIZATIONAL ABBREVIATIONS, April 15, 1951

Description	Boxes

GLOSSARY OF GERMAN ADMINISTRATIVE AND POLITICAL
TERMINOLOGY

ELECTIONS AND POLITICAL PARTIES IN GERMANY, 1945–1952,
June 1, 1952

DOCUMENTS ON THE SAAR, volume II, February 16, 1953

Public Relations Division

DISPLACED POPULATIONS: WELFARE, ASSISTANCE AND
PROBLEMS IN GERMANY TODAY, November 1950

LANDSBERG: A DOCUMENTARY REPORT, January 31, 1951

Historical Division [these are blue cover histories]

THE ESTABLISHMENT OF THE OFFICE OF THE U.S. HIGH
COMMISSIONER FOR GERMANY

THE HISTORY OF U.S. POLICY AND PROGRAM IN THE FIELD OF
RELIGIOUS AFFAIRS UNDER THE OFFICE OF THE U.S. HIGH
COMMISSIONER FOR GERMANY

THE EXCHANGE OF PERSONS PROGRAM IN WESTERN GERMANY

THE HISTORY OF THE DEVELOPMENT OF INFORMATION
SERVICES THROUGH INFORMATION CENTERS AND
DOCUMENTARY FILMS

THE FREE GERMAN YOUTH AND DEUTSCHLANDTREFFEN: A CASE
STUDY OF SOVIET TACTICS IN GERMANY

WOMEN IN WEST GERMANY

FOOD AND AGRICULTURAL PROGRAMS IN WEST GERMANY

LABOR PROBLEMS IN WEST GERMANY

THE LIBERALIZATION OF WEST GERMAN FOREIGN TRADE

THE EMPLOYMENT OF GERMAN NATIONALS BY THE OFFICE OF
THE U.S. HIGH COMMISSIONER FOR GERMANY

FIELD ORGANIZATION OF THE OFFICE OF THE U.S. HIGH
COMMISSIONER FOR GERMANY

DOCUMENTS ON FIELD ORGANIZATION OF THE OFFICE OF THE
U.S. HIGH COMMISSIONER FOR GERMANY, 1949–51

THE SPECIAL PROJECTS PROGRAM OF THE OFFICE OF THE U.S.
HIGH COMMISSIONER FOR GERMANY

ALLIED HIGH COMMISSION RELATIONS WITH THE WEST
GERMAN GOVERNMENT

THE WEST GERMAN BANKING SYSTEM

COMMUNITY AND GROUP LIFE IN WEST GERMANY

REVISION OF THE OCCUPATION STATUTE FOR GERMANY

ECONOMIC ASSISTANCE TO WEST BERLIN, 1949–51

BERLIN: DEVELOPMENT OF ITS GOVERNMENT AND
ADMINISTRATION

STATE AND LOCAL GOVERNMENT IN WEST GERMANY,
1945–53

PRESS, RADIO, AND FILM IN WEST GERMANY

Description	Boxes
THE WEST GERMAN EDUCATIONAL SYSTEM	
GUIDE TO STUDIES OF THE HISTORICAL DIVISION, OFFICE OF THE U.S. HIGH COMMISSIONER FOR GERMANY	

Office of the Executive Director

Description	Boxes
GENERAL RECORDS, 1949–55	114
SECURITY-SEGREGATED GENERAL RECORDS, 1949–55	234
TOP SECRET GENERAL RECORDS, 1953–55	3
DISPATCHES SENT, 1952–53	12
RECORDS PERTAINING TO THE INTERNATIONAL TRACING SERVICE (ITS), 1949–53	1
MISCELLANEOUS FILES MAINTAINED BY COL. H. A. GERHARDT, IOHC, HICOG, 1948–51	6
GENERAL HAY'S FILES, 1949–51	6

Office of the General Counsel
Administration of Justice Division

Description	Boxes
CLASSIFIED NAME FILES, 1947–53	3
CLASSIFIED RECORDS, 1947–54	1
RECORDS OF THE EXECUTION OF WAR CRIMINALS ON JUNE 8, 1951; includes photographs.	1
RECORDS RELATING TO AGREEMENTS BETWEEN THE ALLIED HIGH COMMISSION AND THE FEDERAL REPUBLIC OF GERMANY, 1949–55	17
RECORDS OF THE U.S. REPRESENTATIVE TO THE HICOM LAW COMMITTEE, 1949–55	21
RECORDS PERTAINING TO HICOM LAWS AND REGULATIONS, 1949–55	25

Decartelization and Deconcentration Division

Description	Boxes
GENERAL SUBJECT FILES, 1948–55	16
CARTEL SUBJECT FILES, 1947–55	72
RECORDS RE THE MOTION PICTURE INDUSTRY, 1945–55	16
CLASSIFIED RECORDS RELATING TO I.G. FARBEN, 1945–54	7
RECORDS OF THE TRIPARTITE I.G. FARBEN CONTROL GROUP (TRIFCOG) including files of its predecessor, the BIPARTITE I.G. FARBEN CONTROL OFFICE (BIFCO), 1948–49, and of the committee of German representatives to plan dispersal of the I.G. Farben conglomerate, THE I.G. FARBEN DISPERSAL PANEL (FARDIP), and the latter's successor which executed dispersal, THE I.G. FARBEN LIQUIDATION COMMITTEE (IGLC).	
ARCHIVES SECTION, 1945–53	208
SUBJECT FILES OF THE U.S. SECRETARIAT TO TRIFCOG	46
RECORDS OF THE U.S. CONTROL OFFICER (R. H. NEWMAN) 1945–53	83

Description	Boxes
RECORDS OF THE U.S. CONTROL OFFICER (J. F. TIERNEY) 1946–53	37
RECORDS OF THE U.S. CONTROL OFFICER (W. A. ACTON) 1946–53	106
RECORDS OF THE TRIFCOG FINANCE AND ACCOUNTING SECTION 1946–52	20
SECURITY SEGREGATED RECORDS RE I.G. FARBEN, 1945–54	14

Office of Chief Attorney

SUBJECT FILES, 1949–55	–18
DISTRICT ATTORNEY BLOTTER FILE, 1945–48	3
GENERAL RECORDS, 1949–55	15
REPORTS RECEIVED FROM DISTRICT ATTORNEYS, 1945–49	2

Law Committee

SUBJECT FILES, 1951–55	22

Prisons Division

GENERAL RECORDS, 1945–57	37
SECURITY SEGREGATED RECORDS, 1945–57 (includes Spandau and Landsberg prisons)	16
INSPECTION REPORTS, 1945–54	18
MISCELLANEOUS SUBJECT FILES, 1945–55	18
ADMINISTRATIVE SUBJECT FILES, 1946–55	39
INSTITUTIONS FILES, 1946–54	21
MISCELLANEOUS RECORDS, 1949–55	3
LANDSBERG PRISONER FILES, 1946–57	51
LANDSBERG PRISONER MEDICAL FILES, 1946–57	18
PETITIONS FOR CLEMENCY OR PAROLE AND RELATED RECORDS ON PERSONS CONVICTED BY U.S. MILITARY TRIBUNALS, NUREMBERG, 1947–57	39
CLEMENCY BOARD CASE FILES, 1946–48	18
CLEMENCY PANELS, 1950–55	27
NÜRNBERG TRIALS FILES, 1946–54	9
STATISTICAL REPORTS, 1950–55	1
ISSUES OF *Zeitschrift Für Strafvollzug* (JAN–SEPT, 1950) AND RELATED RECORDS, 1949–53	1

Office of Political Affairs
Passport Control and Security Section

RECORDS RELATING TO THE COMBINED TRAVEL BOARD, 1945–52	12

U.S. Secretariat, Allied High Commission

GENERAL RECORDS, 1949–52	27
ALLIED HIGH COMMISSION DOCUMENT FILE	

Description	Boxes
United States Courts of the Allied High Commission for Germany	
COURT CASE REGISTERS AND INDEXES, 1944–54	172
CRIMINAL CASE FILES, 1949–55	ca. 4,500
COURT OF APPEALS CASE FILES, 1949–55	366
SPECIAL CASE FILES, 1949–55	396
U.S. Element, Combined Travel Board	
U.S. EYES ONLY CORRESPONDENCE, BONN OFFICE, 1949–53	1
COPIES OF CLASSIFIED CORRESPONDENCE OF THE TRAVEL CONTROL DIVISION OF THE OFFICE OF POLITICAL AFFAIRS, 1950–51	
RECORDS RE OFFICE CORRESPONDENCE AND PROCEDURES, 1950–53	2
INCOMING AND OUTGOING CORRESPONDENCE, 1953–54	3
INCOMING AND OUTGOING CABLES, 1949–54	4
MINUTES OF THE MEETINGS, BOARD OF DIRECTORS, 1949–52 PAPERS, 1951–52	
PAPERS SUBMITTED TO THE DEPUTY SECRETARY, POLITICAL AFFAIRS COMMITTEE, ALLIED HIGH COMMISSIONER FOR GERMANY, 1950–52	
MISCELLANEOUS PAPERS, 1949, 1951–52	5
SUBJECT FILES, 1948–53	13
PASSPORT CONTROL AND SECURITY SECTION, 1945–55	1
U.S. Element, Military Security Board	
REPORT ON ACTIVITIES OF U.S. ELEMENT, MSB	6
U.S. Commissioner	
MEMORANDUMS, 1950–54 AGENDA FOR MEETINGS OF THE COMMISSIONERS, 1949–55	1
MINUTES OF THE MEETINGS OF THE COMMISSIONERS, 1949–55	2
PAPERS, 1949–55	2
DISPATCHES, AIRGRAMS, AND CABLES, 1951–54	2
SUBJECT FILES, 1947–55	21
STANDARD OPERATING PROCEDURES, 1950	
MANUAL FOR THE ALLIED HIGH COMMISSION FOR GERMANY, 1950	
BASIC DOCUMENTS PERTAINING TO GERMANY, 1950	1
REPORT ON THE WAR POTENTIAL OF WESTERN GERMANY 1951, and HICOG WEEKLY POLICY REVIEWS, 1951–52	1
HICOG INTELLIGENCE ANALYSES, 1950–51	1
RECORDS RE AERONAUTICAL RESEARCH, GERMANY, 1954–55	1
RECORDS RE PASSIVE AIR DEFENSE, 1950–55	3

Description	Boxes
U.S. Deputy Commissioner	
AGENDA FOR MEETINGS OF COMMITTEE OF DEPUTIES, 1949–51	
MINUTES OF MEETINGS OF COMMITTEE OF DEPUTIES, 1949–50	1
PAPERS, 1949–53	1
U.S. Secretariat	
MONTHLY ACTIVITY REPORTS, 1950–52	1
LETTERS, 1950–55	9
DEPUTY CHIEF SECRETARY (DCS) LETTERS, 1950–55	
NOTICES, 1949–55	2
MEMORANDUMS, 1950–55	1
MISCELLANEOUS ISSUANCES, 1951–53	1
U.S. Element, Industry Division	
AGENDA FOR MEETINGS, 1949–55	1
MINUTES OF MEETINGS, 1949–55	3
MEMORANDUMS, 1950–55	3
PAPERS, 1949–55	1
MSB ISSUANCES PERTAINING TO OR OF INTEREST TO THE INDUSTRY DIVISION, 1950–52	3
MISCELLANEOUS ISSUANCES, 1952–55	4
GENERAL CORRESPONDENCE, 1949–52	1
SUBJECT FILES, 1949–52	2
CLASSIFIED SUBJECT FILES, 1949–53	51
MANUFACTURING APPLICATION FILES, 1951–54	2
DOCUMENTATION RECORDS, 1951–52	1
Statistics Group	
INCOMING STATISTICS AND REPORTS, 1949–52	3
OUTGOING STATISTICS AND REPORTS, 1949–52	1
STATISTICAL PAPERS, 1949–52	3
Chemical Branch	
MINUTES, 1954–55, PAPERS, 1950–55	1
Electronics Branch	
PAPERS, 1951–55	1
Mechanical Engineering Branch	
PAPERS, 1952–55	1
Metals Branch	
PAPERS, 1951	1
Miscellaneous Branch	
MINUTES, 1951, PAPERS, 1951–55	1
Shipbuilding Branch	
MINUTES, 1954, PAPERS, 1952–55	1
U.S. Element, Military Division	
ISSUANCES, 1950–54	4
CLASSIFIED GENERAL RECORDS, 1949–52	4
RESTRICTED GENERAL RECORDS, 1949–52	10
REPORTS AND STATISTICS, 1950–54	6
SECRET GENERAL RECORDS, 1949–55	5

Description	Boxes
U.S. Element, Scientific Research Division	
AGENDA OF MEETINGS, MINUTES OF MEETINGS, LETTERS, MEMORANDUMS, AND PAPERS, 1949–54	2
GENERAL RECORDS, 1949–53	33
SUBJECT FILES, 1948–55	18
RECORDS RE SCIENTIFIC COMPANIES AND ORGANIZATIONS, 1949–53	2
Chemistry Branch	
CHRONOLOGICAL FILES, 1949–52, REPORTS, 1951	1
Engineering Branch	
CHRONOLOGICAL FILES, 1950–52	
CORRESPONDENCE RE INVENTIONS, 1949–52	
REPORTS, 1949–51	1
Patent Branch	
PAPERS, MEMORANDUMS, 1952, REPORTS, 1951–52	1
SUBJECT FILES, 1950–52	1
FORM LETTER CORRESPONDENCE, 1950–52	1
Physics Branch	
MISCELLANEOUS CORRESPONDENCE, 1950–52, REPORTS, 1951	1
U.S. Element, Extradition Board	
MINUTES OF MEETINGS, 1947–54	1
LETTERS, MEMORANDUMS, AND OTHER RECORDS (DAILY FILE), 1947–52	8
GENERAL CORRESPONDENCE, 1948–52	7
WAR CRIMES CORRESPONDENCE, 1945–52	8
SUBJECT FILES, 1947–53	6
COUNTRY SUBJECT FILES, 1946–51	7
REQUESTS FROM HUNGARY FOR EXTRADITIONS IN WAR CRIMES, 1947–51	7
CASE FILES, CRIMES OTHER THAN WAR CRIMES, 1947–55	27
CASE FILES FOR CRIMES OTHER THAN WAR CRIMES OF THE U.S. ELEMENT OF THE JUDICIAL SUB-COMMITTEE (JSC) OF THE LAW COMMITTEE OF THE ALLIED HIGH COMMISSION, 1953–55	20
WAR CRIMES EXTRADITION CASE FILES, 1945–54	192
REGISTERS OF WAR CRIMES EXTRADITIONS, 1945–51	2

U.S. Embassy, Bonn

Since Bonn was an Allied enclave within the British zone, rather than the American, the U.S. Bonn Land Commissioner (LC) really functioned as the housekeeper for HICOG; therefore the records described as Bonn LC are not necessarily local. The following are mainly zonal and interzonal level records:

Description	Boxes
Bonn Land Commissioner	
Legal Adviser	
OMGUS-HICOG Files, 1946–51	27
Telegrams, notes, ordinances, directives, executive decrees, and court cases. Review of German laws, ordinances, decrees, and court decisions for encroachments on areas reserved to the Allies. Also included is information on laws passed by the occupation authorities; arrangement is by case number	
SECRET BRIEFS ON GERMANY: FOUR-POWER TALKS, TRIPARTITE. COUNCIL OF FOREIGN MINISTERS, PARIS; FEDERAL LAW ENFORCEMENT AGENCIES, DOC BKS FMP–CTF, DOCS ON OCCUPATION STATUTE, WEEKLY REVIEWS (BEA), 1949–52	33
TOP SECRET SUBJECT FILES, 1953–58	2
RECORDS OF THE U.S. MEMBER OF THE MIXED PAROLE AND CLEMENCY BOARD, 1953–58	52
CARD INDEXES TO ACTIONS TAKEN ON APPLICATIONS OF GERMAN WAR CRIMINALS FOR PAROLE OR COMMUTATION OF SENTENCE, 1953–58	2
RECORDS RELATING TO THE CASE OF JUDGE WILLIAM CLARK	1

There are also rolls of microfilm of HICOG records prepared by the HICOG Historical Division:[6]

Description	Boxes
Documentary Records of HICOG (McCloy Administration), 1949–52	1 roll
Subject (Card) Index to the Allied General Secretariat, January–May 1952	1 roll

6 These rolls were accessioned in 1962 along with 287 rolls of microfilm of ACC and top-level OMGUS records (see note 2), 1945–48, and 46 rolls of Political Advisor (POLAD) records, 1946–49, prepared by either the OMGUS or HICOG Historical Division, presumably to be retained in Bonn or Berlin as indispensable documentation for continuity of American policy in Germany after the OMGUS records were retired to the continental United States. According to David Langbert, NARA appraisal archivist for State Department records, this compact, chronological collection of the most significant documents and the index cards were prepared by McCloy's direction during 1951–52 by Marie-Louise Acton and Albert M. Frye (memorandum dated January 20, 1987).

Description	Boxes
McCloy Administration	10 rolls

Berlin Element
Office of the Director

RECORDS OF THE OFFICE OF THE AMERICAN REPRESENTATIVE, INTERGOVERNMENTAL STUDY GROUP ON GERMANY, 1950–51	2

Administration Division

CLASSIFIED GENERAL RECORDS, 1949–55	67
CLASSIFIED INFORMATION AND DEPARTMENTAL TELEGRAMS, AIRMAIL LETTERS, AND CIRCULAR LETTERS, 1955	1

Allied Kommandatura (AK)
  Labor Committee

RECORDS OF THE LABOR COMMITTEE OF THE MANPOWER BRANCH, U.S. OFFICE OF MILITARY GOVERNMENT (OMGUS), 1948–49	1
GENERAL RECORDS, 1949	2
RECORDS PERTAINING TO THE MANPOWER WORKING COMMITTEE, 1949	1

  Legal Section

RECORDS PERTAINING TO LEGAL ISSUES AND QUESTIONS, 1951	1

  Eastern Affairs Division

CLASSIFIED GENERAL RECORDS, 1948–52	3

  Labor Affairs Division

SUBJECT FILES, 1948–53	2

  Legal Affairs Division

GENERAL RECORDS, 1945–52	2
MISCELLANEOUS RECORDS, 1945–51	1

  Economic Affairs Division

GENERAL RECORDS, 1949–55	1

  Political Affairs Division

GENERAL RECORDS, 1951	1
CLASSIFIED GENERAL RECORDS, 1949–53	6

  Public Safety Division

CLASSIFIED SUBJECT FILES, 1946–51	1

  Public Affairs Division

CLASSIFIED SUBJECT FILES, 1949–53	12

U.S. Mission Berlin   RG 84
Political Section
Allied Kommandatura Secretariat

MISCELLANEOUS PAPERS AND FILES, 1945–90	53
SUBJECT FILES, 1945–90	43

  Legal Adviser

RUDOLF HESS FILES, 1945–87	6

Description	Boxes
AK Legal Committee	
RECORDS ON POLITICAL AFFAIRS AND RELATIONS, 1945–90	9
SUBJECT FILES, 1945–90	27
INTERNATIONAL TREATIES (K 131 FILE), 1952–90	20
AK Economic Committee	
CLASSIFIED FILES, 1945–90	5
SUBJECT FILES, 1945–90	20
MIXED FILES, 1945–90	12
Berlin Air Safety Center (BASC)	
SUBJECT FILES AND MISCELLANEOUS RECORDS, 1946–90	16
West Berlin Consulate	
GENERAL RECORDS, 1953–55	16
Property Control Division, 1945–52	20
Frankfurt Element	
Office of the Director	
RECORDS OF THE SPECIAL ASSISTANT TO THE DIRECTOR, HENRY C. RAMSEY, 1950–51	1
Peripheral Reporting Unit (PRU)	
REPORTS ON RETURNEE EXPLOITATION GROUP (REG) SOURCES, 1953–55	1
RECORDS RE INTERROGATIONS OF DEFECTORS FROM BULGARIA, CZECHOSLOVAKIA, HUNGARY, POLAND, RUMANIA, AND U.S.S.R., 1953–55	2
Regional Land Commissioners	
Office of the Land Commissioner for Bavaria	
CENTRAL FILES, 1948–52	29
Records of the Intelligence Division	
"EEI" (ESSENTIAL ELEMENTS OF INFORMATION) REPORTS, 1950–51	3
BI-WEEKLY REPORTS OF THE REGENSBURG FIELD OFFICE, 1949–50	1
BI-WEEKLY REPORTS OF THE NÜRNBERG FIELD OFFICE, 1949–50	1
RECORDS RE LOYALTY CHECKS ON GERMAN PERSONNEL, 1949–50	3
LETTERS RECEIVED FROM GERMAN CITIZENS, 1949–51	1
REPORTS OF THE BAVARIAN CUSTOMS POLICE RE: BORDER CROSSINGS, 1950–51	2
MISCELLANEOUS REPORTS, 1950–51	1
Records of the Legal Affairs Division	
SUBJECT FILES, 1946–51	9
INSTITUTIONS FILES, 1945–51	9
German Justice Branch	
CIVIL AND CRIMINAL CASE FILES, 1949–51	45
CASE FILES SUBMITTED TO GERMAN JURISDICTION, 1949–51	10

Description	Boxes
Legislative Branch	
GENERAL RECORDS, 1949–51	1
RECORDS RELATING TO BAVARIAN LEGISLATIVE ORDINANCES, 1949–51	5
Legal Advice Branch	
CIVIL AND CRIMINAL CASE FILES, 1947–50	56
CORRESPONDENCE FILES, 1949–51	4
CRIMINAL INVESTIGATION REPORTS, 1947–48	1
MISCELLANEOUS RECORDS, 1947–50	6
Records of the Political Affairs Division	
Displaced Populations Branch	
CHILDREN'S CASE FILES, 1946–51	11
CLOSED CHILDREN'S CASE FILES, 1946–52	2
CORRESPONDENCE REGARDING DISPLACED CHILDREN, 1946–52	1
Records of the Public Affairs Division	
MONTHLY REPORTS, 1950–52	2
Records of the Field Operations Division	
Office of the Director	
DISTRICT LAND OFFICE ACTIVITY REPORTS, 1950–52	9
District II (Regensburg) Field Office	
CENTRAL FILES, 1947–50	14
RESIDENT OFFICER REPORTS, 1950	1
Munich Consulate General RG 84	
CLASSIFIED GENERAL RECORDS, 1945–55	13
Office of the Land Commissioner for Bremen	
GENERAL RECORDS, 1949–52	8
ADMINISTRATIVE RECORDS, 1951–52	1
COPIES OF LETTERS SENT TO THE BREMEN SENATE, 1945–49	1
LETTERS RECEIVED FROM THE BREMEN SENATE, 1949–51	1
Records of the Deputy Land Commissioner and Executive Officer	
GENERAL RECORDS, 1949–52	7
ADMINISTRATIVE RECORDS, 1947–49	1
RECORDS RE RESTRICTED MATTERS, 1950	1
Records of the Administrative Officer	
GENERAL RECORDS, 1947–49	1
ADMINISTRATIVE RECORDS, 1947–49	1
Reports and Statistics Branch	
ADMINISTRATIVE RECORDS, 1950–52	2
MONTHLY REPORTS OF GERMAN ACTIVITIES, 1950–51	3
Operating Facilities Branch	
GENERAL RECORDS, 1950–51	4
Records of the Political Affairs Division	
GENERAL RECORDS, 1949–51	2
COPIES OF LETTERS SENT, 1951–52	1

Description	Boxes
RECORDS RELATING TO THE CULTURAL EXCHANGE PROGRAMS, 1949–51	5
RECORDS RELATING TO LOCAL GOVERNMENT IN BREMEN, 1950–52	1
RECORDS RELATING TO PUBLIC SAFETY, 1949–52	9
ACCIDENT REPORTS, 1950–52	5
CORRESPONDENCE RELATING TO REQUESTS FOR ASSISTANCE, 1949–52	1
RECORDS RELATING TO OFFICIAL VISITS AND RECEPTIONS, 1950–51	1
LISTS RELATING TO BREMEN RESIDENTS, 1950–52	1

Records of the Legal Affairs Division
Land General Counsel

Description	Boxes
GENERAL RECORDS, 1949–52	9
COPIES OF LETTERS SENT, 1946–52	3
RECORDS RELATING TO LAW CASES, 1946–52	2
REVIEW CASE FILES, 1950–52	3
RECORDS RELATING TO MISCELLANEOUS LEGAL MATTERS, 1950–52	1

Assistant Land General Counsel

Description	Boxes
MISCELLANEOUS RECORDS, 1949–50	1

German Legal Consultant

Description	Boxes
GENERAL RECORDS OF DR. LOHMANN, 1950–52	1

Records of the Economic Affairs Division

Description	Boxes
GENERAL RECORDS, 1951–52	2
RECORDS RELATING TO DECARTELIZATION, 1947–49	4

Finance Advisor

Description	Boxes
GENERAL RECORDS, 1949–50	2

Marine Branch, Maritime Security and Port Observer

Description	Boxes
RECORDS RELATING TO THE BREMERHAVEN PORT OF EMBARKATION, 1949–50	9

Records of the Military Security Division

Description	Boxes
GENERAL RECORDS, 1948–52	1
RECORDS RE SCIENTIFIC RESEARCH, 1949–51	1
RECORDS RE INDUSTRY INSPECTION, 1949–52	1
RECORDS RE MILITARY SECURITY BOARD REPORTS, 1949–52	1

Records of the Field Operations Division, U.S. Resident Officer

Description	Boxes
GENERAL RECORDS, 1949–51	7
COPIES OF LETTERS SENT, 1949–52	2
GENERAL CORRESPONDENCE, 1951–52	1
COPIES OF LETTERS RECEIVED FROM THE LAND COMMISSIONER FOR BREMEN, 1949–52	1
GERMAN EMPLOYEE PERSONNEL FILES, 1947–51	4
RECORDS RE EMPLOYMENT, 1949–51	1

Description	Boxes
RECORDS RE LEGAL AFFAIRS, 1948–52	1
RECORDS RE POLITICAL ACTIVITIES, 1950–51	1
RECORDS RE POLITICAL AFFAIRS, 1949–51	1
RECORDS RE PUBLIC SAFETY, 1949–52	4
LISTS RE MILITARY POLICE BLOTTER INCIDENTS, 1951–52	1
RECORDS RE TRAFFIC ACCIDENTS, 1951–52	1
RECORDS RE CITY ADMINISTRATION AND PUBLIC WELFARE, 1949	1
RECORDS RE HOUSING, 1949–52	1
RECORDS RE HEALTH AFFAIRS, 1949–52	1
RECORDS RE WOMEN'S AFFAIRS, 1949–52	1
RECORDS RE YOUTH AFFAIRS, 1949–52	1
RECORDS RE LABOR AFFAIRS, 1949–52	1
RECORDS RE BUSINESS AND TRADE, 1949–52	1
RECORDS RE THE FILM PROGRAM, 1949–52	1
RECORDS RE MILITARY SECURITY, 1949–52	1
RECORDS RE SPECIAL PROJECTS, 1950–51	1
RECORDS RE CENTRAL WELFARE FUND, 1949–51	1
Bremen Consulate General RG 84	
GENERAL AND RESTRICTED RECORDS, 1946–55	31
SECURITY-CLASSIFIED GENERAL RECORDS, 1954–55	1
Office of the Land Commissioner for Hesse	
GENERAL RECORDS, 1949–51	2
Frankfurt Consulate General RG 84	
GENERAL RECORDS, 1946–55	28
CLASSIFIED GENERAL RECORDS, 1950–52	1
Office of the Land Commissioner for Wuerttemberg-Baden	
CLASSIFIED GENERAL RECORDS, 1949–52	3
MISCELLANEOUS RECORDS, 1950–51	1
Intelligence Division	
CLASSIFIED GENERAL RECORDS, 1948–52	1
Stuttgart Consulate General RG 84	
CLASSIFIED GENERAL RECORDS, 1946–55	4
U.S. Observer for Land – Baden (at Freiburg, French Zone)	
GENERAL RECORDS, 1950–52	1
Düsseldorf Consulate General RG 84 (British Zone)	
GENERAL RECORDS, 1950 52	1
CLASSIFIED GENERAL RECORDS (CONFIDENTIAL), 1950–55	4
TOP SECRET GENERAL RECORDS, 1951–54	1
CLASSIFIED GENERAL RECORDS RELATING TO TRADE AND COMMERCE, 1951–52	1
Hamburg Consulate General RG 84 (British Zone)	
CLASSIFIED GENERAL RECORDS, 1946–55	6

MILITARY RECORDS

Other than the records of overseas U.S. military commands referred to in the preceding sections as containing material relating to postwar Germany, those of the Washington headquarters agencies and commands are found among the geographic files of the following agencies:

Office of the Secretary of Defense (NARG 330), 1947–54;
Office of the Joint Chiefs of Staff (NARG 218), 1945–62;
Department of the Army after 1947 as follows:
  Office of the Secretary of the Army (NARG 335), particularly 20 linear feet of Records relating to Postwar Occupied Areas, 1948–52;
  Plans and Operations Division (NARG 165), 1945–1955;
  Chief of Civil Affairs and Military Government (NARG 319), 1948–64; an undetermined portion pertains to Germany.

One other untapped source of uncertain value needs mention: the records of purely military units other than military government commands stationed in West Germany from 1949 to 1955. How much light they may throw on everyday life in the FRG should, at least eventually, be explored. The records of U.S. commands in Europe during 1949–55, EUCOM (European Command, U.S. Army), 1947–52, renamed USAREUR (U.S. Army, Europe) in 1952 to avoid confusion with the newly created U.S. ground, sea, and air joint European Command, also abbreviated EUCOM, are deposited in NARG 338, U.S. Army, Europe, 1942–60.

ACCESS

Of crucial importance to researchers are the conditions of access to these records. In principle, most records of U.S. federal agencies, civil and military, must be offered to the National Archives by the time they are thirty years old. Archivists must decide, then or earlier, whether such records are of sufficient historical or documentation value to justify their permanent retention, not an easy task because it requires anticipation of what records will be of research interest twenty, fifty, to one hundred years in the future. On the average, only about 2 percent of federal records are permanently retained, but wartime, overseas, and foreign relations records require a much higher retention level, perhaps 20–50 percent.

Records designated as permanent, however, are not always turned over to the National Archives by the end of thirty years, and even those that are may not necessarily be open to public research. Federal agencies may withhold records beyond thirty years on the ground that release might endanger national security. Even when the records are already in the custody of the National Archives, the originating agency or other agencies may assert this exemption from release of such records. But, generally, agencies merely supply guidelines to be applied by National Archives personnel in determining which records can be released and which must be withheld. Once accessioned by NARA, whether thirty years old or less, records may be withheld when in the judgment of NARA archivists release may damage foreign relations, interfere with an ongoing investigation, or constitute an unwarranted invasion of the privacy of an individual.

The U.S. Freedom of Information Act provides any researcher – not just American citizens – with a procedure for appealing the withholding of records. The decision will normally be made by the National Archives if the records in question are more than thirty years old and are identified with sufficient degree of preciseness for efficient retrieval, but in cases of intelligence or foreign-source records, the originating agency will usually be consulted.

The determination whether release of a record would constitute an unwarranted invasion of privacy devolves almost entirely on the National Archives. The principle applied balances, in an open society, the need of the public for timely information as to what its government is doing against the equally important right, in a free and just society, of protection of individual personal privacy. In borderline cases, archivists may differ as to whether public interests override private rights; the balance favors the rights of the private citizen, but less so of public officials and other persons prominent in public life. The pressure on archivists in such decisions is strongest when the researcher is an investigative reporter or journalist, seeking records relevant to a current media story or political controversy.

Unlike most European archives, including those of Germany, the U.S. National Archives is not subject to a statutory privacy law, in our case the U.S. Privacy Act, which is roughly equivalent to West Germany's *Datenschutzgesetz*. Because errors in archival records are "historical errors," so to speak, it is imprudent to alter or destroy permanently valuable documents whenever an alert researcher discovers therein erroneous, derogatory information, even about individuals dead or alive. After all, it would be a falsification of the historical record were government documents to be purged of all erroneous information, inadvertent or deliberate. (The privilege of altering the historical record is reserved to totalitarian states or George Orwell's *1984*.)

The U.S. Privacy Act specifically exempts the National Archives from its provisions, but the Archives has issued and disseminated its own privacy restrictions, which adhere to the *b6* and *b7c* provisions of the Freedom of Information Act (FOIA). These published restrictions conform in essence to the principle of balancing the right of privacy against the public need to know. That right of individual privacy, incidentally, applies equally to all living persons, not just Americans, about whom information by name happens to appear in U.S. Federal records.

The German public has the right and the need to know about the formative years of its second republic. Since a significant part of that history is documented in American diplomatic and military records, the U.S. government and its National Archives intends to do everything feasible to make those records available as soon as possible to German and other researchers.

Select Bibliography

PUBLISHED DOCUMENTS

Akten zur Auswärtigen Politik der Bundesrepublik Deutschland. Ed. Hans-Peter Schwarz on behalf of the Auswärtiges Amt. Vol. 1, *Adenauer und die Hohen Kommissare 1949–1951.* Munich, 1989.
Vol. 2, *Adenauer und die Hohen Kommissare 1952.* Munich, 1990.
Akten zur Vorgeschichte der Bundesrepublik Deutschland, 1945–1949. Ed. Bundesarchiv and Institut für Zeitgeschichte. 5 vols. Munich, 1976–1981.
Flechtheim, Ossip K., ed. *Dokumente zur parteipolitischen Entwicklung in Deutschland seit 1945.* Vol. 2. Berlin, 1963.
Die Kabinettsprotokolle der Bundesregierung 1949ff. Ed. Bundesarchiv. Vol. 1ff. Boppard, 1982ff.
Montanmitbestimmung: Das Gesetz über die Mitbestimmung der Arbeitnehmer in den Aufsichtsräten und Vorständen der Unternehmen des Bergbaus und der Eisen und Stahl erzeugenden Industrie vom 21. Mai 1951. Quellen zur Geschichte des Parlamentarismus und der politischen Parteien, 4. Reihe. Vol. 1. Ed. Gabriele Müller-List. Düsseldorf, 1984.
Der Parlamentarische Rat 1948–1949: Akten und Protokolle. Ed. Deutscher Bundestag and Bundesarchiv. 4 vols. Boppard, 1975–1989.
Pollock, James K., et al., eds. *Germany under Occupation: Illustrative Materials and Documents.* Ann Arbor, Mich., 1947.
Royal Institute of International Affairs, ed. *Documents on International Affairs 1949–1950.* London, 1951.
Ruhm von Oppen, Beate, ed. *Documents on Germany under Occupation, 1945–1954.* London, 1955.
Schubert, Klaus von, ed. *Sicherheitspolitik der Bundesrepublik Deutschland: Dokumentation 1945–1977.* 2 vols. Cologne, 1978.
Smith, Jean Edward, ed. *The Papers of General Lucius D. Clay: Germany 1945–1949.* 2 vols. Bloomington, Ind., 1974.
U.S. Department of State, ed. *Foreign Relations of the United States: The Conference of Berlin (Potsdam) 1945.* 2 vols. Washington, D.C., 1960.
Foreign Relations of the United States 1944. Vol. 1, *General.* Washington, D.C., 1966.
Foreign Relations of the United States 1944. Vol. 2, *General: Economic and Social Matters.* Washington, D.C., 1967.

Foreign Relations of the United States 1945. Vol. 3, *European Advisory Commission; Austria; Germany.* Washington, D.C., 1968.

Foreign Relations of the United States 1947. Vol. 2, *Council of Foreign Ministers; Germany and Austria.* Washington, D.C., 1972.

Foreign Relations of the United States 1947. Vol. 3, *The British Commonwealth; Europe.* Washington, D.C., 1972.

Foreign Relations of the United States 1948. Vol. 2, *Germany and Austria.* Washington, D.C., 1973.

Foreign Relations of the United States 1948. Vol. 3, *Western Europe.* Washington, D.C., 1974.

Foreign Relations of the United States 1949. Vol. 1, *National Security Affairs, Foreign Economic Policy.* Washington, D.C., 1976.

Foreign Relations of the United States 1949. Vol. 3, *Council of Foreign Ministers; Germany and Austria.* Washington, D.C., 1974.

Foreign Relations of the United States 1949. Vol. 4, *Western Europe.* Washington, D.C., 1975.

Foreign Relations of the United States 1950. Vol. 1, *National Security Affairs; Foreign Economic Policy.* Washington, D.C., 1977.

Foreign Relations of the United States 1950. Vol. 3, *Western Europe.* Washington, D.C., 1977.

Foreign Relations of the United States 1950. Vol. 4, *Central and Eastern Europe; The Soviet Union.* Washington, D.C., 1980.

Foreign Relations of the United States 1951. Vol. 3, *European Security and the German Question.* Washington, D.C., 1981.

Foreign Relations of the United States 1951. Vol. 4, *Europe: Political and Economic Developments.* Washington, D.C., 1985.

Foreign Relations of the United States 1952–1954. Vol. 1, *General: Economic and Political Matters.* Washington, D.C., 1983.

Foreign Relations of the United States 1952–1954. Vol 2, *National Security Affairs.* Washington, D.C., 1984.

Foreign Relations of the United States 1952–1954. Vol. 5, *Western European Security.* Washington, D.C., 1983.

Foreign Relations of the United States 1952–1954. Vol. 6, *Western Europe and Canada.* Washington, D.C., 1986.

Foreign Relations of the United States 1952–1954. Vol. 7, *Germany and Austria.* Washington, D.C., 1986.

Foreign Relations of the United States 1952–1954. Vol. 8, *Eastern Europe; Soviet Union; Eastern Mediterranean.* Washington, D.C., 1988.

Foreign Relations of the United States 1955–1957. Vol. 4, *Western European Security and Integration.* Washington, D.C., 1986.

Foreign Relations of the United States 1955–1957. Vol. 5, *Austrian State Treaty; Summit and Foreign Ministers Meetings, 1955.* Washington, D.C., 1988.

Germany 1947–1949: The Story in Documents. Washington, D.C., 1950.

Postwar Foreign Policy Preparations, 1939–1945. Washington, D.C., 1949.

United States Economic Policy toward Germany. Publication 2630. Washington, D.C., 1946.

Die Versorgung der Kriegsopfer in der Bundesrepublik Deutschland: Stand 30.9.1952. Ed. Presse- und Informationsamt der Bundesregierung. Bonn, 1952.

DIARIES, JOURNALS, LETTERS, MEMOIRS

Acheson, Dean. *Present at the Creation.* New York, 1969.
Adenauer, Konrad. *Erinnerungen 1945–1963.* 4 vols. Stuttgart, 1965–1968.
Auriol, Vincent. *Journal du septennat 1947–1954.* 7 vols. Paris, 1970ff.
Blankenhorn, Herbert. *Verständnis und Verständigung: Blätter eines politischen Tagebuchs 1949 bis 1979.* Frankfurt am Main, Berlin, and Vienna, 1980.
Byrnes, James F. *Speaking Frankly.* New York and London, 1947.
Clay, Lucius D. *Decisions in Germany.* Garden City, N.Y., 1950.
Eden, Anthony. *Full Circle.* Boston, 1960.
Eisenhower, Dwight D. *Mandate for Change.* New York, 1963.
Hilgermann, Bernhard. *Der grosse Wandel: Erinnerungen aus den ersten Nachkriegsjahren. Kölns Wirtschaft unter amerikanischer und britischer Militärregierung.* Cologne, 1961.
Jones, Joseph M. *The Fifteen Weeks: An Inside Account of the Genesis of the Marshall Plan.* New York, 1953.
Kennan, George F. *Memoirs, 1925–1950.* Boston, 1967.
Kindleberger, Charles P. *The German Economy 1945–1947: Charles P. Kindleberger's Letters from the Field.* Westport, Conn., 1989.
Marshall Plan Days. Boston and London, 1987.
Maier, Reinhold. *Erinnerungen 1948–1953.* Tübingen, 1966.
Maizière, Ulrich de. *In der Pflicht: Lebensbericht eines deutschen Soldaten im 20. Jahrhundert.* Herford and Bonn, 1989.
Monnet, Jean. *Memoirs.* London, 1978.
From the Morgenthau Diaries. Ed. John Morton Blum. Vol. 3, *Years of War, 1941–1945.* Boston, 1967.
Schmid, Carlo. *Erinnerungen.* Bern, 1979.
Shuckburgh, Evelyn. *Descent to Suez: Diaries 1951–56.* London, 1986.
Sohl, Hans-Günther. *Notizen.* Private publication. Bochum, 1985.
Stimson, Henry L., and McGeorge Bundy. *On Active Service in Peace and War.* New York, 1947.
Truman, Harry S *Memoirs.* 2 vols. Garden City, N.Y., 1956.

BOOKS, ARTICLES, DISSERTATIONS

Abelshauser, Werner. "Hilfe und Selbsthilfe: Zur Funktion des Marshallplans beim westdeutschen Wiederaufbau." *VfZG* 37 (1989):85–113.
Der Ruhrkohlenbergbau seit 1945: Wiederaufbau, Krise, Anpassung. Munich, 1984.
"Wiederaufbau vor dem Marshall-Plan: Westeuropas Wachstumschancen und die Wirtschaftsordnungspolitik in der zweiten Hälfte der vierziger Jahre." *VfZG* 29 (1981):545–78.

Wirtschaft in Westdeutschland 1945–1948: Rekonstruktion und Wachstumsbedingungen in der amerikanischen und britischen Zone. Stuttgart, 1975.

Wirtschaftsgeschichte der Bundesrepublik Deutschland 1945–1980. Frankfurt am Main, 1983.

Abenheim, Donald. *Reforging the Iron Cross: The Search for Tradition in the West German Armed Forces.* Princeton, N.J., 1988.

Adamsen, Heiner. *Investitionshilfe für die Ruhr: Wiederaufbau, Verbände und Soziale Marktwirtschaft 1948–1952.* Wuppertal, 1981.

Ahrens, Hanns D. *Demontage: Nachkriegspolitik der Alliierten.* Munich, 1982.

Almond, Gabriel A. "The Politics of German Business." In Hans Speier and W. Phillips Davison, eds. *West German Leadership and Foreign Policy.* Evanston, Ill., and White Plains, N.Y., 1957, 195–241.

Ambrose, Stephen E. *Eisenhower.* 2 vols. New York, 1983–84.

Anfänge westdeutscher Sicherheitspolitik 1945–1956. Ed. Militärgeschichtliches Forschungsamt. 2 vols. Munich and Vienna, 1982 and 1990.

Auerbach, Hellmuth. "Die politischen Anfänge Carlo Schmids: Kooperation und Konfrontation mit der französischen Besatzungsmacht 1945–1948." *VfZG* 36 (1988):595–648.

Backer, John H. *Priming the German Economy: American Occupational Policies, 1945–1948.* Durham, N.C., 1971.

The Winds of History: The German Years of Lucius DuBignon Clay. New York, 1983.

Bacque, James. *Other Losses: The Shocking Truth behind the Mass Deaths of Disarmed German Soldiers and Civilians under General Eisenhower's Command.* New York, 1991.

Balabkins, Nicholas. *Germany under Direct Controls: Economic Aspects of Industrial Disarmament, 1945–1948.* New Brunswick, N.J., 1964.

Balfour, Michael, and John Mair. *Four Power Control in Germany and Austria, 1945–1946.* New York, 1972.

Ball, George. *The Past Has Another Pattern.* New York and London, 1982.

Barber, Joseph, ed. *American Policy toward Germany.* New York, 1947.

The Marshall Plan as American Policy: A Report on the Views of Community Leaders in 21 Cities. New York, 1948.

Baring, Arnulf. *Aussenpolitik in Adenauers Kanzlerdemokratie: Bonns Beitrag zur Europäischen Verteidigungsgemeinschaft.* Munich and Vienna, 1969.

Bartlett, C. J. *The Long Retreat: A Short History of British Defence Policy, 1945–1970.* London, 1972.

Baumgart, Egon. *Investitionen und ERP-Finanzierung.* Deutsches Institut für Wirtschaftsforschung, Sonderheft 56. Berlin, 1961.

Bédarida, François, and Jean-Pierre Rioux, eds. *Pierre Mendès-France et la Mendésisme.* Paris, 1985.

Belfrage, Cedric. *Seeds of Destruction: The Truth about the U.S. Occupation of Germany.* New York, 1954.

Benz, Wolfgang. *Von der Besatzungsherrschaft zur Bundesrepublik: Stationen einer Staatsgründung 1946–49.* Frankfurt am Main, 1984.

ed. *Neuanfang in Bayern 1945 bis 1949.* Munich, 1988.

Berger, Hugo. *Produktion und Rentabilität der westdeutschen Landwirtschaft nach der Währungsreform.* Hanover, 1949.

Berghahn, Volker. *The Americanization of West German Industry, 1945–1973.* Leamington Spa and New York, 1986.

Unternehmer und Politik in der Bundesrepublik. Frankfurt am Main, 1985.

Birrenbach, Kurt. "Adenauer und die Vereinigten Staaten in der Periode seiner Kanzlerschaft." In Dieter Blumenwitz et al., eds. *Konrad Adenauer und seine Zeit: Politik und Persönlichkeit des ersten Bundeskanzlers.* Vol. 1, *Beiträge von Weg- und Zeitgenossen.* Stuttgart, 1976, 477–509.

Blücher, Fritz. "Financial Situation and Currency Reform in Germany." *The Annals* 260 (Nov. 1948):63–73.

Blumenwitz, Dieter, et al., eds. *Konrad Adenauer und seine Zeit: Politik und Persönlichkeit des ersten Bundeskanzlers.* 2 vols. Stuttgart, 1976.

Boehling, Rebecca. "German Municipal Self-Government and the Personnel Policies of the Local U.S. Military Government in Three Major Cities of the U.S. Zone of Occupation: Frankfurt, Munich, and Stuttgart." *Archiv für Sozialgeschichte* 25 (1985):333–83.

"Die politischen Lageberichte des Frankfurter Oberbürgermeisters Blaum an die amerikanische Militärregierung 1945/1946." *Archiv für Frankfurts Geschichte und Kunst* 59 (1985):678–723.

Bolten, Seymour R. "Military Government and the German Political Parties." *Annals of the American Academy of Political and Social Science* 267 (1950):55–67.

Bonatz, Karl. "Anmerkungen zu den Presseinterviews mit Professor Gropius und zu seinem Vortrag im Titania-Palast am 22. August 1947." *Neue Bauwelt* 2 (1947):550–1.

Borgert, Heinz-Ludger, Walter Stürm, and Norbert Wiggershaus, eds. *Dienstgruppen und westdeutscher Verteidigungsbeitrag.* Boppard, 1982.

Börnsen, Ole, Hans H. Glismann, and Ernst-Jürgen Horn. *Der Technologietransfer zwischen den USA und der Bundesrepublik.* Tübingen, 1985.

Bosch, William J. *Judgement on Nuremberg.* Chapel Hill, N.C., 1970.

Bower, Tom. *Pledge Betrayed: America and Britain and the Nazification of Post-War Germany.* Garden City, N.Y., 1982.

Brünisch, Arthur "Der Wohnungsbau in der Bundesrepublik Deutschland 1945–1955." *Der Architekt* 4 (1955):203–5.

Brunn, Gerhard. "Köln in den Jahren 1945 und 1946: Die Rahmenbedingungen des gesellschaftlichen Lebens." In Otto Dann, ed. *Köln nach dem Nationalsozialismus: Der Beginn des gesellschaftlichen und politischen Lebens in den Jahren 1945/46.* Wuppertal, 1981, 35–72.

Buchheim, Christoph. "Die Währungsreform 1948 in Westdeutschland." *VfZG* 36 (1988): 189–231.

"Die Währungsreform in Westdeuschland im Jahre 1948: Einige ökonomische Aspekte." In Wolfram Fischer, ed. *Währungsreform and Soziale Marktwirtschaft: Erfahrungen und Perspektiven nach 40 Jahren.* Berlin, 1989, 391–402.

Die Wiedereingliederung Westdeutschlands in die Weltwirtschaft 1945–1958. Munich, 1990.

"Die Wirkung der Marshallplan-Hilfe in Schlüsselbranchen der deutschen Wirtschaft." *VfZG* 35 (1987):317–47.

Buczylowski, Ulrich. *Kurt Schumacher und die deutsche Frage: Sicherheitspolitik und strategische Offensivkonzeption von August 1950 bis September 1951.* Stuttgart, 1973.

Bührer, Werner. *Ruhrstahl und Europa: Die Wirtschaftsvereinigung Eisen und Stahl und die Anfänge der europäischen Integration 1945–1952.* Munich, 1986.

Bullen, Roger. "The British Government and the Schuman Plan May 1950–March 1951." In Klaus Schwabe, ed. *Die Anfänge des Schuman-Plans 1950/51–The Beginnings of the Schuman-Plan.* Baden-Baden, 1988, 199–210.

Bullock, Alan. *Ernest Bevin: Foreign Secretary, 1945–1951.* London and New York, 1983.

Buscher, Frank M. *The U.S. War Crimes Trial Program in Germany, 1946–1955.* New York, 1989.

Cairncross, Alec. *The Price of War: British Policy on German Reparations, 1941–1949.* Oxford and New York, 1986.

Carlebach, Emil. "Frankfurts Antifaschisten 1945." In Ulrich Schneider, ed. *Als der Krieg zu Ende war: Hessen 1945.* Frankfurt am Main, 1980, 10–32.

Zensur ohne Schere: Die Gründerjahre der "Frankfurter Rundschau" 1945/47. Frankfurt am Main, 1985.

Clay, Lucius D. "Adenauers Verhältnis zu den Amerikanern und die deutsch-amerikanischen Beziehungen nach 1945." In Dieter Blumenwitz et al., eds. *Konrad Adenauer und seine Zeit: Politik und Persönlichkeit des ersten Bundeskanzlers.* Vol. 1, *Beiträge von Weg- und Zeitgenossen.* Stuttgart, 1976, 466–76.

"Proconsul of a People, by Another People, for Both Peoples." In Robert Wolfe, ed. *Americans as Proconsuls: United States Military Government in Germany and Japan, 1944–1952.* Carbondale, Ill., 1984, 103–13.

Coutrot, Aline. "La politique atomique sous le gouvernement de Mendès-France." In François Bédarida and Jean-Pierre Rioux, eds. *Pierre Mendès-France et la Mendésisme.* Paris, 1985, 310–14.

Dann, Otto, ed. *Köln nach dem Nationalsozialismus: Der Beginn des Gesellschaftlichen und politischen Lebens in den Jahren 1945/46.* Wuppertal, 1981.

Davidson, Eugene. *The Trial of the Germans: An Account of the Twenty-Two Defendants before the International Military Tribunal at Nuremberg.* New York, 1966.

Diebold, William, Jr. *The Schuman Plan: A Study in Economic Cooperation, 1950–1959.* New York, 1959.

Diefendorf, Jeffry M. "Berlin on the Charles, Cambridge on the Spree: Walter Gropius, Martin Wagner, and the Rebuilding of Germany." In Helmut F. Pfanner, ed. *Kulturelle Wechselbeziehungen im Exil–Exile across Cultures.* Bonn, 1986, 343–57.

"Cities of Rubble to Cities in Germany: Postwar Reconstruction Planning in Germany." *Planning History* 12 (1990):19–26.

"Reconstruction Law and Building Law in Post-War Germany." *Planning Perspectives* 1 (1986):107–29.

Diefendorf, Jeffry M., ed. *Rebuilding Europe's Bombed Cities.* London and New York, 1989.

Doering-Manteuffel, Anselm. *Katholizismus und Wiederbewaffnung: Die Haltung der deutschen Katholiken gegenüber der Wehrfrage 1948–1955.* Mainz, 1981.

Dohrn, Klaus. "Das Amerikabild Adenauers." In Dieter Blumenwitz et al., eds. *Konrad Adenauer und seine Zeit: Politik und Persönlichkeit des ersten Bundeskanzlers.* Vol. 1, *Beiträge von Weg- und Zeitgenossen.* Stuttgart, 1976, 510–23.

Dönhoff, Marion. *Foe into Friend.* Trans. Gabriele Annan. London, 1982.

Donovan, Robert J. *Eisenhower: The Inside Story.* New York, 1956.

Dulles, Allen W. "Alternatives for Germany." *Foreign Affairs* 25 (April 1947):421–32.

Eggebrecht, Axel, ed. *Die zornigen alten Männer: Gedanken über Deutschland seit 1945.* Reinbek bei Hamburg, 1975.

Ellis, Howard S. *The Economics of Freedom: The Progress and Future of Aid to Europe.* New York, 1950.

Entmilitarisierung und Aufrüstung in Mitteleuropa 1945–1956. Ed. Militärgeschichtliches Forschungsamt. Herford and Bonn, 1983.

Fait, Barbara. " 'In einer Atmosphäre der Freiheit': Die Rolle der Amerikaner bei der Verfassungsgebung in den Landern der US–Zone 1946." *VfZG* 33 (1985):420–55.

"Auf Befehl der Besatzungsmacht? Der Weg zur Bayerischen Verfassung." In Wolfgang Benz, ed. *Neuanfang in Bayern 1945 bis 1949.* Munich, 1988, 36–63.

Feis, Herbert. *From Trust to Terror: The Onset of the Cold War, 1945–1950.* New York, 1970.

Fichter, Michael. *Besatzungsmacht und Gewerkschaften: Zur Entwicklung und Anwendung der US-Gewerkschaftspolitik in Deutschland 1944–1948.* Opladen, 1982.

"Non-State Organizations and the Problems of Redemocratization." In John H. Herz, ed. *From Dictatorship to Democracy: Coping with the Legacies of Authoritarianism and Totalitarianism.* Westport, Conn., 1982, 36–63.

Fichter, Tilman, and Siegwart Loennendonker, eds. *Freie Universität Berlin 1948–1973: Hochschule im Umbruch.* 5 vols. Berlin, 1973–83.

Fischer, Alexander, ed. *Wiederbewaffnung in Deutschland nach 1945.* Berlin, 1986.

Fischer, Friedhelm. "German Reconstruction as an International Activity." In Jeffry M. Diefendorf, ed. *Rebuilding Europe's Bombed Cities.* London and New York, 1989, 131–44.

Fischer, Wolfram, ed. *Währungsreform und Soziale Marktwirtschaft: Erfahrungen und Perspektiven nach 40 Jahren.* Berlin, 1989.

Foelz-Schröter, Elise. *Föderalistische Politik und nationale Repräsentation 1945–1947.* Stuttgart, 1974.

Freiheit ohne Furcht: Zehn Jahre Heimkehrerverband. Ed. Verband der Heimkehrer, Kriegsgefangenen und Vermisstenangehörigen Deutschlands. Berlin, n.d.

Fried, Hans Ernst. *The Guilt of the German Army.* New York, 1942.

Friedmann, Werner. *The Allied Military Government of Germany.* London, 1947.

Frohn, Axel. *Neutralisierung als Alternative zur Westintegration: Die Deutschlandpolitik der Vereinigten Staaten von Amerika 1945–1949,* Dokumente zur Deutschlandpolitik, Beihefte, vol. 7. Frankfurt am Main, 1985.

"Das Schicksal deutscher Kriegsgefangener in amerikanischen Lagern nach dem Zweiten Weltkrieg: Eine Auseinandersetzung mit den Thesen von James Bacque." *Historisches Jahrbuch* 111,2 (1991):466–92.

Frohn, Axel, ed. *Holocaust and Shilumim: The Policy of "Wiedergutmachung" in the Early 1950s.* German Historical Institute, Occasional Papers Series, vol. 2. Washington, D.C., 1991.

Fünfzehn Jahre Freie Universität Berlin, 1948–1963. Berlin, 1963.

Funk, Albrecht. "Agrarentwicklung und Agrarpolitik." In Wolf-Dieter Narr and Dietrich Thränhardt, eds. *Die Bundesrepublik Deutschland: Entstehung, Entwicklung, Struktur.* Königstein/Taunus, 1979, 214–34.

Gaddis, John Lewis. *Strategies of Containment: A Critical Appraisal of Postwar American National Security Policy.* New York, 1980.

———. *The United States and the Origins of the Cold War, 1941–1947.* New York and London, 1972.

Geiling, Martin. *Aussenpolitik und Nuklearstrategie: Eine Analyse des konzeptionellen Wandels der amerikanischen Sicherheitspolitik gegenüber der Sowjetunion (1945–1963).* Cologne and Vienna, 1975.

Genschel, Dietrich. *Wehrreform und Reaktion: Die Vorbereitung der Inneren Führung 1951–1956.* Hamburg, 1972.

Gillen, J. F. J. *Labor Problems in West Germany.* Bad Godesberg-Mehlem, 1952.

———. *State and Local Government in West Germany, 1945–53.* Historical Division of the Office of HICOG. N.p., 1953.

Gillingham, John. *Coal, Steel, and the Rebirth of Europe, 1945–1955: The Germans and French from Ruhr Conflict to Economic Community.* New York, 1990.

———. "Die französische Ruhrpolitik und die Ursprünge des Schuman-Plans." *VfZG* 35 (1987):1–24.

———. "Solving the Ruhr Problem: German Heavy Industry and the Origins of the Schuman Plan." In Klaus Schwabe, ed. *Die Anfänge des Schuman-Plans 1950/51–the Beginnings of the Schuman-Plan.* Baden-Baden, 1988, 399–436.

Gimbel, John. *The American Occupation of Germany: Politics and the Military, 1945–1949.* Stanford, Calif., 1968.

———. *A German Community under American Occupation: Marburg, 1945–52.* Stanford, Calif., 1961.

———. *The Origins of the Marshall Plan.* Stanford, Calif., 1976.

———. *Science, Technology, and Reparations: Exploitation and Plunder in Postwar Germany.* Stanford, Calif., 1990.

———. "U.S. Policy and German Scientists: The Early Cold War." *Political Science Quarterly* 101 (1986):433–51.

———. "Die Vereinigten Staaten, Frankreich und der amerikanische Vertragsentwurf zur Entmilitarisierung Deutschlands." *VfZG* 22 (1974):258–86.

Göderitz, Johannes, Roland Rainer, and Hubert Hoffmann. *Die gegliederte und aufgelockerte Stadt.* Tübingen, 1957.

Golay, John Ford. *The Founding of the Federal Republic of Germany.* Chicago, 1958.

Grabbe, Hans-Jürgen. "Die deutsch-alliierte Kontroverse um den Grundgesetzentwurf im Frühjahr 1949." *VfZG* 26 (1978):393–418.

Greiner, Christian. "Die alliierten militärstrategischen Planungen zur Verteidigung Westeuropas 1947–1950." In *Anfänge westdeutscher Sicherheitspolitik 1945–1956.*

Haftendorn, Helga. *Sicherheit und Entspannung: Zur Aussenpolitik der Bundesrepublik Deutschland 1955–1982.* Baden-Baden, 1983.

Hardach, Gerd. "The Marshall Plan in Germany, 1948–1952." *Journal of European Economic History* 16 (1987):433–85.

Hartrich, Edwin. *The Fourth and Richest Reich: How the Germans Conquered the Postwar World.* New York and London, 1980.

Heinrichsbauer, August. *Schwerindustrie und Politik.* Essen-Kettwig, 1948.

Henke, Josef. "Das amerikanisch-deutsche OMGUS-Projekt: Erschliessung und Verfilmung der Akten der amerikanischen Militärregierung in Deutschland." *Der Archivar* 35 (1982):149–58.

Herbert, Gilbert. *The Dream of the Factory-Made House: Walter Gropius and Konrad Wachsmann.* Cambridge, Mass., 1984.

Herbst, Ludolf, ed. *Westdeutschland 1945–1955.* Munich, 1986.

Herbst, Ludolf, and Constantin Goschler, eds. *Wiedergutmachung in der Bundesrepublik Deutschland.* Munich, 1989.

Herbst, Ludolf, Werner Bührer, and Hanno Sowade, eds. *Vom Marshallplan zur EWG: Die Eingliederung der Bundesrepublik Deutschland in die westliche Welt.* Munich, 1990.

Hilgermann, Bernhard. *Auf dem Wege aus dem Chaos zum Wirtschaftswunder: Dr. Agartz, der erste Leiter des Zentralamts für Wirtschaft in der britischen Zone.* Cologne, 1979.

Hillgruber, Andreas. *Alliierte Pläne für eine "Neutralisierung" Deutschlands 1945–1955.* Rheinisch-Westfälische Akademie der Wissenschaften, Vorträge G 286. Opladen, 1987.

Hirsch-Weber, Wolfgang. *Gewerkschaften in der Politik: Von der Massenstreikdebatte zum Kampf um das Mitbestimmungsrecht.* Cologne and Opladen, 1959.

The History of the Joint Chiefs of Staff. Vol. 4, Walter S. Poole, *The Joint Chiefs of Staff and National Policy 1950–1952.* Wilmington, Del., 1980.

Vol. 5, Robert J. Watson, *The Joint Chiefs of Staff and National Policy 1953–1954.* Wilmington, Del., 1986.

Hoffmann, Stanley, and Charles Maier, eds. *The Marshall Plan: A Retrospective.* Boulder, Colo., and London, 1984.

Hogan, Michael J. *The Marshall Plan: America, Britain, and the Reconstruction of Western Europe, 1947–1952.* Cambridge, U.K., 1987.

Höhns, Ulrich. " 'Neuaufbau' als Hoffnung, 'Wiederaufbau' als Festschreibung der Misere: Marshallplan und Wohnungsbau in der Bundesrepublik nach dem Kriege." In Bernhard Schulz, ed. *Grauzonen–Farbwelten: Kunst und Zeitbilder 1945–1955.* Berlin, 1983, 85–104.

Horne, Alistaire. *Return to Power.* New York, 1956.

Hudemann, Rainer. *Sozialpolitik im deutschen Südwesten zwischen Tradition und Neuordnung: Sozialversicherung und Kriegsopferversorgung im Rahmen französischer Besatzungspolitik.* Mainz, 1988.

Hughes, Thomas P. *Networks of Power.* Baltimore, 1983.

Die internationale Politik 1955. Ed. Arnold Bergstraesser and Wilhelm Cornides. Munich, 1958.

Jacobmeyer, Wolfgang. "Die Niederlage 1945." In *Westdeutschlands Weg zur Bundesrepublik 1945–1949: Beiträge von Mitarbeitern des Instituts für Zeitgeschichte.* Munich, 1976, 11–24.

Jakab, Elisabeth. "The Council on Foreign Relations." *Book Forum* 3 (1976):418–72.

Jasper, Gotthard. "Wiedergutmachung und Westintegration: Die halbherzige justizielle Aufarbeitung der NS-Vergangenheit in der frühen Bundesrepublik." In
Ludolf Herbst, ed. *Westdeutschland 1945–1955*. Munich, 1986, 183–202.

Johnson, Walter. *The Battle against Isolation*. New York, 1944.

Kellermann, Henry J. *Cultural Relations as an Instrument of U.S. Foreign Policy: The
Educational Exchange Program between the United States and Germany, 1945–1954*.
Cultural Relations Programs of the U.S. Department of State, Historical Stud-
ies, No. 3. Washington, D.C., 1978.

Kleinert, Uwe. *Flüchtlinge und Wirtschaft in Nordrhein-Westfalen 1945–1961*. Düsseldorf, 1988.

Klessmann, Christoph, and Peter Friedemann. *Streiks und Hungermärsche im Ruhrgebiet 1946–1948*. Frankfurt am Main, 1977.

Kluge, Ulrich. *Vierzig Jahre Agrarpolitik in der Bundesrepublik Deutschland*. 2 vols.
Hamburg, 1989.

Koch, Peter. *Konrad Adenauer*. Reinbek bei Hamburg, 1985.

Krammer, Arnold. "Technology Transfer as War Booty: The U.S. Technical Oil
Mission to Europe, 1945." *Technology and Culture* 22 (1981):68–103.

Kreikamp, Hans-Dieter. "Zur Entstehung des Entschädigungsgesetzes der amerikanischen Besatzungszone." In Ludolf Herbst and Constantin Goschler, eds.
Wiedergutmachung in der Bundesrepublik Deutschland. Munich, 1989, 61–75.

Krieger, Leonard. "The Potential for Democratization in Occupied Germany: A
Problem in Historical Projection." *Public Policy* 18 (1968):27–58.

Krieger, Wolfgang. *General Lucius D. Clay und die amerikanische Deutschlandpolitik
1945–1949*. Stuttgart, 1987.

Lademacher, Horst. "Die britische Sozialisierungspolitik im Rhein-Ruhr-Raum
1945–1948." In Claus Scharf and Hans-Jürgen Schröder, eds. *Die Deutschlandpolitik Grossbritanniens und die britische Zone 1945–1949*. Wiesbaden, 1979,
51–92.

Large, David C. "Reckoning without the Past: The HIAG of the Waffen-SS and the
Politics of Rehabilitation in the Bonn Republic." *Journal of Modern History* 59
(1987):79–113.

Lasby, Clarence. *Project Paperclip: German Scientists and the Cold War*. New York,
1971.

Lincoln, Charles. *Auf Befehl der Militärregierung*. Trans. Hans and Elsbeth Herlin.
Munich, 1965.

Link, Arthur S. *American Epoch: A History of the United States since the 1890's*. Vol. 3,
1938–1966, 3rd ed. New York, 1967.

Link, Werner. *Deutsche und amerikanische Gewerkschaften und Geschäftsleute 1945–
1975: Eine Studie über transnationale Beziehungen*. Düsseldorf, 1978.

Lipgens, Walter. "Die Bedeutung des EVG-Vertrages für die politische europäische
Einigungsbewegung." In Hans-Erich Volkmann and Walter Schwengler, eds.
Die Europäische Verteidigungsgemeinschaft: Stand und Probleme der Forschung. Bop-
pard, 1985, 9–30.

Litchfield, Edward H., et al., eds. *Governing Postwar Germany*. Ithaca, N.Y., 1953.

Loth, Wilfried. *Sozialismus und Internationalismus: Die französischen Sozialisten und die
Nachkriegsordnung Europas 1940–1950*. Stuttgart, 1977.

Lüders, Carsten. *Das Ruhrkontrollsystem: Entstehung und Entwicklung im Rahmen der Westintegration Westdeutschlands 1947–1953.* Frankfurt am Main and New York, 1988.

Mai, Gunther. "Der Alliierte Kontrollrat 1945–1948: Von der geteilten Kontrolle zur kontrollierten Teilung." *Aus Politik und Zeitgeschichte* B 23 (1988):3–14.

"Dominanz oder Kooperation im Bündnis? Die Sicherheitspolitik der USA und der Verteidigungsbeitrag Europas 1945–1956." *Historische Zeitschrift* 246 (1988):327–64.

"Osthandel und Westintegration 1947–1957: Die USA, Europa und die Entstehung einer hegemonialen Partnerschaft." In Ludolf Herbst, Werner Bührer, and Hanno Sowade, eds. *Vom Marshallplan zur EWG: Die Eingliederung der Bundesrepublik Deutschland in die westliche Welt.* Munich, 1990, 203–25.

Westliche Sicherheitspolitik im Kalten Krieg: Der Korea-Krieg und die deutsche Wiederbewaffnung 1950. Boppard, 1977.

Mako, William P. *U.S. Ground Forces and the Defense of Central Europe.* Washington, D.C., 1983.

Manchester, William. *The Arms of Krupp.* New York, 1970.

Krupp: Zwölf Generationen. Munich, 1968.

Margairaz, Michel. "Autour des Accords Blum-Byrnes: Jean Monnet entre le consensus national et le consensus atlantique." *Histoire, économie, société* 1 (1982): 440–70.

Martin, James Stewart. *All Honorable Men.* Boston, 1950.

McGeehan, Robert. *The German Rearmament Question: Diplomacy and European Defense after World War II.* Urbana, Ill., 1971.

McIntyre, John R., and Daniel S. Papp, eds. *The Political Economy of International Technology Transfer.* New York, 1986.

Mee, Charles L., Jr. *Meeting at Potsdam.* New York, 1975.

Meier-Dörnberg, Wilhelm. "Die Europäische Verteidigungsgemeinschaft." In Alexander Fischer, ed. *Wiederbewaffnung in Deutschland nach 1945.* Berlin, 1986, 79–91.

"Politische und militärische Faktoren bei der Planung des deutschen Verteidigungsbeitrages im Rahmen der EVG." In Militärgeschichtliches Forschungsamt, ed. *Entmilitarisierung und Aufrüstung in Mitteleuropa 1945–1956.* Herford and Bonn, 1983, 184–208.

Mendelsohn, John. "War Crimes Trials and Clemency in Germany and Japan." In Robert Wolfe, ed. *Americans as Proconsuls: United States Military Government in Germany and Japan, 1944–1952.* Carbondale, Ill., 1984, 226–59.

Merkl, Peter. *The Origins of the West German Republic.* New York, 1963.

Merritt, Anna J., and Richard L. Merritt. *Public Opinion in Occupied Germany: The OMGUS Surveys, 1945–1949.* Urbana, Ill., 1970.

Meyer, Georg. "Zur Situation der deutschen militärischen Führungsschicht im Vorfeld des westdeutschen Verteidigungsbeitrages 1945–1950/51." In *Anfänge westdeutscher Sicherheitspolitik 1945–1956.* Ed. Militärgeschichtliches Forschungsamt. Vol. 1, *Von der Kapitulation bis zum Pleven-Plan.* Munich, 1982, 577–735.

Mielert, Werner. "Die verschenkte Kontrolle: Bestimmungsgründe und Grundsätze der britischen Kohlenpolitik im Ruhrbergbau 1945–1948." In Dietmar Petzina and Walter Euchner, eds. *Wirtschaftspolitik im britischen Besatzungsgebiet 1945–1949*. Düsseldorf, 1984, 105–19.

Miller Lane, Barbara. *Architecture and Politics in Germany, 1918–1945*. Cambridge, Mass., 1968.

"The Berlin Congress Hall, 1955–57." *Perspectives in American History*, new series, 1 (1984):131–85.

Milward, Alan. *The Reconstruction of Western Europe, 1945–51*. London, 1984.

Minter, William M. "The Council on Foreign Relations: A Case Study in the Societal Bases of Foreign Policy Formulation." Ph.D. diss., University of Wisconsin–Madison, 1973.

Möller, Hans, ed. *Zur Vorgeschichte der Deutschen Mark: Die Währungsreformpläne 1945–1948*. Basel, 1961.

Morgenthau, Hans J., ed. *Germany and the Future of Europe*. Chicago, 1951.

Moskowitz, Moses. "The Political Re-education of the Germans: The Emergence of Parties and Politics in Württemberg-Baden (May 1945–June 1946)." *Political Science Quarterly* 61 (1946):535–61.

Müller, Gloria. *Mitbestimmung in der Nachkriegszeit: Britische Besatzungsmacht, Unternehmer, Gewerkschaften*. Düsseldorf, 1987.

Napp-Zinn, Anton Felix. "Wirtschaftsräte und überbetriebliche Mitbestimmung in Deutschland." In Walter Weddigen, ed. *Zur Theorie und Praxis der Mitbestimmung*. Vol. 2. Berlin, 1964, 119–32.

Narr, Wolf-Dieter, and Dietrich Thränhardt, eds. *Die Bundesrepublik Deutschland: Entstehung, Entwicklung, Struktur*. Königstein/Taunus, 1979.

Neuer Wohnbau. 2 vols. Ravensburg, 1952 and 1958.

Die Neuordnung der Eisen- und Stahlindustrie im Gebiet der Bundesrepublik Deutschland: Ein Bericht der Stahltreuhändervereinigung. Munich and Berlin, 1954.

Niethammer, Lutz. "Kampfkomitees und Arbeitsausschüsse in Stuttgart." In Lutz Niethammer et al., eds. *Arbeiterinitiative 1945: Antifaschistische Ausschüsse und Reorganisation der Arbeiterbewegung in Deutschland*. Wuppertal, 1976, 503–602.

Niethammer, Lutz, Ulrich Borsdorf, and Peter Brandt, eds. *Arbeiterinitiative 1945: Antifaschistische Ausschüsse und Reorganisation der Arbeiterbewegung in Deutschland*. Wuppertal, 1976.

Niklas, Wilhelm. *Sorge um das tägliche Brot*. Bonn, 1951.

Noelle, Elisabeth, and Erich Peter Neumann, eds. *The Germans: Public Opinion Polls, 1947–1966*. Allensbach and Bonn, 1967.

Pavitt, Keith. "Technology Transfer among the Industrially Advanced Countries: An Overview." In Nathan Rosenberg and Claudio Frischtak, eds. *International Technology Transfer: Concepts, Methods, and Comparisons*. New York, 1985, 3–23.

Peterson, Edward N. *The American Occupation of Germany: Retreat to Victory*. Detroit, 1978.

Petsch, Joachim. "Neues Bauen und konservative Architektur der 20er und 30er Jahre." *Der Architekt*, no. 4 (1983):188–93.

Petzina, Dietmar, and Walter Euchner, eds. *Wirtschaftspolitik im britischen Besatzungsgebiet 1945–1949*. Düsseldorf, 1984.

Pfanner, Helmut F., ed. *Kulturelle Wechselbeziehungen im Exil–Exile across Cultures*. Bonn, 1986.

Picht, Georg, ed. *Studien zur politischen und gesellschaftlichen Situation der Bundeswehr.* Witten and Berlin, 1965.

Pietsch, Hartmut. *Militärregiergung, Bürokratie und Sozialisierung: Zur Entwicklung des politischen Systems des Ruhrgebietes 1945 bis 1948.* Duisburg, 1978.

Pilgert, Henry P. *The Exchange of Persons Program in Western Germany.* Historical Division, Office of the U.S. High Comissioner for Germany. Washington, D.C., 1951.

Pirker, Theo. *Die blinde Macht: Die Gewerkschaftsbewegung in der Bundesrepublik.* 2 vols. Berlin, 1979.

Plum, Günther. "Versuche gesellschaftspolitischer Neuordnung: Ihr Scheitern im Kräftefeld deutscher und allierter Politik." In *Westdeutschlands Weg zur Bundesrepublik 1945–1949: Beiträge von Mitarbeitern des Instituts für Zeitgeschichte.* Munich, 1976, 90–117.

Poidevin, Raymond. *Robert Schuman: Homme d'Etat, 1886–1963.* Paris, 1986.

Pollard, Robert A. *Economic Security and the Origins of the Cold War.* New York, 1985.

Pöttering, Hans-Gert. *Adenauers Sicherheitspolitik 1955–1963.* Düsseldorf, 1975.

Price, Hoyt, and Carl E. Schorske. *The Problem of Germany.* New York, 1947.

Prowe, Diethelm. "Economic Democracy in Post-World War II Germany: Corporatist Crisis Response, 1945–1948." *Journal of Modern History* 57 (1985): 451–82.

"Im Sturmzentrum: Die Industrie- und Handelskammern in den Nachkriegsjahren 1945–1949." *Zeitschrift für Unternehmensgeschichte,* Beiheft 53, (1987): 91–122.

Rautenberg, Hans-Jürgen, and Norbert Wiggershaus. "Die 'Himmeroder Denkschrift' vom Oktober 1950: Politische und militärische Ueberlegungen für einen Beitrag der Bundesrepublik Deutschland zur westeuropäischen Verteidigung." *MGM* 21 (1977):135–206.

Ritschl, Albrecht. "Die Währungsreform von 1948 und der Wiederaufstieg der westdeutschen Industrie: Zu den Thesen von Mathias Manz und Werner Abelshauser über die Produktionswirkungen der Währungsreform." *VfZG* 33 (1985):136–65.

Rosenberg, Nathan, and Claudio Frischtak, eds. *International Technology Transfer: Concepts, Methods, and Comparisons.* New York, 1985.

Rostow, Walt W. *The Division of Europe after World War II.* Austin, Tex., 1981.

Rudzio, Wolfgang. "Die ausgebliebene Sozialisierung an Rhein und Ruhr: Zur Sozialisierungspolitik von Labour-Regierung und SPD 1945–1948." *Archiv für Sozialgeschichte* 18 (1978):1–39.

Rühland, Helmut. "Entwicklung, heutige Gestaltung und Problematik der Kriegsopferversorgung in der Bundesrepublik Deutschland." Diss. phil., Cologne University, 1957.

Rupieper, Hermann-Josef. *Der besetzte Verbündete: Die amerikanische Deutschlandpolitik 1949–1955.* Opladen, 1991.

"Die Berliner Aussenministerkonferenz von 1954." *VfZG* 34 (1986):427–53.

"Deutsche Frage und europäische Sicherheit: Politisch-strategische Ueberlegungen 1953/1955." In Bruno Thoss and Hans-Erich Volkmann, eds. *Zwischen*

Kaltem Krieg und Entspannung: Sicherheits- und Deutschlandpolitik der Bundesrepublik im Mächtesystem der Jahre 1953–1956. Boppard 1988, 179–209.

"Wiedervereinigung und europäische Sicherheit: Deutsch-amerikanische Ueberlegungen für eine Entmilitarisierte Zone in Europa 1953." *MGM* 39 (1986): 91–130.

Scharf, Claus, and Hans-Jürgen Schröder, eds. *Die Deutschlandpolitik Grossbritanniens und die britische Zone 1945–1949.* Wiesbaden, 1979.

Schenk zu Schweinsberg, Krafft Freiherr. "Die Soldatenverbände in der Bundesrepublik." In Georg Picht, ed. *Studien zur politischen und gesellschaftlichen Situation der Bundeswehr.* Witten and Berlin, 1965, 96–177.

Schillings, Warner R., Paul Y. Hammond, and Glenn H. Snyder, eds. *Strategy, Politics, and Defense Budgets.* New York, 1962.

Schlange-Schöningen, Hans. *Im Schatten des Hungers.* Hamburg, 1955.

Schmidt, Ute, and Tilman Fichter. *Der erzwungene Kapitalismus: Klassenkämpfe in den Westzonen 1945–48.* Berlin, 1971.

Schneider, Ulrich, ed. *Als der Krieg zu Ende war: Hessen 1945.* Frankfurt am Main, 1980.

Schröder, Hans-Jürgen, ed. *Marshallplan und westdeutscher Wiederaufstieg: Positionen-Kontroversen.* Stuttgart, 1990.

Schulz, Bernhard, ed. *Grauzonen–Farbwelten: Kunst und Zeitbilder 1945–1955.* Berlin, 1983.

Schulzinger, Robert D. *The Wise Men of Foreign Affairs: The History of the Council on Foreign Relations.* New York, 1984.

Schwabe, Klaus. " 'Ein Akt konstruktiver Staatskunst': Die USA und die Anfänge des Schuman-Plan." In idem, ed. *Die Anfänge des Schuman-Plans 1950/51–The Beginnings of the Schuman-Plan.* Baden-Baden, 1988, 211–39.

Schwabe, Klaus, ed. *Die Anfänge des Schuman-Plans 1950/51–The Beginnings of the Schuman-Plan.* Baden-Baden, 1988.

Schwartz, Thomas A. *America's Germany: John J. McCloy and the Federal Republic of Germany.* Cambridge, Mass., 1991.

Schwarz, Hans-Peter. *Adenauer: Der Aufstieg, 1876–1952.* Stuttgart, 1986.

"Adenauer und Europa." *VfZG* 27 (1979):471–523.

Die Aera Adenauer 1949–1957. Geschichte der Bundesrepublik Deutschland. Eds. Karl Dietrich Bracher et al. Vol. 2. Stuttgart, 1981.

Shepardson, Whitney H. *Early History of the Council on Foreign Relations.* Stamford, Conn., 1960.

Shoup, Laurence H., and William Minter. *Imperial Brain Trust: The Council on Foreign Relations and United States Foreign Policy.* New York, 1977.

Shuchman, Abraham. *Codetermination: Labor's Middle Way in Germany.* Washington, D.C., 1957.

Simon, Leslie E. *German Research in World War II.* New York, 1947.

Simons, Hans. "The Bonn Constitution and its Government." In Hans J. Morgenthau, ed. *Germany and the Future of Europe.* Chicago, 1951, 114–30.

Smith, Arthur L. *Heimkehr aus dem Zweiten Weltkrieg: Die Entlassung der deutschen Kriegsgefangenen.* Stuttgart, 1985.

Smith, Bradley F. *The Road to Nuremberg.* New York, 1981.

Smith, Glenn H. *Langer of North Dakota.* New York, 1979.

Snyder, Glenn H. "The 'New Look' of 1953." In Warner R. Schillings, Paul Y. Hammond, and Glenn H. Snyder, eds. *Strategy, Politics, and Defense Budgets.* New York, 1962, 379–524.

Snyder, William. *The Politics of British Defence Policy, 1945–1962.* London, 1964.

Sollner, Alfons, ed. *Zur Archäologie der Demokratie in Deutschland.* 2 vols. Frankfurt am Main, 1982.

Soutou, Georges-Henri. "Die Nuklearpolitik der Vierten Republik." *VfZG* 37 (1989):605–10.

Speier, Hans, and W. Phillips Davison, eds. *West German Leadership and Foreign Policy.* Evanston, Ill., and White Plains, N.Y., 1957.

Spiro, Herbert J. *The Politics of German Codetermination.* Cambridge, Mass., 1958.

Spitz, Peter. *Petrochemicals: The Rise of an Industry.* New York, 1988.

Stamm, Thomas. *Zwischen Staat and Selbstverwaltung: Die deutsche Forschung im Wiederaufbau, 1945–1965.* Cologne, 1981.

Starr, Joseph R. *Denazification, Occupation, and Control of Germany, March-July 1945.* Salisbury, N.C., 1977.

Steininger, Rolf. *Eine Chance zur Wiedervereinigung? Die Stalinnote vom 10. März 1952.* Bonn, 1985.

"Ein vereinigtes, unabhängiges Deutschland? Winston Churchill, der Kalte Krieg und die deutsche Frage im Jahre 1953." *MGM* 36 (1984):105–44.

Stimson, Henry L. "The Challenge to Americans." *Foreign Affairs* 26 (Oct. 1947):5–14.

Stokes, Raymond G. *Divide and Prosper: The Heirs of I.G. Farben under Allied Authority, 1945–1951.* Berkeley, Calif., 1988.

"German Energy in the Postwar U.S. Economic Order, 1945–1951." *Journal of European Economic History* 17 (1988):621–39.

Tauber, Kurt. *Beyond Eagle and Swastika: German Nationalism since 1945.* Middletown, Conn., 1967.

Tent, James F. *The Free University of Berlin: A Political History.* Bloomington, Ind., 1988.

Mission on the Rhine: Reeducation and Denazification in American-Occupied Germany. Chicago, 1983.

Thayer, Charles. *The Unquiet Germans.* New York, 1957.

Thoss, Bruno. "Modellfall Österreich? Der österreichische Staatsvertrag und die deutsche Frage 1954/55." In Thoss, Bruno, and Hans-Erich Volkmann, eds. *Zwischen Kaltem Krieg und Entspannung: Sicherheits- und Deutschlandpolitik der Bundesrepublik im Mächtesystem der Jahre 1953–1956.* Boppard, 1988, 93–136.

Thoss, Bruno, and Hans-Erich Volkmann, eds. *Zwischen Kaltem Krieg und Entspannung: Sicherheits- und Deutschlandpolitik der Bundesrepublik im Mächtesystem der Jahre 1953–1956.* Boppard, 1988.

Thum, Horst. *Mitbestimmung in der Montanindustrie: Der Mythos vom Sieg der Gewerkschaften.* Stuttgart, 1982.

Tiedemann, Lotte, and Emmy Bonhöffer. "ECA-Entwicklungsbauten–von ihren Bewohnern und von Frauen gesehen." In Hermann Wandersleb und Georg Günthert, eds. *Neuer Wohnbau.* Vol. 2, *Durchführung von Versuchssiedlungen. Ergebnisse und Erkenntnisse für heute und morgen. Von ECA bis Interbau.* Ravensburg, 1958.

Triffin, Robert. *Europe and the Money Muddle: From Bilateralism to Near-Convertibility, 1947–1956.* New Haven, Conn., and London, 1957.

Vietzen, Hermann. *Chronik der Stadt Stuttgart 1945–1948.* Stuttgart, 1972.

Vogel, Johanna. *Kirche und Wiederbewaffnung: Die Haltung der EKD in den Auseinandersetzungen um die Wiederbewaffnung der Bundesrepublik.* Göttingen, 1978.

Volkmann, Hans-Erich, and Walter Schwengler, ed. *Die Europäische Verteidigungsgemeinschaft: Stand und Probleme der Forschung.* Boppard, 1985.

Wagner, Dieter. *FDP und Wiederbewaffnung: Die wehrpolitische Orientierung der Liberalen in der Bundesrepublik 1949–1955.* Boppard, 1978.

Wala, Michael. "Selling the Marshall Plan at Home: The Committee for the Marshall Plan to Aid European Recovery." *Diplomatic History* 10 (Summer 1986):247–65.

"Selling War and Selling Peace." *Amerikastudien/American Studies* 30 (1985): 91–105.

Winning the Peace: Amerikanische Aussenpolitik und der Council on Foreign Relations, 1945–1950. Stuttgart, 1990.

Wall, Irwin. "Les Accords Blum-Byrnes: La modernisation de la France et la Guerre froide." *Vingtième siècle* 13 (1978):40–62.

Warner, Isabel. "Allied-German Negotiations on the Deconcentration of the West German Steel Industry." In Ian D. Turner, ed. *Reconstruction in Post-War Germany: British Occupation Policy and the Western Zones, 1945–55.* Oxford, New York, and Munich, 1989, 155–85.

Watt, D. Cameron. *Succeeding John Bull: America in Britain's Place, 1900–1975.* Cambridge and New York, 1975.

Weidenfeld, Werner. "Konrad Adenauer und die EVG: Eine Studie zum subjektiven Faktor in der Politik." In Hans-Erich Volkmann and Walter Schwengler, eds. *Die Europäische Verteidigungsgemeinschaft: Stand und Probleme der Forschung.* Boppard, 1985, 255–70.

Weingartner, James J. *Crossroads of Death: The Story of the Malmédy Massacre and Trial.* Berkeley, 1979.

Weisz, Christoph. "Versuch zur Standortbestimmung der Landwirtschaft." In Ludolf Herbst, ed. *Westdeutschland 1945–55.* Munich, 1986, 117–26.

Wengst, Udo. *Beamtentum zwischen Reform und Tradition: Beramtengesetzgebung in der Gründungsphase der Bundesrepublik Deutschland, 1948–1953.* Düsseldorf, 1988.

Westdeutschlands Weg zur Bundesrepublik 1945–1949: Beiträge von Mitarbeitern des Instituts für Zeitgeschichte. Munich, 1976.

Wettig, Gerhard. *Entmilitarisierung und Wiederbewaffnung in Deutschland 1943–1955: Internationale Auseinandersetzungen um die Rolle der Deutschen in Europa.* Munich, 1967.

Wexler, Imanual. *The Marshall Plan Revisited: The European Recovery Program in Economic Perspective.* Westport, Conn., 1983.

Weymar, Paul. *Konrad Adenauer: Die autorisierte Biographie.* Munich, 1955.

Whalen, Robert W. *Bitter Wounds: German Victims of the Great War, 1914–1939.* Ithaca, N.Y., 1984.

Wiggershaus, Norbert. "Zur Frage der Planung für die verdeckte Aufstellung westdeutscher Verteidigungskräfte in Konrad Adenauers sicherheitspolitischer Konzeption 1950." In Heinz-Ludger Borgert, Walter Stürm, and Norbert

Wiggershaus. *Dienstgruppen und westdeutscher Verteidigungsbeitrag.* Boppard, 1982, 11–88.

Williams, Phil. *The Senate and U.S. Troops in Europe.* London, 1985.

Winkel, Harald. *Geschichte der württembergischen Industrie- und Handelskammern Heilbronn, Reutlingen, Stuttgart/Mittlerer Neckar und Ulm 1933–1980.* Stuttgart, 1981.

Wolfe, Robert, ed. *Americans as Proconsuls: United States Military Government in Germany and Japan, 1944–1952.* Carbondale, Ill., 1984.

Young, J. W. "Churchill, the Russians and the Western Alliance: The Three-Power Conference at Bermuda, December 1953." *English Historical Review* 101 (Oct. 1986):889–912.

Ziemke, Earl F. *The U.S. Army in the Occupation of Germany.* Washington, D.C., 1985.

Zink, Harold. *The United States in Germany, 1944–1955.* Princeton, Toronto, London, and New York, 1957.

Index

521

decartelization, 140, 200; on demilitarization of Germany, 412
President's Committee on Foreign Aid, 3
Price, Hoyt, 12
Prisoners of War (POW), 354–6, 360, 363; *see also* veterans, German
Project Solarium, 395–6, 418
Protestant church call for review of Nuremberg cases, 438
Pünder, Hermann, 73

Radford, Arthur William, 397, 415, 430
Radford Plan, 411, 412
Radio Bremen, 474
Radio in the American Sector of Berlin (Rias), 474
Ranger, Richard H., 176
Rangertone and technology exchange, 176, 187
reconstruction of German cities, 331–51; *see also* Gropius, Walter
Red Zone and agricultural development, 168–9
Redslob, Edwin, 240; and formation of Free University of Berlin, 242
refugees and housing shortages, 344
Reichow, Hans Bernhard, 346
Reichswirtschaftsrat, 314, 325, 327
Reinecke, Hermann, 446
Reinhardt, Hans, 452
reparations, 86–93, 113–15, 139, 175–96; Allied Commission on, 177; intellectual, 223; *see also* Plan for Reparations and the Level of Post-War German Industry
Reppe, Walter, 230
Reppe chemistry and chemical technology transfer, 230
reunification, 45–67; *see also* United States; West Germany
Reusch, Hermann, 139, 142, 144
Reuter, Ernst, and formation of Free University of Berlin, 242–3, 245–6, 250; personal papers of, 470
Reuter, Georg, 274, 278
Reynolds, W. H., and technical consultants and missions, 183
Rheinisch–Westfälisches Kohlensyndikat, 199
Rheinische Olefinwerke (ROW), 228, 232–4
Ribbentrop, Joachim von, 135
Riddelberger, James, 8
Ridgway, Matthew, 405

Rimpl, Hermann, 346
Robert Bosch GmbH, 189, 266
Robertson, Sir Brian, 31–3, 35, 42
Rockefeller Foundation, 17
Rohe, Mies van der, 346
Roosevelt, Franklin Delano, 114, 121; and Grand Design for postwar Europe, 111–12
Rosenberg, Ludwig, 263
Ross, Michael, 4
Rostow, Walt W., 116
Rothfels, Hans, personal papers of, 472
Royal, Kenneth, 435
Royal Institute for International Affairs, 2
Ruhr, 11, 14, 27, 88, 90, 93, 111, 131, 324; and France, 128–9, 207; formation of International Authority for, 129; U.S. and industry in, 135–53; impact of deconcentration in, 140; and integration of industry into European industry, 145; coal and U.S. exports, 145–8; and U.S. deconcentration policy, 197–215; and formation of U.K./U.S. Coal Control Group, 202, 204; and formation of German Coal Mines Management (DKBL), 202, 204, 210; and German Coal Sales Agency (DKV), 204, 210, 213–14; and Bergbaubedarf-Beschaffungszentrale, 204; and Law No. 75, 204, 206; labor in, 266, 268, 272–3
Rumania, 53
Rusk, Dean, 55

Saar, 90, 102, 131
Salewski, Wilhelm, 315
Saltzman, Charles E., 191–2
Sandberger, Martin, 449
Schäffer, Fritz, 168; personal papers of, 471–2
Scharnagl, Karl, 288, 300
Scharoun, Hans, 337
Schmid, Carlo, 391–2; and Occupation Statute, 40–1; personal papers, 473
Schmidt, August, 278
Schmoller, Gustav von, 194
Scholl, Inge, 445
Scholle, August, 262
Schorske, Carl E., 12
Schumacher, Kurt, 296, 299–300, 445, 448; and German reunification, 389; personal papers, 473
Schuman, Robert, 39, 131, 132, 377